Communications
in Computer and Information Science · 1438

More information about this series at http://www.springer.com/series/7899

Lorna Uden · I-Hsien Ting · Kai Wang (Eds.)

Knowledge Management in Organizations

15th International Conference, KMO 2021
Kaohsiung, Taiwan, July 20–22, 2021
Proceedings

 Springer

Editors
Lorna Uden
Staffordshire University
Stoke-on-Trent, UK

I-Hsien Ting
National University of Kaohsiung
Kaohsiung, Taiwan

Kai Wang
National University of Kaohsiung
Kaohsiung, Taiwan

ISSN 1865-0929   ISSN 1865-0937 (electronic)
Communications in Computer and Information Science
ISBN 978-3-030-81634-6   ISBN 978-3-030-81635-3 (eBook)
https://doi.org/10.1007/978-3-030-81635-3

This Springer imprint is published by the registered company Springer Nature Switzerland AG
The registered company address is: Gewerbestrasse 11, 6330 Cham, Switzerland

Preface

Welcome to the proceedings of the 15th International Conference on Knowledge Management in Organizations (KMO 2020/2021), held at the National University of Kaohsiung, Kaohsiung, Taiwan during July 20–22 2021. Owing to the unique circumstances brought about by the COVID-19 pandemic, KMO 2020 was postponed and subsequently merged with this year's edition of the conference, which was held in a hybrid format with both in-person and online presentations. KMO 2020/2021 was co-located with the 9th International Conference on Learning Technology for Education Challenges (LTEC 2020/2021).

Knowledge is behind the creation of benchmark products and service. It is power and, when properly harnessed, it gives a competitive advantage. Technology has had a tremendous impact on knowledge management (KM), inspiring the development of robust software platforms to leverage KM strategies. Knowledge management continues to evolve in response to new demands and challenges.

Social media has revolutionized the way we use the Internet. Social elements can be integrated with a variety of application types, including knowledge management. When social media elements are blended with knowledge management the work becomes easier. Knowledge-based systems are becoming more collaborative as seen in social intranets, allowing individuals to work on documents and communicate with each other in real time.

Mobile technology has become a primary means of accessing the Web for both personal and professional reasons. Mobile devices save both money and time, and as a result, mobile technology and KM will soon be inseparable. Today KM software allows us to tag, share, and organize content as soon as we create it. This helps to cut down on confusion and makes knowledge management a more interactive process.

KM today is developing a more robust approach that includes vendors, clients, and customers. Newer knowledge management options must allow for external integration so that internal and external parties can share information more easily. Blockchain and cryptographic technologies allow users in KM to own and control their data, and for data to be trusted by third parties they choose to interact with. There are potential benefits of automating routine knowledge tasks and using powerful algorithms to recommend relevant content and colleagues based on users' personas and the context of their work.

Although technology plays a crucial role in the advancement of KM, it is important to remember that KM will always fail if the end users and stakeholders are not at the centre of the strategy, design, implementation, and operations. KM should also be concerned with human-centred approaches (people, process, content, and culture) and new design methodologies such as design for users' experiences. To effectively manage knowledge in organisations, it is necessary that we address many of the above issues.

KMO 2020/2021 aimed to bring together leading academic researchers and research scholars to exchange and share their experiences and research in all aspects of knowledge management challenges. It also provided an interdisciplinary platform for researchers, practitioners, and educators to present and discuss their most recent work, trends, innovation, and concerns, as well as practical challenges encountered and solutions adopted, in the field of knowledge management in organizations.

This proceeding consists of 37 papers covering various aspects of knowledge management. All of the papers selected for this volume underwent a rigorous review process involving at least four reviewers. The authors of these papers come from 15 different countries including Argentina, Austria, China, Colombia, Ecuador, Finland, France, Hong Kong, Japan, Slovakia, South Africa, Spain, Taiwan, Tunisia, and the USA.

The papers are organised into the following thematic sections:

- Knowledge Management Models & Analysis
- Knowledge Transfer & Learning
- Knowledge & Service Innovation
- Knowledge & Organization
- Information Systems and Information Science
- Privacy and Security
- Intelligent Science & Data Mining
- AI & New Trends in KM

We would like to thank our reviewers and the Program Committee for their contributions and the National University of Kaohsiung, Taiwan, for hosting the conference. Special thanks go to the authors and participants at the conference. Without their efforts, there would be no conference or proceedings.

We hope that these proceedings will be beneficial for your reference and that the information in this volume will be useful for further advancements in both research and industry related to knowledge management.

July 2021   Lorna Uden
                                                                      I-Hsien Ting

Organization

Conference Chair

Lorna Uden   Staffordshire University, UK

Program Chair

Derrick I-Hsien Ting (Diego Lopez)   National University of Kaohsiung, Taiwan

Local Team

Local Chair

Kai Wang	National University of Kaohsiung, Taiwan
Weny Ming-Jun Chen	National University of Kaohsiung, Taiwan
Jahua Chia-Hua Lee	National University of Kaohsiung, Taiwan
Winnie Liu	National University of Kaohsiung, Taiwan

Program Committee

Reinhard C. Bernsteiner	Management Center Innsbruck, Austria
K. Chandrasekaran	National Institute of Technology Karnataka, India
Houn-Gee Chen	National Taiwan University, Taiwan
Juan Manuel Corchado Rodríguez	University of Salamanca, Spain
Sara Rodriguez Gonzalez	University of Salamanca, Spain
Marjan Heričko	University of Maribor, Slovenia
Gan Keng Hoon	Universiti Sains Malaysia, Malaysia
Pei-Hsuan Hsieh	National Chengchi University, Taiwan
Akira Kamoshida	Yokohama City University, Japan
George Karabatis	University of Maryland, Baltimore County, USA
Jari Kaivo-Oja	University of Turku, Finland
Cristian Koliver	Federal University of Santa Catarina, Brazil
Aida Kamišalić Latifić	University of Maribor, Slovenia
Eric Kin-Wai Lau	City University, Hong Kong
Dario Liberona	Universidad Santa Maria, Chile
Furen Lin	National Tsing Hua University, Taiwan
Victor Hugo Medina Garcia	Universidad Distrital Francisco José de Caldas, Colombia

Marja Naaranoja	Vaasa University of Applied Sciences, Finland
Luka Pavlič	University of Maribor, Slovenia
Christian Ploder	Management Center Innsbruck, Austria
Hércules Antonio do Prado	Catholic University of Brasília, Brazil
Fernando De la Prieta	University of Salamanca, Spain
Stephan Schlögl	Management Center Innsbruck, Austria
Dai Senoo	Tokyo Institute of Technology, Japan
Marrara, Stefania	Consorzio C2T, Italy
Marta Silvia Tabares	Universidad EAFIT, Colombia
Derrick Ting	National University of Kaohsiung, Taiwan
Lorna Uden	Staffordshire University, UK
Costas Vassilakis	University of the Peloponnese, Greece
Remy Magnier-Watanabe	University of Tsukuba, Tokyo, Japan
William Wang	University of Waikato, New Zealand
Xianzhi Wang	University of Technology Sydney, Australia
Yuri Zelenkov	Higher School of Economics, Russia
Mariusz Kostrzewski	Warsaw University of Technology, Poland
Kamoun-Chouk Souad	Manouba University, Tunisia
Iraklis Varlamis	Harokopio University of Athens, Greece
Mingzhu Zhu	Apple Inc., USA

Contents

Knowledge and Service Innovation

Knowledge and Organization

Intelligent Science and Data Mining

AI&New Trends in KM

Knowledge Management Models and Analysis

Index Management Design as Knowledge Management Enhancers for the Colombian Swine Industry

Pablo Cesar Gómez-Silva[1]([✉]), Flor Nancy Diaz-Piraquive[1] [iD],
and Johanna Trujillo-Diaz[2] [iD]

[1] Universidad Católica de Colombia, Bogotá, Colombia
{pcgomez21,fndiaz}@ucatolica.edu.co
[2] Fundación Universitaria Internacional de la Rioja, Bogotá, Colombia
johanna.trujillo@unir.net

Abstract. The Colombian Swine Industry (CSI) has a global importance in agriculture as a sustainable objective worldwide, and it is very attractive for farmers for its short productive cycle, if it is compared to other business lines. Thus, the CSI seeks to encourage profitability, to minimize production cost, to open new markets, and to supply local demand. Therefore, they need to search tools for measuring its key indicators. They have important constrains, for instance the lack of technology, economic benefits, and human resources training. With the above, the article objective is to identify pig producers' key indicators which could carry to create and share knowledge management. Pig industry key indicators were extracted from the literature. After that, those indicators were contrasted by 19 companies using a Likert scale; then, those were analyzed and grouped according to the Balance Scorecard perspectives using the main component analysis. Finally, a measuring instrument was designed, it was validated by 15 CSI experts, who then applied it to a representative sample of 62 companies in the agricultural sector. Among the most outstanding results were the list of pig industry key indicators and its validation, its importance and measurement level; CSI sustainable indexes inclusion from literature; knowledge creation in pig farmers using indexes for measuring and making decisions.

Keywords: Knowledge management · Colombian swine sector · Swine industry · Key performance indexes · Sustainable balanced scorecard · Swine management indexes

1 Introduction

1.1 Background

Pork is the most consumed type of meat worldwide, China is the main pork producer, it produces half of the total world production, in second place is the United States of America, and the third place is Germany. The pork consumption average is 37.4% (110 million metric tons), 35.3% chicken; 22.6% cattle, and 4.7% sheep.

L. Uden et al. (Eds.): KMO 2021, CCIS 1438, pp. 3–22, 2021.
https://doi.org/10.1007/978-3-030-81635-3_1

The Colombian livestock sector is the second most important of Colombian agriculture, which has a GDP of 6.5%, 11% correspond to pigs, 43% to cattle, and 46% to poultry. However, pork consumption has been rising in Colombia, in 2009 it was 4.22 kg/inhabitant and in 2017 9.4 kg/inhabitant [1].

In Colombia, pork production is aimed at supplying domestic demand, and it does not have barriers to entry. In 2017, Colombian pig production slaughter was USD $711 million worth, and imports were USD $177 million worth due to free trade agreements [1], out of which 91.2% was from the USA., the rest is from Canada, Chile, Denmark, Portugal, and Spain. Thus, by 2017, the Colombian pork market was composed by 80% of national production, and 20% of imported pork [2].

Colombian importing departments are Cundinamarca, Valle del Cauca, and Bolívar, while the main producers are Cundinamarca, Antioquia, Valle del Cauca, Meta, and Córdoba [3]. Pig producers are classified as technical, semi-technical, and traditional production; and sub-classified by the productive object such as: a) genetic improvement farms, b) breeding farms, and c) commercial breeding and fattening farms.

In the last 10 years, the Colombian Swine Industry (CSI) has been rising more than double with 8.8%, compared to the cattle sector with 4.2%. However, the main problem of the CSI is profitability, since cost average for standing pork production was USD$1.55/kg, and pork meat refrigerated was USD$2.09/kg. In addition, the average price for standing pork was USD$1.57/kg, in hot-channel was USD$2.07/kg, and in the cold-channel was USD$2.13/kg. Thus, Colombia has one of the highest standing pig costs in America, due to the fact that pig farmers try to keep costs under control, but they do not have software and technological tools to make that, and they have low levels of training to avoid the innovation in processes; thus, the purpose of this article is to identify the key indicators as a knowledge management strategy for improving profitability.

The CSI is attractive for farmers because the pig cycle is around 296 days. However, to increase CSI's profitability, pig farmers need to measure and control the processes traceability. CSI's profitability is limited due to: a) price volatility, which is given by slaughter plants published on its platforms; b) feeding cost which represents 73.25% of the total production costs, followed by labor costs (6.04%), the using facilities (3.56%) [4], and promotion fees; c) the absence of benefits, economic incentives, tax reduction, and credit programs for innovation and development [5]; and e) compliance with biosafety regulations.

1.2 Problem Statement

Since a BSC implemented in agro-industrial companies allows to increase productivity, efficiency, sustainability, innovation and new markets identification [4–6]. Some works have demonstrated that BSC reduces rework by 9%, increases productivity by 10% [9]; and specifically in agro-industrial companies, it increases incomes by between 23% and 57% [5]. On the other hand, a sustainable BSC generates value for industries by 58.39% [6], however, studies about indexes swine industry are limited, this article seeks to include control key indicators for sustainable processes and to minimize costs in the CSI, due to the fact that CSI main problem is the high Colombian swine cost production [1].

So, CSI needs urgently to design and implement a tool for knowledge management (KM) such as a sustainable BSC. Firstly, KM promotes automatically competitiveness, the creation of internal and inter-industry cooperation strategies (See axis 1 and 3 - Fig. 1), productivity increasing, high customer service levels and innovation capacity [6]. Secondly, a Balanced Scorecard (BSC) is an efficient tool for planning, decision-making, and controlling profitability and costs [7, 8].

In this research, the BSC has been chosen as a tool for creating knowledge in the CSI, because: a) CSI has not standardized its indicators, and also Colombian pig farmers just have implemented certain indicators; b) most of Colombian pig farmers make decisions intuitively, because they control their costs and processes manually and partially; c) Colombian pig farmers are not interested in implementing sustainable processes despite of high pollutant level of the SI [7, 8]. Thus, this research aimed is to inventory CSI key indicators, as a tool to minimize the cost of production, identify basic indexes for internal and external knowledge management, and control of environmental impact. The research question is *what are the key indicators that would incentivize profitability, cost minimization, and processes traceability in pig companies?*

Therefore, looking to build that indexes inventory for the CSI, which potentiate KD (Sect. 3); Firstly, in the second part of the article is described KM theoretical aspects (Sect. 2.1), KM in the pig sector (Sect. 2.2), KM theoretical model established in [1] for the CSI (Sect. 2.3), and some agribusiness and pig applications in dashboards or Balanced Scorecards (BS) are explained (Sect. 2.4). Finally, the methodology, the results, the discussion, and conclusions are written.

2 Literature Review

To define CSI key indicators list, the literature review was carried out on the Science Direct and Scopus databases, using the next search-query: ("knowledge management") AND ("balanced scorecard OR index*") AND ("agribusiness OR pork OR pig OR hog OR swine").

2.1 Knowledge Management

Knowledge management (KM) was born in 1975 with [6–8] and the classical theories of [9–13]; Most studies in the literature are applied at the organizational level, and those are not in industrial sectors. KM is connected with the concept of knowledge economy, which search to increase profitability, innovation capacity, and knowledge transfer [14].

In the literature, several KM theories have been oriented towards the capitalization of knowledge at the organizational level: i) Nonaka (1996) identified the differences between tacit and explicit knowledge, Nonaka explains knowledge process [15], such as: a) socialization or interaction; b) formalization; c) internalization refers conversion of theory into practice; and d) combination stage, which refers to unification of existing theories [16]. ii) Boisot (1998) adapted Nonaka model, which classifies knowledge at the individual, group, intra-organizational, and inter-organizational level [17]; iii) Finally, other authors established KM cycles that allow identifying the stages of the KM process [18–23].

2.2 Knowledge Management in the Swine Sector

Indexes measurement in the CSI potentiates KM in processes, because these add value, innovation capacity [24], and competitive advantages in global and uncertainty scenarios [25, 26]. However, simply because companies belong to an industrial sector does not mean that they can access indexes, knowledge, and information, and they do not transfer easily information between stakeholders [27].

KM has SI applications, which has been focused on index management design, for instance to improve productivity [28] and profitability [29, 30]; traceability applications and methodologies [31], coordination and integration strategies [32–34], training programs [35], and also, software design [34, 36].

2.3 Theoretical KM Model for the CSI

KM is a set of processes and tools to manage and capitalize on knowledge and best practices for leading competitiveness [37, 38]. First, [1] proposed a KM model which is in the definition phase, it consists of knowing what the CSI must have at the organizational and the sector level, given that pig farming and fathering companies have a broad tacit knowledge [39, 40], which does not easily become explicit intra-organizationally [39, 40]. Second, [1] indicates that the KM cycle for CSI is creation [41, 42], storage [23, 43, 44], transfer [23, 43, 44], and knowledge appropriation [23, 41–44] (See axis 2 – Fig. 1). Thus, in the primary production stage the key management indexes and best practices should be created and known, which encourage the CSI competitiveness (See axis 1 - Fig. 1). Therefore, this article is focused on this identification, but while, in the *creation stage*, there is a need to create an intraorganizational culture, in the *storage stage* the need is an interorganizational culture and technology in this process (See axis 3 – Fig. 1).

KM theories motivate knowledge capitalization and it recognizes its role in the competitive advantage, under criteria such as trust, motivation, culture and education among stakeholders, it makes KM's culture be adopted [45, 46]. The KM culture creation facilitates the organizational policy and training plans design, a KM team configuration [47], best practices identification [37, 38], and processes measurement. So, a trained, committed and motivated stakeholder in this culture improves business processes and decision-making [26]. Since the CSI educational level is low, and there is no interest in training, the axis 1 in Fig. 1 indicates the intra-organizational creation of KM culture in the CSI, which is the main phase to achieve a growth in competitiveness (See axis 1 – Fig. 1).

The sector requires that knowledge will be public [17, 48] and spread [17] (see axis 3 - Fig. 1), which indicates that CSI inter-organizational culture promotes to share best practices and key indicators. However, before that, they need to include technologies in processes [49–51], which allow to create a culture of sharing knowledge intra and inter-organizationally [52–60], indexes, and best practices among stakeholders [24] (suppliers, pig companies, and clients).

Finally, axis 4 (Fig. 1) guarantees knowledge appropriation of previous stages and actors of the CSI KM model [1] that refers to the conversion of theory into practice; and its combination stage [16], there are empowerment strategies of the actors that encourage competitiveness.

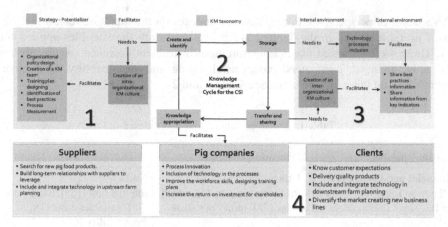

Fig. 1. KM model for SSC

2.4 Balanced Scorecard Applications as a KM Strategy

Balanced Scorecard (BS) is a business tool used to manage organizational knowledge [61, 62] and knowledge transfer [63]. Indeed, organizational development, traceability, profitability and productivity are measured by BS to facilitate decision-making [61, 62, 64, 65], strategic management [66], and to increase competitiveness [67, 68]. BS is focused on four different perspectives relating each other to KM and innovation [63, 69–71] (See Table 1), however, companies must have a previous study of culture to implement it [72–76]. On the other hand, classical BS does not include a sustainable perspective, which involves profitability, environmental, and social aspects. In agricultural sectors such as CSI, it is really relevant, therefore, some studies regarding sustainable BS have been identified on the literature review [69, 71, 77–80], and also, studies applied into CSI [81].

3 Methodology

This study is exploratory and descriptive (see Fig. 2). Firstly, different variables, dimensions and indexes were built based on a literature review (See Table 1), which are financial perspective, customers, processes, learning, R&D, and also sustainability which was added by [69, 71] and proposed for CSI in this article.

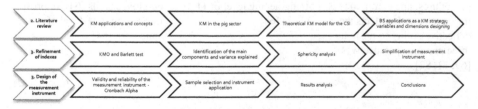

Fig. 2. Methodology

Variables or perspectives, dimensions and indexes on the literature review are presented in Table 1, and in the Table 2 are being used only the variables applied for CSI. Those were validated using a measurement instrument designed specifically for this study, financial, consumers, processes, learning and sustainability perspective, dimensions, and indexes were used (See Table 1 and 2).

Table 1. Variables, dimensions and indexes

Variable - perspectives	Dimension - indexes	
Financial perspective (FP): It is the most important factor in the BS, since shareholders see and evaluate the company's result, it is measured quantitatively [61, 62, 71]	**Utility** Profit margin [78, 81], added value [78], utility per share [81] **Incomes** Turnover [65], increasing profits [64], sales growth [81], foreign sales [81], market share [81] **Expenses** Devaluation expenses [78]	**Costs** Internal costs [65], fixed costs [78], variables costs [78] **Profitability** [65] Global profitability (ROE, ROA) [71, 81], ROI, ROS) [81], stock Price [81], EBITDA [81], term of obligations payment [81], self-financing coefficient [81]
Customer perspective (CP): It is considered the second in importance, because customers define the financial performance. It directs the way customers, products or services offered, and market satisfaction [62, 71, 82]	**Customer Satisfaction** Customer management [64], customer complaints [78], customer satisfaction [64, 65, 71, 81]	Number of customers [64] Product quality [71], customer loyalty level [64]
Process, innovation and development perspective (PIDP): It focuses on the company's CORE processes, efficiency, innovation and operation [61, 71]	**Supply Chain Management** Suppliers [78], number of defective units [78], productivity [78], operating efficiency [81], distribution efficiency [64]	**Innovation and Development (I+D)** Number of patents [81], innovation in processes [81], innovation in processes and products [64]
Development and learning perspective (DLP): It focuses on support processes such as technology, personnel, procedures, and continuous improvement. It reflects the collective ability to push the three previous perspectives [69, 71, 82]	**External** Years in the market [80], product demand [78] **Technology** Strengthening level of IT culture [64]	**Human Management** Employee satisfaction level [71, 78, 81], personnel retention [81], improve employee skills [64], improve motivation [64], level of teamwork [64]

(continued)

Table 1. (*continued*)

Variable - perspectives	Dimension - indexes	
Sustainable perspective (SP): It defines the company's sustainable strategy, based on qualitative and quantitative indicators, own actions or regulations applied linking sustainable objectives with actions and performance results [69, 71]. This is included as a contribution to literature	**Environment** Level of exploitation of natural resources [71, 78], Emission of greenhouse gases [71]	Energy consumption [71], CO_2 emissions [71]

Secondly, the measurement instrument was designed using a Likert scale for quantitative indexes, which are: 5 points (it is important and measured - *IM*); 4 points (it is important and not measured - *INM*); 3 points (indifferent or neutral - IN); 2 points (it is not important and measured - *NIM*); 1 point (it is not important and not measured - *NINM*). Measurement instrument was designed by combining 10 categorical questions which measure variable characteristics and 31 questions of key indexes. Those were contrasted with 19 experts from CSI to reduce indexes in perspectives or variables.

Thirdly, using the previous variables and perspectives in Table 1, the first instrument designed had 42 indexes, and to refine it (see Table 2), an analysis of main components was made. After that, those were classified by perspective or variables, using KMO test (Kaiser-Meyer-Olkin), the KMO result was 0.829, that identifies the relation between variables using correlation coefficients; in addition, Bartlett's level of significance was zero. The indicators were extracted identifying their main components (variables or perspectives - see Table 1), for which, sedimentation graph and components rotated matrix with VARIMAX using six iterations were used, compared with the perspectives (see Table 1). Hence, the indicators were extracted, if the indicator lowered the KMO test or the total variance explained. Thus, nine indexes reduced KMO test and the explained variance, for which, indexes were summarized in 31 key-indexes. To sum up this stage, the graph sedimentation had 6 components and the explained variance was 83.7%, which indicates that it is highly correlated. The VARIMAX association coefficients extracted by factorial analysis are shown in Table 3, these were classified by BSC perspective, main factorial components or variable.

Fourthly, quantitative variables were validated by 15 experts from CSI, to confirm the validity and reliability of the measurement instrument, a Cronbach Alpha was determined, whose result was 0,927; therefore, this measurement instrument is reliable and replicated to be applied into the sample.

Fifthly, to delimitate the representative probabilistic sample, the companies dedicated to *breeding and fattening of pigs* from Antioquia (Colombia) were selected. A database from the Chamber of Commerce of Bogota was used, By April 12th, 2017, it includes 191 companies dedicated to the breeding and fattening of pigs. The applied sampling

Table 2. Design of the measurement instrument. Source. Authors based on information from [3]

Variable	Dimension	Index	Question
Learning (**L**) [69, 71, 82]	Physical infrastructure	Type of production	A1
		Productive capacity [81]	A2.–A4
	Technological infrastructure	Technology	A5
	Human resources	Work-force capacity	A6
Financial (**F**) [61, 62, 71]	Financial process	Manufacture costs [65, 78]	B1.–B3
		Sales and incomes [65, 81]	B4.–B5
		Utility [65]	B6.–B7
		Price	B8
	Leverage [81]	Supplier [81]	B9.–B10
		Customers	B11
Process (**P**) [61, 71]	Productivity [78, 81]	Breeding	C1.–C7
		Breastfeeding	C8
		Fattening	C9.–C12
Customer (**C**) [62, 71, 82]	Quality management [71]	Customers [64]	C13.–C14
		Customer satisfaction [64, 65, 71, 81]	C15
Sustainability (**S**) [69, 71]	Environment	Community	C16
		Energy [71]	C17
		Water	C18
		Fluid waste [71, 78]	C19
		Solid waste	C20
Learning (**L**) [69, 71, 82]	Internal development (**ID**)	Retention programs [81]	D1
		Training [64]	D2
		Education level	D3
	External development (**ED**)	Technical and management knowledge sharing	D4

was of a finite population. Given that the probability of an event happening or not is unknown, a 0.5 probability is handled, a confidence level of 95%, with a Z statistic of 1.645 and an accepted maximum estimation error of 0,08 [83] to select the 63 companies.

Table 3. Results summary

Question	Factorial analysis results*	Category	Result
A1. What kind of swine production does your farm have? [85]	Not apply	**Type of technification**	**Percentage %**
		Traditional	49%
		Semi – Technified	26%
		Technified	25%
A2. How many sows does your farm have?	Not apply	Traditional	52 sows
		Semi-technified	170 sows
		Technified	127 sows
		100 sows 200 sows 300 sows >400 sows	72% 17% 6% 6%
A3. What is the predominant breed of pigs in your pig farm? [84–86]	Not apply	Duroc	19%
		Hampshire	9%
		Landrace	17%
		Landrace-Belgian	11%
		Pietrain	21%
		Yorkshire	23%
		Various	85%
A4. What is the number of piglets born by litter?	Not apply	8 piglets 9 piglets 10 piglets 11 piglets 12 piglets	16% 31% 39% 12% 2%
A5. Do you use any software, application or platform for the measurement, management and control of your farm indicators?	Not Apply	Yes No	23% 77%

(continued)

Table 3. (*continued*)

Question	Factorial analysis results*	Category		Result	
A6. What is the number of operational employees in your company?	Not Apply	Traditional		3 persons per farm	
		Semi-technified		6 persons per farm	
		Technified		7 persons per farm	

Question	Variable or component*	IM	INM	IN	NIM	NINM
B1. Cost of errors of re-processes	F-0,841	15%	72%	0%	5%	8%
B2. Percentage of the administrative cost regarding the pig price	IDL-0,743	25%	66%	0%	2%	8%
B3. **Cost per kilogram produced**	F-0,833	33%	66%	0%	0%	1%
B4. **Income per kilogram produced**	F-0,748	30%	67%	0%	0%	3%
B5. Total monthly sales	F-0,856	38%	59%	0%	2%	2%
B6. Profit per pig or batch produced	F-0,919	36%	62%	0%	0%	2%
B7. Percentage of farm profit	F-0,938	36%	62%	0%	0%	2%
B8. Pig price in the marker per kilogram	F-0,797	33%	64%	0%	0%	3%
B9. Debt or credit time	F-0,906	26%	66%	2%	0%	7%

(*continued*)

Table 3. (*continued*)

Question	Factorial analysis results*	Category		Result	
B10. What is the average of day of debt or credit do you manage with food companies?	Not apply	Cash 30 days 45 days 60 days		7% 43% 30% 20%	
B11. How many days do you credit your customers?	Not apply	Cash 30 days 45 days 90 days		23% 49% 26% 3%	
Question		**IM**	**INM**	**IN**	**NIM**	**NINM**
C1. Male reproductive efficiency	P-0,815	26%	48%	0%	2%	25%
C2. Number of sows selected for replacement	P-0,796	25%	51%	0%	2%	23%
C3. Feed consumption per sow	P-0,869	30%	52%	2%	0%	16%
C4. Amount or percentage of deliveries per sow before replacement [86]	P-0,887	30%	52%	3%	2%	13%
C5. Number of pigs per delivery [86]	P-0,931	34%	49%	3%	2%	11%
C6. Number of pigs born per week	P-0,934	31%	52%	3%	2%	11%
C7. Number of dead born pigs [86]	P-0,897	30%	57%	3%	0%	10%
C8. Number of dead pigs before weaning [85]	P-0,843	28%	57%	3%	0%	11%

(*continued*)

Table 3. (*continued*)

Question	Factorial analysis results*	Category			Result	
C9. Feed consumption per pig or per batch of pigs	P-0,732	26%	62%	0%	0%	11%
C10. Food consumption per week	P-0,781	26%	52%	0%	2%	20%
C11. Kilograms gained in weight per week	P-0,826	21%	62%	0%	5%	11%
C12. Total fattening time per batch before sale	P-0,756	30%	62%	0%	0%	8%
C13. Number of customers lost per year	C-0,607	8%	46%	0%	5%	41%
C14. Number of effective customers	C-0,791	21%	43%	0%	0%	36%
C15. Monitoring customer satisfaction (in terms of color of meat produced, amount of fat and capacity)	C-0,825	18%	39%	0%	2%	41%
C16. Number of complaints from neighboring farms	EDL-0,603	5%	54%	7%	3%	31%
C17. Electricity consumption for each pig	S-0,911	11%	52%	0%	2%	34%
C18. Water consumption for each pig	S-0,867	16%	48%	0%	2%	34%

(*continued*)

Table 3. (*continued*)

Question	Factorial analysis results*	Category			Result	
C19. Destination of wastewater from corral washing	S-0,923	16%	51%	2%	0%	31%
C20. Solid waste management	S-0,797	18%	52%	0%	2%	28%
D1. Personnel turnover level	IDL-0,609	21%	38%	0%	2%	39%
D2. Number of trainings received by personnel per year	IDL-0,585	20%	34%	0%	3%	43%
D3. Employee education level	IDL-0,732	30%	52%	2%	0%	16%
D4. Would you be willing to share the information of the indicators by an online platform oriented to the knowledge management for all actors of the Swine Industry?	Not apply	Yes No			21% 79%	

*Component **F** (Financial); **C** (Customer); **P** (processes); **S** (Sustainability); **IDL** (Internal development learning); **EDL** (External development learning)

4 Results

5 Discussion

Most of pig farms in the CSI has traditional production, indicating a low technological development, even 77% of pig farms do not handle software. However, while the traditional Colombian pig farm has an average of 50 sows, and its workforce is 3 people per farm, a semi-technified Colombian pig farm has more than 150 sows, and its workforce is 6 people per farm. Likewise, 72% of pig farms have between 0 and 100 sows, 85%

of them manage several pig breeds, and its average birth rate is 10 piglets per litter (see Table 3).

For BS the most important is the perspectives measurement. Therefore, the financial perspective consists in costs, incomes, utilities, price measurement, among others. Firstly, the pig costs is important given that it represents 73.25% of the total cost [87], and a farmer's need is cost minimization, for which they search vertical integration upstream to slaughter plants and downstream [88–92]. Thus, according to this study 99% of the pig farms surveyed consider this indicator important, however only 33% measures it. One of the most important indicators is "the cost per kilogram produced", 99% consider it important, although only 33% measure it (see Table 3).

CSI has a strong trend to accounting measurement, thus regarding income and utility indexes, it is evident that 97% of the farms consider these important, although only 34% measure them, being the "total monthly sales" the most measured index, however they think that the most important indexes are utility and price per kilogram, it indicates a strong tendency in which the performance measurement used by the farms is a traditional system which is based on an accounting measurement [65]. On the other hand, 92% of the farms surveyed consider that borrowing time is important, but only 26% measure it. Likewise, 45% of pig farms finance their food and leverage their customers 30 days. Overall, 23% of farms sell cash (see Table 3).

The processes perspective and supply chain management for Colombian pig farms is reflected by productivity, quality management and environmental impact [62, 65], for which the key indicators are the number of pigs by birth and dead, killed pigs before weaning, food consumption efficiency and weight gain. These indexes measure the company CORE, reflected in increased customer satisfaction, and the company's financial performance [71]. In addition, the customer perspective, quality, and management have a high impact on the financial perspective [71], the study shows that only 16% of the farms surveyed measure it and 58% consider it important (see Table 3).

The sustainable perspective is very important in the agribusiness sector [69, 79] consists in avoiding pigs in confinement, which is considered pollutant for soil and air [93], however, in this study, 70% of interviewed answered that solid waste management is the most important index of sustainability, but 13% only measures it (see Table 3).

The CSI is seeking to implement management measurement strategies for new business lines generation [3], for which, knowledge management, learning and development perspective allow creating value [61, 62]. In this perspective only 82% of the farms consider it important, but only 24% measure it (see Table 3). Indeed, they are exposing their pig farms to an outdated employee in terms of processes, care, regulations, improvements, or trends in the sector, etc., because its production is based on tacit knowledge, and not explicit [63]. Thus, only 21% of the farms surveyed are willing to share their knowledge with suppliers, competitors, and customers; it can generate innovation, research, and continuous improvement in their processes [63].

6   Conclusions and Perspectives

This research proposes a KM model based in a sustainable BSC, it included in the literature CSI indexes for measuring production processes, client satisfaction and financial processes. On the other hand, this research showed two novel proposals into that theory: the sustainable and learning perspective. All of indexes were proved using a sampling to build this inventory for CSI. Those will be proved in the future researches, when the BSC will be designed.

Most of the farmers are oriented to measure profit and sales, they do not control the traceability of the process, due to a lack of culture and organizational leadership, staff training, education level, resources, among others. Thus, decision-making of these organizations is done in an uncertainty environment, because there is no strict control of the process indexes and technology which support this process. An clear example is that pig food cost represents 73.25% of the total productive cost [87], however, only 33% of people measured it, and 99% consider it important. In this way, this research permits to consolidate at least the financial perspective for pig farmers, for instance, if they want to measure financial indexes, it could be measured by five key indexes: B3-Cost per kilogram produced; B6-Profit per pig or batch produced; B7-Percentage of farm profit; B5-Total monthly sales; B4-Income per kilogram produced. All of them are organized by importance.

Within the client's perspective, there is not a follow-up on customer satisfaction and their needs. Because little interest was found in knowing the meat quality produced and performing client management. If a pig farmer wants to identify its efficiency; it could be measured by two key indexes: C14-Number of effective customers and C15-Monitoring customer satisfaction (in terms of color of meat produced, amount of fat and capacity), these were identified due to its relevance for respondents.

The lack of innovation, research, and development in the processes is seen in the process perspective; for example, CSI needs to measure fattening process, and new food sources and experimentation to reduce its cost. Currently, a pig farmer breed and combine several pig breeds, and they do not register the efficiency of those decisions. However, if they want to improve their productivity, it research found that it could be raised controlling five key indexes: C12-Total fattening time per batch before sale, C9-Feed consumption per pig or per batch of pigs, C7-Number of dead born pigs; C8-Number of dead pigs before weaning; C5-Number of pigs per delivery.

The largest number of pig farms in Colombia are semi-technified, they considered most of the indicators presented in this research important, however, pig companies need to be aware in order to generate a measurement culture, decision-making with greater certainty, and technologies implementation. There, these aspects are defined such as knowledge management indexes or in BSC theories such as the **learning perspective**. This research found that learning or knowledge perspective could be considered internal or external; for instance, if a pig farm wants to measure its internal perspective, they should **measure**: D3-Employee education level, D1-Personnel turnover level, and D2-Number of trainings received by personnel per year; on the other hand, if they wants to identify external learning, they should consider at least the C16-Number of complaints from neighboring farms, among others which will be not included in the BSC for CSI.

In order to improve the **sustainable processes** of pig companies, they must create new sustainable business lines if they search new treatments of water, new uses for solid wastes, and corral washing. This research includes in the BSC theories two important indexes, as a new sustainable dimension in the BSC for CSI: C20-Solid waste management and C19. Destination of wastewater from corral washing.

BS potentializes the KM in CSI, because the indicators proposed in this article for a sustainable BSC designing are taken from the literature, and complemented by pig farming and fattening indexes; all of them were validated using a representative sample of Colombian pig farmers, and after these will be included in a sustainable BSC which adds to the classic perspectives of BSC, the sustainable dimension, and also there is proposed a learning perspective division between internal and external, which permits to make decisions and response to the market quickly.

References

1. Trujillo-Diaz, J., Diaz-Piraquive, F.N., Herrera, M.M., Gomez, J.: Modeling the Colombian swine supply chain from a knowledge management perspective. In: Uden, L., Ting, I.H., Corchado, J. (eds.) Knowledge Management in Organizations. KMO 2019. Communications in Computer and Information Science, vol. 1027, pp. 25–35. Springer, Cham (2019). https://doi.org/10.1007/978-3-030-21451-7_3
2. DANE. Encuesta de sacrificio de ganado (ESAG) (Departamento Administrativo Nacional de Estadística (DANE) ed.), 25 August 2018. http://www.dane.gov.co/index.php/estadisticas-por-tema/pobreza-y-condiciones-de-vida/encuesta-nacional-del-uso-del-tiempo-enut?id=131&phpMyAdmin=3om27vamm65hhkhrtgc8rrn2g4
3. Trujillo-Diaz, J., Diaz-Piraquive, F.N., Herrera, M.M., Gomez-Acero, J.: Identification of global best practices for increasing competitiveness in pig farms in the Colombian central Andean region. Ciencia y tecnología pecuaria **20**(4), 507–522 (2019)
4. Trujillo-Diaz, J., Diaz-Piraquive, F.N., Herrera, M.M., Gomez, J., Rodriguez, J.A., Sarmiento, H.R.: Design of theoretical dimensions for a knowledge management model applied to the Colombian Swine Industry. Presented at the CONIITI, Universidad Católica de Colombia, Bogota - Colombia, 2nd October 2019 (2019)
5. 3tres3. Economia - Precios del cerdo (3tres3 - Comunidad Profesional Porcina ed.), 15th May. https://www.3tres3.com/cotizaciones-de-porcino/
6. Machlup, F.: The Production and Distribution of Knowledge in the United States. Princeton University Press, Princeton (1962)
7. Bell, D.: The coming of the post-industrial society. In: The Educational Forum, vol. 40, no. 4, pp. 574–579. Taylor & Francis (1973)
8. Drucker, P.: The Age of Discontinuity: Guidelines to Our Changing Society. Routledge, Milton Park (2017)
9. Nonaka, I.: A dynamic theory of organizational knowledge creation. Organ. Sci. **5**(1), 14–37 (1994)
10. Kogut, B., Zander, U.: Knowledge of the firm, combinative capabilities, and the replication of technology. Organ. Sci. **3**(3), 383–397 (1992)
11. Grant, R.M.: Toward a knowledge-based theory of the firm. Strateg. Manag. J. **17**(S2), 109–122 (1996)
12. Nonaka, I., Takeuchi, H.: The Knowledge-Creating Company: How Japanese Companies Create the Dynamics of Innovation. Oxford University Press, Oxford (1995)
13. Davenport, T.H., Prusak, L.: Working Knowledge: How Organizations Manage What They Know. Harvard Business Press, Boston (1998)
14. Castillo, H.G.C.: El modelo de la triple hélice como un medio para la vinculación entre la universidad y empresa. Revista Nacional de administración **1**(1), 85–94 (2010)

15. Nonaka, I., Takeuchi, H.: The knowledge-creating company: how Japanese companies create the dynamics of innovation. Long Range Plan. 4(29), 592 (1996)
16. McAdam, R., McCreedy, S.: A critical review of knowledge management models. Learn. Organ. 6(3), 91–101 (1999)
17. Boisot, M.: Information and Organizations: The Manager as Anthropologist. Fontana, London (1987)
18. Nickols, F.: KM overview (2000). http://home.att.net/~discon/KM/KM_Overview_Context. htm. Accessed 18 Oct 2015
19. Wigg, K.: Knowledge management foundations (1993)
20. McElroy, M.W.: The New Knowledge Management: Complexity, Learning, and Sustainable (2003)
21. Rollett, H.: Knowledge Management: Processes and Technologies. Springer, Heidelberg (2012)
22. Bukowitz, W.R., Williams, R.L.: The Knowledge Management Fieldbook. Financial Times/Prentice Hall (2000)
23. Zack, M.H.: Managing codified knowledge. Sloan Manag. Rev. 40(4), 45–58 (1999)
24. Peng Wong, W., Yew Wong, K.: Supply chain management, knowledge management capability, and their linkages towards firm performance. Bus. Process Manag. J. 17(6), 940–964 (2011)
25. Soto, M.M.: System dynamics in the simulation of the effect of knowledge management on the supply chain of corn agroindustry (Zea mays L.). Revista Técnica de la Facultad de Ingeniería Universidad del Zulia 36(1) (2013)
26. Kant, R., Singh, M.: An integrative framework of knowledge management enabled supply chain management. In: 2008 IEEE International Conference on Industrial Engineering and Engineering Management, pp. 53–57. IEEE (2008)
27. Hoffmann, V.E., Lopes, G.S.C., Medeiros, J.J.: Knowledge transfer among the small businesses of a Brazilian cluster. J. Bus. Res. 67(5), 856–864 (2014)
28. da Silva, E.F., Mafra Pereira, F.C., Guimaraes Rodrigues, E.H.: Creation of organizational knowledge on the basis Von Krogh, Nonaka and Ichijo capacitors: a case study in the grange DF Pork Company. Int. J. Innov. 4(2), 155–172 (2016)
29. AHDB and BPEX. Profitability in the Pig Supply Chain. https://pork.ahdb.org.uk/media/ 2338/profitability_in_the_pig_supply_chain.pdf
30. Duflot, B., Roussillon, M., Rieu, M.: A competitiveness index for national pork chains in Europe: for the years 2010, 2011 and 2012. Cahiers de l'IFIP 1(1), 29–45 (2014)
31. Nogueira, M., Greis, N.: An answer set programming solution for supply chain traceability. In: Fred, A., Dietz, J.L.G., Liu, K., Filipe, J. (eds.) IC3K 2012. CCIS, vol. 415, pp. 211–227. Springer, Heidelberg (2013). https://doi.org/10.1007/978-3-642-54105-6_14
32. Kurtz, D.J., Soriano Sierra, E.J., Varvakis, G.: Fluxo de conhecimento interorganizacional: estudo de múltiplos casos em uma cadeia produtiva. Espacios 34(4), 9 (2013). (in Portuguese)
33. Wognum, N., Wever, M.: Quality and co-ordination in supply chains - the case of pork chains in the Netherlands. In: IEEE International Technology Management Conference, ICE 2008. Institute of Electrical and Electronics Engineers Inc. (2016)
34. Chiran, A., Gîndu, E., Ungureanu, G., Drobotă, B., Jităreanu, A.F.: Designing an informatics' system regarding the technical-economic and financial analysis of integrated agro alimentary units. In: 15th International Business Information Management Association Conference, IBIMA 2010, Cairo, vol. 2, pp. 1160–1165. International Business Information Management Association, IBIMA (2010)
35. Paranhos da Costa, M.J.R., Huertas, S.M., Gallo, C., Dalla Costa, O.A.: Strategies to promote farm animal welfare in Latin America and their effects on carcass and meat quality traits. Meat Sci. 92(3), 221–226 (2012). (in English)

36. Zhang, K., Chai, Y., Weng, D., Zhai, R.: Analysis and design of information traceability system for pork production supply chain. Nongye Gongcheng Xuebao/Trans. Chin. Soc. Agric. Eng. **26**(4), 332–339 (2010). (in Chinese)
37. Arboníes, Á.L., Azúa, S.: Cómo evitar la miopía en la gestión del conocimiento. Díaz de Santos (2001)
38. Marshall, A.: Principles of Economics. Macmillan, London (1920)
39. Nonaka, I.: The Knowledge-Creating Company. Harvard Business Review Press, Boston (2008)
40. Hedlund, G.: A model of knowledge management and the N-form corporation. Strateg. Manag. J. **15**(S2), 73–90 (1994)
41. Johnston, R., Blumentritt, R.: Knowledge moves to center stage. Sci. Commun. **20**(1), 99–105 (1998)
42. Swan, J., Newell, S.: Linking knowledge management and innovation. In: ECIS 2000 Proceedings, p. 173 (2000)
43. Meyer, M., Zack, M.: The design and implementation of information products. Sloan Manag. Rev. **37**(3), 43–59 (1996)
44. Jordan, J., Jones, P.: Assessing your company's knowledge management style. Long Range Plan. **30**(3), 392–398 (1997)
45. Patil, N.Y., Warkhedkar, R.M.: Knowledge management implementation in Indian automobile ancillary industries: an interpretive structural model for productivity. J. Model. Manag. **11**(3), 802–810 (2016)
46. Patil, S.K., Kant, R.: A hybrid approach based on fuzzy DEMATEL and FMCDM to predict success of knowledge management adoption in supply chain. Appl. Soft Comput. **18**, 126–135 (2014)
47. Cyrino, A.B., Parente, R., Dunlap, D., de Góes, B.B.: A critical assessment of Brazilian manufacturing competitiveness in foreign markets. Competitiveness Rev. Int. Bus. J. **27**(3), 253–274 (2017)
48. Wiig, K.: Knowledge Management Foundations: thinking about-how people and organizations create, represent, and use knowledge. Schema, Arlington, Texas (1993)
49. Acar, M.F., Tarim, M., Zaim, H., Zaim, S., Delen, D.: Knowledge management and ERP: complementary or contradictory? Int. J. Inf. Manag. **37**(6), 703–712 (2017)
50. Irani, Z., Sharif, A., Kamal, M.M., Love, P.E.: Visualising a knowledge mapping of information systems investment evaluation. Expert Syst. Appl. **41**(1), 105–125 (2014)
51. Bagheri, M.M.: Investigate the effect of information systems on supply chains with mediation of knowledge management in Iran Khodro Company. Int. Bus. Manag. **10**(18), 4153–4162 (2016)
52. Li, Y., Liu, Y., Liu, H.: Co-opetition, distributor's entrepreneurial orientation and manufacturer's knowledge acquisition: evidence from China. J. Oper. Manag. **29**(1–2), 128–142 (2011)
53. Mazzola, E., Perrone, G.: A strategic needs perspective on operations outsourcing and other inter-firm relationships. Int. J. Prod. Econ. **144**(1), 256–267 (2013)
54. Chong, A.Y.-L., Bai, R.: Predicting open IOS adoption in SMEs: an integrated SEM-neural network approach. Expert Syst. Appl. **41**(1), 221–229 (2014)
55. Chen, Y.-H., Lin, T.-P., Yen, D.C.: How to facilitate inter-organizational knowledge sharing: the impact of trust. Inf. Manag. **51**(5), 568–578 (2014)
56. Maçada, A.C.G., Costa, J.C., Oliveira, M., Curado, C.: Information management and knowledge sharing in supply chains operating in Brazil. Int. J. Automot. Technol. Manag. **13**(1), 18–35 (2013)
57. Machikita, T., Ueki, Y.: Knowledge transfer channels to Vietnam for process improvement. Manag. Decis. **51**(5), 954–972 (2013)

58. Briscoe, G., Dainty, A.R., Millett, S.: Construction supply chain partnerships: skills, knowledge and attitudinal requirements. Eur. J,. Purchasing Supply Manag. **7**(4), 243–255 (2001)
59. Choi, T.Y., Budny, J., Wank, N.: Intellectual property management: a knowledge supply chain perspective. Bus. Horiz. **47**(1), 37–44 (2004)
60. Weiss, D., Minshall, T.: Negative effects of relative proximity and absolute geography on open innovation practices in high-tech SMEs in the UK. In: 2014 IEEE International Conference on Management of Innovation and Technology (ICMIT), pp. 1–6. IEEE (2014)
61. Huang, H.-C.: Designing a knowledge-based system for strategic planning: a balanced scorecard perspective. Expert Syst. Appl. **36**(1), 209–218 (2009)
62. Lesáková, Ľ., Dubcová, K.: Knowledge and use of the balanced scorecard method in the businesses in the Slovak Republic. Procedia-Soc. Behav. Sci. **230**, 39–48 (2016)
63. Manville, G., Karakas, F., Polkinghorne, M., Petford, N.: Supporting open innovation with the use of a balanced scorecard approach: a study on deep smarts and effective knowledge transfer to SMEs. Prod. Plan. Control **30**(10–12), 842–853 (2019)
64. Moraga, J.A., Quezada, L.E., Palominos, P.I., Oddershede, A.M., Silva, H.A.: A quantitative methodology to enhance a strategy map. Int. J. Prod. Econ. **219**, 43–53 (2020)
65. Chytas, P., Glykas, M., Valiris, G.: A proactive balanced scorecard. Int. J. Inf. Manag. **31**(5), 460–468 (2011)
66. Hoque, Z., Kaplan, R.S.: The balanced scorecard: comments on balanced scorecard commentaries. J. Account. Organ. Change **8**, 539–545 (2012)
67. Casas, M., Perez, M., Rojas, J., Alvarez, J.: Strategic planning model to improve competitiveness for service industry SMEs using the balanced scorecard. In: Ahram, T., Taiar, R., Colson, S., Choplin, A. (eds.) IHIET 2019. AISC, vol. 1018, pp. 1001–1006. Springer, Cham (2020). https://doi.org/10.1007/978-3-030-25629-6_155
68. Chong, P., Ong, T., Abdullah, A., Choo, W.: Internationalisation and innovation on balanced scorecard (BSC) among Malaysian small and medium enterprises (SMEs). Manag. Sci. Lett. **9**(10), 1617–1632 (2019)
69. Kalender, Z.T., Vayvay, Ö.: The fifth pillar of the balanced scorecard: sustainability. Procedia-Soc. Behav. Sci. **235**, 76–83 (2016)
70. Hu, Y., Xiao, S., Wen, J., Li, J.: An ANP-multi-criteria-based methodology to construct maintenance networks for agricultural machinery cluster in a balanced scorecard context. Comput. Electron. Agric. **158**, 1–10 (2019)
71. Myung, J.K., An, H.-T., Lee, S.-Y.: Corporate competitiveness index of climate change: a balanced scorecard approach. Sustainability **11**(5), 1445 (2019)
72. Zeng, K., Luo, X.: The balanced scorecard in China: does it work? Bus. Horiz. **56**(5), 611–620 (2013)
73. Harvey, H.B., Sotardi, S.T.: Key performance indicators and the balanced scorecard. J. Am. Coll. Radiol. **15**(7), 1000–1001 (2018)
74. Al-Qubaisi, S.S., Ajmal, M.: Determinants of operational efficiency in the oil and gas sector: a balanced scorecards perspective. Benchmarking Int. J. **25**(9), 3357–3385 (2018)
75. Gibbons, R., Kaplan, R.S.: Formal measures in informal management: can a balanced scorecard change a culture? Am. Econ. Rev. **105**(5), 447–451 (2015)
76. Oliveira, H.C., Lima-Rodrigues, L., Craig, R.: The presence of bureaucracy in the balanced scorecard. Revista de Contabilidad-Spanish Account. Rev. **22**(2), 218–224 (2019)
77. Leksono, E.B., Suparno, S., Vanany, I.: Integration of a balanced scorecard, DEMATEL, and ANP for measuring the performance of a sustainable healthcare supply chain. Sustainability **11**(13), 3626 (2019)
78. Teniwut, Y.K.: Decision support system for increasing sustainable productivity on fishery agroindustry supply chain. In: 2013 International Conference on Advanced Computer Science and Information Systems (ICACSIS), pp. 297–302. IEEE (2013)

79. Valenzuela, L., Maturana, S.: Designing a three-dimensional performance measurement system (SMD3D) for the wine industry: a Chilean example. Agric. Syst. **142**, 112–121 (2016)
80. Hristov, I., Chirico, A., Appolloni, A.: Sustainability value creation, survival, and growth of the company: a critical perspective in the sustainability balanced scorecard (SBSC). Sustainability **11**(7), 2119 (2019)
81. Kuncová, M., Hedija, V., Fiala, R.: Firm size as a determinant of firm performance: the case of swine raising. Agris On-Line Pap. Econ. Inform. **8**(665-2016-45098), 77–89 (2016)
82. Muda, I., Erlina, I.Y., Nasution, A.A.: Performance audit and balanced scorecard perspective. Int. J. Civ. Eng. Technol. **9**(5), 1321–1333 (2018)
83. Sampieri Hernández, R., Fernandez Collado, C., del Pilar Baptista Lucio, M.: Metodología de la Investigación, 6th edn. MrGraw-Hill, México (2014)
84. Kithinji, K.R., Kanui, T.I., Ndathi, A.J., Mwobobia, R.M.: Characterization of pig production systems in Embu west sub county, Embu County, Kenya (2017)
85. Paixão, G., Esteves, A., Payan-Carreira, R.: Characterization of a non-industrial pig production system: the case of Bísaro breed. Revista Brasileira de Zootecnia **47** (2018)
86. Ieda, N., Van Bui, Q., Nguyen, N.T.D., Lapar, L., Marshall, K.: Characterization of smallholder pig breeding practices within a rural commune of North Central Vietnam. Trop. Anim. Health Prod. **47**(6), 1005–1016 (2015). https://doi.org/10.1007/s11250-015-0817-4
87. PorkColombia. Boletín - Ronda de precios # 34 (PorkColombia ed.), 28 August 2018. https://www.miporkcolombia.co/wp-content/uploads/2018/08/Semana34de2018.pdf
88. Selva, G.: Analysis of the Competitiveness of the Pork Industry in Denmark (2005)
89. Hoste, R.: International comparison of pig production costs 2015 (2017). https://library.wur.nl/WebQuery/wurpubs/fulltext/412970
90. Ménard, C.: The economics of hybrid organizations. J. Inst. Theor. Econ. JITE **160**(3), 345–376 (2004)
91. Raynaud, E., Sauvee, L., Valceschini, E.: Alignment between quality enforcement devices and governance structures in the agro-food vertical chains. J. Manag. Gov. **9**(1), 47–77 (2005)
92. Martins, F.M., Trienekens, J., Omta, O.: Differences in quality governance: the case of the Brazilian pork chain. Br. Food J. **119**(12), 2837–2850 (2017)
93. Fernández, M., Millán, G., Calvetty Ramos, M., Basso, M., Mouteira, M.C.: Efectos sobre el suelo de efluentes de producción porcina intensiva. In: XIX Jornadas de Divulgación Técnico-Científicas, VI Jornada Latinoamericana, IV Jornadas de Ciencia y Tecnología y III Reunión Transdisciplinaria en Ciencias Agropecuarias (Facultad de Ciencias Veterinarias y Facultad de Ciencias Agrarias, Universidad Nacional de Rosario) (Casilda y Zavalla, 16 y 17 de agosto de 2018) (2018)

A Practical Taxonomy of Knowledge

Remy Magnier-Watanabe[✉]

Graduate School of Business Sciences, University of Tsukuba, Tokyo, Japan
magnier-watanabe.gt@u.tsukuba.ac.jp

Abstract. Knowledge has not generated the gains in efficiency and competitive advantage promised over the past three decades. One reason lies in the existing taxonomies which remain both abstract and difficult to apply. This research examines knowledge from the perspective of economics. It discusses tacit and explicit knowledge in terms of complements, substitutes, and normal or inferior goods, and consider their elasticity of demand and of supply.

This new model offers a practical matrix based on depth and breadth of knowledge, which can be readily applied by firms in any industry. The proposed model can be used to diagnose the existing stock of knowledge, recognize shortages and the cost to fill them, and identify essential knowledge that should be protected.

Keyword: Knowledge · Taxonomy · Tacit · Explicit · Elasticity

1 Introduction

The knowledge revolution, spurred by innovations in information and communication technologies and subsequent radical changes in the global economy over the past 30 years, has granted knowledge the status of most-sought after resource [1–3].

This resource has been construed as a factor of production at times, on par with land, labor, capital, and entrepreneurship [4]. Indeed, these factors constitute the basis for the production of goods and services in the current knowledge-based economy. Without going as far as elevating knowledge to the status of the fifth factor of production, it probably belongs both to labor and entrepreneurship. Regardless of how it is pigeonholed, it has become the basis for the knowledge economy, which is "highlight[ing] the increasing importance of the informational content of goods and services, the mobilization of knowledge in the production process, the occupational trends toward professionalization, the commercialization of knowledge, and the sectoral shift from an economy based on the manufacturing of industrial goods by production workers to one based on the design of informational goods and services by knowledge workers" [5, p. 31].

Despite the recognition of the growing importance of knowledge, its properties as economic input remain unclear and its applicability uncertain. Past research has neglected to sketch out its basic economic properties (with the exception of [2]), and therefore knowledge has remained an abstract and misunderstood resource to most managers [4]. As a result, this research seeks to ascertain knowledge's economic properties and present a practical taxonomy readily usable by company executives.

© Springer Nature Switzerland AG 2021
L. Uden et al. (Eds.): KMO 2021, CCIS 1438, pp. 23–29, 2021.
https://doi.org/10.1007/978-3-030-81635-3_2

2 Knowledge

2.1 Knowledge Definition

Knowledge has been defined in several ways; in general, it has been construed as either a representation of the world or alternatively as the result of the interplay between people and reality [6]. In essence, knowledge is the building block of reality, which is itself socially constructed. For instance, Berger and Luckmann [7] define knowledge as "certainty that phenomena are real and that they possess specific characteristics" (p. 1). Knowledge is both an ingredient and a product of this constructed reality, and it is not possessed equally by every member of society.

Moreover, because some knowledge can only be acquired over a long learning process and can be intangible and difficult to share, it has come to be perceived as an important source of competitive advantage [8].

2.2 Knowledge Dimensions

When trying to decide the nature of specific knowledge, it is useful to use Baloh et al. [9]'s three contingent elements of task domain, type of knowledge, and volatility of knowledge. Task domain can be either focused or broad and refers to whether employees need to collaborate within their existing teams or beyond even outside of their institution [10]. Knowledge type is divided between informational know-what and procedural know-how; know-what is more easily transferable and is largely explicit, whereas know-how is harder to share because it is mostly tacit [11, 12]. Volatility reflects the short or long shelf life of knowledge. Some knowledge has a very distant expiration date and can therefore be re-used many times, while other spoils fast and should thus be discarded and re-created [13].

Snell et al. [14]'s classification of knowledge can also be useful to most firms. They evaluate knowledge based on how specific, unique, and strategically valuable it is to the organization. Their taxonomy divides up knowledge among that which is unique to the firm and high in strategic value (core knowledge), that which is generic to firms in the industry and of high strategic value (compulsory knowledge), that which is unique to the firm but of low strategic value (idiosyncratic knowledge), and that which is generic and of low strategic value (ancillary knowledge). However, these categories do not provide any implications about the costs associated with acquiring or protecting these types of knowledge.

3 New Dimensions of Knowledge

3.1 Tacit and Explicit Knowledge as Complements

Many have debated whether tacit or explicit knowledge are critical, and whether they are two sides of the same coin. While it is clear that they are different [11], we need to establish the nature of their relationship. In economics terms, they could be construed as substitutes, complements, or normal and inferior goods.

By definition, a substitute is a good that can be consumed in place of another good, a complement is a good that can be consumed in conjunction with another good, and an inferior good is a cheaper substitute to a normal good [15]. When demand and price for a good increase (decrease), demand and price for one of its substitute decrease (increase). When demand and price for a good increase (decrease), demand and price for one of its complements increase (decrease) as well. And when income increases (decreases), demand for an inferior good decreases (increases) [15].

The question therefore becomes whether demand and price for explicit (tacit) knowledge change when demand and price for tacit (explicit) change, and if so, in which direction, and whether, when income increases, demand for explicit or tacit knowledge change. While these questions have neither been asked, nor answered, past research suggests they are both needed as knowledge creation is an outcome of the dyadic interplay between the two [16].

We argue here that tacit and explicit knowledge are complements rather than substitutes. Pisano [10, 17] distinguished problem solving as learning-before-doing, appropriate in a situation with an established knowledge base, and learning-by-doing, suitable in a setting with little reliable knowledge. He contended that both have merits depending on the knowledge environment. It follows that tacit knowledge cannot replace explicit knowledge, or vice-versa, as each is indispensable depending on context. When the firm is seeking specific knowledge, for products or processes, it will search for either or both; however, finding one will be an addition to the other and not a replacement. For instance, knowledge about a competitor's production process can be valuable in explicit form, when captured in documents that are readily sharable for sales and marketing employees; however, related tacit knowledge from a poached engineer will be precious for the R&D department.

Tacit knowledge, such as know-how, is often perceived as more costly and more valuable since its acquisition and transfer requires more time and it is less transferable. Conversely, explicit knowledge can be thought of as less costly and less valuable for the same opposite reasons. These reasons imply that tacit knowledge is a normal good of higher value and in higher demand in good times, while explicit knowledge is an inferior good of lower value and higher demand in lean times. Indeed, their disparity in transferability makes tacit knowledge a superior source of competitive advantage.

3.2   Knowledge Breadth and Depth

The categorization of knowledge remains vague and impractical to most firms, despite the many typologies that have been put forward. Spender [18] divided knowledge based on whether it is tacit or explicit and whether it is individual or social, and proposed the four categories of conscious knowledge (explicit and individual), automatic knowledge (tacit and individual), objectified knowledge (explicit and social), and collective knowledge (implicit and social). He claimed that "collective knowledge, implicit and embedded in organizational practice is a powerful source of economic advantage", which "is context specific, shaped by the particular uncertainties and possibilities of the situation which management faced" [18, p. 362]. These categories are difficult to apply in practice, although they have improved the understanding of knowledge.

Moorthy and Pooley [19] were the first to consider knowledge in terms of its breadth and depth, albeit for technical knowledge only. They based their taxonomy on Wang and von Tunzelmann [20]'s definitions whereby breadth denotes the degree of analytical sophistication, while depth the extent of learning and search across disciplines. Their measures, tailored to assessing technical knowledge, use a firm's granted patents classes of technology. They evaluate the former by studying "the number of technology class[es]" of the patents of the firm, and the latter by examining the "degree to which a firm shuns dispersal of its knowledge, preferring instead to be more knowledgeable in a smaller number of technology classes" (p. 365).

However, their measure is ill-fitting for firms which do not routinely apply for and may be granted patents for their production of knowledge. What about companies in low-tech industries or those which do not produce patents? It is thus critical for many firms to identify practical applications of the taxonomy allowing individuals to assess their knowledge stock and needs.

We similarly conceive knowledge to have both different levels of breadth and depth on a scale from one to three, with one meaning low, two medium, and three high. Breadth denotes the domains of knowledge and whether it is constrained to a single discipline (narrow = 1) or extends over several disciplines (broad = 3). Depth refers to the complexity or sophistication of knowledge and whether it is know-what and explicit (shallow = 1) or know-how and both tacit and explicit (deep = 3). Scores of 2 specify medium dimensions in either breadth or depth. By multiplying the two dimensions, we can calculate scores from 1 (1×1) for narrow and shallow knowledge, to 9 (3×3) for broad and deep knowledge. The range of scores includes 1, 2 (1×2 and 2×1), 3 (1×3 and 3×1), 4, 6 (3×2 and 2×3), and 9. The four major quadrants cover narrow and shallow knowledge (score of 1, quadrant I), broad and shallow knowledge (score of 3, quadrant II), narrow and deep knowledge (score of 3, quadrant III), and broad and deep knowledge (score of 9, quadrant IV) (Fig. 1) [4].

Using illustrations drawn from the automobile industry, specific job titles and associated knowledge and competencies can represent each major quadrant, such as factory machine operator (I), sales representative (II), R&D worker (III), and Chief Operations Officer (IV). A higher score in the taxonomy indicates a higher cost to the firm to acquire or replace that particular knowledge; acquisition can be completed by hiring an employee with that specific knowledge, by developing and growing that particular knowledge within the firm, or by contracting out the services of a consultant or an outsourcing firm. The matrix can be used by the firm to accomplish a three-level knowledge diagnosis. First, the organization can take stock of the knowledge it possesses and classify those bits of knowledge according to their intrinsic characteristics; second, the firm can spot knowledge gaps based on needs against the previously-assessed knowledge stock, and evaluate the costs and ways associated with filling these knowledge gaps; and third, it can recognize the knowledge that is source of competitive advantage and that therefore should be protected against leakages and competitors.

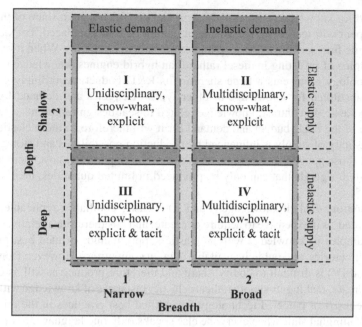

Fig. 1. Knowledge taxonomy

3.3 Knowledge Elasticity

Elasticity is a concept that estimates the relationship between a change in the quantity of a good and a change in its price. Elasticity can refer to that of demand or of supply, with the former calling for the quantity demanded and the latter the quantity supplied [15]. When the numerator exceeds the denominator, the resulting ratio is higher than 1 and denotes elasticity of demand or supply; this is typical of goods that are luxury items, or that are defined narrowly, or whose price changed just recently. When the denominator exceeds the numerator, the resulting ratio is lower than 1 and denotes inelasticity of demand or supply; this is characteristic of goods that are necessities, or that are defined narrowly, or whose price changed a while ago [15].

The elasticity of demand is affected by the availability of substitutes and the share of income spent on this good. For the firm, resources are limited, and it continuously aims to achieve the greatest efficiency possible, thus making sought-after knowledge a necessity. There are few substitutes for necessities, and consequently demand is relatively inelastic. One method to make demand more elastic for certain knowledge is to narrowly define that knowledge because then substitutes will be available. For instance, let's consider the R&D department; while computer-assisted design (CAD) software knowledge is broadly defined and therefore demand for it inelastic, knowledge of specific CAD software such as AutoCAD or AutoDesk is narrowly defined and thus demand for them are more elastic since one can be substituted for another. It follows that demand for broad knowledge (II and IV) is relatively inelastic, whereas that for narrow knowledge (I and III) is relatively elastic.

Demand for knowledge critical to the firm and on which a great share of the firm's budget is spent will tend to be inelastic as it cannot be easily replaced. Let's consider an automobile firm seeking to develop higher gas mileage vehicles. When it makes the strategic choice of investing in diesel rather than hybrid engines, knowledge related to diesel technology represents a large share of its R&D budget; accordingly, it cannot easily be substituted for knowledge of other types of engines and demand for it will be rather inelastic. In contrast, knowledge related to seat design represents a relatively lower share of the R&D budget and demand for it will therefore be more elastic.

The elasticity of supply is influenced by production possibilities and storage possibilities. For those goods that can be made at a constant opportunity cost, their supply is elastic, while for goods that can only be produced in limited quantities, their supply is inelastic [15].

By definition, explicit knowledge (I and II) is easily codifiable, replicable, shared, and transmitted, is inexpensive to acquire or create, and has therefore a relatively elastic supply. Examples of knowledge with an elastic supply include printed best practices, employee directories, and publicly available data on competitors. However, tacit knowledge (III and IV) is difficult to codify, share and therefore produce at will, is costly to acquire or create, making its supply rather inelastic. Instances of knowledge with inelastic supply consist of patented technology, uncodified best practices in the mind of an expert, and bilingual staff when everyone else speaks only one language.

Whether knowledge has an elastic supply also depends on whether it can be easily stored. Goods that can be stored are deemed to have an elastic supply, while those that cannot have an inelastic supply. Explicit knowledge can effortlessly be stored and thus has an elastic supply, while tacit knowledge is challenging to codify and store, and hence has an inelastic supply. This is echoed by Spender [18], who contained that collective firm-specific knowledge, which is both tacit and social, is "perishable" and worthless outside the firm boundary. That type of knowledge is hard to codify and transfer (III and IV), with an inelastic supply.

The scores calculated in the matrix by multiplying a particular knowledge's breadth and depth, ranging from 1 to 9, can provide a cost estimate for acquiring, replacing or protecting it.

4   Conclusion

Knowledge can only be a source of competitive advantage if it is properly valued. However, the assessment of knowledge is sometimes neglected and often overlooked. Drucker [21] famously stated that "only what gets measured, gets managed", highlighting the need to assess knowledge before even considering drawing any benefits from it.

While existing typologies have helped technology firms for instance, they have been impractical or unusable for most companies such as those operating in the service industry. The lens of economics is suitable because it helps clarify the characteristics of knowledge and allows practitioners to evaluate their needs for specific knowledge. We first established that tacit and explicit knowledge are complements instead of substitutes. Second, the taxonomy of knowledge according to its depth and breadth and elasticity of supply and demand allows firms to rapidly and accurately take stock of their knowledge and unmet needs, while also considering its cost. The proposed model can be used to diagnose the existing stock of knowledge, recognize shortages and the cost to fill them, and identify essential knowledge that should be protected.

References

1. Drucker, P.F.: Post-Capitalist Society. Harper Business, New York (1993)
2. Chichilnisky, G.: The knowledge revolution. J. Int. Trade Econ. Dev. **7**(1), 39–54 (1998)
3. Davenport, T.H., Prusak, L.: Working Knowledge: How Organizations Manage What They Know. Harvard Business School Press, Boston (1998)
4. Magnier-Watanabe, R.: Recognizing knowledge as economic factor: a typology. In: 2015 Portland International Conference on Management of Engineering and Technology (PICMET), pp. 1279–1286. IEEE (2015)
5. Kerr, A., Riain, S.O.S.Ó.: Knowledge economy. In: International Encyclopedia of Human Geography, pp. 31–36 (2009)
6. Von Krogh, G.: Care in knowledge creation. Calif. Manag. Rev. **40**(3), 133–153 (1998)
7. Berger, P.L., Luckmann, T.: The Social Construction of Reality: A Treatise in the Sociology of Knowledge. Anchor Books, New York (1966)
8. Teece, D.J.: Capturing value from knowledge assets: the new economy, markets for know-how, and intangible assets. Calif. Manag. Rev. **40**(3), 55–79 (1998)
9. Baloh, P., Desouza, K.C., Hackney, R.: Contextualizing organizational interventions of knowledge management systems: a design science perspective. J. Am. Soc. Inform. Sci. Technol. **63**(5), 948–966 (2012)
10. Pisano, G.P.: Knowledge, integration, and the locus of learning—an empirical—analysis of process-development. Strateg. Manag. J. **15**(S1), 85–100 (1994)
11. Polanyi, M.: Tacit Dimension. Peter Smith, Gloucester (1966)
12. Kogut, B., Zander, U.: Knowledge of the firm, combinative capabilities, and the replication of technology. Organ. Sci. **3**(3), 383–397 (1992)
13. Goodhue, D.L.: Understanding user evaluations of information systems. Manag. Sci. **41**(12), 1827–1844 (1995)
14. Snell, S.A., Lepak, D.P., Youndt, M.A.: Managing the architecture of intellectual capital: implications for strategic human resource management. In: Ferris, G.R. (ed.) Research in Personnel and Human Resources Management, vol. 4, pp. 175–193 (1999)
15. Bade, R., Parkin, M.: Essential Foundations of Economics, 6th edn. Prentice Hall, Upper Saddle River (2013)
16. Nonaka, I., Takeuchi, H.: The Knowledge-Creating Company: How Japanese Companies Create the Dynamics of Innovation. Oxford University Press, New York (1995)
17. Pisano, G.P.: Learning-before-doing in the development of new process technology. Res. Policy **25**(7), 1097–1119 (1996)
18. Spender, J.-C.: Organizational knowledge, collective practice and Penrose rents. Int. Bus. Rev. **3**(4), 353–367 (1994)
19. Moorthy, S., Polley, D.E.: Technological knowledge breadth and depth: performance impacts. J. Knowl. Manag. **14**(3), 359–377 (2010)
20. Wang, Q., von Tunzelmann, N.: Complexity and the functions of the firm: breadth and depth. Res. Policy **29**(7–8), 805–818 (2000)
21. Drucker, P.F.: The Practice of Management. Routledge, London (2007)

Democratic Production and Mobilization of Knowledge in Colombia

Yasser de Jesús Muriel-Perea[1](✉) (iD), Astrid Tibocha-Niño[1](✉) (iD), and Flor Nancy Díaz-Piraquive[2](✉) (iD)

[1] Universidad Santo Tomas, Bogotá, Colombia
yassermuriel@ustadistancia.edu.co,
astridtibocha@usantotomas.edu.co
[2] Universidad Catolica de Colombia, Bogotá, Colombia
fndiaz@ucatolica.edu.co

Abstract. Knowledge is important to the extent it is used. This knowledge use assumes that people know about findings resulting from the investigations that generate it. Production and mobilization of knowledge are not new, nevertheless, such production and mobilization have occurred in developed countries from works and products research. In Colombia, in accordance with the Ministry of Science, Technology and Innovation, 5.772 groups of investigation are recognized by different institutions, and 16.799 researchers. The purpose of this article is to determine what are the means used by researchers in Colombia, to disseminate the results of their investigations. The methodology incorporates primary data, through a validated instrument by experts. Those results confirm that Colombian researchers still use traditional means to spread out such results. Very few of them use the emerging Information and Communication Technology for that purpose. Thus, an opportunity emerges for Researchers regarding the use of ICT in knowledge mobilization.

Keywords: Knowledge adoption · Knowledge Mobilization - KMb · Knowledge production · Knowledge management · ScienTI Colombia

1 Introduction

Today's society of knowledge, should produce, circulate and share the necessary knowledge to leverage human development [1]. Therefore, besides production, a knowledge mobilization is necessary, which is understood as a "set of processes that help to take the results of investigations to society, as well as to bring new ideas to the research world" [2]. "Mobilization of knowledge is given through a social and interactive process, between two or more different groups – researchers, policy makers, teachers, intermediaries and community members" [3]. Knowledge is a public good and "a society of knowledge must guarantee the shared use of knowledge" [1].

The impacts of research results depend on appropriation made by society of those results, and for that, it is necessary that they be known by the different audiences with

L. Uden et al. (Eds.): KMO 2021, CCIS 1438, pp. 30–40, 2021.
https://doi.org/10.1007/978-3-030-81635-3_3

general or specific interests. True value of knowledge comes when it is used [4], and its use is preceded by mobilization.

According to Gibbons, there are two modes of knowledge production. Mode 1, where production and its use occur in different moments, and mode 2, where production and its use go together [5].

Everybody, with no exception, requires the utilization of knowledge, for personal development as well as for society's development. However, production and mobilization of knowledge are concentrated in the northern countries. Not all of them have a democratic access to production, mobilization and use of knowledge.

This analysis conducted in Colombia, answers the following questions: ¿Who generates and has the information and knowledge? ¿How is it valued? ¿How is knowledge disseminated and distributed?

The article is structured as follows: Sects. 2 and 3 describe the concept of mobilization of knowledge, and a general description of the investigation system in Colombia; Sect. 4 analyzes the generation and knowledge possession; Sect. 5 defines the methodology of investigation and the design of the instrument; Sect. 6 shows and analyzes the results of investigation h; Sect. 7 includes discussion about the investigation; Sect. 8 defines proposed route for improvement, focused to researchers and institutions. Finally, Sect. 9 presents the conclusions and proposed future work.

2 Knowledge Mobilization

Knowledge Mobilization is known as a "set of processes that help to take the research results to society, as well as to bring new ideas to the research world" [2], that is to say, it is a two way means, from researchers to knowledge users and vice-versa. With the aim of setting the basis and give context to investigation, it is convenient to define the main concepts associated to the topic.

Mode 1 of Knowledge Production: According to Gibbons [5], in mode 1, is the production mainly given in academic environments – whose use occurs at different times. This method of knowledge production is usually based on a discipline, and the main interest is its production instead of its use.

Mode 2 of Knowledge Production: In mode 2, production and its use go together, production is transdisciplinary, and its main characteristic is that production is given not only in the academic environment, but also out of it, and by the social distribution of knowledge [5].

Adoption of Knowledge: "The process, in all its complexity, of policy makers digesting, accepting and then 'taking on board' research findings; noting their relevance, benefits or future potential" [6].

Policy Makers: Refer to people or organizations, policy makers, in the Colombian instance, they are represented by the National and Territorial Government, and congressmen, who define policies and decide, if, they consider as input the results of investigations.

3   National Science System, Technology and Innovation

In Colombia, In accordance with most recent call (announcement), for recognition and measuring of research groups, technological or innovation development, and for the recognition of researchers, from the National System of Science, Technology and Innovation - SNCTel, 833 out of 2018, conducted by Colciencias - today Ministry of Science, Technology and Innovation - 8.070 investigation groups were analyzed, and 84.316 research resumes, from which 5.772 and 16.799, research groups and researchers were recognized, respectively [7]. Following is a description of the classification of research groups resulting from the call.

3.1   Distribution of Research Groups

Distribution of groups, organized from the highest to the lowest category was as follows: Groups A1: 717, Groups A: 1.203, Groupss B: 1.285, Groups C: 2.328 and recognized – that did not reach classification – 419.

3.2   Researchers Classification

In call 833 of year 2018, 84.316 resumes were analysed, and 16.799 researchers were recognized, distributed from the highest to the lowest category as follows: Senior: 2.437, Associated: 4.349, Junior: 9.921, Emeritus: 56.

4   Generation and Possession of Information and Knowledge

Information, no doubt, is necessary for the generation of knowledge, but it is not enough. "Information will continue to be just an undifferentiated data mass, until all people of the world enjoy equal opportunities, in the educational environment to treat available information with discernment and critical spirit" [1]. Now, the information is presented in large quantities and, in multiple places. This is due, in great measure, to the technology boom of information, and communications – TIC. Today, the percentage of internet access is of about 58.8% [8], while on 2005 it was of 11%. Regarding the generation sources of knowledge, and considering mode 2, the Gibbons production sources, today they are different than what they used to be in the past, for now they are multiple and heterogeneous, such as: researcher, academic institutions, research networks, research centers, research groups and corporations, and alliances between researchers, policy makers and teachers, etc. Nevertheless, if origin countries are analyzed, these sources are, mostly, established in the northern countries. In Latin-America, the low capacity for production and the spread of knowledge are recognized, according to the bibliometric measuring of SCImago Country Rankings, production of Latin-America and the Caribbean, is equivalent only to 3.5% of world communications registered. Of the first 14 countries none corresponds to Latin-America and the Caribbean. Brazil is ranked in the 15th place but it has 11.131.792 documents less than the U.S.A., country that is ranked in the first place [9].

Ownership of information and knowledge fall, in first place, on people generating them and in the second place on countries, organizations and people that, due to their higher access to education and resources, count with a higher capability to analyze information and convert it into knowledge. Also, there is a knowledge in the hands of societies or native cultures, but not less valuable because of that.

4.1 Valuation of Knowledge

Nowadays, with dematerialization of activities of the value chain of organizations, and therefore the dematerialization of individual work, knowledge has become a valuable resource which is above the material world. Societies have understood that knowledge is a source of competitive advantage. "immaterial activities related to investigation, education and services, tend to occupy a place every time more important in the world economy" [1]. Because of the importance of non-material activities, in the GDP (gross domestic product) of countries, there is, every time, a largest destination of the nations spending, for non-material activities. An example to illustrate this statement is evident in Colombia, where the largest percentage of the country's budget for year 2019, was set aside for education [10].

The proportion of non-material activities of Gross Domestic Product (GDP) in the countries, is getting bigger. The proportion of Gross Domestic Product allocated to Research and Development (R+D) has been increasing in both the northern and southern countries. Nevertheless, the gap is still big. For example, Sweden and Switzerland allocate a 3.39% and 3.37% respectively, while southern countries as Argentina and Chile, allocate 0.54% and 0.35% respectively [11].

4.2 Dissemination and Distribution of Knowledge

Regarding dissemination of research results, they are made through multiple channels, such as: books, specialized magazines, television, newspapers, social networks and events. Their main advantage is the coverage, since it allows the democratization of the access. Their main disadvantage is that this is a passive communication, and the analysis shows that they are less effective for the establishment of knowledge mobilization networks, that interaction face to face [3]. Another type of channel is the personal interaction between researchers, policy makers and teachers, through the relational model of knowledge mobilization, determined by people categories, political places [12]. The main advantage is effectiveness which facilitates the set-up of long-term networks. The main disadvantage is the low coverage with respect to interest communities.

Regarding knowledge dissemination, it is necessary to recognize that there is a disconnection between academic researchers, policy makers and teachers [6]. As previously mentioned, this knowledge implementation is made mainly in the northern countries where not only is produced in a largest proportion but also, access to it is bigger.

5 Study

The purpose of this analysis is the identification of means and strategies used by researchers in Colombia, to disseminate the results of investigation and, if results were considered by the policy makers or by teachers in the classroom. In order to define the analysis universe, the total number of researchers recognized by the most recent call from the Ministry of Science, Technology and Innovation was considered. The analysis included a sample of 83 researchers from different regions and Institutions of Higher Education of the country, from different knowledge areas. This is a sample from only a small number of researchers; however, the study is relevant since it is heterogeneous because researchers are from different institutions and regions of the country, condition that provides a strongest support to research.

5.1 Research Methodology

This Study used the quantitative methodology to achieve its objective, through a validated instrument (on-line survey) by experts. The goal is to confirm the research assumption. For calculation of the sample, the probabilistic sampling, a simple random technique was used. For this purpose, and in order to make the sample representative, in a universe of 16.799 researcher in Colombia, the representative sample it would be 376. However, it was assumed that the sample of 83 researchers was representative because includes an important number of cities in the country.

5.2 Research Design

The on-line survey integrates 4 questions. The questions of survey come from, mainly, concepts about Knowledge Mobilization, Knowledge Production and previous studies, such as Studies made by Brown called The Policy – preferences model [6]. The on-line survey was sent to Colombian researchers. Each participant received a link in order to respond the survey. The on-line survey was structured as follows (see Table 1).

5.3 Research Question

The question used for this research is: what means of Knowledge Mobilization are used by Colombian Researchers?

6 Result of the Survey

Following are the survey results applied to 83 colombian researchers:

Regarding the means used for disclosure of the investigation results, 74, 65 and 50 researchers indicated that the mean used for that corresponds to magazine articles, lectures in academic environments, and book chapters, respectively. 39 researchers said that they used books, 22 open lectures, 15 workshops, and 14 face to face communication. Other means, among them social networks, newspapers, mobile applications, according to results, are used by less than 13 researchers. – see Fig. 1.

Table 1. Survey

No	Question	Answer options
1	¿What are the means you use to disseminate the results of your investigations? (multiple answer)	Magazine articles, books, book chapters, face to face communication, conferences in academic environments, open conferences to public in general, web pages, workshops, Researchgate, LinkedIn, mobile applications, Facebook, Twiters, newspapers, government contacts, others
2	¿Has any of your investigations been considered by policy makers?	Yes, No
3	¿Has any of your investigations been incoporated by practitioners in your classrooms?	Yes, No
4	Please select the key factors you consider relevant so that results are adopted by the community (multiple answer)	Effectivity of disclosure, nature of message, source credibility, involve users, access to policy makers, context adaptation, quality of evidence, Community need, Real problem solving, others

Source. Authors

As can be seen, most of researchers use traditional means to disseminate knowledge, and very few of them consider additional strategies.

Regarding the question on whether the investigation results are considered by the policy makers, 75% of people surveyed answered No, and 25% answered Yes. See Fig. 2.

The evidence shows that a great percentage of investigations carried out by researchers surveyed, are not considered by policy makers, these is to say, these research products have not been an input for decision making by policy makers.

Regarding incorporation of results by teachers in the classroom, 71% of surveyed people, answered Yes, investigation is considered. Therefore, it is understood that they are used in teaching activities used or, possibly, in curricular designs. 29% of surveyed people answered No – see Fig. 3.

This study shows that results of investigations made by surveyed people are, mostly considered by teachers.

Regarding key factors required for the research results to be adopted by community [6], 54 surveyed people answered that the main factor is the adaptation to the context. 51 researchers considered that most important of all, will be the effectivity of disclosure. 44 said that the most important thing is to involve users and source credibility, 41, quality of evidence, and 35 access to policy makers. The other factors were less valued. – see Fig. 4.

Select factors you consider to be key so that results of researchers are adopted by the community:

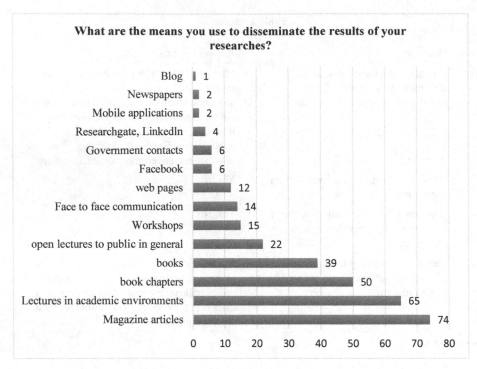

Fig. 1. Means of knowledge dissemination. Source: Authors

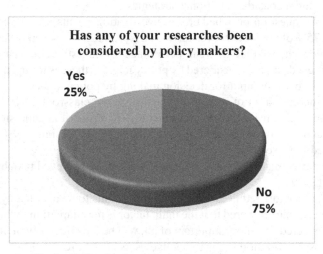

Fig. 2. Utilization by policy makers. Source: Authors.

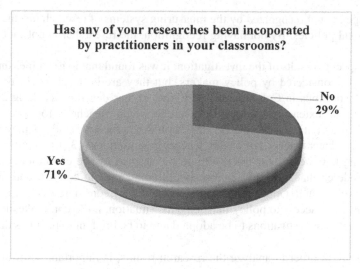

Fig. 3. Utilization by practitioners. Source: Authors

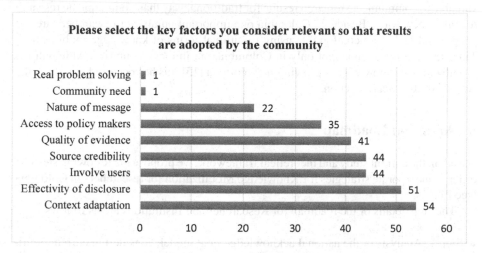

Fig. 4. Key factors. Source: Authors

7 Discussion (Argumentation)

The study or analysis reveals that most of researchers use traditional means to disseminate the results of their investigations. The main means used is magazine articles. This
mechanism, although it is true, as confirmed by work, is widely used, in general its main
audience corresponds to researchers themselves. This situation makes it difficult for
knowledge to be democratic, and to be adopted by community. Knowledge remains in
the environment where it is produced, the researcher's environment. It is evident that ICT
Are not used for knowledge dissemination, probably, because these dissemination spaces

of knowledge are not recognized by the measuring systems of research production, nor by institutional policies. By not having recognition, the researcher is not motivated to use it.

With respect to results of the investigation, it was found that in great measure, those results are not considered by policy makers, but they are by teachers. In the Higher Education Institutions in Colombia, usually, the teacher develops teaching activities, investigation and extension, therefore, researchers being teachers, for sure use their results in their activities. Nevertheless, that would be object of study if they are used only by the producer teacher or by large teacher communities [13, 14].

Regarding key factors, for the results to be adopted by the community, surveyed people considered that the investigation should be adapted to context, and that users should be involved in it. Opposite to what is thought, they considered as less important, the relationship or access to policy makers. This situation, no doubt, makes it difficult for the findings of investigations to be adopted and to be brought to people's day to day activities.

In addition, in order to analyze the research results, is important be aware of this question: ¿Why does the researchers communicate results of research in traditional way? the answer probably is due to the fact that the academic community considers more valuable to communicate research results for traditional way than communicate research results in new ways. Beside, in Colombia one important number of researchers are old people and feel more comfortable using traditional forms of knowledge mobilization. This situation is common, not only in Colombia, but in many countries. Although the mobilization of knowledge is growing in Colombia [15] this has occurred mainly in the type of study-research-action.

8 Adoption Roadmap

Based on the current study and theoretical framework, we propose the following steps, in order to incorporate strategies for Knowledge Mobilization for researchers in Colombia (see Fig. 5).

The step details of the roadmap for Researcher and Institutions are as follows:

- Step 1: Analysis of the national acknowledgement model, considering current political, economic, social, technological, ecological and legal environmental conditions.
- Step 2: Updating of the model, to take advantage of current environmental conditions.
- Step 3: Define guidelines for Higher Education Institutions, to promote and acknowledge the knowledge dissemination through different means.
- Step 4: Researchers training in topics such as ICT, so that they take advantage of this.
- Step 5: Engage policy makers in research projects.
- Step 6: Engage teachers in research projects so that they bring their results to the classroom.

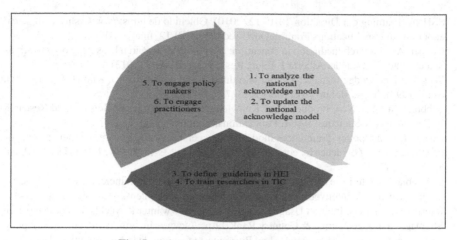

Fig. 5. Adaptation roadmap. Source: Authors

9 Conclusions and Future Works

There are today, many available tools or means to disseminate knowledge, many of them related to social networks, and information and communication technology. If only traditional means continue to be used, no doubt, democratization and use of knowledge will be affected. Use of these means are directly linked to acknowledge to be given by the scientific community to publications done through them. Unless this happens, just as shown by the analysis, researchers will tend to use traditional means.

The research done allows us to propose the following conclusions:

- Most researchers in Colombia do not use new technologies to disseminate their research results.
- A high percentage of investigations in Colombia is not used by policy makers.
- In Colombia, teachers, much more than policy makers, incorporate results of investigations to the classroom.
- The core factor, considered by researchers in Colombia, so that the results of investigations are adopted by the community, is that such results are adapted to context.
- Emerging information and communication technologies represent an opportunity to achieve a greater dissemination of knowledge.
- Social networks, currently, Facebook is one of the most important media used by researchers for disseminating knowledge the researches results.
- Future work needed to confirm and reinforce project conclusions. In the future, it is necessary to expand the study to more researchers in Colombia. In this study it was a limitation since it was conducted with a sample of only 83 researchers in Colombia.

References

1. UNESCO. Hacia las Sociedades del Conocimiento (2005). Obtenido de http://www.lacult.unesco.org/docc/2005_hacia_las_soc_conocimiento.pdf

2. SSHRC. Framing our Direction 2010–12 (2010). Obtenido de https://www.sshrc-crsh.gc.ca/about-au_sujet/publications/FramingOurDirection_2010-12_final_e.pdf
3. Cooper, A.: Research mediation in education: a typology of research brokering organizations that exist across Canada. Alberta J. Educ. Res. **59**(2), 181–207 (2013)
4. Wiig, K.: Knowledge management: an introduction and perspective. J. Knowl. Manag. **1**(1), 6–14 (1997). https://doi.org/10.1108/13673279710800682
5. Gibbons, M.: The New Production of Knowledge: The Dynamics of Science and Research in Contemporary Societies. SAGE Publications, London (1994)
6. Brown, C.: The 'policy-preferences model': a new perspective on how researchers can facilitate the take-up of evidence by educational policy makers. Evid. Policy: J. Res. Debate Pract. **8**, 455–472 (2012)
7. Colombia, Ministerio de Ciencia, Tecnología e Innovación. https://minciencias.gov.co/convocatorias/investigacion/convocatoria-nacional-para-el-reconocimiento-y-medicion-grupos-0
8. Internet World Stats. Internet Usage Statistics. https://www.internetworldstats.com/stats.htm
9. SCImago. Scimago Journal & Country Rank. https://www.scimagojr.com/countryrank.php
10. Colombia, Ministerio de Hacienda. Ley Presupuesto General de la Nación. https://www.minhacienda.gov.co/webcenter/ShowProperty?nodeId=%2FConexionContent%2FWCC_CLUSTER-065977%2F%2FidcPrimaryFile&revision=latestreleased
11. OECD. Key STI Statistics. https://www.oecd.org/innovation/inno/stistatistics.htm
12. Ng-A-Fook, N., Kane, R., Butler, J., Glithero, L., Forte, R.: Brokering knowledge mobilization networks: policy reforms, partnerships, and teacher education. Educ. Policy Anal. Arch. **23**, 122 (2015)
13. Moreno-Monsalve, N.A., Diez-Silva, M., Diaz-Piraquive, F.N., Pérez-Uribe, R.I.: Handbook of Research on Project Management Strategies and Tools for Organizational Success, pp. 1–400. IGI Global, Hershey (2020). https://doi.org/10.4018/978-1-7998-1934-9
14. López-Sevillano, A.M., Díaz-Piraquive, F.N., Crespo, R.G.: Trends in management of TI projects and CEO competence. In: Handbook of Research on Project Management Strategies and Tools for Organizational Success, pp. 19–48. IGI Global (2020). https://doi.org/10.4018/978-1-7998-1934-9.ch002. Accessed 28 Jan 2020
15. Institute for Knowledge Mobilization. Growing Knowledge Mobilization Practice in Colombia. http://www.knowledgemobilization.net/growing-knowledge-mobilization-practice-colombia/

Towards a Knowledge Operationalisation Model for Service Learning in Community Projects in Higher Education

Hanlie Smuts[1]([✉]) [ID], Martina Jordaan[1] [ID], and Corlia Smuts[2]

[1] Department of Informatics, University of Pretoria, Pretoria, South Africa
{hanlie.smuts,martina.jordaan}@up.ac.za
[2] Department of Humanities Education, University of Pretoria, Pretoria, South Africa
U19264217@tuks.co.za

Abstract. Service-learning conjoins academic study with community service and provides a richer, more practical experience for students, while benefitting the community. Students are required to transform their prior knowledge or generate new knowledge through experience into competencies and operational know-how. However, current research indicates concerns such as transfer of homogenous, theoretical-based knowledge only and a low adoption of project-based learning activities. Therefore, the aim of this study was to design a knowledge operationalisation model for service learning in community projects at a higher education institution (HEI). We applied the model in a service-learning module from an HEI using the elements of the model as guide to identify knowledge operationalisation mechanisms. By using the knowledge operationalisation model, service learning may support the effective transformation of knowledge that students can access and apply.

Keywords: Knowledge management · Service learning · Knowledge operationalisation · Knowledge in education

1 Introduction

Educational programmes in higher education institutions (HEI's) that connect a student's real life with prior knowledge, has the prospective to create meaningful learning milieus in which students could develop their creativity, problem solving and innovation skills [1]. One opportunity that combines a focus on curriculum outcomes, real-world engagement and high-impact learning, is HEI facilitated service learning, community projects (CPs) [2, 3]. CPs combine academic study with community service, focusing on fostering meaningful outcomes for communities while achieving academic goals for students [4, 5]. In addition, service-learning is regarded as a high-impact practice that improves student engagement [3, 6]. The aim of service-learning design in an HEI, is to ensure that academic course content and experiential learning create knowledge that students can access and apply in new situations [7]. Researchers established that service-learning and community-based experiences provide a rich context for learning

© Springer Nature Switzerland AG 2021
L. Uden et al. (Eds.): KMO 2021, CCIS 1438, pp. 41–53, 2021.
https://doi.org/10.1007/978-3-030-81635-3_4

[8] and that prior knowledge is reframed into new understanding through reflection and active experimentation [9, 10]. Therefore, service-learning solutions should enable the acquisition of abilities such as active engagement, problem analysis, action orientation and reflection on the entire service-learning experience [7].

However, scholars have identified several difficulties regarding academic service-learning programmes such as; the transfer of homogenous, theoretical-based knowledge only, a lack of academic development measurement, a low adoption of deeper learning approaches such as project-based learning activities, and limited examination of the impact of reflection in service-learning programmes [4, 5, 8, 11]. Therefore, the primary research question that this study aims to address through the design of a model is: "*How can knowledge be operationalised for service learning in community projects in Higher Education?*". The aim of such a model is to ensure that the service learning module effectively transforms knowledge and generates new knowledge through experience into competencies and operational know-how. In addition, such a model enables the measurement of how successfully the module outcomes were met or alternatively, identify module optimisation opportunities.

The paper is structured as follows: the background in Sect. 2 provides an overview of the essence of knowledge, Bloom's taxonomy of learning and knowledge conversion and education. Section 3 presents the research approach and the design of the knowledge operationalisation model (KOM) is shown in Sect. 4. In Sect. 5 we complete a mapping of a CP in higher education to the KOM for education in order to illustrate the proposed model's suitability for application. We summarise the findings and conclude in Sect. 6.

2   Background

Service-learning addresses the theory and practical application of teaching and learning through mechanisms, such; as community and volunteer service projects, work-based learning, field studies and internship programmes [12, 13]. Community engagement is a complex, multi-faceted process that involves relationships in-, for- and with communities [1, 13] and service-learning, in this context, is "an educational methodology that combines community-based experiences with explicit academic learning objectives and deliberate reflection" [6: 1]. The success of service-learning modules in HEIs depends on numerous aspects and interrelationships as these institutions consider module design, implementation and assessment while engaging the community [6, 14]. Some of these factors include the HEI context, the student group involved, the community involved, and the desired learning outcomes [13].

In the following sections we consider the nature of knowledge, as well as Bloom's taxonomy of learning and knowledge conversion in education.

2.1   Knowledge and Student Learning

Polanyi [15] was the first to articulate the concept of two different, mutually exclusive, dimensions of knowledge, namely tacit knowledge and explicit knowledge [15: 601]. *Explicit knowledge* refers to knowledge that has been articulated and formally recorded in handbooks, document databases, program code, manuals and knowledge bases [16].

Implicit knowledge, which is far less tangible than explicit knowledge, is knowledge in a person's internal cognition and refers to deeply embedded knowledge [17]. *Tacit* knowledge refers to implicit knowledge that is difficult to articulate, reproduce or share and includes norms, values and relationships. In this context, the knowing is in the doing [18]. Therefore, learning of a procedural skill may access an explicit description, while knowledge on how the procedure is applied in a specific environment, may only be learnt through doing or socialising, pointing to implicit knowledge [19].

Students must be able to accomplish both the explicit-to-implicit knowledge and the implicit-to-explicit knowledge transitions [20, 21]. In the seminal work on learning objectives, Bloom's taxonomy was created by Dr. Bloom and his associates [22]. The purpose of Bloom's taxonomy was to transition from merely remembering facts to higher-order thinking in education by building up from lower-level cognitive skills. Such transitioning includes the analysis and evaluation of procedures, processes, concepts and principles, rather than just recollecting facts [23].

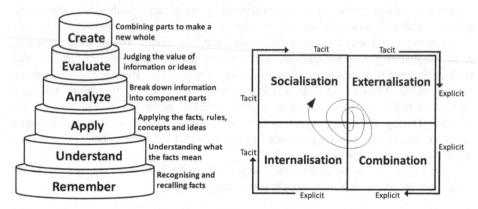

Fig. 1. Bloom's taxonomy of learning [24]   **Fig. 2.** The knowledge conversion model [25]

Through increasingly more complex and abstract mental levels, Bloom's taxonomy identified six levels within the cognitive domain as depicted in Fig. 1. The six levels, each of which is built on a foundation of the previous level, include: the recall of prior learning *(remembering),* comprehension of the meaning of facts *(understanding),* using information *(applying),* drawing connections among ideas *(analysing),* justifying the merit of information *(evaluating)* and producing new or original outputs *(creating)* [23, 24]. Design, in this context, is an evaluation process outcome as a result of analysis. Therefore, evaluation leads to the main objective of the whole process which is to create [26].

2.2 Knowledge Conversion and Education

The aim of service-learning through experience is to increase knowledge and provide a service to the larger community [27, 28]. The role of an HEI in this instance includes the development of cross-boundary knowledge and requires new approaches to knowledge generation and transmission as students must be able to apply knowledge in and outside academic structures [9, 29]. The management of knowledge in this instance is intrinsically connected to knowledge sharing between individuals, as well as the collaborative processes involved [30]. However, personal knowledge can only be created by the individual and in order to create knowledge, an individual needs to perceive a sufficient amount of information [20, 31, 32].

Nonaka and Takeuchi [33] defined a knowledge conversion model (SECI model) that is based on the fundamental assumption that knowledge is created and expanded through social interaction between tacit and explicit knowledge. The process of knowledge conversion advances through four different modes as shown in Fig. 2. *Socialisation (tacit to tacit)* is the conversion of tacit knowledge among individuals through shared information and experiences by means of observation, imitation and practice. *Externalisation (tacit to explicit)* is the process whereby tacit knowledge is articulated as explicit knowledge through collaboration with others using conceptualisation and extraction by means of document management systems, e-mails, and education-, learning- and training interventions. *Combination (explicit to explicit)* is the enrichment of the collected information by re-configuring it or enhancing it by organising, combining or categorising it so that it is more usable. *Internalisation (explicit to tacit)* enables individuals to act on information and creating their own tacit knowledge. The process is closely related to learning-by-doing through studying documents or attending training in order to re-experience to some degree what others have previously learned [25, 33]. Learning actually results from a process in which individual knowledge is transferred, enlarged and shared and is characterised as a spiral of knowledge conversion from tacit to explicit [33, 34]. During this last stage, newly formed knowledge is considered and evaluated in the context of other existing knowledge and personal experience, hence forming an individual's own unique world-view [32].

In the next section we explore the research approach followed to design the KOM for education, and how it may support education in a HEI.

3   Approach Followed to Design the Knowledge Operationalisation Model (KOM) for Service Learning in Education

Our overall objective with this paper was to design a KOM for CPs in higher education. The purpose of such a model is to support the effective transformation of knowledge and generation of new knowledge, through experience, into competencies and operational know-how. The research approach that we followed was educational design, namely; "a genre of research in which the iterative development of solutions to practical and complex educational problems also provides the context for empirical investigation, which yields theoretical understanding that can inform the work of others" [35: 7]. The outcome of educational design research is predominantly concerned with developing practical knowledge that aims to improve educational practices [35, 36] and yields theories and practical educational interventions as its outcomes [37]. Educational design research is guided by five features [35, 36]. The *theoretically orientated* feature frames the research and informs the solution through the use of scientific understanding. The *interventionist* nature of educational design research aims to bring about changes in practice through the design of transformative, real-world solutions. Educational design research entails *collaboration* among many stakeholders associated with the issue being investigated and necessitates *responsively grounded* assumptions anchored in literature, field testing and expert inputs, enabling discovery of the complex realities of teaching and learning contexts. The insights and interventions of educational design research evolve over time through multiple *iterations* of investigation, development, testing and refinement, illustrating the iterative nature of the approach [35]. With these features guiding our research, we built upon prior literature about knowledge conversion and education through a qualitative process in order to create a KOM for the effective operationalisation of knowledge into know-how. The KOM for education is grounded in educational theory and knowledge conversion theory within a real-world context of higher education.

The study was conducted at an HEI in South Africa that offers a credit-bearing, undergraduate community-based project module. In order to evaluate the KOM for HEIs designed from the literature, the CP module was mapped to the proposed KOM (Sect. 4), corroborating the comprehensive nature of the model elements.

In the next section we discuss the KOM for education in detail.

4 Design of the Knowledge Operationalisation Model in Education

The aim of this paper was to design a KOM for CPs in higher education. In order to design the KOM, we considered Bloom's taxonomy (Fig. 1) [24] and the knowledge conversion model (Fig. 2) [25]. Knowledge is continuously converted and created (spiral of knowledge) as students practice, collaborate, interact, and learn. Students firstly acquire new personal knowledge when an overview of the topic of study is observed. An incoherent and disorganised mixture of data and information is formed in the student's mind while listening, watching, reading and sensing. Once different tasks are completed and actions performed in order to organize all pieces of information and connect them with each other and the outcome, initial knowledge is formed. A student's initial knowledge is then enlarged as own opinions are formed during discussions regarding the topic of study. Lastly, the newly formed knowledge is considered and evaluated in the context of other existing knowledge and personal experience, hence forming a student's own unique world-view [32, 38].

By considering each of these steps in the context of the knowledge conversion model (Fig. 2), this process is depicted in Fig. 3 as an expanded spiral with the learning stages indicated on the spiral and the knowledge conversion stages in the centre. In stage 1, *seeking*, the knowledge operationalisation cycle is initiated with prior knowledge held by a student. During stage 2, *absorbing*, conversion of tacit knowledge among individuals through shared information and experiences takes place. Stage 3, *doing*, facilitate the articulation of tacit knowledge as explicit knowledge through collaboration with others using conceptualisation and extraction. In stage 4, *networking*, collected information is enriched by re-configuring it or enhancing it by sorting, adding, combining or categorising it so that it becomes more usable. In the final stage, stage 5 *reflecting*, the knowledge operationalisation cycle is concluded with increased understanding through the process of creating the student's own tacit knowledge [38]. As the objective of this paper is a KOM in education, we considered Bloom's taxonomy (Fig. 1) as it affords a pathway to guide the learning process. By applying the Bloom's spiral taxonomy to our proposed model, we were able to capture the complexity of learning in a more tangible manner within the context of experiential learning at a HEI [39].

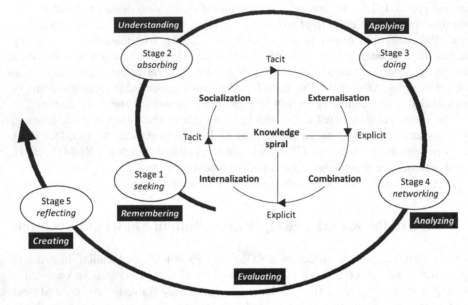

Fig. 3. Proposed knowledge operationalisation model for education (adapted from [24, 25])

The first level of the taxonomy as proposed by Bloom, refers to the *recall* of information. This retrieval of information can refer to conceptual knowledge or recollections from previous experience. Within the context of the KOM, this taxonomic level would directly relate to Stage 1: *seeking,* seeing as the remembering of information would be the catalyst to the initiation of the cycle. Recall or remembering requires a framework of prior knowledge to already be established upon which can be drawn, and said framework is not necessarily complex, dense or sophisticated, or always relevant to the learning taking place. As the spiral develops and the cycle continues, the *seeking* and recalling of knowledge, transitions into the *absorption* of knowledge. Upon the first taxonomic level of *remembering*, Bloom anchored the next level of *understanding*, which is directly related to- and dependent on the *remembering* (and by extension the *seeking*) of information within the required prior knowledge framework. The successful *absorption* of knowledge is dependent on the level, or lack of, *understanding*. During this stage of the cycle, a lack of- or failure to *understand* can cause new knowledge to be lost as it fails to be properly *absorbed* and this will also impact the ability to effectively *recall* partial, prior knowledge at the beginning of the next phase or cycle of learning. However, should the *understanding* of newly acquired knowledge be qualitative in nature, the *absorption* (and later use or expansion) thereof will be all the more successful. Whether Stage 2 was successful or not, the transition into the third stage of *doing* continues when what was *understood*, now needs to be *applied* and articulated as explicit knowledge. The stage of *doing* therefore, also correlates with the third taxonomic level of *application* as identified by Bloom. It must be stressed that the application of knowledge through doing, is not a singular occurrence, but rather numerous events with which the new knowledge acquired through Stages 1 and 2 can be applied across a span of time in a multiplicity of ways. It must also be noted that not all new knowledge will be applied/used, but only what is appropriate or applicable need be accessed. When transitioning into the fourth Stage: *networking*, of the KOM, what was *applied* previously can now closely be examined and compartmentalised. Knowledge that was not *absorbed* during Stage 2, or knowledge that was misunderstood, can also be corrected at this point. It is also within this phase of the KOM, that the related taxonomical level of *analysing* will add value to its process. In order for newly acquired knowledge that has now been *recalled, absorbed and applied*, to be re-applied or adjusted, the close analyses of its contents as described by Bloom, needs to take place. A wide range of information or related variables (whether they be tacit or explicit) should be utilised in order for the process of *analysing* to take place at optimal efficacy. We identified the fifth taxonomical level of *evaluation* as a transitional component rather than a counterpart of the fifth Stage of the KOM. Within this level, the careful evaluation of all new knowledge that has been acquired takes place. Although anchored, and dependent on, the analysis present in the previous level, the evaluation of knowledge seeks to closely inspect the results of the analysis and determine if any irrelevant, unnecessary or incomplete components need be discarded. With this process of *evaluation* acting as transitionary medium, the sixth Stage of the KOM: *reflecting*, ensues. It is at this point where the final taxonomical level of *creation* aids in the culmination of the KOM and the learning cycle. Now that learning has taken place across a variety of levels and dimensions, the creation of unique-, personalised- and tacit knowledge concludes one cycle and may initiate another and fulfil the initial requirement of prior knowledge needed in order to recall/seek as identified above.

It must be noted however, that learning is a vastly complex and personal process that manifests uniquely within each individual and context and is dependent on a myriad of variables. However, this model was constructed and integrated with Blooms' taxonomy to aid in the interpretation of the learning process of a specified situation within the context of service-/experiential learning. It must also be stressed that multiple learning processes can take place simultaneously and one can progress or digress at any point in the cycle. This approach also enabled us to design learning experiences in response to changes in the world students use information in. In this process, all students start at the same point and then progress through Bloom's taxonomy, with the *create* level providing a flexible ceiling that can stretch to meet the needs of even the most advanced understanding, while still acting as a goal for students that might be struggling. In addition, Bloom's spiralling can be used to frame a project-based learning unit [39].

In the next section we apply the model defined in Fig. 3 to a CP module at a HEI.

5   Programme Mapping to the Knowledge Operationalisation Model for Education

An HEI in South Africa presents a compulsory undergraduate module: Joint Community-based Project (JCP). The decision to create the independent course was motivated by the necessity to integrate community service and learning projects, including humanitarian engineering projects, in the curriculum of all the undergraduate programmes in addition to adhering to the University's strategic social responsibility goal [40]. The module's primary objectives include benefit realisation for a relevant section of society by exposing groups of students to real-life challenges. Students do at least 40 h of fieldwork, after which they reflect on their experiences through various assignments, including a final presentation, video and report. It is a macro community engagement course due to the substantial number of enrolled students and projects. Since 2011, more than 1600 students have registered for the course annually, with an average completion rate of 95%. Generally, the students work in 500 groups (4–5 students per group) each year to help more than 370 different community partners. A small budget of ZAR400 is awarded per student and students are allowed to raise additional funds that are required to complete their project. A profile of the 2018 and 2019 service learning projects and community partners are shared in Tables 1 and 2 respectively.

In 2018 more than half of the students (63%) delivered building, renovation and maintenance projects and this increased to 66% in 2019. Skills development and career related initiatives are a priority in SA and in 2018 28% of projects focused on educational resources, career guidance, computer training, skills development, etc., while 27% of projects contributed to this focus area in 2019. A second output from the analysis of the reports, was to apply the KOM and map the JCP programme to the proposed stages as shown in Table 3. Table 3 presents an overview of the stages of our proposed model and for each model element, we provide a brief description as well as the knowledge operationalisation mechanisms that the JCP programme utilises. There is a good spread of mechanisms across all the stages of knowledge operationalisation and the JCP module design is well positioned to achieve the learning outcomes of a service learning programme.

Table 1. Project types

Project types	2018	2019
Building and renovation	59%	62%
Maintenance	4%	4%
Educational resources	1%	5%
Career guidance	7%	4%
Computer repairing	3%	2%
Computer training	3%	6%
Mathematics and Science	12%	5%
Inventory lists	3%	2%
Mentoring	2%	2%
Skills development	3%	5%
Adjudication	1%	1%
Website/Apps/Marketing material	2%	2%
	100%	100%

Table 2. Community partner type

Community partners	2018	2019
Animal sanctuaries/Zoo's	15%	18%
Libraries	1%	0%
Learners with special educational needs schools	4%	3%
Museums	3%	9%
NGOs	25%	11%
Old age homes	2%	1%
Pre-schools	10%	19%
Primary schools	7%	6%
Secondary Schools	22%	10%
Universities	5%	13%
Nature reserves	0%	2%
Children's Homes	2%	3%
Government	3%	3%
	100%	100%

In addition to the knowledge operationalisation mechanisms map presented in Table 3, we analysed 411 reflection reports of the class of 2018 and 442 reflection reports from the class of 2019 in order to establish if increased learning took place (difference between stages 1 and 5 of the proposed model). A summary of increased knowledge elements from the reflection reports is depicted in Table 4.

In 2018 the "other" category included painting skills, financial management, self-confidence, listening skills and problem solving. In 2019 the "other" category included painting skills, problem solving, patience and humility.

Based on this mapping and evaluation of the KOM for CPs in a HEI, we believe that the model provides good coverage of considerations for the effective transformation of knowledge, as well as the generation of new knowledge, into operational competencies and know-how. In addition, Table 3 presents examples of the application of the proposed KOM that may be referenced for service learning module design in order to ensure that increased understanding, learning and knowledge are achieved.

Table 3. Service learning module operationalisation mechanisms

Model component and description	Knowledge operationalisation mechanism	
Stage 1 seeking: Initiate knowledge operationalisation cycle with prior knowledge	• Module description	• Service learning module enrolment
Stage 2 absorbing: Conversion of tacit knowledge among individuals through shared information and experiences	• Module study guide • Face-to-face briefing • Project guidelines document • Security guidelines document	• Learner management system content portal • Community project list • Project scoping and motivation document
Stage 3 doing: Tacit knowledge is articulated as explicit knowledge through collaboration with others using conceptualisation and extraction	• Community partner technical guidance • Community partner mentorship • Alumni mentorship • Alumni projector leader guidance • Project solution brainstorming	• Project meetings • Budget management report • Project progress report • Experiential learning • Project outcome measurement • Project-based learning
Stage 4 networking: Enrichment of the collected information by re-configuring it or enhancing it by sorting, adding, combining or categorising it so that it is more usable	• YouTube video production and upload • Facebook page content update	• Wiki update • Lessons learnt report • Community partner evaluation
Stage 5 reflecting: Complete knowledge operationalisation cycle with increased understanding through process of creating their own tacit knowledge	• Individual reflection report Student module questionnaire	• Student increased knowledge

Table 4. Increased knowledge extracted from 2018 and 2019 student reflection reports

	2018	2019
Leadership	51.2%	60.2%
Project management	63.0%	74.3%
Time management	58.3%	73.5%
Group work/Team work	78.7%	85.4%
Building and renovation skills	50.0%	51.8%
Communication and interpersonal skills	61.8%	71.2%
Working with people from diverse backgrounds and cultures	41.7%	48.2%
Creative thinking	49.6%	54.9%
Computer related skills	16.9%	7.1%
Internet related skills	7.9%	7.1%
Other	5.1%	2.2%

Note: students could indicate more than one learning point

6   Conclusion

Research established that service-learning programmes in higher education provide more practical experience for students while providing benefits for the community. Furthermore, from an HEI perspective, a service-learning module must achieve certain learning outcomes, and classroom knowledge must be turned into practical knowledge and expertise. However, scholars highlighted concerns such as transfer of theoretical knowledge only, low adoption of deeper learning activities and limited consideration of the impact of reflection in service-learning programmes. Therefore, the aim of this study was to design a KOM for service learning in community projects at an HEI. In this study, we developed the model through an education design research process by considering Bloom's taxonomy, knowledge conversion, and learning processes in education. We applied the model to a service-learning module from an HEI identifying knowledge operationalisation mechanisms and highlighting the effective transformation of knowledge and generation of new knowledge, through experience, into competencies and operational proficiency. We established that the service-learning module that was considered aligned well to the elements identified in the KOM.

Future research opportunities include further optimisation of the KOM and testing the application of the KOM for service learning module design.

References

1. Bennett, D., Sunderland, N., Bartleet, B.-L., Power, A.: Implementing and sustaining higher education service-learning initiatives: revisiting Young et al.'s organizational tactics. J. Exp. Educ. **39**(2), 145–163 (2016)
2. Bedford, D.: A case study in knowledge management education - historical challenges and future opportunities. Electron. J. Knowl. Manag. **11**(1), 199–213 (2013)
3. Bennett, E.: A simple, practical framework for organizing relationship-based reciprocity in service-learning experiences: insights from anthropology. IJRSLCE **6**(1), 1–15 (2018)
4. Meyer, M., Wood, L.: A critical reflection on the multiple roles required to facilitate mutual learning during service-learning in creative arts education. Teach. High. Educ. **22**(2), 158–177 (2017)
5. Hébert, A., Hauf, P.: Student learning through service learning: effects on academic development, civic responsibility, interpersonal skills and practical skills. Act. Learn. High. Educ. **16**(1), 37–49 (2015)
6. Gelmon, S.B., Holland, B.A., Spring, A.: Assessing Service-Learning and Civic Engagement: Principles and Techniques, 2nd edn. Campus Compact, Boston (2018)
7. Eyler, J.: Reflection: linking service and learning—linking students and communities. J. Soc. Issues **58**(3), 517–534 (2002)
8. Mitchell, T.D., et al.: Reflective practice that persists: connections between reflection in service-learning programs and in current life. MJCSL **21**, 49–63 (2015)
9. Kuklick, C.R., Gearity, B.T., Thompson, M.: Reflective practice in a university-based coach education program. Int. Sport Coach. J. **2**, 248–260 (2015)
10. Jones, S.R., et al.: The meaning students make as participants in short-term immersion programs. J. Coll. Stud. Dev. **53**(2), 201–220 (2012)
11. Adams Becker, S., et al.: NMC Horizon Report: 2017 Higher Education Edition. The New Media Consortium, Austin (2017)

12. Halberstadt, J., et al.: Learning sustainability entrepreneurship by doing: providing a lecturer-oriented service learning framework. Sustainability **11**, 1–22 (2019)
13. Bednarz, S.W., et al.: Community engagement for student learning in geography. J. Geogr. High. Educ. **32**(1), 87–100 (2008)
14. Bringle, R.G., Clayton, P.H., Price, M.F.: Partnerships in service learning and civic engagement. J. Serv. Learn. Civic Engagem. **1**(1), 1–20 (2009)
15. Polanyi, M.: Tacit knowing: its bearing on some problems of philosophy. Rev. Mod. Phys. **34**(4), 601–606 (1962)
16. Freitas de Azeredo Barros, V., Ramos, I., Perez, G.: Information systems and organizational memory: a literature review. J. Inf. Syst. Technol. Manag. **12**(1), 45–64 (2015)
17. Dalkir, K.: Knowledge Management in Theory and Practice. Elsevier Butterworth–Heinemann, Burlington (2005)
18. Clarke, T., Rollo, C.: Corporate initiatives in knowledge management. Educ. Train. **43**(4/5), 206–214 (2001)
19. Bruning, R.H.: Cognitive Psychology and Instruction, 3rd edn. Prentice-Hall Inc., Upper Saddle River (1999)
20. Kutay, C., Aurum, A.: Knowledge transformation for education in software engineering. Int. J. Mob. Learn. Organ. **1**(1) (2007)
21. Bhusry, M., Ranjan, J., Nagar, R.: Implementing knowledge management in higher educational institutions in India: a conceptual framework. J. High. Educ. Res. **7**(1), 64–82 (2012)
22. Imrie, B.W.: Assessment for learning: quality and taxonomies. Assess. Eval. High. Educ. **20**(2), 175–189 (1995/2008)
23. Hakky, R.: Improving basic design courses through competences of tuning MEDA. J. High. Educ. **4**(1), 21–42 (2016)
24. Krathwohl, D.R.: A revision of bloom's taxonomy: an overview. Theory Into Pract. **41**(4), 212–218 (2002)
25. Nonaka, I., Toyama, R., Konno, N.: SECI, Ba and leadership: a unified model of dynamic knowledge creation. Long Range Plan. **33**, 5–34 (2000)
26. Anderson, L., Krathwohl, D.: A taxonomy for learning, teaching, and assessing: a revision of Bloom's taxonomy of educational objectives. Longman, New York (2001)
27. Harvey, M., et al.: Aligning reflection in the cooperative education. Asia-Pac. J. Coop. Educ. **11**(3), 137–152 (2010)
28. Millican, J., Bourner, T.: Student-community engagement and the changing role and context of higher education. Educ. Train. **53**(2/3), 89–99 (2011)
29. Smuts, H., Kotzé, P.: Client-vendor knowledge transfer mechanisms in the context of information systems outsourcing. In: Uden, L., Heričko, M., Ting, I.-H. (eds.) KMO 2015. LNBIP, vol. 224, pp. 102–119. Springer, Cham (2015). https://doi.org/10.1007/978-3-319-21009-4_9
30. Edersheim, E.H.: The Definitive Drucker. McGraw-Hill, New York (2007)
31. Andreeva, T., Ikhilchik, I.A.: Applicability of the SECI model of knowledge creation in Russian cultural context: theoretical analysis. Knowl. Process. Manag. **18**(1), 56–66 (2011)
32. Lebedeva, O., Prokofjeva, N.: The use of systems for knowledge search in e-learning. In: Nunes, M.B., McPherson, M. (eds.) International Association for Development of the Information Society, pp. 343–348. IADIS Press, Lisbon (2012)
33. Nonaka, I., Takeuchi, H.: The Knowledge Creating Company. Oxford University Press, Oxford (1995)
34. Nonaka, I., Toyama, R., Byosiere, P.: A theory of organisational knowledge creation: understanding the dynamic process of creating knowledge. In: Dierkes, M., et al. (eds.) Handbook of Organizational Learning & Knowledge, pp. 491–517. Oxford University Press, New York (2001)

35. McKenney, S., Reeves, T.C.: Conducting Educational Design Research, 2nd edn. Routledge, New York (2019)
36. Wang, F., Hannafin, M.J.: Design-based research and technology-enhanced learning environments. Educ. Tech. Res. Dev. **53**(4), 5–23 (2005)
37. Edelson, D.C.: Design research: what we learn when we engage in design. J. Learn. Sci. **11**(1), 105–121 (2002)
38. Smuts, H., Hattingh, M.J.: Towards a knowledge conversion model enabling programme design in higher education for shaping industry-ready graduates. In: Kabanda, S., Suleman, H., Gruner, S. (eds.) SACLA 2018. CCIS, vol. 963, pp. 124–139. Springer, Cham (2019). https://doi.org/10.1007/978-3-030-05813-5_9
39. Ursula Fuller, U., et al.: Developing a computer science-specific learning taxonomy. In: Working Group Reports on ITiCSE on Innovation and Technology in Computer Science Education, pp. 152–170. Association for Computing Machinery (2007)
40. Jordaan, M.: Sustainability of a community-based project module. Acta Academica **44**(1), 224–246 (2012)

Analysis of Knowledge Management in the Context of Projects in Colombia
Subject Area: (Knowledge Management and Project Management)

César Rincón-González[1]([✉]), Flor Nancy Díaz-Piraquive[2],
and Rubén González-Crespo[3]

[1] Faculty of Engineering, EAN University, Bogotá, Colombia
crincon2.d@universidadean.edu.co
[2] Fundación Universitaria Internacional de La Rioja UNIR, Logroño, Colombia
flornancy.diaz@unir.edu.co
[3] Universidad Internacional de La Rioja UNIR, Logroño, Spain
ruben.gonzalez@unir.net

Abstract. This research work conducted a meticulous analysis about the Knowledge Management (KM) in the context of projects in Colombia, with the aim of determinate the way organizations carryout related activities and practices about the matter of study. 3 distinctive KM clusters were identified by conducting an extensive fieldwork and deploying a meticulous statistical analysis of the collected data. Firstly; a theoretical framework was built, allowing the identification of concepts about knowledge management. Secondly; a research methodology was constructed, variables of study were identified and integrated into an information gathering instrument, applied randomly on an extensive fieldwork covering more than 500 organizations nationwide, by interviewing project representatives. Subsequently; a detailed statistical analysis was carryout, techniques such as hierarchical clustering, variables factor maps, Principal Components Analysis (PCA), boxplots and Anova tests, were used to identify the KM clusters related to the management of projects in Colombia. Afterwards; the characteristics of each of the clusters of KM in the context of projects in Colombia were documented. And finally; conclusions were established and as future lines of research were outlined.

Keywords: Impact analysis · Knowledge management · Project management · Colombia

1 Introduction

On the scientific literature, several researches target on the analysis of knowledge management in the context of projects form an exploratory perspective, typically by unique or multiple cases of study, without a comprehensive statistical coverage, and developed on geographical contexts dissimilar to the reality of this kind of endeavors conducted in Colombia. This research work developed a meticulous analysis about knowledge management from the perspective of projects, by conducting a detailed analysis of this matter of study in the Colombian enterprise context.

L. Uden et al. (Eds.): KMO 2021, CCIS 1438, pp. 54–64, 2021.
https://doi.org/10.1007/978-3-030-81635-3_5

The main objective of this research is to analyze knowledge management in the context of project in Colombia. As specific objectives of this study, were defined:

- Develop a theoretical framework about main concepts related to knowledge management and project management.
- Define a research methodology in order to analyze KM in the context of project management.
- Conduct a nation-wide fieldwork to analyze knowledge management form the perspective of projects, in the Colombian enterprise context.
- Document the findings about the analysis on KM in the context of project management in Colombia.
- Identify conclusions and define future lines of research about KM as a topic of study on project management.

2 Theoretical Framework

On this heading, main concepts related to KM in the context of project management (refer to Table 1) and variables of study were defined. These elements were included into the research methodology of this investigation.

Rincón-González & Diaz-Piraquive (2019) conducted a detailed scientometric analysis establishing a precise state of the art about KM and project performance. On an extensive literature review, principal topics of research about KM were identified: "project management; knowledge management; project performance and success; information technology (information management, systems, and knowledge based systems); innovation and perspective; knowledge – sharing and knowledge transfer; organizations and firms; models and frameworks; knowledge acquisition; and knowledge engineering" [1; p. 22].

Regarding to KM, several studies illustrate on key topics related to this matter, [5–13] developed on tools for developing KM strategies, identifying KM issues, and managing lessons learned on KM from different industries such as oil & gas, engineering, procurement and construction, and learning; [14, 15] developed KM as a driver for IT projects improvement; [16, 17] analyzed the effect of KM on project performance; and [18, 19] investigated the effect of KM on constructions projects and its impact on the cost of poor quality. All cited studies, concurred on KM as a relevant aspect of project management, and as a promising line of research that requires applied studies for further development.

Variables of study to collect the accumulated score of knowledge management on the fieldwork later on this research, were defined in order to measure KM on main knowledge areas of project management as showed on Table 2 [2, 20]:

3 Methodology

In this section, the methodology for this research work was defined as follow [1, 20–42]: (a.) determination of the variables of study; (b.) compilation of variables into an information gathering instrument to analyze KM; (c.) execution of a rigorous fieldwork

Table 1. Theoretical framework of KM in the context of projects.

Definition	Source
The term knowledge can be defined as "a mixture of experience, values and beliefs, contextual information, intuition, and insight that people use to make sense of new experiences and information" to manage a project properly	[2; p. 709]
Knowledge also is been defined as "the collection of information and experience that an individual possesses. For example, understanding the concept of a Gantt chart might be considered knowledge"	[3; p. 15]
Knowledge is a key component of Project Management (PM), as PM can be defined as "the application of knowledge, skills, tools, and techniques to project activities to meet the project requirements" [2; p. 10]. In a similar way of thinking PM is the use of knowledge as well as skills, abilities, procedures and methods to aim project results [4]	[2; p. 10], [4]
Project knowledge is defined as "the process of using existing knowledge and creating new knowledge to achieve the project's objectives and contribute to organizational learning" [2; p. 70]. Then again, project management relays on "ensuring the creation and the use of the appropriated knowledge to and from the project as necessary"	[2; p. 70–72]
Knowledge, as a valuable organizational process asset, relays on the methodical use of information and learning, from the individual data to collective information in order to be distributed across the organization	[4]
Knowledge management occurs when "organizational knowledge is leveraged to produce or improve the project outcomes, and knowledge created by the project is available to support organizational operations and future projects"	[2; p. 98]
Knowledge is also an enabler of human interaction on projects as "knowledge management tools and techniques connect people so they can work together to create new knowledge, share tactic knowledge, and integrate the knowledge of diverse teams members"	[2; p. 102]

Source: The authors

on 502 organizations that conduct projects in Colombia; (d.) application of a detailed statistical analysis of the information collected on fieldwork; (e.) characterization of KM clusters in Colombia; and (f.) documentation of findings and conclusions.

On the fieldwork of this research, a sample of 502 organizations were included, the selection criteria were that objects of study (organizations) were considered as representative of the Colombian enterprise context, and execute projects as part of its business and were selected randomly. On each organization a face to face semi-structures interview was conducted with project manager, PMOs or project sponsors, were evaluation of aspects of study (refer to Table 2) were gather by using a Likert-type scale. and 100% response rate was archived by assuring interviews with project representatives beforehand.

The variables of study were incorporated into a factor map analysis, with 2 dimensions of the principal components analysis, 57.13% of the variance of data can be explained. In addition the orientation and magnitude of the analyzed variables point

Table 2. Dimensions and aspects of analysis on KM in the context of projects.

Dimensions	Aspects of analysis
(a.) KM within scope	Historical information from previous projects to define requirements, deliverables validation outcomes Organizational Process Assets (OPA) updates relates to scope for future projects
(b.) KM within time	Data from previous projects for activities duration estimations, estimation techniques, buffer appraisal based on historical information, OPA updates related to time management
(c.) KM within cost	Previous project costs estimations; contingency reserves based on historical project cost performance, OPS updates on cost performance for incoming projects
(d.) KM within quality	Data base of quality specifications from past projects, information gathering of quality aspects and issues for future projects, OPA updates on quality management
(e.) KM within resources	Historical information on resource rates for estimations, resource estimation tools, data on utilization and performance of resources to be used on future projects
(f.) KM within communications	Communications information from past projects database, gathering of information flows and procedures for future projects, OPA updates about information management
(g.) KM within risks	Past projects risk logs for incoming projects risk management activities such as risk identification and quantitative analysis, risk probability and impact estimations, OPA updates for risks in future projects
(h.) KM within procurement	Performance of contractors, vendors and suppliers from past projects to be used on procurement processes on incoming ones, OPA updates on procurement for forthcoming projects
(i.) KM within stakeholders	Stakeholders maps from past projects, tools and techniques for stakeholders identification and management, information about stakeholders aspects to be used on upcoming projects
(j.) KM within integration	Business cases, project charters, project management plans, performance reports and closure reports from past projects as historical information
(k.) PM knowledge	Management of existing management and creation of new one for better project performance
(l.) Career path	Career paths for project related roles such as project, program, portfolio and PMO managers
(m.) Lessons learned	Management of lessons learned on previous and current project to be taken into account on yet to come projects
(n.) KM tools	Historical information from past projects, PMO databases, OPA, project repositories, and other sources of information to be used on future projects
(o.) KM Total	An aggregation of measures from previous variables

Source: The authors

out in a coherent directions and can be correctly explained by KM total variables as presented in Fig. 1,

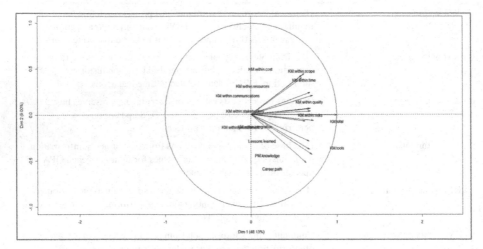

Fig. 1. Variables factor map of KM in Colombia. Source: The authors.

4 Results

Once the analysis instrument was applied to the 502 companies of different economic sectors in Colombia, the data was included into the R statistical software, where a hierarchical clusters analysis was performed, where it was identified that the optimal number of groupings to carry out the analysis of the knowledge management levels, in the context of project management in Colombia, was 3. On Fig. 2, elements of each cluster are similar in knowledge management measures, but dissimilar when comparing to objects of study from other group. Also, dimensions 1 and 2 collect 57.13% of the variance in order to define KM clusters on the analyzed data.

Once the clusters of knowledge management in the Colombian enterprise context were visually identified, an *Anova test* analysis was executed in the R statistical software, with a significance level of ($\alpha = 0.05$); it was noticed a *p_value* $\approx 0,00$ (see Table 3) direct evidence of rejection of the hypothesis of equality of measures between the knowledge management clusters. Therefore, this evidence allows to determinate that, groups have different score levels, and consequently, the clustering conducted on this research discriminates, perfectly, the organizations analyzed.

Figure 3 shows the three levels clearly differentiated about knowledge management in the context of project management in Colombia: (a.) low (in blue color); (b.) medium (in red color); and (c.) high (in green color). The characterization and a diagnosis of each performance level are summarized in Table 4.

Variables of study on KM were identified and validated on a nation-wide and extensive fieldwork analyzing the way more than 500 organizations of the Colombian

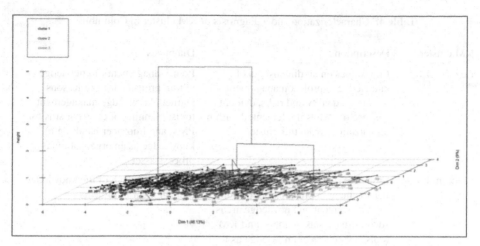

Fig. 2. Hierarchical clustering on the factor map of KM in Colombia. Source: The authors.

Table 3. Variance analysis for knowledge management clusters in Colombia.

Source of variation	Freedom degrees	Sum of squares	Mean square	F	P value
Cluster	2	137.97	68.98	901.5	<2e−16
Residuals	499	38.18	0.08		

Source: The authors

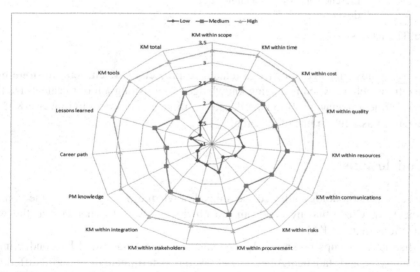

Fig. 3. Comparative of clusters on knowledge management on projects context in Colombia. Source: The authors (color figure online)

Table 4. Characterization and a diagnosis of KM cluster in Colombia.

KM cluster	Description	Diagnosis
Low level	Low values on all dimensions of knowledge in project management, mainly on quality and risks, evident absence of PMOs implemented within organizations from this cluster	Pour management of knowledge within projects, lack of lessons learned, knowledge management tools, planning of careers paths for PMs, and improper handling of knowledge as an organizational process asset
Medium level	Moderate scores on knowledge management in projects, opportunities of improvement on knowledge areas such as risks, stakeholders, and KM tools, awareness of knowledge as a valuable organizational processes asset, and moderate presence of PMOs as knowledge facilitator	Modest approach of the knowledge management in projects
High level	Proper handling of knowledge across all areas of project management, mindfulness of knowledge as an outstanding asset and a competitive advantage to drive business by projects. Use career paths, lessons learned and KM tools, and a strong presence of PMOs as a knowledge driver	Exceptional management of projects knowledge across all dimensions of study; use of advanced techniques and tools for knowledge management

Source: The authors

enterprise context manage knowledge related to projects. KM clusters illustrate how organizations behave when managing knowledge, establishing a tool to categorize this aspect of project management to later develop an integrated model to improve KM on organizations as a future line of research.

5 Conclusions

The research methodology allowed the study knowledge management in the context of projects in Colombia, by conducting a cluster analysis to characterize the way organizations manage KM.

3 distinctive groups of knowledge management were identified by conducting a cluster analysis, and statistical *Anova test* allowed to determinate meaningful difference among elements of study included into each of the aggregations of this research.

On the group of low score, pour practices of KM were observed, lack of lessons learned, knowledge management tools, planning of careers paths for PMs, and improper handling of knowledge as an organizational process asset. On the medium score cluster, a moderate approach of the knowledge management in projects was evident with opportunities of improvement on knowledge areas such as risks, stakeholders, and KM tools, awareness of knowledge as a valuable organizational processes asset. On the high score set, a proper management of projects knowledge across all dimensions of study, as well as the use of advanced techniques and tools for knowledge management was observed.

The results of this research, validated the methodology by conducting a nation-wide study, identifying KM variables with the aim of incorporate them latter on other further applied studies on KM in the context of projects.

As future lines of research, it was proposed to develop this kind of studies in other geographical contexts, in order to compare the impact of KM on project management in other countries by conducting comparative and correlation analyses to build an integrated KM model to improve the way organizations manage knowledge and enhance the performance of this kind of endeavors.

References

1. Rincón-González, C.H., Díaz-Piraquive, F.: Scientometric analysis of knowledge in the context of project management. In: Knowledge Management in Organizations. 14th International Conference, KMO 2019 Zamora, Spain, July 2019.https://doi.org/10.1007/978-3-030-214 51-7. ISSN 1865-0929
2. Project Management Institute (PMI). A guide to the Project Management Body of Knowledge - PMBOK® Guide - Sixth Edition. Pennsylvania, USA (2017)
3. International Project Management Association (IPMA). Individual Competency Baseline ICB 4 (2015)
4. Association for Project Management (APM). APM Body of Knowledge 7th edition (2019)
5. Al-Ghassani, A.M., Kamara, J.M., Anumba, C.J., Carrillo, P.M.: A tool for developing knowledge management strategies. Electron. J. Inf. Technol. Construct. **7**, 69–82 (2002). https://www.scopus.com/inward/record.uri?eid=2-s2.0-3042552726&partnerID= 40&md5=960a5d922e8191a4aaa311f380fc8514
6. Al-Ghassani, A.M., Kamara, J.M., Anumba, C.J., Carrillo, P.M.: An innovative approach to identifying knowledge management problems. Eng. Construct. Architect. Manag. **11**(5), 349–357 (2004). https://doi.org/10.1108/09699980410558548
7. Carrillo, P.: Managing knowledge: lessons from the oil and gas sector. Construct. Manag. Econ. **22**(6), 631–642 (2004). https://doi.org/10.1080/0144619042000226289
8. Carrillo, P.: Lessons learned practices in the engineering, procurement and construction sector. Eng. Construct. Architect. Manag. **12**(3), 236–250 (2005). https://doi.org/10.1108/096999805 10600107
9. Carrillo, P., Chinowsky, P.: Exploiting knowledge management: the engineering and construction perspective. J. Manag. Eng. **22**(1), 2 (2006). https://doi.org/10.1061/(ASCE)0742-597X(2006)22:1(2)
10. Carrillo, P., Ruikar, K., Fuller, P.: When will we learn? Improving lessons learned practice in construction. Int. J. Project Manage. **31**(4), 567–578 (2013). https://doi.org/10.1016/j.ijp roman.2012.10.005
11. Chinowsky, P., Carrillo, P.: Knowledge management to learning organization connection. J. Manag. Eng. **23**(3), 122–130 (2007). https://doi.org/10.1061/(ASCE)0742-597X(2007)23: 3(122)
12. Tan, H.C., Carrillo, P.M., Anumba, C.J.: Case study of knowledge management implementation in a medium-sized construction sector firm. J. Manag. Eng. **28**(3), 338–347 (2012). https://doi.org/10.1061/(ASCE)ME.1943-5479.0000109

13. Udeaja, C.E., et al.: A web-based prototype for live capture and reuse of construction project knowledge. Autom. Construct. **17**(7), 839–851 (2008). https://doi.org/10.1016/j.autcon.2008.02.009

14. Gemino, A., Reich, B.H., Sauer, C.: A temporal model of information technology project performance. J. Manag. Inf. Syst. **24**(3), 9–44 (2007). https://doi.org/10.2753/MIS0742-1222240301

15. Gemino, A., Reich, B.H., Sauer, C.: Plans versus people: comparing knowledge management approaches in IT-enabled business projects. Int. J. Project Manage. **33**(2), 299–310 (2015). https://doi.org/10.1016/j.ijproman.2014.04.012

16. Reich, B.H., Gemino, A., Sauer, C.: Knowledge management and project-based knowledge in it projects: A model and preliminary empirical results. Int. J. Project Manage. **30**(6), 663–674 (2012). https://doi.org/10.1016/j.ijproman.2011.12.003

17. Reich, B.H., Gemino, A., Sauer, C.: How knowledge management impacts performance in projects: An empirical study. Int. J. Project Manage. **32**(4), 590–602 (2014). https://doi.org/10.1016/j.ijproman.2013.09.004

18. Olayinka, R., Suresh, S., Chinyio, E.: Impact of knowledge management on the cost of poor quality. Proc. Inst. Civ. Eng. Manag. Procur. Law **168**(4), 177–188 (2015). https://doi.org/10.1680/mpal.1400035

19. Suresh, S., Olayinka, R., Chinyio, E., Renukappa, S.: Impact of knowledge management on construction projects. Proc. Inst. Civ. Eng. Manag. Procur. Law **170**(1), 27–43 (2017). https://doi.org/10.1680/jmapl.15.00057

20. Rincón-González, C.H., Díaz-Piraquive, F.: Impact of project management offices on knowledge management. The Handbook of Research on Project Management Strategies and Tools for Organizational Success. Chapter 7, pp. 166–195. IGI Global, Hershey (2020). https://doi.org/10.4018/978-1-7998-1934-9. ISBN-13: 9781799819349

21. Acosta, A., Rincón-González, C.H., Nieto, L., Rodríguez, Á., Romero, F., Fajardo, J.: Propuesta para la creación de una oficina de gestión de proyectos (PMO) en una compañía del sector downstream en Colombia Modelos, metodologías y sistemas de gestión de proyectos, pp. 156–170. Ediciones EAN, Bogotá, Colombia (2019). ISBN 978-958-756-614-7

22. Castro-Silva, H.F.C., Rincón-González, C.H., Diez-Silva, H.M.: Sustainability on project management. An analysis of the construction industry in Colombia. The Handbook of Research on Project Management Strategies and Tools for Organizational Success. Chapter 12, pp. 281–304. IGI Global, Hershey (2020). https://doi.org/10.4018/978-1-7998-1934-9.ISBN-13: 9781799819349

23. Díaz-Piraquive, F., Rincón-González, C.H.: Building knowledge in Project Management from the perspective of collaborative learning. Proceedings from the XXIII International Congress on Project Management and Engineering, CIDIP 2019, pp. 300–308. AEIPRO IPMA. Málaga, España (2019). http://dspace.aeipro.com/xmlui/handle/123456789/2259. ISBN-13: 978-84-09-13557-8

24. Rincón-González, C.H.: Las oficinas de gerencia de proyectos un impulsador del desempeño organizacional. Investigación En Administración y Redes Globales de Conocimiento, Cali, Colombia (2014). ISBN 978-958-772-238-3

25. Rincón-González, C.H.: Propuesta de estudio de factibilidad con un enfoque basado en PMI e ISO: Un modelo para la evaluación de proyectos. Face **14**, 91–107 (2014). ISSN 1794-9920

26. Rincón-González, C.H.: Propuesta de un Modelo de Evaluación Económica, Ambiental y Social de Proyectos: Un Enfoque Ético para la Evaluación de Proyectos Sostenibles. Daena **10**(2), 1–24 (2015). ISSN 1870-557X

27. Rincón-González, C.H.: Análisis de la problemática de la gestión de proyectos: estudio en el contexto empresarial colombiano. Revista Ciencias Estratégicas **24**, 35, pp. 119–136 (2016). ISSN 1794-834

28. Rincón-González, C.H.: Caracterización de los stakeholders que se relacionan con las Oficinas de Gerencia de Proyectos. Daena **12**(3), 230–255 (2017). ISSN 1870-557X
29. Rincón-González, C.H.: Diagnóstico de la gerencia de proyectos en Colombia – una investigación aplicada en el contexto empresarial del país. Investigación En Administración y su impacto en comunidades académicas internacionales, Bogotá, Colombia (2017). ISBN: 978-958-772-874-3
30. Rincón-González, C.H.: Las oficinas de gerencia de proyectos y su relacionamiento con los stakeholders de los proyectos bajo su supervisión: un estudio en el contexto empresarial colombiano. Tópicos gerenciales para la gestión de empresas: una mirada desde la investigación, pp. 11–39. Ediciones EAN. Bogotá, Colombia (2018). ISBN 978-958-756-590-4
31. Rincón-González, C.H.: Las oficinas de gerencia de proyectos - un impulsor de la estrategia y el desempeño de los proyectos en las organizaciones. La gerencia de proyectos como impulsor de la estrategia organizacional, pp. 155–171. Ediciones EAN. Bogotá, Colombia (2018). ISBN 978-958-756-586-7
32. Rincón-González, C.H.: Metodología para la creación de oficinas de gestión de proyectos en las organizaciones. Doctoral tesis. Magna Cum Laude, Doctorado en Gerencia de Proyectos. Universidad EAN, Bogotá, Colombia (2018)
33. Rincón-González, C.H., Díaz-Piraquive, F.: Impact analysis of the project management offices in the colombian enterprise context. In: Proceedings from the 22nd International Congress on Project Management and Engineering, Madrid, July 2018, pp. 279–291. IPMA, Madrid, España (2018). http://dspace.aeipro.com/xmlui/handle/123456789/1569. ISBN-13: 978-84-09-05132-8
34. Rincón-González, C.H., Díaz-Piraquive, F.: Análisis cienciométrico de los stakeholders en la gestión de proyectos. El talento humano como factor clave en el éxito de los proyectos, pp. 164–179. Ediciones EAN. Bogotá, Colombia (2019). ISBN 978-958-756-615-4
35. Rincón-González, C.H., Díaz-Piraquive, F., Castro-Silva, H.: Stakeholders impact on the performance of projects in the Colombian Military Forces. In: Proceedings from the XXIII International Congress on Project Management and Engineering, CIDIP 2019, pp. 71–83. AEIPRO IPMA, Málaga, España (2019).http://dspace.aeipro.com/xmlui/handle/123456789/2253. ISBN-13: 978-84-09-13557-8
36. Rincón-González, C.H., Díaz-Piraquive, F., Diez-Silva, M.: Biliometric and impact analysis of the Project Management Offices in Colombia. In: CONIITI 2019 Bogotá, Colombia, September 2019, pp. 1–6 (2019). https://doi.org/10.1109/CONIITI48476.2019.8960626
37. Rincón-González, C.H., Díaz-Piraquive, F., González-Crespo, R.: Analysis and characterization of project management in the Colombian enterprise context. In: CONIITI 2019, Bogotá, Colombia, September 2019, pp. 1–6 (2019). https://doi.org/10.1109/CONIITI48476.2019.8960696
38. Rincón-González, C.H., Rueda Varón, M., Díaz-Piraquive, F.: Determination of the performance levels of project management in Colombia. In: Proceedings from the XXIII International Congress on Project Management and Engineering, CIDIP 2019, pp. 263–275. AEIPRO IPMA. Málaga, España (2019).http://dspace.aeipro.com/xmlui/handle/123456789/2391. ISBN-13: 978-84-09-13557-8
39. Rincón-González, C.H.: Análisis Cienciométrico de la Negociación en el Contexto de los Proyectos. Gerencia de proyectos e interesados. Editorial UPTC, pp. 9–38 (2020). ISBN 978-958-660-387-4
40. Rincón-González, C.H.: Análisis Cienciométrico de los Equipos de Trabajo en el Contexto de los Proyectos. Gerencia de proyectos e interesados, pp. 113–150. Editorial UPTC (2020). ISBN 978-958-660-387-4

41. Rincón-González, C.H.: Los Equipos de Trabajo y su Impacto en el Desempeño de los Proyectos en Colombia. Gerencia de proyectos e interesados, pp. 39–74. Editorial UPTC (2020). ISBN 978-958-660-387-4
42. Rodríguez Marrugo, Y., Rincón-González, C.H.: Equipos de Trabajo y su Incidencia en los Programas de Pregrado de la Escuela Naval de Colombia. Gerencia de proyectos e interesados, pp. 231–283. Editorial UPTC (2020). ISBN 978-958-660-387-4

Knowledge Transfer and Learning

Methodology of Learning Combined: The Use of the Social Networks in the Classroom

Susana A. Arias T.[1], Hector F. Gomez A.[2]([⊠]), Willyams R. Castro D.[3], and Judith C. Nuñez Ramírez[3]

[1] Facultad de Ciencias de la Salud, Carrera de Laboratorio Clinico, Universidad Técnica de Ambato, Ambato, Ecuador
sa.arias@uta.edu.ec
[2] Centro de Posgrados, Universidad Técnica de Ambato, Ambato, Ecuador
hf.gomez@uta.edu.ec
[3] Facultad de Ciencias Humanas y de la Educación, Universidad Técnica de Ambato, Ambato, Ecuador
{williamsrcastrod,judithdnunezr}@uta.edu.ec

Abstract. The Utilization of the new technologies facilitates constructivist and cooperative learning the realization of projects of investigation that generate implementation of the virtual environment in the learning of specific fields, such as the development of the skills of writing and digital in the handle of knowledges. The Students with technophobia causes the outdated in the use of the tools and have freer to express freely, his form to act and think and for this is necessary the integration of the methodology of learning combined and the use of the ones of the social networks in the classroom. The researcher knows the causes and effects to the moment to delimit previous solutions to the done the investigation and research of information. Descriptive knows the problem to describe and the problematic that cries out in the institutions. Before the experiences in the institution like practitioners observe that the methodology that would use to combine the learnings in the social networks would be a success in the students.

Keywords: Education · Social · Network

1 Introduction

In Latin America requires of educational able to confront the challenges of the current world, for like this improve the quality in the education and therefore cooperate in a good life; and have a big responsibility to apply different methodologies in the achievement of the constructivist learning basing us in roads of solution to the problems, to accept and incorporate the educational programs by computer, what will allow that the students visualise and experience the learning with the resources that offers us the new technology [1]. In this regard, (Cobos 2008) self-evident that in the actuality in the (TIC), bring achieve several profits for the education, exist infinities of tools, such is the case of the educational software, these tools can use in the classroom and would facilitate the learning process [2]. The social networks in the Ecuador the same that in other countries have evolved

© Springer Nature Switzerland AG 2021
L. Uden et al. (Eds.): KMO 2021, CCIS 1438, pp. 67–71, 2021.
https://doi.org/10.1007/978-3-030-81635-3_6

totally of social way today in the actuality the need to form citizens in the use of the technologies like something fundamental to be competitive in the global stages and these competitions like digital citizens, are directly related to the capacity and skill to work and interacting with the network. As it can evidence in some works like the ones of (Maldonado 2006; Ochoa 2006; Loyal, Lizcano, Uribe, Connstain, Cardona and López, 2008), (Pineda Ballesteros, Meneses Cabrera, & Téllez Coins, 2013). Utilisation of the new technologies facilitates constructivist and cooperative learning the realisation of projects of investigation that generate implementation of the virtual enviroment in the learning of specific fields, such as the development of the skills of writing and digital in the handle of knowledges [3].

The students have to analyses and do a brief synthesis of the research of information to apply the significant learning in the moment to make a work collaboratively in the current society that live and interacting with educational and electronic means. The investigation or technological innovation has evolved in the society and the daily life of each human being goes turning into evolutionary spirits with the digital era and the current civilization that root like native beings of the current society, the applications created by the man are critical and self-criticism in the development of a subject related to the technology [4]. The demotivation of the student and the ignorance of the methodology of learning combined and the use of the ones of the social networks this problem comports that the students have under academic performance. The inappropriate use of the budgetary resources with the students and the ignorance of the methodology of learning combined and the use of the ones of the social networks, this originates a difficulty in the education of quality, this is to cause to the not having immediate media. The Students with technophobia causes the outdated in the use of the tools and have freer to express freely, his form to act and think and for this is necessary the integration of the methodology of learning combined and the use of the ones of the social networks in the classroom. The following sections detail some research that attempts to provide solutions to the problem, as well as our methodological proposal to mediate the learning scheme based on social networks. It is experienced in some areas and the conclusions of this study are obtained.

2 Methodology

Analytical and synthetic the problem allows previsualization the context of the methodology of learning combined and use of the networks sales in the classroom inductive and deductive allows to inform the contours of a proposal the tasks of sensitization and conscientization on the experiences of the society and of the actors of the present problem. The level of investigation here knows the problematic of the methodology of learning combined and use of the social networks in the classroom. The researcher knows the causes and effects to the moment to delimit previous solutions to the done the investigation and research of information. Descriptive knows the problem to describe and the problematic that cries out in the institutions. Previous to the experiences in the institution like practitioners observe that the methodology that would use to combine the learnings in the social networks would be a success in the students. The recollection of information is confidential because of each one of the users that show his interest and his usual possibilities that strengthen the investigation. The analysis of the information will have the following appearances in the processing of the project:

- Critical review and cleaning of the defective information, contradictory, incomplete, no pertinent, among others.
- Correction of failing by means of the repetition of the recollection of information and; Statistical tabulation.
- Analysis of the results of the questions.

3 Experimentation

It applied on the mastery in educational computing and on the courses of Psicopedagogy 1 and 2 B, matter Methodology of Investigation and Foundations of investigation (Figs. 1, 2, 3 and 4):

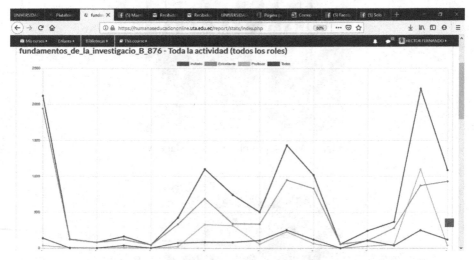

Fig. 1. Activity student course Psicodepagogy

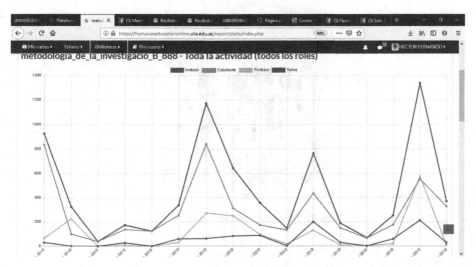

Fig. 2. Activity student course Methodology

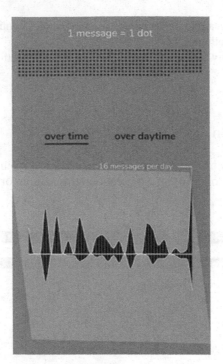

Fig. 3. Whatsapp course Psicopedagogy

Fig. 4. Whatsapp course Methodology

4   Conclusions

In this work develop a methodology that, through the combination of ontologies, allows us to monitor the process of education-learning. The methodology splits of the hypothesis that the style of learning, is the base to attain the necessary skills for the development of the career of a student. When it combines the social networks and the tools tecnopedagógicas obtains a structure of knowledge that allows queries and findings eat: choose a resource in accordance with the styles and skills of learning, the sending of programs of tasks, the place that corresponds with the style and the type of education. In the implementation of the methodology, test our proposal and could identify weaknesses in the development of the processes of education - learning. This has carried us to look for improvements in the conceptualización of the queries to cover so many cases as it was possible. A reason for this is that only we work with an alone subject. It is possible that this error increases if we work with more subjects. We observe the exert of the students afterwards to apply ourselves methodology. The aim of our work is that the monitory converts not only in a tool to help, but also to determine what so good is our proposal. The results showed that for the majority of the students likes them our proposal, although there is some that do it and showed a decrease in the academic performance. For this last, propose a new methodology management and the development of personalized queries that drive to findings that allow us to interpret what success during the process of education-learning.

References

1. Carmona, H.: SlideShare (2011). https://es.slideshare.net/thedarwin10/investigacion-tecnologi ca-1
2. Ortiz, O.: repositorio.educacionsuperior.gob.ec (2013). http://repositorio.educacionsuperior. gob.ec/bitstream/28000/1221/1/t-senescyt-000352.pdf
3. Góngora, R.: Scribd (2015). https://es.scribd.com/document/285940654/aplicacion-de-sof tware-educativo-en-el-proceso-ensenanza-aprendizaje
4. Córdoba, O.L.S.: Electronic Magazine Educated (2013). http://www.scielo.sa.cr/pdf/ree/ v17n3/a14v17n3.pdf
5. Cuevas, R.A., Angelino, F., Arturo, M., Catalan, A.: Common theoretical on learning combined in the education. Magazine Iberoamerica of Sciences (2015)
6. Aguilar, A.: Magazine IIPSI (2012). http://sisbib.unmsm.edu.pe/bvrevistas/investigacion_psic ologia/v15_n1/pdf/a13v15n1.pdf
7. Santos, U.F.: Magazine of Philosophy and Theology Redalyc (2012). http://www.redalyc.org/ articulo.oa?id=291124138004
8. Arias, J., Villasís, M., Miranda, M.: Magazine Allergy Mexico (2016). http://revistaalergia. mx/ojs/index.php/ram/article/view/181/273
9. Nolasco, A.: rua.ua.es (2012). https://rua.ua.es/dspace/bitstream/10045/63629/1/conceptos-basicos-de-estadistica-en-la-investigacion-sanitaria.pdf

Predicting Effects of University Service Quality and Internet Use Motives Towards Study Abroad Students' Depression

Wen-Lin Wang and Gregory Siy Ching(✉)

Graduate Institute of Educational Leadership and Development, Fu Jen Catholic University,
New Taipei City 242, Taiwan, ROC
094478@mail.fju.edu.tw

Abstract. The number of students participating in study abroad programs has been increasing for the past decades. In Taiwan, the rising number of incoming study abroad students have also helped in augmenting the oversupply of higher education. However, it is reported that within study abroad situations culture shock does happens. In the current study, it is assumed that the internet has already created a highly connected society. Hence, study abroad depression should be minimized. In addition, with the current drive for the advancement of service quality within higher education, these perceived positive interactions between the school and students should be able to further lessen study abroad related difficulties. With the trend of knowledge management within university institutional research, the collection and understanding of data with regards to study abroad students is quite important for future policy recommendations. To further understand these assumptions, information from a total of 665 study abroad students in Taiwan are surveyed. Service quality (SERVQUAL), the Study Abroad Internet Use Motives Survey (IUM), and the Center for Epidemiologic Studies Depression Scale (CES-D) were used to collect the information. Results show that IUM factors *online habits* and *online facilitation*, and the SERVQUAL factors *tangibles* and *reliability* are able to predict study abroad students' depression. In essence, for study abroad to become successful universities should make use of such tools and provide the appropriate adjustments within their service provisions.

Keywords: Culture shock · Institutional research · Student recruitment · Survey questionnaire · SERVQUAL

1 Introduction

For the past 25 years, international education has evolved into one of the mainstream components of higher education [1]. From the traditional experience of getting a degree from a foreign country, international education has expanded to encompass short-term study abroad, twinning or dual degree programs, cross-country fieldwork or researches, internship and service learning experiences, study tours, and many other variants that might either be credit earning or not [2]. Similar with Taiwan, internationalization for the

© Springer Nature Switzerland AG 2021
L. Uden et al. (Eds.): KMO 2021, CCIS 1438, pp. 72–84, 2021.
https://doi.org/10.1007/978-3-030-81635-3_7

past few years has been quite deliberate with strategies inclined towards sustainability and quality of programs [3].

These deliberate strategies for the internationalization of higher education in Taiwan have brought about the rapid increase in the number of incoming study abroad students [4–7]. Statistics from the Ministry of Education show that the annual intake of study abroad students has increase from around 10 to 19% and even to as high as 28% per year. However, this rapid growth seems to have reached its peak with the computed annual growth to have gradually slowed down to only around 5% and lower. Some attribute this change to the fact that universities in Taiwan are more focused on recruiting outside the Asian region [8]. To add, major global phenomenon starting from 2013, such as the China's economic slowdown, the exit of UK from the European Union, and the new border policies of the US have all together changed the outlook of global student mobility, hence, brought upon both barriers and new opportunities of collaboration [9].

These new collaboration opportunities have actually opened up the door for more regional cooperation and student mobility [2]. However, within the vast study abroad literature, it is noted that when students are exposed to new situations and environments, they (the students) tend to suffer from various levels of anxiety, confusion, and depression [10, 11]. Hence, in order to better enhance the study abroad student recruitment strategies, the current study shall focus on understanding how depression can be minimize. More important, the data collected can also enhance the capabilities of university institutional research towards knowledge management [12, 13], while at the same time strengthening its role as knowledge managers [14].

2 Service Quality and Study Abroad

Within these past few years, many have started to wonder about the quality and value of participating in a study abroad program [15, 16]. Some say that this is actually a common practice within the academe [17]; denoting the cornucopia of study abroad programs available in the market today. Most primary reasons for study abroad is typically to avail of foreign language gains, however, some studies have shown that only slight improvements are found to be correlated with studying abroad [18–20]. Some even proved that local language immersion program participation and previous foreign language experiences to be far more useful in achieving language performance gain [21, 22]. Even more surprising is that some research have shown that locally held foreign language immersion programs are seem to be more effective than studying abroad [19]. Nonetheless, these only means that student should choose wisely in the type and form of study abroad program they would participate in [23, 24]. Hence, to better understand the inner workings of these programs *service quality* studies have become of high importance.

According to Zeithaml [25], *service quality* can be expressed as the overall consumers' judgment of the product (or services) performance. Consequently, service quality studies have started to become crucial for organizational progress and survival [26]. Furthermore, Gronroos [27] noted that service quality has already become a requirement for firms to become successful and organizations to remain competitive. As with the current competitive nature of higher education, maintaining a competitive advantage is crucial for sustainability [28, 29]. Together with the increasing role of students in having to *fund themselves* in their university education [30], competition is not only within the domestic sector, but as well as within the international education market, which has all together risen [31–33]. More important is that students are now seen as the primary consumers of higher education [34]; ultimately, issues leading to *service quality* and *satisfaction* are seen as the antecedents for making a *differential advantage* over other institutions.

Among the vast literature of service quality dimensions, the SERVQUAL model developed by Parasuraman, Zeithaml, and Berry [35] captures service quality within five dimensions, namely: a) *Tangibles* - the physical facilities, equipment, appearance of personnel; b) *Reliability* - the ability to perform the desired service dependably, accurately, and consistently; c) *Responsiveness* - the willingness to provide prompt service and help to customers; d) *Assurance* - employees' knowledge, courtesy, and ability to convey trust and confidence; and e) *Empathy* - the provision of caring, individualized attention to customers. These are actually a simplified version of the previous ten dimensions (reliability, responsiveness, competence, access, courtesy, communication, credibility, security, understanding, and tangibles). Within the five dimensions, *reliability* and *assurance* are mainly concerned with the *service outcomes*, while *responsiveness* and *empathy* are functions focusing on the *service process* [36].

Besides SERVQUAL, Gronroos [27] proposed that service quality can be measured using six criteria, namely: a) *Professionalism and skill* - customers see the service provider as knowledgeable and able to solve their problems in a professional way; b) *Attitudes and behavior* - customers perceive a genuine, friendly concern for them and their problems; c) *Access and flexibility* - customers feel that they have easy, timely access and that the service provider is prepared to adjust to their needs; d) *Reliability and trustworthiness* - customers can trust the service provider to keep promises and act in their best interests; e) *Recovery* - customers know that immediate corrective action will be taken if anything goes wrong; and lastly f) *Reputation and credibility* - customers believe that the brand image stands for good performance and accepted values. More important is that the service quality is also separated into two sections (similar with SERVQUAL), the *process* dimensions or how the service process functions, and the *output* dimensions or what the service process leads to as a result from the process [37, p. 177].

Comparing the two models, analysis suggests that the SERVQUAL model seems to be more highly used in various service quality studies. Researchers in various countries have actually adapted SERVQUAL to validate their higher education service quality, such as in Turkey [38], Bosnia [39], Singapore [26], Greece [40], Thailand [41], Egypt [42], Tanzania [43], special educations in Turkey [44], business administration program in Jeddah [45], Iran [46], and many others. More important, SERVQUAL is also used in evaluating the service quality of international education programs such as in Australia [47], and Malaysia [48, 49]. While most of the studies use a modified SERVQUAL survey based on contextualizing the five service quality dimensions, quite a few studies also integrated the importance-performance analysis so as to compare the perceived and the actual service quality situation of an organization [50, 51]. In sum, the use of the SERVQUAL model in determining the *service quality situations* of universities seems to be a valid conceptual paradigm. More important, service quality feedbacks should be able to provide university institutional research with valuable quality improvement policy recommendations.

3 Methodology

The current study is conceptualized within a quantitative design, wherein surveys are used to collect the information needed for the analysis [52]. Surveys are very useful in the collection of particular information describing the current issues at hand [53]. A total of 665 volunteer study abroad students in Taiwan participated in an online survey that lasted for around 3 months. The 42-item survey included 3 scales, namely: IUM (3 factors, 11 items) [54], the self-developed SERVQUAL (5 factors, 21 items), and the short depression scale CES-D (20 items) [55]. In addition, nominal data on participants' backgrounds and relevant details are also collected within the survey [56]. Data for the IUM and SERVQUAL is collected in terms of students' perceived agreement within 5 Likert [57] type scale, namely: 1 for strongly disagree, 2 for disagree, 3 for neutral, 4 for agree, and 5 for strongly agree. Overall, Cronbach's [58] Alpha (α) reliability of the survey is computed to be at **.86**, which is considered to be adequate (as a rule of thumb α should be greater than .45) [59, 60].

Table 1 shows the study abroad students background demographics. Data shows that the average age of the study abroad student respondents is around **25** years old with the number of male and female participants almost equal. In addition, the students' average duration of stay is around **14** months. As for their study abroad program types, a little over half or around 51% of the participants are non-degree seeking or short-term exchange students, while the remaining participants are degree seeking students (see Table 1 for more details).

Table 1. Participants' background demographics ($N = 665$).

Gender	Age (years)		Duration (months)		Degree seeking	
	M	SD	M	SD	Yes (%)	No (%)
Female ($n = 332$)	24.52	5.85	13.69	22.69	158 (47.6%)	174 (52.4%)
Male ($n = 333$)	26.22	7.28	15.04	23.70	165 (49.5%)	168 (50.5%)

3.1   Study Abroad Internet Use Motives Survey (IUM)

IUM is composed of 3 factors, namely (together with their original Alpha reliabilities): *Online Benefits* (OB, 4 items, $\alpha = .88$) – these are the notions that internet use is able to help reduce both social and academic difficulties. *Online Habits* (OH, 4 items, $\alpha = .86$) – these are the students' behaviors regarding the use of social networking sites (including messaging apps). Lastly, *Online Facilitation* (OF, 3 items, $\alpha = .82$) – these are the items related to how students use the internet to facilitate both social and cultural activities [54, p. 1208].

Table 2 shows the various IUM factors, together with their current Alpha reliabilities, and item means (M) and standard deviations (SD). Data shows that generally speaking, students are quite adept in using the internet to make their study abroad experience more fruitful. This is further noted with the highest rated item to be "*Look for a place of interest to visit*" with a mean of $M = 4.68$ ($SD = 0.64$), suggesting the facilitation for local tourism in Taiwan. Similarly, the second highest rated item "*Look for a cultural event that I will attend*" with a mean of $M = 4.53$ ($SD = 0.79$), denoting high levels of intention in learning more about the local cultures in Taiwan. In sum, study abroad students in Taiwan are seen as highly capable in using the internet within their social, academic, and leisure activities.

Table 2. IUM factors and items ($N = 665$).

Factor/Items/Cronbach Alpha Reliability	Mean	SD
Online Benefits ($\alpha = .82$)	**4.28**	**0.73**
OB01. Help me feel accepted	4.18	0.95
OB02. Help me feel more confident in interacting with the local Taiwanese culture	4.35	0.88
OB03. Help me perform better in my courses	4.25	0.93
OB04. Help reduce my academic problems	4.34	0.88
Online Habits ($\alpha = .80$)	**4.28**	**0.73**
OH01. Regularly interact with my friends online	4.38	0.89
OH02. Use email, Facebook or any other online services as a way to communicate	4.33	0.90
OH03. Regularly update my online posts	4.11	1.00
OH04. Have an online account that I use regularly	4.32	0.91
Online Facilitation ($\alpha = .73$)	**4.48**	**0.59**
OF01. Look for a cultural event that I will attend	4.53	0.79
OF02. Look for a place of interest to visit	4.68	0.64
OF03. Look for a leisure activity that I can join	4.22	0.75

3.2 Service Quality (SERVQUAL)

To collect the study abroad students' perception of university service quality, a self-made SERVQUAL instrument is developed with the consideration of several previous researches [41, 48, 51]. To validate the instrument, confirmatory factor analysis is accomplished. Factor analysis is a highly used method in checking whether survey items with similar construct are able to successfully group together [53]. The factorability of the proposed 21 items is first subjected to several criteria for factor analysis. First, the items were checked to having a primary factor loading of above .50 and no cross-loading of above .32 [61]. Second, the Kaiser-Meyer-Olkin value was computed to be **.84** well above the acceptable value [62]. Lastly, the Barlett's test of sphericity was computed to be at 4,294.4 with Chi-square to be significant ($p < .000$) and degrees freedom of 210, signifying acceptable values [63].

Table 3 shows the various SERVQUAL factors together with their items, means, SD, including their computed Alpha reliabilities, factor loadings, communalities, and variance explained. It is noted that the study abroad students' perception of service quality is considered to be fairly adequate. This can be seen with the overall mean of SERVQUAL to be computed at $M = 3.59$ ($SD = 54$). In addition, the highest rated item is *"Physical appearance of infrastructures (e.g. buildings, offices, campus grounds)"* with a mean of $M = 4.12$ ($SD = 0.88$), suggesting the effort placed by universities to upgrade their facilities. However, the lowest rated item is *"Faculty provides prompt response to students' inquiries"* with a mean of $M = 2.85$ ($SD = 1.09$), signifying the need for the improvement of quality interactions between students and faculty.

Lastly, to further validate the proposed SERVQUAL instrument, Structured Equation Modelling is used to explain the possibility of relationships among the items and latent variables [64]. Results show that the measurement model has a Chi-square of 5696.35 with $df = 136$, which is significant with $p < .000$ and a root mean square error of approximation (RMSEA) value of .060 all of which are within the acceptable CFA values [64]. Furthermore, several comparative fit indices such as: Normed Fit Index (NFI) = .93, Non-Normed Fit Index (NNFI) = .94, Comparative Fit Index (CFI) = .95, Incremental Fit Index (IFI) = .95, and Relative Fit Index (RFI) = .92 are also computed; all of which are within acceptable values [64–66]. Hence, the proposed SERVQUAL instrument can be said to be an empirically validated scale.

3.3 Center for Epidemiologic Studies Depression Scale (CES-D)

The CES-D is a highly used 20 items short depression scale. For the current study, the average depression score for the study abroad students is computed to be at $M = 12.17$ ($SD = 8.90$), signifying study abroad students in Taiwan are relatively happy (similar to the previous result noted by Lin and Ching [54]). As a rule of thumb depression values greater than or equal to 16 is considered to be depress [55].

Table 3. Proposed SERVQUAL confirmatory factor analysis ($N = 665$).

Factor/Items/Cronbach Alpha/Variance Explained	Mean	SD	Communalities	Factor loading
Tangible ($\alpha = .84$, 16.73%)	**3.88**	**0.70**		
Ta01. Teaching facilities (e.g. classroom, laboratory)	3.93	0.92	.664	.789
Ta02. Campus recreational facilities (e.g. swimming pool, basketball court, gym)	3.97	0.94	.635	.790
Ta03. Library facilities (e.g. collections, digital resources)	3.81	0.96	.519	.689
Ta04. Physical appearance of infrastructures (e.g. buildings, offices, campus grounds)	4.12	0.88	.572	.719
Ta05. Physical appearance of staff (e.g. faculty, non-teaching personnel)	3.78	0.93	.541	.666
Ta06. Professionalism of staff (e.g. faculty, non-teaching personnel)	3.68	1.04	.477	.619
Reliability ($\alpha = .75$, 12.26%)	**3.68**	**0.77**		
Ra01. Providing services as promised (e.g. course offerings)	3.67	1.14	.436	.546
Ra02. Providing on time services as scheduled	3.81	0.99	.644	.760
Ra03. Performing the service right at the first time	3.53	1.13	.548	.723
Ra04. Telling when services will be performed	3.54	1.08	.498	.678
Ra05. Shows sincerity in solving problems	3.86	1.09	.511	.624
Responsiveness ($\alpha = .80$, 11.63%)	**3.42**	**1.08**		
Re01. Staff provides prompt response to students' inquiries	3.08	1.10	.717	.814
Re02. Staff provides appropriate assistance to students' administrative needs	3.45	1.07	.672	.752
Re03. Faculty provides prompt response to students' inquiries	2.85	1.09	.619	.769
Re04. Faculty provides appropriate assistance to students' academic needs	3.71	1.02	.591	.646
Assurance ($\alpha = .58$, 8.73%)	**3.27**	**0.84**		
As01. Value of education from the university	3.72	1.15	.466	.644
As02. Quality of counselling services (e.g. career, psychological)	3.70	1.13	.473	.644
As03. Qualification of faculty	3.52	1.27	.396	.549
As04. Quality of education	3.84	1.09	.556	.703
Empathy ($\alpha = .63$, 7.22%)	**3.70**	**0.77**		
Em01. Place students' interest first	3.43	1.25	.609	.707
Em02. Understand specific needs of students	3.40	1.28	.735	.820

Table 4. Pearson correlations, means, and standard deviation for the factors ($N = 665$).

Factors	1	2	3	4	5	6	7	8	9	10	11
1 Age (Years)	1.00										
2 Duration (Months)	.088*	1.00									
3 Online Benefits	-.067	-.158**	1.00								
4 Online Habits	-.099*	-.007	.446**	1.00							
5 Online Facilitation	-.113**	.043	.390**	.415**	1.00						
6 Tangibles	.092*	-.025	.245**	.213**	.157**	1.00					
7 Reliability	-.006	-.074	.194**	.196**	.132**	.370**	1.00				
8 Empathy	-.033	-.066	.208**	.155**	.124**	.243**	.414**	1.00			
9 Responsiveness	.081*	-.062	.182**	.177**	.079*	.456**	.199**	.174**	1.00		
10 Assurance	-.029	.06	.058	.230**	.178**	.126**	.306**	.290**	.178**	1.00	
11 CES-D	.074	.067	-.093*	-.186**	-.186**	-.197**	-.237**	-.153**	-.102**	-.124**	1.00
Mean	25.37	14.37	4.28	4.28	4.48	3.88	3.68	3.42	3.27	3.70	12.17
Standard Deviation	6.65	23.19	0.73	0.73	0.59	0.70	0.77	1.08	0.84	0.77	8.90

Note. $*p < .05$ level (2-tailed). $**p < .01$ level (2-tailed)

4   Results and Discussions

As for the predictability of IUM and SERVQUAL towards study abroad students' depression, regression analysis is accomplished. Prior to the regression analysis, correlations among the factors are first computed. Table 4 shows the various with almost all of the IUM and SERVQUAL factors correlated with each other, denoting high linear associations each other [67]. In addition, a standard multiple regression analysis was performed between the dependent variable (CES-D; depression) and the independent variables (IUM factors; online benefits, online habits, online facilitation, and SERVQUAL factors; tangibles, reliability, empathy, responsiveness, assurance). Analysis was performed using SPSS regression.

Assumptions were tested by examining the plots and diagrams or residuals with no violations of normality, linearity, or homoscedasticity of residuals were detected [68]. Regression analysis revealed that the model significantly predicted study abroad students' depression, $F(8, 656) = 0.20, p < .000$. R^2 for the model was .10, and adjusted R^2 was .09. Table 5 shows the unstandardized regression coefficients (B), intercept, and standardized regression coefficients (β) for each variable.

Table 5. Regression analysis for study abroad students' depression ($N = 665$).

Factors	B	SE B	β	t	Sig
(Constant)	35.857	3.252		11.026	.000
Online Benefits	0.799	0.536	0.066	1.491	.136
Online Habits	−1.255	0.540	−0.103	**−2.323**	**.020**
Online Facilitation	−1.898	0.644	−0.125	**−2.948**	**.003**
Tangibles	−1.298	0.564	−0.103	**−2.301**	**.022**
Reliability	−1.801	0.508	−0.155	**−3.542**	**.000**
Empathy	−0.356	0.345	−0.043	−1.032	.302
Responsiveness	0.009	0.447	0.001	0.021	.983
Assurance	−0.102	0.471	−0.009	−0.216	.829

For each of the individual predictors (independent variables; IUM and SERVQUAL factors), IUM factors *online habits* ($t = -2.32, p < .020$), *online facilitation* ($t = -2.95, p < .003$) and SERVQUAL factors *tangibles* ($t = -2.30, p < .022$) and *reliability* ($t = -3.54, p < .000$) each significantly predicted depression (see Table 4 for the means and SDs). Note that the t values are negative, hence, the factors are said to be able to significantly minimize study abroad students' depression.

5   Conclusions

The current study used a survey questionnaire and collects information regarding the study abroad students' perceived service quality of their host universities and together with their internet use motives to predict their tendencies to become depress. Results of the study shows that two factors of the internet use motive variable are quite useful in minimizing depression. First, the students' *online habits* which are the tendencies wherein students are able to use the internet (either with their personal computers, laptops, or smartphones) to communicate with their family and friends. This also denotes that students are able to use the technologies that they are familiar with. Hence, availability and accessibility to internet connection would seem crucial. Second, students are able to use the internet to *facilitate* their social and leisure activities. This can be useful as long as the students are able to successfully enjoy or participate in the activities.

As for the study abroad students' perceived university service quality, the results noted that the physical *tangible* properties of the institution matters. This means that the actual infrastructure and facilities should be pleasing to the students. More specifically, these tangibles should have both functionality and appeal to the students. Similarly, study abroad students also values the *reliability* of the services provided. Consistency and accuracy of the services are very important. In essence, these service qualities issues should be continue, while the other non-significant factors should be enhanced. Lastly, findings of the current study shall provide institutional providers and researchers with valuable information with regards to service quality improvement, which ultimately leads to a more fruitful and less stressful study abroad experience.

References

1. Knight, J., de Wit, H.: Internationalization of higher education: past and future. Int. High. Educ. **95**(1), 2–4 (2018). https://doi.org/10.6017/ihe.2018.95.10715
2. Knight, J.: Student mobility and internationalization: trends and tribulations. Res. Comp. Int. Educ. **7**(1), 20–33 (2012). https://doi.org/10.2304/rcie.2012.7.1.20
3. Chen, D.I.-R., Lo, W.Y.W.: Internationalization or commodification? A case study of internationalization practices in Taiwan's higher education. Asia Pac. Educ. Rev. **14**(1), 33–41 (2013). https://doi.org/10.1007/s12564-013-9246-0
4. Chin, J.M.-C., Ching, G.S.: Trends and indicators of Taiwan's higher education internationalization. Asia Pac. Educ. Res. **18**(2), 185–203 (2009). https://doi.org/10.3860/taper.v18i2.1322
5. Chin, J.M.-C., Wu, C.-T., Ching, G.S.: Apple and oranges: comparison of Taiwan higher education institutions' internationalization. Int. J. Res. Stud. Educ. **1**(1), 3–22 (2012). https://doi.org/10.5861/ijrse.2012.v1i2.24
6. Ching, G.S., Chin, J.M.-C.: Managing higher education institution internationalization: contemporary efforts of a university in Taiwan. Int. J. Res. Stud. Manag. **1**(1), 3–16 (2012). https://doi.org/10.5861/ijrsm.2012.v1i1.9
7. Chou, C.P., Ching, G.S.: Taiwan Education at the Crossroad: When Globalization Meets Localization. Palgrave Macmillan, New York (2012). https://doi.org/10.1057/9780230120143
8. Chan, S.-J.: Shifting patterns of student mobility in Asia. High Educ. Pol. **25**(2), 207–224 (2012). https://doi.org/10.1057/hep.2012.3
9. Choudaha, R.: Three waves of international student mobility (1999–2020). Stud. High. Educ. **42**(5), 825–832 (2017). https://doi.org/10.1080/03075079.2017.1293872
10. Ching, G.S., Chao, P.-C., Lien, W.-C.: Acculturative hassles and strategies: relationship between study abroad related depression, anxiety, and stress. Int.J. Res. Stud. Psychol. **3**(5), 3–25 (2014). https://doi.org/10.5861/ijrsp.2014.818

11. Lin, J.-C.G., Yi, J.K.: Asian international students' adjustment: issues and program suggestions. Coll. Stud. J. **31**(4), 473–479 (1997)
12. Santos, J.L.: Institutional research meets knowledge management. In: Metcalfe, A. (ed.) Knowledge Management and Higher Education: A Critical Analysis, pp. 93–114. IGI Global, Hershey (2006). https://doi.org/10.4018/978-1-59140-509-2.ch006
13. Sireteanu, N.-A., Bedrule-Grigoruta, M.V.: Perspectives of knowledge management in universities. SSRN Electron. J. (2007). https://doi.org/10.2139/ssrn.1029990
14. Teodorescu, D.: Institutional researchers as knowledge managers in universities: Envisioning new roles for the IR profession. Tert. Educ. Manag. **12**, 75–88 (2006). https://doi.org/10.1007/s11233-005-4069-0
15. Bok, D.: Our Underachieving Colleges: A Candid Look at How Much Students Learn and Why They Should Be Learning More. Princeton University, Princeton (2006)
16. Vande Berg, M.: Intervening in student learning abroad: a research-based inquiry. Intercult. Educ. **20**(4), 15–27 (2009). https://doi.org/10.1080/14675980903370821
17. Vande Berg, M., Paige, R.M., Lou, K.H.: Student learning abroad: paradigms and assumptions. In: Vande Berg, M., Paige, R.M., Lou, K.H. (eds.) Student Learning Abroad: What Our Students are Learning, What They're not, and What We Can do About It, pp. 3–28. Stylus Publishing, Sterling (2012)
18. Freed, B.F.: An overview of issues and research in language learning in a study-abroad setting. Front. Interdiscip. J. Study Abroad **4**(2), 21–60 (1998)
19. Freed, B.F., Segalowitz, N., Dewey, D.P.: Context of learning and second language fluency in French: Comparing regular classroom, study abroad, and intensive domestic immersion programs. Stud. Second. Lang. Acquis. **26**(2), 275–301 (2004). https://doi.org/10.1017/S0272263104262064
20. Segalowitz, N., Freed, B., Collentine, J., Lafford, B., Lazar, N., Díaz-Campos, M.: A comparison of Spanish second language acquisition in two different learning contexts: study abroad and the domestic classroom. Front. Interdiscip. J. Study Abroad **10**(1), 1–18 (2004). https://doi.org/10.36366/frontiers.v10i1.130
21. Di Silvio, F., Donovan, A., Malone, M.E.: The effect of study abroad homestay placements: participant perspectives and oral proficiency gains. Foreign Lang. Ann. **47**(1), 168–188 (2014). https://doi.org/10.1111/flan.12064
22. Wilkinson, S.: On the nature of immersion during study abroad: some participant perspectives. Front. Interdiscip. J. Study Abroad **4**, 121–138 (1998)
23. Gardner, P., Gross, L., Steglitz, I.: Unpacking your study abroad experience: critical reflection for workplace competencies. CERI Res. Brief **1**(1), 1–10 (2008)
24. Vande Berg, M., Paige, R.M., Lou, K.H. (eds.): Student Learning Abroad: What Our Students are Learning, What They're Not, and What We Can Do About It. Stylus Publishing, Sterling (2012)
25. Zeithaml, V.A.: Consumer perceptions of price, quality, and value: a means-end and synthesis of evidence. J. Mark. **52**(3), 2–22 (1988). https://doi.org/10.1177/002224298805200302
26. Yeo, R.K., Li, J.: Beyond SERVQUAL: the competitive forces of higher education in Singapore. Total Qual. Manag. **25**(2), 95–123 (2014). https://doi.org/10.1080/14783363.2011.637802
27. Gronroos, C.: Service quality: the six criteria of good perceived service. Rev. Bus. **9**(3), 10–13 (1988)
28. Christensen, C.M., Eyring, H.J.: The Innovative University: Changing the DNA of Higher Education from the Inside Out. Jossey-Bass, San Francisco (2011)
29. Cubillo-Pinilla, J.M., Zúñiga, J., Soret, I., Sánchez, J.: Factors influencing international students' evaluations of higher educational programs. J. Acad. Bus. **15**(1), 270–278 (2009)
30. Angell, R.J., Heffernan, T.W., Megicks, P.: Service quality in postgraduate education. Qual. Assur. Educ. **16**(3), 236–254 (2008). https://doi.org/10.1108/09684880810886259

31. Shanka, T., Quintal, V., Taylor, R.: Factors influencing international students' choice of an education destination: a correspondence analysis. J. Mark. High. Educ. **15**(2), 31–46 (2006). https://doi.org/10.1300/J050v15n02_02
32. Mazzarol, T., Soutar, G.N.: Push-pull factors influencing international student destination choice. Int. J. Educ. Manag. **16**(2), 82–90 (2002). https://doi.org/10.1108/09513540210418403
33. Soutar, G.N., McNcil, M.M., Lim, K.: Service quality in educational institutions: a foreign student view. J. Mark. High. Educ. **7**(2), 85–94 (1996). https://doi.org/10.1300/J050v07n02_07
34. Hill, F.M.: Managing service quality in higher education: the role of the student as primary consumer. Qual. Assur. Educ. **3**(3), 10–21 (1995). https://doi.org/10.1108/09684889510093497
35. Parasuraman, A., Zeithaml, V.A., Berry, L.L.: SERVQUAL: a multi-item scale for measuring consumer perceptions of service quality. J. Retail. **64**(1), 12–40 (1988)
36. Parasuraman, A., Berry, L.L., Zeithaml, V.A.: Refinement and reassessment of the SERVQUAL scale. J. Retail. **67**(4), 420–540 (1991)
37. Lloyd, A.E., Luk, S.T.K.: Interaction behaviors leading to comfort in the service encounter. J. Serv. Mark. **25**(3), 176–189 (2011). https://doi.org/10.1108/08876041111129164
38. Atrek, B., Bayraktaroğlu, G.: Is there a need to develop a separate service quality scale for every service sector? Verification of SERVQUAL in higher education services. J. Faculty Econ. Adm. Sci. **17**(1), 423–440 (2012)
39. Donlagic, S., Fazlic, S.: Quality assessment in higher education using the SERVQUAL model. Management **20**(1), 39–57 (2015)
40. Zafiropoulos, C., Vrana, V.: Service quality assessment in a Greek higher education institute. J. Bus. Econ. Manag. **9**(1), 33–45 (2008). https://doi.org/10.3846/1611-1699.2008.9.33-45
41. Yousapronpaiboon, K.: SERVQUAL: measuring higher education service quality in Thailand. Procedia. Soc. Behav. Sci. **116**(21), 1088–1095 (2014). https://doi.org/10.1016/j.sbspro.2014.01.350
42. Mostafa, M.M.: A comparison of SERVQUAL and I-P analysis: measuring and improving service quality in Egyptian private universities. J. Mark. High. Educ. **16**(2), 83–104 (2006). https://doi.org/10.1300/J050v16n02_04
43. Mbise, E.-R., Tuninga, R.S.J.: The application of SERVQUAL to business schools in an emerging market: the case of Tanzania. J. Trans. Manag. **18**(2), 101–124 (2013). https://doi.org/10.1080/15475778.2013.782238
44. Behdioğlu, S., Şener, H.Y.: Improving service quality in special education institutions: SERVQUAL scale. Glob. Bus. Manag. Res. **6**(2), 169–184 (2014)
45. Nasseef, M.A.: Measuring the quality of educational service provided by business administration department using the SERVQUAL instrument at King Abdul-Aziz University Jeddah. J. Bus. Stud. Q. **5**(4), 147–172 (2014)
46. Enayati, T., Modanloo, Y., Behnamfar, R., Rezaei, A.: Measuring service quality of Islamic Azad University of Mazandaran using SERVQUAL model. Iranian J. Manag. Stud. **6**(1), 101–118 (2013)
47. Arambewela, R., Hall, J.: A comparative analysis of international education satisfaction using SERVQUAL. J. Serv. Res. **6**, 141–163 (2006)
48. Rasli, A., Shekarchizadeh, A., Iqbal, M.J.: Perception of service quality in higher education: perspective of Iranian students in Malaysian universities. Int. J. Econ. Manag. **6**(2), 201–220 (2012)
49. Shekarchizadeh, A., Rasli, A., Huam, H.-T.: SERVQUAL in Malaysian universities: perspectives of international students. Bus. Process. Manag. J. **17**(1), 67–81 (2011). https://doi.org/10.1108/14637151111105580

50. O'Neill, M.A., Palmer, A.: Importance-performance analysis: a useful tool for directing continuous quality improvement in higher education. Qual. Assur. Educ. **12**(1), 39–52 (2004). https://doi.org/10.1108/09684880410517423
51. Ibrahim, E., Wang, L.W., Hassan, A.: Expectations and perceptions of overseas students towards service quality of higher education institutions in Scotland. Int. Bus. Res. **6**(6), 20–30 (2013). https://doi.org/10.5539/ibr.v6n6p20
52. Axinn, W.G., Pearce, L.D.: Mixed Method Data Collection Strategies. Cambridge University Press, New York (2006). https://doi.org/10.1017/CBO9780511617898
53. Cohen, L., Manion, L., Morrison, K.: Research Methods in Education. Routledge, New York (2007)
54. Lin, M.-C., Ching, G.S.: The role of internet in study abroad related stress in Taiwan. In: Slykhuis, M., Marks, G. (eds.) Proceedings of Society for Information Technology and Teacher Education International Conference 2015, pp. 1207–1211. AACE, Chesapeake (2015)
55. Radloff, L.S.: The CES-D scale: a self-report depression scale for research in the general population. Appl. Psychol. Meas. **1**(3), 385–401 (1977). https://doi.org/10.1177/014662167700100306
56. Weisberg, H.F., Kronsnick, J.A., Bowen, B.D.: An Introduction to Survey Research, Polling, and Data Analysis, 3rd edn. Sage, Thousand Oaks (1996)
57. Likert, R.: A technique for the measurement of attitudes. Arch. Psychol. **140**, 5–55 (1932)
58. Cronbach, L.J.: Coefficient alpha and the internal structure of tests. Psychometrika **16**(3), 197–334 (1951). https://doi.org/10.1007/BF02310555
59. Carmines, E.G., Zeller, R.A.: Reliability and Viability Assessment. Sage, Thousand Oaks (1991)
60. Nunnally, J.C.: Introduction to Psychological Measurement. McGraw-Hill, New York (1970)
61. Costello, A.B., Osborne, J.W.: Best practices in exploratory factor analysis: four recommendations for getting the most from your analysis. Pract. Assess. Res. Eval. **10**(7), 1–9 (2005)
62. Kaiser, H.F.: An index of factorial simplicity. Psychometrika **39**(1), 31–36 (1974). https://doi.org/10.1007/BF02291575
63. Henson, R.K., Roberts, J.K.: Use of exploratory factor analysis in published research: common errors and some comment on improved practice. Educ. Psychol. Measur. **66**(3), 393–416 (2006). https://doi.org/10.1177/0013164405282485
64. Schreiber, J.B., Stage, F.K., King, J., Nora, A., Barlow, E.A.: Reporting structural equation modeling and confirmatory factor analysis results: a review. J. Educ. Res. **99**(6), 323–337 (2006). https://doi.org/10.3200/JOER.99.6.323-338
65. Hu, L.T., Bentler, P.M.: Cutoff criteria for fit indexes in covariance structure analysis: conventional criteria versus new alternatives. Struct. Equ. Model. **6**(1), 1–55 (1999). https://doi.org/10.1080/10705519909540118
66. MacCallum, R.C., Browne, M.W., Sugawara, H.M.: Power analysis and determination of sample size for covariance structure modeling. Psychol. Methods **1**(2), 130–149 (1996). https://doi.org/10.1037/1082-989X.1.2.130
67. Taylor, R.: Interpretation of the correlation coefficient: a basic review. J. Diagn. Med. Sonogr. **6**(1), 35–39 (1990). https://doi.org/10.1177/875647939000600106
68. Hayes, A.F.: Introduction to Mediation, Moderation, and Conditional Process Analysis: A Regression-Based Approach. Guilford Publications, New York (2018)

Improvement on Attribute Weighting in Attribute Coordinate Comprehensive Evaluation Method

Xiaolin Xu[1](✉) and Jiali Feng[2]

[1] Shanghai Polytechnic University, Shanghai, China
[2] Shanghai Maritime University, Shanghai, China
jlfeng@shmtu.edu.cn

Abstract. Attribute coordinate comprehensive evaluation method is essentially a qualitative evaluation method. Its feature lies in that on the same total score plane, on the basis of considering the comprehensive scores of all attributes, it focuses on considering the weight of certain attributes. The weight of an attribute is obtained by the evaluator's ratings, i.e. several samples are randomly selected from the hyperplane with the same total score for the evaluator to rate. However, the samples can be randomly selected and may not reflect all the characteristics of the entire attribute system, thus the ratings cannot reflect the evaluator's preference well or the comprehensive factors of the attributes, further resulting in unreasonable evaluation results. This paper proposes a new attribute weighting method to fundamentally address this problem. Simulation experiments also verify the effectiveness of this method.

Keywords: Comprehensive evaluation · Attribute weighting · Local satisfactory solution curve · Global satisfaction

1 Introduction

Attribute coordinate comprehensive evaluation method [1–6] is such an evaluation method that evaluators subjectively give weights to the certain attributes of the evaluated objects by way of rating the selected samples. The rating lays evaluators' particular stress on certain attributes, thus to calculate the weight of each attribute. Due to the randomness of the selected samples, there may be sample data with repeated characteristics, or extreme data with a certain attribute value particularly good and a certain attribute value particularly poor, resulting in that the selected samples may not effectively reflect all the characteristics of the attribute system, thus causing the evaluator to fail to give a reasonable rating, thus failing to well reflect the psychological weight level of the evaluator, and further affecting the results of the following processes and the accuracy of the final evaluation.

The work was supported by the Key Disciplines of Computer Science and Technology of Shanghai Polytechnic University (No. XXKZD1604).

L. Uden et al. (Eds.): KMO 2021, CCIS 1438, pp. 85–94, 2021.
https://doi.org/10.1007/978-3-030-81635-3_8

In order to address this problem, this paper improves the rating method of the samples by directly rating the attributes rather than rating the samples to give them different weights, thus reducing the difficulty of rating and more accurately reflecting the psychological weight of the evaluator.

This paper first gives a brief introduction to attribute coordinate comprehensive evaluation method, then introduces the shortcomings of the original rating method, and the improved weighting method, and finally compares the evaluation results obtained by the two methods through simulation experiments.

2   Introduction to Attribute Coordinate Comprehensive Evaluation Method [7–10]

2.1   Barycentric Coordinate

When evaluating the multi-attribute object, the evaluator usually thinks that some attributes are more important than others, and should be endowed with more weights. The importance of attributes can possibly change along with the advantageous or disadvantageous degree of the evaluated objects, and such change reflected in the evaluation model is the dynamic change of the weight of a certain attribute.

One of the main characteristics of the attribute coordinate comprehensive evaluation is to endow attributes with different weights according to the evaluator's preference. The specific method is to give ratings on the given samples. Suppose T_0 is the critical total scores, and T_{max} is the maximum total scores. In the interval $[T_0, T_{max}]$, several scores $T_1, T_2, ..., T_{n-1}$ are uniformly selected according to the requirement for curve fitting. For the total score $T_i(i = 1, 2, 3..., n-1)$, several samples are selected for the evaluator and rated according to the evaluator's preference. Then, the barycentric coordinate with total score of $T_i(i = 1, 2, 3...n-1)$ is calculated by Eq. (1).

$$b\left(\left\{v^h(z)\right\}\right) = \left(\frac{\sum_{h=1}^{t} v_1^h f_1^h}{\sum_{h=1}^{t} v_1^h}, \cdots, \frac{\sum_{h=1}^{t} v_m^h f_m^h}{\sum_{h=1}^{t} v_m^h}\right) \tag{1}$$

Where, $b(\{vh(z)\})$ is the psychological barycentric coordinate of the evaluator z; $\{x_k, k = 1,...,s\}$ is the set of all the samples with total score of T_i, and each sample has m attributes, with the values respectively of f_i, $i = 1...m$. The evaluator selects t sets of samples $\{f_h, h = 1,...,t\}$ which are believed thereby to be satisfactory, and respectively rates as $v^h(f^h)$, which is taken as the evaluator's psychological weight; then, the weighted average method is adopted to find the psychological barycentric coordinate of the evaluator for the total score T_i, and also seen as the evaluator's local satisfactory solution. The process is called as the learning of the evaluator's psychological weight.

2.2   Satisfactory Solution Curve

Obviously, with plenty of training samples and training times, the barycenter $b(\{v^h(z)\})$ will be gradually approximate to the local most satisfactory solution $x*|T$ in total score

T, namely: $\lim_{h\to\infty} b(\{vh(z)\}) \to x * |T$. Through the learning of each total score $T_i(i = 1,$ $2, 3... n-1)$, $b_i(\{vh(z)\})$ can be obtained. After T traverses the interval $[T_0, T_{max}]$, the set $\{b'(\{v^h(z)\})|T \in [T_0, T_{max}]\}$ for all local most satisfactory solutions can be obtained. Generally speaking, the psychological criteria of the evaluator z on different total score T_i are consistent with each other. In other words, $\{b'(\{v^h(z)\})|T \in [T_0, T_{max}]\}$ can form a continuous curve, recorded as $L(b'(\{v^h(z)\}))$, which is called as the local most satisfactory solution curve of the evaluator z. $L(b'(\{v^h(z)\}))$ can be obtained by polynomial curve fitting. For example, three local most satisfactory solutions are taken as the interpolation points and input into Lagrange interpolation Eq. (2) to calculate and the most satisfactory solution curve:

$$g_i(T) = \frac{(T - x_1^*)(T - x_2^*)}{(x_0^* - x_1^*)(x_0^* - x_2^*)}a_{i0} + \frac{(T - x_0^*)(T - x_2^*)}{(x_1^* - x_0^*)(x_1^* - x_2^*)}a_{i1} + \frac{(T - x_0^*)(T - x_1^*)}{(x_2^* - x_0^*)(x_2^* - x_1^*)}a_{i2}$$

(2)

Normally, when T value is larger, the evaluator is better satisfied with the local most satisfactory solution $b'(\{v^h(z)\})$ corresponding to T in $L(b'(\{v^h(z)\}))$.

2.3 Satisfaction Degree for Each Object

With many satisfactory solutions which construct satisfactory solution curve L $(b(\{f^h(z)\}))$, we can calculate the global satisfaction according to (3) for each object to reflect how satisfactory it is compared with the satisfactory solution of the total plane to which the object belongs.

$$sat(f, Z) = \left(\frac{\sum_{ij=1}^{m} f_{ij}}{\sum_{j=1}^{m} F_j}\right)^{\left(\frac{\sum_{i=1}^{m} f_j}{3(\sum_{j=1}^{m} f_{ij})}\right)} * \exp\left(-\frac{\sum_{j=1}^{m} w_j|f_j - b(f^h(z_j)|}{\sum_{j=1}^{m} w_j\delta_j}\right)$$

(3)

Where, $sat(f,Z)$ is the satisfaction of evaluated object f, whose value is expected to be between 0 and 1.f_j is the value of each attribute.$|f_j - b(f^h(z_j)|$ is to measure the difference between each attribute value and the corresponding barycentric value(satisfactory solution).w_j and δ_j are used as the factor which can be adjusted to make the satisfaction comparable value in the case where the original results are not desirable. $\sum_{j=1}^{m} F_j$ is the sum of F_j with each attribute value full score. $\sum_{ij=1}^{m} f_{ij}$ is the sum of the values of all the attributes F_{ij} of F_i.

3   Comparison of Attribute Weighting Methods Before and After Improvement

Before calculating the local satisfactory solution in Sect. 2.1, the evaluator needs to score the samples selected from different total score planes to obtain their preference(or weight) for the attributes. Under this weighting method, there are two kinds of samples that possibly increases the evaluator's difficulty in judging them and causes the inaccuracy of the scoring, which is why we try to improve this method. The weighting methods before and after improvement are respectively explained below.

3.1 The Original Way of Weighting

1. Samples with Duplicated Characteristics

Let $\{x_k, k = 1,...,s\} \subseteq S_T \cap X$ is the sample set with the total score equal to T, z is the evaluator, z randomly selects t sets of samples he considers satisfactory from $\{x_h, h = 1,...,t\}$, and scores $w_h(x_h)$ respectively. However, the data selected in this way may not be representative. As shown in Table 1, the samples are in the same total score plane($T = 412$), and the similarities between samples are calculated by way of Pearson correlation coefficient, which are shown in Table 2. The similarity of sample 2 and 9, sample 10 and 15, and sample 8 and 13 is 1, which shows that the attribute features of these sample pairs are basically the same. If sample 2 is already selected for scoring, 9 can be ignored.

Table 1. The samples with the total score of 412

No.	SubjectA	SubjectB	SubjectC	Total
1	204	98	110	412
2	203	103	106	412
3	207	105	100	412
4	198	105	109	412
5	211	100	101	412
6	200	96	116	412
7	207	100	105	412
8	205	108	99	412
9	205	102	105	412
10	210	107	95	412
11	197	100	115	412
12	196	118	98	412
13	207	107	98	412
14	195	120	97	412
15	202	110	100	412

2. Samples with imbalance

In the same total score plane, the certain samples may appear like this way that some attribute values are very good while some attribute values are very bad, so it is difficult for

Table 2. Similarity between samples

No.	1	2	3	4	5	6	7	8	9	10	11	12	13	14	15
1	1	0.997	0.990	0.998	0.995	0.997	0.998	0.984	0.997	0.980	0.999	0.956	0.984	0.946	0.982
2	0.997	1	0.998	1	1	0.988	1	0.995	1	0.993	0.993	0.976	0.995	0.968	0.993
3	0.990	0.998	1	0.997	0.999	0.975	0.997	0.999	0.998	0.999	0.983	0.988	1	0.983	0.999
4	0.998	1	0.997	1	1	0.990	1	0.993	1	0.991	0.994	0.973	0.994	0.965	0.992
5	0.995	1	0.999	1	1	0.985	0.999	0.996	1	0.995	0.991	0.980	0.997	0.973	0.995
6	0.997	0.988	0.975	0.990	0.985	1	0.990	0.967	0.988	0.962	0.999	0.930	0.967	0.918	0.963
7	0.998	1	0.997	1	0.999	0.990	1	0.993	1	0.991	0.995	0.972	0.993	0.964	0.992
8	0.984	0.995	0.999	0.993	0.995	0.967	0.993	1	0.995	1	0.976	0.993	1	0.989	1
9	0.997	1	0.998	1	1	0.988	1	0.995	1	0.993	0.993	0.976	0.995	0.968	0.993
10	0.980	0.993	0.999	0.991	0.995	0.962	0.991	1	0.993	1	0.972	0.995	1	0.991	1
11	0.999	0.993	0.983	0.994	0.991	0.999	0.995	0.976	0.993	0.972	1	0.943	0.976	0.932	0.973
12	0.956	0.976	0.988	0.973	0.980	0.930	0.972	0.993	0.976	0.995	0.943	1	0.993	1	0.995
13	0.984	0.995	1	0.994	0.997	0.967	0.993	1	0.995	1	0.976	0.993	1	0.989	1
14	0.946	0.968	0.983	0.965	0.973	0.918	0.964	0.989	0.968	0.991	0.932	1	0.989	1	0.991
15	0.982	0.993	0.999	0.992	0.995	0.963	0.992	1	0.993	1	0.973	0.995	1	0.991	1

the evaluator to judge such samples good or not. In the following example, the value of SubjectA is very high and the value of SubjectC is relatively small. With comprehensive consideration, the evaluator usually ratings such sample a low score, thus ignoring the preference for a certain attribute.

No.	SubjectA	SubjectB	SubjectC
14	195	120	97

3.2 Improved Way of Weighting

The purpose of attribute coordinate comprehensive evaluation method is to find out the dynamic weight of the evaluator on some attributes by scoring the sample data on the certain hyperplanes by the evaluator. Based on this principle and drawbacks of the original rating way mentioned above, this paper designs a simpler and more scientific scoring method to give the weight to the specific attribute. Let $\{t_i, k = 1, ..., s\}$ be the attribute system set of the evaluation system, with a total of s attributes, t_i is the ith attribute. In the plane with a total score equal to T, the evaluator can directly score the each specific attribute, and mark it as $v_i(t_i)$, and calculate $w_i(t_i) = v_i / \sum_{i=1}^{s} v_i$, $w_i(t_i)$ is the dynamic weight of the evaluator gives the attribute t_i in the hyperplane, reflecting the evaluator's preference.

4 Simulation Experiment

To verify the rationality of the improved method, simulation experiments are carried out. In the simulation, we take the exam results of a county as sample data, with a total of 2500 samples. We select 412 as the first total hyperplane, and the distribution of samples on this hyperplane is shown in Fig. 1.

The following illustrates attribute coordinate comprehensive evaluation method introduced in 2 by calculating in turn, the barycenter coordinates, local satisfactory solution lines and global satisfaction, through this, compares the two results before and after the improvement of the weighting method, and particularly, the data of three students are selected to verify the effectiveness of the new method by ranking the global satisfactions respectively with the original and new weighting method.

4.1 Comparison of Local Satisfactory Solutions Before and After Improvement of Weighting Method

1. Rating Samples with the Old Weighting Method

First, we randomly select samples and get the evaluator to rate them, which is shown in Table 3 below. Through Pearson correlation coefficient calculation, we find that the features of sample 9 and sample 2, sample 7 are very similar. And we also find that some sample data are not balanced. For example, the SubjectC value of sample 14 is

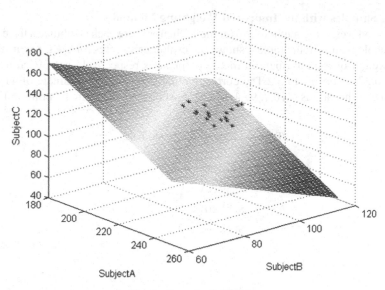

Fig. 1. Sample distribution

poor, so the evaluator gives a low score, the SubjectB value of sample 6 is poor, and the evaluator also gives a low score, thus completely ignoring the increase of the SubjectC value of sample 6 compared to sample 14. Therefore, this kind of weighting method is arbitrary and in some cases fails to consider the comprehensive performance of attributes, or highlight the difference of specific attribute value among samples so that it cannot fully reflect psychological weight of the evaluator in the comprehensive evaluation of attributes.

From the evaluator's scoring, we get the barycentric coordinate on the plane according to Eq. (1) as (204.25, 104, 103.75), shown by the "+"point in Fig. 2.

Table 3. Selected samples and ratings

No.	SubjectA	SubjectB	SubjectC	Rating
5	211	100	101	7
9	205	102	105	8
7	207	100	105	8
2	203	103	106	9
14	195	120	97	7
6	200	96	116	6

2. Rating Samples with the Improved Weighting Method

The improved weighting method is to let the evaluator score each attribute as the evaluator's psychological weight. Table 4 shows the evaluator's scores for the three attributes, and the weight of each attribute in this hyperplane is respectively calculated as 0.33, 0.30 and 0.37 according to 3.2.The corresponding barycentric coordinate of 412 total score plane in the case is (210.2, 97.1,104.6), as shown by the "Circle" point in Fig. 2.

Table 4. Ratings on the attributes

Attribute	Rating
SubjectA	9
SubjectB	8
SubjectC	10

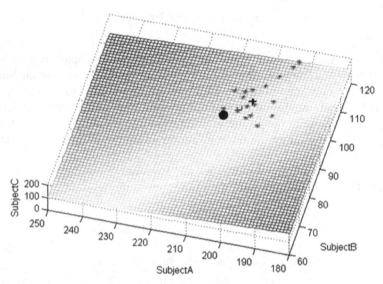

Fig. 2. Barycentric coordinates for the total score 412 using old and improved weighting method

From the distribution of the barycenter, the improved algorithm is closer to the center, which not only reflects the comprehensive consideration of various attributes but also takes into account the evaluator's psychological preference, so the result is more reasonable.

4.2 Comparison of GlobalSatisfaction Before and After Improvement

We further fit the curve through interpolation Eq. (2), and the most satisfactory solution line obtained is shown in Fig. 3.The curve is the most satisfactory solution line obtained by the old method, and the straight line is the most satisfactory solution line obtained by the improved method. The abscissa axis represents the score of SubjectB + SubjectC, and the ordinate axis represents the score of Subject A. From the Fig. 3, it can be seen that the improved satisfactory solution is less obvious in the attribute preference than the old satisfactory solution, and comprehensive consideration of the attribute is also taken when weighting the individual attribute.

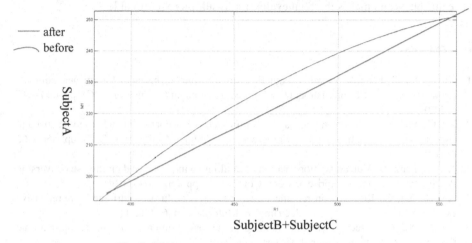

Fig. 3. Fitting curves before and after improvement

Finally, we calculate the global satisfaction of the evaluated data by way of Eq. (3).

Table 5 shows the selected evaluation results obtained by using the original and improved method. The global satisfactions and rankings of the evaluated objects No. 356, 365, 642 with the two methods are specified. Under the same total score, with original method, No. 642 sample is ranked highest and No. 365 is ranked lowest. Basically, they are ranked according to the preference for SubjectC, which is relatively unreasonable and does not reflect the balanced factor of the evaluator's preference for the secondary attribute SubjectA. Comparatively, with improved method, while the SubjectC has the highest weight, the sample 642 is not rated the highest, with the balanced factor of the SubjectA considered, so the sample 356 is rated the highest.

Table 5. Evaluation results using the original and improved weighting method

No.	SubjectA	SubjectB	SubjectC	Satisfaction (original)	Rank (original)	Satisfaction (improved)	Rank (improved)
356	214	105	107	0.8655	2	0.8754	1
365	216	111	99	0.8404	3	0.8608	2
642	206	110	110	0.8871	1	0.8501	3

5   Conclusion

In this paper, the shortcomings of the original method of weighting attributes through the selected samples in attribute coordinate comprehensive evaluation method are analyzed, thereby improved method is proposed, which scores the attributes to embody the different weights for them instead of scoring the samples so as to make the process of weighting easier and more specific. Meanwhile, it reflects the comprehensive considerations on the entire attributes and makes the final evaluation result more reasonable.

References

1. Xu, X., Xu, G., Feng, J.: A kind of synthetic evaluation method based on the attribute computing network. In: IEEE International Conference on Granular Computing (GrC), pp. 644–647 (2009)
2. Xu, G., Min, S.: Research on multi-agent comprehensive evaluation model based on attribute coordinate. In: IEEE International Conference on Granular Computing (GrC), pp. 556–562 (2012)
3. Xu, X., Feng, J.: A quantification method of qualitative indices based on inverse conversion degree functions. In: Enterprise Systems Conference, pp. 261–264 (2014)
4. Xu, X., Xu, G.: Research on ranking model based on multi-user attribute comprehensive evaluation method. In: Applied Mechanics & Materials, pp. 644–650 (2014)
5. Xu, X., Xu, G.: A recommendation ranking model based on credit. In: IEEE International Conference on Granular Computing (GrC), pp. 569–572 (2012)
6. Xu, G., Wang, L.: Evaluation of aberrant methylation gene forecasting tumor risk value in attribute theory. J. Basic Sci. Eng. **16**(2), 234 (2008)
7. Xu, G., Xu, X.: Study on evaluation model of attribute barycentric coordinates. Int. J. Grid Distrib. Comput. **9**(9), 115–128 (2016)
8. Xu, X., Xu, G., Feng, J.: Study on updating algorithm of attribute coordinate evaluation model. In: Huang, D.-S., Hussain, A., Han, K., Gromiha, M.M. (eds.) ICIC 2017. LNCS (LNAI), vol. 10363, pp. 653–662. Springer, Cham (2017). https://doi.org/10.1007/978-3-319-63315-2_57
9. Xu, X., Liu, Y., Feng, J.: Improvement on subjective weighing method in attribute coordinate comprehensive evaluation model. In: Uden, L., Ting, I.-H., Corchado, J.M. (eds.) KMO 2019. CCIS, vol. 1027, pp. 178–186. Springer, Cham (2019). https://doi.org/10.1007/978-3-030-21451-7_15
10. Xu, X., Liu, Y., Feng, J.: Attribute coordinate comprehensive evaluation model combining principal component analysis. In: Shi, Z., Pennartz, C., Huang, T. (eds.) ICIS 2018. IAICT, vol. 539, pp. 60–69. Springer, Cham (2018). https://doi.org/10.1007/978-3-030-01313-4_7

The Effect of System Quality, Knowledge Quality, and Knowledge-Contribution Signals on Members' Knowledge Contribution and -Seeking Behaviors in Professional Virtual Communities

Hui-Min Lai[1] and Pi-Jung Hsieh[2]([✉])

[1] Department of Business Administration, National Taichung University of Science and Technology, Taichung, Taiwan, R.O.C.
[2] Department of Hospital and Health Care Administration, Chia Nan University of Pharmacy and Science, Tainan, Taiwan, R.O.C.
beerun@seed.net.tw

Abstract. Professional virtual communities (PVCs) can serve as knowledge exchange platforms that allow community members to voluntarily contribute and seek knowledge collaboratively. The extant literature suggests that the system design of PVCs may influence community members' knowledge contribution and knowledge-seeking behaviors. Adopting the information system (IS) success model, and signaling theory as a theoretical lens, we propose and examine the direct effects of the system quality, knowledge quality, and knowledge-contribution signals of PVCs on knowledge-contribution and -seeking behaviors. Empirical data were collected from one PVC in Taiwan through survey questionnaires; 77 participants answered the knowledge contribution questionnaire, and 98 answered the knowledge-seeking questionnaire. The results indicated that knowledge content quality, perceived virtual reward mechanism, perceived public recognition mechanism, and perceived knowledge-rating mechanism have significance for knowledge contribution behavior. Knowledge content quality, perceived virtual reward mechanism, and perceived knowledge-rating mechanism have significance for knowledge-seeking behavior. Collectively, the results highlight the differences in the impact of system artifacts on these key behaviors in PVCs.

Keywords: Knowledge contribution · Knowledge seeking · Knowledge contribution signals · Professional virtual communities · Signaling theory

1 Introduction

Virtual communities have emerged as pertinent knowledge-sharing platforms that cross organizational boundaries and overcome geographic constraints, and professional virtual communities (PVCs) represent an important manifestation of this recent phenomenon [1]. PVCs' sustainability relies on user participation [2]; however, many PVCs have

© Springer Nature Switzerland AG 2021
L. Uden et al. (Eds.): KMO 2021, CCIS 1438, pp. 95–110, 2021.
https://doi.org/10.1007/978-3-030-81635-3_9

failed owing to the low willingness of members to share knowledge [3, 4]. Given that user participation is voluntary, successful knowledge sharing depends on attracting more knowledge seekers who continue to reuse and spread shared knowledge and attracting more knowledge contributors who continue to contribute their valuable knowledge and experience [1, 5, 6]. Most PVCs have invested a lot in designing and maintaining their websites and systems to support and incentivize knowledge contribution and knowledge-seeking activities. However, an examination of the extant literature on promoting members' knowledge-seeking and knowledge contribution in virtual communities indicates that most studies focus on the effects of personal motivation and contextual factors [1, 2, 6, 7]. We can further assess how technical infrastructures affect virtual communities [8]. We do not yet understand which PVC system artifacts may benefit the development of knowledge contribution behavior and knowledge-seeking behavior. Thus, we asked the following question: *Which system, knowledge, and knowledge-contribution signals are best designed to promote members' knowledge contribution and knowledge-seeking behaviors in a PVC setting?*

Two issues remain inadequately addressed in the research in this area. First, knowledge sharing is likely to be inhibited when knowledge seekers face high search costs in obtaining the necessary knowledge and when knowledge contributors do not find enough rewards to outweigh the costs of contributing knowledge [9]. Such a scenario often leads to knowledge market inefficiency [9], but design may play a key role in overcoming the associated issues. From the view of the information system (IS) success model, these factors may include knowledge content quality and searchability. According to signal theory, a strong signaling environment between knowledge contributors and seekers is needed to make the knowledge flow efficiently, as knowledge market signals indicate information that shows where the knowledge is and how to gain access to it [9]. In the PVC setting, these signals may include virtual reward, public recognition, and knowledge-rating mechanisms. Specifically, the IS success model may account for system and knowledge quality, while signaling theory may be used to justify the knowledge contribution signals. Thus, the model and the theory may be appropriate for explaining voluntary human behavior in PVCs. Second, questions regarding whether users' perceptions of different system quality, knowledge quality, and knowledge contribution signals can promote the users' knowledge contribution and knowledge-seeking behaviors have not been considered simultaneously and systematically. Accordingly, this paper proposes and empirically tests system quality, knowledge quality, and knowledge contribution signals concurrently to explore the impact on these two behaviors.

2 Literature Review

2.1 Integrating the IS Success Model and Signaling Theory

This study integrates the IS success model [10] and signaling theory [11] to understand PVCs system artifacts. The IS success model is used to examine the knowledge quality and system quality of PVC features. System quality, information quality, use, user satisfaction, individual impact, and organizational impact have been used to evaluate IS success [10]. Signaling theory is used to understand knowledge contribution signals in PVCs. Signaling theory describes the use of different types of information by senders and receivers [11]. One of the parties (the sender) must choose whether or how to communicate and transmit the information, and the other party (the receiver) must choose how to interpret the signal. The fundamental concept is focused on reducing information asymmetry between two parties [12]. Information asymmetries happen when "different people know different things" [13]. Signaling theory has been used in marketing research; potential buyers and sellers must acquire information about each other and about the product [12]. A signal is an extrinsic cue that the seller can use to "convey information credibly about unobservable product quality to the buyer" [14]. This situation is similar to the knowledge market that knowledge contributors use to convey the quality of the knowledge contribution to the knowledge seeker. In Fig. 1, we present the timeline of signaling theory and apply it to the knowledge-sharing market, which includes senders and receivers. The signals shown in the knowledge-sharing market promote further knowledge contribution and knowledge-seeking behavior. Based on signaling theory, we selected popular knowledge contribution signals and understand how they stimulate further knowledge contribution and knowledge-seeking behaviors.

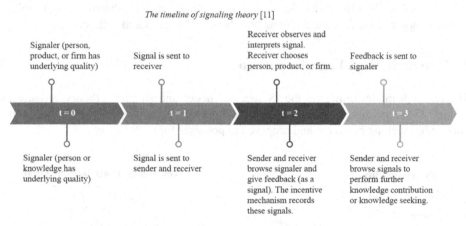

Fig. 1. The signaling timeline in the knowledge market

2.2 Knowledge Contribution Signals in Virtual Communities

Unlike members of organizations, members of PVCs may not know each other at all, and they are not likely to receive tangible rewards such as salaries, bonuses, job promotions, or other favorable benefits that come with organizational membership. In PVCs, strong external signals must flow between contributors and seekers in pursuit of minimizing information uncertainty, which reveals more information about the knowledge contribution quality and credibility, and enables contributors to make more contributions and seekers to find information more effectively. Therefore, understanding the knowledge contribution signals in PVCs will contribute to the involvement of community members in community activities. We reviewed existing PVCs and literature and summarized the common knowledge contribution signals into the following five categories: (1) Moderator application mechanism: Members who make major contributions to a PVC are promoted to moderator status. (2) Virtual reward mechanism: Members can get a certain score or number of points while participating in community activities; any member who has a certain score or number of points (usually through knowledge contribution or browsing) is allowed to convert these virtual rewards into actual gifts [15]. (3) Public recognition mechanism: The community website recognizes members who contribute significantly through a public recognition process such as community levels. Based on members' knowledge contribution experience, they are assigned different levels, such as beginner or expert. With these mechanisms, a member's performance ranking in the community can be raised [16]. Examples are site experts, post rankings, and most recommendations. (4) Knowledge-rating mechanism: Certain scores or points are given to members or comments. The more one participates, the higher one's score, thus allowing contributors to determine whether others make a significant difference to the community [17]. Examples include giving "likes," topic views, and response views. (5) Knowledge-tracking mechanism: Any member who "likes" favorite authors or topics is allowed to collect or subscribe [18]. Examples include collecting articles, subscribing to a topic, following topics or authors, and having "my favorite" articles and authors.

3   Research Model and Hypotheses

The research model draws on the IS success model and signaling theory as shown in Fig. 2. We predicted how each factor would affect knowledge contribution and knowledge-seeking behavior, and proposed hypotheses for each factor.

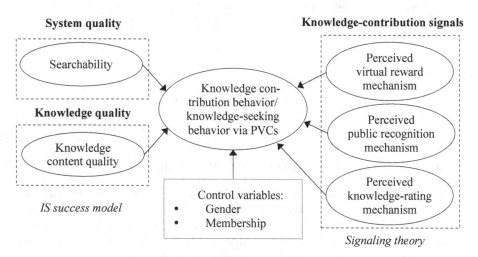

Fig. 2. The research model

Searchability is defined as users' perception of the PVC site's ability to help users search for and reuse certain pieces of knowledge [19]. The most obvious feature of a knowledge management system is the ability to retrieve knowledge [20] so that users can find knowledge easily without feeling overwhelmed [21]. When users can easily control a PVC, they are able to use various interaction forms to exchange knowledge [22]. In the present study, the interaction forms included those for entering search keywords, limiting the search scope, and sorting the search results. The greater the amount of necessary knowledge obtained from a search tool, the more likely users are to seek a greater amount of knowledge from the PVC, thus promoting knowledge contribution behavior while browsing existing knowledge. Due to the limited time for users to find information on a PVC, the increased searchability of a PVC may enhance members' knowledge retrieval abilities [19], thus possibly promoting knowledge-seeking behavior. We hypothesized the following:

H1: In PVCs, Searchability Is Positively Associated with (a) Knowledge Contribution Behavior and (b) Knowledge-Seeking Behavior
Knowledge content quality is defined as the relevance, timeliness, reliability, and accessibility of the knowledge provided in a PVC [19, 23]. The main concern of virtual community users is knowledge quality, because knowledge in a virtual community comes from strangers who are free to express their opinions [23], and the knowledge may or may not be reliable. Higher knowledge content quality can help individuals find more useful knowledge more easy and quickly, and such individuals may follow up and contribute their own knowledge to further enhance the knowledge content quality stored in knowledge repositories [19]. Knowledge quality is especially critical for knowledge seekers, because knowledge enables them to complete their tasks effectively [5], and may lead to user satisfaction with the PVC [19, 23]. Thus, we proposed the following hypothesis:

H2: In PVCs, Knowledge Content Quality Is Positively Associated with (a) Knowledge Contribution Behavior and (b) Knowledge-Seeking Behavior
A virtual reward mechanism is defined as a user's perception of virtual incentives provided for knowledge contribution to PVC. Members can get a certain score or number of points while participating in community activities; any member who has a certain score or number of points is allowed to convert these virtual rewards into actual gifts [15]. These virtual reward attributes may help contributors and seekers understand which topic involved in the topic discussion received high rewards, and subsequently, promote knowledge contribution and -seeking behaviors. A virtual reward mechanism provides a signal to the knowledge contributor and may increase contributors' willingness to contribute. A virtual reward mechanism makes it easier for knowledge seekers to concentrate on hot topics. Thus, we proposed the following:

H3: In PVCs, the Perceived Virtual Reward Mechanism Is Positively Associated with (a) Knowledge Contribution Behavior and (b) Knowledge-Seeking Behavior
A *perceived public recognition mechanism* is defined as a user's perception of the ranking of knowledge contribution activities in a PVC such as hot topics and expert celebrities. Earning a reputation [24] or creating an intelligent image is an important motivator for knowledge contributors [25]. Extant research has shown that PVC systems providing reputation feedback that contain ranking lists promote high-quality and high-quantity

knowledge contributions [15, 16]. The reputation system inspires knowledge contributors to be more generous with their contributions [26] because their contribution behaviors are appreciated and recognized [27, 28]. Many knowledge seekers in a PVC will never meet in person [26], so public recognition features such as the "hottest" issues, celebrity experts, and topic rankings reveal information about the credibility of the contributors and may increase a contributor's further contribution. In addition, through public recognition signals, seekers can find accurate knowledge, which may promote knowledge-seeking behavior. Accordingly, we posited the following:

H4: In PVCs, the Perceived Public Recognition Mechanism Is Positively Associated with (a) Knowledge Contribution Behavior and (b) Knowledge-Seeking Behavior
A *perceived knowledge-rating mechanism* is defined as a user's perception of the interactive features a PVC provides to enable members to rate or evaluate knowledge through "likes," and scores. These rating attributes may promote increasing levels of contribution because knowledge contributors can assess whether they have helped others. When individuals find that their contributed knowledge helped others, it creates a sense of enjoyment that promotes further knowledge contribution behavior [5]. The knowledge-rating mechanism could potentially reveal direct information about the knowledge contribution quality and may represent a contributor's credibility. Thus, we predict that the knowledge-rating mechanism encourages knowledge contribution behavior. This mechanism may assist knowledge seekers in showing their appreciation for the knowledge received and in understanding topics that most users recommend or care about and have effective, high-quality knowledge sources [17, 29, 30]. Thus, we proposed the following:

H5: In PVCs, the Perceived Knowledge-Rating Mechanism Is Positively Associated with (a) Knowledge Contribution Behavior and (b) Knowledge-Seeking Behavior.

4   Research Methodology

4.1   Data Collection

Data were collected via questionnaires distributed to one of the largest programming design-oriented PVCs in Taiwan: BlueShop. The participants were BlueShop members. We chose BlueShop because it is a professional knowledge exchange with mature knowledge-contribution signals, and it has a large number of users and posts. In this study, two questionnaires were used: a knowledge contribution questionnaire and a knowledge-seeking questionnaire. The knowledge contribution questionnaire was administered only to members who had experience contributing solutions or comments to questions. The respondent criteria, detailed definitions, and specific examples of knowledge-contribution signals were presented in the questionnaire. To minimize any potential common method variance, questionnaire data were collected at two time points [31]. For the knowledge contribution and knowledge-seeking questionnaires, at time point 1 (TP1), the participants answered in terms of their perceptions of knowledge content quality, searchability, and perceived virtual reward, public recognition, and knowledge-rating. At time point 2 (TP2), which was three months later, the second set of questionnaires was emailed to the respondents who had submitted valid questionnaires at TP1. Behavioral data were collected from the participants by asking them to report the average time they spent using the selected PVC for knowledge contribution, knowledge seeking, or both. At TP1, 108 participants with knowledge contribution experience completed the knowledge contribution questionnaire, and 139 participants completed the knowledge-seeking questionnaire. At TP2, 77 of the 108 participants completed the knowledge contribution questionnaire, and 98 of the 139 participants completed the knowledge-seeking questionnaire. Table 1 shows the respondents' characteristics.

Table 1. Demographic profiles of respondents

(a) Descriptive statistics of respondents		
	Knowledge contribution (TP2/TP1)	Knowledge seeking (TP2/TP1)
Valid response rate	77/108	98/139
(b) Demographic profile of respondents		
	Knowledge contribution	Knowledge seeking
Category	Frequency (%)	Frequency (%)
Gender		
Male	71 (92.2%)	81 (82.7%)
Female	6 (7.8%)	17 (17.3%)
Age		
20 years or younger	0 (0.0%)	6 (6.1%)
21–30 years	41 (53.2%)	68 (69.4%)
31–40 years	25 (32.5%)	12 (12.2%)
41–50 years	11 (14.3%)	9 (9.2%)
51 years or older	0 (0.0%)	3 (3.1%)
Education		
Senior high school	2 (2.6%)	0 (0.0%)
University or college	46 (59.7%)	92 (93.9%)
Graduate degree or above	29 (37.7%)	6 (6.1%)
Membership history		
Less than 1 month	1 (1.3%)	26 (26.5%)
1–3 months (less)	11 (14.3%)	26 (26.5%)
3–6 months (less)	24 (31.2%)	20 (20.4%)
6 months–1 year (less)	25 (32.5%)	16 (16.3%)
1–2 years	14 (18.2%)	7 (7.1%)
Longer than 2 years	2 (2.6%)	3 (3.1%)

4.2 Measurement

To enhance content validity, we adopted available items from previous studies when available; when items were not available, we developed new items based on literature. We chose to adapt wording to fit the PVC context. To validate the applicability of the questionnaires, we performed a pre-test and a pilot test. Appendix A shows all constructs in the research model. In addition to knowledge contribution or knowledge-seeking behavior, one of the questions measured frequency, which was converted into a five-point Likert scale. The remaining questions were also measured using a five-point Likert scale ranging from 1 = strongly disagree to 5 = strongly agree.

5 Results

5.1 Measurement Model

To assess the validity and reliability of all variables, and to ensure the quality of the questionnaire, we performed confirmatory factor analysis using SmartPLS3.0 software [32]. With this method, validity is evaluated by computing the convergent validity and the discriminant validity. In this study, all factor loadings on the corresponding variables were greater than 0.50 (see Appendix A), and the AVE values exceeded the 0.50 criterion (see Table 2); thus, the convergent validity was satisfactory. Table 2 illustrates that all square roots of the AVE values were greater than the inter-construct correlations; thus, discriminant validity was also satisfactory. Reliability was assessed using Cronbach's alpha and composite reliability. As demonstrated in Table 2, the Cronbach alpha values of the knowledge contribution and knowledge-seeking models ranged from 0.84 to 0.93 and from 0.87 to 0.94, respectively; both values were higher than 0.7 [33]. Similarly, the composite reliability of the knowledge contribution and knowledge-seeking models ranged from 0.90 to 0.96 and from 0.92 to 0.96, respectively; again, both values were higher than 0.7 [34]. In sum, the measurement model showed good validity and reliability, so the model was adequate for conducting further analysis.

5.2 Structural Model

The hypotheses were examined using partial least squares (PLS). A bootstrapping analysis with 500 iterations was used to examine whether the path coefficients were statistically significant [35], with the subsamples set to equal the sample sizes of the knowledge contribution and knowledge-seeking models (n = 77 and n = 98, respectively). Figure 3 and Fig. 4 show the path analysis results of the knowledge contribution and knowledge-seeking models, respectively. Searchability did not have a statistically significant positive effect on knowledge contribution behavior ($\beta = -0.035$, $p = 0.742$) and -seeking behavior ($\beta = 0.137$, $p = 0.220$); thus, H1a and H1b were not supported. Knowledge content quality was statistically significantly related to knowledge contribution behavior ($\beta = 0.239$, $p = 0.026$) and -seeking behavior ($\beta = 0.267$, $p = 0.003$); thus, H2a and H2b were supported, respectively. Because a perceived virtual reward mechanism had a statistically significant positive effect on knowledge contribution behavior ($\beta = 0.271$, $p = 0.025$) and -seeking behavior ($\beta = 0.232$, $p = 0.023$), H3a and H3b were supported,

Table 2. Reliability and validity

(a) Contribution model (N = 77)

	CA	CR	AVE	SEA	KQ	PVR	PPR	PKR	KC
Searchability	0.877	0.961	0.862	**0.928**					
Knowledge content quality	0.918	0.938	0.753	0.603	**0.868**				
Perceived virtual reward	0.929	0.955	0.876	0.346	0.379	**0.936**			
Perceived public recognition	0.908	0.942	0.845	0.315	0.448	0.298	**0.919**		
Perceived knowledge-rating	0.905	0.941	0.841	0.480	0.549	0.384	0.500	**0.917**	
Knowledge contribution	0.836	0.902	0.757	0.412	0.553	0.518	0.554	0.593	**0.870**

(b) Seeking model (N = 98)

	CA	CR	AVE	SEA	KQ	PVR	PPR	PKR	KS
Searchability	0.901	0.930	0.770	**0.904**					
Knowledge content quality	0.938	0.956	0.844	0.355	**0.915**				
Perceived virtual reward	0.887	0.930	0.815	0.517	0.322	**0.924**			
Perceived public recognition	0.868	0.919	0.792	0.324	0.293	0.385	**0.885**		
Perceived knowledge-rating	0.899	0.937	0.832	0.369	0.398	0.480	0.550	**0.905**	
Knowledge seeking	0.891	0.933	0.822	0.463	0.515	0.535	0.487	0.563	**0.911**

Notes. CA = Cronbach's alpha; CR = composite reliability; AVE = average variance extracted; Square root of AVE for each construct is shown in bold

respectively. A perceived public recognition mechanism had a statistically significant positive effect on knowledge contribution behavior ($\beta = 0.279$, $p = 0.020$); H4a was supported. However, a perceived public recognition mechanism it did not have a statistically significant effect on knowledge-seeking behavior ($\beta = 0.129$, $p = 0.171$); H4b was not supported. A perceived knowledge-rating mechanism was statistically significantly related to knowledge contribution behavior ($\beta = 0.254$, $p = 0.040$) and -seeking behavior ($\beta = 0.214$, $p = 0.023$); H5a and H5b were supported, respectively. Finally, several control variables were also included in the data analysis. None of the control variables had a statistically significantly effect on knowledge contribution and -seeking behaviors.

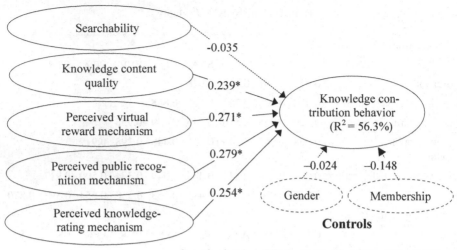

Sample size (n = 77); *$p<0.05$; **$p<0.01$; ***$p<0.001$
Dotted line indicates a lack of significance.

Fig. 3. Results of the knowledge contribution model

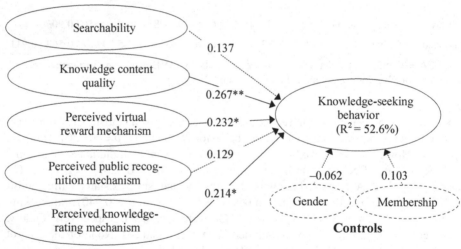

Sample size (n = 98); *$p<0.05$; **$p<0.01$; ***$p<0.001$
Dotted line indicates a lack of significance.

Fig. 4. Results of the knowledge-seeking model

6   Discussion, Implications, and Limitations

6.1   Discussion of Findings

This study aimed to understand the influence of system quality, knowledge quality, and knowledge-contribution signals on the knowledge contribution and knowledge-seeking behaviors of virtual community members. The empirical results showed several important findings. First, the results revealed that the PVC searchability did not increase knowledge contribution and knowledge-seeking behavior. The interaction between members and the PVC becomes easier, because members have previous experience in use of the PVC. Thus, PVC searchability is not a major concern. Second, the results showed that knowledge content quality is an important factor that drives members' knowledge contribution and knowledge-seeking behaviors. The success of a virtual community relies on the high quantity and quality of the knowledge contained in the community [15]. Low-quality content may frustrate users because potential contributors may not want to be associated with a low-quality space, and knowledge seekers may not want to participate actively if they feel that reading low-quality content is a waste of their time [36]. Third, as expected, a perceived virtual reward mechanism significantly affects knowledge contribution behavior and knowledge-seeking behavior. The results showed that similar to physical market transactions, currency in the knowledge market is required. Currency is needed to maintain a contributor–seeker relationship. Fourth, a perceived public recognition mechanism significantly affects knowledge contribution behavior but not knowledge-seeking behavior. A public recognition mechanism that provides various rewards in acknowledgment of users' knowledge contributions, such as reputation or ranking systems, undoubtedly helps members form their own expert identity in particular areas, thus promoting knowledge contribution behavior in virtual communities [37]. This result is consistent with self-determination theory [38], which suggests that a recognition mechanism can incentivize users to contribute knowledge, because it is an extrinsic reward that recognizes active contributors and arouses more contributing behavior [16, 39]. Fifth, the study showed that a perceived knowledge-rating mechanism had a statistically significant influence on knowledge contribution and knowledge-seeking behaviors. A knowledge-rating mechanism can help contributors understand whether they have been of help to others. The enjoyment of helping others is one kind of intrinsic motivation that promotes knowledge contribution behavior [39]. A knowledge-rating mechanism can help seekers find which topics are hot topics. When seekers use a knowledge-rating mechanism, they can easily find the knowledge-seeking activities and authors in which PVC members are interested.

6.2 Implications

This study has several implications for theory. First, there is little clarity about which knowledge-contribution signals of PVC design affect community participation. This study is the first to use the IS success model and the signaling theory perspective to test the role of system, knowledge, and knowledge-contribution signals in knowledge contribution and knowledge-seeking settings. Most previous studies explored knowledge contribution and knowledge-seeking behaviors separately. In contrast, the present study explored the two major activities conducted by professional members in particular, and PVCs should find the results useful for promoting both types of activities simultaneously. Second, previous research related to knowledge contribution and knowledge-seeking behaviors focused mostly on individual motivation, social-contextual, and technological factors. Of these factors, technological factors generally concentrated on perceived usefulness, perceived ease of use, and system reliability. Thus, from the perspective of

PVC design, there was a theoretical gap in extant research. We contributed to knowledge management research by exploring PVC system artifacts: We integrated system quality, knowledge quality, and knowledge-contribution signals that are popular in PVCs and explored how these artifacts affect participation decisions, such as whether to contribute and whether to seek information in a PVC. Finally, we integrated the IS success model and signaling theory, and proposed a model to explain which PVC system drives members to contribute and/or seek knowledge directly. This research model explained 56.3% of the variance in knowledge contribution behavior and 52.6% of the variance in knowledge-seeking behavior. A PVC is an information technology platform, and this study emphasized that as a result of IS success features and knowledge contribution signals, knowledge contribution and knowledge-seeking research might be missing the nuances of the key constructs associated with research in this field.

This study contributes to practice in several ways. First, knowledge content quality is critical for the two behaviors. PVCs need to ensure the quality of their content [23]. The study results suggest that moderators or administrators should monitor, filter, or delete posts that are not trustworthy or that come from advertisers; in these ways, PVCs may help knowledge seekers search or browse for useful posts. Second, PVCs could also use a virtual reward mechanism, to attract members to participate, as the present study showed that a virtual reward mechanism can effectively enhance both types of behaviors; specifically, a virtual reward mechanism encourages contributors' behaviors more effectively and enhances seekers easier to find hot topics. PVCs need to minimize users' efforts to process knowledge [23]. Third, to increase knowledge contribution, PVC designers should provide a public recognition mechanism, such as rankings or expert lists, to strengthen the reputation and recognition of community members. Finally, the provision of a knowledge-rating mechanism enhances knowledge contribution and knowledge-seeking behaviors. PVC designers or developers should implement rating mechanisms to acknowledge users' contributions, which may make users contribute more while also allowing seekers to more easily rate or vote for knowledge they found useful.

6.3 Limitations

This study has several limitations. First, the survey data used in this study came from only 77 valid sample answers to the knowledge contribution questionnaire, and the data were self-reported. Future research could use actual knowledge contribution behavior (e.g., the number of postings or the quality of the postings) in a PVC to reflect knowledge contribution behavior. Second, the knowledge-contribution signals consisted of perceived virtual reward, public recognition, and knowledge-rating mechanisms, which were developed from new scales based on Bhattacherjee [40] from the core concepts of "actual situations," "expectations," and "satisfaction." This system may not be the most appropriate measurement method, and we hope that future researchers refine other scales or manipulations in an experimental system.

Acknowledgements. We would like to acknowledge that the research is supported by the Ministry of Science and Technology of Taiwan under grants NSC 102–2410-H-270–001.

Appendix A. Constructs and Items

Construct and items	Sources	Factor loading*
Knowledge content quality (KQ)		
Knowledge in BlueShop is accurate (KQ1)	Adapted from [19]	0.827 I 0.897
Knowledge in BlueShop is trustworthy (KQ2)	Adapted from [19]	0.907 I 0.891
Knowledge in BlueShop is valuable for my needs (KQ3)	Adapted from [23]	0.844 I 0.913
Knowledge in BlueShop is current (KQ4)	Adapted from [23]	0.892 I 0.939
Knowledge in BlueShop is in-depth for a given topic (KQ5)	Adapted from [23]	0.865 I 0.932
Searchability (SEA)		
BlueShop provides tools to retrieve information easily (e.g., table of contents, categories, and index) (SEA1)	Adapted from [23]	0.930 I 0.871
I can control how I access information (SEA2)	Adapted from [23]	0.931 I 0.896
BlueShop provides quick search response (SEA3)	Adapted from [19]	0.932 I 0.900
BlueShop can filter searches (SEA4)	Adapted from [19]	0.920 I 0.947
Perceived virtual reward mechanism (PVR)		
In the context of BlueShop, the virtual reward mechanism includes virtual points		
My experience with the virtual reward mechanism was better than expected (PVR1)	Developed based on [40]	0.954 I 0.905
Most of my expectations for the virtual reward mechanism were confirmed (PVR2)	Developed based on [40]	0.935 I 0.938
I am very satisfied with the virtual reward mechanism provided by the PVC (PVR3)	Developed independently	0.918 I 0.928
Perceived public recognition mechanism (PPR)		
In the context of BlueShop, the public recognition mechanism includes expert celebrities		
My experience with the public recognition mechanism was better than expected (PPR1)	Developed based on [40]	0.926 I 0.897
Most of my expectations of the public recognition mechanism were confirmed (PPR2)	Developed based on [40]	0.918 I 0.889
I am very satisfied with the public recognition mechanism provided by the PVC (PPR3)	Developed independently	0.914 I 0.869
Perceived knowledge-rating mechanism (PKR)		
In the context of BlueShop, knowledge-rating mechanisms include page views and number of responses		
My experience with the knowledge-rating mechanism was better than expected (PKR1)	Developed based on [40]	0.899 I 0.889

(continued)

(*continued*)

Construct and items	Sources	Factor loading*
Most of my expectations for the knowledge-rating mechanism were confirmed (PKR2)	Developed based on [40]	0.933 I 0.927
I am very satisfied with the knowledge-rating mechanism provided by the PVC (PKR3)	Developed independently	0.919 I 0.898
Knowledge contribution behavior (KC) / Knowledge-seeking behavior (KS)		
I frequently use BlueShop to contribute/seek knowledge	Adapted from [41]	0.937 I 0.948
I regularly use BlueShop to contribute/seek knowledge	Adapted from [41]	0.952 I 0.929
I use BlueShop to contribute/seek knowledge: [once every few months, once a month, many times per month, many times per week, and many times per day]	Adapted from [41]	0.698 I 0.853

Notes: *Contribution model I Seeking model.

References

1. Chen, C.J., Hung, S.W.: To give or to receive? Factors influencing members' knowledge sharing and community promotion in professional virtual communities. Inf. Manag. **47**(4), 226–236 (2010)
2. Hu, M., Zhang, M., Luo, N.: Understanding participation on video sharing communities: the role of self-construal and community interactivity. Comput. Hum. Behav. **62**, 105–115 (2016)
3. Tamjidyamcholo, A., et al.: Evaluation model for knowledge sharing in information security professional virtual community. Comput. Secur. **43**, 19–34 (2014)
4. Lin, M.J.J., Hung, S.W., Chen, C.J.: Fostering the determinants of knowledge sharing in professional virtual communities. Comput. Hum. Behav. **25**(4), 929–939 (2009)
5. Kankanhalli, A., Tan, B.C.Y., Wei, K.K.: Understanding seeking from electronic knowledge repositories: an empirical study. J. Am. Soc. Inform. Sci. Technol. **56**(11), 1156–1166 (2005)
6. Zhao, L., et al.: Cultivating the sense of belonging and motivating user participation in virtual communities: a social capital perspective. Int. J. Inf. Manage. **32**(6), 574–588 (2012)
7. Zhang, Y., et al.: Understanding the formation mechanism of high-quality knowledge in social question and answer communities: a knowledge co-creation perspective. Int. J. Inf. Manage. **48**, 72–84 (2019)
8. Park, J., Gabbard, J.L.: Factors that affect scientists' knowledge sharing behavior in health and life sciences research communities: differences between explicit and implicit knowledge. Comput. Hum. Behav. **78**, 326–335 (2018)
9. Davenport, T.H., Prusak, L.: Working Knowledge: How Organizations Manage What They Know. Harvard Business School Press, Boston (1998)
10. DeLone, W.H., McLean, E.R.: Information systems success: the quest for the dependent variable. Inf. Syst. Res. **3**(1), 60–95 (1992)
11. Connelly, B.L., et al.: Signaling theory: a review and assessment. J. Manag. **37**(1), 39–67 (2011)
12. Spence, M.: Signaling in retrospect and the informational structure of markets. Am. Econ. Rev. **92**(3), 434–459 (2002)

13. Stiglitz, J.E.: Information and the change in the paradigm in economics. Am. Econ. Rev. **92**(3), 460–501 (2002)
14. Rao, A.R., Qu, L., Ruekert, R.W.: Signaling unobservable product quality through a brand ally. J. Mark. Res. **36**(2), 258–268 (1999)
15. Lou, J., et al.: Contributing high quantity and quality knowledge to online Q&A communities. J. Am. Soc. Inf. Sci. **64**(2), 356–371 (2013)
16. Hung, S.Y., et al.: The influence of intrinsic and extrinsic motivation on individuals' knowledge sharing behavior. Int. J. Hum. Comput Stud. **69**(6), 415–427 (2011)
17. Cheung, C.M.K., Lee, M.K.O., Lee, Z.W.Y.: Understanding the continuance intention of knowledge sharing in online communities of practice through the post-knowledge-sharing evaluation processes. J. Am. Soc. Inform. Sci. Technol. **64**(7), 1357–1374 (2013)
18. Phang, C.W., Kankanhalli, A., Sabherwal, R.: Usability and sociability in online communities: a comparative study of knowledge seeking and contribution. J. Assoc. Inf. Syst. **10**(10), 721–747 (2009)
19. Bock, G.W., Sabherwal, R., Qian, Z.: The effect of social context on the success of knowledge repository systems. IEEE Trans. Eng. Manage. **55**(4), 536–551 (2008)
20. Bowman, B.J.: Building knowledge management systems. Inf. Syst. Manag. **19**(3), 32–41 (2002)
21. Alavi, M., Leidner, D.E.: Review: knowledge management and knowledge management systems: conceptual foundations and research issues. MIS Q. **25**(1), 107–136 (2001)
22. Pai, F.-Y., Yeh, T.-M.: The effects of information sharing and interactivity on the intention to use social networking websites. Qual. Quant. **48**(4), 2191–2207 (2013). https://doi.org/10.1007/s11135-013-9886-5
23. Zheng, Y., Zhao, K., Stylianou, A.C.: The impacts of information quality and system quality on users' continuance intention in information-exchange virtual communities: an empirical investigation. Decis. Support Syst. **56**, 513–524 (2013)
24. Wasko, M., Faraj, S.: Why should i share? examining social capital and knowledge contribution in electronic networks of practice. MIS Q. **29**(1), 34–56 (2005)
25. Davenport, T.H., DeLong, D.W., Beers, M.C.: Successful knowledge management projects. Sloan Manag. Rev. **39**(2), 43–57 (1998)
26. Emelo, R.: Why personal reputation matters in virtual knowledge sharing. Ind. Commer. Train. **44**(1), 35–40 (2012)
27. Liu, H., Zhang, J., Liu, R., Li, G.: A model for consumer knowledge contribution behavior: the roles of host firm management practices, technology effectiveness, and social capital. Inf. Technol. Manage. **15**(4), 255–270 (2014). https://doi.org/10.1007/s10799-014-0199-8
28. Pai, P., Tsai, H.-T.: Reciprocity norms and information-sharing behavior in online consumption communities: an empirical investigation of antecedents and moderators. Inf. Manag. **53**(1), 38–52 (2016)
29. Sutanto, J., Jiang, Q.: Knowledge seekers' and contributors' reactions to recommendation mechanisms in knowledge management systems. Inf. Manag. **50**(5), 258–263 (2013)
30. Poston, R.S., Speier, C.: Effective use of knowledge management systems: a process model of content ratings and credibility indicators. MIS Q. **29**(2), 221–244 (2005)
31. Podsakoff, P.M., et al.: Common method biases in behavioral research: a critical review of the literature and recommended remedies. J. Appl. Psychol. **88**(5), 879–903 (2003)
32. Ringle, C.M., Wende, S., Becker, J.-M.: SmartPLS 3. Bönningstedt: SmartPLS (2015)
33. Nunnally, J.C.: Psychometric Theory. McGraw Hill, New York (1978)
34. Fornell, C., Larcker, D.F.: Evaluating structural equation models with unobservable variables and measurement error. J. Mark. Res. **18**(1), 39–50 (1981)
35. Kraut, R.E., et al.: Varieties of social influence: the role of utility and norms in the success of a new communication medium. Organ. Sci. **9**(4), 437–453 (1998)

36. Matschke, C., et al.: Motivational factors of information exchange in social information spaces. Comput. Hum. Behav. **36**, 549–558 (2014)
37. Ma, M., Agarwal, R.: Through a glass darkly: information technology design, identity verification, and knowledge contribution in online communities. Inf. Syst. Res. **18**(1), 42–67 (2007)
38. Deci, E.L., Ryan, R.M.: Intrinsic Motivation and Self-Determination in Human Behavior. Plenum Press, New York (1985)
39. Kankanhalli, A., Tan, B.C.Y., Wei, K.K.: Contributing knowledge to electronic knowledge repositories: an empirical investigation. MIS Q. **29**(1), 113–143 (2005)
40. Bhattacherjee, A.: Understanding information systems continuance: an expectation-confirmation model. MIS Q. **25**(3), 351–370 (2001)
41. Davis, F.D.: Perceived usefulness, perceived ease of use, and user acceptance of information technology. MIS Q. **13**(3), 319–340 (1989)

Public Innovation Through Co-creation Platforms in Response to the Covid-19 Pandemic

Lizeth Fernanda Serrano Cárdenas[1]([⊠]) (iD), Laura Victoria Buitrago Álvarez[2] (iD),
Yessika Lorena Vásquez González[3] (iD), Flor Nancy Díaz-Piraquive[4] (iD),
and Hugo Fernando Castro Silva[2] (iD)

[1] Universidad del Rosario, Bogotá, Colombia
Lizeth.serrano@urosario.edu.co
[2] Universidad Pedagógica y Tecnológica de Colombia, Sogamoso, Colombia
{Laura.buitrago,hugofernando.castro}@uptc.edu.co
[3] Universidad Jorge Tadeo Lozano, Bogotá, Colombia
lorena.vasquezg@utadeo.edu.co
[4] Fundación Universitaria Internacional de la Rioja UNIR, Logroño, Colombia
flornancy.diaz@unir.edu.co

Abstract. The participation of citizens to solve public challenges is a driver to implement public innovation. Addressing new mechanisms and arenas that facilitate citizen participation is one of the challenges on the governments' agenda, especially under changing, complex and social distancing scenarios such as those caused by the Covid-19 Pandemic. Therefore, digital platforms that promote co-creation between citizens, governments, and other actors in the countries' innovation ecosystems, are becoming more and more necessary, but at the same time, there is a need to study their scope and contributions to generate transparent, equitable, inclusive and people-centered citizen participation processes. Indeed, the research aim was to make a trend analysis on the field integrating two methods: a literature review about concepts related to public innovation platforms: co-creation and citizen participation; and finally, a web content analysis on three platforms that generated co-creation exercises to solve challenges in the Covid-19 Pandemic. The main results show the need to study the challenges and contributions of digital platforms to make public innovation the result of a collaborative effort that goes beyond the ideation stages to implement solutions and generate public value.

Keywords: Co-creation · Citizen participation · Public innovation · Digital platforms · Covid-19 pandemic

1 Introduction

The world faces a deep transformation that implies the reinvention of multiple sectors, among them, the public sector. New ways of doing things have been discovered. The development of collaborative solutions between different actors of the innovation ecosystems in societies is becoming increasingly relevant. Within this dynamic, citizens are called to make part of public issues in a conscious and relevant way, and interacting

© Springer Nature Switzerland AG 2021
L. Uden et al. (Eds.): KMO 2021, CCIS 1438, pp. 111–122, 2021.
https://doi.org/10.1007/978-3-030-81635-3_10

under new schemes with governments, to build economic, political and social alternatives to solve wicked problems [1]. In this dynamic, citizens participation strengthens its relevance by becoming a mechanism for making collective concerns more visible. At the same time, this mechanism favors the consolidation of trust networks between citizens and governments and the strengthening of social capital [2, 3]. Elements which all together favour progress of societies. Despite relevance of participative processes, there are still multiple challenges associated to prevalence of top-down schemes, where the design of participative processes, their promotion and results continue to be led exclusively by public institutions [4]. Studying the mechanisms of collaboration and citizen participation mediated by platforms is especially important in the context we live in, where the Covid-19 pandemic has generated two effects: the isolation of the population and the growing demand for public innovation solutions.

The above facts, under the premise that although technology could facilitate participative processes, it could also restrict them out. According to the OECD report [5], there are five challenges of citizen participation developed by digital platforms: 1) the challenge of scale: From citizen perspective, How could technology facilitate to make the individual voice of citizens to be heard, and prevent it from being lost in mass debates?, and from the government perspective, it is required to understand How can technology overcome the challenge of listening and answering to the diversity of demands of the different individuals involved in the process?. 2) the challenge of capabilities development to favour active citizens: How can the information and communication technology help to encourage constructively deliberation of citizens on public issues? 3) the challenge of coherence: How can technology support the reporting, consultation, analysis, feedback, and evaluation to the diversity of demands of the different individuals involved in the public policies process?. 4) The evaluation challenge, with the understanding that as governments integrate the information and communication technology, to mediate citizen participation in matters related to public policies, there is a growing need for evaluation, and analyze if such participation complies with the citizens and the government's objectives, raising questionings such as How to implement this evaluation? and especially about What aspects are vital in the evaluation process? Finally, 5) the challenge of commitment, to ensure that the digital citizen participation, be analyzed, disseminated, transcended, and included in the decision-making process of public policy.

It was found that global initiatives that came up because of Covid-19 pandemic, turned the efforts of public institutions to cooperate with multiple sectors and with citizens, to generate collective knowledge for the designing of co-creative solutions to face the most relevant challenge of the century [6]. Some of the digital platforms implemented with this purpose, and which are object of analysis of this investigation, are as follows: Stop the curve (Frena la Curva), Each day counts (Cada día cuenta) and Hack the Crisis 2020 (Hackea la Crisis). To understand the dynamics behind these new platforms, for co-creation and citizen's participation, a trend analysis is required, to facilitate the comprehension of how this topic has been included in the governments' agenda in different countries. According to Palacin, Nelimarkka, Reynolds-Cuéllar & Becker [7], it is found that it is necessary to study how technology configures out the participative processes. To respond to this challenge, authors suggest the articulation of knowledge fields, oftenly studied independently: technology, engineering, and politics.

Such articulation coincides with Chadwick's proposal [8], who makes evident the need to increase comprehension of how technologies of information and communication are reconfiguring governance, States, and democracy. Considering this research need, this article makes a research trend analysis about the field. This analysis was done in two stages. A systematic review of literature on the knowledge field, and an analysis based on web content techniques of pages from digital platforms, for citizens participation within the frame of the Covid-19 pandemic. The results contribute to outlining the future agenda for the development of participatory scenarios through digital platforms.

2 Methodology

The methodology structure of research is composed of two stages: Systematic literature review, and web content analysis:

2.1 Systematic Literature Review

The systematic literature review is considered as a structured methodology, whose purpose is to identify, evaluate and interpret all available research, being pertinent for a specific research question, subject area, or a phenomenon of interest [9]. According to some authors [10], the purpose of the review is to synthetize relevant literature about a research problem. Since, it is about a coherent criticism, where through a narrative, the knowledge status of a carefully defined topic is interpreted from an argumentative stance, analyzing the relevant literature, selected systematically.

Since knowledge accumulates over time, it is up to researchers to find the relevant information about the knowledge field of interest and use it as a starting point. Ignoring existent knowledge would imply the development of inefficient research processes. That is why the literature review is a good strategy to acquire knowledge about a topic from an analysis exercise of complex theoretical bodies [11]. Based on the above criteria, the methodology proposed by Notar & Cole [10] was considered for this research, which is coherent with the three generic stages of the methodology established by Tranfield [12] Planning, Development and Results Report (See Fig. 1). Hart [13] says that four key elements must be considered for its development: focus on a specific problem or issue of research, be related to the problem for which analysis and deep study is required, relationship between the theoretical, methodological, and practical aspects of the topic. In this case, the purpose of systematic review was to analyze trends about the study of digital platforms for public innovation with special emphasis in the co-creation and citizen participation processes.

Ten relevant initiatives were found for the study, however, in order to make an exhaustive analysis, some selection criteria were defined: integrate Latin American countries in their scope and impact, involve other actors beyond public institutions, integrate the citizen as the center of the process, establish the solution of Covid challenges as a focus, develop co-creation and citizen participation exercises to respond to these public challenges. And finally, to have information available on the process developed and its results. Thus, three platforms that met the established criteria were selected. In addition to the three selected platforms, an initiative from Colombia called *Mincienciaton* was found.

This platform focused its efforts on strategic lines of public health, with 531 proposals submitted with the participation of 26 departments. Despite its relevance, it did not have enough information to answer the research question. Therefore, it was discarded as an object of analysis.

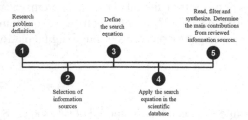

Fig. 1. Systematic literature review process. Source: Authors based on Notar & Cole, 2010 and Tranfield, 2003.

The development stage followed five steps: First, build the search equation and apply it to the data base Web of Science, a total of 110 documents were found. The second stage consisted in the analysis of the 110 documents through data mining software VOSviewer®. After this, a review was done on the correlation between the study fields and the relevance of publications between countries. Subsequently, the reading of titles and summaries of the 52 prioritized documents in the search was done; likewise, 22 documents product of the snowball process were reviewed, documents that showed a direct relationship with the research topics. Finally, in the fifth stage, reading and coding of documents in analytical categories was done, using the qualitative analysis software Maxqda® (See Fig. 2).

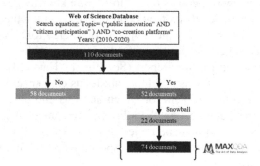

Fig. 2. Systematic literature review process followed.

2.2 Web Content Analysis

Web content analysis is conceptualized as the process of discovering trending information on the Web [14]. For the development of this phase, the information associated with the keywords was downloaded from the web pages of three platforms for public innovation in the context of the Covid-19 pandemic: Stop the curve (Frena la Curva), Each day counts (Cada día cuenta) and Hack the Crisis 2020 (Hackea la Crisis). Subsequently, the information was processed and encoded through the Maxqda® software, verifying the content of keywords and eliminating those that did not make sense by themselves. Finally, relevance maps were built that made it possible to visualize which keywords were predominant on each web page, making it easier to identify the most relevant topics in each of them.

3 Results

3.1 Understanding Public Innovation

Unexpected changes are currently being experienced. However, we need to understand how to act under these changes, and what are the right ways to do it, and it is there when the term innovation makes sense. Innovate means to make a change within a context, For Serrani [15], innovation is understood as "move or alter things by incorporating novelties". Within the change processes, the concept of innovation has also been transferred to the public sector scene, given its relevance to generate transformation in social processes, which promote dynamic learning environments *with* the actors and *for* the actors. Academic studies in the field of public innovation have been carried out since the 70s and 80s, as indicated by Osborne et al. [16], for whom governments must transform themselves by adapting to new challenges. In this scenario, values, attitudes, and spaces that encourage citizen participation become determining elements.

For that reason, it is understood that public innovation is only possible through collaborative efforts from different actors involved in the process. For some authors, public innovation not only generates contributions to the improvement of public services, but also contributes to the legitimacy of governments as value-creating institutions. A value that derives from its receptivity to the needs and aspirations of citizens, who are the users of public services [17]. The interest expressed by organizations in adopting innovative practices reflects the urgency of generating positive responses to new global challenges [18]. It has been shown that public innovation has become a strategy implemented by multiple governments to resolve these demands, a reason that explains the growing interest in its study, both by academics and decision makers within and outside the public sector [19, 20].

Public innovation is defined as the creation and application of new management models, processes, products and services and methods focused on citizens, which lead to significant improvements in efficiency, effectiveness and in the quality of public results [21]. Hence, it is understood that the concept of public innovation is oriented to break political stagnation, reduce costs, and improve services for the benefit of citizens, private companies, and others [22]. The literature on the subject every day increases and consequently the expectations about its results, in terms of quality, efficiency, effectiveness and relevance. According to Potts and Kastelle [23], the inclusion of specialized knowledge in the process will help to understand the complexity of public problems, leaving aside standardized solutions and concentrating on individualized and personalized solutions to citizen challenges.

From another perspective, it is found that if effective public innovation is to be sought, better ways of meeting needs, solving problems, and using resources and technologies must be developed, generating new collaborative governance schemes [24–26]. Collaborative governance requires citizen participation as its fundamental determinant [27, 28]. In this scenario, it is essential to understand the process of strengthening ties, not only of joining isolated efforts, but also of deepening the opening of collective approaches under network bets [29]. In conclusion, public innovation is described as a learning process, where governments, accompanied by citizens, can develop new services, technologies, management approaches, governance processes and approaches for the generation of public solutions [30].

3.2 Co-creation and Citizen Participation in the Development of Public Innovation

Citizen participation is understood as organized civil society initiatives, through social and political movements, developed to manage the inclusion of new alternatives that allow citizens to access quality public services [3]. The concept of participation must be understood from multiple transversal axes, since its concept contains the paradox of simplicity-complexity. Citizen participation is, in essence, a paradigm shifts in the relationship between the people and the government [31]. It has been understood as the opportunity to empower in two ways: those who intervene in this process, and the public institutions that promote it. However, it is evident that historically, the inclusion of citizens in public management has had restrictions. For some authors [3] the participatory process integrates a humanizing value from ethical, political, and educational dimensions. In the literature, it is found that citizen participation is the determining factor to materialize public innovation through co-creation dynamics.

Co-creation is defined as the dissemination of participatory creation through environments that promote interactive processes, where new approaches are proposed on the way in which organizations acquire commitments and the way in which these commitments are organized and structured [32, 33]. Co-creation processes are characterized by being done in a planned manner, tracing a direction, and defining possible actions. Therefore, currently co-creation has uses in different dimensions within public management. Considering the different contexts of application of co-creation, it is necessary that studies on the subject are oriented to understand how this concept is developed in practice, contributing not only to its understanding but also to its integration into government strategies. In particular, Puerari et al. [34], suggest that five aspects associated with their understanding be deepened: 1) the purpose of the co-creation processes; 2) understanding the formal and informal mechanisms for co-creation; 3) analyzing how property rights are established in the co-creation process; 4) the motivation and incentives of the actors for the development of co-creation processes; and finally, they propose as relevant, 5) a deep study of the spaces and mechanisms implemented to materialize co-creation.

3.3 Trends Analysis on Digital Platforms for Co-creation

Citizen participation initiatives and co-creation platforms for public innovation, studied together, are a field of a growing interest within research communities. In particular, the contribution of the United States stands out with 18 documents, followed by Spain (16 documents) and China (10 documents). The presence of European countries such as Austria, Finland, Netherlands, Germany, Sweden, and England within this analysis demonstrates the advantage they have in terms of publications related to the subject under study. The Latin American country that has deepened in this field of study is Brazil. It was identified that the most cited article is aimed at studying new trends in public management, and the challenge of their implementation under new governance schemes [16]. The second most cited article exposes the future challenges of citizen participation, and the potential it has in terms of effectiveness, legitimacy, and social justice. In this study, it is proposed that, with the new strategies of technological inclusion, new paths are generated for participatory innovations that lead to more effective governance [35]. The third featured article reflects the importance of co-creation processes with an innovation approach, where creativity and design by the participants are key. At the same time, it reflects on the dynamics of virtual spaces for participation, posing the challenges so that they become scenarios to generate opportunities in terms of experience and social impact [32].

Finally, the relationship between keywords was studied, building a co-relationship map between keywords. For visualization purposes, only those words that were found in more than 3 articles were represented. As a result of the process, the map shown in Fig. 3 was generated. This map shows that the processes of citizen participation are a growing focus of study. In parallel, new approaches to governance, open innovation, public participation, open government and, in general, processes framed in the transformation of public management are evident as trends. The trend analysis made it possible to show that the new mechanisms of citizen participation, and the new co-creation platforms, are increasingly relevant [36]. For some authors, this explains, considering the social, economic, political, and democratic benefits, that these new mechanisms and these new platforms arise due to the need for governments to open for the generation of fast, relevant, and pertinent solutions, focused on citizen demands. In this scenario, digital platforms that promote interaction and the effective exchange of ideas, knowledge and capabilities are key to making public innovation a reality and to transform the logic of governance from top-down processes to network dynamics [37].

3.4 Co-creation Platforms to Facilitate Citizen Participation in the Context of the COVID-19 Pandemic

The growing interest in the use of digital platforms to solve public challenges was evident in the last months, where the world faced an emergency situation, which challenged governments, citizens, companies, bilateral organizations, and other actors in the social sector, to rapidly develop co-creation mechanisms that would produce fast solutions to face the challenges of Covid-19. To understand the main issues addressed in three digital platforms that were implemented for these purposes, a keyword map for each web page were built, which synthesize the priorities and approaches of each platform.

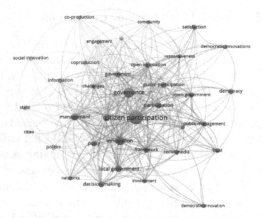

Fig. 3. Co-relationship map between author's keywords using VOSviewer®.

a. Stop the curve (Frena la Curva) [38]: It is a citizen platform, which was born in Spain, with its motto "together we are stronger". It has been successfully replicated in 22 countries worldwide, the participants of the initiative are: volunteers, entrepreneurs, activists, social organizations, changemakers, and public and social innovation laboratories. Its purpose is focused on cooperation to channel and organize social energy and civic resilience to face the challenges of Covid-19. As a result of the initiative, more than 50 projects were generated, 140 responses to common challenges, 900 citizen initiatives, and some spaces for social appropriation of knowledge were developed, such as the Open Innovation Festival, with 12 continuous hours of transmission on YouTube. The map built on the content of its website (Fig. 4) allowed to identify the orientation of the initiative to the consolidation of projects and the laboratory approach, where experimentation is part of the co-creation process. Likewise, they stand out as axes of the innovation process, the active participation of citizens, the breaking down of geographical barriers for the formation of work teams; and finally, practical, and resilient guidance for the development of innovative solutions.

Fig. 4. Keyword map derived from https://frenalacurva.net/.

b. Every day counts (Cada día cuenta) [39]: this initiative has been developed in 18 countries in Latin America, with more than 3,600 participants and generating 210 solutions, built in 48 h of hackathon. The platform is described as a digital space in which "all together" develop, test, and improve solutions to face the challenges of Covid-19. The map built on the content of its website (Fig. 5) facilitated the identification of the initiative's emphasis on developing solutions to the emerging problems in the crisis. Keywords stand out as democratizing knowledge and opportunity in the generation of new leadership of citizens; highlighting the characteristics that define these leaders: enthusiastic, creative, empathetic and action-oriented.

Fig. 5. Keyword map derived from: https://socialabglobal.socialab.com/challenges/cadadiacu enta.

c. Hack the crisis [40]: this initiative consists of the development of six online hackathons, to find solutions within the context of the pandemic. The topics of interest were as follows: women, migrant population, health, education, food, and finally, entrepreneurship and small and medium-sized enterprises. The hackathon development process involves brainstorming, followed by team building and prototyping for 48 h. The process is accompanied by volunteer mentors and in its first version, it generated more than 27 solutions, where more than 218 participants, 78 juries and the representation of 20 countries were involved, to respond to three challenges faced by women and girls during the pandemic: 1) increase in domestic violence, 2) access to products and services, correct information, psychosocial care and timely medical care, and 3) design of solutions that respond to the difficulties women and girls have in asking for and receiving help and protection. The map built on the content of its website (Fig. 6) allowed to validate the initiative's emphasis on providing fast, experimental, and collaborative responses to the challenges brought by the pandemic. The role of citizens is highlighted as mentors and participants who collaborate with other actors to design solutions that are inserted into problems of specific groups in coherence with the prioritized topics.

Fig. 6. Keyword map derived from: https://www.hackealacrisis.net/.

4 Discussion and Conclusions

Fast and unpredictable transformations also generate opportunities. The contribution of this research was oriented to deepen on the context of public innovation within the framework of co-creation processes and citizen participation, through digital platforms, managing to understand the complexity of the new collaboration mechanisms given in the dynamics that complex societies bring. Dynamics that call for new collaborative relationships between citizens, governments, and other actors in the countries' innovation ecosystems. In this research, a theoretical deepening of public innovation was developed. The relationship of this topic with the co-creation processes where citizens are the central actor was discussed in depth. Based on the literature, trends were studied on the study of the field of knowledge that associates public innovation and digital platforms, to finally study how digital platforms implemented by governments and other actors in the context of the Covid-19 pandemic, integrate principles found in the theory to materialize innovation, facing the most relevant public challenge of the millennium.

Despite the advantages identified as contributions of public innovation platforms, challenges were also identified which are suggested to be explored in the future research agenda on the subject, such as: 1) an analysis of the limits and contributions generated in the process of co-creation in digital platforms. To do that, the integration of methodologies under qualitative approaches is required, which will allow exploring the narratives of actors involved in the process, to know beyond what is explicit in the web pages, other aspects that allow analyzing and contrasting the visions of the actors who were part of the process. 2) Longitudinal analyzes on the platforms over time, with the aim of evaluating the scope and impact of the co-creation process, in relation to the implementation of solutions, facing the challenges that the initiatives prioritized, studying with special emphasis the citizen advocacy in the prototype design or solution implementation stages, after the ideation exercises developed on the platforms. Lastly, 3) documenting the cases of the initiatives studied in greater depth, identifying reference practices that contribute to transferring the learning, derived from the co-creation and participation processes for innovation, developed through these platforms to other scenarios and contexts, inside and outside public institutions.

Finally, in the construction of the theoretical framework for analyzing the processes of co-creation and citizen participation, it was found that most of the approaches to the analysis and evaluation of these processes have been constructed for formal and face-to-face scenarios. This finding opens a gap for future studies: the adaptation and resignification of these reference frameworks to integrate new elements of analysis that allow validating that these exercises are truly inclusive, relevant, pertinent, and incident in the contexts where they are implemented.

References

1. Gonzalo, L.A.: La Participación ciudadana: posibilidades y retos. Aposta Rev Ciencias Soc. (Ciencias Sociales), **22**, 1–23 (2005)
2. Velásquez, C.F, González, R.E: Fundación Corona (¿Bogotá C. Qué ha pasado con la participación ciudadana en Colombia? 455 (2003)

3. Araújo, R,O., et al.: Retos de la democracia y de la participación ciudadana [Internet]. Universidad del Rosario, p. 198 (2011). http://repository.urosario.edu.co/handle/10336/8791
4. Sullivan, H.: Modernisation, democratisation and community governance. Local Gov. Stud. **27**(3), 1–24 (2001)
5. Organisation For Economic Co-Operation and Development. Promise and problems of e-democracy: challenges of online citizen engagement. OECD Publishing (2003)
6. Ministerio de salud y protección social. Abecé Nuevo Coronavirus (Covid-19). MinSalud [Internet], 1–5 (2020). https://www.minsalud.gov.co/sites/rid/Lists/BibliotecaDigital/RIDE/VS/PP/ET/abece-coronavirus.pdf
7. Palacin, V., Nelimarkka, M., Reynolds-Cuellar, P., Becker, C.: The Design of pseudo-participation. ACM Int Conf Proc. Ser. **2**, 40–44 (2020)
8. Chadwick, A.: Bringing E-Democracy back in: why it matters for future research On E-Governance. Soc. Sci. Comput. Rev. **21**(4), 443–455 (2003). https://doi.org/10.1177/089443 9303256372
9. Kitchenham, C.: Guidelines for performing Systematic Literature Reviews in Software Engineering (2007)
10. Notar, C.E., North, P.R.A.R.W, Cole, V. Literature Review Organizer, **2**(2), 1–17 (2010)
11. Onwuegbuzie, A.J.: FRELS, Rebecca. Seven steps to a comprehensive literature review: a multimodal and cultural approach (2016)
12. Tranfield, D., Denyer, D., Smart, P.: Towards a Methodology for Developing Evidence-Informed Management Knowledge by Means of Systematic Review. 14 (2003)
13. Hart, C.: Releasing the Social Science Research Imagination. SAGE (1998)
14. Cooley, R., Mobasher, B., Srivastava, J.: Web mining: information and pattern discovery on the World Wide Web. In: Proceedings ninth IEEE international conference on tools with artificial intelligence. IEEE, p. 558–567 (1997)
15. Serrani, E.: El desarrollo económico y los estudios sobre el Estado y los empresarios. Un Constante Desafío Para Las Ciencias Sociales. 127–54 (2012)
16. Osborne, S.P., Radnor, Z., Nasi, G.: The American Review of Public Administration A New Theory for Public (2013)
17. Moore, M., Hartley, J.: The Creation of Public Value through step-change innovation in public organizations. Public value and Public Administration, 82 (2015)
18. Mulgan, G., Tucker, S., Ali, R., Sanders, B.: Social innovation: what it is, why it matters and how it can be accelerated. [Internet]. ©The Young Foundation, editor. London, p. 52 2006; 2007. http://eureka.sbs.ox.ac.uk/761/1/Social_Innovation.pdf
19. Lewis, J.M., Ricard, L.M., Klijn, E.H.: How innovation drivers, networking and leadership shape public sector innovation capacity. Int. Rev. Adm. Sci. 84(2), 288–307 (2018)
20. Serrano Cárdenas, L.F., Vásquez González, Y.L., Díaz-Piraquive, F.N., Guillot Landecker, J.E.: Public innovation: concept and future research agenda. In: Uden, L., Ting, I.-H., Corchado, J.M. (eds.) KMO 2019. CCIS, vol. 1027, pp. 165–177. Springer, Cham (2019). https://doi.org/10.1007/978-3-030-21451-7_14
21. Osborne, S.P., Brown, L.: Handbook of innovation in public services. Handb. Innovation Public Serv. (2013). https://doi.org/10.4337/9781849809757
22. Torfing, J.: Collaborative innovation in the public sector. In: Osborne, S., Brown, L. (eds.) Handbook of Innovation in Public Services, pp. 301–316. Edward Elgar Publishing (2013). https://doi.org/10.4337/9781849809757.00032
23. Potts, J., Kastelle, T.: Public sector innovation research: what's next? Innovation **12**(2), 122–137 (2010). https://doi.org/10.5172/impp.12.2.122
24. De Vries, H., Bekkers, V., Tummers, L.: Innovation in the public sector: a systematic review and future research agenda. Public Adm. **94**(1), 146–166 (2016)
25. Rhodes, R.A.W.: Understanding governance: ten years on. Organ. Stud. **28**(8), 1243–1264 (2007). https://doi.org/10.1177/0170840607076586

26. Angeli, L.A., Delfino, G., Zubieta, E.M.: Participación Ciudadana En La Era Digital : Citizen Participation in the Digital Era : Modalities and Associated (2016)
27. Hartley, J.: Innovation in Governance and public services : past and present. 27–35 (2005)
28. Vercelli, A.: La participación ciudadana en la era digital. VIRTUalis [Internet], **4**(7), 115–29 (2014). http://aplicaciones.ccm.itesm.mx/virtualis/index.php/virtualis/article/view/72/59
29. Macaulay, M., Norris, D.: Ethical innovation in the public services. In: Osborne, S., Brown, L. (eds.) Handbook of Innovation in Public Services, pp. 238–249. Edward Elgar Publishing (2013). https://doi.org/10.4337/9781849809757.00026
30. Bekkers, V., Edelenbos, J., Steijn, B.: An Innovative public sector? embarking on the innovation journey. In: Bekkers, V., Edelenbos, J., Steijn, B. (eds.) Innovation in the Public Sector, pp. 197–221. Palgrave Macmillan UK, London (2011). https://doi.org/10.1057/9780230307520_10
31. Ju, J., Liu, L., Feng, Y.: Public and private value in citizen participation in E-governance: evidence from a government-sponsored green commuting platform. Gov. Inf. Quart. **36**(4), 101400 (2019)
32. Ramaswamy, V., Ozcan, K.: What is co-creation? An interactional creation framework and its implications for value creation (2017)
33. Voorberg, W.H., Bekkers, V.J.J.M., Tummers, L.G.: A systematic review of co-creation and co-production: embarking on the social innovation journey. Public Manage. Rev. **17**(9), 1333–1357 (2014). https://doi.org/10.1080/14719037.2014.930505
34. Puerari, E., de Koning, J., von Wirth, T., Karré, P., Mulder, I., Loorbach, D.: Co-creation dynamics in Urban Living Labs. Sustainability **10**(6), 1893 (2018). https://doi.org/10.3390/su10061893
35. Fung, A.: Putting the Public Back into Governance: Th e Challenges of Citizen Participation and its Future, xx, 1–10 (2015)
36. Bonina, C.: Cocreacion-innovacion-y-datos-abiertos-Bonina. Iniciat Latinoamericana por los Datos Abiertos. **1**, 41 (2015)
37. Issa A, Schumacher S, Hatiboglu B, Groß E, Bauernhansl T. Open Innovation in the Workplace: Future Work Lab as a Living Lab. Procedia CIRP [Internet]. **72**, 629–34 (2018). https://doi.org/10.1016/j.procir.2018.03.149
38. Frena La Curva. Juntos Somos Más Fuertes [Internet] (2020). https://frenalacurva.net/conoce nos-frena-la-curva/
39. Socialab. Cada Día Cuenta Latam Hackaton Soluciones Para El Covid-19 [Internet] (2020). https://cadadiacuenta.org/
40. Impaqto.net. Hackea La Crisis 2020 [Internet] (2020). https://www.hackealacrisis.net/

Knowledge and Service Innovation

Understanding How Patient, Caregiver and Healthcare Professional Come Together During Treatment

Lisa Ribeiro$^{(\boxtimes)}$ and Dai Senoo

Tokyo Institute of Technology, Tokyo, Japan
`ribeiro.l.ac@m.titech.ac.jp`

Abstract. This paper aims at clarifying actors, associations and treatment flow that patient, caregiver and healthcare professional undergo; at identifying shared contexts ("ba") and their overlap for self-transcendence; at looking at the actors and associations as activity systems to understand the activities and actions executed, and expected to be executed, by the actors (division of labor) to visualize boundaries for transformation. Qualitative data was gathered through open-ended questionnaires distributed to healthcare professionals and caregivers in Japan, Singapore and Brazil. Hermeneutic analysis and interpretation of the answers were conducted to draw findings and implications; data generated from these went through framework method of analysis in three levels: Actor-Network Theory to identify actors, associations and treatment flow; Knowledge-Creation Theory's shared context; as activity systems to clarify the division of labor. Three actors were found: patient, healthcare professional, and caregiver. The consultation is central to treatment flow as it is when one shared context emerges among actors, assessment is conducted, and tasks are assigned. This is a preliminary study which lays the foundation for our ongoing research, so the implications are targeted at the researchers: necessity to clarify what sort of negotiations and translations usually take and the role of technology in it; identify where and how actors become attuned to focus on where and how self-transcendence happens; understand actions to visualize boundaries for transformation. This is a first attempt to analyze patient-healthcare professional-caregiver relationship combining the Actor-Network Theory, "ba" and Activity Theory's division of labor.

Keywords: Patient-caregiver-healthcare professional · Associations · Shared context · Division of labor

1 Introduction

Health professionals have started seeing patients as active participants in their treatment, co-creating value and increasing the technical and functional quality of healthcare services and patient well-being [1]. This may be viewed as one of the effects of the caring model of patient care where the patient is seen a "whole by focusing on the treatment of illness, and not just on the removal of the symptoms of a disease" [2]. There

© Springer Nature Switzerland AG 2021
L. Uden et al. (Eds.): KMO 2021, CCIS 1438, pp. 125–137, 2021.
https://doi.org/10.1007/978-3-030-81635-3_11

has been a focus on patient-physician (healthcare professionals) relationship in studies. More recently, with changes in populations' demographics and forms of care delivery, informal caregivers have received attention and studies started looking into their role in the treatment. Next is a review of literature regarding this trend.

2 Literature Review

Prior studies have focused on the patient-physician communication resulting in information exchange between the two, planning of treatment, compliance to the treatment and satisfaction with it [3]. Looking through the lens of Latour's Actor-Network Theory, patient and physician have agency and are actors who associate with one another: each makes or promotes a difference in the other or in the network [4].

More recently, scholars started turning their eyes to informal caregivers and their role in care provision. These are caregivers not by profession and provide care on an unpaid basis [5]. Examples are spouses, partners, family members. Reasons behind these studies are various: change in demographics with a large number of elderly who are cared by a family member [6]; introduction of enhancements for cooperation and coordination of intra- and extra-mural care to improve standard community care [7]; increase in number of consultations where patient is accompanied by another individual [8]; the recognition that decision-making processes during treatment are informed by relationships [9] and the impact of such decisions on both the patient and the caregiver [10]; and the psychological and physical well-being of caregivers during and after caregiving period [11, 12].

The confirmation of the caregiver's key role in day-to-day care provision leads us to see this individual as a new actor in the patient-physician association resulting in a patient-caregiver-physician association where each actor promotes difference in one another or in the network.

These actors interact to combine "technical and trans-disciplinary action schemes" [7], mix and match lay, expert knowledge, and action in a shared context. In Nonaka's terms, the actors are in "ba" - a shared context which serves as the foundation for knowledge creation and is related to shared experiences, mental models, and relationships emersion. It is in "ba" where individuals spiral through Socialization (tacit to tacit knowledge), Externalization (tacit to explicit knowledge), Combination (explicit to explicit knowledge) and Internalization (explicit to tacit knowledge) [13].

Weick [14] explains that people share experience and this may not lead to a shared meaning. This shared experience, when analyzed in retrospect by individuals, rarely has similar meanings; they may, however, be equivalent. The author affirms that what people do share are actions, activities, moments of conversation, and joint tasks. Epstein [9] proposes that from the sharing of thoughts, feelings, perceptions, meanings, and intentions among two or more individuals emerges a shared mind which is both an achievement and an interpersonal process, as the author puts it, a "becoming attuned" process. This "tuning" encompasses the varying degrees of human interaction [9]. Laidsaar-Powell [10] expands the study and proposes a framework in which the caregiver is included in the decision-making process of the patient-physician association based on the notion of shared mind.

The idea of becoming attuned aligns with Nonaka's shared context ("ba") and with Actor-Network Theory's associations and connections among actors through translations [15]. We can argue, then, that different associations result in different interactions and actions which will achieve different shared contexts. They resemble activity systems which are multi-voiced and have a division of labor that creates different positions for its participants [16].

This preliminary study aims at: (1) clarifying actors, associations and treatment flow that patient, caregiver and healthcare professional undergo; (2) identifying contexts shared by actors and their overlap; (3) looking at the findings from analysis (2) and (3) as activity systems to understand the activities and actions executed - and expected to be executed - by actors to understand boundaries for transformation. This lays the foundation for our ongoing research which aims at proposing a model where the actors are active knowledge contributors and creators in the treatment.

3   Methodology

After literature review, empirical collection of qualitative data through two separate questionnaires was conducted during November 2019: one for caregivers and another for healthcare professionals. Both questionnaires had a brief introduction of this research; the caregiver questionnaire had 7 (1 multiple choice and 6 open-ended) questions and respondents were encouraged to freely share their thoughts; the health professional questionnaire had 8 (1 multiple choice and 7 open-ended) questions and, again, respondents were encouraged to freely share as their thoughts (Table 1). The reason why we chose open-ended questions was so that we would not restrain respondents with any researchers' assumption bias.

These were online questionnaires using Google Forms platform for easier diffusion and respondents' comfort who could answer them through their phones or computers. The questions' first language was English, then it was translated into Portuguese and Japanese. Questions 1, 2 and 3 aimed at identifying actors and understanding agency to find out how it takes shape throughout the treatment. Questions 4, and 5 targeted at elucidating the (expected) activities and (expected) actions by the identified actors; in addition, the researchers expected these questions to uncover knowledge creation experiences. Question 6 focused solely on identifying the creation and application of this knowledge back into the patient's treatment. Questions 7 and 8 were there for the purpose of demographics.

Answers were translated into English - with the help of Google Translate - for analysis of their contents to draw findings and comment on their implications. We grouped the questions based on their objective as explained in the previous paragraph, resulting in three groups. We then analyzed healthcare professionals' and caregivers' answers for each question for deeper understanding through hermeneutic analysis and interpretation [12]. The qualitative data generated from it went through framework method of analysis targeting to generate themes which aided us in providing descriptions to crystalize phenomenon under investigation [17].

Table 1. Questionnaires for caregivers and health professionals

Scenario: Think of when you accompany a patient (i.e. family member, partner) as a caregiver to a consultation. Please try to recall how such consultations usually go and answer freely the following questions

Objective	Questions for Caregivers	Questions for Healthcare Professionals
Identifying actors and understanding agency	**1.** For majority of the cases, whose voice do you feel is prioritized by the healthcare professional? a) Voice of the patient b) Voice of the caregiver	**1.** For majority of the cases, do you prioritize the voice of the patient or the voice of the caregiver? a) Patient b) Caregiver
	2. Please share with us situations you feel the voice of patient is prioritized	**2.** Please share with us situations when the voice of patient is prioritized
	3. Please share with us situations you feel the voice of caregiver is prioritized	**3.** Please share with us situations when the voice of caregiver is prioritized
Elucidating the (expected) activities and (expected) actions by the identified actors; knowledge creation experiences	**4.** How do you think the healthcare professional involves the patient in the treatment (role in treatment) and what actions do you think he usually expects from patient?	**4.** How do you involve the patient in the treatment (role in treatment) and what actions do you usually expect from him/her during treatment?
	5. How do you think the healthcare professional involves the caregiver in the treatment (role in treatment) and what actions do you think he usually expects from caregiver?	**5.** How do you involve the caregiver in the treatment and what actions (role in treatment) do you usually expect from him/her during treatment?
Uncovering knowledge creation experiences	**6.** Now, think of the treatment in its entirety (first and subsequence consultations). How do you see the information and knowledge shared by patient and caregiver throughout treatment to be utilized by healthcare professional in practical terms?	**6.** Now, think of the treatment in its entirety (first and subsequence consultations). How do you utilize the information and knowledge shared by patient and caregiver throughout treatment in practical terms?
Demographics	**7.** Country	**7.** Country
		8. Profession

4   Analysis and Findings

Answers to the questionnaires were collected from healthcare professionals and caregivers in Japan, Singapore and Brazil. A total of twelve (12) caregivers and eight (8) healthcare professionals answered the questionnaires. Because the number of answers was small, we conducted a manual analysis of their contents.

We have no intentions of conducting a cross-nations analysis and the reason to send out to respondents in different countries was access to them and the intent to obtain a general view to base our analysis. To aid in our interpretation of the answers, we:

1. Looked through Actor-Network Theory's lens to clarify actors, associations and treatment flow;
2. Looked through the eyes of Knowledge-Creation Theory's shared context ("ba") to identify it/them;
3. Looked at the identified associations and shared contexts as activity systems to understand the activities and actions executed, and expected to be executed, by the actors (division of labor).

4.1   First Analysis: Clarifying Actors, Associations and Treatment Flow

When enquired about which voice is prioritized during treatment, majority of answers on both ends (healthcare professionals and caregivers) replied the voice of the patient was favored, except when the patient is unable to communicate the condition or feedback on developments, then the voice of the caregiver was favored. Caregivers mentioned their close contact with the patient and active participation in the daily care activities.

Technology (e.g. medication, shower chair, information system) was briefly mentioned by caregivers and healthcare professionals and its use throughout the treatment: it was interesting that the use of an information system with database for medical knowledge diffusion (with permission of patient and caregiver) was pointed out by a caregiver and not by any of the healthcare professionals.

With the mentions to technology and having a service provider (i.e. healthcare professional, caregiver) and a service recipient (i.e. patient), this encounter can be analyzed through Froehle and Roth's [18] Modes of Customer Contact with Technology framework (Fig. 1). The authors separate customer contact into face-to-face and face-to-screen. Within each, they identify the different roles technology plays in the encounter.

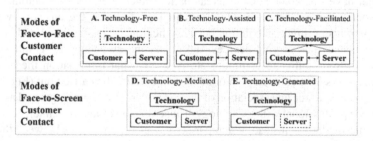

Fig. 1. Role of technology in service encounter. Source: Froehle and Roth [18]

The questionnaire sets the scenario of this study as the consultation where we assumed the patient, caregiver and healthcare professional would meet. Then, under Froehle and Roth's framework, the research is placed in face-to-face mode of contact.

We were able to see patient, healthcare professional and caregiver under a technology-assisted contact (Fig. 2) where both have face-to-face contact with patient and both employ the technology to improve this contact [18].

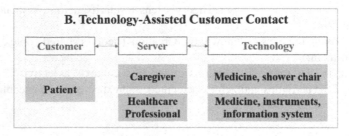

Fig. 2. Technology-assisted customer contact

The theme generated through Froehle and Roth's framework crystallized and supported our interpretation of the respondents' inputs through the lens of Actor-Network Theory is illustrated in Fig. 2.

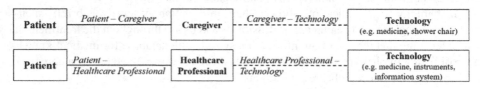

Fig. 3. Actors and their associations.

Three actors were clear: patient (prioritized voice), healthcare professional (voice of medicine [7]) and caregiver (prioritized voice when patient voice cannot be prioritized). Each promotes a difference in the other or in the network. However, patient and healthcare professional have one association whereas patient and caregiver have another. These strong associations are the continuous lines in Fig. 1. From the answers, we could not see a permanent direct association between healthcare professional and caregiver. Caregiver's agency has varying degrees: full or secondary agency is "granted" by the patient's condition, ability to communicate it or by what information the healthcare professional looks for treatment plan or action expected to be carried out (Fig. 2).

It was possible to see an association of the caregiver with technology, and another of the healthcare professional with technology. These responses led us to interpret technology as an intermediary – instead of another actor – as it only passes between these two actors and defines their relationship [19]. Particularly for these two associations, technology assisted the service encounter: the healthcare professional makes use of exams, medicine, electronic health records of the patient to assess him/her; for the caregiver, it assisted when deploying the daily care (e.g. medication, showering the patient) [18]. It was not seen an actor-intermediary association between patient and technology.

The only time the three actors associate themselves is during consultation, as illustrated in Fig. 4. It is during consultation when they interact, feedback and problems are shared, ideas are translated, negotiations happen, deviations are corrected, and orders are given. It resembles what Callon calls 'obligatory passage point' in the network of relationships being built [20].

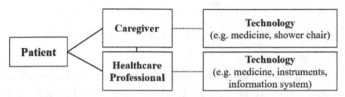

Fig. 4. Actors and associations during consultation.

4.2 Second Analysis: Identifying Shared Contexts

With actors and associations clarified, we sought out to understand the shared contexts ("ba"). "Ba" is a shared space, a shared context which serves as the foundation for knowledge creation and is related to shared experiences, mental models, spaces where relationships emerge [13].

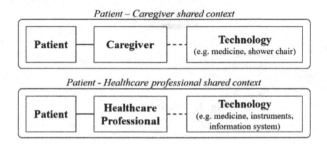

Fig. 5. Shared contexts

Initially, two separate shared contexts were found as illustrated in Fig. 5. As Epstein [9] puts it, it is through it that actors become attuned. From the answers, we could see one shared context where health professional and patient become attuned and another where patient and caregiver do. Technology item was included as respondents mentioned their own experience with it during treatment.

Once again, it was during the consultation when the three actors shared one same context in one same space and their relationship emerges through interactions as illustrated in Fig. 6.

The consultation is important because it is when separate shared contexts overlap giving rise to a context shared by all identified actors. It is the patient and his/her well-being which binds the other two actors, placing him at the center of the association. It was evident when one caregiver mentioned about being taught on how to apply vaccines; another, the knowledge gained during an episode when the shower chair needed to be

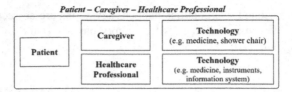

Fig. 6. Patient - Caregiver - Health professional shared context

adjusted due to patient's height which the caregiver shared judged important to share with the healthcare professional. Healthcare professionals mentioned patient's compliance to treatment monitoring checks with caregiver.

4.3 Third Analysis: Understanding the Division of Labor

With the interpretation and understanding gained in the previous analyses, we were able to combine the concepts and illustrate the flow of the treatment (Fig. 7).

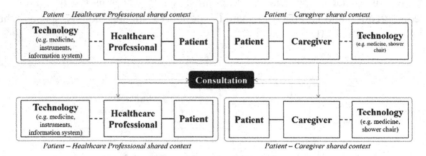

Fig. 7. Treatment flow

The patient is key to all associations and shared contexts. Looking at the consultation through magnifying glass, it is central to the flow of treatment, because it is where patient, healthcare professional and caregiver interact, share and create knowledge. Healthcare professional can assess patient's well-being through it, indicate following steps and teach the caregiver about how to deploy them (Fig. 8).

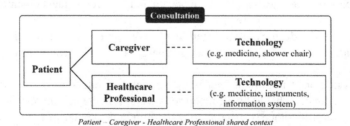

Fig. 8. The consultation

It was possible to understand the activities and actions executed, and expected to be executed, by the actors (division of labor), consolidated in Table 2. These seem to influence caregiver's varying degrees of agency granted throughout the treatment as healthcare professionals and patient's needs expect specific actions by the caregiver.

Table 2. Activities and actions of actors

Actor	Activities and actions	Expected activities and actions by caregiver	Expected activities and actions by healthcare professional
Healthcare professional	Leads the treatment ("voice of medicine") Listens to patient Assesses patient well-being based on patient's (sometimes, caregiver's) feedback Explains treatment options Explains the need for treatment Assigns tasks, prescribes medication and sets next treatment steps based on assessment and information provided by patient (some-times, by caregiver) Motivates patient about life and well-being Hears caregiver when patient is unable to communicate Teaches caregivers about medication and how to apply it	Leadership in treatment ("voice of medicine") Listening to patient Listening to caregiver about details of patient and treatment due to his/her neutrality concerning illness Teaching of medication and how to apply it	
Patient	Joins healthcare professional and caregiver together Makes decisions about treatment Provides information for assessment and deviations detection in treatment		Decisions about treatment option Adherence to treatment Collaboration in treatment Understanding of treatment's importance Motivation

(*continued*)

Table 2. (*continued*)

Actor	Activities and actions	Expected activities and actions by caregiver	Expected activities and actions by healthcare professional
Caregiver	Deploys the day-to-day treatment Applies medication Provides information about operational side of treatment Accompanies patient to consultations Supports patient Supervises treatment adherence		Companion to consultations Communication of condition when patient is unable to do so Aid and support to patient and treatment Compliance to medical orientations about treatment Patient adherence supervision Medication application Psychoeducation and attention to patient

Understanding these will help us identify boundaries and study their maintenance, question them, or transform their qualities [21] so actors can transcend them [22].

5 Conclusion

This study aimed at clarifying actors, associations and treatment flow that patient, caregiver and healthcare professional undergo; at identifying shared contexts ("ba") and their overlap; and at understanding (expected) activities and actions (to be) executed by actors to understand boundaries for transformation. Open-ended questionnaires were answered in Japan, Singapore and Brazil by a total of 12 caregivers and 8 healthcare professionals. Hermeneutic analysis and interpretation of the answers were conducted to draw findings and implications; data generated from these went through framework method of analysis in three levels: through Actor-Network Theory to identify actors, associations and treatment flow; through the Nonaka's shared context ("ba"); lastly, we looked at them as activity systems to clarify the division of labor. Three actors were found: patient, caregiver and healthcare professional. Technology assists the caregiver and the healthcare professional. The consultation is central to the flow as it is where one shared context emerges among actors, assessment is conducted, and orders are given. It is also in the consultation where activities and actions are determined.

A three levels analysis was preferred over an overall analysis to gain deeper understanding of actors, agency, associations, shared contexts, their overlap, flow of treatment and the dynamics within identified associations. Nonaka's "ba" focuses on interactions between humans and does not look at technology as a possible actor. On the other hand, Actor-Network Theory sees humans and non-humans (e.g. technology) as actors if any promotes difference in others or in the network: during treatment, technology is used extensively. The division of labor sheds light on the inner dynamics of the associations by breaking down (expected) activities and actions, helping us understand roles, expectations, process of agency, care deployment and knowledge creation among the actors.

Due to limited financial and time resources, the sample size is small. The authors acknowledge this as a limitation of this study. However slight and a preliminary study which lays the foundation for our ongoing research, the sample analyzed helped us gather insights and implications for future studies.

The first set of implications comprise the first analysis and its findings. The consultation is central to the flow of the treatment. It is where all actors associate with one another and where information is shared, knowledge is created, ideas are translated, negotiations happen, deviations are detected, and next steps are decided on. It is necessary to clarify what sort of negotiations and translations usually take place among actors and measure again the role of technology to see whether it remains as a plain assistant to healthcare professional and caregiver or shifts to be a facilitator in the encounter and, if it does, what exactly it facilitates in these negotiations and translations, as per Froehle and Roth's framework [18]. One unexpected finding was to see varying degrees of caregiver's agency in the treatment: future studies can go deeper to map its reasons and progression throughout the treatment – this may give a clue on the changes the associations undergo throughout.

The second set of implications concerns the second analysis and its findings. Identifying where separate context overlap and a common shared context arises is crucial to so we can understand the situation where knowledge is created. It is about looking at the specific position where associations' components as what they are: actors (or intermediaries) who promote difference in others or in the network. Understanding where and how actors become attuned helps us focus our following study on where and how self-transcendence happens. Some caregivers mentioned that healthcare professionals "do not listen to details": we interpret these "details" as contextual knowledge the caregiver feels important to share. We are inclined to see this as a conflict of priorities: caregiver has one set of priorities and healthcare professional has another. Through the study of shared context, future research could tackle the processes of "tuning" of priorities to minimize misfit.

The last set implications pertain the third analysis and its implications. With associations clarified and the identification of when separate contexts overlap and a common shared one emerges among actors, we were able to identify some of the actors' actions (or tasks) and the excepted actions other actors have towards each other. We still need to dig deeper and understand how expected actions define boundaries so we may transform or, even, encourage actors to transcend and redefine them. These seem to be one of the reasons for varying degree of caregiver's agency, but we believe there are others and it requires more evidence to understand its effects on the knowledge creating activity of the system.

These implications set the ground for our following study which targets to obtain the answers to the implications described previously. We aim at proposing a model where all actors are active knowledge contributors and creators in the treatment. Basically, our model desires to be a roadmap to guide the identified actors in their path to transcend and transform their boundaries.

References

1. Zhao, J., Wang, T., Fan, X.: Patient value co-creation in online health communities: social identity effects on customer knowledge contributions and membership continuance intentions in online health communities. J. Serv. Manag. **26**(1), 72–96 (2015)
2. Hojat, M.: The interpersonal dynamics in clinician–patient relationships. In: Hojat, M. (ed.) Empathy in Patient Care: Antecedents, Development, Measurement, and Outcomes, pp. 117–139. Springer, New York (2007). https://doi.org/10.1007/0-387-33608-7_8
3. Sakai, E.Y., Carpenter, B.D.: Linguistic features of power dynamics in triadic dementia diagnostic conversations. Patient Educ. Couns. **85**(2), 295–298 (2011)
4. Sayes, E.: Actor-network theory and methodology: just what does it mean to say that nonhumans have agency? Soc. Stud. Sci. **44**(1), 134–149 (2014)
5. Saito, M.: Current issues regarding family caregiving and gender equality in Japan: male caregivers and the interplay between caregiving and masculinities. Japan Labor Rev. **14**(1), 92–111 (2017)
6. Kusaba, T., et al.: Influence of family dynamics on burden among family caregivers in aging Japan. Fam. Pract. **33**(5), 466–470 (2016)
7. Vasconcellos-Silva, P.R., Rivera, F.J.U., Siebeneichler, F.B.: Healthcare organizations, linguistic communities, and the emblematic model of palliative care. Cad. Saude Publica **23**(7), 1529–1538 (2007)
8. Mazer, B.L., Cameron, R.A., DeLuca, J.M., Mohile, S.G., Epstein, R.M.: "Speaking-for" and "speaking-as": Pseudo-surrogacy in physician–patient–companion medical encounters about advanced cancer. Patient Educ. Couns. **96**(1), 36–42 (2014)
9. Epstein, R.M., Street, R.L.: Shared mind: communication, decision making, and autonomy in serious illness. Ann. Family Med. **9**(5), 454–461 (2011)
10. Laidsaar-Powell, R., et al.: The TRIO framework: conceptual insights into family caregiver involvement and influence throughout cancer treatment decision-making. Patient Educ. Couns. **100**(11), 2035–2046 (2017)
11. Mendes, V.L.F., Molini-Avejonas, D.R., Ribeiro, A., Souza, L.A.P.: The collective construction of a guide for caregivers of bedridden patients: experience report. J. Soc. Bras. Fonoaudiol. **23**(3), 281–287 (2011). http://www.scielo.br/scielo.php?script=sci_arttext&pid=S2179-64912011000300016&lng=en&nrm=iso
12. Linderholm, M., Friedrichsen, M.: A desire to be seen: family caregivers' experiences of their caring role in palliative home care. Cancer Nurs. **33**(1), 28–36 (2010)
13. Nonaka, I., Reinmoeller, P., Senoo, D.: The 'ART' of knowledge: systems to capitalize on market knowledge. Eur. Manag. J. **16**(6), 673–684 (1998)
14. Weick, K.E.: Sensemaking in Organizations. Sage Publications, Thousand Oaks (1995)
15. Latour, B.: On Actor-network Theory: A Few Clarifications. Soziale Welt **47**(4), 369–381 (1996)
16. Engestrom, Y.: The new generation of expertise. Seven theses. In: Rainbird, H., Fuller, A., Munro, A. (eds.) Workplace Learning in Context, pp. 145–165. Routledge, London (2004)
17. Gale, N.K., Heath, G., Cameron, E., Rashid, S., Redwood, S.: Using the framework method for the analysis of qualitative data in multi-disciplinary health research. BMC Med. Res. Methodol. **13**, 117 (2013)
18. Froehle, C.M., Roth, A.V.: New measurement scales for evaluating perceptions of the technology-mediated customer service experience. J. Oper. Manag. **22**(1), 1–21 (2004)

19. Callon, M.: Techno-economic networks and irreversibility. Sociol. Rev. **38**(1_suppl), 132–161 (1990)
20. Callon, M.: Some elements of a sociology of translation: domestication of the scallops and the fishermen of St Brieuc Bay. Sociol. Rev. **32**(1_suppl), 196–233 (1984)
21. Kerosuo, H.: Boundaries in health care discussions: an activity theoretical approach to the analysis of boundaries. In: Paulsen, N., Hernes, T. (eds.) Managing Boundaries in Organizations: Multiple Perspectives. Palgrave Macmillan, London (2003)
22. Nonaka, I., Konno, N.: The concept of "Ba": Building a foundation for knowledge creation. Calif. Manag. Rev. **40**(3), 40–54 (1998)

Knowledge Gain in Production Planning and Execution Systems

Christian Ploder[✉], David Weber, Reinhard Bernsteiner, and Stephan Schlögl

Management, Communication and IT; MCI Entrepreneurial School,
Universitätsstraße 15, 6020 Innsbruck, Austria
christian.ploder@mci.edu

Abstract. The aim of this work is to identify use cases supporting production planning and execution with big data mining in make to order (MTO) based manufacturing companies. MTO manufacturers are described by a variety of characteristics. Due to the production in the context of customer orders, adherence to delivery dates, production quality, flexibility and the knowledge of production managers are key success factors. A suitable production planning and execution system is required. In addition to Workload Control, which was specially developed for MTO manufacturing, manufacturing resource planning, enterprise resource planning or the theory of constraints can also be considered. These systems are collecting increasing amounts of data in the production process. Consultants for production planning systems and production experts were interviewed so as to obtain a deep and integrated understanding of the topic, and in parallel an internal, context-dependent view of the processes. The evaluation using deductive and inductive category based coding shows that Workload Control and Theory of Constraints are not used as production planning and control systems. The theoretically developed use cases were critically discussed and their usefulness for production managers evaluated, while two additional application cases were identified. Furthermore, limitations in the data mining process could be determined.

Keywords: Production planning and execution · Predictive data mining · Knowledge gain in PPS · Make to order manufacturers

1 Introduction

Information systems, such as Enterprise Resource Planning (ERP) systems, generate a lot of data that can be evaluated [11, pp. 1891–1892]. Also Internet of Things (IoT) technologies provide a wide variety of data structures that can be used in the production process [3, p. 2]. Production managers use this data to provide accurate forecasts regarding product quality and production times, while real-time analysis is used to execute the production process [3, p. 1].

The term 'big data' is becoming increasingly important for small and medium-sized enterprises (SME). It offers the chance to create a sustainable

© Springer Nature Switzerland AG 2021
L. Uden et al. (Eds.): KMO 2021, CCIS 1438, pp. 138–146, 2021.
https://doi.org/10.1007/978-3-030-81635-3_12

competitive advantage, especially for make to order (MTO) manufacturers who have to act within various framework constraints in order to remain competitive [3] . Using predictive data mining methods, valuable information can be found to make optimal decisions [3, p. 1].

Even if numerous production planning and control systems (PPS) are suitable for MTO manufacturers, none can be named that covers all requirements [20]. In addition, MTO manufacturers are subject to a number of challenges that have a significant impact on the competitiveness of these companies. The importance of adherence to delivery dates, product quality and flexibility is only a small part of the framework in which the MTO manufacturers operate [5,10]. Production managers can be seen as knowledge workers [13,19] and have to deal with many different information streams so as to establish the most efficient production plan according to the current order situation [9], which is much more flexible in the case of MTO SMEs. This challenge has to be tackled with dedicated support form a management perspective as from a technical perspective. However, many of the different data streams in production can be meaningfully analyzed [17]. By identifying patterns in this data, information can be created that may lead to significant benefits. These advantages of analyzing big data help companies remain competitive and act within their framework.

In order to add to this field, the work presented in this paper discusses predictive big data mining use cases supporting production managers. So far use cases for big data in production have undergone little examination. Hence, our goal was to first use the literature to identify, examine, and critically discuss uses cases and then reflect their challenges with experts. To this end, the following research question served as an umbrella for our work: *What are predictive big data mining use cases to gain knowledge in production planning and execution systems in make to order producing SMEs?*

The remainder of this paper first starts with the relevant theoretical background discussed in Sect. 2 followed by a description of our research methodology in Sect. 3. Results in form of different use case descriptions are then given in Sect. 4 and will be critically discussed in Sect. 5. Finally, Sect. 6 closes the paper, highlighting limitations and potential future work.

2   Theoretical Background

This section of the paper presents the theoretical concepts of the current literature. The goal is to provide an overview of production planning and execution systems for MTO manufacturers and to identify the terms 'big data' and 'predictive big data mining' to address use cases. Some of the companies produce in large series or mass production and can therefore align their production much easier to production programs. However, there is a number of companies that can be categorized as MTO manufacturers or individual manufacturers and therefore have special requirements for PPS systems. The majority of these companies are designated as SMEs. There is currently no precise definition of this term, however the European Commission refers to SMEs as companies with fewer than

250 employees who generate annual sales of up to 50 million euros or have a balance sheet total of no more than 43 million euros[1].

The main characteristic of MTO manufacturing is production based on customer orders, possibly with special adjustments [10]. Thus, all activities of the operational PPS are based on the individual customer orders, whereby the customer request with regard to delivery date, quantity and adjustments should always be the focus [10]. The use of a suitable PPS system for SME MTO manufacturers has to meet certain requirements that are unique in the MTO environment. An order from an individual manufacturer can otherwise be on hold for up to 90% of the time before it is actually produced [8, p. 580]. Kingsman and Hendry further mention factors such as fluctuating demand, a small number of standard products or the importance of holding deadlines in order to satisfy customers [8]. Furthermore, a suitable system depends on the individualization of the products, the configuration of the production facility and the size of the company [20, p. 871]. Therefore, requirements for a PPS system can be named as follows [20, p. 873]:

- Possibility of integrating customer inquiries for planning delivery dates and capacities
- Possibility of integrating order entry and release with a focus on adherence to delivery dates
- Ability to map non-repeating or limited-repeating production
- Ability to react to variable production routes
- Applicability for SMEs

Kurbel also mentions adherence to delivery dates and product quality as important competitive factors [10]. In addition, the dominance of order processing results in the requirement that current information and details about the order must be known at all times. This emphasizes the importance of the information architecture behind the corresponding concept. In addition, there is a requirement for companies that are highly MTO oriented to be able to plan appointments, quantities and capacity allocations, even if important basic data are sometimes missing [10]. This affects the planning security, because when a work plan or a product modification is implemented by an order, there is no guarantee that no errors or weaknesses will occur.

SME MTO companies also experience the difficulty of a high level of control complexity, which arises from the high variability in many ways [6, p. 192]. This includes indicators such as the widely differing frequency of customer orders, exact or many different delivery dates, variable production times through variable products and variable production routes and times.

There are different methods that are used in an MTO environment to deal with the complexity caused by variability. One of these concepts is Workload Control (WLC), a PPS method specifically designed for the requirements of the

---

[1] European Commission recommendation on the definition of small and small and medium-sized enterprises - 20.05.2003.

MTO manufacturing industry [20, p. 878]. However, methods such as Manufacturing Resource Planning (MRP II), ERP or Theory of Constraints (TOC) can also be applied in certain cases and under certain circumstances [20, p. 886].

MRP II is a further development of the MRP concept, which is defined as a periodic push-based system and is used in complex production environments [20, p. 873]. Many advantages are associated with the concept, including better production planning, shorter throughput times, higher inventory turnover, better cost control and better capacity planning [18, p. 332]. MRP II systems began to develop into ERP systems in 1988 [16, p. 852]. ERP systems are systems that plan and handle all company-internal resources and processes. Furthermore, given today's age of e-business, ERP systems increasingly tend to not only control internal processes but rather focus on cross-business processes instead [7].

The TOC originated in the production context in the 1970s as a bottleneck-oriented solution, but developed further into a management and leadership theory [12]. The concept behind TOC takes bottlenecks in production into account [20, p. 876]. Thus, companies with applied TOC can notice various improvements, such as reduced throughput times, reduced cycle times and increased sales [12, p. 580].

The emergence of big data enables the generation of valuable information and better decisions through advanced data mining methods [3, p. 2–3]. Big data in particular is dealing with advanced data mining techniques to meet the requirements of structured, unstructured, production and process-relevant data to support production planning managers. According to Cheng and colleagues [3, p. 2], using advanced data mining methods is helpful because:

- Problems and unknown changes are found
- Useful and efficient patterns are recognized
- Production plans are adjusted
- Intelligence and automation of production are improved
- Efficiency and quality of production are improved

To elaborate on this work and find out more about the specific use cases that may help increase the production planning and execution of system quality, we used a research methodology based on expert interviews. This methodology was used to gain new insights from experts across multiple contexts.

3 Methodology

People are considered experts because it is assumed that they have knowledge that is not yet accessible [1, p. 37]. Experts are thus often involved so as to answer research questions and gain new knowledge [4, p. 12].

In addition, experts have exclusive positions that give them their knowledge [4, p. 13]. For example, production managers are interviewed because they have internal process and technology knowledge due to their exclusive position.

3.1 Selection of Experts

Following the definition of Bogner et al. [2, p. 13], experts are people which are able to structure the concrete field of action in a meaningful and guiding manner for others. For this particular study, experts were divided in two different groups:

- Consulting Experts, i.e., Senior Consultants or Partners (C1–C5)
- Experts in SMEs, i.e., Heads of Production or CEOs (E1–E6)

In total, 11 experts were interviewed. Five experts were not part of a manufacturing company, but rather in an advisory capacity. They offered an external view on the topic and provided deeply integrated knowledge. This knowledge is company-independent, since their experience in the various industries enables generalization and comparability. Every chosen consultant had more than 15 years of experience. The other six interviewees were experts from MTO based SMEs. They provided in-depth knowledge of the production process in the company and possible uses of predictive big data mining. This internal perspective allowed for the description of context-dependent processes. Every expert of the second group had more than 20 years of experience.

3.2 Interview Procedure

The main goal of the exploratory expert interviews was to discuss existing use cases and to identify new ones. Therefore, the interviews were investigative interviews, aimed at generating additional information about the area of investigation [2, p. 23]. In addition, it was not a question of closing information gaps, but rather one of generating as much knowledge as possible so as to allow for exploration [2, p. 24].

Meuser and Nagel [14, p. 454] differentiate between operational and contextual knowledge in connection with exploratory interviews. To this end, our expert interviews represent a mixture of operational knowledge and contextual knowledge, since these relate to the action context of the experts as actors [2, p. 23].

After we had carried out two pre-tests to verify the comprehensibility of the questions, the content of the answers and the duration of the interview, interviews were conducted within a six week period in spring 2019. Subsequently they were transcribed, paraphrased and coded based on a deductively and inductively created categorization schema [15, p. 56]. During the final theoretical generalization, categories were arranged by their context [15, p. 57]. The following presentation of results is thus guided by a theoretically informed perspective, whereby sensory connections are linked to typologies.

4 Results

The following subsections present the categories related to the information gathered by the experts. Statements are referenced in the text followed by the expert identification number. Results focus on the information based on the categories which were most relevant for the given research question.

4.1   Category 1: Production Planning and Execution

As part of the interviews, respondents named various MTO manufacturers characteristics. Those include:

- Highly customized products
- Delivery date is determined by customers
- Use of backwards scheduling
- High flexibility
- Small lot sizes
- Delivery reliability is of great importance
- Production planning is triggered by sales order

Expert E6 additionally described that due to increasing customer requirements, limits are being reached in the manufacturing of the products.

Different IT support in the processes of the MTO manufacturers were also explained. According to C2, C3, C4 and C5, ERP systems are increasingly being used. ERP systems are becoming more and more flexible (C4; C5), but *"it is definitely the case that a system is only as good as it is managed"* (C5). The aspect of master data maintenance is also explained as an important factor (C5; E2; E6). Expert C5 developed a system that enables communication from machines, controls and control systems. This means that information returned from the machine can be used more effectively and consequently that the system is easier to use for SMEs.

Expert C1, on the other hand, did not see any benefit in using other IT systems in SMEs as his/her company is considered lean. But all respondents from SMEs mentioned using an ERP system at least as support (E2; E3; E4; E5; E6). A system for operating data acquisition is also used by two respondents (E2; E5). According to C2 and C4, today's systems have an MRP character. Due to their flexibility, newer approaches are sometimes included as well (C4).

4.2   Category 2: Scheduling Rules

Forward and backward scheduling is used accordingly (C1; C3; E5). The respondents stated different prerequisites so that the application can be used to gain advantages. Expert C2 mentioned the amount of in-house and third-party production. If there is a high proportion of contribution by the producer and a certain degree of product standardization, then forecasting models can be used more easily. Higher individualization increases the complexity of a model. In addition, it is not a decision between ERP or data mining, but a combination of both (C2). C3 complemented the applicability depending on production structures such as parts lists, organizational and work plan structures. The selection of the right features also plays an important role (C2). C4 further mentioned the difficulty of using appropriate tools and automating them. If the proportion of third-party production is high, it would also be more interesting to analyze data from the supply chain across companies (C2).

None of the respondents explicitly applies this use case. Expert E1, however, could imagine an application, in cases where the customer is difficult and thus processes may be optimized. E3 and E5 see coverage by the ERP system. E4 could not think of an application and had no experience in this regard. Nevertheless, according to the respondent, there is room for improvement (E4).

4.3   Category 3: Forecasting of Lead Times

In order to apply a lead time forecasting successfully, the right data has to be recorded, analyzed and operated continuously (C4). The method is also heavily dependent on the product and location (C2). C3 also mentioned that orders can only be compared to a limited extent. It is therefore important to find the right data and build the model accordingly. The larger the lot size, the easier. C1 sees *"an evolution and not a revolution"* through the analysis of existing data.

C5 mentioned the importance of the application for the re-ordering of special tools. That is, special tools may be ordered in a timely manner based on historical data, so that with the right combination and control, all orders can be processed seamlessly (C5). One company is currently implementing the forecast of throughput times (E2). The main goal here is to improve throughput times and to summarize work steps. Experts E3, E4 and E5, however, see this covered by the ERP system.

4.4   Category 4: New Use Cases

Two of the experts were able to identify new use cases for predictive big data mining. C3 named the use case of bottleneck optimization. In their case, the entire production was restructured, machines were chained together differently so that the machine with a bottleneck could be used more efficiently (C3). Such led to an increase in production by over 80 percent.

A second identified use case deals with the topic of energy management (C5). Many companies require a lot of energy (C5). Electricity suppliers impose fines if trends in electricity consumption rise above a certain limit. This is where data mining comes into play, i.e. if these trends would be analyzed in a targeted manner irrelevant consumers could easily be switched off. Such may be implemented using priorities (C5). In addition, cold stores could pre-produce at night consequently smooth consumption curves (C5).

5   Summary and Discussion

Adding to known use cases of predictive data mining reported in the literature, two new use cases could be identified during the interviews.

That is, C3 explained the use case of bottleneck optimization based on existing ERP data. There was a significant advantage from an increase in production of around 80%, but the application was only used in one company so far. A prerequisite for an implementation could be high system intensity and low product diversity. In addition, *"it was something we only did once"* (C3). Nevertheless, the use case may be classified as predominantly predictive, since existing data was used to achieve future improvements. Furthermore, C5 explained the application of energy management. The generalized explanation of the use case suggests a potential application by many companies (C5). The analysis of consumption curves, in particular, promises the advantage of cost savings by smoothing consumption curves and avoiding fines.

In contrast to the given literature, the empirical results show that, ERP systems based on MRP and MRP II are more often used than WLC or TOC based systems. However, these also have weaknesses in terms of data volumes and flexibility. The setting of scheduling rules is examined more critically in practice than in theory. Even if the use case has some advantages, none of the respondents did actually use it.

The literature explains both advantages and challenges for the forecast of throughput times. These are supplemented by our interviews, with the respondents primarily providing information on the requirements of the application. It can thus be summarized, that the use of a suitable PPS system in the literature is described differently than it is in practice for MTO based SMEs. Limitations in the process were particularly supplemented by the statements of the experts. There is no most suitable use case identified by the experts, although there may be dependencies concerning company and production structures in which cases fit better than others.

6 Limitations and Potential Future Work

While the above described use cases for big data and predictive big data analytics may be seen as a starting point, their applicability is somewhat limited. That is, in order to establish a framework for the use of big data in production planning and execution systems, we focused exclusively on MTO based SMEs. Further, only production experts in German speaking countries were interviewed. As confirmed by an expert, these results cannot easily be extended to other regions. Finally, future research projects should focus on the integration of predictive maintenance to address the challenges according to production planning and execution systems.

References

1. Bogner, A., Littig, B., Menz, W. (eds.): Experteninterviews: Theorien, Methoden, Anwendungsfelder. VS Verlag für Sozialwissenschaften, Wiesbaden, 3, grundlegend überarbeitete auflage edn. (2009)
2. Interviews mit Experten. QS, Springer, Wiesbaden (2014). https://doi.org/10. 1007/978-3-531-19416-5
3. Cheng, Y., Chen, K., Sun, H., Zhang, Y., Tao, F.: Data and knowledge mining with big data towards smart production. J. Ind. Inf. Integr. **9**, 1–13 (2018)

4. Gläser, J., Laudel, G.: Experteninterviews und qualitative Inhaltsanalyse als Instrumente rekonstruierender Untersuchungen. Lehrbuch, VS Verlag für Sozialwissenschaften, Wiesbaden, 3, überarb. aufl. edn. (2009)
5. Hendry, L.C., Kingsman, B.G.: Production planning systems and their applicability to make-to-order companies. Eur. J. Oper. Res. **40**(1), 1–15 (1989)
6. Henrich, P., Land, M., Gaalman, G.: Exploring applicability of the workload control concept. Int. J. Prod. Econ. **90**(2), 187–198 (2004)
7. Kehoe, D.F., Boughton, N.J.: New paradigms in planning and control across manufacturing supply chains: the utilisation of internet technologies. Int. J. Oper. Prod. Manage. **21**(5/6), 582–593 (2001)
8. Kingsman, B., Hendry, L.: The relative contributions of input and output controls on the performance of a workload control system in make-to-order companies. Prod. Plan. Control **13**(7), 579–590 (2002)
9. Kohlegger, M., Ploder, C.: Data driven knowledge discovery for continuous process improvement. In: Knowledge Management in Digital Change, pp. 65–81. Springer (2018)
10. Kurbel, K.: Produktionsplanung und -steuerung im Enterprise Resource Planning und Supply Chain Management // Produktionsplanung und -steuerung: Methodische Grundlagen von PPS-Systemen und Erweiterungen, 6th edn. Oldenbourg Wissenschaftsverlag, München (2005)
11. Li, L., Zijin, S., Jiacheng, N., Fei, Q.: Data-based scheduling framework and adaptive dispatching rule of complex manufacturing systems. Int. J. Adv. Manuf. Technol. **66**(9–12), 1891–1905 (2013). https://doi.org/10.1007/s00170-012-4468-6
12. Mabin, V.J., Balderstone, S.J.: The performance of the theory of constraints methodology. Int. J. Oper. Prod. Manage. **23**(6), 568–595 (2003)
13. Maier, R., Hädrich, T., Peinl, R.: Enterprise knowledge infrastructures. Springer, Heidelberg (2009)
14. Meuser, M., Nagel, U.: Expertinneninterviews - vielfach erprobt, wenig bedacht: Ein beitrag zur qualitativen methodendiskussion. In: Garz, D., Kraimer, K. (eds.) Qualitativ-empirische Sozialforschung, pp. 441–471. Westdeutscher Verlag, Opladen (1991)
15. Meuser, M., Nagel, U.: Experteninterview und der wandel der wissensproduktion. In: Bogner, A., Littig, B., Menz, W. (eds.) Experteninterviews, pp. 35–60. VS Verlag für Sozialwissenschaften, Wiesbaden (2009)
16. Muscatello, J.R., Small, M.H., Chen, I.J.: Implementing enterprise resource planning (ERP) systems in small and midsize manufacturing firms. Int. J. Oper. Prod. Manage. **23**(8), 850–871 (2003)
17. Öztürk, A., Kayalıgil, S., Özdemirel, N.E.: Manufacturing lead time estimation using data mining. Eur. J. Oper. Research **173**(2), 683–700 (2006)
18. Petroni, A.: Critical factors of MRP implementation in small and medium-sized firms. Int. J. Oper. Prod. Manage. **22**(3), 329–348 (2002)
19. Pyöriä, P.: The concept of knowledge work revisited. J. Knowl. Manage. **9**(3), 116–127 (2005)
20. Stevenson, M., Hendry, L.C., Kingsman, B.G.: A review of production planning and control: the applicability of key concepts to the make-to-order industry. Int. J. Prod. Res. **43**(5), 869–898 (2005)

Fuzzy Evaluation System for Innovation Ability of Science and Technology Enterprises

Wenpei Shao[1], Xiangyang Feng[1(✉)], Ming Zhu[1], Ran Tao[1], Yi Lv[2], and Youqun Shi[1]

[1] School of Computer Science and Technology, Donghua University, Shanghai 201620, China
{fengxy,zhuming,taoran,yqshi}@dhu.edu.cn
[2] Xinsheng'an Internet Technology (DaLian) Co., Ltd., Dalian, China
ly20001010@Sina.com

Abstract. Innovation ability is the core competitiveness of science and technology enterprises. Regular monitoring and evaluation of enterprise innovation capabilities can help management departments accurately grasp the enterprise's research and development (R&D) and market expansion capabilities, and help enterprises understand their own development potential. Referring to relevant national science and technology innovation enterprise evaluation standards, an innovation index evaluation system was established for science and technology innovation enterprises. In this paper, the innovation capability of science and technology enterprises was modeled and evaluated from the point of view of medical device companies. It made use of fuzzy comprehensive evaluation on enterprise innovation capability, used relatively objective entropy method to determine weight, and applied weighted geometric mean method to further optimize the weight value of wide-ranging data. Thus, it ensured the scientificity and stability of the weight value. In order to verify the rationality and correntness of our model, 218 representative science and technology enterprises in the medical machinery industry were selected as evaluation samples. Based on entropy method, their respective index weights were determined, while their innovation capabilities in the industry were evaluated comprehensively.

Keywords: Innovation ability · Evaluation index system · Entropy method · Evaluation model

1 Introduction

The concept of innovation ability was proposed by Schumpeter [1] in "Economic Development Theory" in 1912. He believed that the process of social development is a dynamic development process. As China's economic construction progresses from high-speed growth to high-quality growth, the demand for scientific and technological innovation is becoming more and more urgent. The enterprise innovation ability [2] refers to its ability to complete various activities related to innovation. It contains three aspects: whether the concept can be transformed into a product, whether the product can be recognized by users, corporate management and financial returns situation.

© Springer Nature Switzerland AG 2021
L. Uden et al. (Eds.): KMO 2021, CCIS 1438, pp. 147–159, 2021.
https://doi.org/10.1007/978-3-030-81635-3_13

Science and technology enterprises [3] refer to knowledge-intensive enterprises with high product technology content, high proportion of scientific and technological professionals, and high returns and high growth.

To accurately evaluate the innovation ability of an enterprise, it is necessary to build a scientific, reasonable, effective and accurate evaluation index system for science and technology innovation ability, and to construct a corresponding evaluation model for the index system.

The research on the evaluation indexes of enterprises' innovation ability abroad started earlier and more mature. In the 1980s, Porter classified the strategic development affecting the enterprise into five major forces, built the Porter Five Force Model [4], and summarized the factors affecting the competitiveness of the enterprise. Burgelman [5] incorporated resources and allocation, industry technology understanding ability and management ability into the evaluation index of enterprise innovation ability. Kotabe [6] proposed that knowledge exchange with suppliers could improve innovation capabilities. Pittaway L [7] believed that government policy factors would indirectly or even directly affect the results of corporate innovation.

China's innovation evaluation system research began in the mid-to-late 1980s. Li Husheng [8] proposed the concept of a universal innovation capability evaluation index system to promote the development of innovation in various fields. Zhang Jinhua [9] constructed the evaluation index system from the aspects of industrial input, output, technology and market efficiency, so as to evaluate the innovation ability of manufacturing industry in Jiangsu Province. Zhao Yanyun [10] carried out dynamic index evaluation from the perspective of enterprise regional distribution, enterprise scale status, technical structure and enterprise type.

For the evaluation model of scientific and technological innovation capabilities, the commonly used methods include Factor Analysis (FA) [11], Analytic Hierarchy Process (AHP) [12], Gray Relationla Analysis (GRA) [13], Entropy Method [14] and so on. Many Chinese scholars have improved these basic methods for the specific problems of the evaluation of technological innovation ability of enterprises, and achieved some results. Li Zuowei [15] used FA to evaluate the technological innovation capabilities of listed companies in Jinzhou manufacturing industry, and attributed their low innovation capability scores to the lack of capital chain and R&D investment insufficient. Zhao Jiaxin [16] applied AHP to evaluate the comprehensive innovation ability of 20 high-tech enterprises in Wuhan. Wang Zhibo [17] evaluated the technological innovation ability of enterprises from the seven stages of enterprise innovation by using GRA.

The key to solve the evaluation model of technological innovation ability is to determine the weight of each index. When integrating each index into a comprehensive conclusion, it is necessary to consider the relative importance of each index in the enterprise innovation evaluation system, that is to give different weights according to its importance. According to the way of empowerment, it can be divided into subjective empowerment and objective empowerment.

The technological innovation ability of enterprises is a systematic ability with many influencing factors. It is difficult to evaluate qualitatively through subjective judgment. Entropy Method can objectively reflect the orderliness of various indexes in the process of enterprise technological innovation. That is, through the entropy value of each index in the process of technological innovation, it is possible to relatively accurately assess the innovation ability of the enterprise.

At present, Entropy Method is widely applied in regional economic analysis and evaluation of urban innovation ability [18], and is also found in the evaluation of university innovation ability [19]. However, there are few researches on the evaluation of innovation ability of scientific and technological enterprises by using Entropy Method.

In this paper, 218 representative scientific and technological innovation enterprises in medical machinery industry are selected as evaluation samples, and the evaluation system of innovation ability is constructed by referring to relevant national evaluation standards of scientific and technological innovation enterprises. By using Entropy Method, according to the difference degree of the index, give the appropriate weight to each index in the index system with the size of entropy, and evaluate the technological innovation ability based on the determined index weight.

2 Construction of Evaluation Index System

Whether the evaluation index system is scientific or not will not only affect the evaluation results, but also affect the development of innovative enterprises and the improvement of innovation capabilities. The whole process from conception to production should be considered in the evaluation of innovation ability of scientific and technological enterprises. China's science and technology enterprises have the characteristics of fierce market competition, a large proportion of intangible assets, high technology, and senior intellectuals as the core. Based on the analysis of the factors affecting the technological innovation ability of enterprises, following the principles of systematization, rationality, and accuracy of the establishment of the index system, referring to the "Measures for the Evaluation of Science and Technology Small and Medium-sized Enterprises" issued by the Ministry of Science and Technology and other relevant official documents, the factor set is sorted out and adjusted. Considering the characteristics of long scientific research cycle, innovative development is added to the evaluation system to evaluate the growth rate of innovative enterprises. The part of innovation income is used to measure the knowledge intensive degree and technology content of innovative enterprises.

Based on the study of 218 enterprises in domestic medical machinery industry, combined with the availability of data, the evaluation system of scientific and technological innovation index established in this paper includes 5 first-level indexes and 18 second-level indexes. The system comprehensively considers the innovation capabilities of innovative enterprises from five aspects, including funding, manpower, results, benefits, and development. The innovation funding shows the state of innovation investment. The innovation manpower refers to the manpower composition of the enterprise. The innovation results show the total knowledge and intensity of the enterprise. The innovation income refers to the degree of the company's core technology. Innovation development reflects R&D cycle and investment value of a unit project. The factor set of innovative enterprises in the medical industry is shown in Table 1:

Table 1. Index of innovation ability evaluation

First-level indexes	Secondary indexes	Subscript
Innovation funding	Net profit (100 million)	Y1
	Business income (100 million)	Y2
	Proportion of innovation investment in main business income (%)	Y3
Innovative manpower	Number of employees (person)	Y4
	Proportion of R&D personnel in employment (%)	Y5
	Proportion of employees with B.S. or above (%)	Y6
	Proportion of graduate with employment (%)	Y7
	Proportion of M.D. in employment (%)	Y8
	Proportion of employees aged 30 and under. (%)	Y9
Innovation achievements	Number of patent applications	Y10
	Proportion of utility model patents in all patents (%)	Y11
	The average number of patents per 100 employees	Y12
	Implemented invention patents/invention patents (%)	Y13
Innovation income	Proportion of core product profit (%)	Y14
	Proportion of overseas sales (%)	Y15
	Proportion of operating revenue of core products (%)	Y16
Innovative development	Average funding for ongoing project (100 million)	Y17
	Cooperative Innovation Enterprises/Cooperative Enterprises (%)	Y18

3 Establishment of Evaluation Model

On the basis of quantitative description and correlation analysis of quantitative and qualitative changes of technological innovation ability evaluation indexes, according to the degree of difference of indexes, each index in the index system is given proper weight with the size of entropy value. Then, based on the determined index weight, Entropy Method evaluation model is established to evaluate the technological innovation ability. For the evaluation of the innovation ability of technology-based enterprises, the problem is abstracted and described. Y is the mapping of X to R.

$$Y = RX \tag{1}$$

$X = \{x_1, x_2 \ldots x_m\}$ is the factor set, and $Y = \{y_1, y_2 \ldots y_n\}$ is the evaluation result set. R represents the calculation process. The paper mainly needs to solve three problems. 1) Selection of factor set. 2) The establishment and calculation of evaluation models, especially the calculation of weight sets. 3) Model optimization. The entire system architecture is shown in Fig. 1 below:

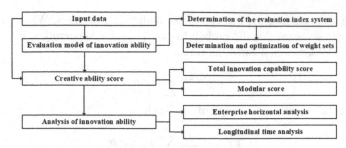

Fig. 1. Model construction diagram

The modeling process includes clarifying the purpose of enterprise evaluation, determining the evaluation index system, comparing and determining the evaluation index system model, screening and enriching the evaluation index system, determining the calculation method of the weight, and further optimizing the change of the weight to obtain the evaluation result. This paper completes the establishment of the factor set by referring to relevant domestic and foreign literature and standards. A fuzzy evaluation model based on the entropy method was used for modeling. The weighted geometric mean method is used for weight optimization.

3.1 Determine Weights by Entropy Method

The contribution should contain no more than four levels of headings. In the entropy method, the data is regarded as molecules, and the importance of the molecules to the system is judged by the degree of chaos. More chaotic molecules carry more information. An event with a greater probability of occurrence carries a smaller amount of information, and a smaller probability of an event has a larger amount of information.

1. Standardize and classify indicators of different orders of magnitude into the same order of magnitude. The value of i represents the i-th company. The value of j represents the j-th factor set. Yij represents the value of the j-th factor of the i-th company.

   1) Normalize the positive index by comparing with the minimum value of this factor to obtain the positive degree of difference.

$$Z_{ij} = \frac{Y_{ij} - \text{MIN}(Y_{ij})}{\text{MAX}(Y_{ij}) - \text{MIN}(Y_{ij})} \tag{2}$$

   2) Normalize the reverse index by comparing with the maximum value of this factor to get the reverse difference.

$$Z_{ij} = \frac{\text{MAX}(Y_{ij}) - Y_{ij}}{\text{MAX}(Y_{ij}) - \text{MIN}(Y_{ij})} \tag{3}$$

2. Pij is the proportion of the i-th enterprise under the j-th index. When the value of Pij is larger, it means that the probability of this value appearing is larger, and the amount of information it carries is smaller.

$$P_{ij} = \frac{Z_{ij}}{\sum_{i=1}^{n} Z_{ij}} \tag{4}$$

Calculate the information entropy of the j-th index.

$$E_j = -\frac{1}{\ln n} \sum_{i=1}^{n} P_{ij} \ln(P_{ij}) \tag{5}$$

3. Calculate the coefficient of difference for the j-th index. The value range of the information entropy is between 0–1, and the difference coefficient is obtained through the difference operation. The larger the difference coefficient, the greater the influence of this factor on the overall evaluation, and the larger the weight value.

$$G_j = 1 - E_j \tag{6}$$

4. Normalize the weights:

$$W_j = \frac{G_j}{\sum_{j=1}^{m} G_j} \tag{7}$$

The weight calculation pseudo code is shown in Table 2:

Table 2. Weights calculated by entropy method

Algorithm 1:The Learning Algorithm of Entropy generation method
Input: P = {d1,d2...dn}, Output: w={w1,w2...wn} :

```
Begin
    for i = 1:n
        for j = 1:m
            p(i,j)=X(i,j)/sum(X(:,j));//standardized
        k=1/log(n);
    for j=1:m
        e(j)=-k*sum(p(: ,j).*log(p(:,j))); //Calculate information entropy
        d=ones(1 ,m)-e; //Calculate the information entropy redundancy
        w=d./sum(d);  //Calculate the weight
End
```

3.2 Fuzzy Evaluation Model

The evaluation and analysis of enterprise innovation ability is a relatively complicated system. The indicators need to be divided into levels and categories. Fuzzy comprehensive evaluation is a very effective method for multi-factor decision making. This paper uses fuzzy evaluation to model the innovation ability of enterprises.

$$Y = (U, R, V, W) \tag{8}$$

$U = \{u1, u2 \ldots un\}$ is the factor set, $V = \{V1, V2 \ldots Vm\}$ is the evaluation set, $W = \{w1, w2 \ldots wn\}$ is the weight set, and R is the evaluation matrix. The factor set is divided into two levels, with 5 first-level factors and 18 s-level factors. The rij represents the membership of the enterprise at the j-th comment Vj of the i-th index.

$$R = \begin{bmatrix} r11 & r12 & \ldots & r1m \\ r21 & r22 & \ldots & r2m \\ rn1 & rn2 & \ldots & rnm \end{bmatrix} \qquad (9)$$

B is the fuzzy evaluation set. The weight W and the fuzzy matrix R are calculated by weighted average.

$$B = W * R \qquad (10)$$

The weight in W is divided into two levels, the first level weight is $W = \{w1, w2 \ldots wn\}$, and the corresponding second level weight is $Wi = \{wi1, wi2 \ldots wim\}$ ($i = 1, 2, 3, 4, 5$). The following is the calculation process of the membership of the secondary index.

$$B_i = W_i * R_i = [W_{i1} \quad W_{i2} \ldots W_{in}] * \begin{bmatrix} R_{i1} & \ldots & R_{i5} \\ \vdots & \vdots & \vdots \\ R_{in} & \ldots & 1 \end{bmatrix} \qquad (11)$$

The final evaluation matrix for the primary indicators is calculated as follows.

$$B' = [W_1 \ W_2 \ldots W_5] * \begin{bmatrix} B_1 \\ \vdots \\ B5 \end{bmatrix} = [B'_1 \ldots B'_5] \qquad (12)$$

The evaluation model calculation pseudo code is shown in Table 3:

Table 3. Evaluation model calculation

Algorithm 2:The Learning Algorithm of Fuzzy evaluation modeling
Input: W={w1,w2...,wn} , R={r1,r2,...rn} , V={v1,v2...,vn} Output: : Y={y1,y2...,yn}
Begin
for i <- 0 to length[w]
for j <-0 to length[R]
Bi=Wi*Rij
bi={vl|vl->max bj} //Calculate the maximum membership
for i <-0 to length[W]
Yi = Bi
End

3.3 Determination of Membership Matrix

The characteristic of fuzzy evaluation is not to directly classify the values, but to express the degree by the membership of the values. This paper divides the review set into five levels, which are (excellent, good, moderate, pass, and poor). We consider the data corresponding to the first 15% of an indicator to be an excellent range, the first (15%–35%) value range is considered good, the value at (35%–65%) is better, and the previous (65%–85%) is qualified, the last 15% is poor. The membership matrix is determined by the membership function based on the principle of maximum membership (Fig. 2).

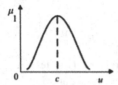

Fig. 2. Gaussian membership function

Commonly used membership functions are rectangular, trapezoidal, and curved. According to the principle that the membership function must be a convex fuzzy set and pairwise balanced, this evaluation model uses a two-terminal trapezoidal distribution and a middle curve distribution. The curve part uses a Gaussian membership function, and c is the center of the curve.

$$\mu(u) = e^{\frac{-(u-c)^2}{2\sigma^2}} \tag{13}$$

3.4 Weight Optimization

The change in weight is determined by the indicator information. When the amount of data changes, the weight will also change. As the amount of data increases, the weight values tend to stabilize. Optimizing the weight is to use the weight change trend to make the weight value more reasonable. We categorize the weight dataset and save the core of each class. This process is a hash clustering process. This paper uses the weighted geometric mean method for optimization [20]. Multiply each value by the corresponding weight, then add up and sum to get the overall value, and then divide by the total number of units.

$$W' = \sum_{i=1}^{n} \sqrt[fi]{\prod_{i=1}^{n} wi^{fi}} = \sum_{i=1}^{n} \sqrt[fi]{w1^{f1}w2^{f2}w3^{f3}\ldots wn^{fn}} \tag{14}$$

The set of W is determined by the amount of data. The corresponding weighting factor fi is the proportion of all data sets occupied by xi. When the content of the data set is larger, fi is higher, and the weight is considered to be closer to a reasonable value (Table 4).

Table 4. Geometric mean calculation

```
Algorithm 3:The weighted geometric mean method
Input: f={f1,f2...fn}, w={w1,w2...wn} Output: w':
Begin
   result = 1
   num =0
   for i=1:m
      for j=1:fj
         result * = wi;
      num++;
   w'= Math.Pow(result,1.0/num);
End
```

4 Evaluation Model Verification and Analysis

4.1 Data Sources

The data in this paper is mainly data for 218 medical companies with a time span of (2008–2019), which is derived from Oriental Fortune Network, Baidu Patent Database, Yearbook and Enterprise Website.

4.2 Calculation Results and Optimization of Weight Sets

This paper calculates the entropy value according to the formula (2–7) set, and divides the collected data set into three total (30%, 60%, 100%) calculations. The change of each weight value is shown in Fig. 3. We can find that the three trends are basically the same. In Y_7, Y_8, and Y_{18}, there are relatively large differences. This paper adopts the method of weighted geometric mean to further optimize. The weight value calculated according to formula 14 is shown in Table 5. The proportion of the first-level indicators is shown in Fig. 4:

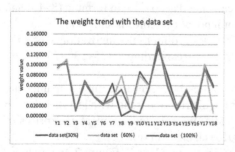

Fig. 3. Trend of weight change   **Fig. 4.** Weight ratio

From the data we can find that the weight distribution in the first-level indicators is innovation funding (0.211), innovation manpower (0.229), innovation results (0.342), innovation gains (0.171), and innovation development (0.148).

Table 5. Weight values of first and second level indicators

First-level indexes	X value	Subscript	Y value
Innovation funding	0.210806	Y1	0.098013
		Y2	0.102116
		Y3	0.010677
Innovative manpower	0.228977	Y4	0.068762
		Y5	0.038111
		Y6	0.024548
		Y7	0.034708
		Y8	0.051813
		Y9	0.011035
Innovation achievements	0.342171	Y10	0.075377
		Y11	0.055704
		Y12	0.151395
		Y13	0.059695
Innovation income	0.170546	Y14	0.012305
		Y15	0.05031
		Y16	0.01601
Innovative development	0.147625	Y17	0.091921
		Y18	0.055704

Among the secondary indicators, the most significant impact on the company's innovation ability is the average number of patents per 100 employees, followed by operating income. The per capita creativity of science and technology innovation personnel and the total investment of enterprise funds are crucial to the development of innovative enterprises.

After determining the weight index, it is calculated according to formula (8–13) and the score interval is 1–100. The distribution of innovation scores is shown in Fig. 6. The main scores are concentrated between (15, 30). According to the innovation score, the company is divided into five levels (A, B, C, D, E) corresponding to (75+, 30–75, 15–30, 5–15, 5-).

From Fig. 5 and 6, we can find that the scores between different companies are significantly different. The scores show a normal distribution trend with less distribution at both ends and more distribution in the middle. We selected 7 typical enterprises of different magnitudes and observed (2008–2019) changes in time.

Selected companies are represented in this paper by C1–C7. Figure 7 and 8 shows the vertical change of the innovation capability scores of 7 companies. There is a gap in the total score between the companies. From Fig. 8, we find that the growth rate of innovation capabilities of C2 companies in the second echelon is the highest, for medium

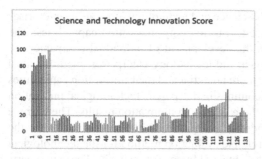

Fig. 5. Innovation scores

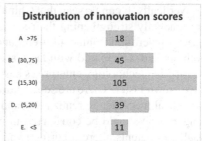

Fig. 6. Level distribution

Fig. 7. Comparison of innovation scores

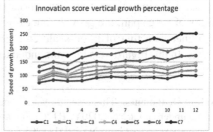

Fig. 8. Growth rates of innovation scores

Innovative companies have the greatest development potential. The innovation ability of enterprises is going up and down. In the early stage, the development and change were rapid, and the growth rate gradually decreased.

5 Summary

Through data analysis, we find that the innovation results in the evaluation index system have the greatest impact on the innovation ability of enterprises. The per capita number of intellectual property rights and the rate of conversion of intellectual property rights need to be given full attention. In terms of innovation funding, there is not much difference in the proportion of R&D funding in corporate income. However, the magnitude of the amount is large, so the total R&D expenditure needs to be increased. In terms of innovative manpower, the higher the degree, the greater the contribution to the innovation ability of the enterprise. The talent structure should be optimized and expanded to ensure a good academic level, and doctoral students are better than master students than undergraduates. In terms of innovation results, increase the total amount of intellectual property rights. While expanding personnel, increase the corresponding number of intellectual property rights and increase the rate of intellectual property rights conversion. In terms of innovation revenue, increase the proportion of overseas sales and increase market recognition. In terms of innovation and development, we should increase the average research funding of the project and actively cooperate with scientific research units such as schools, research institutes, and high-tech enterprises.

Vertically, it can be seen that China's science and technology innovation enterprises are gradually strengthening their science and technology innovation capabilities. The general macro-environmental trend and the development of individual companies are both upward. Compared with large science and technology enterprises, medium-sized science and technology enterprises have more potential and their innovation capabilities have grown faster. There are some shortcomings in this paper. Technological innovation is cyclical from idea to realization, and there is a lag in innovation results. Therefore, a longer cycle should be considered in judging innovation. At the same time, as for the quality of patents, there is currently no reliable evaluation method for the technological leadership in the field, which can only be obtained by expert analysis. These two parts are future development trends.

Horizontally, large enterprises are superior to medium-sized enterprises in terms of innovation capabilities. Large enterprises have relatively large innovation advantages. In terms of time span, the growth rate of innovation capacity of medium-sized enterprises is higher than that of large-scale enterprises, especially those of medium-sized enterprises. In this regard, it is recommended to increase support for medium-sized innovative enterprises.

Acknowledgments. This research was supported in part by the National Key R&D Program of China under Grant No. 2020YFB1707700, and the Fundamental Research Funds for the Central Universities under Grant No.19D111201.

References

1. Schumpeter, J.: The Theory of Economic Development. 1st Ed, pp. 63–283. Business Printing Museum, Beijing (1990)
2. Jia, M.: Research on the investment and loan linkage of Chinese commercial banks. Heilongjiang University (2018)
3. Ni, Z., Zhang, K., Zong, Y.: Financialization of enterprise and enterprise innovation ability. Bus. Res. (10), 31–42 (2019)
4. Research and Markets; Canada's Biotechnology Industry - Porter's Five Forces Strategy Analysis, Along With a Brief Overview of the Market -Research And Markets.com. Biotech Business Week (2018)
5. Burgelman, R.A., Christensen, C.M., Wheel Wright, S.C.: Strategic Management of Technology and Innovation, pp. 55–61. McGraw-Hill, New York (2008)
6. Kotabe, M., Martin, X., Domoto, H.: Gaining from vertical partnerships: knowledge transfer, relationship duration, and supplier performance improvement in the U.S. and Japanese automotive industries. Strateg. Manag. J. **24**(4), 293–316 (2003)
7. Pittaway, L., Robertson, M., Munir, K., et al.: Networking and innovation: a systematic review of the evidence. Int. J. Manag. Rev. **5**(3–4), 137–168 (2004)
8. Li, H., Yang, P.: Social evaluation of the benefits of technological innovation—thinking about the evaluation indexes of technological innovation. J. Int. Technol. Econ. Res. (01), 38–41 (1990)
9. Zhang, J., Yu, J.: Analysis on regional competitiveness of manufacturing industry in Jiangsu Province. Jiangsu Stat. (3), 20–22 (2002)
10. Zhao, Y., Zhang, M.: Evaluation and analysis of China's manufacturing industry competitiveness. Econ. Theory Econ. Manag. (5), 23–30 (2005)

11. Dolan, C.V.: Investigating Spearman's hypothesis by means of multi-group confirmatory factor analysis. Multivariate Behav. Res. **35**(1), 21–50 (2000)
12. The analytic hierarchy process: how to measure intangibles in a meaningful way side by side with tangibles. In: Transactions from International Symposium on Quality Function Deployment, 19th Symposium, pp. 113–135 (2007)
13. Lumeij, J.T.: Relation of plasma calcium to total protein and albumin in African grey (Psittacus erithacus) and Amazon (Amazona spp.) parrots. Avian Pathol. J. W.V.P.A, **19**(4), 661–667 (1990)
14. Fu, W., Diez, J.R., Schiller, D.: Regional innovation systems within a transitional context: evolutionary comparison of the electronics industry in Shenzhen and Dongguan since the opening of china. J. Econ. Surv. **26**(3), 534–550 (2012)
15. Li, Z., Peng, W., Li, W.: Research on evaluation of technological innovation ability of listed companies in Jinzhou City. J. Bohai Univ. (Philos. Soc. Sci. Ed.), **41**(05), 99–103+144 (2019)
16. Zhao, J.: Research on comprehensive innovation of high-tech enterprises. Wuhan University of Technology (2007)
17. Wang, Z.: Evaluation of enterprise technology innovation capability based on AHP-grey relevance model. Stat. Decis. (04), 51–53 (2013)
18. Li, B., Tian, X., Zhang, S., Zhao, H.: Research on the evaluation of urban innovation capability and the spatiotemporal pattern evolution. Math. Stat. Manag. 1–15 (2019)
19. Xie, Y., Li, H., Zou, Q.: Research on innovation index of resource-based cities in China—a case study of 116 prefecture-level cities. J. Peking Univ. (Philos. Soc. Sci.) **54**(05), 146–158 (2017)
20. Drnovšek, R., Peperko, A.: Inequalities for the hadamard weighted geometric mean of positive kernel operators on Banach function spaces. Positivity **10**(4), 613–626 (2006)

A Study on Profit Generation Model by Service Innovation of Electronic Manufacturers in the Age of IoT Digitization

Toru Fujii[1]([email]) and Akira Kamoshida[2]

[1] Kitami Institute of Technology, Kitami, Hokkaido, Japan
toru-fujii@live.jp
[2] Yokohama City University, Yokohama, Japan
mail@akirakamoshida.jp

Abstract. The competitiveness of electronics manufacturers has shifted from traditional product competitiveness to service competitiveness, including products. The purpose of this paper is how a new generation of IoT and digitalization will change Toru Fujii (2010) with a "profit generation model through service innovation". The goal is to review this framework.

Keywords: Electronics manufacturers · Service Innovation · IoT digitalization

1 Introduction

The competitiveness of electronics manufacturers has shifted from traditional product competitiveness to service competitiveness, including products. In addition, as a de-commercialization strategy, the service business that provides the demanding functions of customers by increasing the added value of existing services and packaging products and services is essential for high profitability. In recent years, the service business, which is mainly carried out by electromechanical manufacturers, sells goods to customers (assets moved to customers), the usual form of business in which traders perform maintenance services from the outside, and the customer's own business (assets owned by traders) are so-called There is a business form that only provides solution. The benefits of these service businesses vary greatly depending on whether the customer or trader owns the assets of the goods themselves. In addition, there are many cases where several things, such as engineering services, are linked as systems, and the service strategy can vary greatly depending on whether the entire system has coordinate values (the coordinate value between assets). Similarly, Business Transformation Outsourcing (BTO) services, where suppliers contract the entire customer's business in bulk, is also an important strategy for electronics manufacturers. The purpose of this paper is how a new generation of IoT and digitalization will change Toru Fujii (2010) with a "profit generation model through service innovation". The goal is to review this framework.

© Springer Nature Switzerland AG 2021
L. Uden et al. (Eds.): KMO 2021, CCIS 1438, pp. 160–169, 2021.
https://doi.org/10.1007/978-3-030-81635-3_14

2 Study Background

2.1 "Profit Generation Model Through Service Innovation"

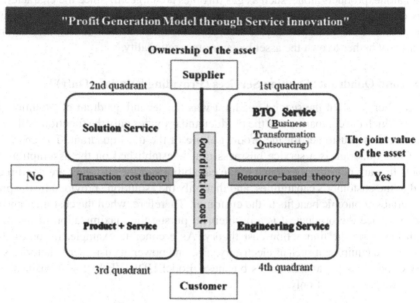

(Source) TORU FUJII(2010) Annual Report of Chuo University Graduate School of Science and Technology

Fig. 1. "Profit generation model through service innovation" [1]

The "Profit Generation Model through Service Innovation" proposed by Toru Fujii (2010) is as shown in Fig. 1. As this framework suggests, the service innovation business of electronics manufacturers about 10 years ago (2010) was carried out in four quadrants in Fig. 1. Figure 1 shows that when a customer purchases a product service, the determination of whether to own the entire product alone or the entire multi-product system that is the asset is simply calculated the total cost of owning the asset based on economic rationality and selects the lower "transaction cost theory" developed in two frameworks: "resource-based theory" that takes into account the capabilities within the customer. Therefore, Fig. 1 shows the classification framework for profit generation from the customer's point of view by taking "the joint value of the asset" in the X-axis and "ownership of the asset" on the Y-axis. The "joint value of the asset", and when the product is functioned alone and the service is added value, these products are accompanied by a service in the aggregate (including the customer's mobile it therein) system, it compares the case where the value is added. In addition, "asset ownership" compares the case where the customer has ownership of the hardware itself of the product and the system and the case where the trader has it.

2.2   Third Quadrant "Product Alone + Service"

The service business first developed by a supplier (electrical manufacturer) is a service business that provide maintenance, and other services from outside the customer to a single product sold to customers in the third quadrant. This quadrant, and elevator is a product alone, products alone, such as gas turbines are targeted. Since the characteristic of this quadrant is a product that is not directly related to the capabilities of the customer, based on the "transaction cost theory" at the time of introduction, the customer determines whether to own the asset by economic rationality.

2.3   Second Quadrant "Solution Services (Providing Solutions Only)"

"Solution Services" of the second quadrant was the second quadrant of "solution services" in which the company owns the product and provides only the function "solution" from outside the customer for the product alone of the third quadrant. The characteristic of this quadrant is a service business that is established on the assumption that products that are not directly related to the capabilities of the customer are not directly related to the customer's capabilities, and that only the "solution" provided by the product generates economic benefits to the customer. Therefore, when the customer and the trader introduce the product, it is a problem to pursue the maximization of the profit of both based on the transaction cost theory. As a concrete example, it comes from utility-related equipment such as electricity, gas, and power at customer's factories such as ESCO business [2] and Hitachi's business model HDRIVE [3]. in a business that requires the provision of only.

2.4   Fourth Quadrant "Engineering Services"

The engineering service of the fourth quadrant is a business that has been systemized (including capabilities in the customer's production process) by combining the product alone of the third quadrant. The characteristic sofaofing of this product system is that it has the coordinated value of the asset, so it is possible to explain it in "resource-based theory" (X-axis). In addition, (Y-axis) is the coordination cost (adjustment cost) for the "cooperation of assets" to choose whether the customer purchases a third quadrant product alone + service, engineering on their own, or one-stop consignment to the supplier. Considered to economic rationality based on However, with regard to engineering services, there are many cases that depend on the special summary ability (capability) of the trader side. Specifically, it is a study of plant construction in petrochemical manufacturers and energy saving of piping equipment spanning petrochemical complexes. With regard to plant construction, since the customer's capabilities are included in this, assets are owned by the customer, but it is a comprehensive engineering service business, etc. that the supplier entrusts design, construction, maintenance, and maintenance in one stop. It is a service model that permanently performs maintenance and maintenance services related to operation by permanently installing the contractor's site office on the customer's premises. As a result of the current equipment improvement, customers present issues such as "CO_2 reduction -10%", and it is a package-type service model that performs all the services from consulting to plant construction for equipment improvement to realize it.

2.5   First Elephant Limit "BTO (Business Transformation Outsourcing) Service"

Table 1. "Service innovation strategies of electronics manufacturers around 2010".

Quadrant	Characteristic
1st quadrant BTO service	Maximize corporate value by transferring customer businesses to suppliers ■ UK High Speed Rail Project (Hitachi, Ltd.) ■ Fukushima Prefecture Minamisoma City Sol ar Mega Solar Project (Toshiba)
2nd quadrant Solution Service	Providing only "solutions" for commodity products ■ ESCO business, HDRIVE solution business (Hitachi, Ltd.)
3rd quadrant Product + Service	Product alone + service (maintenance, etc.) ■ Elevators, gas turbines, etc. (each company)
4th quadrant Engineering Service	One-stop engineering ■ Consolidation of petrochemical plant construction (all companies) ■ System integration for smart community (each company)

The BTO of the first quadrant is an outsourcing service in which the contractor entrusts the entire business of the customer in one lump sum. This project is often found in the information systems department, etc., where real-time services by specialized SE are required. Since the target service is a business that is not directly related to the customer's main business (capability), it is not necessary to own assets within the customer, such as the fourth quadrant "Engineering Service", so it is possible to easily outsource to the business-by-business operator. For this reason, there is a merit of the customer side that the customer can focus on the main business by entrusting each business to the trader in one lump sum. The feature is that "the coordinate value of the asset" is high, but because it is a business that is not a capability for the customer, "ownership of the asset" is moved to the trader. IBM is developing BPOs that accept customer information systems departments in bulk, including human resources (Table 1).

Therefore, the determination of whether to select the service of the fourth quadrant "engineering service" and the first quadrant "BTO" from the customer's point of view, in the target business (product system), the customer it is determined by whether to include the capabilities of the customer.

3   Proposition of This Study

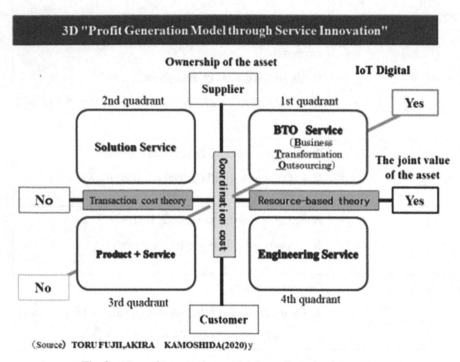

(Source) **TORU FUJII,AKIRA KAMOSHIDA(2020)**y

Fig. 2. 3D profit generation model through service innovation

In recent years, with the emergence of IoT digitalization, electronics manufacturers are conducting a new service business called digital solutions using their own platform. The characteristic of this business is the business of co-creating and developing digital applications with customers. The process is co-creation marketing of B to B to C. With the development of this new service business, The proposition of this study is whether it is possible to classify "IoT digitization (yes)" (no) in "Profit generation model by service innovation" Business decisions for "IoT digitization (yes)" are applied only when the business efficiency of customers is improved and the possibility of entering new businesses is high by performing AI, AR, and big data analysis. It is determined by whether or not it is possible to "customer cooperative service business" that takes place between the trader and the customer. We will introduce the efforts of Japanese electronics manufacturers to digitize IoT.

4 "Customer Co-creation Service Business" of Electronics Manufacturers

4.1 Changes in Japanese Industry (Manufacturing) and Distribution Market

Traditional manufacturing marketing methods are used to meet consumer needs (socalled 4P;Product, Price, Place, Promotion) We plan advertising and advertising strategies and sales and sales strategies by conducting analysis based on The main concern is positioning with competitors, the superiority of the products and technologies we offer, or the selling price. However, with the dawn of the IoT era, the industrial and distribution markets are changing rapidly. Consumer needs are changing dramatically, from "from things to things, from ownership to share, from closed to open, from individual optimum to overall optimum". Marketing activities that follow this need to be followed. In addition, the needs of countless "individuals" such as age, sex, family structure, lifestyle, behavior pattern, health, illness, worries, desire, joy, joy, excitement, etc. of consumer (use) persons, digitalization and data conversion, Active involvement in consumers has also had a significant impact on marketing activities.

In such an era of environmental upheaval, marketing strategies in the industrial (manufacturing) and distribution markets have also changed drastically.

4.2 Customer-Sponsored Service Business "IoT Digitization"

"Co-creation-type marketing" is booming in the marketing field today. The purpose of this is to "co-create" to create new technologies and business innovations. "Co-creation" is not just a technology development, but a practice of business creation, and the "co-creation process" defined by Hitachi, Ltd. is as follows. "We will work with a division that is well versed in one business domain to determine where to enter with a sense of management. (Go To Market Strategy Planning). (2) Share your vision with customers by identifying customer issues from social changes that are the background to the business ecosystem. (3) Design new concepts for services and business models, and expect profitability through prototypes and simulations. (4) One Hitachi will widely discover Hitachi Group technologies and products to realize solutions and demonstrate effectiveness. The human resources who promote these collaborative creation activities are "Service Business Creators [5]". "IoT Platform Business" is a business that continuously provides various service businesses to the cloud environment (platform) owned by an electronics manufacturer through the application of service provision developed by customers and "co-creation". In doing so, it is a business that consists logically from the upstream of the business value chain (vision, strategy, service design, business plan) to the middle stream (concept formulation, systemization consideration, requirement definition, basic design, application development), downstream (service operation, maintenance, and enhancement) from the perspective of consumers (users) by "co-creation" between companies. Today, many companies have established the IoT Promotion Office and the New Business Development Office, with the aim of promoting new business development by utilizing IoT and AI technologies, and are promoting "co-creation projects. This initiative is a theme that includes management, production, and logistics reforms throughout the company, so executives are often appointed as leaders. The common problem with each company is that by utilizing IoT and AI technologies, "I want to do something new, but I don't know how to proceed with it. I don't know where to start. I have a trouble such as. Therefore, the first issue to do in the "co-creation process" is to have an image of how the business environment of each company changes with the advent of the digital society. On top of that, we need to identify the existing capabilities of each company, and design a specific service business model that will be used by each company, and how much money will be invested in which business, what applications to create, and what kind of profit to be generated continuously from the utilization of ioT platforms. When building this service business model, it is important to clearly assess where the profit generation of each company (customer) and the profit generation of the electric manufacturer is in the target business, and it is necessary to create a mechanism to build a WIN-WIN relationship. Therefore, the most important thing in b-to-B-to-C co-creation marketing is the activity that B (electrical manufacturer) and B (company) "co-create" and find what benefits (benefits) for the C (consumption) person in the future. As a concrete example of co-creation, we will explain the collaborative marketing strategy of electronics manufacturers and automobile manufacturers.

In Japan, automobile manufacturers have shifted from marketing centered on conventional manufacturing and sales to structures centered on consumer (use) people. With the dawn of the IoT era, the car itself will be made into a module (EV/PHV) in the future. Along with this, the manufacturing and technology of the car will be open from the closed. It is thought that a lot of information can be obtained from the digitized car, and the thing of the car becomes various information processing and transmission, and even intelligence (AI) by the introduction of AI technology. On the other hand, the needs of consumers (use) people for cars are changing from the joy they have had so far to share them. The first to respond to this change in consumers is the emergence of a "sureing economy" like Uber. Until now, automakers have been in marketing strategies to get cars owned. For this reason, by owning a car, we conducted advertising activities that provided a comfortable lifestyle, and the source of profit creation was limited to car sales and after-sales service. The marketing activities of automobile manufacturers were to find rational production methods to meet the needs of consumers (use) when manufacturing products such as manufacturing plans, procurement inventory plans, r&d research plans, equipment control plans, environmental measures, and quality control plans. In addition, the sales department is a demand forecasting, sales campaign plan, and recall preventive maintenance plan. This is a promotion strategy that tailors the needs of consumers to meet the needs of consumers. However, it will be difficult to follow the rapidly changing consumer needs of the IoT era with these marketing activities. Then, it is co-creation type marketing that is attracting attention. In cooperative marketing, we aim to build a digital business model in peripheral businesses that use automobiles such as car sharing, automobile insurance, refueling charging, garage storage, automatic driving, consumables, accessories, leisure travel, etc., starting from consumer (use) persons. The environment surrounding automobile manufacturers, which have been extracted through collaborative marketing activities, is a new car society called "Connected Urban Mobility". This is (1) it is possible for the car itself to perform data processing by transmitting various data from the cloud environment to the car. (2) By introducing a car sensor, the car comrades will communicate to prevent collisions and avoid danger. (3) By information sharing of

Table 2. "Service innovation strategies of electronics manufacturers in the IoT era".

Quadrant	Characteristic
1st quadrant BTO service	Maximize corporate value by transferring customer businesses to suppliers ■ UK High Speed Rail Project (Hitachi, Ltd.) ■ Fukushima Prefecture Minamisoma City Solar Mega Solar Project (Toshiba)
2nd quadrant solution·service	Providing only "solutions" for commodity products ■ ESCO business, HDRIVE solution business (Hitachi, Ltd.)
3rd quadrant Product + Service	Product alone + service (maintenance, etc.) ■ Elevators, gas turbines, etc. (each company)
4th quadrant engineering service	One-stop engineering ■ Consolidation of petrochemical plant construction (all companies) ■ System integration for smart community (each company)
Fifth quadrant IoT Digital BTO Services	"IoT Digital Platform Outsourcing" in the Customer Business ■ Digital marketing of customer co -creation service business (BtoBtoC) Co-creation of new businesses on customer digital platforms
Sixth quadrant IoT Digital Solutions & Service	Development of general -purpose applications such as predictive diagnosis and GPS operation diagnosis (open data) Home management use case app development business for couriers Truck distribution use case app development business for logistics companies
Seventh quadrant IoT Digital Products + Services	Commoditization products alone + maintenance and maintenance service business Private cloud such as predictive diagnosis, GPS operation diagnosis (close data) Elevators, gas turbines, construction equipment, etc. (each company)
Eighth Quadrant IoT Digital Engineering & Service	IoT Digital Platform Private Cloud Business for Systems Including Customer Capabilities Bulk digitization of factories (private cloud) Development of yield improvement application by pharmaceutical manufacturing big data analysis

the city block (signals and signs, etc.), it is possible to control the position information and traffic flow. (4) It is possible to transmit information to pedestrians by introducing a walking information system. (5) charging station is installed. (6) Various changes in the environment of the automotive society can be considered, such as the introduction of a logistics system by the advanced supply chain by the introduction of IoT technology. In collaborative marketing, it is necessary to create a competitive-dominated application (business model) based on "IoT platform business" ahead of the rest of the world, with a view to these near-future image of car society.

Such a customer cooperative type service business is also carried out in NEC, IBM Japan, etc. NEC and the University of Tokyo have concluded a strategic partnership of industry-academia co-creation as an effort to explore and implement various social issues facing Japan. IBM Japan opened the Strategic Co-Creation Center in October 2015 in the Marunouchi Eiraku Building as a base for creating the future together with customers. In this way, with regard to the development of IoT digital applications, it is necessary to cooperate consistently not only in research and development of specific technologies, but also from the creation of a vision for solving social issues to the implementation of research and development, human resource development, and social implementation. Hitachi, Ltd. is also developing an "industry-academia co-creation strategy" based on AI, and by entering into partnerships with specific national universities, the role and challenges of "Service Business Co-Creator (12)" are very important, as we have established a cooperative creation strategy that not only develops research and development of specific technologies, but also creates a vision for solving social issues, as well as implementation of research and development, human resource development, and social implementation.

5 Conclusion

The development of the customer co-creation service business of Japanese electronics manufacturers (Hitachi, NEC, IBM Japan) introduced above is shown in Fig. 1. Toru Fujii(2010) "Profit Generation Model through Service Innovation" is considered to be possible to classify it as "IoT digitization (yes)" (no). As shown in Table 2, the 5th Quadrant "IoT Digital BTO Service", the 6th Quadrant "IoT Digital Solution Service", the 7th Quadrant "IoT Digital Product + Service", It is thought that it is possible to classify the business of the electronics manufacturer into the eighth quadrant "IoT digital engineering service". In the future, we would like to conduct interviews with electronics manufacturers, including overseas, for the classification of specific businesses.In this paper, when electronics manufacturers conduct customer-co-creation service business for IoT digitalization with customers, whether or not to build a cooperative relationship is the development of IoT digital applications. It should be emphasized that it is determined by whether or not there is a benefit for both the supplier and the customer.

6 Summary

In this paper, the introduction of the "Customer Co-creation Service Business", in which the service innovation strategy of electric manufacturers due to the emerging ioT digitalization has been developing digital applications with customers, IoT digitization" suggested the possibility. Future research topics will examine the case studies of specific service businesses in each quadrant of the "3D Service Innovation Model" in Fig. 2. To this end, we plan to conduct interviews with executives and managers of electronics manufacturers, including overseas.

References

1. Fujii, T.: Framework of classification of profit generation by service innovation: a study from transaction cost theory and resource-based theory. (Reviewed Paper) (Single Work) Annual Report of Chuo University Graduate School of Science and Technology, pp. 59–75 (2010)
2. ESCO business stands for Energy Service Company and is an "energy-saving service business" that began in Europe and the United States in the 1970s. A business form that provides comprehensive energy-saving services and covers the expenses required for renovation from energy reduction. In Japan, esco business has been attracting attention rapidly since 1996, and it has been adopted by companies in various fields and has achieved great results. In order to guarantee energy-saving effects, esco business enters into performance agreements (success compensation agreements) between ESCO operators and customers
3. Hitachi's HDRIVE is a high-efficiency motor, high-voltage inverter, and monitoring system.equipment to the customer's factory for free, and the energy saving benefits obtained by operating the equipment at a certain rate, It is a solution business to collect as HDRIVE usage fee. Unlike the conventional idea of product sales business, it is to sell the energy saving of the product in the form of a service. Because it is a payment from the merit amount by the energy effect, Monthly payments vary.Customers can introduce new equipment withno initial costs, and can save energy and reduce costs. And help with energy saving and profit generation at customer's factory, and because the introduction and maintenance of remote monitoring systems are included in the usage fee, the factory can also reduce maintenance personnel
4. Hirai, C., Furuya, J.: Service Business through Customer Collaboration. Hitachi Review. Hitachi, Ltd. (2015)
5. Fujii, T.: Collaborative (co-creation) strategy for realizing a super smart society (SOCIETY 5.0) and a study on the relationship between hospitality management. J. Nejimento Soc. Hospit. **27**, 55–64 (2018)
6. Shimada, Y., Sato, T.: Successful "digital" use use cases to promote quickly without worrying, without waste. In: 2018 Diamond Corporation, 14 November 2010. Hitachi Consulting Co., Ltd. (2018)
7. Fujii, T.: Marketing strategies in the industry and distribution market in the IoT Era-B (Electrical IoT)Corporate) to B (automaker) to (consumer). In: PTU Forum 2018, Vocational ability Development Research Presentation S.A. (20-K-5), pp. 17–18. College of Vocational Ability Development (2018)

The Deficit's Threat of Contextual Intelligence and KM in the Coaching Process of an Academic and Scientific Incubator for the Survival of Start-Ups

Zeineb Ayari[✉] and Souad Kamoun Chouk

ESCT, LIGUE, Univ. Manouba, Campus Manouba, 2010 Manouba, Tunisia
`Zeineb.ayari@etu.unice.fr`, `souad.kamoun@esct.uma.tn`

Abstract. In the context of this research work, we committed a reflection on the contribution of the contextual Intelligence (CI) and Knowledge Management (KM) in the survival of some start-ups housed to an Academic and Scientific Incubator (ASI) of the National School of Engineers (ENISO) at the University of Sousse in Tunisia). The study KM in the context of entrepreneurship: in particular, how entrepreneurs utilize and create knowledge, and build on knowledge as a core competency. The starting point of this reflection is the vulnerability of start-ups in their launch phase from which ensues the question of research relative to the capacity of the contextual intelligence to favor the survival of these young companies. In this paper, we used the investigation made in our master's thesis which mobilized a qualitative method coherent with the exploratory character of the study. The results allowed noticing that the practice of contextual intelligence by the incubated start-ups seems, in the light of this first result, to have a mattering weight compared with the conditions of incubation and to the intrinsic factors of survival of the start-up.

This exploration of the causes of failure of some start-ups incubated in an ASI allowed verifying the importance of KM in this context. It especially allowed bringing out two factors for avoiding failure: the cohesion between the team members and their ability to co-create value and the perseverance and the obstinacy of the entrepreneur. We highlight that, at the micro-level (IAS), start-up entrepreneurs are floundering with too much irrelevant and timely less information. Few tools and skills are available to deal with information effectively and convert them into knowledge. Through the SECI model of Nonaka and Takeuchi (1994), we try to explore the actual reasons for the failure of some incubated start-ups and verify the proposition of the attribution of this failure to the lack of KM and co-creation of value.

Keywords: Knowledge Management (KM) · Contextual Intelligence (CI) · Co-creation of value · Academic and Scientific Incubator (ASI) · SECI model

1 Introduction

Contextual intelligence deals with the practical application of knowledge and information to a real-world situation. So, what is contextual intelligence? According to Kutz

L. Uden et al. (Eds.): KMO 2021, CCIS 1438, pp. 170–183, 2021.
https://doi.org/10.1007/978-3-030-81635-3_15

(2017), It can be described, rather simply, as the ability to influence anyone, in any place, at any time by accurately diagnosing the surroundings. Knowledge management is the systematic management of an organization's knowledge assets for the purpose of creating value and meeting tactical and strategic requirements. It consists of the process of creating, sharing, using, and managing the knowledge and information of an organization. It refers to a multidisciplinary approach to achieve organizational objectives by making the best use of knowledge. Through this research work, we aim at developing a reflection on the contribution of CI and KM in the survival of some incubated startups. Our study will be conducted within the Tunisian academic and scientific incubator of ENISO (National School of Engineers of Sousse). Non-profit-making academic and scientific incubators oriented towards the valorization of technologies. These structures emerged under the impulse of public programs, they present themselves, through their territorial anchoring, as the natural extension of a socio-responsible commitment in the development of the territories and the country. This article proceeds with a review of the principals' concepts of this study: Contextual Intelligence (CI), the co-creation of value as the process of knowledge, and then the KM. The next section describes the research approach of this study. The fifth section discusses the findings. The paper concludes with suggestions for future research.

2 Contextual Intelligence (CI)

2.1 What is Contextual Intelligence?

An important key to understanding CI is the use of the two words context and intelligence. Chouk and Uden (2016) highlight that the context presents everything that shapes and gives meaning to a situation we find ourselves in. This contains factors like physical, natural, social, and psychological realities and dynamics (Chouk and Uden 2016). Context includes all the external, internal, interpersonal, and intrapersonal factors that contribute to the uniqueness of each situation and circumstance (Kutz 2008). Context is the background in which an event takes place. Contexts come in various forms and involve any set of circumstances surrounding an event. What is "intelligence?" Intelligence is the ability to transform data into useful information, information into knowledge, and then assimilate that knowledge into practice (Chouk and Uden 2016).

Considering the above descriptions of context and intelligence and by combining the two concepts Kutz (2017) described the term contextual intelligence which operationally means: "the ability to quickly and intuitively recognize and diagnose the dynamic contextual variables inherent in an event or circumstance which results in an intentional adjustment of behavior in order to exert appropriate influence in that context". Therefore, the start-ups must be contextually intelligent and need specific skills to be able to function in uncertainty, embrace complexity, remain calm in volatile situation, and adapt to ambiguity (Kutz and Bamford – Wade 2013). These elements constitute the VUCA world that indicates the context in which start-ups visualize their current and future state. They draw the lines of policy planning and management. They try to confound decisions or enhance the ability to anticipate, plan and move forward.

VUCA determines the conditions for managing and leading. Kutz (2013) highlight that CI is a concept which can be applied in VUCA contexts. CI can add value anyplace, anytime, with anyone. The specific relevance of CI and the VUCA approach is often related to how people perceive the conditions under which they make decisions, solve problems, analyze the consequences of these problems, appreciate the interdependence of Variables, anticipate emerging issues, manage risks, prepare for other realities and challenges, and identify relevant opportunities in a defined territory.

Thus, it is associated with Territorial Intelligence (TI) (Girardot 2000). The author defined TI as «a means for the researchers, for the actors and for the territorial community to get a better knowledge of the territory, but also to better control its development. The appropriation of information and communication technologies is an indispensable step so the actors enter the learning process that will allow them to act in a relevant and efficient way. Territorial intelligence is especially useful to help the territorial actors planning, defining, animating, and evaluating the policies and actions of sustainable territorial development». Therefore, CI could emerge within a territory and can add value to the startups housed in this territory. In our case, the context is the territory where the startups are housed which is the Academic and Scientific Incubator (ASI). It represents the territory for CI.

2.2 Contextual Intelligence and Territory

Sternberg (1988) has used CI as a synonym for his concept of practical intelligence, a subtheme within his theory of Triarchic Intelligence. According to Sternberg (1988), CI signifies the ability to apply intelligence practically in specific time, specific space and with specific material, which includes considering social, cultural, and historical backgrounds. He maintained that individuals who have a high level of CI easily adapt to their surroundings can fit into new surroundings easily and can fix their surroundings when they perceive it to be necessary. In fact, CI is the ability to understand the limits of our knowledge and to adapt that knowledge to an environment different from the one in which it was developed. Time, material, and space are key dimensions of contextual intelligence.

The concept of territory has been used under several names such as "cluster", place-based, Ba, etc. Speaking of cluster policy, Daubert (2008) introduced the term "clusters". The latter can refer to "territory" in the sense that it has been used to refer to "A group of the same or similar elements gathered or occurring closely together". It is "a geographical concentration of firms and institutions whose activities are interconnected and interdependent in a particular economic sector". (Michael E. Porter 1998). Also, the concept of territory is presented under the name "place-based". In his article on "Food Safety in Tunisia", Chouk (2010) indicates that the authors Hans J et al. (2005) use the word "place" from which they derive the concept of place-based management.

Nonaka and Takeuchi, for their part, used the concept of "Ba" in their SECI model, which aims to theorize the phenomenon of production, use, and dissemination of knowledge within an organization, particularly in the industrial sector. The Ba is a foundation for knowledge creation within SECI. It is a commonplace of transfer, a "learning base", a place for inter-individual interactions that create new knowledge that can be translated literally as "place". Thus, according to Bakkali et al. (2011), the ASI is a shared space in which the exchange of information and relationships between entrepreneurs, university, and incubator takes place. It is at the focal point of two policies: innovation and entrepreneurship. They are structures within the university that support students in creating their entrepreneurial projects. The university incubator is then a place to welcome and support innovative projects.

The learning process could only be built on a 'territory' (Chouk et al. 2017). The ASI as a territory would allow the entrepreneurs and stakeholders to hold complementary knowledge and expertise (researchers, organizations, and associations) and would allow them also to co-construct and co-create coherent representations of their common interest object, the environment (Chouk 2012). While, in each territory, start-ups are being created and others disappearing (Ayari 2018). This issue of early exit is due to many obstacles and problems (Smida et al. 2010). How do we overcome this problem? We believe that using co-creation of value can reduce the early death of some start-ups.

3 Co-creation of Value

What is co-creation? Co-creation as a term has multiple meanings. Co-creation is used in several disciplines, including marketing, innovation management, information systems, design, and public management. and public management. Roser et al. (2013) propose a definition of co-creation as an interactive, creative, and social process between stakeholders. interactive, creative, and social process between stakeholders, initiated by a company at different stages of value creation (Suvi Konsti-Laakso 2018, p. 24). «Co-creation is a process where users consciously and actively engage in an innovation process and take over activities traditionally executed by an organization, so the user and organization interact jointly» (Suvi Konsti-Laakso 2018, p. 24).

What is the value? Value is determined by the experiences that products and services provide and not by what they are. Organizational performance is determined by the ability to integrate the knowledge, skills, and capabilities of an organization with the knowledge, skills, and capabilities of its customers to co-create an experience those customers can successfully co-produce (Chouk and Uden 2016). In our context, the value is determined by the ability to integrate the knowledge, skills, and capabilities of the entrepreneurs (between each other also) and the knowledge, skills, and capabilities of the stakeholders. Chouk and Uden (2016) concur with these authors that whether an organization manufactures a physical product or provides an intangible service experience, it is what is co-created with the customer that produces value. And in the context of ASI, the start-ups-stakeholders model today has been replaced by the notion of co-creation of value.

The study of Meglino and Ravlin, (1998) showed that values not only predict motivational behavior, but they also show a person´s perspective of life. This is because values are initially developed through social interactions about the perspective of a culture. The values of a human being can be seen as a normative view of what is good and desirable (Kast and Rosenwieg 1974). Because values are developed through social interactions, there tends to be congruence in value patterns within cultures, as shared values are passed from generation to generation (Meglino and Ravlin 1998). These values, which are passed on from generation to generation can be considered having an enduring and autonomous influence on society (Inglehart and Baker 2000). By identifying the patterns of how the different participants work, their attitudes, the language used, and the structure of the organization would help the smooth process of dialogue, access, risk, and transparency in co-creation (Chouk and Uden 2016). Mahr et al. (2014) consider the co-creation of value in a startup as the co-production of knowledge with consumers. As defined, co-creation occurs through a process of communication between users and innovation teams on innovation-related issues such as ideas and user needs (Mahr et al. 2014).

According to Prahalad and Ramaswamy (2004), the value creation process is based on experience co-creation that enables the co-creation of experiences of valued outcomes. Innovation and efficiency are about facilitating compelling experiences of value through interacting processes in experience environments, supported by networks of start-ups and communities of individuals, including the stakeholders. The innovation process is centered on the co-creation of knowledge. Based on Magnusson et al. (2003) and Grabher et al. (2008), knowledge represents the central ingredient for innovation and the entrepreneurs are considered as knowledge co-creators: they manage the phases of the development process of innovation and act as knowledge sources and creators. Knowledge management (KM) is then the process of creating, sharing, using, and managing the knowledge and information of start-ups. Its efforts typically focus on organizational objectives such as improved performance, competitive advantage, innovation, the sharing of lessons learned... (Girard et.al 2015).

4   Knowledge Management (KM)

4.1   What's KM?

Alavi and Leidner (2001) declare knowledge as a key resource in business. Knowledge is seen to be entrenched and embedded in the organization, as it is found in its culture, routines, systems, policies, and the individual employee (Pillay et al. 2019). Serrat (2017) defined knowledge as: "A combination of data and information, to which is added expert opinion, skills, and experience, resulting in an asset that aids decision making. In organizational terms, knowledge is generally thought of as being know-how, applied information, information with judgment, or the capacity for effective action. Knowledge may be tacit, explicit, individual, and/or collective. It is intrinsically linked to people".

According to Nonaka and al. (2000), «Information becomes knowledge when it's interpreted by individuals and given a context and anchored in the beliefs and commitments of individuals». Egbu and al. consider knowledge as the most important resource in organizations and as a key differentiating factor in business today (Chouk and al. 2017). A combination of skills and knowledge is needed to succeed in an entrepreneurial project (Schmitt and et al. 2004). Knowledge Management (KM) has been an established discipline since 1995. The knowledge movement spawned through managements' realization that what an organization and its employees know is central to an organization's success (Davenport and Prusak 1998). The study of Artail (2006) showed that the KM is the systematic and organizationally specified process of acquiring, organizing, and communicating knowledge so that entrepreneurs can use it to become more effective and productive in their work.

Moreover, the KM, according to King (2009), is the planning, organizing, motivating, and controlling of people, processes, and systems in the organization to ensure that its knowledge-related assets are improved and effectively employed. According to Wu et al. (2018) "Knowledge management can be broadly referred to as the process of creating, utilizing, sharing, storing, and managing knowledge and information within an organization to achieve its objectives. It draws upon interdisciplinary literature from business administration, information systems, management, and library and information sciences". Whereas, in our study, at the micro-level, entrepreneurs are floundering with too much information readily available, too little relevant, and timely information when they need it, and with few tools or skills to deal with information effectively which caused difficulties to survive for some start-ups in an academic and scientific incubator. Therefore, Tsoukas underlines the "crucial roles of human interpretation, communication, and skills in the conversion of internalized tacit knowledge into explicit codified knowledge for successful knowledge sharing and consequently for generating effective organizational action".

4.2 SECI Model

In 1995, two Japanese academics, Ikujiro Nonaka and Hirotaka Takeuchi (1995) developed, in their book 'The Knowledge-Creating Company' a model for knowledge conversion, called SECI (Socialization, Externalization, Combination, and Internalization). Many taxonomies specify various kinds of knowledge. The most fundamental distinction is between "tacit" and "explicit" knowledge. The SECI model explains how tacit and explicit knowledge are converted into organizational knowledge. It distinguishes four knowledge dimensions – socialization, externalization, combination, and internalization (Fig. 1).

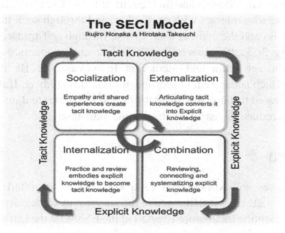

Fig. 1. SECI model (Nonaka and Takeuchi 1995)

Socialization involves the process of acquiring and sharing tacit knowledge between individuals, emphasizing capturing knowledge through apprenticeship and conversations. Externalization involves the transforming of tacit knowledge to explicit knowledge into a comprehensible form understood by others. The combination involves the process of combining all explicit sources for creating new knowledge. Internalization involves the conversion of explicit knowledge into tacit knowledge, which is actionable, i.e., developing skills and experience by learning from existing explicit knowledge. These modes present knowledge as context-specific and depend on time, space, and relationship with others (Nonaka and Toyama 2000). Nonaka and Konno (1998) subsequently developed the SECI model by introducing the Japanese concept of 'Ba', which roughly translates as 'place'. Ba is a shared context or shared space in which knowledge is shared, created, and utilized. It is a concept that unifies physical space such as an office space, virtual, and mental space such as shared ideas.

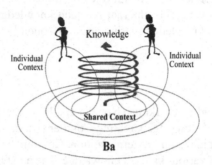

Fig. 2. Ba as shared context (Nonaka et al. 2000)

The key concept in understanding Ba is 'interaction' (Nonaka et al. 2000). According to Nonaka et al. (2000), knowledge is created through the interactions amongst individuals or between individuals and their environments. Therefore, Ba can be the context shared by those who interact with each other, and through such interactions, those who participate in Ba and the context itself evolve through self-transcendence to create knowledge (see Fig. 2). Participants of Ba cannot be mere onlookers. Although, they are committed to Ba through action and interaction. In our case, the 'Ba' presents the territory of our study which is the ASI. Our proposition in this study is: If the entrepreneurs see the value co-created through the interactions and the contextual intelligence process in a 'Ba', they can reduce the early death of some start-ups.

5   Methodology

In the context of the research work of our master's thesis, we committed a reflection on the contribution of the contextual intelligence in the survival of some start-ups incubated to an Academic and scientific Incubator (The ASI of the ENISO at the University of Sousse). In this respect, the ASI form the anchor territory for newly created startups. However, in each territory, new companies are being created and others disappearing (Gasse 2003). This issue of early exit is of concern to governments (Smida et al. 2010). As researchers, we are called upon to explore the field and identify development levers likely to curb this phenomenon. After having developed all the theoretical concepts, we will present the methodological framework of our research while exposing the exploratory study that was conducted with four startups that were incubated in the ENISO incubator. In our master's thesis, we have positioned ourselves within the framework of an interpretative reflection.

5.1 The Research Designs

According to Wacheux (1996), our strategy of access to the real world was based on an abductive qualitative approach, using mainly in the data collection process semi-directive interviews. We conducted semi-structured interviews with the founders of the startups which lasted between They lasted between 45 min and 1 h 15 min. They were conducted in a relaxed atmosphere conducive to discussion. For Wacheux (1996), this technique is not sufficient on its own, the triangulation of sources is a requirement in case studies as well as the use of data collection and techniques of data collection and analysis can strengthen the validity of the research. In this context, we have triangulated the methods of data collection.

We used semi-structured interviews, the collection of internal documents and consultation of the official websites of the startups and of the IAS ENISO. These qualitative collection tools were deployed in the framework of an exploratory case study that focused on four Tunisian startups incubated within the ENISO incubator. We conducted our exploratory research with the startups incubated in the academic and scientific incubator ENISO. It should be noted that our interviewees found it preferable to anonymize them for reasons of confidentiality: Startup 1: (SR); Startup 2: (SCS); Startup 3: (SJV); Startup 4: (SRA).

5.2 The Instrumentation of the Data Collection

Our data are descriptive information gathered through interviews. They are qualitative and not quantitative data. These qualitative collection tools were deployed in the framework of an exploratory case study that focused on four Tunisian startups incubated within the ENISO incubator. The data collected were analyzed (processed and coded) using the Nvivo'12 plus software. This tool enabled us to construct comparative matrices facilitating the analysis and to focus on the relationships between themes.

In the framework of our research, the number of cases is limited to the number of startups incubated in the ENISO incubator we have chosen to use the method convenience sampling. The latter is in a way a choice that is arbitrated by the researcher. It is generally chosen for constraints related to practicality, accessibility, and cost. The investigation period lasted 11 months. The interviews took place at the offices of the interviewees and each interview lasted an average of one hour. All interviews were recorded after permission was granted. In addition, we brought the printed interview guide with us during the interviews so that the interviewee can read the questions.

5.3 Presentation of the Cases Studied

The information on Tunisian incubated startups was collected during the interviews and from their official websites. Case 1: Startup Robots (SR): is a Tunisian technology startup founded in 2016. It develops didactic robotic solutions for primary, secondary, and university education. The founders contribute to the improvement of the educational system. They provide high-technology tools that facilitate learning. It is indeed a project that develops robots that meet educational needs. (SR) is to date (date of publication of research results) incubated within IAS ENISO. Case 2: Startup Connected Solutions (SCS): is a Tunisian technology startup launched in 2016. It has worked on the connected industry. One of its main objectives was to find solutions for all its customers by synchronizing embedded systems engineering, mobile, and web development. The project stopped after 6 months of work and the startup left the incubator. Case 3: Video Games Startup (SJV): is a Tunisian technology startup launched in 2016. (SJV) is to date (date publication of research results) incubated within IAS ENISO. It designs and develops gaming technologies in such an innovative way. These founders believe that video games have the power to engage users in a more effective way. communication experience that stimulates their passion. They began operating in education because they believe in its highest priority. Case 4: Augmented Reality Startup (ARS): is a Tunisian technology startup founded in 2016. It was incubated for 9 months and then she left IAS ENISO to move to her own premises in Tunis. It is a startup that seeks, through new technologies, to make following possible Tunisia's cultural heritage more attractive while developing a reality helmet virtual augmented allowing you to visit museums and archaeological sites at distance. The sample was selected according to the following criteria: The territory of Sousse ENISO's Incubator, to be an ENISO student or graduate of ENISO, to be a founder or co-founder of a startup incubated in ENISO's incubator or who has already left the incubator.

6   Findings

The interpretation of the individual responses of participants to questions from the questionnaire has identified the following deductions:

The startup SCS: we notice a relatively weak practice of CI (quasi absence of territorial communication, relatively weak practice of federation of competences, valorization of individual competencies). The lack of positive synergy between the project team members (war of equals, exacerbated individuality). SCS could not survive more than 6 months despite its chances of survival (strong human capital and good social capital). The startup SJV: We notice that SJV practices a lot of CI while developing especially its relational network by multiplying its partners. Although in the beginning, its social capital is not developed (absence of the informal network, a relatively weak institutional network). Despite the relatively limited chances of survival compared to the other cases, this startup is still alive. The investigation showed that it wished to extend its incubation period to expand its territorial network and strengthen its chances of survival through this network.

The startup SR: From the responses, we can see that SR has more positive indicators of survival for a less intense CI practice for SJV. However, the low practice of CI is due to the reduced number of partnerships and the quasi absence of territorial communication and informational sharing.

The startup SRA: We notice an intense practice of CI and high chances of survival. We then notice the strong correlation between the practice of CI and the chances of survival of the startup. A company that wants to survive and which wants to impose itself must have developed a relational network, intense territorial communication, the strong practice of skills federation, frequent informational sharing, as intense as potentialities of survival.

7 Discussion and Implications

This analysis leads to the identification of two categories of startups under identical conditions of unsatisfactory support: Startups that are not active in contextual intelligence and knowledge management with a high risk of early death for lack of satisfactory support (SCS and SR). Startups that are active in CI and KM with a strong relational network and chances of survival (SJV and SRA). The practice of CI and KM proves to be positive discriminatory conditions in the survival of the startup while the lack of support proves to be a negative condition in all cases. The results of this research, reveal that contextual intelligence practice can counterbalance the lack of support at the ASI, the startup that we can consider as a success story (SRA) certainly relied on its intrinsic success factors (a persevering and persistent entrepreneur, family and institutional support, co-creation of value between the team members and the stakeholders) but it also showed a perceptible interest in knowledge management (developed relational network, intense territorial communication, the strong practice of skills federation, frequent information sharing, creating and managing knowledge).

The case of failure (SCS) shows that the combination of a lack of support, a low intelligence practice, a low practice of KM, and a deficit of co-creation of value does not favor the startup's survival in the incubation phase. The two other companies (SR, SJV) are in an intermediate situation: they have less autonomy and intrinsic potential than the success case and more predisposition to KM and intelligence practices but remain highly dependent on incubation conditions for their survival more specifically, the time frame (1 year) which is like what is in force in the other territories (2 to 2.5 years) and the degree of compliance with the stages of the support process.

The practice of CI and the use of KM by incubated startups seems to have an important contribution to the survival of some start-ups incubated. The factors retained as predictors of failure in our study resemble the causes of failure found in the paper of Chouk (2014) in the same Tunisian context "Computer Supported Collaborative Environmental Scanning: Diagnostic Framework and Its Application for a Tunisian Case Study". In that case, Chouk and Lorna (2016) proposed the concept of co-creation of value and a model for the Tunisian case to avoid the barriers and the obstacles of collaborative work. The exploration of the conditions and factors of survival of startups incubated in an ASI has allowed us to verify the conditions and factors that we found in the literature review and that we mobilized in the context of our field survey. Above all, however, it allowed us to bring out two factors that contextualize our results: **the co-creation of value and the cohesion between the members of the team** and **the perseverance and the obstinacy of the entrepreneur.** These factors emerged in the specific context of an academic and scientific incubator. We do not know whether they will emerge in an institutional or private sector? This question is just as valid for the results above regarding the quality of the support perceived very much in line with the expectations of the 4 startups. This study used the SECI (KM) Model. We propose an integrated one that we modeled on an academic and scientific incubator (Fig. 3).

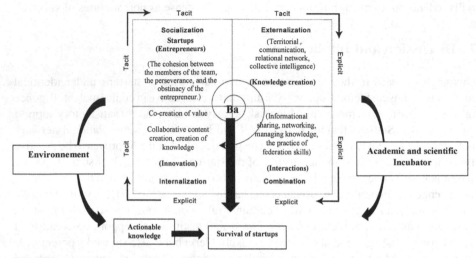

Fig. 3. Proposed knowledge operationalization model for startups housed to an Academic and Scientific Incubator

8   Conclusion

At the beginning of this research, we asked the question: CI and KM: what contribution to the survival of start-ups housed in an academic and scientific incubator?

To answer this question, we conducted a field investigation of university incubator and obtained results, some of which are consistent with those we identified in the literature review and others that emerged from our context as specific components.

The results and their discussion reveal a response that yes, the CI and KM contributed to the survival of start-ups housed in an academic and scientific incubator. In fact, the practice of CI and KM can counterbalance the lack of accompaniment at ASI, the startup that we can consider a success story (SRA) has success factors (a persevering entrepreneur and an entrepreneurial spirit), but it has also expressed an interest in the perceptible for CI and KM practices (developed relational network, communication, creating and sharing knowledge, strong practice of skills federation, frequent information sharing and intense co-creation of value). The case of failure (SCS) shows that the combination of deficit sharing knowledge with a low intelligence practice and no creation of value causes the failure of the startup in the incubation phase. The co-creation of value is in deficit in this startup. According to Chouk and Uden (2016), we can provide value to each of the entrepreneurs involved. Startups must work on a co-creation of value for the collaborative system that we believe will overcome the cause of failure identified in the case study. The proposed model shows the contribution of contextual intelligence, knowledge management, and co-creation of value in the survival of startups.

We conclude that values are developed through social interactions. Nonaka, I. (1994) represented these interactions through his "spiral of knowledge" that leads to new knowledge that reflects the collective intelligence of the company. It is a loop that is never closed, which is very much in line with the characteristic of an "ongoing" continuous process, of the creation of meaning (Chouk 2005). The next step, beyond the scope of this paper, is to continue and replicate the investigation in other incubation contexts than ASI and other establishments than ENISO and in other territories than Sousse to advance towards a certain theoretical generalization.

Like all research, ours is not without limits. These are related to the sample size related to the choice of ENISO's incubator. We cannot talk here about theoretical saturation. The second limit is related to the fact that we were limited to interviewing Start uppers. Only, and for not having collected the perceptions of the incubator which does not give us a complete view of the incubation situation.

References

Alavi, M., Leidner, D.E.: Knowledge management and knowledge management systems: conceptual foundations and research issues. MIS Q. 107–136 (2001)

Artail, H.A.: Application of KM measures to the impact of a specialized groupware system on corporate productivity and operations. Inf. Manage. 43(4), 551–561 (2006)

Ayari: Pratiques d'intelligence territoriale et conditions contextuelles de survie de startups en phase d'incubation. Master's thesis presented ans publicly supported on December 2018 (2018)

Chaffk, B., Karim, M.M., Sylvie, S.: Towards a typology of incubators based on HRM. ICSB, Stockholm, June 2011

Davenport, T.H., Prusak, L.: Working Knowledge: How Organizations Manage What They Know. Harvard Business School Press (1998). 27,061 Reads. https://doi.org/10.1145/348772.348775

Girard, J.P., Girard, J.L.: Defining knowledge management: toward an applied compendium (PDF). Online J. Appl. Knowl. Manage. 3(1), 14 (2015)

Grabher, G., Ibert, O., Flohr, S.: The neglected king: the customer in the new knowledge ecology of innovation. Econ. Geogr. 84(3), 253–280 (2008)

Gasse, Y.: L'influence du milieu dans la création d'entreprises. Centre d'Entrepreneuriat et de PME, Québec, Université Laval: Organisations et Territoires, 12(2), 49–56 (2003)

Schellnhuber, H.J., Crutzen, P.J., Clark, W.C., Hunt, J.: Earth system analysis for sustainability. Environ.: Sci. Policy Sustain. Dev. 47(8), 10–25 (2005). https://doi.org/10.3200/ENVT.47.8. 10-25

Inglehart, R., Baker, W.E.: Modernization, cultural Change, and the persistence of traditional values. Am. Sociol. Rev. 65, 19–51 (2000)

Kamoun-Chouk, S., Berger, H., Sie, B.H.: Towards integrated model of big data (BD), business intelligence (BI) and knowledge management (KM). In: Uden, L., Lu, W., Ting, I.-H. (eds.) KMO 2017. CCIS, vol. 731, pp. 482–493. Springer, Cham (2017). https://doi.org/10.1007/978-3-319-62698-7_40

Kamoun Chouk, S., Uden, U.: Co-creation of value for Tunisian environmental scanning agriculture observatory. In: KMO 2016, 25–28 July 2016, Hagen, Germany. ACM (2016). ISBN 978-1-4503-4064-9/16/07…$15.00. https://doi.org/10.1145/2925995.2926041

Kamoun Chouk, S.: Sécurité Sanitaire des Aliments en Tunisie: L'apport différentiel de l'Intelligence territoriale pour une gouvernance à plusieurs dans une logique de développement durable. Ediemar 2010 (2010)

Kamoun Chouk, S.: veille anticipative stratégique: processus d'attention à l'environnement application à des PMI tunisiennes. Thesis presented and publicly supported on 16 June 2005 (2005)

Kamoun Chouk, S.: Territorial intelligence as a knowledge creation process: the tunisian national food safety system experience. IUP J. Knowl. Manage. **X**(3), 53–72 (2012). Available at SSRN: https://ssrn.com/abstract=2170287

Kamoun-Chouk, S.: Computer supported collaborative environmental scanning: diagnostic framework and its application for a tunisian case study. J. Inf. Knowl. Manage. **13**(04), 1450034 (2014). https://doi.org/10.1142/S0219649214500348

Kast, F.F., Rosenzweig, J.E.: Organization and Management: A Systems Approach. McGraw-Hill, New York (1974)

King, W.R.: Knowledge management and organizational learning. In: King, W. (ed.) Knowledge Management and Organizational Learning, vol. 4, pp. 3–13. Springer, Boston (2009)

Kutz, M.: Toward a conceptual model of contextual intelligence: a transferable leadership construct. Transferable Leadership Construct. Kravis Leadership Institute, Leadership Review, Winter 2008, vol. 8, pp. 18–31 (2008)

Kutz, M.: Contextual Intelligence How Thinking in 3D Can Help Resolve Complexity, Uncertainty and Ambiguity (2017). ISBN 978-3-319-44997-5, ISBN 978-3-319-44998-2 (eBook). Library of Congress Control Number: 2016957718. https://doi.org/10.1007/978-3-319-44998-2

Kutz, M.R., Bamford-Wade, A.: Understanding contextual intelligence: a critical competency for today's leaders. Emergence Complexity Organ. **15**(3), 55–80 (2013)

Magnusson, P.R., Matthing, J., Kristensson, P.: Managing user involvement in service innovation: experiments with innovating end users. J. Serv. Res. **6**(2), 111–124 (2003)

Mahr, D., Lievens, A., Blazevic, V.: The value of customer co-created knowledge during the innovation process. J. Prod. Innov. Manage. **31**(3), 599–615 (2014)

Meglino, B.M., Ravlin, E.C.: Individual values in organizations: concepts, controversies, and research. J. Manag. **24**, 351–389 (1998)

Nonaka, I., Takeuchi, H.: The Knowledge-Creating Company: How Japanese Companies Create the Dynamics of Innovation. Oxford University Press, New York (1995)

Nonaka, I., Konno, N.: The concept of Ba: building a foundation for knowledge creation. Calif. Manage. Rev. **40**(3), 45 (1998)

Nonaka, I., Toyama, R., Konno, N.: SECI, Ba, and leadership: a unified model of dynamic knowledge creation. Long Range Plan. **33**, 5–34 (2000). https://doi.org/10.1016/S0024-6301(99)001 15-6. ISSN 0024-6301

Nonaka, I., Takeuchi, H.: The knowledge-creating company: how japanese companies create the dynamics of innovation. Oxford University Press, New York (1994)

Pillay, D., Barnard, B.: Entrepreneurship and knowledge management: knowledge requirements, utility, creation, and competency. Expert J. Bus. Manage. **7**(1), 44–81 (2019). ISSN 2344-6781. http://Business.ExpertJournals.com

Prahalad, C.K., Ramaswamy, V.: Co-creation experiences: the next practice in value creation. J. Interact. Mark. **18**(3), 5–14 (2004)

Porter, M.E.: Clusters and the New Economics of Competition. Harvard Business Review, Harvard Business School Press (1998). https://hbr.org/1998/11/clusters-and-the-new-economics-of-competition. On Competition

Roser, T., DeFillippi, R., Samson, A.: Managing your co-creation mix: co-creation ventures in distinctive contexts. Eur. Bus. Rev. **25**(1), 20–41 (2013)

Serrat, O.: Building a learning organization. In: Serrat, O. (ed.) Knowledge Solutions, pp. 57–67. Springer, Singapore (2017). Print ISBN 978-981-10-0982-2. https://doi.org/10.1007/978-981-10-0983-9_11

Smida, A., Khelil, N.: Repenser l'échec entrepreneurial des nouvelles entreprises: proposition d'une typologie s'appuyant sur une approche intégrative. 9 ième Conférence du CIFEPME, Louvain-la-Neuve (2010)

Schmitt, C., Berger-Douce, S., Bayad, M.: les incubateurs universitaires et le paradoxe de la relation entre université et entrepreneuriat., acte du 7ème Congrès International Froncophone sur la PME., Montpellier, octobre (2004)

Sternberg, R.J.: The Triarchic Mind: A New Theory of Human Intelligence. Viki, New York (1988)

Konsti-Laakso, S.: Co-creation, brokering and innovation networks: a model for innovating with users, 58 p. Acta Universitatis Lappeenrantaensis 816 Diss. Lappeenranta University of Technology (2018). ISBN 978-952-335-275-9, ISBN 978-952-335-276-6 (PDF), ISSN-L 1456-4491, ISSN 1456-4491

Wacheux, F.: Méthodes qualitatives et recherche en gestion. Economica, Paris (1996)

Wu, J., Lo, M.F., Ng, A.W.: Knowledge management and sustainable development. Encycl. Sustain. High. Educ. 1–9 (2018). https://doi.org/10.1007/978-3-319-63951-2_175-1

Knowledge and Organization

Relationship Between a Company's Knowledge Management Strategy and Its Business Sustainability

Eric Kin-Wai Lau[✉]

Lee Shau Kee School of Business and Administration, The Open University of Hong Kong, Hong Kong, China
ekwlau@ouhk.edu.hk

Abstract. The current business environment is dynamic, and organizations' learning capability is critical. In order to gain sustainable competitive advantage, a company's organizational knowledge base must be well protected and cultivated, and it must be shared among its employees. Knowledge management (KM) has become critical for the success of every organization. Importantly, KM is more than information technology and is not just a technical concept. Building on previous studies of KM and organizational performance, the paper provides a framework for investigating the relationship between a company's KM strategy and its business sustainability.

Keywords: Knowledge management · Business sustainability · Dynamic business environment

1 Introduction

Davenport and Prusak [1] defined knowledge as "a fluid mix of framed experience, contextual information, values and expert insight that provides a framework for evaluating and incorporating new experiences and information" (p. 5). In the words of Penrose [2], "this increase in knowledge not only causes the productive opportunity of a firm to change in ways unrelated to changes in the environment, but also contributes to the 'uniqueness' of the opportunity of each individual firm" (pp. 52–53). Gordon and Grant [3] suggested that knowledge management (KM) has been a popular research topic since 1994. They found thousands of articles indexed with the keywords "knowledge management" published between 1986 and 2004. The keywords "strategy" and "organizational learning" are also linked to their study. Bo [4] highlighted that the management of knowledge can be a "strategic objective" of an organization wishing to gain competitive advantage. It is believed that KM strategies can help companies to secure a long-term sustainable competitive advantage [5]. Andriani, Samadhi, Siswanto, and Suryadi [6] also proposed a KM strategy model that aligns with the different growth stages of organizations.

© Springer Nature Switzerland AG 2021
L. Uden et al. (Eds.): KMO 2021, CCIS 1438, pp. 187–196, 2021.
https://doi.org/10.1007/978-3-030-81635-3_16

2 Literature Review

Knowledge management is defined as "managing information flow; getting the right information to the people who need it so they can act on it quickly" [7]. According to Jennex, Smolnik and Croasdell [8], "KM success is a multidimensional concept. It is defined by capturing the right knowledge, getting the right knowledge to the right user, and using this knowledge to improve organizational and/or individual performance. KM success is measured using the dimensions of impact on business processes, strategy, leadership, efficiency and effectiveness of KM processes, efficiency and effectiveness of the KM system, organizational culture, and knowledge content (p. 183)". Gao, Li and Clarke [9] suggested that both substance knowledge and process knowledge in organizations need to be managed for KM success.

Andreeva and Kianto [10] questioned whether it is necessary for organizations to invest in knowledge management. They hypothesized that organizations' ICT (information and communication technologies) practices for managing knowledge have a positive relationship with their competitiveness and their economic performance. In their study, both human resources management (HRM) and ICT practices were found have positive relationships with an organization's competitiveness. However, they also found a negative relationship between ICT practices and financial performance. They argued that an organization's financial performance can be affected by factors other than KM. In an earlier study by Liao [11], it was suggested that managers can leverage their company's performance by aligning their HRM control system with a particular KM strategy. Using a sample of 111 computer and peripheral equipment manufacturing industries in Taiwan, Liao [11] found that the use of behaviour control enhanced firm performance in cases in which the firm emphasized a personalization strategy.

Kim, Lee, Chun, and Benbasat [12] tried to define four different KM strategies commonly used in organizations: external codification, internal codification, external personalization, and internal personalization. Using a sample of 141 companies, they found that the effectiveness of these strategies depended on both external and internal contextual conditions, namely, environmental knowledge intensity and organizational information systems (IS) maturity.

A structural equation model was constructed by Ul Rehman, Ilyas and Asghar [13] to test the inter-correlations between explicit knowledge sharing, tacit knowledge sharing, system-oriented strategy, human-oriented strategy and company performance (including operational and financial performance, customer satisfaction and product development). With 810 respondents from banking industries in India, they found that knowledge sharing practices have significant impacts on system-oriented strategies and a bank's performance.

Kumar and Mishra [14] tried to sum up the benefits of KM, stating that it fostered an organization's innovation, improved customer service, increased sales revenues, enhanced employee retention rates and cut costs.

3   Conceptual Framework

Knowledge management can provide business benefits in organizations [15]. Kivits and Furneaux [16] suggested that KM can facilitate sustainability. In a case study, Wagner and Svensson [17] emphasized that business sustainability is a multi-dimensional construct between a company and its stakeholders. As defined by Buranapin and Ratthawatankul [18], business sustainability is "the activities of companies demonstrating the inclusion of social and environmental concerns in business operations, and in interactions with stakeholders (p. 117)".

It is necessary for people in an organization to translate their experience into knowledge that is shared and adopted in the organization. Therefore, organizations' strategies for knowledge creation and knowledge sharing are popular research perspectives.

Hosseini, Tekmedash, Karami and Jabarzadeh [19] hypothesized that the KM strategies of knowledge creation, knowledge transfer, knowledge storage and knowledge application have positive relationships with an organization's service innovation performance. Using a sample of 169 respondents in public and private hospitals in the Iranian city of Tabriz, they found that knowledge creation and knowledge application have positive impacts on service innovation performance in the sample of private hospitals.

Based on the empirical studies discussed above, the conceptual framework for this study is presented in Fig. 1.

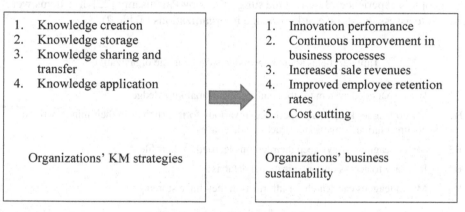

1. Knowledge creation
2. Knowledge storage
3. Knowledge sharing and transfer
4. Knowledge application

Organizations' KM strategies

1. Innovation performance
2. Continuous improvement in business processes
3. Increased sale revenues
4. Improved employee retention rates
5. Cost cutting

Organizations' business sustainability

Fig. 1. The conceptual model

4   Questionnaire Design

The questionnaire consisted of three sections, which covered the organization's KM strategies, the organization's business sustainability indicators and the organization's business profile. The first section assessed the organization's current KM strategies. Nine items were adopted from the scale developed by Ram and Gupta [20] dealing with knowledge creation (Table 1).

Table 1. Items about knowledge creation in the organization

A1	My colleagues take initiatives to develop new knowledge
A2	My colleagues actively spend resources (time, effort) on acquiring new knowledge
A3	My colleagues are aware of the latest developments in their field
A4	My colleagues implement best practices adopted from outside the team
A5	My colleagues develop knowledge, keeping in mind a long-term perspective
A6	My colleagues continuously rethink their work processes
A7	My section managers are appreciative of my team members' efforts to create new knowledge
A8	My colleagues show an interest in solving challenging problems
A9	My colleagues search outside the team (Internet, books, friends, etc.) for efficient work processes

As suggested by Chen [21], a knowledge base includes the storage of tacit and explicit knowledge in both individuals and groups. Palanisamy [22] further suggested that organizational memory is the collection of the memory of all the individuals within the organization. Therefore, this would include all written documents, structured databases and people's experience. Based on the suggestions by Palanisamy [22], five items were created to assess the storage of knowledge in organizations (Table 2).

Table 2. Items about knowledge storage in the organization

B1	We have a good system to store our organizational knowledge
B2	My colleagues keep their experience in various forms, such as in their minds, written documentation, e-mails and structured databases
B3	My colleagues always keep their lessons learned in their files
B4	It is easy to access our organizational databases
B5	My colleagues can search for information they have stored

Eight items were adapted from the scale developed by Ram and Gupta [20] dealing with knowledge sharing and transfer (Table 3).

Alavi and Leidner [23] suggested that knowledge management systems (KMS) are IT-based systems used to manage organizational knowledge. Three common KM applications include: "coding and sharing of the organization's best practices"; "creation of the organization's knowledge directory" and "creation of a knowledge network". According to Palanisamy [22], "knowledge application refers to the integration of the organizations knowledge into their products, processes, and services (p. 105)". Ten items were borrowed from the scale developed by Martelo-Landroguez and Martin-Ruiz [24] dealing with the application of knowledge in organizations (Table 4).

Table 3. Items about knowledge creation and sharing

C1	When my colleagues develop some know-how, it is shared in their team
C2	My colleagues willingly share knowledge
C3	My colleagues do not keep knowledge to themselves
C4	My colleagues share information on problem-solving strategies that have worked well
C5	My colleagues help others understand knowledge embedded in work processes
C6	My colleagues clearly discuss project details when a new project is initiated
C7	My colleagues are able to optimally utilize competencies of their individual subordinates
C8	We have regular meetings where people share their knowledge

Table 4. Items about the application of knowledge in organizations

D1	My organization has processes for applying knowledge learned from mistakes
D2	My organization has processes for applying knowledge learned from experience
D3	My organization has processes for using knowledge in the development of new services
D4	My organization has processes for using knowledge to solve problems
D5	My organization matches sources of knowledge to problems and challenges
D6	My organization uses knowledge to improve efficiency
D7	My organization uses knowledge to adjust strategic direction
D8	My organization makes knowledge accessible to those who need it
D9	My organization takes advantage of new knowledge
D10	My organization applies knowledge to critical competitive needs

The second section is about the organization's business sustainability. It includes the organization's innovation performance, continuous improvement, increased sales revenues (expected % change), changes in employee retention rates (expected % change), and cost cutting in the organization (expected % change). According to Byoung, Hyoung and Ko [25], "The organization's innovation is defined as the employees' perception of the degree of the organization's efforts to differentiate products or services compared with its competitors (p. 1260)". Six items were borrowed from Scott and Bruce [26] to measure an organization's innovation (Table 5).

Continuous improvement is necessary for business sustainability [27]. Business process innovation can even improve productivity. Six items were adapted from the scale developed by Nadarajah and Kadir [28] dealing with continuous improvement in business processes (Table 6).

The last section required all respondents to indicate their organization's business profile and basic information (i.e. company size, main business category, age, major market).

Table 5. Items about the innovation performance of the organization

E1	My organization searches out new technologies, processes, techniques, and/or ideas
E2	My organization develops adequate plans and schedules for the implementation of new ideas
E3	There is a steady stream of innovative products/services being developed, which competitors cannot conceive
E4	My organization is open and responsive to change
E5	My organization has adequate resources devoted to innovation
E6	My organization encourages innovation

Table 6. Items about the organization's continuous improvement in business processes

F1	My organization will definitely continue with process improvement initiatives
F2	The overall experience with process improvement initiatives has generally been positive in my organization
F3	The process improvement initiatives contribute to bottom line improvement in my organization
F4	The number of process improvement initiatives has increased annually in the last three years in my organization
F5	There is an increase in the number of employees involved in process improvement initiatives in the last three years
F6	My organization has a formal methodology in place to guide process improvement initiatives

5   Research Samples

Eight hundred Hong Kong companies were randomly selected from the public database provided by the Hong Kong Trade Development Council. Questionnaires were mailed in October 2019 to the managing director of these eight hundred companies, which were of different sizes and natures of business. The respondents represented a wide range of industries, including accounting and finance, education, electronics, food supply, information technology, retail and trade.

6   Pilot Test

An exploratory factor analysis of pilot data, using principal factors extraction with varimax rotation, was used to assess the factor structure of the constructs. Six factors were identified (Table 7). These results indicate that the constructs in the study were adequately operationalized. The reliability and internal consistency of the scale-type constructs were measured using Cronbach's alpha. All constructs had acceptable values above 0.70.

Table 7. A pre-test of the measures of the scale-type variables in the pilot test

Item	1	2	3	4	5	6
A1	**.823**	.127	.389	.218	.125	.291
A2	**.823**	.127	.389	.218	.125	.291
A3	**.781**	.114	.347	.344	.106	.267
A4	**.745**	.261	.340	.429	−.049	.210
A5	**.618**	.365	.389	.384	.252	.280
A6	**.603**	.345	.359	.489	.231	.264
A7	**.691**	.268	.337	.232	.364	.356
A8	**.824**	.207	.369	.198	.048	.308
A9	**.824**	.207	.369	.198	.048	.308
B1	.260	**.673**	.506	.378	.175	.148
B2	.323	**.495**	.639	.459	−.044	.042
B3	.306	**.718**	.355	.404	.227	.198
B4	.325	**.753**	.323	.370	.209	.147
B5	.325	**.753**	.323	.370	.209	.147
C1	.323	.483	**.578**	.181	.429	.217
C2	.334	.217	**.797**	.310	.274	.160
C3	.334	.217	**.797**	.310	.274	.160
C4	.413	.165	**.781**	.103	.338	.245
C5	.358	.139	**.842**	.087	.282	.197
C6	.358	.139	**.842**	.087	.282	.197
C7	.334	.217	**.797**	.310	.274	.160
C8	.282	.186	**.861**	.278	.219	.115
D1	.226	.105	.206	**.885**	.261	.200
D2	.226	.105	.206	**.885**	.261	.200
D3	.226	.105	.206	**.885**	.261	.200
D4	.226	.105	.206	**.885**	.261	.200
D5	.234	.300	.184	**.769**	.374	.291
D6	.234	.300	.184	**.769**	.374	.291
D7	.234	.300	.184	**.769**	.374	.291
D8	.234	.300	.184	**.769**	.374	.291
D9	.234	.300	.184	**.769**	.374	.291
D10	.149	.225	.165	**.793**	.444	.254

(continued)

Table 7. (*continued*)

Item	1	2	3	4	5	6
E1	.153	.055	.291	.343	**.865**	.105
E2	.153	.055	.291	.343	**.865**	.105
E3	.084	.163	.225	.304	**.893**	.156
E4	.084	.163	.225	.304	**.893**	.156
E5	.084	.163	.225	.304	**.893**	.156
E6	-.003	.066	.151	.390	**.848**	.246
F1	.228	.094	.148	.229	.149	**.918**
F2	.228	.094	.148	.229	.149	**.918**
F3	.228	.094	.148	.229	.149	**.918**
F4	.228	.094	.148	.229	.149	**.918**
F5	.228	.094	.148	.229	.149	**.918**
F6	.228	.094	.148	.229	.149	**.918**

Remarks: N = 20 (Pilot test)

7 Discussion

Knowledge management is a continuous process through which companies may gain competitive advantage. Organizations need to be aware of their knowledge management strategies and whether they are well-fitted to their existing business strategies. This framework also provides some direction for future research on the assessment of the knowledge management strategy of organizations. The paper describes the initial development of the instrument used in the main study, including scale construction, evaluation, and exploratory pilot testing. The operationalization of the six main dimensions of the model was presented.

References

1. Davenport, T., Prusak, L.: Working Knowledge. Harvard Business School Press, Boston (1998)
2. Penrose, E.: The Theory of the Growth of the Firm. Oxford University Press, New York (1959)
3. Gordon, R., Grant, D.: Knowledge management or management of knowledge? Why people interested in knowledge management need to consider Foucault and the construct of power. Tamara: J. Crit. Postmod. Organ. Sci. **3**(2), 27–38 (2005)
4. Bo, B.N.: Strategic knowledge management research: tracing the co-evolution of strategic management and knowledge management perspectives. Compet. Rev. **15**(1), 1–13 (2005). https://doi.org/10.1108/10595420510818722
5. Storey, C., Kahn, K.B.: The role of knowledge management strategies and task knowledge in stimulating service innovation. J. Serv. Res. **13**(4), 397–410 (2010)
6. Andriani, M., Samadhi, T.M.A.A., Siswanto, J., Suryadi, K.: Knowledge management strategy: an organisational development approach. Bus. Process. Manag. J. **25**(7), 1474–1490 (2019). https://doi.org/10.1108/BPMJ-07-2018-0191

7. Gates, B.: Business@ the Speed of Thought: Using a Digital Nervous System. Warner Books, New York, NY (1999)
8. Jennex, M.E., Smolnik, S., Croasdell, D.T.: Towards a consensus knowledge management success definition: very informal newsletter on library automation. Vine **39**(2), 174–188 (2009). https://doi.org/10.1108/03055720910988878
9. Gao, F., Li, M., Clarke, S.: Knowledge, management, and knowledge management in business operations. J. Knowl. Manag. **12**(2), 3–17 (2008). https://doi.org/10.1108/136732708 10859479
10. Andreeva, T., Kianto, A.: Does knowledge management really matter? Linking knowledge management practices, competitiveness and economic performance. J. Knowl. Manag. **16**(4), 617–636 (2012). https://doi.org/10.1108/13673271211246185
11. Liao, Y.S.: The effect of human resource management control systems on the relationship between knowledge management strategy and firm performance. Int. J. Manpow. **32**(5), 494–511 (2011). https://doi.org/10.1108/01437721111158170
12. Kim, T.H., Lee, J., Chun, J.U., Benbasat, I.: Understanding the effect of knowledge management strategies on knowledge management performance: a contingency perspective. Inf. Manage. **51**(4), 398 (2014)
13. Ul Rehman, W., Ilyas, M., Asghar, N.: Knowledge sharing, knowledge management strategy and performance: a knowledge based view. Pak. Econ. Soc. Rev. **53**(2), 177–202 (2015)
14. Kumar, S., Mishra, B.: Knowledge management: important tool for the success of an organization. Int. J. Manage. Res. Rev. **2**(5), 697–701 (2012)
15. Pina, P., Romão, M., Oliveira, M.: Using benefits management to link knowledge management to business objectives: very informal newsletter on library automation. Vine **43**(1), 22–38 (2013). https://doi.org/10.1108/03055721311302124
16. Kivits, R.A., Furneaux, C.: BIM: enabling sustainability and asset management through knowledge management. Sci. World J. **2013**, 1–14 (2013). https://doi.org/10.1155/2013/983721
17. Wagner, B., Svensson, G.: A framework to navigate sustainability in business networks. Eur. Bus. Rev. **26**(4), 340–367 (2014). https://doi.org/10.1108/EBR-12-2013-0146
18. Buranapin, S., Ratthawatankul, T.: Philosophy of sufficiency economy and business sustainability: a framework for operational implications. J. Bus. Behav. Sci. **27**(1), 115–141 (2015)
19. Hosseini, S.S., Tekmedash, Y.N., Karami, A., Jabarzadeh, Y.: The impact of knowledge management strategy on service innovation performance in private and public hospitals. Iran. J. Manage. Stud. **12**(1), 1–24 (2019). https://doi.org/10.22059/ijms.2018.249784.672966
20. Ram, M.S., Gupta, M.: Knowledge management in teams: empirical integration and development of a scale. J. Knowl. Manag. **18**(4), 777–794 (2014). https://doi.org/10.1108/JKM-11-2013-0450
21. Chen, C.: Analysis of the knowledge creation process: an organizational change perspective. Int. J. Organ. Theory Behav. **10**(3), 287–313 (2007). https://doi.org/10.1108/IJOTB-10-03-2007-B001
22. Palanisamy, R.: Organizational culture and knowledge management in ERP implementation: an empirical study. J. Comput. Inf. Syst. **48**(2), 100–120 (2008)
23. Alavi, M., Leidner, D.E.: Review: Knowledge management and knowledge management systems: conceptual foundations and research issues. MIS Q. **25**(1), 107–136 (2001)
24. Martelo-Landroguez, S., Martin-Ruiz, D.: Managing knowledge to create customer service value. J. Serv. Theory Pract. **26**(4), 471–496 (2016). https://doi.org/10.1108/JSTP-06-2014-0137
25. Byoung, K.C., Hyoung, K.M., Ko, W.: An organization's ethical climate, innovation, and performance: effects of support for innovation and performance evaluation. Manag. Decis. **51**(6), 1250–1275 (2013). https://doi.org/10.1108/MD-Sep-2011-0334

26. Scott, S.G., Bruce, R.A.: Determinants of innovative behavior: a path model of individual innovation in the workplace. Acad. Manag. J. **37**(3), 580–607 (1994)
27. Fleaca, E., Fleaca, B., Maiduc, S.: Fostering organizational innovation based on modeling the marketing research process through event-driven process chain (EPC). TEM J. **5**(4), 460–466 (2016). https://doi.org/10.18421/TEM54-08
28. Nadarajah, D., Kadir, S.L.S.A.: Measuring business process management using business process orientation and process improvement initiatives. Bus. Process. Manag. J. **22**(6), 1069–1078 (2016). https://doi.org/10.1108/BPMJ-01-2014-0001

Project Management in Small and Medium Enterprises to Improve Management Knowledge

Bolívar Arturo-Delgado[1,2] and Flor Nancy Díaz-Piraquive[3(✉)]

[1] Universidad Internacional Iberoamericana, Campeche, México
[2] Universidad Mariana, Pasto, Colombia
barturo@umariana.edu.co
[3] Fundación Universitaria Internacional de La Rioja UNIR, Bogotá, Colombia
flornancy.diaz@unir.edu.co

Abstract. This article presents the research results of the bibliographic review, done about the application of project management processes, in small and medium size enterprises worldwide, with the aim of knowing the current state of investigative productivity that is addressed in them and thus increasing knowledge management in the organization's operations. In this sense, a qualitative research with descriptive scope was carried out. With the analysis of information from existent literature, four thematic units were constructed: administrative, operational, strategic and external, which by the authors judgment, explain the disclosure about investigations carried out in organizations of this nature.

As a result, it was found that, despite the heterogeneity of research in this type of companies, in the field of knowledge management and project management it is limited, an aspect that is considered later in detail, given that it is a relevant factor. in the research that generates this article and that will enable the articulation of knowledge management and project management. The investigations, as a result of the review, reach the highest concentration in the administrative category, with problems centered on the administrative process: planning, organizing, directing and controlling; and financial and accounting aspects.

Keywords: Bibliometry · Scientific production · PYME · Project management · Knowledge management · Small and medium size enterprises (**SME**)

1 Introduction

The objective of this article seeks to know the current state of research productivity advanced in small and medium-sized enterprises (SME), from the characterization of bibliographic records, with the aim of suggesting to researchers, the possibility of emphasizing untreated problems and raising Value propositions that optimize project and knowledge management and, with it, market competitiveness in this type of organization.

The SME concept changes, depending on the specific needs of each country or entity. Some authors highlight, among other criteria to classify a company, the number of workers, sales and assets, from which policies and strategies are applied to develop these types

© Springer Nature Switzerland AG 2021
L. Uden et al. (Eds.): KMO 2021, CCIS 1438, pp. 197–211, 2021.
https://doi.org/10.1007/978-3-030-81635-3_17

of organizations, which represent an important role in the economy, contributing considerably to the growth and economic development of a country; therefore, its processes and procedures must be in continuous improvement.

Hence, each of the processes investigated in this type of organization constitutes a valuable tool that minimizes disadvantages, enables subsistence over time and provides opportunities for improvement. SME play an important role in the national economy, they contribute in great measure to growth and economic development of the country, representing 35% of the gross domestic product (GDP), 80% of employment and 90% of the national productive sector, according to information from the National Department of Statistics [1], therefore, their processes and procedures (SME) must be in continuous improvement, since based on their progress and competitiveness, many factors of the Colombian economy depend on them. Thereby each of the researched processes, in this type of organizations, becomes a valuable tool, that minimizes disadvantages, and makes it possible their long-term survival. On that respect, and considering the purpose of this investigation, Toro [2], says that small companies have more difficulty to find an adequate financing in terms of costs and time, due to their higher risk; Beltrán [3], says that other disadvantages that this type of organizations present, are their great structural weakness, due to the lack of strategy and planning, their difficult access to credit lines which restrict their investment in technology, working capital and knowledge; administrative management shortcomings, financial, accounting and operational failures. In this same part, emphasis is placed on knowledge management and particularly on project management.

A second phase considers the characterization of the bibliographic records of the Scopus database, published in the period 2010–2019: authors, citations, institutions, countries and keywords used in the publications, so that the study evidences a contribution to the scientific community.

To achieve the objective, a bibliometric analysis was carried out based on the review of scientific articles published in the period 2000–2019, in two databases: Ebsco and Scopus, whose approach was aimed at research related to SME companies worldwide. A total of 323 articles from Ebsco and 219 from Scopus were identified, from which the investigative productivity was studied.

2 Methodology

For the development of this article, a qualitative type research was prepared, with descriptive scope, based on the review of scientific articles published in the period between 2000 and 2019, in two databases: Ebsco and Scopus, whose approach was addressed to investigations related to diverse SME factors, on a worldwide level. To obtain the documents, a search was filtered towards those documents related to advanced investigations, in small and medium size enterprises; published in indexed journals (reviewed by pairs), including in the title the word used as a key criterion for search (SME); and Spanish. Journals, opinions and degree thesis that were not subject to review by external pairs, were restricted, which takes away from them the academic characteristic desired to be impregnated in the analysis.

The search and analysis of the literature was made in two phases. The first one gathers information from 323 scientific articles, from the Ebsco database, during the period 2000 – 2019. List which is exported to the Excel software, in which duplicated files were eliminated, and the information was organized in four categories. The second phase considers the search of literature in the database Scopus, 219 results. Data are exported to the Excel program, and from there to the software VOS viewer (version 16.13) from which a set of metadata is established to allow the analysis through co-author networks by authors, countries and institutions, and finally, by co-occurrence networks or keywords, which facilitated studying and analyzing the trend of scientific activity or the thematic contents more studied or developed in research work, in this type of organization.

First Phase Results

For the first phase, the identification of representative elements in each of the reviewed articles took place, which allowed the definition of 4 thematic areas, approached in the investigations as proposed by Okpara and Winn [4] and Apia [5] who categorize common problems, faced by businessmen of small companies, in the administrative, operational, strategic and external area.

As a result of the search strategy, 323 scientific articles were obtained that make up the bank of gross articles; subsequently, the sample is debugged selecting those works presenting pertinent information, about small and medium companies (SME), in the title. For the review, 87 articles were eliminated which did not comply with the search criteria, 7 duplicates and 8 which do not allow access to the summary, therefore, the documental analysis was affected from 221 articles onwards.

Research works in advanced SME enterprises, according to the database, have been developed, on international level, in countries such as Spain (15.38%); at Latin-American level, stand out countries like Colombia (33.03%), México (16.74%), Venezuela (7.24%) and Argentina (5.43%), data that can be seen in Fig. 1.

As a relevant information for the researcher, in the regional environment, (Nariño – Colombia) and local environment (Pasto – Nariño), according to bibliographic tracking, no investigations were found, worrying aspect, even more if SME enterprises, as previously stated, make up in one of the productive sectors more significant of the economy, specially of emerging countries.

Regarding time for research, out of the 221 articles written between years 2000 and 2009, 62 were published; and between 2010 and 2019 (June), 160 articles were published related, in their title, with small and medium size enterprises. Years 2014 and 2018 are the periods during which a higher number of investigations of this type of organizations has been conducted, with percentages equivalent to 13.12% each year (see Fig. 2).

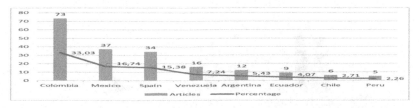

Fig. 1. Advanced research in small and medium enterprises. Source. Authors

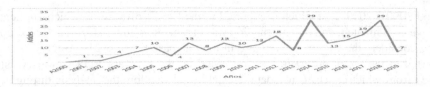

Fig. 2. Percentage of publication, SME investigations, per year

Remembering aspects previously addressed, analysis of small and medium size enterprises (SME), show that contexts of accomplishment are addressed from different categories or problem cores: administrative, operational and external investigations, and finally, the category of strategic investigations, which as a last resort becomes the most valuable one for the analysis, considering that they are investigations that focus on the object of analysis more directly. Following is a conceptualization of each one them, to group the 221 articles tracked.

The first category **Administrative Factors** refers to those investigations focused on the organizational structure and skills, to obtain and develop the necessary resources for the development of the organization. They provide information, and a favourable environment for the fulfillment of the strategic factors of the company. Within the administrative category, the more important identified topics are related to information and communication technology (IT), aspects related to own administration activities, human resources and finally financing and accounting aspects (see Fig. 3).

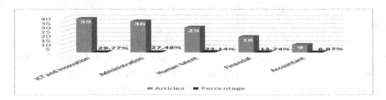

Fig. 3. Investigations by category. Administrative factors

The second category, **Operational Factors**, identify those investigations related to the efficient use of resources, in the functional areas of the organization. This category presents investigations that analyze problems related to quality and control of production (63,33%), marketing and entrepreneurship (see Fig. 4).

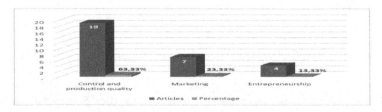

Fig. 4. Investigations by category. Operational factors

The third category – **External Factors**, presents investigations that include internationality issues, networks and associativity and regulatory aspects, for the organizations to adjust themselves to demands of each country. Figure 5 shows 30 related investigations.

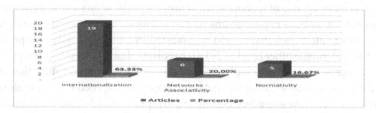

Fig. 5. Investigations by category. External factors

The fourth category – **Strategic Factors**, deals with investigations focused on the skill analysis of SME entrepreneurs, to adjust their products and/or services to external demand (vision, diversification, marketing development). In this factor bibliographic tracking is included, related to management (environmental, technological and knowledge among others); the strategic thinking and an additional classification called project management, because of direct relationship with the object of investigation. Figure 6 presents the bibliographic tracking.

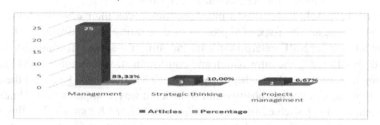

Fig. 6. Investigations by category – Strategic factors

Keeping in mind that the object of this investigation is focused on project management, defined according to PRIN (2006) as "planning, supervision and control of all aspects of the project, as well as motivation of all people involved in the project, to reach the project's goals, in terms of time, specific cost, quality and performance", tracked investigations become an important progress, however, the researcher looks at the need to deepen on findings related to management and, particularly on project management. For this, starting from the recovery of 30 articles of complete text of the category – strategic factors, it is pretended to enrich management articulated to the needs of small and medium size enterprises (SME), and the modernization of practice from the identified trends and conclusions.

There are different jobs focused on analyzing management of SME enterprises. Their tracking allowed the identification of investigations oriented to organizational management (7), knowledge management (6), technology management, innovation, communication and information (6), quality management (3), human resources management

(2), environmental management (2), project management (2) and business intelligence (1), which tacitly or explicitly are focused on strengthening, growth, productivity and competitiveness of SME enterprises.

Works from [6–11], show that business management based on creativity, changes produced by the emergence of technological knowledge, innovation and communication must be present in modern organizations of any sector of economy, above all, in small and medium size enterprises that should be inserted in an increasingly competitive and demanding world; on the other hand [12–14], highlight that any business result reflects a previous management process, which requires an organizational structure that provides form and action to communication and decision processes, agreed in turn, to the interior of the formal figure. Investigations conducted by [4, 6, 9, 15–18], are framed in the concept of innovation, its analysis and interpretation, the need to incorporate indicators which are essential tools in the decision-making processes, and its relationship with competitiveness.

On the other hand, [19–23], specify, among other strategic factors for success to be considered in small enterprises: the technological resources (including technology stock, experience in its application, scientific and technical human resources for its development); added to above concept, innovation associated to three fundamental management pillars, workers and cooperation with other enterprises (new services, products, processes responding to customer's needs, and adaptation to the environment), and the need to manage the human resources, relying on the good working environment, motivation, communication facilitating the scope of achievements.

In return, proposals from several investigations focus their efforts, on the importance of knowledge and its associated process of generating new knowledge, topic of an increasing interest for SME enterprises, with the aim of assuring its long-term survival and growth. For [23, 24], the information and communication technology (IT) become a determining factor for growth; for Marulanda, López M. and López F (2016), the organizational culture moderates in a positive and significant way, competences for knowledge management. For [11], such culture is a fundamental factor for survival of this type of organizations. [25], propose a model of generation and transfer of knowledge, for direction and human management, from the strategic addressing of organizations focused on two key factors for success: organizational culture and training, factors which contribute in the development of new skills and knowledge, to optimize and qualify systems and processes of the organization. Authors such as [5, 6], explicitly, raise the need to analyze the skills of knowledge management as a basis to generate competitiveness skills in the small and medium size enterprises (SME). Legendre's investigation (2005), poses that business intelligence (BI) not only should be oriented towards big corporations, but also to SME companies which can perfectly apply BI (business intelligence) and organize the knowledge management, thus assuring important benefits.

The human resources management, related to administrative aspects (payroll, contracting and layoffs) and legal aspects (law enforcement), is another type of investigations conducted by [25, 26] and oriented towards achieving efficiency, effectiveness and productivity in the organization, associated to satisfaction of workers and customers, innovation, development and brand building, that contribute in the talent attraction and conservation.

Authors such as [17, 18] report analysis regarding the quality management, as an important element for the managerial decision making, for which the entrepreneur may appeal to different options: implement innovation processes, invest in human resources, improve internal technology capabilities, establish alliances, reduce operational costs, improve quality of products and services, among others, which at the same time, will allow the acquisition of competitive advantages.

Meanwhile, [27] developed an administration model. a project portfolio for SME, about engineering services; considering as fundamental elements, the definition of internal procedures for a feedback of completed projects information, and a support structure to the portfolio management, for the appropriate assignment and control of resources. Researchers base their model on the standard PMBOK, and PRINCE2 methodology, since they think that they are aligned and complemented among them, due to needs and limitations of SME. The implementation of this model is done by means of computer tools (IT), Microsoft Excel and Microsoft Access, which can be used as information dissemination tools, and Microsoft Project as a support tool to manage the different projects, from their beginning to their formal closure. Above authors state that, in case of resistance to change, by the members of the organization, it can be overcome by strategies for the change process, by explaining the functionality and benefits of the new system.

Conducted [21] a research work on 2018, that contains valuable information about Project Management, in the small and medium size companies, from an epistemological vision, offering conceptual elements that generate a deep knowledge about this technique in SME. Theoretically, it is based on different approaches from different authors: Kwak (2005), MacLachlan (1996), PMBOK (2008), Páez (2004), Tejada (2003), Doménico (2010), among others. The article presents as a fundamental conclusion, the absence of project management in SME companies, according to the researcher, originated due to scarce resources for the company itself, lack of knowledge, lack of academic training and discipline practice. The Above authors suggest that SME management pay attention to innovation, continuous improvement, opening new markets and internalization, and the need to cooperate with other companies and institutions in major projects.

These aspects confirm the need to inquire, deepen, analyze and make proposals for project management knowledge for SME, to facilitate planning, organization, management and control of assigned activities and resources for the execution of a project, using knowledge, skills, tools and techniques in such a way that the project complies with the scope, time and cost established by activity.

As noticed, the analysis conducted stands out for its wide heterogeneity, and diversity of studies in management processes, supported by several theories, presenting interpretation of their investigations results, in the identified categories. However, each one of them, highlights the importance to include management processes, in order to obtain better levels of effectiveness, efficiency and productivity in the small and medium size enterprises.

Evidently SME lacks of studies related to management and/or project administration, absence of resources oriented towards project management, knowledge and training, aspects which are linked to an uncertainty environment, nonetheless, the related information to other management processes, allow the identification of a series of common factors which limit the growth and survival of this type of companies. Following is a summary of main conclusions:

[4, 10, 15] highlight a poor technological knowledge in the SME organizations, that makes the organizational change difficult, in that sense, [7] concludes that such a change is limited to the use of a text processor, a spreadsheet, accounting software and internet, and he recommends that this type of organizations should use a system of enterprise resources planning, with a free software, since they need key information in the processes for sales, customers, inventory, payments, taxes, procurement and accounting, as well as indicators to facilitate a reliable management, efficient, economical, ecological and ethics contributing to social responsibility.

Investigations, such as the one made [6, 8, 13, 22], conclude that there is a definite or incipient failure of strategies and processes that otherwise should help in the knowledge management in SME organizations. The investigation conducted by [11], from the review of literature, identified seven dimensions: procurement, aspect that may become a potential factor for the generation of competitive advantages and added value: creation, capture, organization, transmission, application and knowledge evaluation. This last one transcends much more than any other element in the organization. Meanwhile, [20], points out that culture moderates competences in a positive and significant way, for knowledge management.

Regarding management of human resources in SME, [25], states that it is weak, it does not have a direct relationship with the business strategy, it is done informally and executed directly by the company's owner. The existence of human resources in this type of organizations, is related to administrative aspects (payroll, hiring and layoff), and fulfillment of legal aspects. On the other hand, [28, 29] concludes that the utilization of a model of knowledge generation and transfer, allows the small and medium size enterprises, the optimization of resources and capabilities available; aspect reflected in better levels of competitiveness. The investigation conducted by [26] considers that, for development of new innovating projects, the need for good relationships between the members of the company and the creation of an adequate working environment are key factors.

In front of the investigations addressed to quality management, among the most relevant results, the review of backgrounds came out with, according to [18], weaknesses in the quality management system. The due importance is not given to it, and quality management tools are used routinely; on the other hand, [17] points out that the lack of coherence among the directive actions, and results of the organizations. Therefore, it is necessary to create a quality center to face competitors [30–32].

From the above, the generation of an organizational culture is highlighted, in which the role of planned change becomes a dynamizing factor, and the project management a basic pillar, both in this type or organizations, focused to make individuals, equipment and organizations, achieve the execution of the different projects in the best possible way, complying with the requirements of quality, cost and scheduled time.

Results of Second Phase

The second phase, considers the characterization of bibliographic registrations of 306 scientific articles related to the topic, listed in the Scopus database, and published during the period 2010–2018. Following is an analysis of the diverse information units, contained in the bibliographic registrations (authors, mentions, institutions, countries and key words). In the domain of SME in a worldwide level, contributions related to investigations of small and medium size enterprises are diverse. However, the bibliometric analysis allowed to know the knowledge level gap, in the specific field of project management, and knowledge of this type of organizations.

Productivity by Authors

To analyze productivity, authors were listed according to the number of articles produced, keeping in mind the key word - SME. A total of 306 articles were identified, out of which 42 were obtained with frequency in production and mentions higher or equal to 2. It is noticed that in those articles 85,71% have produced two documents. The highest production (4 articles) is presented by two authors, Briozzo A. and Muñoz M., 30,95% has been referenced in more than 10 opportunities, and Larrán J. López M. stand out with 18 and 17 mentions respectively. Table 1 shows the most representative and mentioned authors.

On the bibliometric map, the size of the cluster was determined by the number of links, among authors. In Fig. 8, 20 clusters were identified, randomly coloured. Out of them, four groups on the map with red colour, green, blue and yellow show greater co-authorship, made up by three links (four authors). Two linked between three authors; 5 related to one author, and 8 are not connected to the network (Fig. 7).

Productivity by Countries

Among the most outstanding countries in scientific production about the topic, with 127, 80 and 34 documents are Spain, Colombia and México, respectively. A second group is made up by Ecuador with 22 productions, Chile and Venezuela, each one with 15. In these six countries, 85,92% of analyzed publications is concentrated (see Fig. 8). On the other hand, the countries with the highest number of mentions are Spain, Colombia and México, followed by Chile and Argentina. Countries like Perú, Costa Rica, Brasil, Malasia and Netherlands, have no mentions.

On the bibliometric map, the size of clusters was determined by the number of links in countries related to the topic subject of analysis (SME). Figure 9 identifies 13 clusters highlighted by a random colour. Out of them, two highlighted with golden and blue colour (each one related to 11 countries) which show the greatest links, and as outstanding countries are: Spain, Colombia, México and Ecuador. The green cluster links Ecuador with five countries (Spain, Colombia, Argentina, Cuba and Perú). The red cluster links Venezuela with 4 countries (Colombia, Spain, Chile and the United Kingdom). On the other hand, 9 countries located on the periphery are not connected to the network: Brazil, Portugal, Costa Rica, Panamá.

Productivity by Institutions

Universities with the largest number of publications are Universidad del Norte, (Colombia) and Universidad Politecnica from Cartagena (Spain), each one with 5 documents; subsequently, with 3 documents are: for Spain, Universities of Rioja, Cantabria, Sevilla and Valencia, and for Colombia: Universidad Nacional. The biggest mention is for Universidad Politecnica of Cartagena, Spain (26), followed by Universidad de Valencia Spain (17); eight universities did not reach the average of 5 mentions, and the rest of them have one or two mentions.

Table 1. Productivity Authors, SME topic

Author	Documents	Mentions
Muñoz M.	4	15
Briozzo A.	4	7
Larrán Jorge M.	3	18
Pérez-González D.	3	8
Díaz A.C.	3	6
Vanegas J.G.	3	2
López M.	2	17
Herrera Madueño J.	2	16
Lechuga Sancho M.P.	2	16
Martínez-Martínez D.	2	16

Source. Authors

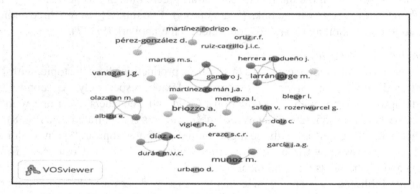

Fig. 7. Productivity by authors 2000–2018. Source: Scopus database 08/12/2019

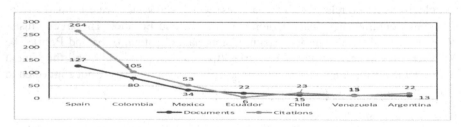

Fig. 8. Productivity by countries

The bibliometric map shows 30 universities selected from the minimum parameter of 2 documents per organization. Out of them, 23 clusters are made up; where the red presents three links of Spanish universities: Politecnica from Cartagena and Cantabria;

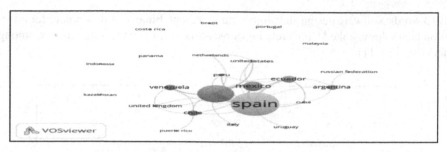

Fig. 9. Productivity by countries 2000–2018. Source: Database Scopus 08/12/2019

5 groups present 1 link, and the rest of universities are not linked to the network (see Fig. 10).

Co-occurrence Key Words

Finally, but as a vital element of investigation, object of analysis, is about co-words, by which the documentary similarity is measured through the word analysis and their relationship with documents in which the words appear according to their co-occurrence frequency.

After applying the cluster's algorithm, with a 5 value resolution parameter, 23 key words are generated among which the following stand out: SME concept 31,89% (129) of occurrences; others with less use: innovation (32), competitivity (22), information system (16), administrative knowledge (13), etc.; on the other hand, words as: project management (6), strategic planning (6), communication (5), profitability (5), financing (5), added up do not reach 2% of repetition.

Fig. 10. Productivity by institutions 2000–2018. Source: Database Scopus 08/12/2019

The resulting thematic groups are visualized on the bibliometric map, sorted through 5 clusters, with parameter adjustments, to the VOS viewer software, of minimum 5 co-occurrences. The first node, SME (purple colour) groups 22 relationships: innovation, competitiveness among others; two nodes, innovation (red colour) and competence (blue colour) grouped each one by 14 lines: where words competitivity, productivity, management, etc. are highlighted. The fourth group, information system (green colour) linked with 13 words: software design and project management. Finally, yellow colour for information technology, linked with 7 relationships: strategic planning, competitivity, among others (see Fig. 11).

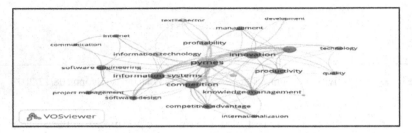

Fig. 11. Productivity by authors 2000–2018. Source: Database Scopus 08/12/2019

3 Conclusions

It can be noticed that despite finding heterogeneous and diverse information, investigations carried out in SME organizations, did not show lots of analysis oriented towards the field of project management. However, found information becomes a base line to conduct research processes, with the aim of helping this type of organizations to boost appropriation of knowledge, in order to improve their competitive positioning.

The evaluation of the thematic, investigations in SME, through the study of literature, from databases EBSCO and Scopus, in the period 2000–2019, allows the comprehension of the thematic structure of investigation lines conducted by the small and medium size enterprises; which on the one hand brings a working tool for researchers, and on the other hand, it brings trends for future development to strengthen the knowledge management.

The research shows the leadership in SME investigations on a worldwide level in Spain and, outstanding at a Latin-American level, Colombia and México; likewise, Spanish universities that have the highest productivity and mentions, helping SME, to improve results on project management and the same time on the knowledge management, by applying best practices.

The bibliometric analysis made along with the bibliometric maps, become a pioneering reference for SME investigations, improving the comprehension of this field of action.

References

1. DANE: Departamento Administrativo Nacional de Estadísticas. Boletín informativo. Colombia (2018)
2. Toro, J., Rosas, K.: Las decisiones financieras en las gerencias de las PYME. Estudio de caso –San Juan de Pasto, Colombia. Rev. Digital Obs. de la Econ. Latinoam., (163), Disponible en. http://www.eumed.net/cursecon/ecolat/co/12/tdre.Html

3. Beltrán, A.: Pyme: un reto a la competitividad. La Universidad, Universidad Externado de Colombia (2004)
4. Castiblanco, A.M.O., Jáuregui, E.M., Peláez, J.E.R., Hoyos, L.H.R.: Relación de la norma técnica colombiana icontec ntc5801 con los procesos de gestión de la innovación en las pyme del sector textil y de confección de Manizales-Colombia. Rev. Ing. Ind. **11**(2), 57–69 (2012). http://search.ebscohost.com.ezproxy.umng.edu.co/login.aspx?direct=true&db=asn&AN=89472265&site=ehost-live
5. Apia, R.A., Díaz, M.D.R.G.: Estrategias De Gestión Del Conocimiento Para Generar Ventajas Competitivas en Pequeñas Y Medianas Empresas en El Estado De México. Gestión y Estrategia, (46), 55–71 (2014). http://search.ebscohost.com.ezproxy.umng.edu.co/login.aspx?direct=true&db=asn&AN=110194839&site=ehost-live
6. Hernández, A., Marulanda, C.E., López, M.: Análisis de capacidades de gestión del conocimiento para la competitividad de PYME en Colombia. Inf. Tecnol. **25**(2), 111–122 (2014). https://doi-org.ezproxy.umng.edu.co/https://doi.org/10.4067/S0718-076420140 00200013
7. Quispe-Otacoma, A.L., Padilla-Martínez, M.P., Telot-González, J.A., Nogueira-Rivera, D.: Tecnologías de información y comunicación en la gestión empresarial de Pyme comerciales. Ing. Ind. **38**(1), 81–92 (2017). http://search.ebscohost.com.ezproxy.umng.edu.co/login.aspx?direct=true&db=asn&AN=122026286&site=ehost-live
8. Barrios-Hernández, K.D.C., Salinas, J.A.C., Olivero-Vega, E.: La gestión por procesos en las pyme de barranquilla: factor diferenciador de la competitividad organizacional. Inf. Tecnol. **30**(2), 103–113 (2019). https://doi-org.ezproxy.umng.edu.co/https://doi.org/10.4067/S0718-07642019000200103
9. Bustos, M., Arias, A.C.C., Bernal, M.C.P.: Un caso de gestión de la comunicación y la información en la Pyme manufacturera de calzado chiquitines. Rev. EAN, (69), 168–175 (2010). http://search.ebscohost.com.ezproxy.umng.edu.co/login.aspx?direct=true&db=asn&AN=82981352&site=ehost-live
10. Tañski, N.C., Fernandez-Jardón, C.M.: El Conocimiento tecnológico y la comunicación interempresarial como elementos del cambio en la gestión asociativa de las pyme de la foresto-industria. Brazilian J. Manage./Rev. de Adm. Da UFSM, **11**(1), 153–171 (2018). https://doi-org.ezproxy.umng.edu.co/https://doi.org/10.5902/19834659.13629
11. Gutiérrez-Diez, M.D.C., Aguilar, A.L.S., Howlet, L.C.P.: Gestión de conocimiento en PyME del sector servicios en la ciudad de Chihuahua. Nova Sci. **7**(15), 499–513 (2015). https://doi-org.ezproxy.umng.edu.co/https://doi.org/10.21640/ns.v7i15.314
12. Mejía, S.I.S., Peña, R.J.I., Moreno, M.C.E.: Modelo de sistema de información para apoyar la gestión ambiental proactiva en Pyme. Rev. EAN, (73), 116–135 (2012). http://search.ebscohost.com.ezproxy.umng.edu.co/login.aspx?direct=true&db=asn&AN=90462252&site=ehost-live
13. Mantulak-Stachuk, M.J., Hernández-Pérez, G.D.: Capacidades que contribuyen al pensamiento estratégico. Un enfoque en la gestión tecnológica en Pyme de la madera. Ing. Ind. **39**(2), 160–169 (2018). http://search.ebscohost.com.ezproxy.umng.edu.co/login.aspx?direct=true&db=asn&AN=130249422&site=ehost-live
14. La gestión ambiental preventiva en la actividad de las PYME prestadoras de servicios alimentarios para contribuir al desarrollo turístico del municipio de La Libertad. Masferrer Investiga: Revista Científica de La Universidad Salvadoreña Alberto Masferrer, **9**(2), 15–31 (2019). http://search.ebscohost.com.ezproxy.umng.edu.co/login.aspx?direct=true&db=asn&AN=136780425&site=ehost-live
15. Quezada-Torres, W.D., Hernández-Pérez, G.D., Suárez, E.G., Comas-Rodríguez, R., Quezada-Moreno, W.F., Molina-Borja, F.: Gestión de la tecnología y su proceso de transferencia en pequeñas y medianas empresas metalmecánicas del ecuador. Ing. Ind. **39**(3), 303–314

(2018). http://search.ebscohost.com.ezproxy.umng.edu.co/login.aspx?direct=true&db=asn& AN=132586093&site=ehost-live

16. Legendre, R.: Es La Inteligencia de negocio aplicable a las pyme? PUZZLE: Revista Hispana de La Inteligencia Competitiva **4**(17), 4–9 (2005). http://search.ebscohost.com.ezproxy.umng. edu.co/login.aspx?direct=true&db=asn&AN=25502979&site=ehost-live

17. Parra, C.M., Villa, V.M., Restrepo, J.W.: Gestión de la calidad con el modelo efqm en 10 pyme metalmecánicas de medellín. Rev. EIA, (11), 9–19 (2009). http://search.ebscohost.com.ezp roxy.umng.edu.co/login.aspx?direct=true&db=asn&AN=45266814&site=ehost-live

18. Delgado, J.V.L., Lima, M.E.C.: Gestión de calidad y toma de decisiones en pyme's del sector de medios impresos regionales del estado Lara, Venezuela. Compendium, **17**(32), 27–53 (2014). http://search.ebscohost.com.ezproxy.umng.edu.co/login.aspx?direct=true&db=asn& AN=103192230&site=ehost-live

19. Bañón, A.R., Sánchez, A.A.: Competitividad y recursos estratégicos en las Pyme. Rev. de Empresa, (17), 32–47 (2006). http://search.ebscohost.com.ezproxy.umng.edu.co/login.aspx? direct=true&db=asn&AN=23004542&site=ehost-live

20. Marulanda, C., López, M., López, F.: La cultura organizacional y las competencias para la gestión del conocimiento en las pequeñas y medianas empresas (Pyme) de Colombia. Inf. Tecnol. **27**(6), 3–10 (2016). https://doi-org.ezproxy.umng.edu.co/https://doi.org/10.4067/ S0718-07642016000600002

21. Mazurkiewicz, I.: The Management of projects in the small and medium-sized enterprise from an epistemological perspective. Rev. Negotium, **14**(40), 64–76 (2018). http://search.ebscohost.com.ezproxy.umng.edu.co/login.aspx?direct=true&db=asn& AN=132376825&site=ehost-live

22. Morantes, M.E.L., Ferrer, N.J.L., Parra, O.D.S.B., de Hernández, V.E.V.: Gestión tecnológica en pyme del sector textil del municipio maracaibo-estado zulia-venezuela. Utopia y Praxis Latinoamericana **23**(82), 64–84 (2018). http://search.ebscohost.com.ezproxy.umng.edu.co/ login.aspx?direct=true&db=asn&AN=132310870&site=ehost-live

23. Juárez, L.E.V., de Lema, D.G.P., Guzmán, G.M.: TIC y la gestión del conocimiento como elementos determinantes del crecimiento de la PyME. Investigación y Ciencia de La Universidad Autónoma de Aguascalientes **25**(70), 50–62 (2017). http://search.ebscohost.com.ezp roxy.umng.edu.co/login.aspx?direct=true&db=asn&AN=125767304&site=ehost-live

24. Rodríguez, N.(s.f.): Factores que limitan el crecimiento de las micro y pequeñas empresas en el Perú (Mypes). Recuperada de https://www.academia.edu/32847592/Factores_que_lim itan_el_crecimiento_de_las_micro_y_peque%C3%B1as_empresas_en_el_Per%C3%BA_ MYPES_

25. Torres, C.C.: Tarea pendiente: la gestión de recursos humanos en las pyme. Debates IESA, **19**(4), 22–25 (2014). http://search.ebscohost.com.ezproxy.umng.edu.co/login.aspx?direct= true&db=asn&AN=108920455&site=ehost-live

26. Urbano, D., Toledano, N., Ribeiro-Soriano, D.: Prácticas de gestión de recursos humanos y desarrollo de nuevos proyectos innovadores: un estudio de casos en las Pyme. Univ. Bus. Rev. (29), 116–130 (2011). http://search.ebscohost.com.ezproxy.umng.edu.co/login.aspx?direct= true&db=asn&AN=60840258&site=ehost-live

27. González, D.V., Hornig, E.S.: Modelo de administración de proyectos en pyme de servicios de ingeniería. Rev. Ing. Ind., **11**(2), 5–18 (2012). http://search.ebscohost.com.ezproxy.umng. edu.co/login.aspx?direct=true&db=asn&AN=89472262&site=ehost-live

28. Rodríguez, M.V.: Modelo de generación y transferencia de conocimiento para los procesos de dirección y gestión humana en pyme del sector cárnicos de la ciudad de cali. Ing. Ind. **30**(3), 1–6 (2009). http://search.ebscohost.com.ezproxy.umng.edu.co/login.aspx?direct=true&db= asn&AN=60258555&site=ehost-live

29. Rojas, W.O., Uribe, R.I.P.: Efectos de la gestión organizacional en la rentabilidad en pyme: evidencias empíricas y algunas consideraciones teóricas. Rev. EAN (69), 88–109 (2010). http://search.ebscohost.com.ezproxy.umng.edu.co/login.aspx?direct=true&db=asn& AN=82981347&site=ehost-live
30. López-Sevillano, A.M., Díaz-Piraquive, F.N., Rubén, G.C.: Trends in management of TI projects and CEO competence. Handbook of Research on Project Management Strategies and Tools for Organizational Success. IGI Global, 2020, p. 19–48. Web. 28 January 2020. https://doi.org/10.4018/978-1-7998-1934-9.ch002
31. Moreno-Monsalve, N.A., Diez-Silva, M., Diaz-Piraquive, F.N., Pérez-Uribe, R.I.: Handbook of Research on Project Management Strategies and Tools for Organizational Success, pp. 1–400 (2020). Hershey, PA: IGI Global. https://doi.org/10.4018/978-1-7998-1934-9
32. Rincón-González, C.H., Díaz-Piraquive, F.N.: Impact of project management offices on knowledge management. In: Moreno-Monsalve, N., Diez-Silva, H., Diaz-Piraquive, F., Perez-Uribe, R. (Eds.) Handbook of Research on Project Management Strategies and Tools for Organizational Success, pp. 166–195 (2020). Hershey, PA: IGI Global. https://doi.org/10. 4018/978-1-7998-1934-9.ch007

Benchmarking in Colombian Sterilization Departments

Mayra Samara Ordoñez-Díaz[1]([⊠]) (iD), Flor Nancy Díaz-Piraquive[2]([⊠]) (iD), and Yasser de Jesús Muriel-Perea[2]([⊠]) (iD)

[1] Fundación Universitaria de Ciencias de la Salud-FUCS and Sociedad de Cirugía de Bogotá-Hospital de San José, Bogotá, Colombia
msordonez@fucsalud.edu.co
[2] Universidad Catolica de Colombia, Bogotá, Colombia
{fndiaz,yjmuriel}@ucatolica.edu.co

Abstract. Quality tools allow improving health attention processes. Benchmarking is an effective tool because allows recognize success key factors to be replied in a specific sector. The sterilization department is the area in charge of reprocessing the necessary supplies for the care of patients in the institutions providing health services, hence good practices are important in this sector to guarantee patient safety and efficiency in the hospital service provision.

This investigation pretends to identify success key factors and high quality in eight sterilization departments in Colombia, from a comparative study. A multiple case study was carried out in recognized sterilization departments, with the application of a comparative evaluation tool based on AAMI and adjusted to the objectives, highlighting quality management, human talent management, information management and technology and process management. Results show the sterilization departments adaptation in quality management, human talent management, information and technology management and process management.

Sterilization departments in Colombia are adapting to the quality requirements of the environment, adjusting the operation to be cost-effective and consistent with the reality of the country. Leaders have a challenge to manage with quality and efficiency, although there is still progress in technological development and provide greater resources to the sector, the quality of the process and patient safety are guaranteed.

Keywords: Sterilization · Management · Benchmarking · Quality

1 Introduction

The sterilization department (SD) is defined as the unit of a health institution responsible for reprocessing the surgical medical supplies necessary for the provision health service, therefore, this department receives, inspects, conditions and sterilizes each device that allow his reuse [1]. The characteristics of this service allow it to be recognized as a functional unit at the hospital and independent level that requires quality tools that permit its efficiency and integration with other areas of knowledge [2].

© Springer Nature Switzerland AG 2021
L. Uden et al. (Eds.): KMO 2021, CCIS 1438, pp. 212–224, 2021.
https://doi.org/10.1007/978-3-030-81635-3_18

In Colombia, both the execution of the processes of the SD and the preparation of the professionals who lead this area are evolved according to technology worldwide development [3]. Today, leaders in charge of managing the SD are professional nurses or operating room nurses as it is called in European countries and in the United States, in Colombia and Latin America these professionals are called surgical assistants [4]. The development of strategies to adapt to technological change, have generated in Colombia a migration towards the systematization of the SD processes, both operational and administrative, for the optimization of decision making with the opportunity required by the clients, which is evidenced in positioned management models that can become references both nationally and internationally [5].

Within this framework Colombia has built a state of art used as a Latin American reference, on sterilization processes management, where the use and appropriation of information and communication technologies, has permeated its performance in collaborative environments that adapt to the technological and quality context, which demands globalization and the demand of the users it serves [6]. The interdisciplinarity required by the SD management reveals that benchmarking in health sector is an effective tool for quality improvement, [7] in Brazil the use of this tool improved the quality indicators of greater impact in SD, such as production and customer satisfaction, [8] and has been used successfully in other health sector areas and is considered a novel tool in this context [9].

In Colombia, health institutions must qualify their services through the national regulatory entity who establishes the minimum parameters for the provision of the service, this regulation is established with Resolution 2003 of 2009, which specifies minimum conditions of SD provision. [10] On the other hand, the institutions searching quality excellence in the services provision tend for the accreditation of the services, in Colombia it is done through ICONTEC which is recognized at Latin American level as the entity endorsed to carry out in addition, determine and control the high quality standards for the service provision [11]. In accordance with the regulation, quality processes and patient safety, an exploration was carried out in institutions providing health services in Colombia, with the purpose of identifying the key factors that have a high impact on quality processes to measure how it is the current competitive environment of the SD processes within the practice carried out in the institutions that have the prestige and high quality certifications in this country.

Within the methodology for quality improvement contemplated for SD in Colombia, the first phase executed is benchmarking with which the key factors of competition are defined, in a next phase these results of these factors will be applied in the SD that want to improve their structure and the processes quality with which to measure the impact of these factors. In studied cases, SD are strategically located near the operating rooms or has a direct channel of communication with this area and supports the hospital process or other processes that require decontaminated and sterilized supplies or instruments, provides its services to ambulatory processes, emergency and hospital of the chosen institutions daily throughout the year. It manages the reception, disinfection, processing, control and distribution of textiles (clothing, gauze, dressings, etc.), biomedical equipment and instruments sterilized in optimal conditions to all hospital services to be used on the patient. Institutions have documented operating procedures in the Quality

Management System, among which specifically three, refer to each sterilization method describing the activities to be carried out for each cycle, in order to ensure that activities are standardized and complied with by all the operators assigned to the process. These sterilization plants operate 24 h a day, 365 days a year.

1.1 Benchmarking

Benchmarking is defined as a quality tool that allows the comparison of key success factors, and has been used to improve efficiency, cost-effectiveness and quality in health services [12] This tool provides a clear signal of success or failure. In the 90s benchmarking has become one of the most popular tools of business management (Cox and Thompson, 1998; Foster, 1992; MacNeil and Rimmer, 1993; Richardson and Taylor, 1993) [13]. Benchmarking cycle begins with the identification of the benchmark, which should be highlighted in the studied area, then the selection of the relevant factors for comparison. The collection tool for the organization data is designed, the reference points are established, gap is analyzed and the actions for improvement are carried out. The collection tool for the data organization is designed, reference points are established, gap is analyzed and finally the actions for improvement are carried out (see Fig. 1), [14].

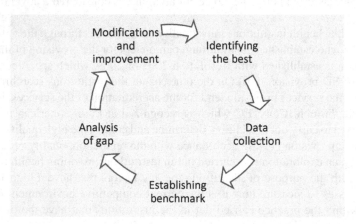

Fig. 1. Benchmarking cycle based on Harrington and Harrington. Source [15].

1.2 Comparison Attributes

The comparison attributes that are determined as key competition factors in the health sector within the sterilization area are related to the existence of a defined and structured quality system within the institution, as well as a process management that allows activities to be standardized within the service provision, a clear definition of the competence, preparation and personnel training in charge of the processes at all levels [16] and information management for traceability, generation of indicators and reports in a timely way and not least the technology management with preventive and corrective tools that contribute to service technovigilance (see Fig. 2), [17].

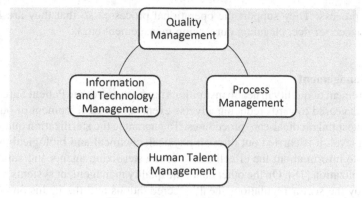

Fig. 2. Key competition factors

1.3 Process Management

A formulation of the process that facilitates its correct subsequent development is essential. Processes are the key activities that are managed to manage and/or direct an organization. The process map established for the S.D is exposed in Fig. 3.

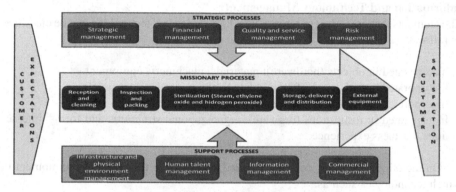

Fig. 3. Sterilization department process map [6]

- Strategic processes: Necessary for the maintenance and progress of the organization. (Strategic plan, quality plan, training plan).
- Missionary process: The care process that directly affects the user-patient is developed. (Global activities of clinical-assistance care).

- Support process: They support the operational processes so that they are fulfilled. (Maintenance service, cleaning, purchasing management etc.).

Quality Management

The measurement of quality in health institutions has been one of the Patient Safety Policy pillars and is geared towards reducing adverse events in the development of outpatient, surgical or hospital medical-care procedures. To guarantee the sterilization quality at the operational level, it is carried out through physical, chemical and biological indicators or controls to inform about the effectiveness of the sterilizing agents and validates the product sterilization [18]. On the other hand, the quality management systems have been supported by the sector regulations, health accreditations and the inclusion of quality tools and methodologies such as the evaluation of adverse events, risk management, Lean Healthcare and benchmarking [19].

Human Talent Management

This function determines how well a institution recruits, hires, trains, motivates, rewards, retains and replaces its human talent. People are a significant source of value, so businesses can create a competitive advantage with good human talent practices [20].

Information and Technology Management

The elements that are linked to information, knowledge and technology can be classified as follows:

- Incorporated in objects (hardware): materials, machinery, equipment.
- Incorporated in registers (software): data banks, procedures, manuals.
- Incorporated in man (humanware): knowledge, skills.
- Incorporated in institutions (orgware): organizational structures and forms, interactions, business experience.

On the other hand, they can be organized according to the phase or the moment in which technologies such as:

- Product technology: standards and specifications related to composition, configuration, properties or mechanical design, as well as quality requirements, presentation, among others.
- Process technology: conditions, procedures, details and forms of organization, necessary to combine inputs, human resources and basic means for the adequate production or provision of the service.
- Distribution technology: norms, procedures and specifications on packaging conditions, storage -temperature, humidity, maximum storage time, its form, among others-, as well as transportation and marketing.
- Consumer technology: instructions on the form or process of using a good service; responds to the requirements of the product, habits and traditions, among other factors [21].

2 Methodology

2.1 Objective

Identify success key factors and high quality in eight SD in Colombia, based on a comparative study in the best positioned institutions in the country, which will reveal the progress in the sterilization sector in accordance with global references and the regulatory guidelines state in national and international standards, in order to document the evolution, opportunities for improvement and adaptive methods that these services present in compliance with quality standards, in accordance with the resources that are managed from the Colombian health system.

2.2 Type of Study

A multiple case study was conducted in which the data obtained from each institution was compared. An investigation is carried out using methodological triangulation integrating the researcher's perspective and the data sources of the process in 8 SD of complex level IV health institutions that provide hospitalization, surgery, outpatient and diagnostic support services. It has a sterilization center that disinfects and uses three methods to sterilize medical instruments and supplies: hydrogen peroxide, ethylene oxide and autoclave.

2.3 Population

Population target was eight SD of health care institutions in Colombia. The inclusion criteria were SD recognized in the sector that had certification and/or accreditation of the sterilization process.

2.4 Instruments

An instrument designed by the AAMI (Association for the Advancement of Medical Instrumentation) was implemented, which identifies the success factors and allows a comparison between SD, next step was to adjust according to the key factors for the corresponding study. The survey was designed through the ®LimeSurvey tool. The survey had a total of 44 questions divided into four dimensions, institution identification, learning and growth, internal processes and stakeholders. The four dimensions of the survey

- Institution identification: Complex, localization, capacity.
- Learning and growth: Employees, induction and training, staff training and participation.
- Internal processes: Sterilization methods, production volume, management tools.
- Stakeholders: Clients, supplier selection, community impact.

2.5 Procedure

In total, 4 institutions were visited in the Bogotá city, 2 institutions in Cali, 2 institutions in Medellin, 1 institution in Bucaramanga. Subsequently, an approach was made with the institutions to obtain the necessary permits to gather the information and carry out the field visit to SD and the process leader.

3 Results

3.1 Institution Characterization

Institutions consulted are of medium and high level, all are located in the urban area and meet the minimum quality requirement through qualification, 4 of them are accredited, 2 with ISO certification and 2 with international accreditation (Joint Commission) (Table 1).

Table 1. Institution characterization

Complexity level	4 (62.5%) 3 (37.5)
Location zone	Urban (100%)
Certification level	Qualified (100%) Accredited (50%) ISO certified (25%) International certificate (25%)
Average beds	328.3
Average surgery rooms	11.2
Average surgical procedure (annual)	17.827
Number of workers in SD	Between 5 y 15

Source: Authors

The average number of beds of the institutions surveyed is 328.3, which reflects the large capacity and volume of patients, in the same way an average of 11.2 qualified surgery rooms, for a significant volume of surgery of 17,827 average. 75% of the institutions provide all medical-surgical services and the remaining 15% do not provide cardiovascular and ophthalmologic surgery.

3.2 Process Management

All SD consulted provide sterilization services for surgical instruments, including procedures for cleaning, decontamination, preparation and packaging, and sterilization of all surgical instruments in the operating room, distribution of supplies to other services, guarantee of transportation to their destination final, disinfection of transport pails of dirty or sterile material and support disinfection processes in the different hospital services to which the supplies are distributed. The sterilization methods used in these institutions are steam, hydrogen peroxide plasma, ethylene oxide and less frequent glutaraldehyde (see Fig. 4), with an average production of 1610 monthly packages and approximately 2147 annual loads.

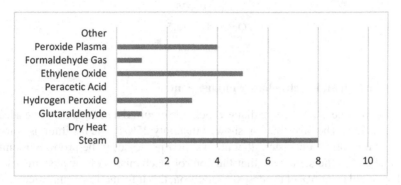

Fig. 4. Sterilization methods Source: authors

Information collection about SD operational process management, it was identified that the monitoring through the biological indicators in the loads is the method that guarantees the correct functioning of the sterilizers, it is only performed in the First load of the day in 62.5% institutions and only 37.5% institutions consulted use the biological indicators in all loads. Regarding the use of this monitoring in the implantable material (osteosynthesis material and joint replacements) 75% use it when an implantable material is processed and the remaining 25%, only do it when this material is used in an articular replacement.

3.3 Talent Human Management

SD consulted are mostly between 5 and 15 workers (75%) and those which has a bigger demand 20 workers or more. All institutions focus on training and updating staff, frequency which this training is carried out is monthly at 87.5% and remaining 12.5% every fifteen days. Topics explained in these activities are related with sterilization procedures (management of new technologies and training in process concepts, followed by training in patient safety, technology transfer and finally, less frequently, the issues of regulation are covered. of the sector, accreditation and management indicators, [22].

Monitoring used to guarantee workers' competence is an evaluation, which is carried out periodically according to institutional policies (Table 2). It is important to follow up as more than 60% of the plants delegate management and supervision responsibilities to at least one of the workers in the sterilization plant.

About training of the SD coordinators, identified that only 25% have training at specialization level in administrative areas. On the other hand, the most frequent postgraduate training of these professionals is in no formal continuing education since 87.5% have training in courses, 75% in knowledge upgrade and 62.5% in reinforcement workshops.

Table 2. SD workers competence evaluation

Frecuency	%
Anual	37,5
Montlhy	25
Biannual	25
Quarterly	12,5

Source: Authors

3.4 Information and Technology Management

Information volume and the immediacy which it is required demands SD have adequate data management. The investigation showed that only 25% of the institutions consulted have a digital information system that allows their processes to be properly monitored in real time and in the same way that the control mechanisms of the systems used are manual or verbal in 87.5% of the cases. In addition, this information is analyzed monthly and only 25% make improvement plans.

Leaders of the process must be a communication channel of the service with the environment, so that more than 80% of the leaders of the SD are members of committees or associations that regulate and train in this sector. Although SD has a direct relationship with other in-hospital areas, only 37.5% of the leaders hold or participate in committees or informational meetings of the processes, such as purchases, occupational health infections committee or institutional quality. All institutions at the head of the coordinator have a communication with the other dependencies for the improvement of service, being the main recipient the surgical service most of these verbally.

Technology management is an activity that is carried out exhaustively in SD since the supplies and instruments used in the different surgical procedures must be reprocessed, hence it is involved in the processes of selection and acquisition of related technologies with sterilization and devices for medical-surgical use, this participation is actively carried out in 87.5% institutions.

3.5 Quality Management

Frequent clients to whom the sterile material is provided are the surgical unit, intensive care unit, emergency department and the outpatient clinic (see Fig. 5). All S.D have a clear understanding of the customers' needs and goals and focus their management indicators towards achieving these objectives. In the same way, 75% SD uses the management indicators to define their improvement plans.

To ensure national and international standards are met, 87% of the institutions regularly review the policies and procedures with the current standards of regulatory entities in health and all of them are used as a basis for practices recommended by international entities such as AORN, AAMI, APIC, ISO, NFPA.

It is essential that SD has control over the quality of the inputs it receives for both, the area's own operation, such as the instruments and biomedical equipment that are

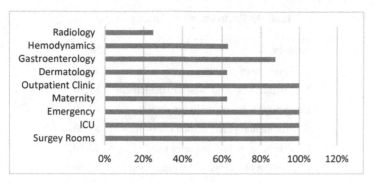

Fig. 5. SD clients. Source: authors

managed from there, the SD consulted require 75% quality certifications (INVIMA) to critical suppliers.

Reuse is a critical issue in sterilization, because the reprocessing of single-use devices implies a legal responsibility in the institutions providing health services, but it is also a way to lower operation costs. Regarding this issue, the institutions consulted carry out reprocessing of single-use inputs by 87.5%, and to ensure regularity in this process they have established an institutional reuse protocol.

To measure customer satisfaction, the SD have documented procedures for reporting compliance problems or complaints. 87.5% report adverse events related to the sterilization process and devices that come from this area in institutional formats that are based on the guidance provided by regulatory entities.

Actions realized in SD to reduce the environmental impact are mainly focused on the rational use of resources, management of dangerous and non-dangerous solid waste, measurement of environmental performance, strategies for reducing paper use, installation of energy saver equipment and make green purchases (Table 3). In the same way a direct impact on the population has been sought with the development of strategies for social promotion, 62.5% SD participates in activities such as days of surgical procedures for the vulnerable population, hands washing and patient safety campaigns, recycling and training on specific issues in institutions of less complexity.

4 Discussion/Conclusion

SD in Colombia are in process of transitioning from the management of manual information to the systematization of processes, to guarantee the quality processes required by national and international standards. Workers training in this area is essential to consolidate technology transfer, because even with the information management systems that were acquired by the institutions, it has not been possible to fully implement them due to resistance to change of tool.

Although the institutions take international standards as referents and seek high quality certification and accreditation in their process, the reality of the sector does not allow them to fully adhere to each good practices that are required for this, so it is still there is reprocessing or re-sterilization of single-use devices to operate with

Table 3. Environmental impact strategies

Strategy	%
Rational use of resources	100
Non-dangerous solid waste management	87,50
Dangerous solid waste management	87,50
Environmental performance measurement	87,50
Strategies for reducing paper use	62,50
Installation of energy saver equipment	62,50
Green purchases	50
Other technologies	0

Source. Authors

greater cost-effectiveness, and although the institutions try to make this process safe, they cannot guarantee devices suitability under the same conditions as guaranteed by the manufacturer.

SD are a high-cost center for institutions providing health services and functionally operation of these institutions depends to a large extent on the proper functioning of this area, due to the direct relationship in the sterile devices provision for procedures and service of the majority dependencies in institution. Training in administrative areas of the SD leaders can contribute to the improvement in process and quality management, although the sector deals with continuing education through participation in courses, workshops and upgrades, it is relevant raise awareness of the importance of deepening administrative knowledge, which allows finding efficient solutions to the problems of the sector.

Another remarkable attribute in the SD quality is the concern for the environmental impact that is generated from there, and the strategies that are developed to improve the waste disposal, the waste of the products necessary for the operation, and the management in the green purchases made for this area.

The dimensions in which the survey is framed allow us to explore the key factors of competition, so the dimensions of identification of the institution and internal processes account for the quality management and internal processes of the SD, while the dimension of learning and growth, identifies the characteristics of the factor of human talent management and stakeholders and finally within the four dimensions' information and technology management is evaluated.

It is important to recognize this work explores the best practices carried out in the most representative SD and presents the description of the results obtained against the reality of the institutions and the requirements of the high quality standards identified in literature, with conclusions according to this process, but it is necessary to continue with the application of the results in the institutions concerned, with the aim of measuring the effectiveness in each of the dimensions and comparing it with the starting point. This work is a reference for the implementation of key competition factors.

References

1. Acosta-Gnass, S., Stempliuk, V.: Manual de esterilización para centros de salud (2008)
2. Seavey, R.E.: Sterile processing accreditation surveys: risk reduction and process improvement. AORN J. **102**, 358–368 (2015). https://doi.org/10.1016/j.aorn.2015.07.005
3. Niel-Laine, J., et al.: Interest of the preliminary risk analysis method in a central sterile supply department. BMJ Qual. Saf. **20**, 698–703 (2011). https://doi.org/10.1136/bmjqs.2010.048074
4. ACITEQ, ACFIQ, COLDINSQUI: Perfil y Competencias del Profesional en Instrumentación Quirúrgica en Colombia. 52 (2014). https://doi.org/10.1017/CBO9781107415324.004
5. Carr, S., Mak, Y.T., Needham, J.E.: Differences in strategy, quality management practices and performance reporting systems between ISO accredited and non-ISO accredited companies. Manag. Account. Res. **8**, 383–403 (1997). https://doi.org/10.1006/mare.1996.0053
6. Rozo Rojas, I., et al.: Identification of key factors in the implementation of quality management practices in sterilization centers. In: Proceedings of the LACCEI international Multi-conference for Engineering, Education and TeCHIology (2017)
7. Rojas, I.R., et al.: Identificación de factores clave en la implementación de prácticas de gestión de calidad en centrales de esterilización. In: 15th LACCEI International Multi-Conference for Engineering, Education and Technology "Global Partnerships Development and Engineering Education, pp. 19–21 (2017). https://doi.org/10.18687/LACCEI2017.1.1.279
8. de Fátima Benato, F.S., Wilza Carla, S.: Analysis of quality indicators of central sterile supply departments at accredited public hospitals. Texto Context. - Enferm. **23**, 426–433 (2014)
9. Ettorchi-Tardy, A., Levif, M., Michel, P.: Benchmarking: a method for continuous quality improvement in health. Healthc. Policy **7**, 101–119 (2012). https://doi.org/10.12927/hcpol.2012.22872
10. Ministerio de Salud y Proteccion social: Resolucion 2003 de 2014 (2014)
11. Ministerio de Salud y Protección Social: Decreto Numero 903 De 2014 (2014)
12. Naranjo-Gil, D., Ruiz-Muñoz, D.: Aplicación del benchmarking en la gestión de la cadena de aprovisionamiento sanitaria: efectos sobre el coste y la calidad de las compras. Gac. Sanit. **29**, 118–122 (2015). https://doi.org/10.1016/j.gaceta.2014.11.003
13. Elmuti, D., Kathawala, Y.: An overview of benchmarking process: a tool for continuous improvement and competitive advantage. Benchmark. Qual. Manag. Technol. **4**, 229–243 (1997). https://doi.org/10.1108/14635779710195087
14. Dacosta-Claro, I., Lapierre, S.D.: Benchmarking as a tool for the improvement of health services' supply departments. Heal. Serv Manag. Res. **16**, 211–223 (2003). https://doi.org/10.1258/095148403322488919
15. Staiger, R.D., Schwandt, H., Puhan, M.A., Clavien, P.A.: Improving surgical outcomes through benchmarking. Br. J. Surg. **106**, 59–64 (2019). https://doi.org/10.1002/bjs.10976
16. Rozo-Rojas, I., Díaz-Piraquive, F.N., Ordoñez-Díaz, M.S., de Jesús Muriel-Perea, Y.: Quality measurement in sterilization processes at healthcare organization in Colombia using six sigma metrics. In: Uden, L., Ting, I.-H., Corchado, J.M. (eds.) KMO 2019. CCIS, vol. 1027, pp. 297–306. Springer, Cham (2019). https://doi.org/10.1007/978-3-030-21451-7_25
17. Sangthong, K., Soparat, P., Moongtui, W., Danchaivijitr, S.: Development of quality indicators for sterilization practices of the central sterile supply department. J. Med. Assoc. Thail. = Chotmaihet thangphaet. **88**(Suppl 1) (2005)
18. Stefan, R., Hermann, T., Mracek, M., Kopp, S., Steil, J.: Supporting workers and quality management in sterilization departments. In: van Berlo, A., Hallenborg, K., Rodríguez, J., Tapia, D., Novais, P. (eds.) Ambient Intelligence - Software and Applications. Advances in Intelligent Systems and Computing, vol. 219, pp. 137–145. Springer, Heidelberg (2013). https://doi.org/10.1007/978-3-319-00566-9

19. Ciarapica, F.E., Bevilacqua, M., Mazzuto, G., Paciarotti, C.: Business process re-engineering of surgical instruments sterilization process: a case study. Int. J. RF Technol. Res. Appl. **7**, 1–29 (2016). https://doi.org/10.3233/RFT-150070

20. Piteres Redondo, R., Cabarcas Velázques, M., Hernández Gaspar, H.: The human resource factor of competitiveness in the health sector. Investig. Innov. Ing. **6**, 93–101 (2018). https://doi.org/10.17081/invinno.6.1.2778

21. Guerrero Pupo, J.C., Amell Muñoz, I., Cañedo Andalia, R.: Tecnología, tecnología médica y tecnoslogía de la salud: algunas consideraciones básicas. Acimed **12**, 1–16 (2004)

22. Díaz-Piraquive, F.N., Rincón-Gonzalez, C.: Análisis cienciométrico de los stakeholders en la gestión de proyectos. In: "El talento humano como factor clave en el éxito de los proyectos" Editorial Publicaciones EAN, Bogotá (2019)

Global Export Strategy of the "Born Global" Companies, Business Modeling, and Dynamic Capabilities: Eight Knowledge Management Cases of Country and City Data Analytics

Jari Kaivo-oja[1,2], Theresa Lauraeus[1], and Mikkel Stein Knudsen[1,2(✉)]

[1] Kaziemieras Simonavicius University, Vilnius, Lithuania
[2] Finland Futures Research Centre, Turku School of Economics,
University of Turku, Turku, Finland
mikkel.knudsen@utu.fi

Abstract. In this article, we will discuss the export strategy of a company seeking to export its products and services to global markets. We note that the export strategy is always linked to the company's dynamic capabilities and business model. In this article, we present four basic business models, Business-to-Consumer, Business-to-Business, Business-to-Government and Business-to-Digital business models. As a company seeks to export its products and services overseas, it is worthwhile to implement an information management strategy that serves the export business strategy that links the export market to the business models and dynamic capabilities of the company. This article presents 8 different case examples of how the business model and export market analysis are combined. It should be emphasized that each company needs its own customized export strategy, where its export-related resources are realistic in relation to its export choices and scale. If there are not enough human and material resources, it is better to stay in the home market.

Keywords: Export strategy · Dynamic capabilities · Business model · Data filtering · Knowledge management

1 Introduction

Over the last decades, increasing internationalization of the market place has co-evolved with a flourishing scholarly interest how companies organize their export activities. However, quite weak theoretical foundations characterize traditional export strategy research. Today the most promising theoretical foundation is the dynamic capabilities perspective and its links to business modeling [1, 2]. The strategic choice of export country focus is very important, as it always affects what is the preferable business model design [2–4]. Key business model elements are: (1) value proposition (product and service, customer needs and geography/logistics), (2) revenue model (pricing logic, channels, and customer interaction), and (3) cost model (core assets and capabilities, core activities, and partner network).

© Springer Nature Switzerland AG 2021
L. Uden et al. (Eds.): KMO 2021, CCIS 1438, pp. 225–236, 2021.
https://doi.org/10.1007/978-3-030-81635-3_19

Companies that want to be successful in the challenging global business environment need to be able to react fast and flexibly to changes hard to predict beforehand. The global business environment has become a VUCA-environment: Volatile, uncertain, complex, and ambiguous [5]. The value of resilience and dynamism has been mightily illustrated during the COVID-19 crisis. Companies need strategic flexibility to understand changes in both demand and supply. Modularity is a means to gain this strategic flexibility. Modularity can be built, among many other things, on smart knowledge management of export strategy, business modeling, and dynamic capabilities.

Key elements of dynamic capabilities are [2]: (1) capability of sense (identify opportunities), (2) capability of seizing (design and refine the business model and commit resources) and (3) capability of transfer and deliver products and services (realign structure and culture).

In this way, export strategies, business models, and associated dynamic capabilities are interlinked.

2   Export Strategy, Business Models and Dynamic Capabilities

In recent years, there has been an emerging interest in the theory of *effectuation* [6, 7]. This theory suggests that entrepreneurs and new businesses choose their goals and actions with the use of given means under high uncertainty. Another key theme is firms need for continuous learning. The interest in effectuation illustrates the need for business research to find new answers for the new paradigms of modern operational VUCA environments. There is also need to find operational links between business modeling and export strategy formulations, in particular for newly established companies.

These links are often crucial to building a sustainable new business. In this article, we therefore look at different ways to evaluate export-oriented businesses' choices of choosing the right destination countries. A key research question is to find a strategic connection between business modeling, business models, dynamic capabilities and spatial export markets (Fig. 1).

Our article is motivated also by the surprisingly sparse amount of current literature linking effectuation with "learning by exporting". Both of these concepts have received significant attention in the academic business literature, yet very few studies attempt to link these concepts.

We illustrate aspects of this model with examples of initial analyses. The starting point for this article is a variety of alternative business models that a "born-global" company can choose to base its export business and strategy on [8, 9]. Such basic models are (1) Business-to-Business, (2) Business-to-Consumer, (3) Business-to-Government and (4) Business-to-Digital networks (e-business).

It is important for a company to plan its business model and export strategy carefully. Export operations always involve different business risks; it can be difficult, costly, and time-consuming. Few companies succeed perfectly in their export business. Economics and business literature have dedicated very much attention to international trade studies at the firm level, and there is a significant knowledge base on motivations and dynamics of when "born-global" companies decide to engage in international markets. Key issues in export strategy are (1) strong joint strategic decision and leadership about export,

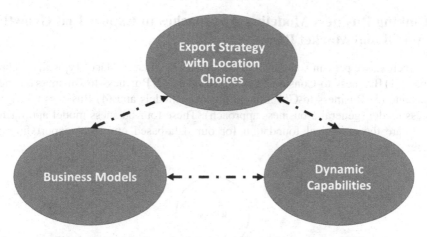

Fig. 1. Export strategy, business models and dynamic capabilities.

(2) knowledge management system of export strategy, (3) Blue ocean market segment (not Red Ocean market segment), (4) clear target market and segment definition, (5) good understanding of business model elements, (6) dynamic capabilities to implement company's export strategy, and (7) realistic budget for export strategy [2, 10–13].

Our study is tailored for "born global" companies, which adopt a global market approach from the beginning of their business management. Because markets are dynamic, companies need to have updated export filtering data analyses (see e.g. [14]). In this article, we have used data sets of the World Bank (2019), International Monetary Fund (2019) and the Economists Intelligence Unit (2019) [15–18]. Due to space limitations, we provide eight export filtering analyses for different business modeling purposes. Our aim is to demonstrate empirically power and usefulness of the export filtering analysis for companies.

On the basis of previous research we know that (1) economics of scale is fostered by exports, (2) higher competitive pressures in international markets leads to production and management improvements, (3) the improvement of innovation capabilities happens due to better access to technology and the possibility of cooperation with foreign companies in the production chain [19–22] (4) economies of scale derived from international trade dilutes fixed costs of innovation, especially R&D projects [23].

In general, knowledge-seeking is an elementary part of the export activities of companies. One key issue for "born global" companies to seek information and knowledge of foreign markets and understand market demand potential for their products. To scale innovations, production and service volume requires a broad understanding of the size of markets and potential demand. Careful knowledge-based analysis of export markets can reduce business risks and keep them manageable. Current research findings inform us that many sizes, efficiency and productivity gains occur before a company starts to export [24]. The learning-by-exporting processes of firms should always include knowledge management of demand-side potentials.

This is a key research question in this article.

3   Linking Business Modeling Approaches to Export-Led Growth and Global Market Place

In this section, we present some insight into the global market place. Typically companies have (1) Business-to-Consumer business models, (2) Business-to-Business business models and (3) Business-to-Government business models and (4) Business-to-Digital business model (general e-business approach). These four business model approaches (Fig. 2) are the analytical foundation for our data-based empirical export filtering analyses.

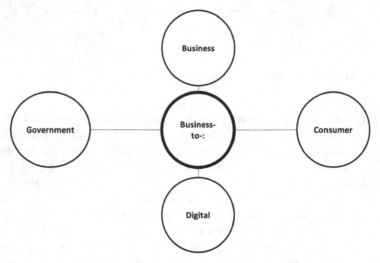

Fig. 2. Business models based filtering approach.

During the latest decades, much of business research has focused on business model innovation [25]. In recent years, this has also led to an academic focus on business model innovation through Industry 4.0 (e.g. [26–28] or "platform thinking" [29]. Forward-looking and inspired business modeling approaches are also looking towards "happiness based business models" [30] or "sustainable socially responsible and ethically oriented" business models [31]. These novel business modeling approaches can be integrated into our data-driven export filtering approaches with B-C, B-C, B-G and B-to-D business models.

4   Typical "Born Global" Business Models of Export Activity

It is good to remember that firms can select different approaches to their business model. In Table 1 we can see typical business models for exporting companies [13]. One elementary part of the export-led business strategy is to identify different business models.

When one or some of these business models are selected by a business owner, the key question is to define the spatial country-level focus of business strategy and business model.

Table 1. Business models of export-oriented firm

Business model	Definition
Direct sales	The company itself sells directly to foreign end customers either from the home country or locally
Resale	The company sells to resellers who sell directly or through intermediaries to the end customer
Licensing	The technology (or equivalent) is made available to another company to package it into a product or service to be sold for a license fee
Franchising	Foreign, the local operator operates in accordance with the business concept developed in the home country
Associated company	A foreign-owned company with a minority share sells a product or service locally to foreign customers
Joint venture	Equally owned (50/50) foreign company that sells in the local market
Subsidiary	Wholly owned (or majority-owned). The parent company has a majority of the shares, participations or other voting rights in the subsidiary company. The parent company is required to prepare a consolidated financial statement, which records the profit or loss generated by the foreign affiliate

5   Export-Focused Market Filtering: Eight Cases of Business-Model Based Filtering

In this section, we present a Business Model-Based Filtering Analysis (cf. [32]), based on three main criteria: The absolute size of the market, the size of the market per capita, and the examined sectors' shares of the total economy. This is an illustration of the first crude step of establishing a data-driven business-model based export strategy.

First export-focused filtering analysis is focused on *B-to-C-filtering*, where we use GDP, current prices (Purchasing power parity; billions of international dollars) as a filtering variable. In this market filtering we use IMF's future forecasting results are filtering data (IMF forecasts for 2019–2014, [17]). In Table 2, we report the filtering results of world regions.

In Table 3 we report potential GDP PPP filtering results of the world's top countries of potential GDP for years 2019–2024. This generic export filtering is based on the forecasting data of IMF for years 2019–2014 (IMF 2019).

The third filtering analysis is focused on B-to-C-filtering. In this case, we analyze the average % level of merchandise trade. This export filtering is based on the merchandise data of the World Bank (World Bank 2019) (Table 4).

Fourth filtering analysis is also focused on B-to-C-filtering. In this case, we analyze average mobile cellular subscriptions per 100 people in the world. The data is from the World Bank (2019). The results of this merchandise trade export filtering are the following. In Table 5 we report the top 20 countries. This filter is relevant when we discuss the challenges and hotspots of digital transformation in the world.

Table 2. Filtering 1. World regions. Average GDP PPP Potential, years 2019–2024, billions of dollars. Average GDP PPP Potential, 2019–2024, billions of dollars GDP, purchasing power parity (PPP), billions of international dollars, relevant B-to-C- and B-to-B and B-to-G models. Source: [17]

	World	163991
1	Emerging market and developing economies	101250
2	Asia and Pacific	78807
3	Advanced economies	62741
4	Emerging and Developing Asia	60181
5	Major advanced economies (G7)	46005
6	East Asia	44250
7	Western Hemisphere (Region)	37466
8	China, People's Republic of	33497
9	Europe	31936
10	North America	28711
12	European Union	25026
13	United States	23511
14	Western Europe	22341
15	South Asia	17602
16	India	14709
17	Latin America and the Caribbean	11729
18	Middle East, North Africa, Afghanistan, and Pakistan	11681
19	Southeast Asia	10983
20	Middle East and North Africa	10241

Fifth filtering analysis is also focused on B-to-C, B-to-B, B-to-G- and B-to-D export filterings. Typically economic risks are very diverse in high growth countries. In this special export trade case, we analyze the average real growth rate (%) in 2011–2020 in the world (IMF 2019). In Table 6, we again report the top 20 countries.

Sixth filtering analysis is also focused on B-to-B filtering. In this special case, we analyze the average size of the industrial market in relation to GDP in 2000–2017 in the world. The results of this filtering, shown in Table 7, are relevant for B-to-B- business modeling.

Sixth filtering analysis is also focused on *B-to-B filtering*. In this special case, we analyze average foreign direct investments (FDIs) in 2000–2018 in the world [16]. Table 8 shows the results of this filtering, which are relevant for B-to-B- business modeling. Typically high FDI level indicates good possibilities to B-to-B business activity in particular country and market.

Table 3. Filtering 2. Top countries. Average GDP PPP Potential, years 2019–2024, billions of dollars, average GDP PPP Potential, 2019–2024, billions of dollars GDP, purchasing power parity (PPP), billions of international dollars, relevant B-to-C- and B-to-B, B-to-G, and to B-D models. Source: IMF 2019.

1	Japan	6135	11	Turkey	2584
2	Germany	4880	12	Korea, Republic of	2528
3	Russian Federation	4789	13	Saudi Arabia	2146
4	Indonesia	4510	14	Spain	2136
5	Brazil	3908	15	Canada	2091
6	United Kingdom	3425	16	Australia and New Zealand	1780
7	France	3342	17	Egypt	1709
8	North Africa	3102	18	Iran	1652
9	Mexico	2975	19	Thailand	1604
10	Italy	2621	20	Australia	1547

Table 4. Filtering 3. Average % level of merchandise trade, B-to-C Business models, Merchandise trade (% of GDP), Average level in 2000–2018. Source: World Bank 2019.

1	Hong Kong SAR, China	331.6	11	Estonia	130.1
2	Singapore	277.0	12	United Arab Emirates	128.7
3	Aruba	238.4	13	Czech Republic	127.5
4	Belgium	167.8	14	Netherlands	124.5
5	American Samoa	157.9	15	Slovenia	121.7
6	Malaysia	154.6	16	Seychelles	119.2
7	Vietnam	139.0	17	Guyana	117.2
8	Hungary	135.8	18	Belarus	116.8
9	Slovak Republic	135.0	19	Lithuania	113.8
10	Lesotho	131.2	20	Cambodia	110.9

Seventh filtering analysis is also focused on *B-to-C filtering,* but in this special case, on expensive luxury goods and services. This city-level export filtering analysis provides information and knowledge about big cities, where consumers are rich and have a very high potential to buy luxury goods and adopt luxury brands. Results are shown in Table 9.

The eight and final filtering analysis is also focused on *B-to-C filtering,* but in this special case illustrates the market for very cheap consumer goods and services in cities. Table 10 shows the ten cheapest major cities in the world.

Table 5. Filtering 4. Mobile cellular subscriptions, B-to-C e-business models. Mobile cellular subscriptions (per 100 people), the average level in 2000–2018. Source: World Bank 2019.

1	Sint Maarten (Dutch part)	195.9	11	Lithuania	123.2
2	Macao SAR, China	190.4	12	Antigua and Barbuda	122.8
3	Hong Kong SAR, China	174.3	13	Singapore	122.3
4	British Virgin Islands	155.1	14	Austria	121.9
5	Montenegro	155.0	15	Finland	121.6
6	Cayman Islands	133.6	16	Israel	117.4
7	Italy	133.1	17	Estonia	113.8
8	Luxembourg	129.2	18	Bahrain	113.2
9	United Arab Emirates	128.7	19	Czech Republic	111.4
10	Curacao	128.6	20	Saudi Arabia	110.7

Table 6. Filtering 5: Real GDP growth (Annual percent change,), B-to-C, B-to-B, and B-to- G business models. Generic approach. The average real growth rate in 2000–2010. IMF database 2019. Source: IMF 2019.

1	Nauru	10.6	11	Côte d'Ivoire	7.1
2	Ethiopia	9.8	12	Cambodia	7.1
3	Turkmenistan	8.4	13	Bangladesh	6.9
4	Mongolia	7.6	14	Myanmar	6.7
5	Rwanda	7.5	15	Tajikistan	6.6
6	Uzbekistan	7.4	16	Ireland	6.5
7	Lao P.D.R	7.3	17	Guyana	6.5
8	China, People's Republic of	7.2	18	Panama	6.5
9	India	7.1	19	Philippines	6.3
10	Ghana	7.1	20	Vietnam	6.3

We have demonstrated eight cases of export-focused filtering. These are relevant examples of first steps towards data-based filters, which can help export-oriented firms to decide target countries and regions of export strategy. Of course, all companies need tailored filtering calculations of export regions and plans depending on their own business models and dynamic capabilities.

The very big challenge in the export strategy is separating the Blue Ocean Strategy from the Red Ocean Strategy [11]. As a logical result of this strategic dilemma, companies have to think carefully about the export portfolio of destination countries. As a result, exports are usually decentralized to several countries and regions. Also, a firm's product and brand portfolio of export can be decentralized. Often a firm's export strategy

Table 7. Filtering 6. Size of the industrial market in a relation to GDP. The average industry (including construction), value-added, % of GDP, years 2000–2017 (%), relevant B-to-B Industrial business models.

1	Libya	77.1	11	Angola	55.0
2	Equatorial Guinea	72.4	12	Azerbaijan	54.5
3	Congo, Rep	68.1	13	Gabon	53.9
4	Brunei Darussalam	67.2	14	United Arab Emirates	52.0
5	Qatar	66.2	15	Turkmenistan	50.3
6	Kuwait	66.1	16	Trinidad and Tobago	50.3
7	Timor-Leste	62.0	17	Algeria	49.7
8	Iraq	61.7	18	Puerto Rico	48.9
9	Oman	60.3	19	Venezuela, RB	47.1
10	Saudi Arabia	56.8	20	Bahrain	45.5

Table 8. Filtering 6. Foreign direct investment (FDI), net inflows (bn. BoP, current US$), average level, years 2000–2018 [16].

1	United States	260,630	11	Singapore	42,119
2	Netherlands	179,021	12	Belgium	41,206
3	China	160,631	13	The British Virgin Islands	37,416
4	United Kingdom	102,553	14	Spain	36,241
5	Germany	70,784	15	Australia	35,600
6	Hong Kong SAR, China	70,680	16	Russian Federation	29,830
7	Brazil	51,219	17	Mexico	27.519
8	Ireland	48,874	18	Cayman Islands	24,882
9	France	47,157	19	India	23,958
10	Canada	45,158	20	Switzerland	22,953

depends on the willingness of a firm to take risks in the short and long run. In the export filtering process, these strategic aspects can be taken into consideration by (1) filtering country rankings with different time-horizon data and calculating alternative forecasting scenarios of historical data sets and (2) classifying destination countries and regions to Red Ocean and Blue Ocean countries and regions.

Table 9. Filtering 7. The worldwide cost of living, luxury goods and services and luxury brands. B-C filtering, luxury goods and services in cities. The ten most expensive cities in the world. A ranking of the world's major cities. A report by the Economist Intelligence Unit (2019), Data year 2018.

Country	City	WCOL index (New York = 100)	Rank	Rank movement
Singapore	Singapore	107	1	0
France	Paris	107	1	1
China	Hong Kong	107	1	3
Switzerland	Zurich	106	4	−2
Switzerland	Geneva	101	5	1
Japan	Osaka	101	5	6
South Korea	Seoul	100	7	−1
Denmark	Copenhagen	100	7	1
US	New York	100	7	6
Israel	Tel Aviv	99	10	−1
US	Los Angeles	99	10	4

Table 10. Filtering 8. Worldwide cost of living, basic very cheap consumer goods and services in cities. B-C filtering, basic consumer goods, and services in cities. The ten cheapest cities in the world. A ranking of the world's major cities [19].

Country	City	WCOL index (New York = 100)	Rank	Rank movement
Venezuela	Caracas	15	133	−1
Syria	Damascus	25	133	1
Uzbekistan	Tashkent	33	131	−19
Kazakhstan	Almany	35	130	1
India	Bangalore	39	129	0
Pakistan	Karachi	40	127	0
Nigeria	Lagos	40	127	3
Argentina	Buenos Aires	41	125	−48
India	Chennai	41	125	1
India	New Delhi	41	123	1

6 Conclusions

Based on the 2018–2019 statistics (World Bank, IMF, the Economist Intelligence Unit), this article presents a variety of case studies of lists that can help business decision-makers reflect on a company's export strategy. These reported lists are a demonstration of knowledge management operation when a firm and especially "born global" firm wants to build a data-driven export strategy, which is tailored to their own business models.

This article states that a business model can be a Business-to-Consumer Model, a Business-to-Business Model, a Business-to-Government, or a Business-to-Digital Networks. These four alternative business model templates help business decision-makers develop a knowledge management system of different types of data filters linked to business models and associated dynamic capabilities.

It is good to find out information and knowledge about spatial and global market demand, especially as the company hopes to be a "born global" company. Unless the various demand-side aspects of the global market are properly addressed, the company can easily take too big business risks and expose itself to serious business failure.

It is always worthwhile for a company to tailor its own export strategy and data accounting systems carefully, already because of the strategic need to distinguish between Blue Ocean and Red Ocean strategies. Export filtering database must be updated regularly and results must be compared to previous filtering results to create a rolling export destination filtering system.

Acknowledgments. Authors gratefully acknowledge financial support from the Research Council of Lithuania (LMTLT) and the European Regional Development Fund implementing the project "Platforms of Big Data Foresight (PLATBIDAFO)" (project No. 01.2.2-LMT-K-718-02-0019).

References

1. Knudsen, T., Madsen, T.K.: Export strategy: a dynamic capabilities perspective. Scand. J. Manag. **18**, 475–502 (2002)
2. Teece, D.: Business models and dynamic capabilities. Long Range Plan. **51**, 40–49 (2018)
3. Osterwalder, A., Pigneur, Y.: Business Model Generation. A Handbook for Visionaries, Game Changers and Challengers. Oxford University Press, New York (2010)
4. Schön, O.: Business model modularity – a way to gain strategic flexibility. Controll. Manage. Rev. **56**(2), 73–78 (2012)
5. Kaivo-oja, J., Lauraéus, T.: The VUCA approach as a solution to corporate foresight challenges and global technological disruption. Foresight **20**, 27–49 (2018)
6. Djuricic, K., Bootz, J.-P.: Effectuation and foresight – an exploratory study of the implicit links between the two concepts. Technol. Forecast. Soc. Chang. **140**, 115–128 (2019)
7. Guo, R., Lv, X., Wang, Y., Chaudry, P.E., Chaudry, S.S.: Decision-making logics and high-tech entrepreneurial opportunity identification: the mediating role of strategic knowledge integration. Syst. Res. Behav. Sci. **37**, 719–733 (2020)
8. Gabrielsson, M., Manek Kirpalani, V.H.: Born globals: how to reach new business space rapidly. Int. Bus. Rev. **13**(5), 555–571 (2004)
9. Braunerhjelm, P., Halldin, T.: Born globals – presence, performance and prospects. Int. Bus. Rev. **28**(1), 60–73 (2019)
10. Chan, K., Mauborgne, R.: Blue Ocean Strategy. How to Create Uncontested Market Space and Make the Competition Irrelevant. Harvard Business School Press, Boston (2005)
11. Chan, K., Mauborgne, R.: Blue Ocean Shift. Beyond Competing. Hachette Books, New York (2017)

12. Lindič, J., Bavdaž, M., Kovačič, H.: Higher growth through the blue ocean strategy: implications for economic policy. Res. Policy **41**(5), 928–938 (2012)
13. Väisänen, K.: Väärää vientiä. Mene itään tai länteen, mutta tee kotiläksysi [Wrong export strategy. Go to East or to West, but make your homeworks]. Alma Talent, Helsinki (2018)
14. Dikova, D., Jaklic, A., Burger, A., Kuncic, A.: What is beneficial for first-time SME-exporters from a transition economy: a diversified or a focused export-strategy? J. World Bus. **51**(2), 185–199 (2016)
15. World Bank. Open Data (2019). https://data.worldbank.org/. Accessed 15 Oct 2019
16. International Monetary Fund (IMF). World Economic Outlook Databases and IMF Data Mapper (2019). https://www.imf.org/en/Publications/SPROLLS/world-economic-outlook-databases#sort=%40imfdate%20descending and https://www.imf.org/external/datamapper/NGDP_RPCH@WEO/OEMDC/ADVEC/WEOWORLD
17. International Monetary Fund (IMF). Coordinated Investment Survey (2019). http://data.imf.org/?sk=40313609-F037-48C1-84B1-E1F1CE54D6D5
18. The Economist Intelligence Unit. Worldwide cost of living. A ranking of the world's major cities. A report by The Economicst Intelligence Unit (2019). https://www.eiu.com/topic/worldwide-cost-of-living
19. Araújo, B.C., Salerno, M.S.: Technological strategies and learning-by-exporting: the case of Brazilian manufacturing firms, 2006–2008. Int. Bus. Rev. **24**, 725–738 (2015)
20. Aw, B.Y., Hwang, A.R.: Productivity and export market: a firm-level analysis. J. Dev. Econ. **47**, 313–332 (1995)
21. Clerides, S., Lauch, S., Tybout, J.R.: Is learning by exporting important? Microdynamic evidence from Colombia, Mexico and Marocco. Q. J. Econ. **113**(3), 903–947 (1998)
22. World Bank. East Asia Miracle. Oxford University Press, New York (1993)
23. Aw, B.Y., Roberts, M.J., Xu, D.Y.: R&D investments, exporting, and the evolution of firm productivity. Am. Econ. Rev. **98**, 451–456 (2008)
24. Wagner, J.: Exports and productivity. A survey of evidence from firm-level data. World Econ. **30**(1), 60–82 (2007)
25. Chesbrough, H.: Business model innovation. Opportunities and barriers. Long-Range Plann. **43**, 354–363 (2010)
26. Ibarra, D., Ganzarain, J., Igartua-Lopez, J.: Business model innovation through industry 4.0: a review. Proc. Manuf. **22**, 4–10 (2018)
27. Müller, J.M.: Business model innovation in small- and medium-sized enterprises: strategies for Industry 4.0 providers and users. J. Manuf. Technol. Manag. **30**(8), 1127–1141 (2019)
28. Müller, J.M., Buliga, O., Voigt, K.-I.: The role of absorptive capacity and innovation strategy in the design of Industry 4.0 business model: a comparison between SMEs and large enterprises. Eur. Manage. J. **39**(3), 333–343 (2021)
29. Hakanen, E.: Platform-based Exchange: new business models in technology industries. Aalto University Publication Series, Doctoral dissertations 250/2018. Aalto University, Helsinki (2018)
30. Fagerström, A., Cunningham, G. (eds.): A good life for all: essays on sustainability celebrating 60 years of making life better. Atremi AB, Mjölby (2017)
31. Geissdoerfer, M., Vladimirova, D., Evans, S.: Sustainable business model innovation: a review. J. Clean. Prod. **198**(10), 401–416 (2018)
32. Kaivo-oja, J., Knudsen, M.S., Lauraeus, T.: Coping with technological changes: regional and national preparedness in face of technical change. In: Collan, M., Michelsen, K.-E. (eds.) Technical, Economic and Societal Effects of Manufacturing 4.0: Automation, Adaption and Manufacturing in Finland and Beyond. Palgrave McMillan, Cham (2020)

The Moderator Effect of Emotional Labor Among Organizational Innovation and Perceived Organizational Support on Department Store Floor Managers' Job Performance

Yun Wang[✉]

Department of Fashion Design and Management, National Pingtung University of Science and Technology, Pingtung, Taiwan, R.O.C.
yunw@mail.npust.edu.tw

Abstract. In the face of rapid changes environments, department stores must seek ways to survive in the market. This study addressed the topic on the influence of organizational innovation (OI), perceived organizational support (POS), and emotional labor (EL) on department store floor managers' job performance (JP). The participants of this study were department store floor managers from Southern Taiwan. Data were collected by using purposive and snowball sampling method, total 251 effective questionnaires were returned. Data analysis included descriptive data analysis, factor analysis and reliability analysis, Pearson's correlation and regression analysis. The main results were as follows: 1. Department stores' organizational innovation and floor managers perceived organizational support have positive effects on their job performance. 2. Department store floor managers' deep acting of emotional labor has a moderating effect on OI and JP relationship. 3. Department store floor managers' deep acting of emotional labor has a moderating effect on POS and JP relationship.

Keywords: Organizational innovation · Perceived organizational support · Job performance · Emotional labor · Surface acting · Deep acting · Department store floor managers

1 Introduction

As the global economic trend has changed, Taiwan has shifted from traditional agriculture to construction and production industries, and then to service industries. There were 6.79 million employed in the service industry accounting for 59.38% of the total employment in 2018 [1]. Department stores in Taiwan have been increasing their turnover since 2009. Turnover in 2015 was NT\$ 318.9 billion, an increase of 4.2% per year, which is growing for 7 consecutive years [2]. Department stores belong to the general merchandise sales industry, which is defined as: "a retail store engaged in the sale of a variety of merchandise products in a non-specific monopoly form" [3]. Taiwan's business mode of

© Springer Nature Switzerland AG 2021
L. Uden et al. (Eds.): KMO 2021, CCIS 1438, pp. 237–251, 2021.
https://doi.org/10.1007/978-3-030-81635-3_20

department store is based on the "counter system" which the store public facilities, environmental atmosphere creation and counter investment promotion plan are integrated and planned by department store. Department store would draft strategies such as target customers, product combinations, floor composition, service functions, etc., and draft contracts according to their set conditions and solicit cooperative partners to participate in operations. Participating manufacturers must accept the management supervision of the department store and cooperate with the overall operating policy. They should bear the assigned business goals and pay management costs at the same time. If the partner company violates the department store's policies or fails to achieve the expected business goals, the department store has the right to terminate their contracts [4]. Due to market competition department stores are stressing in satisfy customer, consequently, the department store floor managers not only need to manage, communicate with the partner companies' business but also assist to settle the customers complain. In order to achieve the corporate emotional norms such as "be polite, keep smiling, customer is always right", even in unpleasant situations with unreasonable customers' requests they must pretend and show appropriate emotional state. Once they fail to meet the needs of customers, they will encounter emotional conflicts. Emotional labor is the process of managing feelings and expressions to fulfill the emotional requirements of a job [5]. In order to achieve the desired performance of the organization, they must express appropriate emotional behaviors. When the emotions felt by employees go against the concept of emotional expression required by the company, they will express their true emotions through "surface acting" or "deep acting."

In the era of the knowledge economy, the competitive advantage of an organization comes from the organization's continuous generation and application of new knowledge in order to respond to the rapidly changing environment. Organizational innovation (OI) is a novel concept that can be used to initiate or promote a product, process, or service to enhance organizational effectiveness [6]. For department store floor managers, the interactive interpersonal networks are the directors and colleagues in the organization. By caring for each other would influence behavior, the higher the organizational support perceived by employees, the higher the positive mood they feel. A study found perceived organizational support (POS) can increase employee happiness and affect JP. If an enterprise expects sustainable operations and employees work harder for enterprise, they should be rewarded, cared and respected. Employees must be given the necessary support and assistance to achieve good job performance [7]. A study of retail service firms found POS attenuated the negative effects of the emotional labor/job satisfaction and emotional labor/performance relationships [8].

This research takes department store floor managers as the research object and explores the impact of department store organizational innovation and POS of floor managers on job performance. In addition, whether the emotional labor of floor managers have moderating effects on the relationships between OI/JP and POS/JP. It is hoped that this research will provide retail industry and academia with a reference basis for evaluating human resource management and create the best benefits for the department store industry.

2 Literature Review

2.1 Organizational Innovation (OI)

The most effective way to maintain an organization's competitive advantage in order to enable the organization to operate sustainably is through constant change and innovation while facing rapid changes in the environment. "Innovation" is not only an important ability of an individual, but also the key to the survival of an organization. Therefore, OI is mainly to improve the work efficiency of the organization's employees or achieve the goals, and then improve or enhance organizational performance. OI is the intentional introduction and application of new methods in the ideas, processes, products, and procedures of roles, groups or organizations [9]. In the process of solving the problem, OI activities involved product design, product innovation functions, department coordination, company resources, structure and strategy coordination, etc. [10]. OI is the overall behavioral manifestation of employees in the organization to find, establish, execute, and successfully implement ideas for new technologies, techniques, or new products to become useful products or services [11]. Researchers summarized the research on organizational innovation, and considered that OI is divided into four perspectives as follows:

1. Product Perspective: New products produced or designed by the organization. Product perspectives measure organizational innovation by tangible and specific products. Scholars even prejudged organizational innovation with new products, technologies, and services [12, 13].
2. Process perspective: Identify organizational innovation as the "process" of overall innovation, not the "outcome" of the product perspective. The OI process is divided into five stages: setting an agenda, setting procedures, drawing up detailed execution goals and generating ideas, creative testing and implementation, and results evaluation [14]· Scholars believed that the process of organizational innovation includes multiple stages such as problem discovery, seeking assistance from resources, and completing problem solving [15].
3. Binary perspective: Using a dual view of products and processes to define OI, it's a complex problem-solving process that includes diverse concepts, not only products but also creative processes. Therefore, organizational innovation is defined by the process of the organization's new products, services, and creation, or the creativity of existing technologies, concepts, and methods [16].
4. Multiple perspectives: Scholars consider that OI from the perspective of products or processes is mostly focused on the technological innovation, however the management innovation of policies or programs are ignored. OI should include multiple indicators. It should be one of the activities that is naturally generated within the organization. The activity should be new to the organization, and it can be equipment, systems, policies, programs, processes, products and services [17]. Therefore, scholars advocate technological innovation (including products, processes, and equipment) and management innovation (including systems, policies, programs, and services) to define OI. The pattern of OI in the service industry was divided into four aspects: product/service innovation, process innovation, internal organization innovation, and external relationship innovation [18].

2.2 Perceived Organizational Support (POS)

Organizational support is a concept of loyalty. The organization's commitment and loyalty to employees does affect employee behavior. Based on the theory of social exchange, POS was whether the organization would reward employees' efforts and to meet the needs of employees' appreciation and recognition [19]. Its organization attaches importance to employee contributions and cares for employees' well-being will serve as a basis for employees to measure organizational support. POS was defined as the overall perception aggregate formed by employees' awareness of their contributions in organization, and whether the organization truly cares about employee benefits. It is also believed that POS will enable employees to (1) perform their duties, (2) perform emotional and computational investment in the organization, and (3) innovate to meet organizational expectations even in the absence of direct rewards or praise. POS is a subjective judgment and cognition of employees. When employees perceive the organization's support, whether the organization provides real compensation or emotional needs, the employee's feelings and induction can evaluate the level of support provided. This will cause employees perform in favor of their organizational behavior [20].

2.2.1 Theory of Perceived Organization Support

The underlying psychological mechanisms of POS are the concepts of "social exchange theory", "psychological contract theory", "effort-reward expectation theory" and "social emotional demand theory" [19].

1. Social-exchange theory was first proposed by Homans scholars at Harvard University to explore the exchange behavior between people. Human beings are willing to continue certain behaviors in order to survive, because these behaviors have been proven to be rewarded in experience. Regardless of whether this reward is tangible or intangible, the process of exchange behavior is exchanging rewards. The core of the theory of social-exchange is the norm of reciprocity. To get good treatment from others, it is also necessary to actively respond to each other [21]. Therefore, based on the relationship of the principle of reciprocity, employees will give effort and show loyalty to the organization as a substantial reward. Such as raises, benefits, or social emotional responses, such as being cared for and appreciated by supervisors.
2. Psychological contract theory is generally divided into transactional contracts and relational contracts. The psychological contract is "the beliefs and expectations that employees hold about mutual responsibilities and obligations between employees and the organization." Employees think what they should do for the organization, what the organization should do for employees, and what should be paid back to employees [22]. Transactional contracts are stable and narrow; Relational contracts are deeply embedded in social relations networks, especially in considerations related to interpersonal relationships, social emotions, and value bases [23].
3. Effort-reward expectation theory proposed that when employees POS, they will increase employee participation and performance through two effort-reward expectancy and affective attachment to achieve organizational goals. The expected reward will in turn make employees think that the organization attaches importance to employees' contributions, so that employees will have a psychological reward

for the organization. When employees have a positive emotional attachment to the organization, they'll be willing to contribute to the organization [20].

4. Need for social emotion theory: Based on the social-exchange theory, receiving social emotional support will increase personal work effort, and perceived organizational support can meet a variety of need for social emotion. And whether individuals will reward the organization with good performance will increase as social emotional needs increase [20]. When the individual's emotional needs are stronger, the value of POS and the individual's obligation to reciprocate the organization with good performance are also higher. Therefore, meeting the social and emotional needs of employees will motivate employees to work harder to give back to the organization's obligations, and this obligation will drive the employees' performance.

2.3   Emotional Labor (EL)

Emotional labor is the process of managing feelings and expressions to fulfill the emotional requirements of a job. More specifically, workers are expected to regulate their emotions during interactions with customers, co-workers and superiors [5]. Hochschild believes that under organizational norms, when service personnel are required to express an emotional state that is biased from their actual feelings, they will have emotional dissonance. At this time, in order to meet the requirements of the organization, employees must engage in some degree of disguise. According to the degree of disguise, it can be divided into "surface acting and deep acting". Surface acting occurs when employees display the emotions required for a job without changing how they actually feel [5]. Deep acting is an effortful process through which employees change their internal feelings to align with organizational expectations, producing more natural and genuine emotional displays [24]. Emotional regulation theory defines the emotional labor as employees regulate emotions feelings and emotional expression, the emotional labor is emphasizing on the process of how employees experience and express emotions as a physiological arousal and awareness [25]. Surface acting employees change themselves in external emotional performance, which shows behaviors that conform to organizational norms; deep acting employees will find ways to control their inner self-feelings and adjust their performance of external and internal emotions to be consistent. The emotional regulation involved behind the two psychological mechanism is not the same, surface acting is less likely to have an impact on inner emotions. Although the underlying processes differ, the objective of both is typically to show positive emotions, which are presumed to impact the feelings of customers and bottom-line outcomes (e.g. sales, positive recommendations, and repeat business) [24, 25].

2.4   Job Performance (JP)

Job performance (JP) is the criterion for assessing the achievement of an organization's goals which has been an issue of concern to organizations from the 19th century to the present day. Enterprises are composed of employees, and whether employees can reach their full potential has a great impact on the productivity and profitability of enterprises. However, at different points in time, even for the same organization, there will be different performance measures and value judgments of effectiveness. JP is the behavior all about organizational goals which is based on the individual's contribution. It has five approaches to express performances: (1) Achieve the organization's tasks; (2) Voluntarily engage in work outside of his or her own status; (3) Become assisting peers or customers; (4) Follow the organization's work rules and operating procedures; (5) Fully support the organization's policies and goals [26]. Others believed that job performance is based on the standards set by the employees. Evaluate the effectiveness of the tasks or roles given to the corporate group or organization by showing whether the quality or quantity of work achieved the goal [27].

2.4.1 Evaluation of JP

The goal of business operation is to improve business performance. It is not only the direction that managers strive to pursue, but also the overall performance of the company's goals. In order to maximize the effectiveness, performance evaluation plays an important role in management. There are several ways to evaluate employee performance [28]:

1. The JP of the employees evaluated by their direct supervisor. It is a common method in the workplace. Supervisors have the best position to observe employees.
2. The JP of the superior evaluated by subordinates. Employees have frequent contact with supervisors, it is feasible to evaluate supervisors' management performance. However, there must be a complete anonymous supporting plan to protect subordinates due to concerns about retaliation by the supervisor afterwards.
3. Peer evaluation- The most frequently interacted employees are colleagues in the same team. Peer review is the most direct JP evaluation. However, it should be considered that employees are less trained in JP evaluation, and there may be situations where colleagues shield each other.
4. Employee self-evaluation- Employees themselves evaluate their performance at work, so that employees clearly understand what they expect to achieve. If the criteria are set, employees are suitable for self-evaluation, but this method often causes employees to overestimate self-performance and cause errors.
5. Employees evaluated by customers- Customer response has a decisive influence on the company's development. It is necessary for customers to evaluate employees, so customer opinions should be included in job performance evaluation.
6. 360° feedback- A "multiple-source multiple-rater feedback" technology which through the process of collection and analysis of multiple data to assist individuals to grow, develop or act as a way to evaluate individual performance in order to achieve a fairer evaluation. 360-degree feedback pays more attention to the skills needs of cross-department and organization, because the evaluation targets include themselves, superiors, subordinates, colleagues and external related personnel [29].

In the study of organizational behavior, the individual employee's contribution level is often measured by the employee's JP. Everyone's perception or emphasis on JP is different, and the organization will set an equitable reward and punishment system based on the employee's JP. If the employees' efforts within their ability can be rewarded with satisfactory results under the performance evaluation, they can achieve the expected results.

2.5 Relevant Research

A study of selected manufacturing companies in Lagos metropolis, Nigeria confirmed that organizational learning had a positive correlation with OI; OI in turn had positive correlation with organizational performance and organizational learning also had positive correlation with organizational performances [30]. An empirical study provide support for the direct impact of POS on JP [31], other studies reveal mediation roles underlying the relationships between POS to performance outcomes, such as work engagement and organization identification [32, 33]. Other research found POS would improve employees' happiness, while happiness is an intermediary variable between POS and JP of full-time employees in Taiwan [7]. A study of retail service firms found perceived organization support (POS) attenuated the negative effects of the emotional/job satisfaction and emotional labor/performance relationships [8]. Chi examined various types of service firms and found: (1) when perceived supervisor support was high, surface acting (SA) was positively related to customer consideration in service; (2) high coworker support can strengthen the positive relationship between deep acting (DA) and adequate responses; and (3) the negative relationship between DA and turnover intentions [34].

Other study found the higher the employee's recognition of their role at work, the more they will have DA in emotional labor at work, and therefore show better innovative behavior. Additionally, SA in emotional labor has no relationship with innovative behavior. However, members working in a high-competitive organization will have a higher positive impact on SA and innovative behavior than members working in a low-competitive atmosphere [35].

Base on previous review of literature, the research hypotheses would state as:

H1: Department store OI would have a significant positive impact on employees' JP
H2: Department store employees' POS would have significant positive impact on JP
H3: Department store employees' emotional labor of surface/deep acting would have moderating effects on OI and JP relationship.
H4: Department store employees' emotional labor of surface/deep acting would have moderating effects on POS and JP relationship.

3 Research Methods

3.1 Research Framework

Based on the review of literature, this research would examine the moderation roles of surface/deep acting of EL between OI and POS independent variables and JP dependent variable. The research hypotheses are depicted in Fig. 1.

3.2 Sample and Questionnaire

The subjects are employees who have worked more than three months in department store floor management units in Tainan, Kaohsiung and Pingtung cities which locate in southern Taiwan. Data were collected from seven department stores during November 7th through December 16th, 2017, using purposive and snowball sampling methods. A

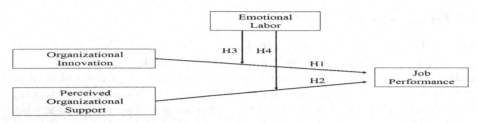

Fig. 1. Research framework

total of 280 questionnaires were sent out and 251 valid questionnaires return with the effective questionnaire rate was 89.6%. All the questionnaire was measured by using a seven-point Likert scale from 1 (*very disagreeable*) to 7 (*very agreement*). OI scale was adopted from previous research with total 15 questions which were divided into technological and management innovation factors [36]. POS scale was adopted from Shanock and Eisenberger [37] short version which was developed by selected some questions from original Eisenberger and Huntington scale [19]. It consists 6 questions of organizational support implications which including organizational care, employee well-being and objectives etc. EL scale was adopted from Grandey [25] with 5 questions in surface acting and 6 questions in deep acting. Twelve questions in JP scale were divided into task performance and contextual performance [38].

4   Results and Analysis

4.1   Sample Characteristics

According to the sample demographic, the majority employees work in department store are female (70.9%) age between 26–32 years old (51%), not married (74.1%). Most of them have College degree (92.8%) with average monthly salary less than NT$30,000 (49.8%) with job tenure less than 3 years (46.6%) follow by 4–8 years (35.1%).

4.2   Factor Analysis and Reliability

The exploratory factor analysis with oblique rotation was conducted to determine an appropriate number of factors and the pattern of factor loadings primarily from the data. The result of OI for Bartlett spherical analysis ($X^2 = 2224.919$, p $< .001$) is significant, and the KMO value equal to .931, indicating that it is suitable for factor analysis. Items 5 and 6 were deleted because cross-loading. Two factors were extracted, "Management Innovation" which had 41.81% variance explained and "Environmental Process Innovation" which had 29.5% variance explained, and the overall cumulative variation was 71.31%. The management innovation α value was 0.93, the environment process innovation's α value was 0.83, all greater than 0.7 indicating a high degree of confidence in this research variable. The result of POS for Bartlett spherical analysis ($X^2 = 889.674$, p $< .001$) was significant, and the KMO value equal to .897, indicating that it is suitable for factor analysis. One factor was extracted with total 68.23% variance. The α value of POS was 0.91, indicating a high degree of confidence.

The result of EL for Bartlett spherical analysis ($X^2 = 1429.695$, p < .001)is significant, and the KMO value equal to .848, indicating that it is suitable for factor analysis. Two factors were extracted namely "surface acting" and "deep acting". The variance explained by surface acting was 32.91%, deep acting was 30.94%, and the overall cumulative variation was 63.86%. The surface acting α value was 0.89 and the deep acting α value was 0.85 indicating a high degree of confidence in this research variable. The result JP for Bartlett spherical analysis ($X^2 = 1538.442$, p < .001) is significant, and the KMO value equal to .896, indicating that it is suitable for factor analysis. Items 7 was deleted because cross-loading in two factors. The results extracted two factors, named "task performance" with 36.12% variance explained and "contextual performance" with 26.17% variance explained and 62.29% of the overall cumulative variation was 71.31%. The task performance α value was 0.90, the contextual performance α value was 0.79, all greater than 0.7 indicating a high degree of confidence.

4.3 Pearson Correlation Analysis

The means, standard deviations, and bivariate correlations of research variables are presented in Table 1. Research variables' means are between 3.13 and 5.79 which indicating most department store employees believe that their company is highly innovative, perceives high level of organization support and evaluate themselves have high job performance. Significant relationships were found among the research variables: The dependent variables, OI and POS, were positively correlated with the dependent variable JP (OIr = .50, p < .01; POSr = .44, p < .01) and EL DA (OIr = .51, p < .01; POSr = .47, p < .01). Emotional labor SA had negative relationships with OI (OIr = −.26, p < .01), POS (POSr = −.31, p < .01), and EL DA (r = −.29, p < .01).

Table 1. Means, standard deviations and correlations among variables

Variable	Mean	SD	1	1a	1b	2	3a	3b	4
1. OI	5.64	0.67	1						
1a. OI1	5.79	0.69	.88**	1					
1b. OI2	5.55	0.75	.96**	.71**	1				
2. POS	5.60	0.72	.66**	.58**	.62**	1			
3a. EL SA	3.13	0.87	−.26**	−.27**	−.23**	−.31**	1		
3b. EL DA	5.74	0.59	.51**	.48**	.47**	.47**	−.29**	1	
4. JP	5.99	0.52	.50**	.46**	.44**	.44**	−.33**	.46**	1

Note: Listwise excluded, **p < .01, two-tailed. OI1- Environmental Process Innovation, OI2-Management Innovation; EL SA- emotional labor surface acting, EL DA- emotional labor deep acting

4.4 Regression Analysis

Simple regression analysis was conducted to examine hypotheses 1 and 2. Results are shown in Table 2 indicated that both OI and POS have significant positive effects on job performance, therefore hypotheses 1 and 2 are supported. Afterward, hierarchical moderated multiple regression analysis [39] was used to test hypotheses 3 and 4. We first entered OI and POS independent variables to perform regression analysis on JP, and then entered SA/DA of the EL as the moderators. In the final step we entered the interaction term (centered SA/DA * centered OI/POS) to examine the moderating effects.

Table 2. Regression analysis of OI and POS on Job Performance

Variable	df	β	F	R2
Independent variable: OI	248	.284***	45.768***	.270
Independent variable: POS		.143**		

Note: $N = 251$. Unstandardized regression coefficients from the last step. ***$p < .001$, **$p < .01$

1) SA/DA of EL and OI have an interactive effect on JP
(a) Surface acting of EL: The results are shown in Table 3, both the OI ($\Delta R^2 = .247$, $p < .001$) and surface acting of EL ($\Delta R^2 = .045$, $p < .001$) had main effects on employees' job performance. The interaction term of OI and SA didn't have significant incremental portion of variance ($\Delta R^2 = .007, p > .05$).

Table 3. Hierarchical moderated regression analysis of SA on Job Performance

Variable	β	df	F	R2	ΔR^2
Step 1: Independent variable OI	.224***	249	81.79***	.247	.247***
Step 2a: Moderator variable surface acting	−.122***	248	51.15***	.292	.045***
Step 3: Interaction term OI * SA Constant	.042 5.999***	247	35.09***	.299	.007

Note: $N = 251$. Unstandardized regression coefficients from the last step. ***p < .001

(b) Deep acting of EL: The results are shown in Table 4, both the OI ($\Delta R^2 = .247$, $p < .001$) and deep acting of EL ($\Delta R^2 = .056$, $p < .001$) had main effects on employees' job performance. The interaction term of OI and DA explained a significant incremental portion of variance ($\Delta R^2 = .014, p < .05$) in job performance.

Therefore, hypothesis 3 was partial supported, the employee's job performance was dependent upon the level of organization innovation, employees' emotional labor in both surface and deep acting; and was moderated by the OI and DA interactive effect.

Table 4. Hierarchical moderated regression analysis of DA on Job Performance

Variable	β	df	F	R2	ΔR^2
Step 1: Independent variable OI	$.182^{***}$	249	$.81.79^{***}$	.247	$.247^{***}$
Step 2: Moderator variable surface acting	$.153^{***}$	248	$.53.92^{***}$	.303	$.056^{***}$
Step 3: Interaction term OI * SA	$-.059^{*}$	247	$.38.20^{*}$	.317	$.014^{*}$
Constant	6.018^{***}				

Note: N = 251. Unstandardized regression coefficients from the last step. $^{***}p < .001$, $^{*}p < .05$

To explore the form of the interaction, we plotted Fig. 2, showing the relationship between OI and employees' JP in both high and low levels of employees' deep action of EL, following the procedures described by Aiken and West [40]. The interactive graph illustrated that high OI and employees who have high deep acting of EL would have the highest level of JP. While the lowest level of JP was reported by those low in OI and low in deep acting of EL. Interesting, while the OI is low, employees' low/high deep acting would affect their JP dramatically.

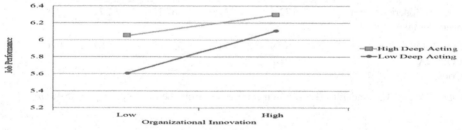

Fig. 2. Interactive effect of deep acting and organization innovation on JP. $Y = 6.018 + .182(Oi) + .153(Da) - .059(Oi*da)$

2) SA/DA of EL and POS have an interactive effect on JP

(a) Surface acting of EL: The results are shown in Table 5, both the POS ($\Delta R^2 = .193, p < .001$) and surface acting of EL ($\Delta R^2 = .043, p < .001$) had main effects on employees' job performance. The interaction term of POS and SA didn't have significant incremental portion of variance ($\Delta R^2 = .003, p > .05$).

Table 5. Hierarchical moderated regression analysis of SA on Job Performance

Variable	β	df	F	R2	ΔR^2
Step 1: Independent variable POS	.190***	249	59.45***	.193	.193***
Step 2a: Moderator variable surface acting	−.117***	248	38.31***	.236	.043***
Step 3: Interaction term POS * SA Constant	.027 5.996***	247	25.84***	.239	.003

Note: N = 251. Unstandardized regression coefficients from the last step. ***$p < .001$

(b) Deep acting of EL: The results are shown in Table 6, both the POS ($\Delta R^2 = .247$, $p < .001$) a deep acting of EL ($\Delta R^2 = .056$, $p < .001$) had main effects on employees' JP. The interaction term of OI and DA explained a significant incremental portion of variance ($\Delta R^2 = .016$, $p < .05$) in JP. Therefore, hypothesis 4 was partial supported, the employee's JP was dependent upon the level of POS, employees' EL in both surface and deep acting; and was moderated by the POS and DA interactive effect.

Table 6. Hierarchical moderated regression analysis of DA on Job Performance

Variable	β	df	F	R2	ΔR^2
Step 1: Independent variable POS	.144***	249	59.45***	.193	.193***
Step 2: Moderator variable deep acting	.172***	248	46.21***	.271	.079***
Step 3: Interaction term POS*DA Constant	−.059* 6.016***	247	33.16*	.287	.016*

Note: N = 251. Unstandardized regression coefficients from the last step. ***$p < .001$, *$p < .05$

To explore the form of the interaction, we plotted Fig. 3, showing the relationship between POS and employees' job performance in both high and low levels of employees' deep action of EL. The interactive graph illustrated that high POS and employees who have high deep acting of EL would have the highest level of JP. While the lowest level of job performance was reported by those low in OI and low in deep acting of EL.

5 Conclusion

The majority department store managers in southern Taiwan are single female age between 26–32 years old with College degree. Their job tenure are less than 3 years and most of them average monthly salaries are less than NT$30,000. The purpose of this

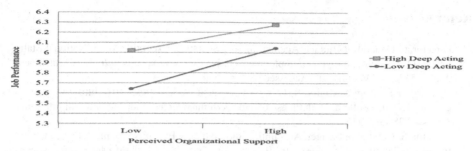

Fig. 3. Interactive effect of deep acting and POS on JP. $Y = 6.016 + .144(Pos) + .172(Da) - .059(Pos*da)$

study is to examine the impact of the department stores' OI and employees' POS on their JP; additionally, explore the interactive effects of the EL in surface/deep acting on OI/JP and POS/JP relationships. The results indicated OI, POS and deep acting of EL have positive significant impacts on employees' JP, while employees' surface acting of EL has significant negative relationships with OI, POS, and JP. Employees' job performance was dependent upon the level of OI, employees POS, deep acting of EL, and was moderated by OI/DA and POS/DA interactive effects. Similar with previous research [34, 35], our research found emotional labor in deep acting of department stores' floor managers effectively enhance the effects of OI and POS on their JP. While department stores' managers perceived high level of organizational support with newly application methods in the ideas, processes, technologies, and procedures to improve the work efficiency, they would execute with effortful to align with organizational expectations from the heart, producing more natural and genuine emotional displays which would positively affects the employee's job performance.

Based on the social exchange theory, when department store emphasize OI in management and environmental process and employees' POS whether it is the substantive reward or feel the organization's high care and attention, the employee will show a high performance, maintain good service quality, in order to repay the organization's support, and thus enhance the employee's recognition and commitment to the organization. Since our results indicated employees who have high deep acting of EL and high OI/POS presumed the highest level of JP. While the lowest level of JP was reputed by those low in OI/POS and low in deep acting of EL. For sustainable development we suggest organization should always cares about employee benefits and support employees whether the real compensation or emotional needs, these would advance employee behavior manifestation in the organization to find, establish, execute, and successfully implement ideas for new technologies, or techniques, to become useful products or services. The result of this research gives the contribution to academic and also for the retail industry, even though previously research had been found positive relationships among OI, POS and JP, there is no research conduct using Asia department stores' floors manager as subjects.

References

1. Directorate-General of Budget, Accounting and Statistics, Executive Yuan: National Statistics, R. O. C. of unemployment/employment. https://www.dgbas.gov.tw/public/Attachment/93251651438VPAVQ8D.pdf. Accessed 28 Jan 2020
2. Ministry of Economic Affairs, R. O. C., Department of Statistics, 2016: http://www.moea.gov.tw/MNS/dos/bulletin/Bulletin.aspx?kind=9&html=1&menu_id=18808&bull_id=2587. Accessed 28 Jan 2020
3. Directorate-General of Budget, Accounting and Statistics, Executive Yuan, R. O. C. Standard Industrial Classification System of the Republic of China, 2016 (10th Ed.). https://www.dgbas.gov.tw/lp.asp?CtNode=3111&CtUnit=566&BaseDSD=7&mp=1. Accessed 28 Jan 2020
4. Lin, C.H.: The conceptual model and development of measurement scale for service-innovation quality in fashion clothing of department store. Master thesis in Fu Jen Catholic University, Graduate Institute of Textiles and Clothing (2010)
5. Hochschild, A.R.: The Managed Heart: Commercialization of Human Feeling. University of California Press, Berkeley, CA (1983)
6. Robbins, S.P.: Organizational Behavior, 9th edn. Prentice-Hall, Englewood Cliffs (2001)
7. Lin, H.Y., Lu, L., Wu, P.Y., Wu, W.Y.: Are happy workers more productive? The dual influences of organizational support and work attitudes. Chin. J. Psychol. 54(4), 451–469 (2012)
8. Duke, A.B., Goodman, J.M., Treadway, D.C., Breland, J.W.: Perceived organizational support as a moderator of emotional labor/outcomes relationships. J. Appl. Soc. Psychol. 39(5), 1013–1034 (2009)
9. West, M., Farr, J.L.: Innovation and Creativity at Work: Psychological and Organizational Strategies. Wiley, New York (1990)
10. Dougherty, D., Bowman, E.H.: The effects of organizational downsizing of product innovation. California Manage. Revive 37(4), 28–44 (1995)
11. Tsai, C.T.: Intrinsic motivation and employee creativity: tests of Amabile's three-way interaction effect and shin's mediation effect. J. Manage. 25(5), 549–575 (2008)
12. Kelm, K.M., Narayanan, V.K., Pinches, G.E.: Shareholder value creation during R&D innovation and commercialization stages. Acad. Manage. J. 38(3), 770–786 (1995)
13. Kochhar, R., David, P.: Institutional investors and firm innovation: a test of competing hypotheses. Strateg. Manage. J. 17, 73–84 (1996)
14. Amabile, T.M.: A model of creativity and innovation in organization. Res. Organ. Behav. 10, 123–167 (1998)
15. Scott, S.G., Bruce, R.A.: Determinants of innovative behavior: a path model of individual innovation in the workplace. Acad. Manage. J. 37(3), 580–607 (1994)
16. Dougherty, D., Bowman, E.H.: The effects of organizational downsizing of product innovation. Calif. Manage. Rev. 37(4), 28–44 (1995)
17. Damanpour, F.: Organizational innovation: a meta-analysis of effects of determinants and moderators. Acad. Manage. J. 34(3), 555–590 (1991)
18. Djellal, F., Gallouj, F.: Innovation in services, patterns of innovation organization in service firms: postal survey results and theoretical models. Sci. Publ. Pol. 28(1), 57–67 (2001)
19. Eisenberger, R., Huntington, R., Hutchison, S., Sowa, D.: Perceived organizational support. J. Appl. Psychol. 71(3), 500–507 (1986)
20. Eisenberger, R., Fasolo, P., Davis-LaMastro, V.: Perceived organizational support and employee diligence, commitment, and innovation. J. Appl. Psychol. 75(1), 51–59 (1990)
21. Eisenberger, R., Cummings, J., Armeli, S., Lynch, P.: Perceived organizational support discretionary treatment and job satisfaction. J. Appl. Psychol. 82(5), 812–820 (1997)

22. Hill, C.A.: Affiliation motivation: people who need people but in different ways. J. Pers. Soc. Psychol. **52**, 1008–1018 (1987)
23. Rousseau, D.M., Parks, J.M.: The contracts of individuals and organizations. Res. Organ. Behav. **15**, 1–43 (1993)
24. Grandey, A., Diefendorff, J. M., Rupp, D.E.: Emotional Labor in the 21st Century: Diverse Perspectives on Emotion Regulation at Work, pp. 3–17. Routledge (2013)
25. Grandey, A.A.: Emotional regulation in the workplace: A new way to conceptualize emotional labor. J. Occup. Health Psychol. **5**(1), 95–110 (2000)
26. Borman, W.C., Motowidlo, S.J.: Expanding the criterion domain to include element of context performance. In: Schmit, N., Borman, W.C. (eds.) Personal Selection in Organization, pp. 71–98. Jossey-Bass Press, SF (1993)
27. Huang, X.F., Lin, X.B.: The impact of organizational change on staff's morale and job performance: the K corporation as the example. Manage. Inf. Comput. **3**, 54–76 (2014)
28. Cardy, R.L., Dobbins, G.H.: Organizational Behavior and Human Decision Processes. McGraw-Hill Press, NY (1994)
29. Bailey, C., Fletcher, C.: The impact of multiple source feedback on management development: Findings from a longitudinal study. J. Organ. Behav. **23**, 853–867 (2002)
30. Bello, O.B., Adeoye, A.O.: Organizational learning, organizational innovation and organizational performance: empirical evidence among selected manufacturing companies in Lagos metropolis Nigeria. J. Econ. Manage. **33**, 25–38 (2018). https://doi.org/10.22367/jem.2018.33.02
31. Oh, J.-E., Rutherford, B.N., Parki, J.K.: The interplay of salesperson's job performance and satisfaction in the financial services industry. J. Financ. Serv. Market. **19**(2), 104–117 (2014)
32. Karatepe, O.M., Aga, M.: The effects of organization mission fulfillment and perceived organizational support on job performance: the mediating role of work engagement. Int. J. Bank Market. **34**(3), 368–387 (2016)
33. Shen, Y., et al.: Linking perceived organizational support with employee outcomes in a Chinese context: organizational identification as a mediator. Eur. Manage. J. **32**(3), 406–412 (2014)
34. Chi, N.W.: Helpful or harmful? Exploring the moderating effects of supervisory and coworker support on the relationships between emotional labor, service performance and turnover intentions. Organ. Manage. **7**(1), 115–160 (2014)
35. Hou, S.T., Fan, H.L., Lien, W.C.: Sincere or insincere? exploring the relationship between emotional labor and innovative behavior. NTU Manage. Rev. **25**(3), 67–99 (2015)
36. Tsai, C.T., Huang, K.L., Kao, C.F.: The relationship among organizational factors, creativity of organizational members and organizational innovation. J. Manage. Bus. Res. **18**(4), 527–566 (2001)
37. Shanock, L.R., Eisenberger, R.: When supervisors feel supported: relationships with subordinates' perceived supervisor support, perceived organizational support, and performance. J. Appl. Psychol. **91**, 689–695 (2006)
38. Motowidlo, S.J., Van Scotter, J.R.: Evidence that task performance should be distinguished from contextual performance. J. Appl. Psychol. **79**(4), 475–480 (1994)
39. Cohen, J., Cohen, P.: Applied Multiple Regression/Correlation Analysis for the Behavioral Sciences. Erlbaum, Hillsdale (1983)
40. Aiken, L.S., West, S.: Multiple Regression: Testing and Interpreting Interactions. Sage Publications (1991)

The Use of Scenarios in Company's Planning

Veronika Šramová[(⊠)], Tatiana Čorejová, Andrea Čorejová, and Jaroslav Jaroš

University of Žilina, Univerzitná, 8215/1, 01026 Žilina, Slovakia
{veronika.sramova,andrea.corejova,jaroslav.jaros}@uvp.uniza.sk,
tatiana.corejova@fpedas.uniza.sk

Abstract. The current business environment is full of constant and rapid changes, to which companies must respond adequately and promptly if they want to maintain their market position. Most changes in the environment cannot be directly influenced by companies, they can only adapt to the new situation. The current changes are so rapid and surprising that it is not enough to stick to best practices and proven strategies in business management. Many strategic planning tools are too static and deal with the past and present of companies, but not with their future. Therefore, it is necessary to look for tools that will be compatible with the strategy and direction of the company, help it prepare for the future - better and worse, and give the company the opportunity to survive the difficult periods that regularly occur in the global economic environment. One of the methods that can be used for this purpose is scenario planning. This paper will address the importance of scenario planning in strategic business planning. The created General model of scenario planning environment explains how to incorporate scenarios into the strategy management system. Empirical research was conducted that assesses the readiness rate of companies to use scenarios for long-term planning in Slovakia.

Keywords: Scenario planning · Scenario · Strategy · Business planning · Enterprise · Model

1 Introduction

The occurrence of crisis situations as well as the need for consistent strategic decisions for the development of the company's future requires the adoption of various measures and changes in the corporate activities management [13]. Most managers expect that the changes they introduce will bring positive business results, such as profit growth, increase in the number of customers, increase in process efficiency and others. However, the results of measures and changes can be arbitrary in unpredictable situations, despite expectations. The company may strengthen its position and increase its market share or it will have to reduce its activities, lay off employees or close down, as was the case of many global and Slovak companies during the economic crisis. The period of crisis is usually accompanied by the emergence of many new businesses and the emergence of new innovations and ideas, because the confusion and emerging gaps in the market offer space for these activities. Businesses are either very flexible and adaptable, they

© Springer Nature Switzerland AG 2021
L. Uden et al. (Eds.): KMO 2021, CCIS 1438, pp. 252–263, 2021.
https://doi.org/10.1007/978-3-030-81635-3_21

are "wise" and know how to take advantage of new situations and opportunities, they are simply lucky or they are prepared for something unexpected to happen.

The planning process has an irreplaceable function in the company system. Without planning, the implementation of business processes would be confusing and often would not even be implemented at all. Planning itself is a system and represents the important existence of interconnected elements and activities that take place in a constant cycle. It is also important to keep in mind the decision-making process that is part of every step of planning, as well as other management processes. The role of business managers is to ensure that the company survives and is successful in a highly competitive environment based on thorough planning and the right decisions.

Market development, the speed of changes in the company's internal and external environment, market volatility and factors whose impact on the company cannot ultimately be precisely determined. One of the tasks of planning is not only to prescribe the implementation of processes in the company, but also to create a possible future for the company, about which no one can say for sure what it will actually be. The future of the company deals with long-term planning and affects all activities of the company. Managers have at their disposal many different techniques and methods that enable quality implementation of the entire planning process. Many of these methods are a means of traditional planning path. The rapid development of the market, the turbulence of the environment, where there are big changes that business managers could not even imagine a few years ago, the influence of customers on business activities has a growing tendency and customers are involved in many processes, requires new non-traditional practices.

Scenario planning, when properly applied, helps a company prepare for unforeseen events. The scenario planning process is not simple, so it is necessary to thoroughly incorporate scenarios into the long-term business planning system, create a corporate climate that will be acceptable for the implementation of created scenarios and especially to attract managers and employees and involve all stakeholders in the whole process.

The method of creating scenarios intended for long-term planning is not new at all. Scenarios focus primarily on creating several possible futures and have many uses. Their main purpose is to build a resilient strategy and a company that can withstand the effects of the environment by being prepared for them. Scenarios help solve crisis situations, test existing business strategies, and serve to develop business proactivity, creativity, and the imagination of managers about what they will do when a situation arises and they have to deal with it.

In terms of the focus of scenarios and the purpose of their use, they need to be closely linked to the strategy management system. Therefore, it is necessary to appeal to the level of business processes and basic elements that are necessary for the company to be able to implement its strategy. The intention is therefore to create a suitable environment for the implementation of scenarios and their successful use.

It is important to find and develop a suitable scenario planning process for the company that plans to use this method. Business managers should focus on linking scenario planning process with the strategy management system. Both processes should be as compatible as possible. It is important to monitor the reasons for which scenarios are used and to look for their weaknesses, which could be complemented by other available planning methods. The purpose of introducing the scenario method into the company's management system is to reduce the company's uncertainty in the necessary decisions and to create an apparatus that will be relatively easy to apply and beneficial in its procedures. Scenarios are often confused with forecasting, which is one of the possible tools used to create scenarios. Managers can view scenarios with great distrust that stem from the uncertainty of what will happen in the future and are reluctant to try new unknown practices in business planning.

Due to the complexity of the examined area of scenario planning, it is therefore necessary to monitor the development of the scenario method and look for advantages and benefits that will be usable in the conditions of companies. The intention of the created proposals is to set the basic process of introducing the method of scenarios into the company management system so that scenarios can be implemented into the planning systems of companies in Slovakia and abroad. In the event of a crisis situation, the company will be ready and will be able to draw up a specific scenario according to which it will proceed in its activities in order to be able to respond to the crisis in a timely manner. For this purpose, a research was carried out on the readiness of companies in Slovakia for the possible implementation of scenario planning. Research and its results can be used in the process of sharing knowledge between managers in Slovakia and abroad. Based on knowledge from the world literature, knowledge of business planning, creation and implementation of business strategy and research results, a general model of the scenario planning environment was created.

2 Literature Review

The first mention in the history of the future that could occur is divination. Futurology - the science of the future denies divination and deals with the use of various scientific methods. Flechthaim authored the term and first introduced it in a article in the Atlantic University of Phylon (1943) entitled: Toynbee and the Webers: Remarks on Their Theories of History. According to Flechtheim, "futurology consists of futuristic, forecasting and planning. Futurology includes the philosophy, politics and pedagogy of the future [2]. I. Klinec states that "futurology is the science of exploring the future. Creates alternative scenarios of possible future development of the company [4, p. 229]. He expressed the opinion that "futurology was a politically undesirable science and for this reason a prognosis was made [4, p. 210]. Scenario planning is part of the scientific field: Futurology, which is part of strategic planning. Strategic foresight has emerged as an attempt to distinguish between futurology and futurological studies. The difference between strategic foresight and futurology is that strategic foresight results in several alternative scenarios for a possible future, while futurology provides a definitive picture of the future.

2.1 Scenario Planning Process

As the business environment becomes increasingly volatile and new uncertainties emerge, the need for more rigorous preparation for the future increases. Therefore, there is space for the involvement of scenario planning in long-term business planning.

According to Schoemaker (1995), scenario planning is the difference between chaos and business management day after day with certainty and foresight [9, 11]. This view is very similar to the characteristics of planning as such. The concept of foresight appears here, which is a feature of scenario planning. Ringland combines scenario planning with an apparatus designed for its implementation. According to him, scenario planning is the part of strategic planning that is associated with tools and techniques designed to manage the uncertainties of the future [7, p. 4]. The definition precisely defines that scenario planning is only considered as part of strategic planning, so that its very existence is not possible and it includes methods, techniques and procedures by which the company prepares for the future. According to De Geus, scenarios are tools designed to discuss predictions and documents that are not intended to be a prediction or a plan, but a change in the minds of the people who use them [1]. Kahane argues that scenario planning is primarily a diagnostic tool designed for conditions in which uncertainty prevails [8]. It states that scenario planning not only uses various tools and techniques, but itself is a targeted tool in the hands of managers, which is designed to reveal uncertainties in the company's environment. Porter (1985) looked at scenario planning more comprehensively, arguing that it was: an internally consistent view of how the future might turn out - not a prediction, but one possible outcome of the future [5, 6]. Schwartz (1991) focuses on deciding on a possible future from the perspective of the individual, and according to him, scenario planning is a tool designed to organize the perception of an alternative future in one person's environment in which his decisions can take place [10]. The importance and essence of decision-making, which is part of all management processes, is emphasized.

All the mentioned definitions and opinions are very diverse, each author focuses on a certain meaning and purpose of scenario planning. The authors complement each other or, on the contrary, partially contradict each other, so it is possible to state the following from the overall overview of the problem: "Scenario planning as a part of long-term planning is a means of creating several possible images of the future of the company's environment in the form of scenarios that could support the implementation of the company's strategy after their implementation." [12].

If managers want to use scenario planning, they must see the scenario planning process in an organizational context and they must understand how scenario planning fits into the organizational system as a subsystem with its own inputs, processes, outputs, and feedback loops. At the Fig. 1 it is shown the performance-based scenario system where it is described shortly the process of scenario creating. The system consists of 5 phases [3, p. 66]: 1. Project preparation, 2. Scenario exploration, 3. Scenario development, 4. Scenario implementation, 5. Project assessment.

3   Research Methodology

The research was carried out in order to obtain data and their subsequent interpretation in the field of long-term business planning and their preparation for the future through the use of various available tools and techniques. The research was mainly focused on examining the degree of readiness of companies for the use of scenario planning procedures in long-term planning of companies. All phases of the research were carried

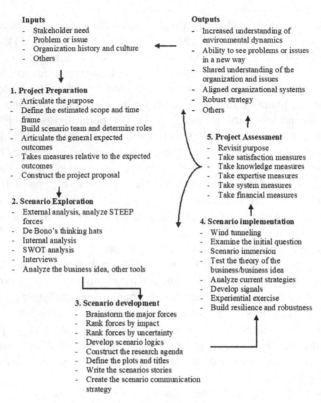

Inputs
- Stakeholder need
- Problem or issue
- Organization history and culture
- Others

↓

1. Project Preparation
- Articulate the purpose
- Define the estimated scope and time frame
- Build scenario team and determine roles
- Articulate the general expected outcomes
- Takes measures relative to the expected outcomes
- Construct the project proposal

↓

2. Scenario Exploration
- External analysis, analyze STEEP forces
- De Bono's thinking hats
- Internal analysis
- SWOT analysis
- Interviews
- Analyze the business idea, other tools

3. Scenario development
- Brainstorm the major forces
- Rank forces by impact
- Rank forces by uncertainty
- Develop scenario logics
- Construct the research agenda
- Define the plots and titles
- Write the scenarios stories
- Create the scenario communication strategy

Outputs
- Increased understanding of environmental dynamics
- Ability to see problems or issues in a new way
- Shared understanding of the organization and issues
- Aligned organizational systems
- Robust strategy
- Others

↑

5. Project Assessment
- Revisit purpose
- Take satisfaction measures
- Take knowledge measures
- Take expertise measures
- Take system measures
- Take financial measures

↑

4. Scenario implementation
- Wind tunneling
- Examine the initial question
- Scenario immersion
- Test the theory of the business/business idea
- Analyze current strategies
- Develop signals
- Experiential exercise
- Build resilience and robustness

Fig. 1. The performance-based scenario system [3]

out in the period from July 2012 to December 2012. 4969 companies were contacted for research purposes. 133 directors were involved and cooperated in the research.

Data were obtained through an electronic questionnaire, personal interviews and also through a secondary survey (analysis of available written and Internet sources). In addition to the basic programs MS Word and Excel, the program SPSS 2.0 (Software package used for statistical analysis) from IBM was used for data processing. Primary data were obtained from a questionnaire survey conducted on a certain sample of respondents and from personal interviews that took place in selected companies. The questionnaire contained 48 claims divided into five research areas. The questions that have become the subject of quantitative research are linked to individual hypotheses so that the answers to them clearly confirm or refute the stated hypotheses of the research. In personal interviews, the method of semi-structured interview was used to clarify the situation in the company and the important relationships between some key business elements. Secondary data were obtained mainly from the Internet, professional literature, scientific articles, etc. Further data were drawn from the Statistical Office of the Slovak Republic.

The research problem was identified as: *Insufficient control and application of the principle of scenario planning in the strategic management of the company, which causes a reduced ability of the company to respond to the effects of external environments.*

The aim of the research was *to identify, evaluate procedures and techniques that help companies work with the strategy and assess the degree of their readiness to use scenarios in long-term planning.* Based on the tent goal of the research, 5 areas of research were determined: 1. Criteria of success and development of the company, 2. Personnel capacity in creating a company strategy, 3. Work with the company's strategy, 4. Critical areas of company management, 5. Identification of the company. Based on the stated goal of the research and the intentions of the research areas, the following research hypotheses were established:

H1: More than 60% of business managers are prepared to apply scenario planning procedures at least at an acceptable level.

H2: The current state of application of scenario planning procedures in medium-sized enterprises is comparable to the state of application of scenario planning procedures in large enterprises.

H3: More than 60% of managers of large and medium-sized companies consider the most important prerequisites for creating a strategy using scenario planning of employee knowledge and management systems in the company.

H4: There is a significant dependence between the degree of readiness of medium and large enterprises to apply scenario planning procedures and the long-term direction of enterprises.

Experts who participated in the research, based on their experience, evaluated that as a representative sample and a critical measure of the overall readiness of the surveyed companies in Slovakia will be a sufficient number of 60% of managers of the surveyed companies (accepted for hypotheses H1 and H3). The data is indicative and provides an idea and measure of the state of preparedness of companies.

4   Analyses

Before starting the scenario planning process, it is necessary to verify whether the process is suitable for the company and the company is able to perform all process activities in a form that makes sense and will show the desired results. Companies are encouraged to start creating scenarios in their comprehensive form if:

– the company is well placed to implement the scenarios,
– the company has a sophisticated system of work with strategy or a system of long-term planning,
– there are no other facts that could prevent or devalue the correct creation of scenarios and their implementation.

In order to achieve the intentions and expectations from the implementation of scenario planning in the corporate strategy, it will be necessary to eliminate problems that the company already knows about or which will be identified in the initial stages of the scenario creation process. Depending on the situation, some issues may need to be addressed immediately or during the planning process or may be resolved during scenario implementation. Some of the problems, which were identified as key for the company and should be gradually eliminated, have been the subject of quantitative research in companies. Identified problems are:

- a problem with the company's strategy, e. g. the strategy is vaguely formulated, the goals of the company are incorrectly set, problems in terms of implementation of individual activities, incorrectly divided competencies of employees, etc.,
- absence of competent and responsible staff,
- absent or malfunctioning enterprise information system,
- absent or malfunctioning controlling system,
- incorrect, resp. improperly functioning organizational structure of the company,
- insufficient cooperation between the various departments of the undertaking,
- individual (supportive) activities of the company are inefficient, or they don't make sense at all,
- missing, resp. inappropriately set up motivation system of the company.

The large number of identified problems and the low level of the company's ability to solve them leads to the assumption that companies will not have a satisfactory level of strategic planning and this may prevent managers from implementing the main processes related to the process of preparing the company environment for scenario planning and final implementation of scenarios in the company environment.

On this assumption, complex elements were selected, which cover the most important areas for an adequately prepared company environment for scenario planning. Selected elements were included in the first version of the General model of scenario planning environment. Parts of the model together with the identified problems were broken down into research questions, which were asked by the manager during the research. Based on the used analytical methods and statistical processing of the research, parts of the model were modified and its final version is the subject of discussion in Sect. 5.

Micro (32.33%), small (17.29%), medium-sized (24.06%) and large enterprises (26.32%) participated in the research. All hypotheses that were the subject of the research were confirmed by statistical processing.

H1 verification: Based on the use of the enterprise readiness index for scenario planning, it was found that 68.42% of enterprises are ready for the application of scenario planning procedures.

H2 verification: Based on the test of agreement of two proportion of the basic sets, it can be argued that the current state of application of scenario planning procedures in medium-sized enterprises is comparable to the state of application of scenario planning procedures in large enterprises.

H3 verification: Cluster analysis was used to verify this hypothesis. The research confirmed that the managers of the surveyed companies consider the knowledge of employees and company management systems to be most important for the creation of a strategy using scenario planning.

H4 verification: The hypothesis was accepted on the basis of a test of the independence of quantitative features. There was a significant dependence between the degree of readiness of medium-sized and large enterprises to apply scenario planning procedures and their long-term direction. Acceptance of this hypothesis is important, because it can be concluded that companies are preparing for the future precisely because of the desired change, in which they see great potential and begin to identify with ideas that will allow them to adopt new ways of dealing with situations.

The comprehensive processing of research is an extensive part of the processed dissertation thesis focused on the Using of scenarios in company's planning [12].

5   Design of a Model of Compatible Use of Scenario Planning in the Process of Creating a Business Strategy

The proposed solution, processed into a model, focuses on determining the conditions, procedures and possibilities for the effective use of the scenario method in long- term business planning. For its use and further elaboration, it was necessary to identify relevant elements influencing the scenario planning process. Relevant elements were selected on the basis of an analysis of the current state of the research problem and incorporated into the general model of scenario planning (see Fig. 2). Selected elements of the proposed general model were used in the research. Thus, a survey was conducted on the readiness of companies for scenario planning, and at the same time the importance and the current state of the incorporated components of the model was verified in advance. Based on the findings, the model was modified to the form that is presented in this discussion.

The model shows the interconnection of the scenario creation process, strategy management system, key success factors of the company, stakeholders and involved people (people directly influencing the creation of scenarios). Captured changes based on external and interactive environments can cause many problems. Scenario planning is a tool designed to prevent them.

The scenario planning system is part of the strategic planning of the company. Therefore, another condition for the possible creation and implementation of scenarios as a tool for shaping the future of the company is a functional strategic system or a system for long-term planning (hereinafter a system for working with strategy). The systems should be interconnected and their activities must be interlinked and consecutive. This will prevent the implementation of duplicate and redundant activities in individual stages of processes.

Figure 3 illustrates a simple strategy process linked to a scenario creation process that represents the basic idea and function of using scenarios in enterprise planning. The scenario creation process has a simplified form compared to the whole system, because it takes into account only the influences of the external environment and does not include internal influences. The model serves to simply represent the two principles of the systems on which further proposals are based. The mentioned model of the scenario creation process can also be connected with the model of the planning process. This means that the scenario method is applicable in different systems and activities depending on its adaptation.

If a company has decided to use a scenario planning system but has found that it does not have a functioning strategy system, it will be necessary to create a new one or modify the original strategy system of the company.

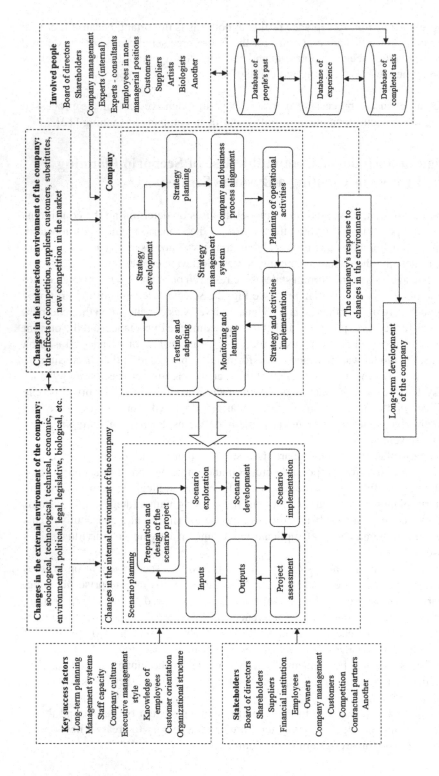

Fig. 2. General model of scenario planning environment [6]

Figure 4 shows a model situation where two systems are interconnected: a strategy management system and scenario planning. Both systems are created synchronously (or the functionality of the strategy management system is restored) under certain conditions. From the point of view of time and implementation of processes in the company, it may be more advantageous to perform some activities continuously and gradually supplement them as needed. The phases of the strategy management system are designated from 1 to 6 (F1–F6) and the phases of the scenario planning system are designated from 1a to 5a (F1a–F5a).

If the company is interested in the possibility of implementing scenarios in the strategic planning, its main goals may be the following:

– reducing the degree of business uncertainty,
– trying to find out about the possible future of the company,
– creating a more resilient strategy,
– building a more resilient company,
– increasing the flexibility of the company,
– increasing or maintaining the competitiveness of the undertaking,
– developing the creativity of employees and promoting their open thinking, and others.

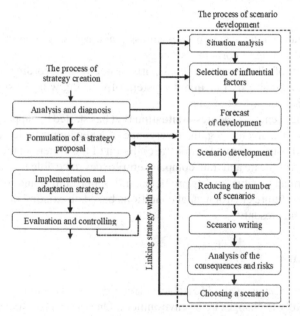

Fig. 3. Scenarios in the strategy management process [6]

Based on the analysis of the phases of the strategy management systems and scenario planning, it can be argued that the scenario planning system can be used for the following purposes:

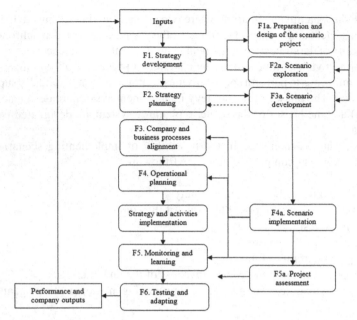

Fig. 4. BSC-based strategy management system model with link to scenario planning [6]

– Creation of a new strategic system of business planning using scenarios.
– Evaluation and testing of corporate strategy.
– Implementation of all scenarios or their parts at one time according to the needs of the company in the already functioning system of working with the strategy.
– Use of scenarios for project testing.
– Using a specific scenario to address a situation that has started to happen and for which a scenario has been created, e.g. the emergence of a new opportunity, the increase in the influence of some external factors, the collision of the system in the company, etc.
– Use scenarios to educate and train company employees to be able to comprehensively assess the company's situation, its problems and opportunities and to learn to better plan and predict future environmental conditions based on existing factors that can be monitored in the present.

6   Conclusion

The success of a company is to build a stable and resilient company that can move forward and respond flexibly to changes in the environment. One of the tools that managers have available for these purposes is the Scenario planning. The issue of scenario planning is demanding especially on the harmonization of individual processes and their subsequent implementation. In order to illustrate the environment in which scenario planning is incorporated into the processes of strategic management of companies, General model of scenario planning environment was created. The model was compiled on the basis of a study of the literature and the knowledge of various experts in the field of strategic management. Research was carried out to verify the correctness of the general model and also to verify a comprehensive study of the readiness of Slovakia companies to integrate scenario planning into their strategic management system. The research was focused on verifying the assumptions of the correctness of the inclusion of individual elements in the General model of the scenario planning environment (Fig. 2) and also a series of questions which, after their statistical processing, led to the confirmation of the established research hypotheses. The primary purpose of this paper is to draw attention to the complexity of the processes of integrating scenario planning into the strategic management of companies and to illustrate the primary processes designed for these purposes. These processes can be developed into many other sub-models according to the type of integrated scenarios or according to the situations to which the company is interested to apply the scenarios [12]. The created data are also intended for modeling processes for researchers in the field of strategic business management.

References

1. Geus, D.: The Living Company. Harvard Business School Press, Boston (1997)
2. Futurologia.sk. Online portal, 19 Feb 2021. https://futurologia.sk/
3. Chermack, T.J.: Scenario planning in organizations. How to create, use, and assess scenarios. Berrett-Koehler Publishers, Inc., San Francisco (2011)
4. Klinec, I.: Na prahu civilizácie Tretej vlny: futurologistické reflexie 1991–2002. SR: Iris, p. 229, 210 (2003)
5. Porter, M., E.: Competitive advantage. Free Press, New York (1980)
6. Porter, M.E.: Competitive Advantage. Free Press, New York (1985)
7. Ringland, G.: Scenario Planning: Managing for the Future. John Wiley & Sons, Ltd., England (2006)
8. Kahane, A.: Transformative Scenario Planning: Working Together to Change the Future. Berrett-Koehler Publishers Inc., San Francisco (2012)
9. Schoemaker, P.J.H.: Scenario planning: s tool for strategic thinking. Sloan Manage. Rev. **37**(2), 25–40 (1995)
10. Schwartz, P.: The Art of the Long View. Doubleday, New York (1991)
11. Schwenker, B., Wulf, T.: Scenario-Based Strategic Planning: Developing Strategies in an Uncertain World. Roland Berger School of Strategy and Economics. Springer (2016)
12. Šramová, V.: The use of scenarios in company's planning. [Dissertation Thesis] University of Žilina, FRI ŽU in Žilina (2013)
13. Titko, M., Ristvej, J.: Assessing importance of disaster preparedness factors for sustainable disaster risk management: the case of the Slovak Republic. J.: Sustain. **12**(21) (2020). Article Number: 9121

Information Systems and Information Science

Prototype Framework for the Implementation of Telemedicine Platforms

Olguer Morales[✉] and Giovanny Tarazona

Faculty of Engineering, Francisco Jose de Caldas District University, Bogotá D.C, Colombia
osmoralesv@correo.udistrital.edu.co, gtarazona@udistrital.edu.co

Abstract. The level of overcrowding of hospitals and health care centers in Colombia and especially in the cities far away from the main capitals has had an increase in recent years, this problem generates a constant and growing discomfort in the Colombian population due to the delayed or lack of provision of various medical services and access difficulties, especially in remote areas. With the aim of providing health centers with tools to make virtual appointments and avoid overcrowding of patients who do not need to go to hospitals due the characteristics of their illness and also to improve the implementation of technologies in the Colombian health system, we propose a framework to develop telemonitoring platforms with dynamic processing capabilities. The tests are carried out using cloud computing and free programming tools. Through the tests carried out on the proposed modeling, we determined that it can be implemented in a simple, fast and easy way.

Keywords: Telemedicine · Remote monitoring · Processing · Biomedical signals · AWS · Framework · Prototype · Python · IoT

1 Introduction

The demographic picture in Colombia is not encouraging, according to the statistics provided by the National Administrative Department of Statistics (DANE) of the last census conducted in 2018 the Colombian population is aging, 9.23% of the population is over 60 years old [1]. The population of 60 years or more has growth rates higher than the growth of the total population, which means that the aging rate defined as the weight of the adult population regarding to the child and adolescent population tripled in the last decades. As highlighted in [2], the goal is to prevent complications and help the elderly maintain their independence in the daily life activities using technology, otherwise taking care of the elderly will require more expenditure and time of the economically active population.

By 2019, date in which this document was development, different approaches to reference frames for smart cities can be found in the bibliography, which describe in a general and high-level way the parameters and essential components to implement the new technologies and tendency of the 4th industrial revolution for the benefit and improvement in the quality of life of citizens. But there is no detailed guide for the

© Springer Nature Switzerland AG 2021
L. Uden et al. (Eds.): KMO 2021, CCIS 1438, pp. 267–279, 2021.
https://doi.org/10.1007/978-3-030-81635-3_22

implementation of technological platforms focused on telemonitoring operating in the cloud, therefore this is one of the main motivations to develop this work.

This paper is divided in five sections, in the first one we made an introduction to the complex system that is desired to model and the needs that gave rise to this work are stated. In the second section, the methodology and the steps followed to develop the prototype are described. Section three shows the results obtained from the tests performed on the prototype developed in Python locally and on the Amazon Web Services server (AWS). Then in section four a comparison is made with some reference works found in the literature and finally in section five the conclusions of the work carried out are described.

2 Materials and Methods

To carry out the design and development of the model of the telemonitoring platform of biomedical signals in real time proposed in this document, five methodological phases were followed. The first step is to make an abstraction of reality to model the complex system that we want to solve, then generate a prototype using this model and finally perform a validation of this prototype with unit tests and performance tests in the cloud through a virtual server. The five phases are listed below:

Data source: three data sources were used, the databases of the Ministry of Health of Colombia MINSALUD, the PPG, EMG and ECG databases of Physionet and the databases repository of machine learning of the University of California, School of Information and Science of Computing.

System modeling: five different types of models were developed to simulate the complex system.

Design of a prototype: one of the models designed in the previous phase was selected and a prototype was designed using the Python programming language. This software was chosen for its power, scalability and easy way of programming.

Prototype tests: through the databases, the correct operation of the prototype was proved and the first results of the local processing were obtained.

Assembly of the system in the cloud: using the powerful infrastructure of Amazon Web Services (AWS), a server machine was created, the prototype programs were loaded, and the correct functioning of the system was validated processing in the cloud.

2.1 Modeling the Complex System

To make an abstraction of reality by contemplating the most relevant elements of the complex system that we want to model, five models are proposed: analogical, conceptual, graphic, statistical and by processes. This last model was used as the basis to build the prototype in the Python programming language.

Analogical Model: An analogous model can be used which allows modeling the complex system that is going to be developed. An analogous system is an Enterprise Resource Planning System (ERP), just as in the complex system that is being worked on, there is an objective user that is constantly monitored (patient) to detect any anomaly and in case of any failure (biomedical signals outside of specific ranges) take the respective control/alert actions to return to the appropriate conditions. All information (patient data) is stored in a database in the cloud for further analysis and possible prediction processes.

In an ERP system, constantly different users with different roles consult the information in the database to use it as input in other processes. As in the complex system, doctors and/or relatives will constantly consult these databases to make decisions.

Conceptual Model: A conceptual model can be used, describing the key elements of the complex system, their characteristics and the relationships between them:

– Complex system key elements:

   Patients: people who need to be monitored remotely in their homes for any medical condition.
   The Colombian government (through the ministry of health): in charge of guaranteeing the provision of the health system to 100% of the Colombian population.
   Patients' relatives: people interested in having information on the status of their loved ones in real time 7/24.
   Health Promoting Entities (HPE): link between the government and Colombian citizens in terms of providing health services.
   Institutions providing health services: entities that are in direct contact with patients. They hire doctors from different disciplines to provide services in different specialties.
   SIMORETE (Remote Patient Monitoring System): project that will oversee supporting HPE and guarantee quality monitoring to patients who require it.

– **Graphic Model:** the relationships between the main entities that make up the system are graphically identified. In Fig. 1, the main components of the complex system can be observed at a high-level description.
– **Statistical Model:** this model can be used to propose an equation or set of equations with different components (technical, financial, social) that allow finding a financially viable and sustainable model over time for the Colombian health model.

   Some parameters that should be considered:

- Contribution to health by people
- Contribution to health by companies
- Moderator fee (additional money paid by people each time they go to a general medical appointment, specialist or to claim medication)
- Prepaid medicine
- Projections of the state funding budget for the health system
- Technological infrastructure for telemedicine
- Bandwidth available for people according to their socio-economic situation.
- Number of contributors to the health system. Average age/demographic bonus

Process Model: The complex system is analyzed as a process of different actors and relationships. The complex system is modeled using the Enterprise Architect software

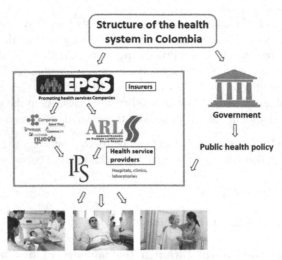

Fig. 1. Structure of the Colombian health system (Own Elaboration).

by BPMN v2.0 notation. This model allows to observe the main and secondary elements of the system and their different relationships. In Fig. 2 you can see the actors and their interactions through the process diagram.

Actor 1: Patient. They must register in the system and use the sensors that allow them to capture different biomedical signals to send it to the remote monitoring system.

Actor 2: Remote Patient Monitoring System (SIMORETE). Responsible for encrypting all information, send it to the server in the cloud, decrypt it, analyze it and take control actions. Additionally, the system must save all this information in a database.

Actor 3: Monitor Stations. They can be doctors enrolled in the system or relatives who are interested in having real-time information of the patient or see historical data to make a more detailed analysis.

2.2 Development of the Prototype in Python

The proposed system has three main blocks:

Block 1: Loading data, in this module the system obtains data from different sources and in different formats, for example:.txt,.csv,.json, among others. At the same time, it obtains real-time information about web services through Python add-ins and libraries.

Block 2: Conditioning and processing through several Python libraries, among which stand out: wfdb, Numpy, Sympy, Scipy, Pandas and Scikit-learn for machine learning.

Block 3: Graphs and results, this module makes use many graphics libraries, among which the Matplotlib library stands out and the graphics complement of the wfdb library.

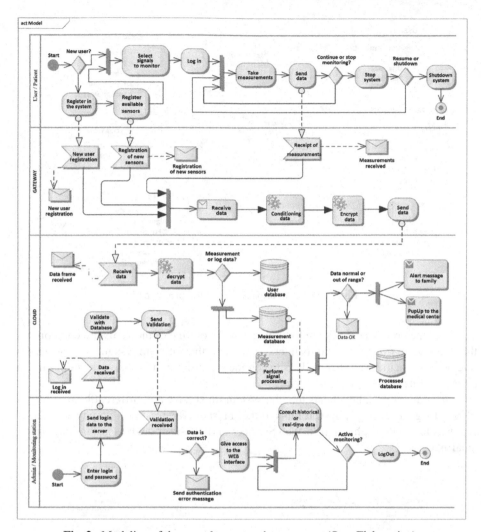

Fig. 2. Modeling of the complex system by processes (Own Elaboration).

After having modeled the complex system the design was done by classes in a program in Python. The prototype consists mainly of 6 packages within you can find several associated classes (see Fig. 3).

The main packages are:

- Users and Sensors
- Health professionals
- Type of monitoring
- Data conditioning
- Monitoring stations.

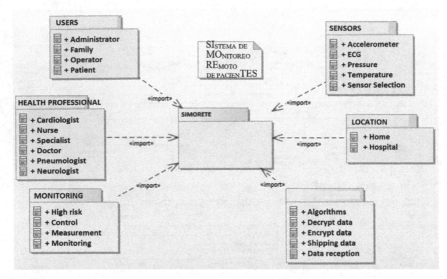

Fig. 3. Diagram of packages of the prototype.

After the prototype design in Python, a general outline of the hardware components that the system must have and its interactions with the software was made (Fig. 4). An interaction scheme was also made between the potential users of the system through a diagram of use cases (Fig. 5).

The main physical elements that the system must have are: different kind of physiological signal sensors, physical links to the Internet (Router, WiFi), a physical server that was tested through Amazon Web Services and end-user devices such as laptops or smartphones.

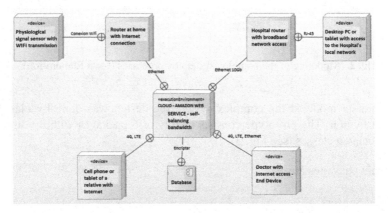

Fig. 4. Prototype component diagram.

The main users of the modeled system are patients, relatives of patients, doctors and health specialists and administrators of the technological platform.

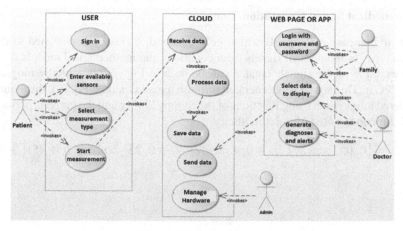

Fig. 5. Use case diagram.

The entire system is designed and tested locally. Finally, it is embedded in an Amazon Web Services (AWS) virtual machine and will be available in real time in the internet cloud.

3   Test Case Results

Different tests were performed on the prototype using different data sources. These tests were done locally and finally tests were performed on a server in the cloud. Some of the results obtained are described below:

3.1   Web Services Data Acquisition Test

To have useful information in the platform on topics of telemedicine, good health habits, advice from experts in nutrition and health-related topics, a class was designed to connect to Twitter and filter by keywords related contents and save them in a .json file to be used later.

Figure 6 shows the programming baselines and the record of the data saved.

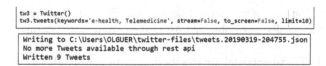

Fig. 6. Acquisition of Twitter web service data.

3.2 Biomedical Signal Generation Test

In order to compare real signals with a gold standard, a class was designed to create different types of biomedical signals from equations and mathematical models.

An example of the signals created can be seen in Fig. 7 (photoplethysmographic signal (PPG)). This signal was generated through a mathematical Eq. (1), this equation was entered into Python using functions of the Sympy library and the graph is performed through functions of the Matplotlib library.

$$PPG_{sim} = \left[0,05 \cdot sen(2\pi f 3t) + 0,4 \cdot sen(2\pi ft) + 0,25 \cdot sen(2\pi f 2t + 45)\right] + 0,5$$

$$(1)$$

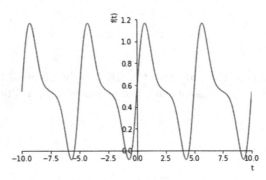

Fig. 7. Simulated plethysmographic signal.

3.3 Conditioning Test, Processing and Graphics of Biomedical Signals

All the data acquired from the different databases must be conditioned, processed and graphed. Two working examples of the design classes are mentioned: a class of spectral analysis of electrocardiographic (ECG) signals and an automatic learning class for the classification of hand movements through electromyographic (EMG) signals.

- **Class for spectral analysis of electrocardiographic signals (ECG):**

The spectral analysis of biomedical signals was performed using functions of the Scipy library, the results were obtained using data from electrocardiographic (ECG) signals.

Data from the Physionet database was used, specifically the file named "100" which contains two channels of ECG signals.

One of the channels has an ECG with Arrhythmia and the other channel has an ECG with normal characteristics. The data was imported and plotted by functions of the waveform-database library (wfdb) (see Fig. 8).

Then entering the appropriate parameters to the FFT (fast discrete Fourier transform) function of the Scipy library is the frequency spectrum of the two EEG signals

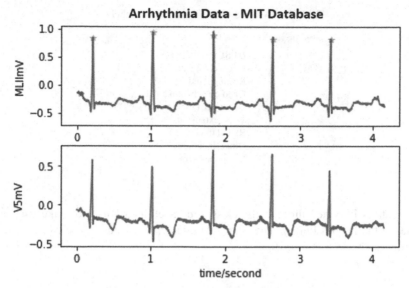

Fig. 8. Graph of Electrocardiographic signals.

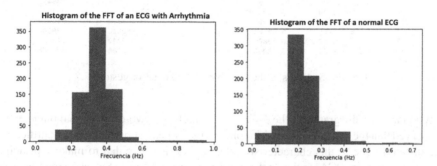

Fig. 9. Histogram of the frequency spectrum of electrocardiographic signals.

and a histogram is made with the results obtained to perform analyzes and subsequent observations (see Fig. 9).

- **Class for machine learning: classification of hand movements by means of electromyography signals (EMG)**

A Dataset called **"EMG Data for Gestures Data Set"** was used, which contains a record of electromyography signals from 36 volunteers. Each file of a volunteer is made up of 10 columns with the following description:

- Column 1: Time in (ms)
- Column 2 to 9: EMG Channels (8 Channels of the MYO Thalmic -bracelet).
- Column 10: Movement label. The movement labels are detailed in Table 1.

Table 1. EMG - 8 Channel movement labels.

DATA LABEL	
LABEL	**DESCRIPTION**
0	Unchecked data
1	Resting hand
2	Hand clenched in a fist
3	Bending of the wrist
4	Wrist extension
5	Radial deviations
6	Ulnar deviations
7	Extended palm

The data is imported through the class and saved as a Panel to make use of the potential of the Pandas library. The basic statistics of the Data Set are calculated, and the results can be seen in Fig. 10.

```
         channel1       channel2      ...          channel8          class
count  343038.000000  343038.000000   ...      343038.000000  343038.000000
mean       -0.364127      -0.425427   ...          -0.575789       3.550548
std        17.944188      13.961548   ...          18.297931       1.746432
min      -128.000000    -128.000000   ...        -128.000000       1.000000
25%        -0.000050      -0.000050   ...          -0.000060       2.000000
50%        -0.000010      -0.000010   ...          -0.000010       4.000000
75%         0.000040       0.000030   ...           0.000040       5.000000
max       127.000000     127.000000   ...         127.000000       7.000000
```

Fig. 10. Statistics of the Data Set "EMG data for gestures".

When making the graphs of the different channels in a two-dimensional plane, it can be observed that the data are very overlapping, which makes separation and identification quite difficult. Due to this characteristic of the data, it is decided to make a principal component analysis (PCA) to detect the main patterns of the Data Set using the functions of the Scikit-learn library (see Fig. 11).

3.4 Tests Case in the AWS Cloud

A professional account was created in Amazon Web Services (AWS) and a server machine was created where a free distribution of Linux was installed. Subsequently, Anaconda was installed on the server and the correct performance of the classes that make up the prototype was verified.

Figure 12 shows the results of testing a class on the AWS server in real time. The instructions are sent to the server through an open console through an SSH connection. In this class, a large volume of data is imported, processed through the functions of the Pandas library and reports of the results obtained are generated.

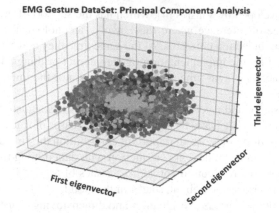

Fig. 11. Result of the PCA applied to the Data Set.

Fig. 12. Testing classes on the Amazon Web Services server.

4 Discussion

In this section a comparison of the literature with the prototype proposed in this document is made. The positive aspects and the most relevant contributions are highlighted and the advantages of the proposed model compared to these solutions are stated.

Joshi, Saxena, Godbole, & Shreyad [2] identify six pillars to develop a frame of reference: Social, Administration, Economic, Legal, Technology and Sustainability (SMELTS), the article describes how the integration of these factors could make the initiative of smart cities be a successful project, however they do not describe how these elements interact when making a technological implementation.

Barth et al. [3] present a conceptual framework conformed by seven pillars: information and knowledge, infrastructures, economy, politics (electronic governance) and administration (electronic government), spaces (spaces of services and spaces of places), location factors, the behavior of information of people, and problem areas. In this case hardware or software technological components are not detailed, and there is no practical validation of the proposed framework.

In the work developed by Vlasios [4], which has the support of the United Nations, it proposes a frame of reference where they involve technological aspects and detail parameters of communication protocols. At the same time they make a state of the art of the main tools used for the implementation of the internet of things. However, they do not contemplate factors of real-time processing design, nor the impact of an adequate use of bandwidth.

In [5] they describe and determine the relevance of the adequate handling of large volumes of information (Big Data) by applying it to two cases of study: analysis of medical images and bioinformatics. As an important contribution they use and mention tools for handling large volumes of data in conjunction with data mining tools. They mainly work on the processing layer but do not address issues of acquisition and presentation of results in local interfaces or web interfaces in the cloud.

In [6] they do the performance evaluation and dimensioning of a convergent access network, based on Metro-Ethernet standards, with a high number of devices (terminals, smartphones and IoT devices) that inject traffic into the environment of a Smart City. This analysis is carried out in a simulation environment through the SimulCity program. As a main contribution, they propose with a methodological approach, some key indicators of medical services associated with citizen welfare and a delay analysis for services in real time. This work contemplates a first important step in the modeling of complex systems of telemedicine platforms: the transmission of high volumes of data, however some external parameters must be modeled in following phases.

In [7] and [8] they propose a real-time monitoring system through an Arduino module, a temperature and heart rate sensor. In [7] they use a GSM wireless transmission module and a GPS positioning module. The information from the sensors is sent to a platform developed using HTML5, CSS, PHP and a database developed in MySQL. As a main contribution, they use wireless transmission technologies and geolocation. In [8] they perform data storage locally using an SDCard and develop a mobile application for Android to visualize the information.

Neither of the two proposed systems performs information processing either locally or in the cloud. They do not perform a data traffic analysis which presents a relevant challenge when are analyzed systems that are going to be used by many people at the same time continuously.

In [9] they propose an architecture for a monitoring system in smart cities based on the Internet of things. The main contribution is the identification of the main network requirements in a monitoring system in terms of updating real-time events, bandwidth requirements and data generation. This architecture provides key guidelines for the implementation of telemonitoring platforms which are also taken into account in the present work.

In [10] they propose an architecture based on the NGeH (next generation e-Health) paradigm as an extension of the ETSI (European Telecommunications Standards Institute) standard. The proposed architecture integrates mechanisms of sensor networks, profiling mechanisms and security mechanisms that allow to easily take advantage of the central capacities so that reliable NGeH services can be built. The main contribution is made through the implementation of an e-Health telemonitoring service in an intelligent home environment applying the proposed architecture. This architecture contemplates several essential elements for the implementation of telemedicine platforms including an international standard.

5 Conclusions

There are many more initiatives, proposals and approaches to developments of biomedical systems that implement new technologies, but all are general and no work has been found aimed at telemonitoring services or dynamic processing of biomedical signals. In the present work, a holistic prototype was designed to take into account the internal and external factors of the hardware and software that are involved in the telemonitoring process. The prototype is equipped with tools to perform several agile validation tests both in local environments and in the cloud in a fast and scalable way.

The system modeled through BPMN v2.0 and UML diagrams manages to generate a complete prototype, which evaluates the main components of signal acquisition, processing, and generation of valid results to allow a group of experts to generate actions according to the profile and information obtained from the data of each patient.

The prototype developed in the present work allows to evaluate the essential technical and structural factors of a remote monitoring platform in real time.

Reference

1. El espectador, «Colombia se está envejeciendo: el 9,23% de la población tiene más de 60 años,» El Espectador, 4 Septiembre 2018
2. Berrío Valencia, M.I.: Colombian J. Anesthesiol. (40) (2012)
3. Joshi, S., Saxena, S., Godbole y Shreyad, T.: Developing smart cities: an integrated framework. ScienceDirect 8 (2016)
4. Barth, J., et al.: Informational urbanism. a conceptual framework of smart cities. In: Proceedings of the 50th Hawaii International Conference on System Sciences, p. 10 (2017)
5. Vlasios, T., et al.: Real-time iot stream processing and large-scale data analytics for smart city applications. City Pulse (2013)
6. Kumaran Nair, S.S., Ganesh, N.: An exploratory study on Big data processing: a case study from a biomedical informatics. In: 3rd MEC International Conference on Big Data and Smart City, p. 4 (2016)
7. Sacristan, A.G., Hernandez, M.A.R.: Communications for sanitary teleservices in a smart city. In: 2018 Global Medical Engineering Physics Exchanges, p. 4 (2018)
8. Aziz, K., Tarapiah, S., Ismail, S.H., Atalla, S.: Smart real-time healthcare monitoring and tracking system using GSM/GPS technologies. In: 3rd MEC International Conference on Big Data and Smart City, p. 7 (2016)
9. Khan, T., Chattopadhyay, M.K.: Smart health monitoring system. In: IEEE, International Conference on Information, Communication, Instrumentation and Control (ICICIC 2017), p. 6 (2017)
10. Khoi, N.M., Saguna, S., Mitra, K., Ahlund, C.: IReHMo: an efficient iot-based remote health monitoring system for smart regions. In: 17th International Conference on E-health Networking, Application & Services (HealthCom), p. 6 (2015)
11. Fengou, M.-A., Mantas, G., Lymberopoulos, D., Komninos, N., Fengos, S., Lazarou, N.: A new framework architecture for next generation e-Health services. IEEE J. Biomed. Health Inform. **17**(1), 10 (2013)

Implementation of the Management System of Knowledge for the Process Management of a Sterilization Central

Flor Nancy Díaz-Piraquive[1]([⊠]) [iD], Yasser de Jesús Muriel-Perea[1] [iD], and Mayra Samara Ordoñez-Díaz[2]

[1] Universidad Catolica de Colombia, Bogotá, Colombia
{fndiaz,yjmuriel}@ucatolica.edu.co
[2] Fundación Universitaria de Ciencias de La Salud FUCS and Sociedad de Cirugía de Bogotá-Hospital de San José, Bogotá, Colombia
msordonez@fucsalud.edu.co

Abstract. The purpose of this article is to present the display of the Management System of Knowledge for the Process Management of a Sterilization Center (KMOS), specifically applied in San José Hospital, located in the City of Bogotá, Colombia, including in the process, the necessary technological dimensions for its operation.

Regarding the process perspective, the information system supports the management indicators process of the sterilization center. This process is a key factor for decision making, and to produce the necessary actions to reduce the percentage of health care-associated infections (HCAIs), since surveys on epidemiology have shown that approximately 5% of people using the surgical intervention services present HCAIs and, as a final outcome, they die.

Regarding the technological component, main contributions are found in the implementation of the information system, using as a method, integration, the development methodology and the management methodology of service. For access to information, primary sources were used directly related to the process, through the double interview technique that is to say, a first interview producing initial information and, a second interview, confirming its declarations in the validation.

Results show that automation of the management indicators allows the development, effectively and reliably, of a key process for the decision making in the sterilization center. The analysis concludes that the use of the KMOS System in the sterilization center, helps to generate pertinent information for data collection, intended to reduce the death rates, as well as health care-associated infections (HCAIs), thanks to the efficient follow up of equipment sterilization, materials, accessories and other items used in the intervention process.

Keywords: Asepsis · Antisepsis · Sterilization center · Management indicators · Load log

L. Uden et al. (Eds.): KMO 2021, CCIS 1438, pp. 280–291, 2021.
https://doi.org/10.1007/978-3-030-81635-3_23

1 Introduction

The research conducted is a contribution to the management of sterilization centers in Colombia, and it enriches the existent literature on those centers. To do that, the development of work was focused from strategic, missionary and support levels, in order for the coordinators or process leaders, to have the management and operation tools required for the optimal performance of the Sterilization Centers, which have now ceased to be a support unit to give them their corresponding importance within the chain of health services provision. Sterilization of instruments, equipment, accessories and the necessary supplies to render medical-assistance services, in the Health Provider Institutions (HPI), make a big impact on the patient's reliability, since within this process, the control of infections associated to health assistance is immersed, and the techno-surveillance of devices used in the different procedures. Therefore, quality of health services provider institutions is directly affected due to the proper functioning of this unit.

Considering that the sterilization center becomes a main axis to manage the sterile product, and that the operation costs are high due to the use of high technology, resources and inherent risks of processes thereon performed, an adequate management is required in order to make of this area a productive resource for institutions and, giving added value to services rendered to patients. Actually, in Colombia, surgical instruments are those who lead the process and for this reason, it is important to offer support tools helping in the complementation of training in healthcare assistance.

Reports from the Administrative Department of National Statistics [1], reveal that, on 2015, approximately a 5% of people presenting HCAIs during the surgery, die. The surgical unit and the sterilization center are units within a healthcare provider institution that require a constant development of personnel, and, a high investment in technology and supplies to grant the correct operation, as well as their competitiveness in the market. Therefore, this research was focused on gathering the required documentation to develop processes, with the aim of achieving a more effective performance, reliable and pertinent.

The importance of the asepsis and antisepsis processes appear since before Christ, since by then it was noticeable the high mortality rates due to infections, Hippocrates (460–377 a.c.). In addition, Galen (130–200 a.c.), used a technique with boiled water to clean the instruments used to cure gladiators that fell on combat. In this way he showed that not only it was a faster recovery, but that the death rate was lower [2]. On XIX century, Ignaz Semmelweis (1818–1865), a Hungarian Doctor who was in charge of hospital births, through observation he could detect that 30% of women who gave birth on 1840, died due to puerperal fever, since the same doctors who made necropsies to deceased people in a near hospital place, were the same ones who took care of births, considering this, as a possible risk factor, [3]. The sterilization center of "San José Hospital" of Bogotá, provides the reception service, washing, packing, sterilization, storage and delivery of required equipment, accessories and clothing for surgical procedures developed by the hospital, as well as for its users. Most of these processes in the sterilization center, although they are developed under the highest quality standards, are done manually with reprocessing and with a low automation level. The hypothesis raised reveals shortcomings in the process development of the sterilization center. Therefore, the main purpose of the work is analysis, designing, developing, testing and implementation of an information system and of knowledge for the process management of the sterilization center, in order to optimize the management indicators.

2 Conceptual Framework

Sterilization is vital for the success of surgical operations and prevention of infections associated to health care. A sterilizer is understood as an equipment used to destroy germs which can cause an infection. Sterilization is "the destruction of all germs, pathogens and non-pathogens by different ways (physical and chemical). It is applicable only to inanimate objects" [4]. The first concept of sterilization center was given on 1982 by Dr. John Perkins, who defined the Center as a processing service that distributes and controls sterile and non-sterile medical items and equipment, for care and safety of patients, [5]. Following are the main technical and sterilization process concepts, which allow to count with a context and reference for the research basis.

Sterilization Center: "is the hospital service that receives, conditions, processes, controls and distributes textiles (clothing, gauze, dressings, etc.), medical and bio-medical equipment, to all sectors of the hospital, with the final aim of obtaining a safe input to be used with the patient" [6].

Sterilization Area: place where autoclaves vapor, ethylene oxide (EtO), dry heat stoves and any other sterilizer equipment are placed: formaldehyde, hydrogen peroxide plasma; including the space to load and unload the trucks [7].

Sterilization Process: The set of required procedures for sterilization of any item, including the operation of the sterilization cycle, and any necessary treatment of the load before and after the sterilization cycle operation [8].

Enterprise Architecture: TOGAF. It is a reference framework, and a methodology of enterprise architecture. It facilitates the aligning between the business and the information and communication technologies [9]. According to Scot, the enterprise architecture is made up of strategy, processes and information systems [10]. An enterprise architecture explains how all "the information technologies elements in an organization, processes, systems, the organizational structure and people, get integrated and work together as a whole unit" [11]. The enterprise architecture is understood as a business strategy which allows the aligning of technology with the strategic goals of the organization [11].

Surgical Instruments: This is the set of items used in the surgical procedures; they must be subjected to a process of decontamination, cleaning and sterilization [12].

Management Indicators in the Sterilization Center: They are performance meters of the sterilization process, during processing or when they are handed out to the professional who makes the surgical procedure.

Another relevant concept is the one about loading, corresponding to equipment and accessories to be used according to the storing method for sterilization (Ethylene oxide, hydrogen peroxide, humid heat). The name given to the information system of process management of the sterilization center, was KMOS, which produces information for the sterilization center, and for the quality information system of Hospital San José, called ALMERA [13].

According to the qualitative research approach the sampling strategy is called criterion – based selection, because the researcher develops inclusion criteria to be used in selecting people or other units [14]. There are many types of sampling. In this paper was used critical case sampling, this sampling consists in selecting what the researcher considers to be particularly important case, which allows say that that if it happens there, it will happen anywhere [15]. The Sterilization Central in San Jose Hospital is a critical case; hence, this case can add to the knowledge and other places, in or out of Colombia.

3   Problem Statement

The epidemiology health care-associated infections (HCAIs), has shown that, an important percentage of in-hospital infections, acquired by a patient during the post-operative period or after any invasive procedure, are greatly associated to an inadequate disinfection and sterilization of reusable objects, including endoscopic equipment, respiratory equipment, transducers and hemo analysis equipment, among others. Table 1 shows number of infections and disinfections per HCAIs.

Table 1. Deaths by HCAIs

Year	Total infections, caused by HCAIs	Total deaths caused by HCAIs	Percentage of deaths caused by HCAIs
2015	13,045	679	5,2%

Source. Authors based on the bulletin from DANE[1]

In the sterilization center of Hospital San José, the average of load registrations through sterilization is of 1.500 approximately. This information is registered by the operators, after the process and, they do it manually, in many cases appealing to the memory capacity. This situation causes inefficiencies in the registration (the reduced process and reliability) and, subsequent generation of management indicators and statistics which allow the analysis and improvement of the process. In addition, the early alarms generation and the knowledge management around the process gets difficult.

Therefore, it becomes necessary the implementation of an information system to support key activities of processes in the sterilization center, with its corresponding tracking.

4   Methodology

For the integration of the business processes, and the development of the automation to use technology, the TOGAF reference framework was used. For this methodology, to start with, the information principles, applications and technology were defined. Then, the business architecture, the architecture of information system and, ultimately, the technology architecture. Everything keeping in mind the as is, and the to be.

For the analysis, design, development, tests and implementation of the application, the methodology based on the cascade model was used (see Fig. 1). Therefore, being coherent with the life cycle of the system, the cascade methodology was used, and articulated within it, the concepts of business architecture for the provision of services, TOGAF, were integrated.

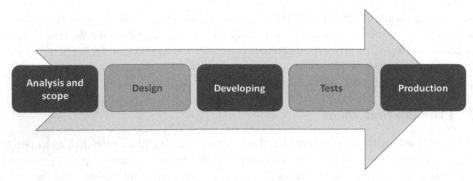

Fig. 1. Implementation Methodology. Source: the authors

4.1 Analysis and Scope

With the aim of making an analysis of processes, define their hierarchy and determine which process starts automation, two tools were used: the impact and criticality matrix and, the difficulty contribution matrix.

For definition of the scope, the use cases technique was used, and the requirements specification according to standard IEEE830 [16]. As information gathering, primary and secondary sources were used. For primary sources, interviews with stakeholders were done, mainly with the surgical instruments. Secondary sources consisted of consultations to physical and digital documentation from Hospital San José and, from the sterilization center.

4.2 Design

In this stage, according to the reference framework TOGAF, the as is and the to be of the data architecture and applications, were defined.

4.3 Development

For the development, installation and display of the system, the following technological tools were used, in coherence with the available infrastructure in Hospital San José: Server with support for PHP/7.1.7, Applications Server: Apache/2.4.26. Server with data base motor: MySQL. 5.7.19. Operating System Linux or Solaris.

4.4 Tests

For the definition of functionality tests of the software, the test protocol was used according to ISO-IEC-IEEE 29119 [10–14], while for documentation of the test results, the international standard for software tests ISO/IEC/IEEE 29119 [16] was used.

4.5 Production

For this activity the information related to equipment inventory, materials, instruments and accessories, among others, previously identified and documented in accordance with the identity requirements of the Hospital and, it is now in process, together with the information technology management office of Hospital San José.

5 Results

Results are presented in accordance with the suggested methodology stages.

5.1 Analysis and Scope

According to processes developed in the Sterilization Center, candidates for automation, which were identified with a character, are as follows:

A: reception and washing. B: storage. C: packing. D: sterilization with humid heat. E: sterilization with ethylene oxide. F: sterilization with hydrogen peroxide. G: reuse procedure and, H: management indicators.

With the purpose of following a priority order in the implementation of processes, in the management system of knowledge, for the process management of the sterilization center, the first step consisted of the application of the importance criticality matrix, applied under the technique of an expert's judgment, by the project team members, and it came out with the following result: see Table 2.

Results show that processes related to construction of management indicators, reuse, reception and washing, storage and sterilization with heat, were the first ones to be automated.

The second step consisted of determining the contribution with the project's goals and the difficulty, understood, as the access difficulty to resources for the management or improvement of them, see Fig. 2.

Based on the application of the two matrices, it was decided that the process to be automated was H: management indicators. Once the process was defined, the use cases were determined, see Fig. 3.

5.2 Design

5.2.1 Data Architecture

The base line found, shows a manual process. The loads are registered in a physical format. The indicators are consolidated manually, and they are loaded to the quality management system ALMERA, through an Excel file. The following is the logical data model proposed. See Fig. 4.

Table 2. Importance and criticality Matrix

Processes		Improvement impact			Response time			Relationship with the management system of knowledge		Weighted total
Weighting (qualification)		High (5)	Medium (3)	Low (1)	High (5)	Medium (3)	Low (1)	Direct (5)	Indirect (1)	
		5	3	1	5	3	1	5	1	
A	Reception and washing	4			4			3	1	56
B	Storage		4		4			3	1	48
C	Packing			4		4			4	20
D	Sterilization with humid heat	4			4				4	44
E	Sterilization with ethylene oxide		1	3			4		4	14
F	Sterilization with hydrogen peroxide		4		4				4	36
G	Reuse procedure	4			4			4		60
H	Management indicators	4			4			4		60

Source. the authors

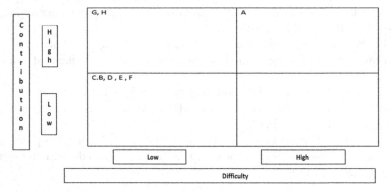

Fig. 2. Difficulty contribution matrix. Source: the authors

5.2.2 Applications Architecture

The process of load registration, basis for the generation process of management indicators, is done manually. This causes errors not only in the registration, but in the consolidation and in the generation of management indicators, making the preventive and corrective activities difficult, since they could allow the process to be more effective. Besides that, great part of the load registration process depends on knowledge and memory of people, an automated process does not exist through an information system to allow the operators to support and keep record before registration. Likewise, it happens with the consolidation and analysis activity of the Center´s coordinator. This causes

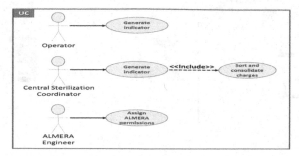

Fig. 3. Use cases. Source: the authors

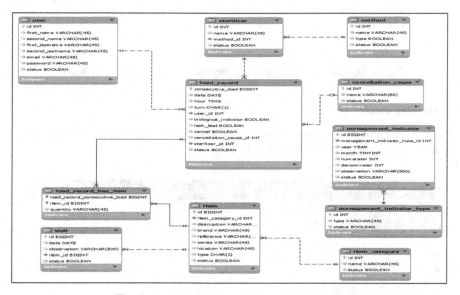

Fig. 4. Logical data model. Source. the authors

inefficiencies in the reporting process of management indicators, from the Sterilization Center to Hospital San José. Classification of the load registration by method, cause of cancellation or other concepts, is done by memory by the coordinator of the sterilization center. Eventually, this can cause involuntary errors or prevent them, it represents a very expensive job. The process basically consists of the load registrations done by the operators phisically. Later, the Center's coordinator makes the counting, consolidation and registration in Excel of the indicators information requested from the Sterilization Center by the Hospital. Then, the coordinator enters the system ALMERA and loads the information. Finally, it is found that the access to historical information is very slow and ineffective and, delivery of indicators is not appropriate.

Thus, the physical view of the applications architecture proposed by the research, would be as follows, see Fig. 5.

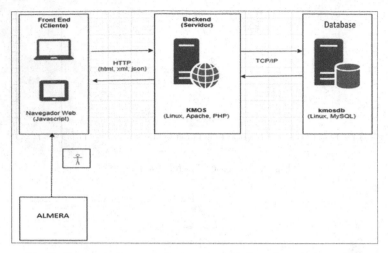

Fig. 5. Diagram of general display, physical view. Source: the authors

5.3 Development

Once the Management System of Knowledge for the Process Management is developed, one of its main screens can be seen. See Fig. 6.

Fig. 6. Load registration. Source: the authors

5.4 Tests

5.4.1 Risk Identification

The main threats, functional and non-functional, detected, are shown on Table 3.

The occurrence probability of threats is defined as high, medium and low, for more than 70%, between 30% and - 70%, and less than 30% respectively. The Test Plan was generated with the risk identification and the probability and impact matrix. See Table 4.

Table 3. Threats

Category	Threat
Functional Code i01	I01–01: The load registration does not persist in the data base I01–02: The equipment does not persist in the data base I01–03: The accessory does not persist in the data base I01–04: The indicator´s calculation for cancellation by cycle does not produce an accurate result I01–05: The indicator´s calculation for returns of non-conformity does not generate an accurate result
Non- functional Code i02	I02–01: Reports are produced inefficiently I02–02: The back-up cannot be recovered

Source: the authors

Table 4. Test plan.

Risk	Action	Responsible person
I01–04: The indicator´s calculation for cancellation by cycle, does not generate an accurate result,	Test of use cases. Precision analysis	Surgical instrumenter
I01–05: The indicator´s calculation of returns for non-conformity does not generate an accurate result	Test of use cases. Precision analysis	Surgical instrumenter
I02–01: Reports are produced inefficiently	Stress test	Systems engineer

Source: the authors

6 Discussion

Although in the beginning methodologies seemed to be distant, it is possible to develop a methodology to integrate the Cascade development methodology, with the reference framework TOGAF. No doubt, automation of the management indicators process contributes to the knowledge management in the sterilization central and, it could be said that it contributes directly to the information generation for the decision making in a critical process, which influences on the success of surgical interventions. Nevertheless, effectiveness of the KMOS system does not only depend on the technological tool but, it really depends on the use given to it [17–20].

The system initially automated the management indicators process, there is a restriction. If it is true that the Hospital is largely automated in its processes, there is also a sterilization center that manages a great number of processes manually and, in some measure, there is no automation culture. Additionally, the amount of the project resources (people, time), are scarce compared with the number of automations needs of the sterilization center. What is suggested is to implement the processes gradually, in accordance with the priorization done and, as long as resources allow it and the organization keeps maturing on this new culture for the organization [17–20].

7 Conclusions

The investigation allowed to establish the following conclusions:

- The implementation of KMOS impacts the quality of medical services because the management indicators are a key factor for decision making, and to produce the necessary actions to reduce the percentage of health care-associated infections (HCAIs).
- The reference framework TOGAF may be worked integrally with the development methodologies of traditional software, optimizing the management processes oriented towards improvement of competitiveness.
- Keeping in mind that the organizational culture in the sterilization center, is a based on handwork, it becomes necessary to develop management actions for change, with the aim of achieving a greater benefit from the KMOS System
- As a future works, it would be important to study about prediction markets as forecasting tools, in order to leverage the sterilization center and to take advantage of KMOS. It is necessary to continue with the automation of the rest of processes of the sterilization center.

References

1. Departamento Administrativo Nacional de Estadísticas. DANE. Boletín Técnico. Estadísticas Vitales 2014–2015. Publicado el 30 de marzo de 2016 en. https://www.dane.gov.co/files/inv estigaciones/poblacion/bt_estadisticasvitales_2014p-2015p-30-03-2016.pdf
2. Santos, F.: Central de Equipos y Esterilización. Recuperado de la página. http://es.slideshare. net/fersantos/esterelizacin-historia. el día 15 de mayo de 2016
3. Costa, B., Soares, E., de Silva, A.Y.C.: Evolución de las centrales de material y esterilización: historia, actualidad y perspectivas de la enfermería. Enfermería Global **15**, 1–6 (2009)
4. Mejías, M.R.: El personal auxiliar de enfermería en el área quirúrgica (2a. ed.). Recuperado de (2014). https://ebookcentral.proquest.com
5. CODEINEP: Conceptos actuales de esterilización hospitalaria y su organización. Recuperado de. https://codeinep.org/portfolio-item/esterilizacion-hospitalaria/. el día 12 de marzo de 2019
6. Social, M.D.S.Y.P.: Resolución 02183, de julio. Por la cual se adopta el Manual de Buenas Prácticas de Esterilización (2004)
7. Riveros, S.: Conceptos Modernos en Esterilización. Recuperado de la página. http://enferm eraspabelonyesterilización.cl/eventos/conceptos_modernos.pdf. el día 13 de marzo de 2019
8. The Open Group. TOGAF 9.2. Recuperado de la página. http://opengroup.org/togaf. el día 13 de marzo de 2019
9. Scott, B.: An Introduction To Enterprise Architecture, Bloomington: Authorhouse, 2005, Recuperado de la página. http://opengroup.org/togaf. el día 13 de marzo de (2019)
10. Revista Ingeniería Universidad de Medellín. Arquitectura empresarial - una visión general recuperado de]. <http://www.scielo.org.co/scielo.php?pid=S1692-33242010000100009& script=sci_arttext>. el día 11 de noviembre de 2019

11. Ross, J.W.: Creating a Strategic It Architecture Competency: Learning in Stages (April 2003). MIT Sloan Working Paper No. 4314–03; Center for Information Systems Research Working Paper No. 335. Available at SSRN: https://ssrn.com/abstract=416180 or https://doi.org/10.2139/ssrn.416180

12. Sarria, S., Lidia, O., Yaima, G.D., Dávila, H., Manuel, C., de Villa, D.C., Evangelina: Manual de instrumental quirúrgico. MediSur, 12(5), undefined-undefined. [fecha de Consulta 11 de noviembre de 2019]. Disponible en (2014). https://www.redalyc.org/articulo.oa?id=1800/180032796014

13. FUCS. Sistema de gestión documental ALMERA. Recuperado de la página. https://sgi.almeraim.com/sgi/index.php?conid=sgifucs&clean=t el día 11 de noviembre de 2019

14. LeCompte, M.D., Preissle, J.: Ethnography and Qualitative Design in Educational Research. Academic Press, New York, NY (1993)

15. Johnson, B., Christensen, L.: Educational Research : Quantitative, Qualitative, and Mixed Approaches, 5th edn., p. 2014. Sage Publications, Los Angeles (2014)

16. IEEE: IEEStandars Association. Recuperado de la página. https://standars.ieee.org/standard/830-1998.html. el día 14 de marzo de 2019

17. Rozo-Rojas, I., Díaz-Piraquive, F.N., Ordoñez-Díaz, M.S., de Jesús Muriel-Perea, Y.: Quality measurement in sterilization processes at healthcare organization in colombia using six sigma metrics. In: Uden, L., Ting, I.-H., Corchado, J.M. (eds.) KMO 2019. CCIS, vol. 1027, pp. 297–306. Springer, Cham (2019). https://doi.org/10.1007/978-3-030-21451-7_25

18. Díaz-Piraquive, F.N., García, V.H.M., Bermúdez, G.M.T.: Modelo de Gestión del Conocimiento como apoyo a la Gestión de Proyectos. Colombia. ed: Universidad Distrital Francisco José de Caldas 2019. ISBN: 978–958–787–097–8 v.1 págs. 476

19. Díaz-Piraquive, F.N., Rozo-Rojas, I., Serrano-Cárdenas, L.F.Y.: Revisión de la literatura de prácticas para evaluar la calidad del servicio en instituciones de salud. Hacia un enfoque de Lean Healtcare. En: Medellín Antioquia. En: Desarrollo e Innovación en Ingeniería, (3ra Edición) ISBN: 978–958–59127–9–3 ed: Instituto Antioqueño de Investigación. Pág. 270–278 (2018)

20. Perkins, J.: Principles and methods of sterilization in health sciences (Segundo ed.) (2008)

The Usability Evaluation Method of E-learning Platform Based on Fuzzy Comprehensive Evaluation

Ran Tao, Lili Zhu$^{(\boxtimes)}$, Qinqin Wen, Youqun Shi, and Xiangyang Feng

School of Computer Science and Technology, Donghua University, Shanghai 201620, China
{taoran,yqshi,fengxy}@dhu.edu.cn

Abstract. E-learning platform provides an online learning environment for teachers and students. The high usability of e-learning platform plays an important role in product competitiveness, user learning effect and so on. However, as the usability of e-learning platform is affected by many factors, it is challenging to analyze the usability of e-learning platform. In this paper, the analytic hierarchy process and fuzzy comprehensive evaluation are used to propose an e-learning platform usability fuzzy evaluation method, which includes evaluation index, weight, comprehensive evaluation matrix and usability evaluation algorithm, and its effectiveness is verified by a case. Experimental results show that this method can be used to evaluate the e-learning platform as a whole and its first-level evaluation indicators. The fuzzy evaluation method presented in this paper provides a quantitative evaluation reference of software usability for software development and users, which can be used in software project planning, comparison, selection, testing, acceptance and other scenarios.

Keywords: E-learning platform · Software usability · Fuzzy comprehensive evaluation · Analytic hierarchy process

1 Introduction

E-learning platform mainly refers to the network platform that can carry out learning and teaching activities [1]. It can effectively integrate and process various teaching resources [2], and help teachers and students prepare lessons and learn anytime, anywhere. The e-learning platform is playing an increasingly important role in the learning process. A survey on corporate e-learning pointed out that most employees used to learn by face-to-face training, but later turned into a half-open situation of e-learning and face-to-face training. Now, the proportion of employees who use e-learning platform for learning has accounted for the majority.

Usability is especially important for e-learning platforms. Improving the usability of the software can not only improve user experience and product competitiveness, but also save the cost of training and technical support [5]. In order to better realize the function and value of the e-learning platform and improve the usability of the e-learning platform, it is necessary to conduct quantitative analysis on the usability of e-learning platform.

© Springer Nature Switzerland AG 2021
L. Uden et al. (Eds.): KMO 2021, CCIS 1438, pp. 292–304, 2021.
https://doi.org/10.1007/978-3-030-81635-3_24

Although most users have subjective feelings about the usability of the e-learning platform, software evaluation experts will also give reasonable suggestions for improving the usability of the e-learning platform based on their own experience. However, since the selection of indicators by users is not comprehensive, these evaluations and suggestions are often one-sided. In addition, when performing comprehensive evaluation, the calculation method is relatively simple, and the weight of the index is not taken into account, so it is difficult to get an objective comprehensive evaluation. However, from the perspective of the usability of e-learning platform, it is of great significance for the design and development of e-learning platform to find out the deficiencies in the use of e-learning platform and put forward reasonable improvement suggestions.

In view of the above problems, this paper proposes a usability evaluation method of e-learning platform based on fuzzy comprehensive evaluation (FCE) to quantify the usability of the e-learning platform and obtain the evaluation results.

The rest of the paper is organized as follows. The following section provides a brief literature review of software usability evaluation and FCE. Section 3 introduces the usability evaluation method of e-learning platform based on FCE. Section 4 presents a case study that uses this method to evaluate the usability of an e-learning platform. Finally, conclusions and ideas for future research are offered.

2 Related Literature Review

2.1 Software Usability Evaluation

Software usability refers to the ability of a software product to be understood, learned, used, and attracted to users under specific use cases [5]. The software usability assessment is based on these elements. Software usability evaluation mainly uses various evaluation methods to obtain evaluation data in the process of completing specific goals by specific users in specific use environments, and then analyzes the quantitative results of software product usability through scientific methods. And use this as a basis to evaluate the usability of software products [4]. At present, the methods used in software usability evaluation mainly include principal component analysis [15], analytic hierarchy process (AHP) [16], BP neural network method [17], FCE [6], gray correlation degree [18], etc. M. r. h. Iman and others developed a fuzzy expert system for quantitative evaluation of software usability [19], but the laboratory only evaluated software usability from the perspective of software user interface, without considering other factors affecting software usability. Jiang Shan from Beijing University of Posts and Telecommunications constructed the e-learning platform's usability evaluation index system, and on this basis, discussed how to use the AHP to compare, rank and evaluate the indicators [4]. However, the experiment only verified the rationality of the evaluation index system, and did not mention the method of quantitative evaluation of software usability.

2.2 Fuzzy Comprehensive Evaluation

In 1965, Professor L.A. Zadeh, an American computer and control expert, proposed the important concept of fuzzy sets in the journal Information and Control [7]. On this basis,

FCE is produced. The FCE is a specific application method based on fuzzy mathematics. It is a reasonable overall evaluation of things with multiple attributes or things whose overall strength is affected by multiple factors. It can well solve fuzzy and difficult to quantify problems [8]. Many scholars have researched using FCE. Huang L C constructed a new management talent evaluation model for the evaluators, and used the fuzzy analytic hierarchy process for evaluation, which can obtain management activity information more systematically and effectively [9]. Using the paired comparison survey method of expert pairs, s. Roy proposed a storage-as-a-service (SaaS) based on the fuzzy analytic hierarchy process model to evaluate the usability of commercial websites [10]. However, the whole process of the study took too long and consumed too much manpower. R. k. Harshan proposed a framework for evaluating the usability of library websites, which involves fuzzy analytic hierarchy process and extensive evaluation techniques, and can be used to evaluate the overall usability score, as well as the score of each evaluation dimension of any type of website [11]. In addition, FCE is also widely used in operational capability [12], energy conservation and emission reduction [13], employability [14] and other different fields.

To sum up, there is still a lack of quantitative evaluation on the usability of e-learning platform. Although FCE has been used in many fields, it has not been used in the usability evaluation of e-learning platform. The above studies provide important references for the study of e-learning platform usability evaluation.

When evaluating the usability of e-learning platform, there will be a large number of "unclear" or "uncertain" in obtaining the evaluation information of various evaluation indicators, which brings certain ambiguity to the evaluation. In order to improve the accuracy of usability evaluation results, it is necessary to deal with the ambiguity of evaluation information. By using the principle of fuzzy linear transformation and the principle of maximum membership degree, the FCE can not only effectively deal with the fuzziness of usability evaluation, but also obtain its comprehensive evaluation based on various factors related to the thing being evaluated. Therefore, this study uses FCE to evaluate the usability of e-learning platform.

3   The Usability Evaluation Method of e-learning Platform Based on FCE

Based on FCE and AHP, this section designs a usability evaluation method of e-learning Platform Based on FCE as shown in Fig. 1.

This method includes evaluation index, weight, comprehensive evaluation matrix and usability evaluation algorithm. The specific steps are as follows.

1. Select e-learning platform to be evaluated;
2. Design first-level and second-level indicators for the evaluated e-learning platform;

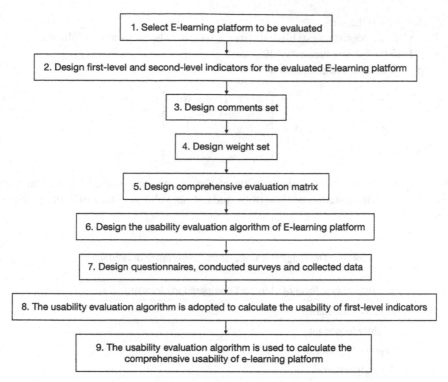

Fig. 1. The usability evaluation method of e-learning platform based on FCE

According to the influential ISO/IEC 25010 [5], and based on the analysis of the characteristics of e-learning platform being evaluated, the indicators are formulated. It is assumed that there are m indicators related to the usability evaluation of e-learning platform, and set the first-level indicator set as:

$$U = \{U_1, U_2, \cdots, U_m\}.$$

Due to the complexity of e-learning platform, it is often a little rough to evaluate only the first-level indicators, and meaningful evaluation results cannot be obtained. Therefore, the first-level indicators are further divided into the second-level indicators. Set the second-level indicator sets as:

$$U_1 = \{U_{11}, U_{12}, \cdots, U_{1p}\},$$
$$U_2 = \{U_{21}, U_{22}, \cdots, U_{2q}\},$$
$$\vdots$$
$$U_m = \{U_{m1}, U_{m2}, \cdots, U_{mr}\}.$$

3. Design comments set;

The rating is based on expert advice. It is assumed that the comments of e-learning platform evaluated are divided into n levels, and the comments set is set as:

$$V = \{V_1, V_2, \cdots, V_n\}$$

4. Design weight set;

The AHP is adopted to establish the index weight. The steps are as follows.

Step 1: Establish the hierarchy diagram

Step 2: Construct judgment matrix

$$A = \begin{bmatrix} a_{11} & a_{11} & \cdots & a_{1n} \\ a_{21} & a_{22} & & a_{2n} \\ \vdots & & \ddots & \vdots \\ a_{m1} & a_{m2} & \cdots & a_{mn} \end{bmatrix}$$

Where, a_{ij} represents the judgment value of the importance of element i relative to element j. The determination method of the judgement value is shown in Table 1, where $a_{ji} = 1/a_{ij}$.

Table 1. The judgment value of the importance of the factor

The importance level of element i compared to element j	a_{ij}
Equally important	1
Slightly important	3
Obviously important	5
Strongly important	7
Absolutely important	9
Between levels	2, 4, 6, 8
The importance of element j compared to element i	Reciprocal

Step 3: Find the maximum eigenvalue λ_{max} of the judgment matrix A and the corresponding eigenvector ω.

Step 4: Verify the compatibility of the judgment matrix

$$C(A) = \frac{\lambda_{max} - n}{n - 1} \tag{1}$$

When $C(A) \leq 0.1$, it is considered that the compatibility of the judgment matrix A is good, and the eigenvector ω corresponding to the maximum eigenvalue λ_{max} of A can be used as the weight vector. Otherwise you need to readjust the judgment matrix.

Set the weight set of the first-level indicator obtained by AHP as

$$\omega = (\omega_1, \omega_2, \cdots, \omega_m), \quad where \ \omega_1 + \omega_2 + \cdots + \omega_m = 1.$$

Set the weight sets of the second-level indicator as

$$\omega_1 = (\omega_{11}, \omega_{12}, \cdots, \omega_{1p}), \quad where \ \omega_{11} + \omega_{12} + \cdots + \omega_{1p} = 1,$$
$$\omega_2 = (\omega_{21}, \omega_{22}, \cdots, \omega_{2q}), \quad where \ \omega_{21} + \omega_{22} + \cdots + \omega_{2q} = 1,$$

$$\vdots$$

$$\omega_m = (\omega_{m1}, \omega_{m2}, \cdots, \omega_{mr}), \quad where \ \omega_{m1} + \omega_{m2} + \cdots + \omega_{mr} = 1.$$

5. Design comprehensive evaluation matrix;

Membership is determined by fuzzy statistics to determine. That is, if y of x participants think that indicator U_1 belongs to comment V_1, then y/x is the membership of U_1 to V_1. After determining the membership of each index to the comments set, the comprehensive evaluation matrix can be obtained. For example, the comprehensive evaluation matrix of U is:

$$
R = \begin{bmatrix} r_{11} & r_{12} & \cdots & r_{1n} \\ r_{21} & r_{22} & & r_{2n} \\ \vdots & & \ddots & \vdots \\ r_{m1} & r_{m2} & \cdots & r_{mn} \end{bmatrix}
$$

Where r_{ij} is the membership of indicator $U_i(i = 1, 2, \cdots, m)$ to comment $V_j(j = 1, 2, \ldots, n)$.

6. Design the usability evaluation algorithm of e-learning platform;

When the index weight set ω and comprehensive evaluation matrix R are known,

$$
B = \omega * R = (b_1, b_2, \cdots, b_n)
$$

can be obtained. Where "*" represents the generalized fuzzy synthesis operation. When evaluating the usability of e-learning platform, the overall indicators should be considered, and all factors should be balanced according to the weight. Therefore, the model $M(\cdot, \oplus)$ is used to perform generalized fuzzy synthesis operation on the weight set and comprehensive judgment matrix, that is

$$
b_j = min\left\{ 1, \sum_{i=1}^{m} \omega_i \cdot r_{ij} \right\}, \quad where\ (j = 1, 2, \cdots, n) \tag{2}
$$

According to the principle of maximum membership degree, the V_j corresponding to the maximum b_j in fuzzy comprehensive evaluation set $B = (b_1, b_2, \cdots, b_n)$ is selected as the result of comprehensive evaluation. The designed Usability Evaluation Algorithm is shown in Table 2.

7. Design questionnaires, conducted surveys and collected data;

In the usability evaluation process, questionnaires were used to obtain scoring data. According to the developed second-level indicators, e-learning platform usability questionnaire is designed. Each second-level indicator sets a question, and a 5-point scale is used to score the question. For example, a question in the questionnaire can be designed as: what do you think about the function recognition of the e-learning platform? The corresponding scoring scales are: 1 – very low, 2 – low, 3 – average, 4 – high, 5 – very high. Then several participants were invited to use the e-learning platform of the evaluated object. In order to ensure the reasonable and accurate experimental results, participants independently used the e-learning platform of the evaluation object, with the use cycle of one month. Finally, on the premise of ensuring that each participant knows the meaning of each score item, participants are asked to score the assessed object on e-learning platform according to the designed questionnaire.

Table 2. Usability evaluation algorithm

Input: MATRIX w(Index weight set), MATRIX R(Comprehensive evaluation matrix), MATRIX V(Comments set)
Output: Usability rating

1. **Begin**
2.   Call w.csv to initializes the index weight set w
3.   Call r.csv to initialize the synthetic evaluation matrix R
4.   Call v.csv to initialize the evaluation matrix V
5.   sum = 0
6.   **For** j = 1:n
7.   **For** i = 1:m
8.   sum += w[i] * R[i,j]
9.   **End**
10.   B[j] = min(1,sum) // Taking the value that's smaller than 1 and sum
11.   **End**
12.   k = 1
13.   **For** q = 1:n
14.   **If** (B[k] < B[q])
15.   k = q
16.   **End**
17.   **End**
18.   return Usability rating is V[k]
19. **End**

8. The usability evaluation algorithm is adopted to calculate the usability of first-level indicators;

Taking the weight set ω_1 and the comprehensive evaluation matrix R_1 as the input of the usability evaluation algorithm, the usability evaluation level of U_1 and its fuzzy comprehensive evaluation set B_1 are obtained. Similarly, the usability evaluation grades of $U_2, \cdots, U_m$ and corresponding fuzzy comprehensive evaluation sets $B_2, \cdots, B_m$ can be obtained.

9. The usability evaluation algorithm is used to calculate the comprehensive usability of e-learning platform;

Based on the above fuzzy comprehensive evaluation sets $B_1, B_2, B_3, B_4,$ and B_5 as the comprehensive evaluation matrix R of U, ω and R are input into the usability evaluation algorithm to obtain the comprehensive usability evaluation level of e-learning platform and the corresponding fuzzy comprehensive evaluation set B.

4   Case Study

Using the e-learning platform usability evaluation method mentioned above, we conducted usability evaluation with an e-learning platform as the evaluation object, and established an e-learning platform usability evaluation index system with 5 first-level indicators and 19 s-level indicators, as shown in Table 3.

Table 3. E-learning platform usability evaluation index system

First-level indicators	Second-level indicators
Appropriateness recognizability U_1	Recognizability of function U_{11}
	Comprehensibility of function U_{12}
	Comprehensibility of function descriptions U_{13}
	Recognizability of interface elements U_{14}
	Comprehensibility of input and output U_{15}
	Recognizability of prompt messages U_{16}
Learnability U_2	Ease of functional learning U_{21}
	Integrity of the functional description U_{22}
	Validity of the help document U_{23}
	Integrity of the prompt message U_{24}
Operability U_3	Difficulty of operating tasks U_{31}
	Complexity of operating tasks U_{32}
	Matches the user's expectations U_{33}
	Cancelability of user actions U_{34}
	Consistency of operation U_{35}
User error protection U_4	Fault tolerance of operations (free from human error)U_{34}
	Recoverability of running errors U_{42}
	False influence U_{43}
User interface aesthetics U_5	User interface aesthetics U_{51}

Therefore, we determined that the first-level index set of e-learning platform usability evaluation is

$$U = \{U_1, U_2, U_3, U_4, U_5\},$$

and the second-level index sets are

$$U_1 = \{U_{11}, U_{12}, U_{13}, U_{14}, U_{15}, U_{16}\},$$
$$U_2 = \{U_{21}, U_{22}, U_{23}, U_{24}\},$$
$$U_3 = \{U_{31}, U_{32}, U_{33}, U_{34}, U_{35}\},$$
$$U_4 = \{U_{41}, U_{42}, U_{43}\},$$
$$U_5 = \{U_{51}\}.$$

According to expert opinions, we divided the comments on e-learning platform usability into five grades: "extremely low", "low", "average", "high" and "extremely high", and set the comment set as

$$V = \{\text{extremely low, low, average, high, extremely high}\}.$$

The weight set of the first-level index obtained by AHP is

$$\omega = (\omega_1, \omega_2, \omega_3, \omega_4, \omega_5) = (0.321, 0.140, 0.263, 0.170, 0.106),$$

The weight sets of each second-level index are

$$\omega_1 = (\omega_{11}, \omega_{12}, \omega_{13}, \omega_{14}, \omega_{15}, \omega_{16}) = (0.254, 0.147, 0.062, 0.342, 0.109, 0.086),$$
$$\omega_2 = (\omega_{21}, \omega_{22}, \omega_{23}, \omega_{24}) = (0.467, 0.095, 0.160, 0.278),$$
$$\omega_3 = (\omega_{31}, \omega_{32}, \omega_{33}, \omega_{34}, \omega_{35}) = (0.257, 0.153, 0.413, 0.076, 0.101),$$
$$\omega_4 = (\omega_{41}, \omega_{42}, \omega_{43}) = (0.547, 0.263, 0.170),$$
$$\omega_5 = (\omega_{51}) = (1).$$

According to 19s-level indicators, we designed a questionnaire with 19 questions. Then, according to the requirements mentioned in point 7 of Chap. 3, 10 participants ($P_i(i = 1, 2, \cdots, 10)$, 5 men and 5 women, with an average age of 23) were invited to use and score the e-learning platform of the evaluation object. The score data obtained are shown in Table 4.

Further, we obtained the comprehensive evaluation matrix of the first-level indexes U_1, U_2, U_3, U_4, and U_5. For example, the comprehensive evaluation matrix of U_1 is

$$R_1 = \begin{bmatrix} 0 & 0.1 & 0.3 & 0.5 & 0.1 \\ 0 & 0.1 & 0.1 & 0.7 & 0.1 \\ 0 & 0 & 0.4 & 0.6 & 0 \\ 0 & 0.1 & 0.3 & 0.6 & 0 \\ 0 & 0.1 & 0.5 & 0.4 & 0 \\ 0 & 0 & 0.3 & 0.5 & 0.2 \end{bmatrix}$$

Taking the evaluation of U_1 in the first row as an example, the meaning of this matrix is: among the 10 participants, 0%, 10%, 30%, 30%, and 10% of the participants consider the feature to be very low in its recognizability.

The fuzzy comprehensive evaluation sets of $U_1, \cdots, U_m$ are

$$B_1 = (0, 0.085, 0.299, 0.599, 0.057),$$
$$B_2 = (0.047, 0.093, 0.541, 0.272, 0.047),$$
$$B_3 = (0, 0.152, 0.424, 0.399, 0.025),$$
$$B_4 = (0.043, 0.087, 0.366, 0.403, 0.081),$$
$$B_5 = (0, 0.1, 0.3, 0.5, 0.1).$$

The usability evaluation grade of each first-level indicator is shown in Fig. 2.

Table 4. E-learning platform usability score data

Second-level indicators	Participants									
	P_1	P_2	P_3	P_4	P_5	P_6	P_7	P_8	P_9	P_{10}
U_{11}	3	2	4	4	5	4	4	3	4	3
U_{12}	4	4	2	3	5	4	4	4	4	4
U_{13}	4	4	4	3	3	4	4	4	3	3
U_{14}	4	3	3	4	4	4	3	4	4	2
U_{15}	2	3	3	3	4	4	3	4	3	4
U_{16}	4	4	5	4	3	3	4	3	5	4
U_{21}	3	1	3	2	4	3	3	5	3	4
U_{22}	3	4	2	3	3	3	3	4	3	2
U_{23}	3	4	3	4	3	3	3	4	3	3
U_{24}	4	3	4	3	2	3	4	3	4	3
U_{31}	2	3	2	3	2	3	3	3	3	3
U_{32}	3	4	2	3	4	5	3	4	3	4
U_{33}	3	2	4	3	4	3	4	4	3	4
U_{34}	4	4	3	4	4	4	4	4	2	4
U_{35}	4	5	4	4	3	4	2	4	4	4
U_{41}	3	4	3	4	5	4	3	3	4	4
U_{42}	4	3	4	2	1	3	4	2	3	5
U_{43}	2	1	3	3	4	4	3	4	3	2
U_{51}	4	4	5	3	2	3	4	4	3	3

The vertical axis represents the usability rating, 1 represents very low, 2 represents low, 3 represents average, 4 represents high, and 5 represents very high. As can be seen from the figure, the evaluation level of the e-learning platform is "high" for its appropriateness recognizability, user error protection and user interface aesthetics, while the evaluation level of learnability and operability is "average". Therefore, the platform can be improved from the aspects of learnability and operability in the future.

Then we got the fuzzy comprehensive evaluation set of e-learning platform as

$$B = (0.014, 0.106, 0.377, 0.444, 0.056).$$

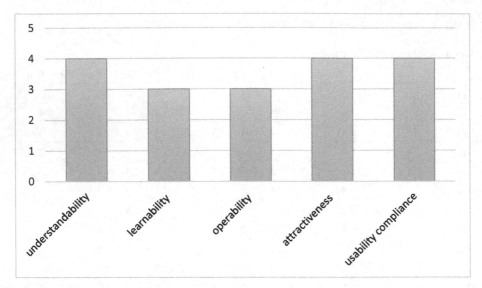

Fig. 2. The usability evaluation grades of each first-level indicators

The comprehensive usability evaluation level of e-learning platform is shown in Fig. 3.

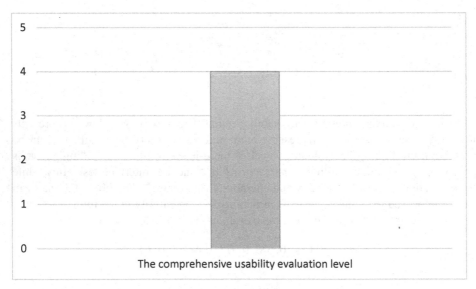

The comprehensive usability evaluation level

Fig. 3. The comprehensive usability evaluation level

The meaning of the vertical axis is as shown in Fig. 2. As can be seen from the figure, the comprehensive usability rating of the e-learning platform is "high", but it does not reach "extremely high" level, and there is still room for improvement.

5 Conclusion

In order to evaluate the usability of e-learning platform, this paper proposes a usability evaluation method of e-learning platform based on FCE. The experimental cases show that this method can be used to quantitatively evaluate the e-learning platform as a whole and its first-level evaluation indicators, such as the dependence of appropriateness recognizability, learnability, operability, user error protection and user interface aesthetics adopted in this case. This method provides a quantitative evaluation reference for software development and users, and can be used in software project planning, comparison, selection, testing, acceptance and other scenarios.

The evaluation indexes, weights, comprehensive evaluation matrix and usability evaluation algorithm presented in this paper need to be combined with specific cases and expert opinions for data accumulation and optimization to gradually improve the accuracy of evaluation results.

Acknowledgments. This research was supported in part by the National Key R&D Program of China under Grant No. 2020YFB1707700, and the Fundamental Research Funds for the Central Universities under Grant No. 19D111201. The authors would like to acknowledge Mr. Lixin Ruan and Mr Zhenggeng Tao for help in the case study.

References

1. Zhang, J., Xu, X.S., Cui, X.X., Song, G.Z.: Development and enlightenment of e-learning platform. J. Guangzhou Radio Telev. Univ. **14**(01), 23–26+107 (2014)
2. Han, X.Q.: A brief discussion on problems existing in online education platform and improvement strategies. Distance Educ. China (Compr. Ed.). **12**, 49–54 (2010)
3. Jiang, F.J., Wu, H.B., Wu, F.: Development analysis and enlightenment of e-learning in the United States, South Korea and Taiwan. Distance Educ. China **9**, 83–91+96 (2012)
4. Jiang, S.: Research and application of e-learning platform usability evaluation system. Beijing University of Posts and Telecommunications (2014)
5. ISO/IEC 25010: Systems and software engineering—Systems and software Quality Requirements and Evaluation (SQuaRE)—System and software quality models (2011)
6. Wang, P.Z.: Fuzzy Set Theory and Its Application. Shanghai Science and Technology Press, Shanghai (1983)
7. Zadeh, L.A.: Fuzzy sets. Inf. Control **8**, 338–353 (1965)
8. Chen, S.L., Li, J.G., Wang, X.G.: Fuzzy Set Theory and Its Application, vol. 9. Science Press, Beijing (2005)
9. Huang, L.C., Wu, P., Jaw, B.S., et al.: A study of applying fuzzy analytic hierarchy process on management talent evaluation model. In: IFSA World Congress & NAFIPS International Conference (2001)
10. Roy, S., Pattnaik, P.K., Mall, R.: Quality assurance of academic websites using usability testing: an experimental study with AHP. Int. J. Syst. Assur. Eng. Manage. **8**(1), 1–11 (2016). https://doi.org/10.1007/s13198-016-0436-0
11. Harshan, R.K., Chen, X., Shi, B.: UNSCALE: multi-criteria usability evaluation framework for library websites in a fuzzy environment. In: 2018 IEEE 22nd International Conference on Computer Supported Cooperative Work in Design (CSCWD), Nanjing, pp. 235–240 (2018)

12. Xia, W., Liu, X.X., Fan, Y.T., Fan, J.L.: Evaluation of urban system combat capability based on hybrid genetic BP neural network. Syst. Eng. Electron. Technol. **39**(01), 107–113 (2017)
13. Lu, Z.G., Cao, L.J.: Research on energy conservation and emission reduction based on comprehensive fuzzy assessment. In: Academic Annual Conference on Power System and Automation in Chinese Universities (2008)
14. Lu, Y.R.: Fuzzy evaluation model of employability of college graduates. Chin. New Technol. New Prod. **16**, 253–254 (2010)
15. Baldi, P., Hornik, K.: Neural networks and principal component analysis: learning from examples without local minima. Neural Nerw. **2**(1), 53–58 (1989)
16. Satty, T.L.: The Analytic Hierarchy Process. Mc Graw-Hill, New York (1980)
17. Zhou, Z.H., Cao, C.G.: Neural Network and Its Application, Tsinghua University Press. Beijing (2004)
18. Dang, Y.G., Liu, S.F., Wang, Z.X., Xia, L.: Research on Grey Prediction and Decision Model. Science Press, Beijing (2009)
19. Iman, M.R.H., Rasoolzadegan, A.: Quantitative evaluation of software usability with a fuzzy expert system. In: 2015 5th International Conference on Computer and Knowledge Engineering (ICCKE), Mashhad, pp. 325–330 (2015)

Critical Success Factors of Hybrid-ERP Implementations

Christian Ploder[✉], Reinhard Bernsteiner, Stephan Schlögl,
and Johannes Walter

Management, Communication and IT, MCI Entrepreneurial School,
Universitätsstraße 15, 6020 Innsbruck, Austria
christian.ploder@mci.edu

Abstract. The idea of combining the advantages of ERP systems with
the benefits of cloud computing is being taken up by more and more
companies. ERP systems are seen as the primary systems to provide
a single source of information/knowledge. Yet today, companies often
decide to switch from on-premise ERP solutions to cloud-ERP solutions
or to a combination of cloud-ERP in a group structure in addition to an
on-premise system in group branches. A variety of factors influence cloud-
ERP implementations. To be able to carry out an application successfully
and with maximum efficiency, it thus makes sense to investigate critical
success factors influencing their application as an addition to on-premise
systems. Eight critical success factors were selected from the literature
and checked for their relevance and importance in practice. To structure
these factors, a distinction was made between organizational and technological success factors. Furthermore, using interviews and subsequent
qualitative content analysis, the feedback of consultants and company
experts, who already completed cloud based ERP implementations, was
integrated.

Keywords: ERP systems · Cloud-ERP systems · Hybrid-ERP
systems · Expert interviews · Critical success factors

1 Introduction

With the advent of cloud computing, which is a concept for accessing remote
servers to manage, process, and store data instead of using local servers or computers, many companies have decided to jump on the bandwagon and join the
cloud business either as providers or as respective consumers [19].

Cloud-based IT services have also made a significant contribution to relocat-
ing Enterprise Resource Planning (ERP) systems. With the resulting cloud-ERP
systems, companies can take advantage of an ERP system and pay for the service
without installing local IT hardware [10]. To this end, the software as a service
(SaaS) model is increasingly becoming a cost-effective way to provide business
applications for companies [6]. Furthermore, due to potential advantages such as

© Springer Nature Switzerland AG 2021
L. Uden et al. (Eds.): KMO 2021, CCIS 1438, pp. 305–315, 2021.
https://doi.org/10.1007/978-3-030-81635-3_25

reduced costs, easy access to global innovations, and scalability [42], cloud-ERP systems offer an attractive option to deal with problems such as resource constraints and the complexity of the business processes involved with traditional on-premise solutions [34].

According to market research company Statista [38], the global cloud-ERP market is expected to reach USD 28 billion in 2022 and will have an annual growth rate of eight percent between 2016 and 2022. There is also increasing interest, mostly from large companies, to implement cloud-ERP solutions in their branches in addition to their on-premise ERP system so as to gain advantages such as access to global innovations or simple scalability [42] for themselves. Companies from different industries with different sizes often have no in-house cloud-ERP experts. Thus, the challenge for companies implementing cloud-ERP is to carry out the implementation in conjunction with an on-premise ERP solution as efficiently and effectively as possible, without being able to rely on internal experts.

Aiming to add to the body of knowledge in this field, the work presented in this paper deals with critical success factors of cloud-ERP implementations, whereby a selection of existing factors from the literature are discussed with experts. All this is guided by the following research question: *What are the critical success factors of cloud-ERP implementations in connection with an on-premise ERP solution?* The question is further divided into two different perspectives, i.e. *(1) What is the organizational perspective,* and *(2) what is the technological perspective.*

To report on this analysis Sect. 2 will first provide an overview of related topics based on a literature review. Terms and definitions such as cloud computing, as well as ERP and its execution on-premise, in the cloud or as a two tier, as well as critical success factors, are given. Next, Sect. 3 elaborates on the used empirical methodology followed by Sect. 4 discussing our results. Finally, Sect. 5 closes the paper highlighting limitations and pointing to potential future research activities.

2   Theoretical Background

Cloud computing is a model for the ubiquitous, convenient on-demand network access to a shared pool of configurable computer resources (e.g., servers, storage, networks, applications, and services) that are quickly made available and released, demanding little administration effort and consultation with service providers [25]. There are three service models commonly used in cloud computing [25]: (1) Software as a Service (SaaS), (2) Platform as a Service (PaaS), and (3) Infrastructure as a Service (IaaS).

2.1   ERP Systems

Enterprise Resource Planning is an integrated application package consisting of several components that support the operational processes in all essential operational and functional areas of a company. The integration is supported by a central database, which avoids data redundancies and enables integrated business processes [20].

ERP systems are of crucial importance for the business activity if the aim is to increase productivity, efficiency, and general business performance [41]. Traditional ERP systems can be divided into two categories, on-premise ERP and hosted ERP [11]. On-premise ERP is operated via a company's infrastructure, such as servers, networks, platforms, or computers. The company operates and manages the ERP system according to a given software license model. Running costs, operating costs, and maintenance costs are covered by the company [11]. Hosted ERP can be defined as a software service that is offered to an individual or organization by a provider who hosts the physical servers and runs this service elsewhere. The service is usually offered via direct, Internet based, network connection [11].

Cloud-ERP solutions are provided via the SaaS model. There are various cloud-ERP systems available on the market [33]. The ERP in a SaaS model is accessed via the Internet, while the application and data are controlled by the cloud service provider and offered to the customer as a 'ready to use' product for a monthly subscription fee [16]. An ERP system is considered cloud-based if the properties of cloud computing influence it. That is, via browser software the user should be able to access the cloud-ERP system, without the need for any installation or configuration tasks performed on the system. One of the best-known cloud-ERP systems in the software market is SAP Business ByDesign [1].

2.2   Two Tier ERP Sytems Implementations

The research and consulting company Gartner introduced the concept of bimodal IT in 2014. This concept deals with the IT landscape of a company that works in two different modes. Mode 1 focuses on the stable and traditional areas of business processes, requiring stability, and Mode 2 supports the innovative and disruptive aspects of the company, requiring agility. Both modes must exist in parallel to ensure the success of a company's digital transformation [39]. In case of ERP systems, two-tier systems are referred to as hybrid-ERP systems.

In branches or group branches, the use of a group-wide ERP solution is often not sensible, since only a fraction of the function is required, the mapping of processes or business models does not fit, or regional flexibility is needed. The parallel operation of a second ERP solution can be an advantage here. This is referred to as a two-tier ERP strategy. Here, for example, an on-premise solution at the group level can be coupled with a cloud solution in the group's branches [30].

2.3   Critical Success Factors of Information Systems

The approach of critical success factors in the area of information systems was introduced by Rockart [32]. Critical success factors are a limited number of factors that, if implemented effectively and in good time, can give the executing company an advantage over competing companies and can significantly improve organizational performance [32]. According to Ram et al. [15], critical success factors are a systematic way to identify essential factors or business areas that require constant management attention. These critical success factors are as follows:

Organizational Success Factors

- Top management support: Can be defined as leadership involvement in areas related to ERP implementation [35]. Ngai et al. [26] argued that executives play an important role in the success of ERP implementations, with top management being responsible for two essential tasks, i.e. the provision of funds and the assumption of management tasks [46].
- Project team and project strategy: The literature repeatedly mentions that a solid, central implementation team should be set up, composed of the best and most competent people in the company [9]. These people should have a proven reputation [8], and there should be an agreement to 'release' these people to the project on a full-time basis [29].
- Change Management: Successful implementation requires that people, processes, and departments in the company change [40]. Change management encompasses both human resource management and social change. Effective communication is an important factor when it comes to these changes and is thus required across the entire business process at all levels [13].
- Support by the cloud-ERP Provider: The support given by the cloud-ERP provider includes various training courses, extended technical support, maintenance, and updates, both during and after implementation. Also, the providers offer analytical advice on the selection of suitable ERP software [37,44]. Companies that transition to cloud-ERP to meet their business needs must be able to rely on cloud providers [22].

Factors	Authors				
Customizing	Gupta et al., 2018	Abd Elmonem et al., 2016	Venkatraman & Fahd, 2016	Leyh & Sander, 2015	Haddara & Zach, 2011
Service Level Agreements	Gupta et al., 2018	Abd Elmonem et al., 2016	Appandairajan, Khan & Madiajagan, 2012	Salleh, Teoh & Chan, 2012	Saini, Saini, Yousif & Khandage, 2011
Cloud-Security	Gupta et al., 2018	Habahbeh, Fadiya & Akkaya, 2018	Gupta, Misra, Singh, Kumar & Kumar, 2017	Gupta & Misra, 2016	Abd Elmonem et al., 2016
System Integration and Compatibility	Habahbeh et al., 2018	Gupta, Misra, Singh, Kumar & Kumar, 2017	Abd Elmonem et al., 2016	Leyh & Sander, 2015	J. Ram, D. Corkindale and M.L. Wu, 2013

Fig. 1. Organizational success factors matrix

Technical Success Factors

– Customizing: Cloud-ERP customers usually have to develop or adapt functions to meet their specific company requirements. Cloud-ERP manufacturers offer ERP solutions with generic core functions and do not invest in individual adjustments, which is why cloud-ERP customers face the challenge of customizing [1]. Customizing cloud-based services can increase the ability to meet current user requirements. Regular system maintenance and software updates increase flexibility in adapting to changing user requirements [21].

– Service Level Agreements: The Service Level Agreement (SLA) is defined as an agreement between a service provider and a service customer about the required Quality-of-Service (QoS) characteristics of some services that the provider delivers to the customer. The agreement, as such, represents a vague understanding of the agreement that exists between the provider and the customer [45]. Achieving a general understanding of the SLA problem between cloud-ERP providers and customers is a must to facilitate the implementation and maintenance of cloud-ERP systems [1].

– Cloud Security: Different countries have different types of security and data/ privacy protection laws and regulations. These laws must be observed at the local, state, and national levels, which is a very complex topic for cloud computing [14]. Information security is an important concern when making decisions for companies wishing to switch to cloud-based services [2]. Companies are often not aware of how data is processed by a cloud-ERP provider [27].

– System Integration: Lee et al. [18] define system integration as the ability to integrate a variety of different system functionalities and to ensure their compatibility. Ideally, companies view ERP as a single solution that covers all business functions. When implementing ERP, it is not uncommon to keep existing specialized software packages [4], so it may be necessary to integrate ERP with these applications. However, this required integration is a complex process, especially given the modular structure of ERP solutions [26].

Factors	Authors				
Top Management Support	Hentschel, Leyh & Baumhauer, 2019	Gupta et al., 2018	Chatzoglou, Fragidis, Chatzoudes & Symeonidis, 2016	Venkatraman & Fahd, 2016	Claude Doom, Koen Milis, Stephan Poelmans & Eric Bloemen, 2010
Project-Team & Strategy	Hentschel et al., 2019	Chatzoglou et al., 2016	Venkatraman & Fahd, 2016	Claude Doom et al., 2010	Shanks et al., 2000
Change Management	Hentschel et al., 2019	Gupta et al., 2018	Chatzoglou et al., 2016	Venkatraman & Fahd, 2016	Claude Doom et al., 2010
Support via Cloud-ERP Provider	Hentschel et al., 2019	Chatzoglou et al., 2016	Leyh, 2014	Goni, Gholamzadeh Chofreh & Sahran, 2011	Claude Doom et al., 2010

Fig. 2. Technical success factors matrix

Since some of these success factors aim for the same meaning but are named differently in the literature or combined with other factors, we decided to present them in concept matrices, illustrating the publications in which they are discussed. Figure 1 shows the concept matrix for the organizational factors described in Sect. 2, and Fig. 2 shows the concept matrix for the technical factors deducted from the literature.

3   Methodology

To re-check an validate the above described success factors, we interviewed 10 industry experts. Although the validity of expert interviews, with respect to their distinct form, and analysis method, may vary from case to case, there are still several convincing reasons highlighting their relevance in research [5]. According to Meuser Nagel [23], experts are people who take responsibility for the design, implementation, and monitoring of problem solutions, or those who have excellent access to information about groups of people and decision-making processes. Expert knowledge is therefore related to a function or a professional role [17].

In our case, the selected experts can be divided into three groups: (1) Group A experts from companies with a focus on cloud-ERP implementation in two-tier ERP systems; (2) Group B experts from companies with a focus on cloud-ERP implementation when changing from on-premise ERP to cloud-ERP; and (3) Group C experts with a focus on cloud-ERP implementation consulting. For the empirical study, three Group A experts with over ten years of experience each, four Group B experts with over 15 years of experience each, and three Group C experts with over eight years of experience were interviewed. The experts cover different industries in international operating companies.

Following predefined guidelines, all interviews were conducted in spring 2019 during a 7-week time-frame. They followed the strict rules of exploratory interviews [5]. After a pre-test [17] with three interviewees and the necessary adaptions, all interviews were recorded and subsequently transcribed, following the methodology put forward by Meuser and Nagel [24]. The inter-rater reliability was implemented following the principles of inter-coding.

The literature based deductive categorization schema, which was used to code interview transcripts, contained the eight success factors described earlier, i.e.: (1) Top Management Support, (2) Project team and project strategy, (3) Change Management, (4) Support by the cloud-ERP system provider, (5) Customizing, (6) SLAs, (7) Cloud-security and (8) System Integration. In addition, two inductively defined categories emerged from the transcribed data, i.e.: (1) Performance of the cloud-ERP system and (2) Market position and strategy of the cloud-ERP system provider.

4   Results and Discussion

Following we summarize the experts' view with respect to the above defined success factor categories and elaborate on the two inductively created categories.

(1) Top management support has been described in all expert groups as one of the most critical success factors. Challenges related to other critical success factors are often associated with this factor. Additions regarding the correct assessment and knowledge of the scope of an implementation project (A1; B4), and the possibilities and restrictions resulting from cloud-ERP (B4; C3) by the top management, were also mentioned.

(2) Experts also described the project team and strategy as critical to success. The composition of the project team with qualified people, as well as the selection and implementation of a suitable strategy, are essential. In the company of the Two-Tier Expert Group, a separate methodology with different phases, milestones, stress tests, and user acceptance tests were developed for a cloud-ERP implementation in 28 group branches (A1). The group of experts on the change from on-premise to cloud-ERP worked in the implementation strategy with a milestone plan (B1, 50) or very closely with the implementation partner and implemented a rapid prototyping approach with review cycles (B4).

(3) Expert interviews also confirmed the importance of the change management process as a success factor. Also Child [7] describes the importance of employees to participate in the design of their work environment. Successful implementations require full employee involvement [3,28]. To this end, people may resist for various reasons, such as lack of top management support [43]. Experts A1 and A3 confirm the connection between increasing resistance, and a lack in management support. Understanding the cause of the resistance with a corresponding reaction (A2), creating facts and demonstrating advantages (B1), and clear communication (C1; C2) are considered by experts a solutions for how to deal with resistance in change management.

(4) The support from the cloud-ERP provider as a critical success factor depends on the size and complexity of the project. In the literature, close cooperation is seen as a decisive factor for successful implementations. In practice, there were differences in the statements made by the two-tier ERP experts and experts regarding the change from on-premise to cloud-ERP. Companies must be able to rely on the cloud provider [22], and the future partnership should be focused on during the selection process [36]. Close cooperation is a crucial factor for the successful implementation of a cloud-ERP system [43]. Experts A1, A2, and A3 confirmed the importance of good cooperation and support. Expert C2 described the cooperation with qualified contacts at the provider as an essential requirement for a successful implementation.

(5) With a focus on the selection of the cloud-ERP provider, customizing cannot be described as a critical success factor. Differences in priority, depending on the size of the company, are described in the literature. The same result could be determined by differences in the statements made by the company expert groups. A large company wants the processes to be adapted to its needs. Small businesses, on the other hand, have to use the services offered by the cloud provider, whereby the scope for adaptation is smaller than in big companies [12]. Expert A1 emphasized that customizing was not a critical

success factor in the selection, while B4 and C1 described customizing in the selection of the cloud-ERP provider as an absolute priority and success factor.

(6) The importance of the service level agreement was confirmed both in the literature and in the expert interviews. Specific SLAs were of great importance for all respondents, and other SLAs were more or less prioritized on a company-specific basis. Cloud-ERP providers often have the opinion that SLAs are a sufficient contract for what the customer has bought and the level of service that the customer expects [1]. Experts A1 and C3 confirm the importance of this success factor, which represents an intangible agreement between provider and customer [45]. Expert A3 describes that an extensive catalog of SLAs has been defined.

(7) Cloud security is a critical success factor. The importance of data encryption is pointed out in the literature. In practice, it is added that there must be no compromise between secure data and performance and that the geographical location of the data centers plays a central role. Security is an important topic and thus should be focused on with every cloud solution (A1; A2; C1; C2; C3). When choosing a cloud-ERP system, companies commit to entrusting sensitive third-party business information [12]. Cloud-ERP providers should thus strengthen the trust customers have in them by providing data encryption services [31].

(8) System integration was described as a high priority with a focus on clearly defined interfaces. Besides, the consistency of the interfaces was described as important in the case of frequent release changes. Ideally, companies view ERP as a single solution that covers all business functions [18]. However, it is not uncommon for companies to prefer to maintain specialized software packages [4]. Experts B3 and C1 emphasized the importance of communication between the cloud-ERP system and other systems. Clearly defined interfaces have the highest priority (A1; A2; A3; B1; B3; C1; C2; C3).

(9+10) Further success factors, which were mentioned by our experts, are on the one hand the performance of the cloud-ERP system (A2; A3; B1), which depends on several factors and is essential for the use of the system. On the other hand, the market position and the strategy of the cloud-ERP provider were described by experts A1, B4, and C1, whereby the size of the provider and the understanding of the strategy were mentioned.

In summary, it can be said that the eight selected success factors from the literature were tested and described for their relevance in practice. Six of the eight selected success factors were deemed important by our experts, while the other two factors (i.e., customization and support by the cloud-ERP provider) could not generally be confirmed. Instead, the interviews pointed to two additional relevant factors, i.e. the performance of the cloud-ERP system and the market position and strategy of the cloud-ERP system provider.

5 Limitations and Potential Future Work

The scope of the above presented study may be perceived limited as it focused on eight critical success factors selected from the literature and two factors inductively generated by the interviews. Also, the choice of company experts can be criticized, as the three two tier experts came from the same company. Furthermore, all experts were acquired without prior knowledge of the topic, which does not exclude a certain heterogeneity of the interview partners. Finally, they came from four different countries, i.e. Austria, Liechtenstein, Switzerland and Norway, and worked in different industries. Thus, results may not easily transfer to other countries or industries.

Consequently, it is recommended that future work should follow up on our results and aim at validating them through other qualitative as well as quantitative analyses. In particular, studies should focus on other countries and industries as well as respective geographic and sector specific differences.

References

1. Abd Elmonem, M.A., Nasr, E.S., Geith, M.H.: Benefits and challenges of cloud ERP systems - a systematic literature review. Future Comput. Inform. J. **1**(1–2), 1–9 (2016). https://doi.org/10.1016/j.fcij.2017.03.003
2. Benlian, A., Hess, T.: Opportunities and risks of software-as-a-service: findings from a survey of it executives. Decis. Support Syst. **52**(1), 232–246 (2011)
3. Bernroider, E., Koch, S.: ERP selection process in midsize and large organizations. Bus. Process. Manag. J. **7**(3), 251–257 (2001). https://doi.org/10.1108/14637150110392746
4. Bingi, P., Sharma, M.K., Godla, J.K.: Critical issues affecting an ERP implementation. IS Manag. **16**(3), 7–14 (1999)
5. Bogner, A., Littig, B., Menz, W.: Interviews mit Experten. QS, Springer, Wiesbaden (2014). https://doi.org/10.1007/978-3-531-19416-5
6. Haselmann, T., Vossen, G.: Software-as-a-service in small and medium enterprises: an empirical attitude assessment. In: Bouguettaya, A., Hauswirth, M., Liu, L. (eds.) WISE 2011. LNCS, vol. 6997, pp. 43–56. Springer, Heidelberg (2011). https://doi.org/10.1007/978-3-642-24434-6_4
7. Child, J.: Strategic choice in the analysis of action, structure, organizations and environment: retrospect and prospect. Organ. Stud. **18**(1), 43–76 (1997). https://doi.org/10.1177/017084069701800104
8. Cliffe, S.: ERP implementation. Harv. Bus. Rev. **77**(1), 16–17 (1999)
9. Finney, S., Corbett, M.: ERP implementation: a compilation and analysis of critical success factors. Bus. Process Manag. J. **13** (2007). https://doi.org/10.1108/14637150710752272
10. Fosso Wamba, S., Akter, S., Coltman, T., Ngai, E.W.T.: Information technology-enabled supply chain management. Prod. Plan. Control **26**(12), 933–944 (2015). https://doi.org/10.1080/09537287.2014.1002025
11. Fripp, C., Owen S.: Cloud vs. hosted services: what's the difference? IT News Africa (2011)

12. Gupta, S., Misra, S.C., Singh, A., Kumar, V., Kumar, U.: Identification of challenges and their ranking in the implementation of cloud ERP: a comparative study for SMEs and large organizations. Int. J. Qual. Reliab. Manag. **34**(7), 1056–1072 (2017). https://doi.org/10.1108/IJQRM-09-2015-0133
13. Harmon, P., Trends, B.P.: Business Process Change: A Guide for Business Managers and BPM and Six Sigma Professionals. Elsevier (2010)
14. Hogan, M., Liu, F., Sokol, A., Tong, J.: NIST cloud computing standards roadmap. NIST Spec. Publ. **35**, 6–11 (2011)
15. Ram, J., Corkindale, D., Wu, M.L.: Implementation critical success factors (CSFs) for ERP: do they contribute to implementation success and post-implementation performance? Int. J. Prod. Econ. **144**(1), 157–174 (2013). https://doi.org/10.1016/j.ijpe.2013.01.032
16. Johansson, B., Ruivo, P.: Exploring factors for adopting ERP as SaaS. Procedia Technol. **9**, 94–99 (2013). https://doi.org/10.1016/j.protcy.2013.12.010
17. Kaiser, R.: Qualitative Experteninterviews. EP, Springer, Wiesbaden (2014). https://doi.org/10.1007/978-3-658-02479-6
18. Lee, J., Siau, K., Hong, S.: Enterprise integration with ERP and EAI. Commun. ACM **46**(2), 54–60 (2003). https://doi.org/10.1145/606272.606273
19. Lin, N.C.C.: Cloud computing as an innovation: percepetion, attitude, and adoption: guest editorial. Int. J. Inf. Manag. **32**(6), 533–540 (2012). https://doi.org/10.1016/j.ijinfomgt.2012.04.001
20. Maier, R., Hädrich, T., Peinl, R.: Enterprise Knowledge Infrastructures. Springer, Heidelberg (2009)
21. May, J., Dhillon, G., Caldeira, M.: Defining value-based objectives for ERP systems planning. Decis. Support Syst. **55** (2013). https://doi.org/10.1016/j.dss.2012.12.036
22. McCabe, B.: Cloud Computing: Australian Lessons and Experiences: KPMG it Advisory: KPMG (2009)
23. Meuser, M., Nagel, U.: Experteninterview, 2005. Das Experteninterview-vielfach erprobt, wenig bedacht. Ein Beitrag zur qualitativen Methoden diskussion. In: Bogner, A., Littig, B., Menz, W. (Hg.): Das Experteninterview. Theorie, Methode, Anwendung. Opladen 71, 94 (2005)
24. Meuser, M., Nagel, U.: Das experteninterview-konzeptionelle grundlagen und methodische anlage. In: Pickel, S., Pickel, G., Lauth, H.J., Jahn, D. (eds.) Methoden der vergleichenden Politik-und Sozialwissenschaft, pp. 465–479. Springer, Heidelberg (2009). https://doi.org/10.1007/978-3-531-91826-6_23
25. National Institute of Standards and Technology (ed.): The NIST Definition of Cloud Computing: Recommendations of the National Institute of Standards and Technology: Special Publication 800–145 (2011)
26. Ngai, E.W.T., Law, C.C.H., Wat, F.K.T.: Examining the critical success factors in the adoption of enterprise resource planning. Comput. Ind. **59**(6), 548–564 (2008). https://doi.org/10.1016/j.compind.2007.12.001
27. Niebuhr, J., Holt, M.W., Aichberger, T., Rosiello, A.: Cloud Computing: An Information Security Perspective. Strategy, New York (2011)
28. Olsen, K.A., Sætre, P.: ERP for SMEs - is proprietary software an alternative? Bus. Process. Manag. J. **13**(3), 379–389 (2007). https://doi.org/10.1108/14637150710752290
29. Parr, A., Shanks, G.: A model of ERP project implementation. J. Inf. Technol. **15**(4), 289–303 (2000). https://doi.org/10.1080/02683960010009051

30. Redaktion IT-Onlinemagazin: Two-tier sap: On-premise und cloud-erp-lösungen kombinieren (2018). https://it-onlinemagazin.de/two-tier-sap-on-premise-und-cloud-erp-loesungen-kombinieren/
31. Rimal, B.P., Choi, E.: A service-oriented taxonomical spectrum, cloudy challenges and opportunities of cloud computing. Int. J. Commun. Syst. **25**(6), 796–819 (2012)
32. Rockart, J.F.: Chief executives define their own data needs. Harv. Bus. Rev. **57**(2), 81–93 (1979)
33. Scavo, F., Newton, B., Longwell, M.: Choosing between cloud and hosted ERP, and why it matters. Comput. Econ. Rep. **34**(8) (2012)
34. Seethamraju, R.: Adoption of software as a service (SaaS) enterprise resource planning (ERP) systems in small and medium sized enterprises (SMEs). Inf. Syst. Front. **17**(3), 475–492 (2014). https://doi.org/10.1007/s10796-014-9506-5
35. Sharma, R., Yetton, P.: The contingent effects of management support and task interdependence on successful information systems implementation. MIS Q. 533–556 (2003)
36. Soliman, F.: Evaluation of cloud system success factors in supply-demand chains. In: Web-Based Services: Concepts, Methodologies, Tools, and Applications, pp. 90–104 (2015). https://doi.org/10.4018/978-1-4666-9466-8.ch033
37. El Sawah, S., Tharwat, A.A.E.F., Rasmy, M.H.: A quantitative model to predict the Egyptian ERP implementation success index. Bus. Process. Manag. J. **14**(3), 288–306 (2008). https://doi.org/10.1108/14637150810876643
38. Statista: Global cloud ERP software revenue 2016–2022—statistic: zitiert nach (2016). https://www.statista.com/statistics/681753/worldwide-cloud-erp-software-revenue/
39. Chakraborty, S., Dixit, A., Prakash, K.M.: Two-tier ERP with SAP S/4HANA cloud and deployment possibilities: SAP S/4HANA cloud product management & co-innovation (2018)
40. Umble, E.J., Umble, M.M.: Avoiding ERP implementation failure. Ind. Manag. **44**(1), 25 (2002)
41. Hedau, V., Malviya, A., Chakraborty, N.: Cloud based ERP for small and medium scale enterprises. Int. J. Eng. Res. Technol. (IJERT) (2013)
42. Venkatachalam, N., Fielt, E., Rosemann, M., Mathews, S.: Software as a service (SaaS) for small and medium enterprises (SMEs): the role of intermediaries. In: Proceedings of the 24th Australasian Conference on Information Systems (2013)
43. Venkatraman, S., Fahd, K.: Challenges and success factors of ERP systems in Australian SMEs. Systems **4**(2), 20 (2016). https://doi.org/10.3390/systems4020020
44. Wang, E.T., Chia-Lin Lin, C., Jiang, J.J., Klein, G.: Improving enterprise resource planning (ERP) fit to organizational process through knowledge transfer. Int. J. Inf. Manag. **27**(3), 200–212 (2007). https://doi.org/10.1016/j.ijinfomgt.2007.02.002
45. Wieder, P., Butler, J.M., Theilmann, W., Yahyapour, R.: Service Level Agreements for Cloud Computing. Springer, New York (2011). https://doi.org/10.1007/978-1-4614-1614-2
46. Zhang, Z., Lee, M.K.O., Huang, P., Zhang, L., Huang, X.: A framework of ERP systems implementation success in China: an empirical study. Int. J. Prod. Econ. **98**(1), 56–80 (2005)

Investigating Trust in Expert System Advice for Business Ethics Audits

Tobias Kirchebner[1,2], Stephan Schlögl[1](✉) , Erin Bass[2] ,
and Thomas Dilger[1]

[1] Management, Communication and IT, MCI – The Entrepreneurial School,
Innsbruck, Austria
`stephan.schloegl@mci.edu`
[2] College of Business Administration, University of Nebraska Omaha,
Omaha, NE, USA
`aebass@unomaha.edu`
`https://www.mci.edu`
`https://www.unomaha.edu`

Abstract. The last decade has seen an uptake of Artificial Intelligence technology in many fields. In particular, we have witnessed the proliferation of so-called Expert Systems (i.e., algorithm-based recommender engines), which are increasingly used to support decision making processes. To this end, trust in technology plays a significant role, as without such people are unwilling to rely on this type of tool support. The goal of the research presented in this paper was thus to investigate said trust in 'expert system advice' when received in the context of a business ethics audit. We report on the results of a scenario-focused survey aimed at understanding people's preference for an advice giver, and whether such is connected to their general trust behavior, as well as their affinity for technology. Results show that participants' willingness to depend on machine advice is approximately similar to their willingness to depend on human advice, the trust they put into the artificial advice giver, however, increases with their affinity for technology.

Keywords: Artificial intelligence · Expert systems · Business ethics audits · Trust · Decision-making

1 Introduction

During the last decade, Artificial Intelligence (AI) features have been embedded into an increasing number of applications and services, showing that computing technology has eventually reached a point where machines are considered (more or less) 'intelligent' actors [22]. Such does not only concern the technology sector, with its software companies and hardware providers, but also other types of businesses, as well as people, who progressively rely on AI supporting their daily activities and operations. It leads to tasks being automated and consequently increases a company's efficiency. To this end, technology supported

L. Uden et al. (Eds.): KMO 2021, CCIS 1438, pp. 316–328, 2021.
https://doi.org/10.1007/978-3-030-81635-3_26

decision making counts as one of the most relevant fields of application. So-called Expert Systems (ES) use AI to provide data-driven information and respective suggestions to humans so as to support them in their (sometimes rather difficult) decision making processes. This trend has been particularly visible in the field of accounting audits, where respective systems often support employees in time consuming data collection and processing tasks [10]. The increasing dependence on AI, however, becomes discerning in cases where not only numbers, but rather human behavior has to be judged. Business ethics audits, for example, require the understanding and correct interpretation of guidelines so as to ensure a company's and their employees' compliance with ethical regulations and standards. Here, (as in many other areas) those emerging technologies only proofs beneficial if people show sufficient trust in the underlying procedures and consequently in the performance of the used system(s). Thus, the question emerges whether decision makers believe that an AI-driven ES is capable of judging people's ethical or unethical behaviour, and consequently provide adequate suggestions for action. Driven by this, our study was guided by the following research question:

"To what extent do people trust an Expert System during their decision making process in business ethics audits?"

Our report starts with a discussion of the relevant theoretical constructs underpinning the research (cf. Sect. 2), followed by a description of the employed research methodology (cf. Sect. 3), and its results (cf. Sect. 4). The final section concludes with some prospective future research directions (cf. Sect. 6).

2   Background and Theoretical Foundation

Following, we provide the necessary theoretical background for the conducted analysis by describing **the link between business ethics and decision making**, and how such is connected to **audits, expert systems**, and **trust**.

2.1   Business Ethics and Its Link to Decision Making

Business ethics depicts an extensive and often rather subjective area of research. Depending on people's individual backgrounds and cultures we may find significant differences in what one considers ethical and thus correct, or unethical and thus disputable behaviour. Looking at Greek philosophy, it may be presumed that ethics generally looks at the character of a person and the morality in how decisions are taken under defined circumstances [29]. The need for an ethical investigation exists in cases where the perception of a given situation varies and thus requires the choosing from a number of different problem-solving approaches. Employees, particularly those in leading positions, are consistently confronted with ethical decision making; where previous research has shown that a person's decision is highly influenced by different biases, such as for example the confirmation bias, where someone only uses information that agrees with their own values and believes [1], the halo effect, which occurs when positive attributes of one person influence other people's opinions even if they are not related [15], or the availability bias, which estimates the probability of an upcoming event mainly by recalling past experiences [27]. Furthermore, humans make decisions based on their individual experiences and beliefs, and they are influenced by the given context and how it is perceived. Hence, one may argue that the ethical decision making process is influenced by two primary constructs: the individual and the given situation [26].

2.2   Business Ethics Audits

Audits ensure that organizations follow respective rules and regulations, and may therefore be considered as judgement for past decision making. While traditionally audits focus on core business aspects, such as accounting [14], human resources [9] or social work [23], an organization's ethical behaviour has lately also become an important area of application [9,18].

The aim of an audit may be seen in producing a third-party expert opinion on the reliability and validity of the information provided by a company [20]. This third-person perspective allows for the critical and open evaluation of decision processes and behaviour and thus supports the potential exposure of mismanagement [11]. In this, ethics audits often face equivocation, as their responsibility lies in the assessment and evaluation of human behavior. The necessary data is thereby collected via observations and surveys, but also through personal interviews; the purpose being, continuous business improvement and consequent risk management [8]. As such, business ethics audits are tedious and their procedure is rather expensive, for which smaller organizations often fail to reserve the necessary funds required to carry them out [18]. Respective technology support in the form of an ES for business ethics decisions may thus be helpful.

2.3   Expert Systems

AI technology has become ubiquitous and moved from impacting business trends [21] (even outside the tech industry [24]) to shaping society [5]. ES, a sub-field of AI, has matured to the point where respective systems fulfill tasks at the same, or an even better, performance level as their human expert counterparts [13,28]. As such, they may help objectify decision making in situations where no human advice giver is available [2,3]. In other words, they are able to replicate the expertise and consequent behavior of a human expert, as long as they have been sufficiently trained (using supervised and/or unsupervised machine learning techniques), and are thus capable of efficiently finding solutions in a given problem space. The more data/information (e.g., books, databases, but also previous decisions made by human experts) the ES has access to, the better its produced outcome [28]. The goal is to simulate humans' thought processes and thus arrive at solid and profound decisions [19]. While initially ES have mainly been used in the financial sector, it is other areas which have recently provided breeding grounds for technological progress. Among those, business ethics audits seem of particular relevance as they depict a field which requires the analysis and processing of usually unstructured data.

2.4 Trust

Trust is a multidimensional, volatile and rather subjective, individual characteristic. McKnight and colleagues have defined it as a multi-dimensional construct, which consists of mainly two coherent components: (1) *Trusting Beliefs* and (2) *Trusting Intentions* [17]. Trusting beliefs describe a person's viewpoint on the integrity, benevolence, and capabilities of a specific tool or person. In contrast, trusting intentions refer to the sole willingness to depend on somebody or something [17]. Hence, trusting beliefs are rather explicit, focusing on the capabilities as well as the goodwill of one party, whereas trusting intentions are rather implicit, representing a person's willingness to depend.

Trust is a ubiquitous trait which influences our daily life. Sans trust people are unwilling to share and exchange information, let alone interact with each other. One may thus refer to trust as a sort of security, for as soon as one puts trust in the certainty of an outcome, they will be more confident when making a decision. In nearly any type of situation which is characterized by either the possibility of an undesirable result or dominated by uncertainty, trust is viewed as a necessity [16]. The significance of trust is thus underlined by numerous research endeavours, including those relevant for the here presented investigation; i.e. organisational studies [25], AI [12] and business ethics audits [8].

3 Methodology

Aiming to shed some light on this connection between business ethics audits, expert systems and trust, we designed a scenario-based questionnaire survey investigating the influence an advice giver has on the trust people put into the given advice. In other words, we wanted to understand whether the advice provided by an ES is perceived differently (and potentially trusted less) than the advice provided by a human. To do so, we probed participants with **seven different business ethics problem scenarios** and asked for each of the scenarios to choose one among three possible actions. All actions had labels attached to them, making participants believe that the advice giver was either a business ethics professional (i.e., a *Human Expert*), an *Expert System*, or a *Friend*. Labels were counterbalanced so as to evaluate if people's selection behaviour would change depending on who they believe the advice came from. In addition, we collected data on participants' general trusting behaviour [17], their affinity for technology [7] as well as their demographics. Based on previous work, we considered the following hypotheses as relevant for our evaluations:

- H-01: People's age is negatively connected to their *Affinity for Technology* [6].
- H-02: People's *Affinity for Technology* is positively connected to their trust in new technology [16].

- H-03: A high level of *Trusting Intention* is positively connected to people's intention to rely on the advise given by an ES [17].
- H-04: A high level of *Trusting Beliefs* is positively connected to people's intention to rely on the advise given by an ES [4].

3.1 Sampling

While ethical decision making concerns all professions and hierarchy levels, one may argue that its foundation is often laid during education. Hence, our study focused on 1st and 2nd year master students of business or related subjects. They were approached via email and social media channels. In addition, we used Amazon MTurk[1] and relevant filters so as to increase our reach for suitable participants.

3.2 Business Ethics Problem Scenarios

In order to evaluate people's preference for an advice giver we used the following business ethics problem scenarios and recommendations, and asked them to choose one advice to be followed with each scenario.

Scenario 1 – Integrity: The ethics audit uncovered that in the last quarterly meeting, two employees embellished the numbers and figures on the first quarterly report in order to meet the standards that are required. This backlog can be corrected by the next meeting. The project's deadline is at the end of the year. Please choose one of the recommended actions to deal with the situation.

- **Expert System:** Because lying and any other kind of misbehavior is not acceptable, those employees should be withdrawn from the project and sent to a seminar to refresh their perceptions on ethics.
- **Human Expert:** Such a behavior is unacceptable and can be harmful for the company. For that reason, their manager should talk with them and clarify the details on the roots of their behavior to make sure that this does not happen again.
- **Friend:** Lying and any other kind of misbehavior is unacceptable. Hence, the first step is to look at the root cause and ensure that they are in a safe environment. Building trust is more important than punishment.

Scenario 2 – Esteem: The ethics audit revealed that false information about a new employee at GTA Inc. is spread by their co-workers. This person has been working at a competitor company before but was now headhunted by your HR. Please choose one of the recommended actions to deal with the situation.

- **Expert System:** Talking bad about someone behind their back is not tolerable and has to stop. The responsible employees have to be sent on probation.

---

[1] https://www.mturk.com/ [Accessed: January 27th 2021].

- **Human Expert:** This is a very common behavior when new employees come into companies. The employees need to be aware that this is not acceptable and receive a warning.
- **Friend:** Above all, the involved people have to come together and talk about this in an informal environment. If this does not solve the problem, managers have to be involved.

Scenario 3 – Confidentiality: The ethics audit found that confidential information about a small, but important project in the IT department was leaked during a social summer party. Please choose one of the recommended actions to deal with the situation.

- **Expert System:** Revealing crucial information about a project is very harmful for its further success. After making the responsible person aware of their mistake, it is crucial to discuss this in an open environment so that also the others see what consequences such behavior has.
- **Human Expert:** The manager has to talk to the subordinate in order to make clear that such behavior is not acceptable and might result in being replaced.
- **Friend:** Talking about crucial information in a private environment is not suitable. Hence, they should be put on probation. Without severe consequences this might happen again.

Scenario 4 – Regulations: The ethics audit detected that an employee went on vacation and took the business computer with them, and used it for personal use (e.g. to watch a movie) without asking for permission beforehand. Please choose one of the recommended actions to deal with the situation.

- **Expert System:** Using business-related devices for private usage and in open networks results in a big privacy issue for the company. Tracking down the person that defied the company rules and warning them is the least action to take - if not more.
- **Human Expert:** The usage of devices that are directly related to a company in open networks is a high risk for the business security. For that reason, the responsible manager needs to have a clear conversation with the culprit and ensure that such behavior does not happen again.
- **Friend:** Unconsciously putting the company into danger solely because of laziness is just not acceptable and needs to be punished. Sending this person on probation or giving them some time off to think about the consequences might be suitable.

Scenario 5 – Workshop: The ethics audit identified a manager who failed to complete the mandatory ethics webinar which has to be done by every employee until the end of each year. Please choose one of the recommended actions to deal with the situation.

- **Expert System:** Rules have to be followed, especially when it is everyone's own responsibility. However, a warning should be enough in case of a first violation.
- **Human Expert:** Such behavior is often seen in companies, but requires a warning in case it is the first time, or even further actions if this has happened already before.
- **Friend:** Underlining the importance of these activities is crucial, so that the employees want to partake in them. The first violation can be punished by a warning.

Scenario 6 – Reputation: The ethics audit found that an employee at GTA Inc. spoke negatively of the company to a competitor, and the information was reported back to a manager of GTA Inc. Please choose one of the recommended actions to deal with the situation.

- **Expert System:** To badmouth the company's name is not OK and further investigation looking at the root cause is necessary. Hence, the manager, the subordinate as well as an ethics coach have to come together before more harm is done.
- **Human Expert:** It is very important that the subordinate gets to talk with an experienced coach in order to find the root cause for this problem before more damage is done to the company's reputation.
- **Friend:** Harming the name of the company is strictly against the code of conduct. For this reason, an investigative meeting has to be held with the subordinate, the manager and a coach so as to find out the root cause of this problem.

Scenario 7 – Assurance: The ethics audit found that a new manager has failed to speak up on several quality management issues which led to difficulties for the future success of GTA Inc. Please choose one of the recommended actions to deal with the situation.

- **Expert System:** Reducing the fear of speaking up is one of the most important goals a company has to pursue. Therefore, an announcement needs to be made that ensures that no one has to be afraid of speaking up, especially when it is for the greater good.
- **Human Expert:** Ensuring that everyone's voice is heard is the number one goal. Hence, this needs to be openly communicated by the management to nurture critical thinking.
- **Friend:** Speaking up is crucial for the development of companies. An announcement of the responsible managers helps reduce this fear.

3.3   Measuring Trust

In order to analyze a person's trusting behaviour, we followed McKnight and colleagues' [17] advice on distinguishing between *Trusting Beliefs* and *Trusting Intentions*. They propose 11 question items to explore a person's trusting beliefs, out of which we used eight as the remaining three would not align with our ES focused research question (cf. Table 1). All items were evaluated based on a 5-point Likert scale running from *1 = Completely Disagree* to *5 = Completely Agree*.

Table 1. Survey items on *Trusting Beliefs* inspired by McKnight et al. [17].

TB1 –	*I believe that expert systems would advise in my best interest*
TB2 –	*If required help, an expert system would do its best to help me*
TB3 –	*An expert system is truthful in their meaning with me*
TB4 –	*I would characterize an expert system as being honest*
TB5 –	*An expert system is competent and effective in providing advice*
TB6 –	*An expert system performs its role of giving suggestions in business ethics audits very well*
TB7 –	*Overall, an expert system is a capable and proficient tool as advice provider*
TB8 –	*In general, an expert system is very knowledgeable about making suggestions*

With respect to participant's intention to trust we used all of the five questions proposed by McKnight et al. [17] (cf. Table 2). Also here, scales ran *1=Completely Disagree* to *5=Completely Agree*.

Table 2. Survey items on *Trusting Intentions* inspired by McKnight et al. [17].

TI1 –	*When an important issue or problem arises, I would feel comfortable depending on the information provided by an expert system*
TI2 –	*I can always rely on an expert system in a tough decision making situation*
TI3 –	*I feel that I could count on an expert system to help with a crucial decision making problem*
TI4 –	*Faced with a difficult decision that required me to make a further step, I would use the firm backing an expert system*
TI5 –	*If I had a challenging problem, I would want to use an expert system*

3.4 Measuring Affinity for Technology

In order to measure people's affinity for technology we used the ATI scale proposed by Franke and colleagues [7]. The scale aims to assess a person's tendency to interact with a given technology, and thus allows to discriminate very technology affine individuals from less technology affine ones (cf. Table 3). Participants were asked to rate the ATI questions on a 6-point Likert scale ranging from $1 = $ *Completely disagree* to $6 = $ *Completely agree*[2].

Table 3. Survey items on *Affinity for Technology* inspired by Franke et al. [7].

ATI1 –	*I like to occupy myself in greater detail with technical systems*
ATI2 –	*I like testing the functions of new technical systems*
ATI3 –	*I predominantly deal with technical systems because I have to*
ATI4 –	*When I have a new technical system in front of me, I try it out intensively*
ATI5 –	*I enjoy spending time becoming acquainted with a new technical system*
ATI6 –	*It is enough for me that a technical system works; I don't care how or why*
ATI7 –	*I try to understand how a technical system exactly works*
ATI8 –	*It is enough for me to know the basic functions of a technical system*
ATI9 –	*I try to make full use of the capabilities of a technical system*

4 Results

We received a total of $n = 133$ completed surveys. All responses were categorized and reduced to numerical values. In line with previous research, we treated Likert scale data as being metric [7,17] and accounted for all items which had to be reverse coded (cf., questions 3, 6 and 8 from the ATI survey). A *Cronbach* α analysis points to a high construct reliability for all the employed survey items: *Trusting Beliefs* ($\alpha = 0.88$), *Trusting Intentions* ($\alpha = 0.83$) and *Affinity for Technology* ($\alpha = 0.85$). Gender-wise, our responses were slightly unequal, with 75 respondents identifying themselves as males, 57 as females and 1 as non-binary. Approximately two-third of them ($64,7\%$) declared to be aged between 18 and 35, which may be due to the use of an online distribution channel. Participants came predominantly from the U.S. (76.7%) and from Austria (21.8%), and had a rather high educational level, with 86% of them stating to have obtained at least an undergraduate college degree.

4.1 Hypotheses

Following we present the results with respect to the hypotheses outlined in Sect. 3. For the performed correlation analyses we used the coefficients of either Bravais-Pearson or Spearman, depending on the given data type and distribution. Confidence levels were set to 95%.

---

[2] Note: These scales did not offer a middle point for which participants had to choose whether they would rather agree or disagree with a statement.

H-01: People's age is negatively connected to their *Affinity for Technology* – In support of H-01, we found a small, but still significant negative correlation between the age of the study participants and their ATI score ($r_s = -0.18; p = 0.040$). That is, the data shows a drop in technology affinity with increasing age.

H-02: People's *Affinity for Technology* is positively connected to their trust in new technology – As for H-02, the data shows a small but highly significant positive connection between one's trusting beliefs and their affinity for technology interaction ($r_s = 0.40; p = 0.000$).

H-03: A high level of *Trusting Intention* is positively connected to people's intention to rely on the advise given by an ES – In order to evaluate H-03, we looked at each of the scenarios separately. Three scenarios show unique characteristics. First, the scenario which concerned **Esteem** had a high number of responses in favor of the Human Expert (i.e., 56% of all responses). The mean *Trusting Intentions* score (i.e., the overall score computed through the trust model which allows for max. 25 points) of those who chose the Human Expert was $AVG = 18.7$ (*Median* $= 19.0$). Those who preferred the advice of the ES (20% of all responses) were, however, even more confident, $AVG = 18.9$ (*Median* $= 19.5$). People choosing the advice of a friend (24% of all responses) showed the lowest score, $AVG = 17.0$ (*Median* $= 17.0$).

Second, looking at the scenario concerning **Confidentiality** we see the ES taking the lead in popularity (41% of all responses; *Trusting Intentions* score: $AVG = 19.0$; *Median* $= 19.0$), closely followed by the human expert (38 % of all responses; *Trusting Intentions* score: $AVG = 17.8$; *Median* $= 18.0$). The advice of a friend only reaches a 21% endorsement level (*Trusting Intentions* score: $AVG = 18.0$; *Median* $= 18.5$).

Finally, the **Workshop** scenario further increases the distance between the ES (47% preference; *Trusting Intentions* score: $AVG = 19.4$; *Median* $= 20.0$) and the human expert (36% preference; *Trusting Intentions* score: $AVG = 17.3$; *Median* $= 17.5$) and puts the friend even further behind (17% preference; *Trusting Intentions* score: $AVG = 17.5$; *Median* $= 18.0$).

While those three scenarios particularly highlighted participants' preferences, similar (although less pronounced) characteristics were found with the other four scenarios.

H-04: A high level of *Trusting Beliefs* is positively connected to people's intention to rely on the advise given by an ES – Looking at *Trusting Believes* one can see similarities to *Trusting Intentions*. Even if the scale for trusting beliefs has more characteristics (i.e., max. 40 points), median values are rather close. Hence, it was again the Human Expert who received by far the highest preference in the scenario on **Esteem** (56% preference; *Trusting Beliefs* score: $AVG = 32.7$; *Median* $= 33.0$), followed by the ES (20% preference; *Trusting Beliefs* score: $AVG = 31.0$; *Median* $= 32.5$), and the Friend (24% preference; *Trusting Beliefs* score: $AVG = 30.4$; *Median* $= 30.5$).

The scenario focusing on **Confidentiality** is also characterized by a value distribution similar to what was observed with the *Trusting Intention* scores, i.e. Human Expert (38% preference; *Trusting Beliefs* score: $AVG = 30.7$; $Median = 32.0$), ES (41% preference; *Trusting Beliefs* score: $AVG = 33.6$; $Median = 33.5$) and Friend (21% preference; *Trusting Beliefs* score: $AVG = 30.5$; $Median = 30.0$).

And also the **Workshop** scenario received similar values as before, yet here the ES took the lead (47% preference; *Trusting Beliefs* score: $AVG = 33.2$; $Median = 33.0$) followed by the Human Expert (36% preference; *Trusting Beliefs* score: $AVG = 30.6$; $Median = 31.0$) and the Friend (17% preference; *Trusting Beliefs* score: $AVG = 30.7$; $Median = 31.0$).

Again, those three scenarios described participants' selection behaviour best, yet the other four showed similar, although less pronounced, characteristics.

5   Discussion

Our results confirm previous findings both with respect to H-01 (e.g. [6]) and H-02 (cf. [16]), although concerning age and its connection to affinity for technology, we are not able to tell whether this also applies to children or teenagers, since our study did not involve any under-aged participants. Concerning our main interest, i.e. the trust people put into the advice of an ES, we found that participants did choose the advice of an expert rather than that of a friend, independent of whether this expert was human or artificial. However, we did not find a significant connection between people's *Trusting Intention* scores and this selection behavior. And also with respect to *Trusting Beliefs* our data does not support such a connection. Hence, overall, we may argue that a person's preference was rather based on the level of expertise which was attached to the advice giver (i.e., the label 'expert') than on their individual trusting beliefs.

6   Conclusion and Future Prospects

The above presented work focused on business ethics audits and investigated a potential connection between people's affinity for technology and the trust they put into expert opinions; comparing preferences for human and artificial advice. Results confirm previous work in that technology affinity is connected to age and that it correlates with people's overall Trusting Believes. Yet, whether and how different stances of trust influence people's preference for a human or an artificial advice giver, requires further investigations. To this end, we suggest long-term analyses of people's actual behavior when using an ES in business ethics audits. We further recommend comparing behaviour with different types of ES, as business ethics may depict a special uses case due to its often rather delicate topics. Finally, we propose investigations into whether trust in technology can be treated similar to trust in humans. Our research has assumed for this to be true. Yet, an alternative trust model may be more suitable to explain people's preferences.

Past research has underlined the usefulness of ES in many areas (cf. Sect. 2.3). However, investigations into what lets people trust ES advice and how such may be connected to individual characteristics are needed so as to create a better understanding of this type of AI technology acceptance.

References

1. Bazerman, M., Moore, D.: Improving decision making. In: Judgement in Managerial Decision Making, pp. 179–199 (2009)
2. Buchanan, B., Sutherland, G., Feigenbaum, E.: Heuristic dendral: a program for generating explanatory hypotheses. Organ. Chem., 209–254 (1969)
3. Buchanan, B.G., Shortliffe, E.H.: Rule-based expert systems: the MYCIN experiments of the Stanford heuristic programming project. CUMINCAD (1984)
4. Chen, L., Pu, P.: Trust building in recommender agents. In: Proceedings of the Workshop on Web Personalization, Recommender Systems and Intelligent User Interfaces at the 2nd International Conference on E-Business and Telecommunication Networks, pp. 135–145. Citeseer (2005)
5. Dignum, V.: Ethics in artificial intelligence: introduction to the special issue (2018)
6. Edison, S.W., Geissler, G.L.: Measuring attitudes towards general technology: antecedents, hypotheses and scale development. J. Target. Meas. Anal. Mark. **12**(2), 137–156 (2003)
7. Franke, T., Attig, C., Wessel, D.: A personal resource for technology interaction: development and validation of the affinity for technology interaction (ATI) scale. Int. J. Hum.-Comput. Interact. **35**(6), 456–467 (2019)
8. García-Marzá, D.: Trust and dialogue: theoretical approaches to ethics auditing. J. Bus. Ethics **57**(3), 209–219 (2005)
9. Gheorghiu, A.: Performance auditing-a complex concept. Hyperion Int. J. Econ. New Econ. **5**(1), 159–176 (2012)
10. Greenman, C.: Exploring the impact of artificial intelligence on the accounting profession. J. Res. Bus. Econ. Manage. **8**(3), 1451 (2017)
11. Hay, D., Knechel, W.R., Willekens, M.: The Routledge Companion to Auditing. Routledge (2014)
12. Hengstler, M., Enkel, E., Duelli, S.: Applied artificial intelligence and trust-the case of autonomous vehicles and medical assistance devices. Technol. Forecast. Soc. Change **105**, 105–120 (2016)
13. Horvitz, E.J., Breese, J.S., Henrion, M.: Decision theory in expert systems and artificial intelligence. Int. J. Approx. Reason. **2**(3), 247–302 (1988)
14. Imhoff, G.: Accounting quality, auditing and corporate governance. Audit. Corporate Govern. (2003). https://papers.ssrn.com/sol3/papers.cfm?abstract_id=374380#references-widget
15. Lucker, G.W., Beane, W.E., Helmreich, R.L.: The strength of the halo effect in physical attractiveness research. J. Psychol. **107**(1), 69–75 (1981)
16. Mcknight, D.H., Carter, M., Thatcher, J.B., Clay, P.F.: Trust in a specific technology: an investigation of its components and measures. ACM Trans. Manage. Inf. Syst. (TMIS) **2**(2), 1–25 (2011)
17. McKnight, D.H., Choudhury, V., Kacmar, C.: The impact of initial consumer trust on intentions to transact with a web site: a trust building model. J. Strateg. Inf. Syst. **11**(3–4), 297–323 (2002)

18. McNamee, M.J., Fleming, S.: Ethics audits and corporate governance: the case of public sector sports organizations. J. Bus. Ethics **73**(4), 425–437 (2007)
19. Naveen, G., Naidu, M.A., Rao, B.T., Radha, K.: A comparative study on artificial intelligence and expert systems. Int. Res. J. Eng. Technol. **6**(2), 1980–1986 (2019)
20. Omoteso, K.: The application of artificial intelligence in auditing: looking back to the future. Expert Syst. Appl. **39**(9), 8490–8495 (2012)
21. Pavaloiu, A.: The impact of artificial intelligence on global trends. J. Multidiscip. Dev. **1**(1), 21–37 (2016)
22. Poole, D.L., Mackworth, A.K.: Artificial Intelligence: Foundations of Computational Agents. Cambridge University Press, Cambridge (2010)
23. Reamer, F.G.: The social work ethics audit: a risk-management strategy. Soc. Work **45**(4), 355–366 (2000)
24. Saponaro, M., Le Gal, D., Gao, M., Guisiano, M., Maniere, I.C.: Challenges and opportunities of artificial intelligence in the fashion world. In: 2018 International Conference on Intelligent and Innovative Computing Applications (ICONIC), pp. 1–5. IEEE (2018)
25. Schoorman, F.D., Mayer, R.C., Davis, J.H.: An integrative model of organizational trust: past, present, and future (2007)
26. Schwartz, M.S.: Business Ethics: An Ethical Decision-Making Approach. Wiley, Hoboken (2017)
27. Tversky, A., Kahneman, D.: Availability: a heuristic for judging frequency and probability. Cogn. Psychol. **5**(2), 207–232 (1973)
28. Tzafestas, S.G., Kokkinaki, A.I., Valavanis, K.P.: An overview of expert systems. In: Tzafestas S. (ed.) Expert Systems in Engineering Applications. Springer, Heidelberg (1993). https://doi.org/10.1007/978-3-642-84048-7_1
29. Wade, D.T.: Ethics, audit, and research: all shades of grey. BMJ **330**(7489), 468–471 (2005)

Privacy and Security

Analysis of WEB Browsers of HSTS Security Under the MITM Management Environment

Raúl Bareño-Gutiérrez[1](✉), Alexandra María López Sevillano[1](✉),
Flor Nancy Díaz-Piraquive[2](✉) (iD), and Ruben González-Crespo[3](✉) (iD)

[1] Universidad Catolica de Colombia, Bogotá, Colombia
{rbareno,amlopez}@ucatolica.edu.co
[2] Fundación Universitaria Internacional de La Rioja, UNIR, Bogotá, Colombia
flornancy.diaz@unir.edu.co
[3] Universidad Internacional de La Rioja, La Rioja, Spain
ruben.gonzalez@unir.net

Abstract. The transactional websites and services on the cloud, have actually become the most used browsers, thanks to their portability and ease of use, with a significant increase in the development of cloud solutions, implementing digital contexts under the 4.0 web, which generated an increase of possibilities for transactions of different types. However, every time more security issues arise. Due to this problem, the computer security is a rising trend, generating new possibilities to mitigate vulnerabilities when handling the information in a transactional web site; an analysis is made of performance, weaknesses and strengths of the HSTS standard, as a security complement of the SSL/TLS protocol.

Different tests scenarios are verified under a man attack in the MITM environment, to intercept or capture the traffic sent and received during web transactions. That is how we identify if the standard can prevent that intrusion, which is of vital importance for the different transactional environments actually used, such as bank entities or online purchases; vulnerabilities of the standard are verified upon making the first request to a website, which strengthens and secures transactions done from the beginning of the transaction to its ending, in an encrypted way. Browsers analyzed - Mozilla Firefox, Google Chrome and internet Explorer, under controlled corporate and personal environments; The security importance of the browser is outlined, Google Chrome being the best one in performance under an internet hacking. The other browsers present some shortcomings during the first interconnection request, during some milliseconds under the point to point model, for the initial phase of information interchange.

Keywords: WEB browsers · HSTS complement · A hacker in the MITM environment · Security

1 Introduction

Actual browsers in their different versions use the SSL/TLS protocol, with continuous improvements regarding the HSTS complement, which allows the minimization of vulnerabilities during different periods of time, to intercept and/or modify data sent in a

© Springer Nature Switzerland AG 2021
L. Uden et al. (Eds.): KMO 2021, CCIS 1438, pp. 331–344, 2021.
https://doi.org/10.1007/978-3-030-81635-3_27

customer/server connection, giving place to mistrust among users, when making online transactions, which are becoming popular due, among other reasons, to their ease of use and displacement elimination [1–4].

One of the biggest mistakes that users frequently do, is writing the URL on the address bar without the corresponding security protocol (http://ejemplo.com, or simply ejemplo.com, instead of https://www.ejemplo.com), allowing the browser to assume that the connection was done through HTTP and in this way, send the initial request through an insecure channel; even if the website forwards immediately the request to a secure connection, any active hacker in the network of the victim, can intercept and modify that initial answer, preventing the user from getting updated and navigate reliably, in this case, it will exist the probability of the absence of a little lock icon in the interphase of the user's browser [5–8]. The transactional website is considered as a virtual platform that allows you to carry out monetary and non-monetary transactions through the internet, with high standards of security and quality from your computer or cell phone. Through the transactional portal you will be able to carry out the following transactions: Internet purchases; online payments for public services, mobile telephony, air tickets, among others; transfers between crediservir accounts; transfers to accounts of cooperatives affiliated with the Coopcentral Network; transfers between interbank accounts; movement inquiry and balance inquiry.

This problem boosted Jeff Hodges, Thomas C. Jackson and Adam Barth [9–11] to make a security proposal of HTTP transport, strict (HSTS). Their approach allow any website in internet tell the browser that all future requests, made on behalf of a host, or a particular domain, should always use a secure channel SSL/TLS, and that all the HTTP traffic should get updated automatically, and be submitted only through this one Without this security mechanism, the forcing of a security protocol to another one, will not be done during the first connection, and would leave the user exposed to any kind of attack, looking to see or manipulate the connection established with the server.

Five scenarios were checked over on a controlled environment, which intends to look for the evidence of the HSTS performance, under a man attack in the MITM [12, 13] environment, with the aim of proving if it is possible to induce an insecure connection, and thus obtain data transmitted without any kind of encryption. Finally, with the collected information, through a comparative method a system is established so that web browsers allow to exploit HSTS vulnerabilities, and some security recommendations are determined in order to avoid being a victim of this type of attack.

Actually, each of the different existent browsers, count with different security policies, with the aim of mitigating the different risks present in the web [14–16]; despite this, and although day by day new policies are implemented to seek the improvement of data security and protection, these browsers are not completely protected, due to failures present in some of the necessary protocols for their correct operation.

One of the protocols used on the web is the HTTPS protocol, which is based on its predecessor HTTP, and seeks to transfer, in a safe way, data through the network; such protocol, is based in itself on the cryptographic protocols SSL/TLS, with the purpose of establishing safe communications between the customer and the server.

With the passing of time vulnerabilities have been found of the cryptographic protocols above mentioned, which left with no effect their use, and they allowed all the traffic between the customer and the server, to be seen and treated without inconvenient; due to that, the need arose to create a security mechanism to mitigate some of these deficiencies and, it is just there where HSTS born, which would take care to grant at any moment, secure connections in the architecture customer/server.

Based on the above, the question is: What are the potential vulnerabilities of the HSTS security mechanism and, how can their effect be mitigated? Under this problem question, a series of technical tests are sought to be developed, in order to determine the scope of possible vulnerabilities of the HSTS protocol, through making one of the most frequent hacking on internet, man in the (MITM) environment, suggesting recommendations to reduce to the minimum the repercussion under this vulnerability.

Actually, there are many browsers in the market and, each one of them counts with its own characteristics, strengths and weaknesses; during most of year 2016, more than 50% of the traffic, registered in hundreds of web pages, was done through the Google Chrome browser, leaving others relegated such as Internet Explorer and Mozilla Firefox [17, 18].

It is necessary to know what type of vulnerabilities are the ones approached by actual systems, in order to assure each one of them in the best possible way, and, successfully mitigate the risks to which all web systems are exposed, a task that is not easy. However, over the years, mistakes present in the different security protocols have been tried to be corrected, and some others affecting browsers or web servers directly. One of these efforts to maintain the web safer is the HSTS standard, security mechanism developed to improve secure connections and, access to the different websites, not only to websites of bank entities that use secure channels, but also those requiring simple authentication, such as social networks, educational platforms, etc.

The purpose of all of the above is to identify if the HSTS security mechanism is implemented in any web environment, providing that additional layer of security that the Internet needs, ensuring that the data that travels through the network is not exposed to suffer any type of interception or alteration that could put the user's information at risk. This seeks to ensure that reliable data supports the generation and appropriation of knowledge in the implementation of best security practices.

2 Materials and Methodology

This investigation was of quantitative type, using a monitored scenario for corresponding tests and, through the man attack in the MITM [19, 20] environment; the hacker was positioned in the network path, between the browser and the web server (see Fig. 1). A stage assembly was made based on virtual machines and monitored with Wireshark, where the hacking was made, capturing the traffic and eliminating the HSTS policies through kali linux, using the SSLStrip tool, which deactivated the HSTS policy, causing the absence of the SSL/TLS certificate in the web with all tests. It was noticed that session HTTPS was disabled using SSLStrip.

This tool captures the HTTP traffic in a network transparently, it finds the HTTPS links and redirects them, mapping the found links in a similar one, in HTTP. The efficiency lies in the fact that it does not attack the security protocols directly, but on the contrary, it is capable of redirecting all the traffic from the victim's machine, through a proxy, allowing to capture data that normally go encrypted in the communication, between the customer and the server.

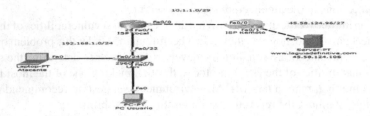

Fig. 1. Test scenarios. Source: Authors [21] Used infrastructure (see Table 1).

Table 1. Infrastructure used

Hardware	Software	Components
PC Customer	Ram: 8 GB Proc: ADM FX 8320 Syst.Ope: Win 10	Browsers Internet explorer Chrome Mozilla
PC Attacker	Ram: 8 GB Proc: ADM FX 8320 Syst.Ope: Win 10	Kali Linux with better cap and SSL
PC Traffic analysis	Ram: 8 GB Proc: ADM FX 8320 Syst.Ope: Win 10	Wireshark
Server	Ram: 8 GB Proc: ADM FX 8320 Syst.Ope: Win 10	Apache version 2.4.23 with Linux operating system with the TLC service active

Source: Authors [21].

The test scenarios were:

1. Access to website through HTTP
2. Access to website through HTTPS
3. Access to website through a secure link
4. Access to website through an insecure link
5. Access to website on the pre-load list HSTS [22–24].

The different browsers [25–28] used were:

- Google Chrome, version v. 58.0.3029.81.
- Mozilla Firefox (v. 53.0)
- Internet Explorer (v. 11.0.9600.18638)

3 Discussion

It is important to critically review the known security problems, due to the constant dynamics of systems, distributed on a large scale. Applications based on the web and other corporate services, invite to redesign security aspects, reviewing in parallel between the new and old computational approaches [5]. According to security experts, HSTS [18] corrects some design shortcomings, SSL, see 3.0/TLS, see 1.2, such as dependence on warnings of certificates that users may ignore.

The HSTS [12, 13] complement is not a security characteristic; it is actually widely spread on the internet, but few websites use it. Some companies such as Twitter, PayPal, Google, Blog spot and Etsy, use this security characteristic. Most of the browsers of personal computers are not compatible with this characteristic and depend on the browser version. Some of them share a domain pre-list HSTS [19], preconfigured, even before the first HTTPS connection, in order for users to be protected after a new installation, or after re-starting the browser [14].

This new security mechanism, described as HTTP Strict Transport Security [RFC6797] (known as HSTS) helps to mitigate, among others, attacks made by SSLstrip [29, 30]. Through HSTS, this change of protocol, HTTPS to HTTP, is detected automatically by the browser and does not allow that connection to happen.

After a first connection is done between the customer and the server, the browser was able to remind the domain and subdomains belonging to that domain, that all intents for connection should be done through a secure channel. For that, the server sends a headboard where time during which the secure connection should be kept in operation is established. At the time, even though HSTS covered in some way certain vulnerabilities, used in most of the web attacks, this browser had also its own vulnerabilities.

One of the problems that HSTS [27, 28] presented was that, it was restricted with the first use of the web page, or when the maximum age appearing on the transport headboard expires. For the first connection intent with the website, the browser must rely against its first use, since it has not received a previous HSTS header, and since that header of the website is not in the HSTS list of the browser, an attack as a SSLstrip would continue taking effect.

In order to avoid this problem, Google developed an HSTS preload list, through which the browser knows in advance that the connection, even if it is the first one, should have been done through a secure connection.

After the publication of HSTS, the improved version of SSL strip quickly emerged, called SSLstrip+ o SSLstrip2. This version is capable to avoid this security mechanism, with the help of the dns2proxy tool, which helps to revert changes made by the proxy (SSLstrip2) and makes the connection to be completely transparent for the user. Thus, HTTPS to HTTP in the HTML code of the website, avoids the HSTS [29, 30] policy.

Given that HSTS is compatible with most of the browsers, Chrome and Mozilla Firefox [31, 32] keep an HSTS preload list, which informs the browser automatically that access to the website can only be made through HTTPS. One of the vulnerabilities mostly known of HSTS lays on the possibility to deny the HTTPS connection, during the first negotiation between the customer and the server, because there is no previous knowledge by the Directive browser; as a consequence, a hacker in the environment, may be successful, managing to register communications, which apparently go through a secure channel. This problem, although it was solved by the browsers upon creating preload lists, which contain the websites that wish to avoid that inconvenient, there are still many websites to be included, and which are exposed to this failure. Besides that, according to the same specification of the security mechanism, HSTS, there are some threats that are approached and, others that. although they affect security of communications, there is no way on how to treat them properly [33–38].

4 Results

Each test scenario is revised as follows:

1. Access to the WEBSITE by HTTP: During the login session between the customer and the server, for each one of the browsers. For Chrome, the hacker cannot obtain data, thanks to the HSTS complement which prevents the communication from being supplanted. See Fig. 2.

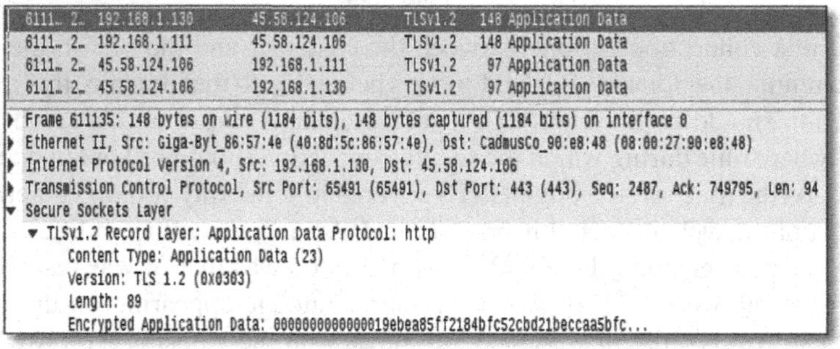

```
6111. 2. 192.168.1.130      45.58.124.106      TLSv1.2   148 Application Data
6111. 2. 192.168.1.111      45.58.124.106      TLSv1.2   148 Application Data
6111. 2. 45.58.124.106      192.168.1.111      TLSv1.2    97 Application Data
6111. 2. 45.58.124.106      192.168.1.130      TLSv1.2    97 Application Data
▶ Frame 611135: 148 bytes on wire (1184 bits), 148 bytes captured (1184 bits) on interface 0
▶ Ethernet II, Src: Giga-Byt_86:57:4e (40:8d:5c:86:57:4e), Dst: CadmusCo_90:e8:48 (08:00:27:90:e8:48)
▶ Internet Protocol Version 4, Src: 192.168.1.130, Dst: 45.58.124.106
▶ Transmission Control Protocol, Src Port: 65491 (65491), Dst Port: 443 (443), Seq: 2487, Ack: 749795, Len: 94
▼ Secure Sockets Layer
  ▼ TLSv1.2 Record Layer: Application Data Protocol: http
      Content Type: Application Data (23)
      Version: TLS 1.2 (0x0303)
      Length: 89
      Encrypted Application Data: 0000000000000019ebea85ff2184bfc52cbd21beccaa5bfc...
```

Fig. 2. Analysis of the Chrome Browser Source: Authors.

On the other hand, the hacker tool does not allow the Mozilla Firefox browser to update a secure protocol and makes it possible to capture the access data to the website during the session with the server. See Fig. 3.

Likewise, through the Internet Explorer browser, the hacker manages to intercept the established data, in the session between the customer and the server, easily preventing the HSTS protocol from establishing it as a protection mechanism. See Fig. 4.

Two requests sent to the web server are evident, since the hacker acts as mediator in the established communications, between the customer and the server, he receives the requests from the customer himself, and later, he sends them to the server. In this way, the hacker can obtain data sent through the Mozilla Firefox and Internet Explorer browsers.

Fig. 3. Analysis of the Mozilla Firefox browser. Source: Authors.

Fig. 4. Analysis of the Mozilla Firefox browser. Source: Authors

2. Access to the WEBSITE by HTTPS: during the logging between the customer and the server, for browsers, it stands out that none of the browsers allows a successful hacking. Making a direct request by writing the secure protocol, does not allow the hacker to mislead the customer making to believe that he is communicated with a true and secure server.

Although in the first connection with the server, the browser does not know the HSTS header, the hacker is unable to make the request through HTTP, to capture data in transit. Thereby, the Mozilla Firefox server allows the data interchange to flow through a secure channel. See Fig. 5.

In the same way, the Google Chrome browser prevents the hacker from capturing data found in the actual session, between the customer and the server. Even after this first connection, the user will keep browsing safely, since the directive is already established. Finally, the Explorer Internet Browser, has the same performance as the other two browsers, encrypting data sent by the customer, and making the hacker fail on his intent to read data easily.

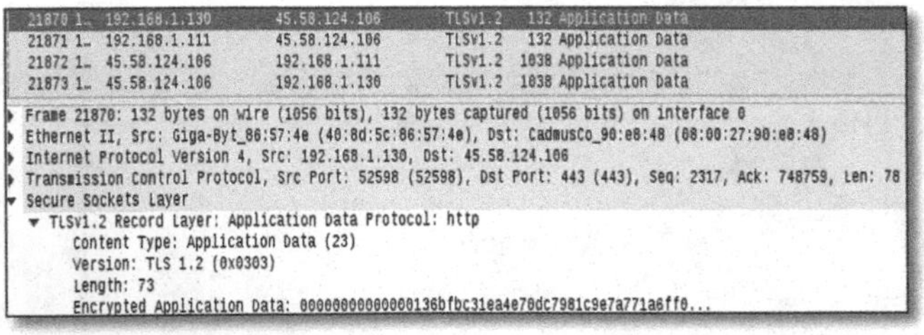

Fig. 5. Analysis of Firefox through HTTPS. Source: Authors.

3. Access to the WEBSITE through an insecure link: it stands out the fact that the Google Chrome browser was the only one capable of keeping a secure connection. See Fig. 6.

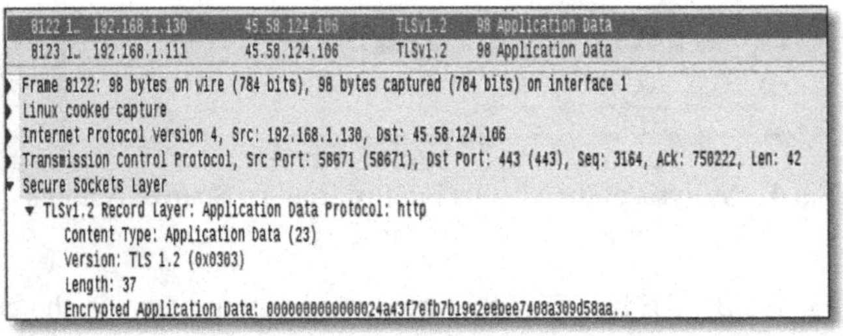

Fig. 6. Chrome browser through an insecure link. Source: Authors.

The Internet Explorer browser, and Mozilla Firefox, on the contrary, allow to establish an insecure communication with the hacker and a communication between the hacker and the legitimate server. In this way, all requests from the browser are intercepted by the hacking tool, and later sent to the secure server. See Fig. 7.

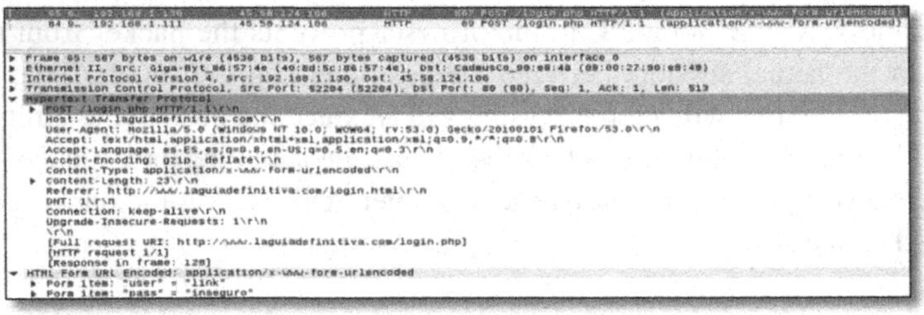

Fig. 7. Mozilla browser through insecure link. Source. Authors.

4. Access to the WEBSITE through insecure link: During this test it stands out that none of the browsers allow the hacker to establish the session through HTTP, and to

capture the session's data. See Fig. 8. The user accesses the website safely through the Mozilla Firefox. Browser.

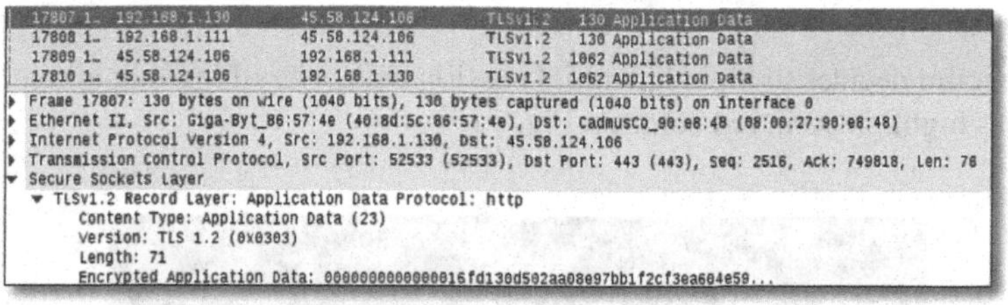

Fig. 8. Access to the WEBSITE through a secure link. Source. Authors.

In a similar way, Internet Explorer, and Google Chrome present the same behavior, preventing the hacker from vulnerating the security of the website, and likewise obtain the incoming data from the user, in the actual connection between the customer and the server.

5. Access to the website in the HSTS preload list: The website www.facebook.com is reviewed, it stands out that none of the servers allow the hacker to capture data sent. See Fig. 9.

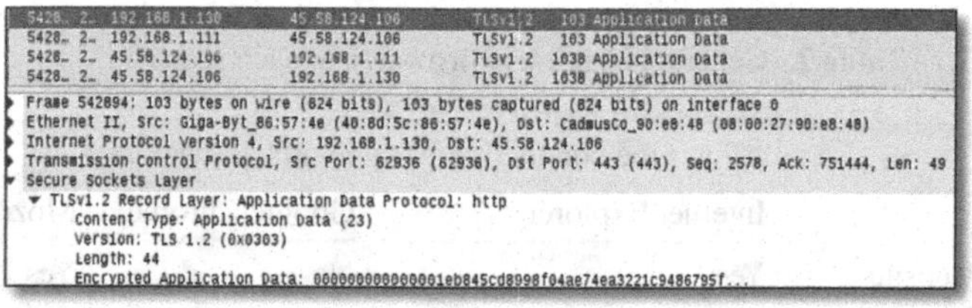

Fig. 9. Browser Explorer with preload list HSTS. Source: Authors.

In a similar way, the hacking tool becomes useless when trying to compromise the security policies of the website, through Google Chrome. Finally, Internet Explorer, thanks to the preload list, obtains the same result, scripting the connection between the customer and the server. Although the test had no effect, a little modification to the URL allows the Mozilla Firefox and Internet Explorer browsers, cannot maintain a secure connection. Upon making a request to http://es-es.facebook.com, the hacking tool makes the connection to be made through HTTP. See Fig. 10.

It stands out after an initial request to website http://es-es.facebook.com, the server makes a temporary redirection (302) to its HTTPS version. However, it inhibits the updating to a secure protocol, and it also replaces the HTTPS links by one corresponding to its HTTP version. Thus, the browsing through the website will keep being insecure.

```
[DESKTOP-TP4RES6/192.168.1.130] GET http://es-es.facebook.com/ ( text/html )
[DESKTOP-TP4RES6/192.168.1.130] GET https://es-es.facebook.com/ ( text/html )
[I] [SSLSTRIP 192.168.1.130] Stripping 37 HTTPS links inside 'https://es-es.facebook.com/'.
```

Fig. 10. Removing HTTPS links by HTTP. Source: Authors.

Once the victim decides to login his initial session data, everything that is sent, may be captured, as highlighted in red color on Fig. 11.

Fig. 11. Analysis of Mozilla Firefox and Internet Explorer browsers. Source: Authors. (Color figure online)

In general, the HSTS complement under each one of the cyberattacks is shown on Table 2.

Table 2. General behavior of browsers in each scenario.

Scenario	Allows the conducting of cyberattack (hacking)		
	Internet Explorer	Google Chrome	Mozilla Firefox
Access to the website through HTTP	Yes	No	Yes
Access to the website through HTTPS	No	No	No
Access to the website through an incoming insecure link	Yes	No	Yes
Access to the website through an incoming secure link	No	No	No
Access to an external website included in the HSTS preload list of web browsers	No	No	No

Source: Authors.

Finally, some strengths and weaknesses are established about the HSTS complement. See Table 3.

Table 3. Strengths and weaknesses of HSTS according to environment used.

HSTS Strengths and weaknesses	
Strengths	Weaknesses
Capable of keeping the HTTPS session during the browsing, if the clause including SubDomains is correctly established	In internet Explorer and Mozilla Firefox is not capable of protecting the first request of the customer to the server
Included in the HSTS preload list. It is a condition that could diminish the possibility of an access through HTTP	If the clause Preload is not included, the website will not be validated if the website is in the HSTS preload list
The Google Chrome browser, HSTS is not vulnerable	Incorrect implementation of the max-age clause may generate vulnerability in the website

Source: Authors.

5 Conclusions

In the development and implementation of information and communication technologies, ensuring integrity and confidentiality of data sent through internet has been tried. However, the problem of hacking HSTS directly, is not focused in the behavior or in the correct application of security protocols, since it is pretended to establish security mechanisms exclusively for the customer-website browser. HSTS is in its first adoption and orientation phases of its utilization. However, this complement has already improved a lot the security in several websites.

The biggest weakness of the HSTS policy is unusual, during the first connection between the customer and the server, it is vulnerable to an attack of traffic interception. In any other case, when the browser knows about the HSTS directive, it will reject all insecure requests, whether the user is under the same policy, or because the website does not have correctly configured the TLS certificate.

The most common web tools of communication on internet have been analyzed, web browsers, and it is evident that none of them is exempt from problems, nor it allows to completely solve the compromise problem, upon initiating the session between a customer and the server. The most realistic proposal is the one implemented by the Chrome web browser, under a series of limitations. Finally, one more protection layer is defined which is not perfect, and even so it provides greater guarantees in the use of most privileged services. That is why it could keep a secure connection, even with no previous knowledge about the HSTS directive. However, delegating all responsibility of the web communications to HSTS, or to a browser, is something that cannot be considered. Due to these reasons, security must be encouraged in the applications to the web developers, to the IT infrastructure departments, who should provide more resources to strengthen protection and improve their security policies; since it seems that they do not fully understand the origin policy in itself, and the relation of sub-domains among themselves. The same policy should apply to HSTS where policies to be applied to sub-domains should exist in a pre- determined way, with an option to deactivate it in specific subdomains. That would be a more secure design.

Nevertheless, more than simply determining if the HSTS mechanism has most of the responsibility, or if the browsers are the ones that should improve their security mechanisms, and how they can be implemented, so that the HSTS mechanism operates without difficulties under a man attack in the environment, is something really important, following certain recommendations, so that our internet connections are a little safer. Finally, it becomes interesting that for future investigations, tests be performed with a domain feasible to be sent to the preload list of browsers, in which no alternate security measures are established in the same test, and in this way determine the behavior of the hacking, when using the preload parameter in the HSTS headboard.

References

1. Fernandes, D.A.B., Soares, L.F.B., Gomes, J.V., Freire, M.M., Inácio, P.R.M.: Security issues in cloud environments: a survey. Int. J. Inf. Secur. **13**(2), 113–170 (2013). https://doi.org/10.1007/s10207-013-0208-7
2. Kiljan, S., Simoens, K., Cock, D.D., Eekelen, M.V., Vranken, H.: A survey of authentication and communications security in online banking. ACM Comput. Surv. (CSUR) **49**(4), 61 (2017)
3. Wang, Y.Q.: Discussion on the security and reliability in network transactions. Appl. Mech. Mater. **427–429**, 2321–2324 (2013).
4. Jarauta Sánchez, J., Prado Montes, Á.: Seguridad en sistemas de comunicación (2017)
5. Cenci, K.M., Matteis, L.D., Ardenghi, J.R.: Arquitectura en capas para acceso remoto sad. In: XVIII Congreso Argentino de Ciencias de la Computación (2013)
6. Cenci, K.M., Matteis, L.D., Ardenghi, J.R.: Tiered architecture for remote access to data sources. J. Comput. Sci. Technol. **14**, 67–72 (2014)
7. Trejo Alfaro, Y.G.: Prueba de penetración de la caja gris realizada a la solución Redborder versión cloud (2017)
8. Vázquez Sanisidro, A.: Optimización de Páginas Web: Visión teórica y análisis práctico (2017)
9. Hodges, J., Jackson, C., Barth, A.: Http strict transport security (hsts) (No. RFC 6797) (2012)
10. Hodges, J., Jackson, C., Barth, A.: Rfc 6797: Http strict transport security (hsts). IETF (2012). https://tools.Ietf.org/html/rfc6797
11. Selvi, J.: Bypassing HTTP strict transport security. Black Hat Europe (2014)
12. Cajiao, G., Fabricio, E.: Método para la detección y prevención de ataques web mediante la parametrización de un proxy reverso basado en software libre (Master's thesis, Escuela Superior Politécnica de Chimborazo) (2018)
13. Raharjo, W.S., Bajuadji, A.A.: Analisa Implementasi Protokol HTTPS pada Situs Web Perguruan Tinggi di Pulau Jawa. J. ULTIMATICS **8**(2), 102–111 (2017). https://doi.org/10.31937/ti.v8i2.518
14. Ortega, M., Santiago, A.: Metodología de hacking ético para instituciones financieras, aplicación de un caso práctico (Master's thesis) (2017)

15. Winter, P., Köwer, R., Mulazzani, M., Huber, M., Schrittwieser, S., Lindskog, S., Weippl, E.: Spoiled onions: exposing malicious Tor exit relays. In: De Cristofaro, E., Murdoch, S.J. (eds.) Privacy Enhancing Technologies: 14th International Symposium, PETS 2014, Amsterdam, The Netherlands, July 16-18, 2014. Proceedings, pp. 304–331. Springer International Publishing, Cham (2014). https://doi.org/10.1007/978-3-319-08506-7_16

16. Muñoz, A., Guzmán, A., Santos, S.D.L.: Contramedidas en la suplantación de autoridades de certificación. Certificate pinning (2014)

17. Sivakorn, S., Polakis, I., Keromytis, A.D.: The cracked cookie jar: HTTP cookie hijacking and the exposure of private information. In: 2016 IEEE Symposium on Security and Privacy (SP), pp. 724–742. IEEE (May 2016)

18. Kalyanam, R., Yang, B.: Try-CybSI: an extensible cybersecurity learning and demonstration platform. In: Proceedings of the 18th Annual Conference on Information Technology Education, pp. 41–46. ACM (September 2017)

19. Bujlow, T., Carela-español, V., Solé-Pareta, J., Barlet-Ros, P.: Web tracking: mechanisms, implications, and defenses. arXiv preprint arXiv:1507.07872 (2015)

20. Bujlow, T., Carela-español, V., Sole-Pareta, J., Barlet-Ros, P.: A survey on web tracking: Mechanisms, implications, and defenses. Proc. IEEE **105**(8), 1476–1510 (2017)

21. Raúl, B.G., Sevillano, A.M.L.: Services cloud under HSTS, Strengths and weakness before an attack of man in the middle MITM. In: 2017 Congreso Internacional de Innovación y Tendencias en Ingeniería (CONIITI), pp. 1–5. IEEE (October 2017)

22. Evans, C., Palmer, C., Sleevi, R.: Public key pinning extension for HTTP (No. RFC 7469) (2015)

23. Parmar, H., Gosai, A.: Analysis and study of network security at transport layer. Int. J. Comput. Appl. **121**(13), 35–40 (2015). https://doi.org/10.5120/21604-4716

24. Sullivan, N.T., Sharma, R.D., Lackey, R., Lin, Z.: U.S. Patent Application No. 14/967,156 (2017)

25. Sugavanesh, B., Hari Prasath, R., Selvakumar, S.: SHS-HTTPS enforcer: enforcing HTTPS and preventing MITM attacks. ACM SIGSOFT Softw. Eng. Notes **38**(6), 1–4 (2013)

26. Vikan, D.E.: TLS and the future of authentication (master's thesis, NTNU) (2015)

27. Buchanan, W.J., Helme, S., Woodward, A.: Analysis of the adoption of security headers in HTTP. IET Information Security (2017)

28. Adeloye, B.: HTTP man-in-the-middle code execution (2013)

29. Swanink, R., Poll, E., Schwabe, P.: Persistent Effects of Man-in-the-Middle Attacks, pp. 1–43. Radboud University (2016)

30. Park, S., Park, S., Yun, I., Kim, D., Kim, Y.: Analyzing security of Korean USIM-based PKI certificate service. In: Rhee, K.-H., Yi, J.H. (eds.) Information Security Applications, pp. 95–106. Springer, Cham (2015). https://doi.org/10.1007/978-3-319-15087-1_8

31. Kranch, M., Bonneau, J.: Upgrading HTTPS in mid-air: an empirical study of strict transport security and key pinning. In: NDSS (February 2015)

32. Dolnák, I., Litvik, J.: Introduction to HTTP security headers and implementation of HTTP strict transport security (HSTS) header for HTTPS enforcing. In: 2017 15th International Conference on Emerging eLearning Technologies and Applications (ICETA), pp. 1–4. IEEE (October 2017)

33. de los Santos, S., Torrano, C., Rubio, Y., Brezo, F.: Implementation state of HSTS and HPKP in both browsers and servers. In: Foresti, S., Persiano, G. (eds.) CANS 2016. LNCS, vol. 10052, pp. 192–207. Springer, Cham (2016). https://doi.org/10.1007/978-3-319-48965-0_12

34. Pineda, S., Matta, J., Torres, J., Díaz-Piraquive, F.N.: Blockchain: Estrategia en la Seguridad e Integridad de los Sistemas de Información de la Policía Nacional. In: Desafíos en Ingeniería: Investigación Aplicada. Ediciones Fundación Tecnológica Antonio Arévalo TECNAR (2019)

35. De La Espriella, L., García, J., Díaz-Piraquive, F.N.: La Sextorsión: Prácticas de Ingeniería Social en las Redes Sociales. In: Desafíos en Ingeniería: Investigación Aplicada. Ediciones Fundación Tecnológica Antonio Arévalo TECNAR (2019)

36. Bautista, V., López, A., Díaz-Piraquive, F.N.: Modelo ISO/IEC 25010 en el Proceso de Evaluación de la Calidad del Software en la Empresa Obras Civiles de Bogotá en el Área de Tecnología de la Información y Comunicación. In: Desafíos en Ingeniería: Investigación Aplicada. Ediciones Fundación Tecnológica Antonio Arévalo TECNAR (2019)

37. Zubieta, K., López, A., Díaz-Piraquive, F.N.: Auditoría para los Procesos de Pruebas y Calidad del Software del Proyecto Comisiones Callidus Accenture Colombia basada en la Norma ISO 9001:2015. In: Desafíos en Ingeniería: Investigación Aplicada. Ediciones Fundación Tecnológica Antonio Arévalo TECNAR (2019)

38. Pisso, A., López, A., Díaz-Piraquive, F.N.: Plan de mejoramiento para el fortalecimiento de competencias del auditor mediante el uso de tecnologías de la información. In: Desafíos en Ingeniería: Investigación Aplicada. Ediciones Fundación Tecnológica Antonio Arévalo TECNAR (2019)

The Importance of the Digital Preservation of Data and Its Application in Universities

Juan Santillán Lima[1]([⊠]), Fernando Molina-Granja[2], Raul Lozada-Yanez[3], Danny Velasco[2], Gonzalo Allauca Peñafiel[2], and Lourdes Paredes Castelo[4]

[1] Fcaulty of Infromatics -LEICI, Faculty of Engineering, National University of La Plata, La Plata, Argentina
juancarlos.santillan@infor.unlp.edu.ar
[2] Facultad de Ingenieria, Universidad Nacional de Chimborazo, Riobamba, Ecuador
{fmolina,dvelasco,gallauca}@unach.edu.ec
[3] Facultad de Informatica y Electrónica, Escuela Superior Politécnica de Chimborazo, Riobamba, Ecuador
raul.lozada@espoch.edu.ec
[4] Facultad de Ciencias, Escuela Superior Politécnica de Chimborazo, Riobamba, Ecuador
lparedes@espoch.edu.ec

Abstract. The article is the result of a documentary investigation concerning the digital preservation of data and the generation of data and its importance in educational institutions. Digital information has important economic value as a cultural product and as a source of knowledge, but this generated information must be preserved, without information, there is no inheritance or culture. Digital heritage is not subject to temporal, geographic, cultural or format limits. But the digital heritage of the world is in danger of being lost for posterity, which is why it is important to preserve them in an adequate manner so that they are accessible, authentic and usable in the long term, under international professional standards. Data in digital form is the main source of knowledge for our students. The repositories in the educational institutions allow not only to store the intellectual production but also the documentation created by the administrative part of the universities. The intellectual capital of universities should not only be stored but also preserved and made known to the community. It is important to investigate adequate techniques for the digital preservation of data in universities, applying or generating digital preservation models that adapt to the unique characteristics of universities.

Keywords: Preservation of data · Intellectual capital · Digital preservation · PREDECI

1 Introduction

With today's society, information is prioritized as a very important capital of companies and even of humanity, a compendium of criteria on Intellectual Capital tells us that "it is constituted by all those knowledge or ideas possessed by the members of a company

© Springer Nature Switzerland AG 2021
L. Uden et al. (Eds.): KMO 2021, CCIS 1438, pp. 345–353, 2021.
https://doi.org/10.1007/978-3-030-81635-3_28

and that is put into practice to contribute to give you competitive advantages within the market in which it operates" [1–3]. Demonstrating in this way the importance not only of material goods but also of knowledge and ideas embodied in information or data.

The main source of knowledge and ideas are universities, either with research projects or links with society that result in the creation of relevant works, or through the transmission of knowledge to their students, this transmission of knowledge is reflected in the conception of pre and postgraduate graduation work, as well as in the grades that are generated semester to semester and that are part of the file of each of the students.

Another type of information generated in the universities is the administrative one embodied in trades, emails, contracts, projects, class plans, syllabus, payment forms, distributive, regulations, statutes, resolutions, schedules, accountability and other documents vital to the management of a university and its evaluation by CEAACES.

Once the information has been generated in the universities "it is very important to maintain and preserve such information...... to ensure that there is no contamination, damage, alteration or manipulation and in this way maintain reliability" [4] of the information stored by higher education institutions.

At present, the resources that are generated as a result of people's knowledge and their expressions "are born", increasingly, in digital forms, be cultural, educational, or include information from different areas of knowledge.

Products of digital origin may not have a physical backup, for example on paper [5].

Many of these resources are valuable and constitute a true heritage to be preserved in the future for society. It is necessary to ensure that they are available and accessible in the long term" [6] Given this background and because a university campus has unique characteristics for which it has different needs, [7, 8] and based on these needs the question arises: Is it important to preserve the information generated by the universities?

2   Methodology Research

In order to carry out research, a theoretical analysis of the preservation of digital data and its applications was used as a starting point, as well as the analysis of its application in university environments. Next, the analysis of the importance of data preservation in Ecuadorian university environments was carried out. Table 1 shows the aspects considered in the methodology used in the present investigation in greater detail.

From these documents a manual review is carried out, repeated or duplicate works that resulted from the search in a more search engine are discarded, then the abstracts are read and the documents that are framed in the proposed exclusion criteria are discarded. Finally, there is a chain of authors that are cited in the selected articles.

3   Results

When analyzing different texts resulting from the application of the methodology described above we can find the following criteria on the importance of data preservation:

We currently live in a society focused on the importance of information, day by day we produce hundreds of documents with relevant information for our culture, education,

Table 1. Research methodology

Aspect	Explanation
Research question	This research seeks to answer the following research question: Is it important to preserve the information generated by universities?
Research strategies	Area: Data preservation, Digital data preservation, Information, University information, Purpose of the search: To determine the importance of the digital preservation of data applied in Ecuadorian universities
Information sources	Thesis, Scientific articles, Books, Papers
search engines	IEEE Xplorer Google Scholars
Search criteria	'Data preservation', 'preservation of data in education', 'educational repositories', 'preservation of educational information'
Inclusion Criteria	Documents containing information on the importance of digital data preservation Documents containing information on the digital preservation of data applied in universities
Exclusion Criteria	Documents that do not contain information on the importance of digital data preservation are excluded Documents that do not contain information on the digital preservation of data applied in universities
Evaluation of the content of the criteria	Accuracy, objectivity, coverage, relevance according to the research questions It is investigated in the chain of authors who have made contributions to the items seen
Information analysis	An overview of the digital preservation of data and its importance is provided, its applications in education are also examined

Prepared by: The authors

work, technology and general information that we apply for our lifestyle. "The information society today constitutes a form of social organization around information and communication technologies" [9], being this society "as a social relations plot" (Redón, 2001), understanding that Internet-based social relationships are not only interconnected people but also the system that hosts and provides the required services, [10] as well as the information that is transmitted by that system.

Redón Rojas (2001) defines information societies "From a holistic approach is the set of social relationships in a highly dynamic, open, globalized social space (institutionality) that are supported and realized through information; which is equally dynamic, open, globalized, technological as well as commercialized. Thus, in order for individuals to exist, they must be receivers, transmitters, consumers and an elite of creators of this type of information" [11]. Emphasizing in this way the importance and importance of information in our current society. Digital information has important economic value as a cultural product and as a source of knowledge. It also plays a very significant role in sustainable development at the national level, taking into account that usually personal, governmental and commercial data are created in digital form. The disappearance of this heritage will generate economic and cultural impoverishment and hinder the advancement of knowledge [12].

But all this information generated must be preserved since "without information (digital or not) that is guarded, there is no inheritance or culture" [13] and "at present, the resources that are generated as a result of the knowledge of the people and their expressions "are born", increasingly, in digital forms [6] that is why "without technology that allows the preservation or recovery of such information, there would be no inheritance or culture" [14] and many of these resources or information are valuable and constitute a true heritage to keep for the future for society [5]. Therefore, it is necessary to ensure that they are available and accessible in the long term [6].

One of the main criteria on the importance of digital data preservation is found in "The Charter on Digital Preservation" issued by UNESCO (2003), "Digital heritage is not subject to temporal, geographical, cultural or format limits. Although specific to a culture, anyone in the world is a potential user. Minorities can target majorities and individuals to a worldwide audience. The digital heritage of all regions, nations, and communities must be preserved and made available to anyone in order to promote, over time, a representation of all peoples, nations, cultures, and languages" [15].

UNESCO emphasizes the importance not only of preserving information but also that this information is accessible and can be used in the long term, it also states that "The world's digital heritage is in danger of being lost for posterity" [15] Therefore, we have the obligation to investigate techniques and models that allow such information not to be lost.

Anne Thurston (2012) tells us in reference to the ways of preserving data that, "... if we want digital archives ... ..to be accessible, authentic and usable in the long term, international professional standards must be met." [16]. Within the most important models, we can find DataNet, CLASS, PODDS, CASPAR, INTERPares, PREMIS, OAIS, PADI, PLANETS, LOCKSS, Digital.CSIC, PREDECI. [4]. The characteristics are briefly analyzed in Table 2.

The preservation of world documentary heritage is not just a matter of creating and storing digital information. It involves repositioning and strengthening the work of information professionals to fulfill a key role in global development. These professionals have already worked internationally to create the standards, laws, practices, and technologies necessary to make good management of digital archives. The current challenge is to foster the political will to move forward" [16].

Digital preservation requires that active measures be taken throughout the life cycle of the resource, so preservation policies must be established in the long term. Research is constantly necessary to apply the most advanced and safe technical solutions at all times [17].

Table 2. Basic characteristics of digital preservation models

Modelos	Características
PREMIS [24]	It focuses on strategies for implementing metadata preservation in Digital Archives
	PREMIS metadata concentrates only on the elements that directly affect preservation, it does not maintain links with access metadata, information retrieval, or even with information on rights
OAIS	It is a reference model that is used for the conservation of digital files
ISO 14721:2003	The OAIS model incorporates technological surveillance, digital preservation and all those processes that require that existing digital documents in a data center cannot be subjected to alterations, modifications or losses
Consultative Committee for Space Data Systems. [25]	Its functions are Ingestion, Storage, Data management, Access, Preservation, Common services
[26] DAMM (Tessella, 2013)	The key characteristics of the Preservation Information are: Identification of the file formats and conceptual objects (object of information that includes many files) that make up the ingested information. Extract the characteristics of these objects for future validation. Ability to identify file formats at risk and in need of attention
	Perform minor loss migration to new "Digital Master" Files, and to validate the migration. Carry out the migration with losses to the presentation quality formats suitable for dissemination. Keep the original information plus all relevant representations created later. Continually add new tools to keep Preservation Information active
NDSA - National Digital Stewardship Alliance [9]	A staggered set of guidelines and practices designed to offer clear reference instructions in preserving digital content in four progressive levels of sophistication through five different functional areas

(*continued*)

Table 2. (*continued*)

Modelos	Características
PREDECI [13]	A reference model for the preservation of digital evidence in criminal investigation institutions that are responsible for long-term custody in order to increase the admissibility of digital evidence in court or the availability of evidence to a community designated for management of evidence, and guarantees its fidelity and integrity in the long term. It responds to a set of responsibilities determined in-laws and regulations for this environment, based on the OAIS preservation model and metadata concepts

Prepared by: The authors

It is also important the following criteria on the digital preservation of data applied in universities and where this information is generated:

Taking into consideration that "at present, the resources that are generated as a result of people's knowledge and their expressions" are born ", increasingly, in digital forms [6] it is necessary to analyze where they" consume "Or where" the digital information "users of universities go up according to this Santillán (2017) determined the main services consumed in a university network being these" internet, virtual libraries, virtual classrooms, online academic services, IP telephony, Institutional mail " [8].

Santillán (2017) determined in their study on the universities of the center of Ecuador that the internet for research/task completion is given by 80.2% of university students, and Ólafsson et al., (2013) states that In Europe, the internet is a priority for school tasks, with a percentage of 85%. Demonstrating that not only in Ecuadorian reality but in much of the planet, digital data is the main source of knowledge directly for our students [18].

According to Pineda, it is necessary to "take advantage of the technology of the globalized world and reduce in some way, the gap between rich and informed poor, to enable everyone to participate in the information society and create a culture of individuals with the ability to work with information, for your personal and professional development" [19].

Repositories reach great importance, as they allow enriching the vision of the authors regarding the dissemination and preservation of their research data and thus guarantee long-term access. From the consolidation and increase of these in universities the visibility of the academic and scientific production of professionals is increased [20].

The repositories are of great importance in the educational institutions since they allow not only to store the intellectual production but also the documentation created by the administrative part of the universities. The "intellectual capital" of universities must not only be stored but also preserved and made known to the community.

States that a digital repository must have four fundamental characteristics: Self-archiving, Interoperability, Free and free access to the full text, Long-term preservation [21].

We can classify repositories according to their main objective [22]:

1) Institutional digital repositories: which are those developed by an academic institution whose objective is to store, preserve, disseminate and give access to intellectual production to the members of that institution (university, research center). In this sense, the type of content can be the most varied; since it can contain only intellectual or scientific production (articles, thesis, etc.), or also gather special collections, administrative documentation, etc. 2) Thematic or disciplinary repositories: whose main objective is to disseminate scientific production in certain areas of knowledge [21, 22].

2) Orphan repositories: established for the work of authors who do not have access to another repository. 3) Aggregators/Collectors: aggregators or portals that collect content from institutional or thematic repositories.

The university institutional repositories "collect part of the intellectual production of the universities, being understood as the" place "where the production of digital documents derived from the academic work of the universities is organized, preserved and disseminated" [23].

The information stored in these university institutional repositories is generated or "born" from the academy and the administrative part, within the academic part the virtual classrooms have become a primary tool for both face-to-face and distance education, as a form of Delivery of reports and works. Virtual libraries and digital libraries present a large number of books, magazines, and theses available to the university community even if this information is located on the other side of the world, thus facilitating access to information to universities and educational institutions [8].

Within the administrative part, the online academic services give access to the academic information of each student, as well as facilitate the registration of student grades and attendance, thus being a significant contribution to the presentation of learning outcomes. And the institutional email gives official character to the communications sent by email, taking a big step towards minimizing the use of the papers [18].

4 Conclusions

We currently live in a society focused on the importance of information, day by day we produce hundreds of documents with relevant information for our culture, education, work, technology and general information that we apply for our lifestyle. In universities, not only material goods are important, but also the knowledge and ideas embodied in information or data.

It is necessary to preserve the intellectual capital of our universities whether or not they were born digitally since without information there is no inheritance or culture, the information is valuable and constitutes a true heritage to be preserved for society in the future, ensuring that they are accessible and available for Posterity.

It is important to investigate appropriate techniques for the digital preservation of data in universities, applying or generating digital preservation models that adapt to the unique characteristics of universities. After carrying out the documentary research, the following research questions arise as references to future research. What is the most appropriate way for the digital preservation of data generated by universities? How to discern which information should be preserved and which not? What parameters to consider for adequate preservation of long-term data? We hope in the future that these doubts can be resolved by the authors of this work.

References

1. Edvinsson, L., Malone, M.: "El capital intelectual". Bogotá: Norma (1998)
2. Stewart, T.: "La nueva riqueza de las organizaciones: el capital intelectual". Granica, Buenos Aires (1998)
3. Román, N.: Capital intelectual: generador de éxito en las empresas. Vis. Gerenc. **2**, 67–79 (2004)
4. Molina, F., Rodriguez, G.: The preservation of digital evidence and its admissibility in the court. Int. J. Electron. Secur. Digital Forens. **9**(1), 1–18 (2017)
5. Molina, F., Rodriguez, G.: Preservation of digital evidence: application in criminal investigation. In: Science and Information Conference, pp. 1284–1292. Springer, London, United Kingdom (2015). https://doi.org/10.1109/SAI.2015.7237309
6. De Giusti, M.R.:"Las dificultades de la preservación digital: problemas, desafíos y propuestas para los repositorios. "VI Conferencia Internacional BIREDIAL-ISTEC (San Luis Potosí, México, 17 al 19 de octubre) (2016)
7. Santillán-Lima, J.C.: Diseño de una infraestructura de telecomunicaciones que optimice el acceso a los servicios para el creciente tráfico de datos del Campus La Dolorosa de la UNACH (Tesis de maestría). Pontificia Universidad Católica del Ecuador, Quito (2013)
8. Santillán-Lima, J.C., Rocha-Jacome, C., Guerrero-Morejón, K., Llanga-Vargas, A., Vásconez-Barrera, F., Molina- Granja, F.: "El Impacto De Los Servicios De Telecomunicaciones y Las Tics En Las Necesidades De La Educación Superior". IV Congreso Internacional de Ciencia Tecnología Innovación y Emprendimiento Cite 2017. Universidad Estatal de Bolívar, Guaranda (2017)
9. National Digital Stewardship Alliance: NDSA National Agenda for Digital Stewardship (2014). http://www.digitalpreservation.gov/ndsa/documents/2014NationalAgenda.pdf. Accessed 28 October 2014
10. Valenzuela, A.R.: Las redes sociales y su aplicación. Revista Digital Univ. **14**(4) 1–14 (2013)
11. Redón Rojas, M.A.: Un análisis del concepto de sociedad de la información desde el enfoque holístico. Inf. C. Soc. **4**, 16 (2001)
12. Duranti, L., Shaffer, E.: The memory of the world in the digital age: digitization and preservation. In: Vancouver: UNESCO Conference Proceedings (2012)
13. Molina, F., Rodriguez, G.: Model for digital evidence preservation in criminal research institutions – predeci. Int. J. Electron. Secur. Digital Forens. **9**(2), 150–166 (2017)
14. Granja, F.M., Rodríguez, G.: Digital preservation and criminal investigation: a pending subject. In: Rocha, A., Correia, A., Costanzo, S., Reis, L. (eds.) New Contributions in Information Systems and Technologies. Advances in Intelligent Systems and Computing, vol. 353, pp 299–309. Springer, Cham (2015). https://doi.org/10.1007/978-3-319-16486-1_30. 978-3-319-16485-4
15. UNESCO: Carta sobre la preservación del patrimonio digital, 15 de octubre de (2003)
16. Thurston, A.C.: "La Memoria del Mundo en la era digital: digitalización y preservación", Vancouver Declaration (Canadá) (2012)
17. Conselho Nacional de Arquivos: Modelo de Requisitos para Sistemas Informatizados de Gestão Arquivística de Documentos. Rio de Janeiro: Câmara Técnica de Documentos Eletrônicos (2011)

18. Santillán-Lima, J.C., et al.: LAS REDES SOCIALES COMO HERRAMIENTA ACADÉMICA EN LAS UNIVERSIDADES DEL CENTRO DEL PAIS. Revista investigar, 5ta Edición, ESPOCH (2017)
19. Pineda, J.M.: El rol del bibliotecólogo en la sociedad de la información (2005)
20. Cabrera, E.D., et al.: Importance of repositories for preserving and recovering information.MEDISAN **19**(10), 1283–1290 (2015). http://scielo.sld.cu/scielo.php?script=sci_art text&pid=S1029-30192015001000014&lng=es&tlng=en. Recuperado en 03 de noviembre de 2017, de
21. López, F.A.: Visibilidad e impacto de los repositorios digitales en acceso abierto. De bibliotecas y bibliotecarios... Boletín electrónico ABGRA, 2013 (5), 1–12 (2013). [Journal article (On-line/Unpaginated)]
22. Abadal, E.: Acceso abierto a la ciencia. Barcelona: editorial UOC. Colección El Profesional de la información, no. 5 (2012). http://eprints.rclis.org/bitstream/10760/16863/1/2012-acceso-abierto-epi-uoc-vfinalautor.pdf
23. Calderón, A., Ruiz, E.: Participación y visibilidad web de los repositorios digitales universitarios en el contexto europeo. Comunicar. **XX**(40), 193–201 (2013)
24. Caplan, P.: Understanding premis. D-Lib Mag. **15**(¾) (2009)
25. Consultative Committee for Space Data Systems: Reference Model for an Open Archival Information System (OAIS) (2012). https://public.ccsds.org/pubs/650x0m2.pdf
26. Tessella: Digital Preservation Maturity Model - White Paper (2013)

Knowledge Management Applied in the Comparative Study of the IRETE Intrusion Methodology to Access to the Computer Systems

Flor Nancy Diaz-Piraquive[1](✉), Emanuel Ortiz-Ruiz[2](✉),
Jansen Jair González-Aragón[2](✉), Harlinzo Hernan Avila-Bermeo[2](✉),
and Wilmer David Parada-Jaimes[2](✉)

[1] Fundación Universitaria Internacional de la Rioja UNIR, Logroño, Colombia
flornancy.diaz@unir.edu.co
[2] Escuela de Tecnologías de la Información y las Comunicaciones ESTIC, Policía Nacional de Colombia, Bogotá, Colombia
emanuel.ortiz@policia.edu.co, {jansen.gonzalez,harlinzo.avila,
wilmer.parada2746}@correo.policia.gov.co

Abstract. The threats in cyberspace materialize big digital security threats for any organization. New computer incidents are permanently reported, visualizing the advanced technical skills of cybercriminals and the cybersecurity professionals' response limitations. Most expensive digital security products are based on the treatment of known threats and are vulnerable to new threats known as zero-day attacks. Likewise, the human factor continues to be one of the main weaknesses when deploying IT security strategies and policies. In this way the tests or computer penetration tests are one of the most appropriate techniques to know and establish digital security mechanisms according to each organization. Therefore, the present work analyzes international standards to carry out computer vulnerability tests and proposes a methodology of ethical hacking under the postulates of gratuity and resources availability. Suggestions on the scalability of cybersecurity strategies are presented at the end of the document, considering that each organization is different and requires adaptability in the use of the available infrastructure to manage known and unknown digital risks.

IRETE's research is based on the management that must be carried out in the creation, distribution and appropriation of knowledge, through the methodology that guides the assurance of information through the PenTESTING phases. Likewise, it proposes a process that integrally integrates the collection of information from any operating system, indicating that IRETE generates information more simply and accurately from the inspection, track, examination, testing and exfiltration phases. IRETE presents a complete methodology to approach the knowledge management of a vulnerable system, which allows an in-depth review of the factors that affect the handling of information.

Keywords: Computer vulnerabilities · Cybersecurity · Digital security · Ethical hacking · IT security policies · Pen-testing · Penetration tests

L. Uden et al. (Eds.): KMO 2021, CCIS 1438, pp. 354–365, 2021.
https://doi.org/10.1007/978-3-030-81635-3_29

1   Introduction

Cyberspace, a term developed by Gibson [1], is today an unlimited field where time and distance are not measurable in the way it is done in the non-digital world [2]. Cyber interactions don't know about traditional borders, a person can send a message from any country through a server of a social network hosted in different countries and that message can be read by multiple users on the planet, who are located in time zones totally asynchronous [3]. This new poly-spatial perspective becomes a constraint in regulating and implementing regulatory frameworks to prevent deviant online behaviors or criminal behavior. Similarly, there are new ways of data transmission with encryption technologies and protection of communications that allow options of anonymity or concealment of the location for any user of the network [2]. From this complexity, cybercriminals and criminals find strategies to prevent their prosecution and increase impunity rates that allow them to keep active by learning and perfecting their intrusion techniques in computer science.

Although the classification of cyber threats is very broad, the cybercriminology and cybersecurity research network [4], presents five relevant categories. First, the threats to the victim's economy are grouped together, second, those that attack the vital infrastructure of a society, third, those that victimize children and adolescents, fourth, those that have an interpersonal environment; and fifth, those that attack new technologies, wearable devices or internet of things (Iot). Some threats may be combined with more than one category or may be specialized in only one, depending on the target of the attack or the profile of the cybercriminal [2]. According to Shoemaker and Kennedy [5] there are twelve different profiles of cyber criminals and according to Choi [6]; different forms of malicious code are used to violate cyber security.

These intrusions are attempted permanently; when the machine capabilities (i.e. processing and storage on computer equipment) increase, those attacks can be automated to optimize the attackers' times. It should be noted that attackers can focus efforts on a single target or multiple victims, however, the first form of attack, also known as targeted attacks, are the ones that materialize the greatest cybercriminal expertise. Cyber-offenders use intrusion techniques and share information about possible vulnerabilities to exploit through different methods, for this reason, cyber security professionals cannot rely on the protection of an organization's digital assets just taking into account the installation of antivirus software or configuration of firewalls. Malicious intrusion techniques usually exceed these basic computer security measures. For this reason, it is advisable to simulate these kinds of attacks in order to detect weaknesses in the cyber security scheme before cybercriminals do. These simulated and controlled attacks, carried out with the knowledge of the organization, are known as tests of penetration, pentesting or ethical hacking.

This document conceptualizes the different cyber threats used to illegally access a technological infrastructure, also lists certain pentesting methodologies available to verify the digital security of an organization, finally, this paper proposes the methodology IRETE [7–10], acronym resulting from five phases: Inspect, Track, Examine, Test and Exfilter, which seeks to improve cybersecurity strategies and optimize the information resources of an organization.

1.1 Cyber Threats and Computer Vulnerability Assessment Methodologies

The cybernetic interactions are not limited to the space and time of the non-digital world, as well as, the cybercrime operates against geographical boundaries and applies multiple techniques to use timelessness and antispatiality in virtual environment, in addition, it allows the anonymity that increases the impunity and indirectly motivates new computer criminals [11]. In this digital environment, cybernauts use social media to share experiences and graphic material and cyber-offenders share malicious code and invite others to improve computer tools to materialise complex cyber-attacks [4].

The level of complexity of an attack increases as the malicious code is developed and is used by the victim. For example, a basic attack may not require a telematic infrastructure to be executed; social engineering techniques are enough. According to Choi and Toro-Alvarez [2], social engineering is the methodology that allows to obtain access to passwords or sensitive information through techniques that stimulate qualities or defects of human nature. That is, envy, solidarity, curiosity, among others. When the information is obtained, cybercriminals can enter an organization's computer infrastructure without the need to use technological tools or combine them to ensure the success of their intrusion. A common case of social engineering is the entry of a courier from a florist's shop to a company building assuring to bring a bouquet for the chief clerk, the gender solidarity of the receptionist allows the entry of the messenger without any problem. Once in the administrative department, the supposed courier takes advantage to look at the passwords of access that are located in the desks of the workers and the names of the employees published in the billboards of the company. After the visit the attacker tests by making fictitious calls to the technical support area of the company with the information collected or tests the passwords obtained and accesses the email accounts that appear in the company contact information, succeeding the intrusion target [4].

In an advanced level of attack, social engineering may require impersonation of websites where false forms are published and seek to capture sensitive data (phishing) or allow the download of contaminated files with malicious software (malware) which can have multiple purposes. This malware can be replicated through other actions performed by the victim and can be known as virus, even it can replicate itself like computer worms or logic bombs [2]. In other scenarios, this malware can be downloaded separately into a victim system and it can surpass cyber security settings or infect the mobile teams of workers, then replicate itself on computers of others to reach the desired system. Most of the time this infection takes advantage of vulnerabilities known by cyber-attackers but unknown by computer incident response teams (CSIRT) of the victim organizations. In this waym the tests of intrusion or computer penetration (pentesting) are appropriate techniques to close the door to cybercriminals [4]. However, pentesting is sometimes limited to testing entry to the technological infrastructure, in addition, it does not test internal organizational scenarios. Ethical hacking or ethical computer intrusion tests are considered pentesting tasks that include the authorization of entry and controlled manipulation of information and files of the organization.

Among the most widely used methodologies at the international level for ethical hacking or ethical hacking are the following five. The Open Security Testing Methodology (OSSTMM), NIST SP 800-42 also known as the Guide to Testing Network Security,

Risk Assessment Work Guide (TRAWG), Operationally Critical Threat, Active and Vulnerability Assessment (OCTAVE), The Standard of Performing Penetration Tests (PTES) [12–15].

OSSTMM is a standard created in 2001 by the Institute for Safety and Open Methodologies (ISECOM) to provide a framework for conducting computer security tests. It is based on compliance with technical standards such as those of the International Organization for Standardization (ISO) 27001–27002 and best practices of the American National Institute of Standards and Technology (NIST). One of the main characteristics of this methodology is the route of the capacities to be evaluated from the internal part of the organization [16].

On the other hand, TRAWG guides the cybersecurity professional to assess the threats and risks of an existing technological system. This guide identifies the critical assets most likely to be at risk and makes recommendations for the safety and management of those threats. It is noteworthy that this methodology defines objectives of desired levels of security and establishes the potential impacts in case a cyber threat is materialized [4].

The NIST SP 800-42 methodology proposes activities to provide information of the integrity of the organization's networks and systems through network mapping, vulnerability scanning, password decryption and security check. In this way, the methodology provides guidance for security experts, technical support officers and technical and functional managers responsible for the implementation of computer security policies [17–19].

OCTAVE focuses on the identification and management of information security risks, defines an evaluation method to label information assets that are important for the mission of the organization, it also labels the threats to those assets and the vulnerabilities that those assets may exhibit. With this information, OCTAVE serves as a guide for proposing strategies for the protection and mitigation of threats (Alberts, et al., 1999). The PTES standard addresses intrusion testing, including an organization's information gathering phase and a threat modeling phase that seeks to gain reasonable knowledge of the corporation under test. This methodology highlights the inclusion of a post-exploitation phase where the level of commitment is documented, and protective measures are suggested [20].

Finally, a local application methodology called ITETE (Inspect, Track, Examine, Test and Exfilter) was analyzed; it was created with the purpose of providing a practical tool for responsable staff in computer security; public and private sectors. It also serves as a frame of reference in processes of auditing and assurance of security infrastructures of the organizations [4]. It should be noted that the official who applies the methodology or pentester is referred by this methodology as an "Investigator".

By breaking down the parts of this methodology it is possible to identify that the "Inspect" is the phase where the investigator plans the intrusion test, identifies the organization's digital assets and makes preliminary maps of the infrastructure to be threatened, i.e., obtains internet protocol (IP) address ranges of the relevant servers and equipment of the organization that can be accessed from the internet. This phase can be of two classes: passive and active.

Passive inspection does not generate direct interaction with the organization under assessment. For example, in this phase is possible to consult on the Internet the name of the target company and obtain the address of the website as well as the IP addresses of the servers where the site is hosted. On the other hand, in active inspection there is an interaction between the investigator and the target organization. For example, using social engineering or using commands from the console mode of the researcher's equipment to the object infrastructure.

Followed by this phase, the "Track" goes deep the level of knowledge of the object organization, identifying vulnerable services and likely access points. The researcher outlines the infrastructure map and determines the operating systems used by the organization's machines. This information is relevant to move on to the next phase; "Examine" explores known vulnerabilities and uses the information collected so far, it means, it uses the data collected through social engineering, the organization's public information on the Internet, common failures reported from identified operating systems and depending on the degree of testing may attempt an infection with malicious software under controlled environments. In this way, it uses intrusive techniques, validation of active user accounts, listing shared files, identification of vulnerable applications and poorly protected resources.

The fourth phase; "Testing" is aimed to achieve access to information systems, obtain a level of privileges higher than those acquired, finally, implement the control or instruction tasks planned at the beginning of the test "The last stage Exfiltrate"; this phase evaluates the possibility of digital asset extraction by cyber criminals, it allows the installation of malicious remote control software and tests the digital security of the organization internally. Among the most used techniques to carry out this phase is the deletion of logs, hiding, creation of access accounts, programs tasks, file infection, introduction of remote-control services and recording evidence of intrusion for the final test report.

1.2 Comparison and Methodological Approximation Variables

Taking into account the computer security testing environments implemented by the Police Academy of Information and Communications Technologies, in Colombia, it was possible to identify, 12 common factors of the methodologies described above were identified. The definitions of these factors are presented below as comparator variables:

- Variable 1 (v1). Guide for the recognition of technological infrastructure: The methodology has a guide to explain the procedure for the recognition of the infrastructure of information systems.
- Variable 2 (v2). Guide for the identification of open network ports: The methodology has a guide to explain the procedure to identify open network ports in the information systems infrastructure.
- Variable 3 (v3). Protocol for the scanning of vulnerabilities: The methodology has a guide to explain the procedure to recognize the infrastructure of the information systems.
- Variable 4 (v4). Guide for the exploitation of vulnerabilities found: The methodology has a guide to know how to exploit vulnerabilities in information systems.

- Variable 5 (v5). Guide to identify procedures for extracting logical assets the methodology has a guide to explaining the procedure to extract assets from information systems.
- Variable 6 (v6). Validity of the methodology: the methodology must have less than 10 years of issuance, creation or updating.
- Variable 7 (v7). Support from the creator of the methodology: The creator of the methodology provides support in Latin America on the implementation of the methodology.
- Variable 8 (v8). Methodology documentation available from closed source: The methodology documentation is on pages that require registration or user authentication.
- Variable 9 (v9). Open source methodology documentation: The methodology documentation is available to the user without authentication by the user.
- Variable 10 (v10). Language of the open source documentation: The language in the methodology documentation is available in open sources
- Variable 11 (v11). Closed source documentation language: the language in the methodology documentation is available in closed sources.
- Variable 12 (v12). The use of the methodology requires the authorization of the creator.

The declaration of the above variables allowed to investigate in literature related to cybersecurity tests and institutions that create or promote standards, related to the aforementioned methodologies. It means, the documentation issued by the ISECOM, creator of the OSSTMM methodology, the American National Institute of Standards and Technology (NIST) owner of the NIST SP 800-42 standard, etc. [17, 18]. Three values were parameterized for all variables except v11 and v12 where the answers are presented with the names of the languages of availability of the compared methodology. In this way, the value for positive response variables is "1", "0" for the negative response to the variable's approach and "no data" for investigations with little documentary support or ambiguous evidence in the literature consulted. For example, v7 inquiries about the availability of the methodology to provide support in Latin America about the implementation of the methodology. The PTES methodology obtained 1 considering that there is reported support, NIST SP 800-42 does not support, therefore, this variable obtained "0", and the OSSTMM methodology does not report information that supports any answer to this question, in this way, this variable recorded "no data" (see Table 1).

It should be noted that the results reported in the matrix of Table 1, are partial due to the documentation consulted in Russian was not readable because of the proficient limitations of the researchers who are all native Spanish speakers.

The findings found show differences between English speakers and Spanish speakers, because cybercriminals have a structure to communicate, to relate and to execute attacks against their victims, in this sense they differ and take on fundamental value when evaluating the methodology with integrity. raised for Spanish speakers.

Another equivalent reason for this methodology is important to highlight that there are different cybercriminal phenomena in other countries and the different methodologies or standards are not adequate to study Spanish-speaking computer systems. In this sense, it is vital to understand a context, a situation, a fact or a primary reason to be able to deploy IRETE based on actions that integrate results of equivalence, trust and sensitivity of the

Table 1. Matrix for comparison of methodologies

	OSSTMM	NIST SP 800-42	TRAWG	OCTAVE	PTES	IRETE
v1	1	1	0	1	1	1
v2	1	1	0	1	1	1
v3	1	1	1	1	1	1
v4	1	1	1	1	1	1
v5	0	0	0	0	1	1
v6	1	0	0	1	1	1
v7	No data	No data	No data	1	1	1
v8	No data		1	1	1	0
v9	1	1	1	1	1	1
v10	English-Spanish	English-Russian	English	English	English	Spanish
v11	No data	English	0	English	English	0
v12	1	1	1	X	1	0

Source: Developed by the authors

information you want to obtain. Based on this, we have several applicable standards, but not in greater depth as IRETE offers, which allows us to determine simpler, more complete actions applied to the Spanish-speaking cybercriminal context; as suggested by its preliminary scientific bases.

2 Methodology

In order to build an article that validates the concept that through innovation, the use and appropriation of ICTs, it is possible to produce knowledge for organizational management, a process of identifying, locating, selecting and analyzing information was carried out. This process began with the formulation of the question that guided the search for documents in the collection of this study, afterwards sources were identified and a strategy to selected documents was defined. Next, analysis and assessment of information was carried out and finally the publication.

The importance of fostering situations and training to guide a continuous process of use and appropriation of ICTs for innovation is reported. Importantly, the literature review and observation of the management of small and medium enterprises were essential in aligning the answers. In order to build an article that validates the concept that through innovation, the use and appropriation of ICTs, it is possible to produce knowledge for organizational management, a process of identifying, locating, selecting and analyzing information was carried out. This process began with the formulation of the question that guided the search for documents in the collection of this study, afterwards sources were identified and a strategy to selected documents was defined. Next, analysis and assessment of information was carried out and finally the publication.

The importance of fostering situations and training to guide a continuous process of use and appropriation of ICTs for innovation is reported. Importantly, the literature review and observation of the management of small and medium enterprises were essential in aligning the answers.

3   Preliminary Analysis of Results

According to the different approaches of the analyzed methodologies, it is difficult to find evaluation constants to determine which of them has better usability or implementation capacity, however, the preliminary results show that OSSTMM is a methodology widely known by the English speakers and it is also recognized by different security firms and cybersecurity corporations.

On the other hand, although NIST SP 800-42 is a widely disseminated methodology, is no longer in force, version 800-115 replaced it since 2008. However, many professionals continue to apply the obsolete version without knowing its validity as assessed in variable v6. According to TRAWG, this methodology has a corporate approach that serves as a frame of reference for designing security and risk management policies, however, its support and documentation is restricted to certain users and this is the reason why its validity cannot be assured [17, 18].

According to OCTAVE and PTES, the comparison made places them very close to each other in terms of dissemination, support, availability to the English language and English community, definition of guidelines for infrastructure recognition procedures and vulnerabilities. However, the OCTAVE lacks sequential instructions used for extracting digital assets from the object organization [21–25].

It is possible to stablish preliminarily, that the PTES methodology obtained the best evaluation for corporate dissemination and it can be used as a good reference for the English speakers and community, similarly it can be assured that there is a good evaluation for the IRETE methodology and its implementation among Spanish digital security professionals. However, from a corporate perspective, IRETE [8–10] does not have support information from closed sources or private sector. This disadvantage, compared to the methodologies most used and described in this study, opens the door to the coloring work of free software communities and organizations with little available resources to carry out computer intrusion tests.

The results presented through the comparison in the use of the IRETE methodology are closely related to Knowledge Management, since each of its aspects is focused on the way in which Pentesters PTES use it to take advantage of vulnerabilities in the affected information systems. It is important to highlight that, it is plated through the comparison from the generation of additional knowledge that allows to strengthen the results of the identification, detection and exploitation of the vulnerabilities of the exploited systems.

Considering that security is an expectation for computer systems, IRETE proposes a reliable methodological organization for the different communities at the international level, for this reason, it ensures the results by measuring the failures that Cybersecurity can present at a global level. These Cybercrime scenarios require comprehensive professionals in the field of computer security, therefore, IRETE reflects the pressing needs for this purpose and consequences.

The methodologies are focused on the strengthening of the information systems are consistent with a training on tools, which only reach a midpoint of depth in the required results; for this reason, the consequence of looking for alternatives that structure the analyst's thinking and allow better consolidation of results.

For Security professionals, it is vital to understand how a computer system works holistically, therefore, the infrastructures and shortcomings found from an analysis through phases, allow the elaboration of a more effective matrix. Because it affects the management of knowledge in what is related to its study and the objective to be achieved. In this sense, "the knowledge" of the cybersecurity professional must have generalized but comprehensive thinking in order to act; which in turn allows you to make the obtaining of as much information as possible effective in order to guarantee the delivery of reliable, comprehensive and scientifically-oriented results.

4 Conclusions

The proliferation of multiple cyber threats and their unpredictable behavior, given the innovation in cybercriminal techniques and the increase in the technological capabilities of computers and mobile devices; they don't allow to devise a cyber security strategy; to respond to the risks they pose. In this way, computer intrusion testing is an indispensable tool to anticipate cyber-attacks.

Multiple standards and methodologies propose courses of action to conduct vulnerability testing in the field of digital security, but most of them provide targeted support to English speakers and community and focus on corporate perspectives that limit access to organizations with limited security budgets. The evaluation of methodologies allows cyber security professionals to approach different selection criteria, among them, the availability and applicability of the methodology, according to the nature and resources of the organization being tested for computer security.

Computer penetration tests, "pentests" or intrusion tests, and evaluations with ethical hacking, are common terms in cybersecurity, but their practice differs. While the pentest only evaluate the organization's external security, ethical hacking involves a complex procedure that is not limited to prove the possibility to breach digital security, as pentest does. On the other hand, ethical hacking tests not only external security but also internal authentication policies and protection against the leakage of digital assets or intellectual property from the organization evaluated.

Computer risk management should be a preliminary phase to the application of any of the methodologies described above. In other words, the assessment of threats, the identification of potential risks and the implementation of computer vulnerability tests must be complemented and adapted to the nature and characteristics of each organization under assessment.

IRETE is an ethical hacking methodology that is gradually spread among cyber security professionals. Its method can be applied openly and as an independent guide for small and medium-sized organizations. Its implementation is supported by a participatory framework that links academics and public sector professionals but with a higher impact in the private sector.

The five phases aim to obtain: identification. Elaboration of a valuation scheme of the critical assets of the computer system, organization or objective in order to guarantee the corresponding actions before the possible tools to be used; taking into account that an initial context is elaborated, a certain investigation model which will allow to carry out the criticality work of these critical assets or vulnerable infrastructure. Recognition. Applies to be able to trace and examine, which allows and facilitates the creation of flags or identifiers of presence in security, or false expectation of security in the organization or possible objective; based on this, define the operational tactics of the team or pentester to be able to act on this already identified scenario. Execution. The testing or that related to generating actions on the objective or computer system, allows the elaboration of a line of errors or possible elements that redirect towards lateral or unreliable objectives; for this reason, the activity in elaboration of a definitive mechanism to be able to understand the infrastructure, know its weak points, and be able to obtain the desired information. Results. The exfiltration stage suggests a tangible and efficient obtaining of the previous stages and clearly allows us to extract as much information as possible against specific objectives, without limiting ourselves to a relationship line or a methodology that limits its effectiveness.

IRETE allows, in addition to efficiency in the actions carried out, it also adds elements of reliability when preparing a report with the results obtained; and from the phases following the identification of the objective, it allows evaluating the degree of effectiveness. Objective that in several of the proposed or compared methodologies, it is not allowed to achieve.

In the same way, it allows having a comprehensive knowledge of the objective (computer system), without thinking that it is not vulnerable, on the contrary, arguing that it is increasingly has better elements to obtain confidential or sensitive information to be able to remedy and correct.

From this writing of this article, it is important to determine the context in which IRETE unfolds; therefore, it is important to define its scope, which will allow security professionals not to limit themselves to the evidence found; if not they can have the flexibility when using tools.

- **Limitations of the study**

The results presented are preliminary since the present work is a technical progress report within the research project "Cybercriminology applied to improve cyber surveillance and counter cyber security threats".

The literature consulted is available in different languages to the Spanish language, native language of the researchers; reason why a later evaluation by researchers proficient in languages such as Russian can ratify the results of this study or provide more evaluation criteria.

References

1. Gibson, W.: Neuromancer. ACE, New York (1984)
2. Choi, K.-S., Toro-Alvarez, M.M.: Cibercriminología: Guía para la investigación del ciber-crimen y mejores prácticas en seguridad digital. Bogotá: Fondo Editorial UAN (2017)
3. Choi, K.: Cybercriminology and Digital Investigation. LFB Scholarly Publishing LLC, El Paso. TX (2015)

4. RedCiber: Diagnóstico del cibercrimen, delitos informáticos y comportamiento desviado en el ciberespacio en Colombia. Bogotá: RedCiber (2018)
5. Shoemaker, D., Kennedy, D.: Criminal profiling and cyber-criminal investigations. In: Schmalleger, F., Pittaro, M. (eds.) Crimes of the Internet, pp. 456–476. Prentice Hall, Upper Saddle River, NJ (2009)
6. Choi, K.: Risk Factors in Computer-Crime Victimization. LFB Scholarly Publishing, El Paso, TX (2014)
7. IC3: Annual Report on Internet Crime 2004. Internet Crime Complaint Center. Recuperado el 15 de Agosto, 2015 de (2005). https://www.ic3.gov/media/annualreports.aspx
8. IC3: Internet Crime Report. Internet Crime Complaint Center. Recuperado el 15 de Agosto, 2015 de (2009). www.nw3c.org/docs/downloads/2008_ic3_annual-report_3_27_09_small.pdf
9. IC3: Annual Report on Internet Crime Released. Internet Crime Complaint Center. Identity Theft 2013 Bureau of Justice Statistics. U.S. Government Printing Office (2014)
10. IC3: Annual Report on Internet Crime Released. Internet Crime Complaint Center. Identity Theft 2014 Bureau of Justice Statistics. U.S. Government Printing Office (2015)
11. Toro-Alvarez, M.M.: Programa de entrenamiento integral de prevención y contención del cibercrimen contra niños, niñas y adolescentes. Bogotá. Escuela de Postgrados de Policía (ESPOL) (2018)
12. APWG: The Global Phishing Survey. Anti-Phishing Working Group. Recuperado el 1 de mayo, 2010 (2009)
13. Barber, R.: Hackers profiled: ¿Who are they and what are their motivations? Comput. Fraud Secur. **2001**(2), 14–17 (2001). https://doi.org/10.1016/S1361-3723(01)02017-6
14. Comando de entrenamiento y doctrina del ejército estadounidense: DCSINT Handbook No. 1.02, Critical Infrastructure Threats and Terrorism. Recuperado el 10 de agosto, 2010, de (2006). https://fas.org/irp/threat/terrorism/sup2.pdf
15. García, L.E., Gómez, C.P., Cortés, Y.L.: Policing Strengthen for knowledge society challenges: Series 1-Policing Beliefs, 11, December, 2018. Technical report PSKSC-S1-20181211, p. 14 (2018). https://doi.org/10.13140/RG.2.2.23479.57766. https://www.researchgate.net/publication/329574001_Policing_Strengthen_for_knowledge_society_challenges_Series_1-Policing_Beliefs
16. Valdez, A.: OSSTMM 3. RITS. Revista de Inf. Tecnol. y Soc. **8**, 29–30 (2013)
17. NIST: Special publication 800-42. Computer security resource center. Disponible en (2003). https://csrc.nist.gov/publications/detail/sp/800/final
18. NIST: Federal guidelines for searching and seizing computers, Recommendations of the National Institute of Standards and Technology. National Institute of Standards and Technology. Recuperado el 23 de marzo, 2015, de (2006). http://nvlpubs.nist.gov/nistpubs/Legacy/SP/nistspecialpublication800-86.pdf
19. Symantec: Corporate profile. Recuperado el 1 de mayo, 2010, de (2016). http://www.symantec.com/about/profile/index.jsp
20. Liu, B., Shi, L., Cai, Z., Li, M.: Software vulnerability discovery techniques: a survey. In: Multimedia Information Networking and Security (MINES), 2012 Fourth International Conference on, pp. 152–156, IEEE, November, 2012
21. Microsoft: Microsoft, the FBI, Europol and industry partners disrupt the notorious ZeroAccess botnet. Microsoft News Center. Recuperado de (2013). https://news.microsoft.com/2013/12/05/microsoft-the-fbi-europol-and-industry-partners-disrupt-the-notorious-zeroaccess-botnet/
22. Motta, D., Toro-Alvarez, M.M.: Social innovation articulators to counter threats to public safety (2017). https://doi.org/10.22335/rlct.v8i2.315
23. Wilson, C.: Computer Attack and Cyberterrorism: Vulnerabilities and policy issues for Congress, Congressional Research Service Report for Congress (2005)

24. De La Espriella, L., García, J., Díaz-Piraquive, F.N.: La sextorsión: prácticas de ingeniería social en las redes sociales. In: "Desafíos en Ingeniería: Investigación Aplicada" Ediciones Fundación Tecnológica Antonio Arévalo TECNAR (2019)
25. Pineda, S., Matta, J., Torres, J., Díaz-Piraquive, F.N.: Blockchain: estrategia en la seguridad e integridad de los sistemas de información de la policía nacional. In: "Desafíos en Ingeniería: Investigación Aplicada" Ediciones Fundación Tecnológica Antonio Arévalo TECNAR (2019)

Intelligent Science and Data Mining

An Integrated Time-Aware Collaborative Filtering Algorithm

Yongquan Wan[1], Yizhou Chen[2], and Cairong Yan[2(✉)]

[1] Department of Computer Science and Technology, Shanghai Jian Qiao
University, Shanghai, China
[2] School of Computer Science and Technology, Donghua University, Shanghai, China
cryan@dhu.edu.cn

Abstract. Collaborative filtering is the type of algorithm that has the most variants
and is currently the most widely used in recommender systems. The advantage is
that it does not require much domain knowledge, and can help to get better recommendation by machine learning. In this paper, a time-aware user&item-based
collaborative filtering algorithm and a time-aware latent factor model recommendation algorithm are proposed. Because the two types of algorithms reflect the time
dynamics in different ways, the effects are also different. We then put forward an
integrated time-aware collaborative filtering algorithm ITCF by integrating them
together to compensate for each other's shortcomings. The experimental results
show that the proposed two single time-aware algorithms can both obtain good
recommendation effect, and the integrated algorithm ITCF gets higher accuracy
than the single models with time factors.

Keywords: Recommender systems · Time-aware recommendation · Latent
factor Model · Collaborative filtering

1 Introduction

Since recommender systems can effectively solve the information overloads problem,
they have received extensive attention from academia and industry [1]. Among all the
recommendation methods, collaborative filtering is currently the most widely used one.
The main idea of neighbor-based collaborative filtering is to find similar users, or similar items, and recommendation is based on similarity results. It includes user-based
collaborative filtering and item-based collaborative filtering. As collaborative filtering
has no special requirements for the type of recommended items, it can handle objects
such as music and movies that are difficult to describe texts. Therefore, it is widely used
in recommender systems and has achieved remarkable achievements, especially for
the e-commerce field and commercial interests. According to VentureBeat, Amazon's
recommender systems provide 35% of merchandise sales [2].

Although the collaborative filtering algorithms have been widely used, there are still
some issues that remain to be resolved, such as poor time-sensitive data and information
explanatory [3]. For the timeliness and explanatory of information, researchers proposed

© Springer Nature Switzerland AG 2021
L. Uden et al. (Eds.): KMO 2021, CCIS 1438, pp. 369–379, 2021.
https://doi.org/10.1007/978-3-030-81635-3_30

a series of time-aware recommendation algorithms, including adding a time decay function or a periodic function in the similarity calculation based on neighbor collaborative filtering [4], and adding a time factor in the model-based collaborative filtering loss function [5]. These methods can improve time-aware ability and can improve the problem of poor time sensitivity of recommendation.

In this paper, by comparing and analyzing the existing time-aware user-based and item-based collaborative filtering algorithms, we designed a new time decay function and a new algorithm. A new loss function is designed for the latent factor model, which can reflect the time dynamics of the model. Correspondingly, a new time-aware latent factor model based collaborative filtering algorithm is proposed. Then an integrated time-aware collaborative filtering algorithm is also proposed, which integrates two different types of collaborative filtering together to compensate for each other's shortcomings. The experimental results show that when recommending items for users, the time-aware algorithm proposed in this paper can better integrate the long-term and short-term interests of users, and has an objective improvement in recommendation accuracy.

2   Related Work

2.1   Collaborative Filtering

The papers most closely related to our work are collaborative filtering algorithms and recommended algorithm papers involving time-aware capabilities.

Collaborative filtering algorithms compare a user' behaviors (rating, clicks, etc.) to the target users to infer the current user's preference for a particular item, and then make recommendations based on this preference [6]. Currently, there are two main types of collaborative filtering recommendation algorithms.

Neighbor-based collaborative filtering is a common recommendation method for product sales, and it is divided into two cases: user-based [7] and item-based [8]. The idea of collaborative filtering is to find the similarity of users (or items) from the historical commodity data purchased by users based on existing sales records, and make recommendations to users based on the similarity of users (or items). User-based Collaborative filtering is to calculate the similarity between users. For a target user, the algorithm will recommend the products purchased by the user who has the highest similarity to him. Collaborative filtering based on items is to find the similarity between products and then recommend the most similar items to the target user.

Currently, model-based algorithms mainly include clustering algorithm [9], probability correlation algorithm [10], latent factor model algorithm [11], and Bayesian hierarchical algorithm [12].

Recently, due to the need to deal with big data, Salakhutdinov et al. proposed the use of low-dimensional approximation matrix the decomposition model performs the recommended probability matrix decomposition algorithm. They generally assumed that a user's interest is only affected by a few factors, and then mapped the user (item) to the low-dimensional feature space and learns by the user (item) rating information. The feature vector of the user (item), thereby reconstructing the rating matrix, using the reconstructed low-dimensional matrix to predict the user's rating of the product, and making corresponding recommendations. Since the feature vector dimension of the user and the product is relatively low, the gradient can be lowered. The method is solved efficiently [13].

2.2 Time-Aware Collaborative Filtering

The recommender systems have made great progress in both academia and business, especially in the fields of e-commerce and network marketing, mobile applications, Internet advertising and information retrieval. Among the recommendation algorithms applied in these fields, collaborative filtering algorithms are widely used. However, most collaborative filtering algorithms only use the user's historical behaviors of the item to generate recommendation list [14]. In this case, the user's interest preference is considered to be static, regardless of the time at which the user's historical rate is generated, its role in the recommendation is equal. In real life, the user's interest or information often change drastically over time. Different historical rate has great differences in the ability to describe the user's current interests and then generate user interest concept drifting problem [15]. Unlike other contextual information (such as location, weather, mood, etc.), time information does not require additional user or device resources, and the standard recommender systems already include the user's rating time for the item. Therefore, more and more scholars are now paying attention to the drift of user interest concepts, and considering the time factor in the recommender systems. Xia et al. introduced the concept of time decay, and proposed an algorithm for calculating the similarity of items by integrating the time decay function, which improved the accuracy of project-based collaborative filtering recommendation to some extent [16]. Bakir et al. proposed to add time weight function to predict the score to improve the accuracy of collaborative recommendation based on the neighborhood-based collaborative filtering algorithm and the change of group user preferences with time [17]. Zhang et al. divided the user's historical rate into several periods, analyzed the user's interest distribution in each period, and set the time window to find the user's recent interest [3]. These algorithms improve the recommendation accuracy to a certain extent after considering the time factor.

2.3 Time-Aware Latent Model

The model-based time-aware recommendation algorithm adds time series information to the existing recommendation algorithm, so that the algorithm can learn the dynamic changes of the data and optimize the recommendation effect. Koren et al. proposed TimeSVD++ algorithm, which adds time information in SVD model so that in the feature vector of the user or product the problem of interest drift is effectively solved and good results are obtained [18]. Zhang et al. took the time information as the third dimension, and used the tensor decomposition method to model the time dynamics [5]. According to the evolutionary co-clustering method, Koshneshin et al. proposed to dynamically assigned user or item the unused clusters for further recommendation [19]. Ren et al. believed that in the existing recommender systems, the user preference pattern and the preference dynamic effect are ignored [4]. Taking this as a starting point, they regularized the user's preference pattern into a sparse matrix, and then used subspace to gradually model the personalized and global preference patterns. Zhao et al. composed different information according to the time segmentation. The main matrix is combined into a joint matrix for decomposition and prediction, but the joint matrix decomposition is computationally complex and computationally inefficient [20]. Sun et al. weighted the rating matrix by time weight based on the forgetting function, and then used the singular value method to decompose and predict the unknown scoring items [21]. The algorithm simplifies the computational complexity.

Different from the above related work, this paper applies the time decay function to both movie heat attenuation and user interest attenuation. The movie heat decay function increases the sensitivity of the algorithm to time. The user's interest attenuation function selects the piecewise attenuation function, which can better simulate the user's long-term interest and short-term interest changes, and the accuracy of the recommendation is improved.

3 Time-Aware Collaborative Filtering Model

3.1 A Time-Aware User&Item-Based Filtering Collaborative Algorithm

Neighbor-based collaborative filtering has good scalability and stability. User-based collaborative filtering and item-based collaborative filtering have very similar algorithms. In this paper we add a time-aware function to both algorithms. The following content uses item-based time-aware collaborative filtering algorithm as an example. The algorithm is mainly divided into three steps: the first step is information preprocessing, the second step is to construct a set of similar items that are time-aware, and the last step is prediction and recommendation.

(1) Information preprocessing. We suppose a user set $U = \{U_1, U_2, \ldots, U_m\}$, the number of users is m, an item set $I = \{I_1, I_2, \ldots, I_n\}$, and the number of item is n, shown as Table 1. R_{ui} indicates whether U_u has viewed I_i. Value 1 indicates that user U_u has viewed item I_i, and value 0 indicates that user U_u has not viewed item I_i.

Table 1. Dataset summary

	I_1	I_2	I_i	$\ldots$	I_n
U_1	R_{11}	$\ldots$	R_{1i}	$\ldots$	R_{1n}
U_2	$\ldots$	$\ldots$	$\ldots$	$\ldots$	$\ldots$
U_u	R_{u1}	$\ldots$	R_{ui}	$\ldots$	R_{un}
$\ldots$	$\ldots$	$\ldots$	$\ldots$	$\ldots$	
U_m	R_{m1}	$\ldots$	R_{mi}	$\ldots$	R_{mn}

(2) Constructing time-aware nearest neighbor sets. There are many similarity measurements between vectors. The Cosine similarity method is widely used in recommender systems fields. If the rate value in the rating matrix R is empty, it is recorded as 0.

When time-aware functions are added to the user-based and item-based collaborative filtering algorithms, most of them are embedded in the similarity function. The following shows how a time-aware function is added to the cosine similarity function.

$$sim(i,j) = f(t)\frac{\vec{i} * \vec{j}}{\left\|\vec{i}\right\|_2 * \left\|\vec{j}\right\|_2} = f(t)\frac{\sum_{u \in U_{ij}} R_{u,i} R_{u,j}}{\sqrt{\sum_{u \in U_i} R_{u,i}^2}\sqrt{\sum_{u \in U_j} R_{u,j}^2}} \qquad (1)$$

Four types of functions that are now widely used, $f_1(t) = e^{\frac{t}{\lambda}}, f_2(t) = \frac{2}{1+t^k}, f_3(t) =$
$\begin{cases} 1, t < k \\ \left(\frac{t}{k}\right)^{-a}, t > k \end{cases}$, and $f_4(t) = \frac{1}{1+e^{\frac{t}{k}-b}}$. These four functions are linear functions or piecewise decay functions based on the time difference between two rating behaviors.

Through research and experiments, we found that $f_1(t)$ has the best performance. However, we also found a problem that it might cause. When the time difference increases, the function will decay quickly, and it can well reflect the short-term interests of users, and it does not perform well in reflecting the long-term interests of users. In this paper, we have made further adjustments to $f_1(t)$. The segmented time decay function can be used to better simulate the short-term interest and long-term interest of the user, and achieve better recommendation results. The new function is shown below.

$$f_1'(t) = \begin{cases} e^{\frac{t}{\lambda}}, & t < k \\ e^{\frac{t}{\lambda}} * 0.5 + b, & t > k \end{cases} \qquad (2)$$

In the new function, when the time difference increases, the function performances in line with expectations, which will be shown in the experimental section.

(3) Predicting & recommending. After the nearest neighbor set NN_i of item I_i is obtained, the behavior probability $P_{u,i}$ of U_u to item I_i is predicted by the target user for the behavior data of items in the nearest neighbor set NN_i.

$$P_{u,i} = \frac{\sum_{u \in U_{ij}} sim(i,j)}{\sum_{j \in NN_i} |sim(i,j)|} \qquad (3)$$

where $sim(i,j)$ represents the similarity between items I_i and I_j.

According to the above steps, all the non-behavior items of the target user U_u are predicted, and the first top-k items with higher prediction scores are selected and recommended to the target user U_u.

3.2 A Time-Aware Latent Factor Model

In latent factor models, each user corresponds to a vector, and each item also corresponds to a vector. It is assumed that d is the dimension of the vector and also the number of potential factors. Then the behavioral probability prediction of user u for item i can be expressed as follows:

$$\hat{r}_{ui} = q_i^T p_u = \left(\sum_{j=1}^{d} q_i[j] * p_u[j] \right) \tag{4}$$

where p is the feature matrix of user, q is the feature matrix of item. To learn the parameters in this equation, we can minimize the loss on the validation set of the score.

$$loss = \sum_{(u,i) \in D} \left(r_{ui} - q_i^T P_u \right)^2 + \lambda \left(\|q_i\|^2 + \|p_u\|^2 \right) \tag{5}$$

where D is the dataset, λ is the penalty factor. The purpose of the penalty parameter is to prevent the algorithm from being overfit.

In practical applications, we find that user preferences and item popularities change over time. In order to reflect the impact of time dynamics, e.g., users' passion for a movie will decrease over time. For this problem, we propose a new loss function where a time-aware factor $f_{ui}(t)$ is added according to of the movie's release time to the user's viewing time to simulate the attenuation of the movie heat. It is modified as follows.

$$loss = \sum_{(u,i) \in K} f_{ui}(t)(r_{ui} - q_i^T P_u)^2 + \lambda \left(\|q_i\|^2 * \|p_u\|^2 \right) \tag{6}$$

The time-aware function is defined as:

$$f_{ui}(t) = 1 / \left(1 + e^{-\gamma(t - t_{ui})} \right) \tag{7}$$

where parameter γ is used to control the decay rate, and $(t - t_{ui})$ is the difference between the release time of movie i and the current time t. Their difference determines the degree of influence on the recommendation result. Since the current recommend time is definitely after the movie is released, the value of $(t - t_{ui})$ must be greater than 0, which makes the function value range from 0 to 1, and is monotonically decreasing. This feature is suitable for the function as an important reason for the attenuation function.

There are two ways to minimize the formula which are gradient descent and alternating least squares. In general, the gradient descent method can achieve good prediction accuracy in a short time while the alternating least squares can achieve better prediction accuracy in some cases, but it takes longer to calculate. In this paper, we use gradient descent method to train the parameters. The implementation of gradient descent is as follows:

First, for each given training instance, the algorithm prepends the value of r and calculates the difference between the predicted value and the actual value as a formula.

$$e_{ui} = r_{ui} - q_i^T p_u \tag{8}$$

Then, the algorithm adjusts the parameters of q_i and P_u according to the deviation between the predicted value and the actual value. The parameter adjustment formula is as follows:

$$q_i \leftarrow q_i + \gamma(e_{ui} p_u - \lambda q_i), p_u \leftarrow p_u + \gamma(e_{ui} q_i - \lambda p_u) \tag{9}$$

where γ is the learning rate and λ is the penalty. Smaller learning rate leads to better prediction accuracy, but at the same time require more learning time. The purpose of adding a penalty factor is to prevent the algorithm from being overfit.

3.3   Integration of Time-Aware Algorithms

According to the representation information of Algorithm 1 and Algorithm 2, it can be seen that the user and item-based collaborative filtering algorithm added with time awareness can effectively simulate the long-term and short-term interests of users. After adding the time perception function to the latent factor model, it can effectively simulate the change in heat after the movie is released. In order to be able to synthesize the mutual advantages of the three algorithms, we use the weighted fusion method to fuse the algorithms, and the algorithm is improved. Weighted fusion weights will be obtained by training using multiple linear regression. This method can have algorithms that can get good accuracy when facing different data sets.

This paper uses the method of multiple linear regression to fuse the three algorithms. Define the prediction value of the user-based collaborative filtering recommendation algorithm with the time-aware factor added as x_1, the prediction value of the item-based collaborative filtering recommendation algorithm with the time-aware factor added as x_2, the prediction value of Latent Factor Model with the time-aware factor added as x_3.

$$h_\theta(x) = \theta_0 x_0 + \theta_1 x_1 + \theta_2 x_2 + \theta_3 x_3$$

In the function, θ_0 is a constant term of multiple linear regression, and x_0 has a fixed value of 1, θ_1, θ_2, θ_3 is the weight of x_1, x_2, and x_3.

Define the number of users as m and the number of items as n. The loss function of multivariate linear regression is as follows, and using the gradient descent method is the objective function to obtain the optimal result.

$$J(\theta_0, \theta_1, \theta_2, \theta_3) := \frac{1}{2m*n} \sum_{i=1}^{m} \sum_{j=1}^{n} \left(h_\theta\left(x^{(i,j)}\right) - y^{(i,j)} \right)^2$$

$$\theta_k := \theta_k - \alpha \frac{1}{2m*n} \sum_{i=1}^{m} \sum_{j=1}^{n} \left(h_\theta\left(x^{(i,j)}\right) - y^{(i,j)} \right) x_k^{(i,j)}$$

The value of k in the function is 0 to 3. After obtaining the weights of the three algorithms, the final recommendation algorithm is as follows. The result of time-aware user-based, item-based collaborative filtering algorithms Latent factor model are represented as result_T_UBCF, result_T_IBCF and result_T_LFM, respectively. θ is the corresponding weight parameter obtained by multiple linear regression. ResLists is the final recommendation.

ALGORITHM 1: Integrated time-aware collaborative filtering algorithm

---

Input: *result_T_UBCF*, *result_T_IBCF*, *result_T_LFM*, θ
Output: *recLists*
1.   **for each** *result* **in** [*result_T_UBCF*, *result_T_IBCF*, *result_T_LFM*] **do**
2.   **for each** (*user*, *item*) **in** *result* **do**
3.   *merge_result*[*user*, *item*] $\leftarrow$ *merge_result*[*user*, *item*] + θ * *result*[*user*, *item*]
4.   **end for**
5.   **for each** *user* **in** *merge_result* **do**
6.   *sort*(*merge_result*[*user*])
7.   *recLists* $\leftarrow$ (user, top-k(*merge_result*[*user*]))
8.   **end for**
9.   **end for**

---

4 Experiments and Evaluation

4.1 Experimental Environment

In the experiment, we used dataset Movielens (ml–100K) and dataset Netflix as test datasets to validate the prediction accuracy of algorithm ITCF. There are several different subsets of Movielens. In dataset ml-100K, there are 1,682 movies for 943 users. It also contains some additional information such as release time for each movie. Dataset Netflix is from the movie website Netflix, which contains the scores of approximately 17,770 movies for 48,189 anonymous users. It also includes the additional information of release time for each movie.

The evaluation criteria used in the experiment include recommendation precision and recall. Generally, the higher the precision and recall, the better the performance of the algorithms, and the higher the precision of the recommendation. These two measurements are defined as

$$precision = \frac{\sum_{u \in U} |R(u) \cap T(u)|}{\sum_{u \in U} |T(u)|}, recall = \frac{\sum_{u \in U} |R(u) \cap T(u)|}{\sum_{u \in U} |T(u)|} \tag{11}$$

where R(u) is the recommendation list after training and T(u) is the test set, which contains the real viewing behavior of test users.

The hardware platform running all the experiments is Intel Core i5–4460 cpu @ 3.20 GHz, 15.6 GB memory, 967 GB hard disk, 64-bit Ubuntu 16.04 operating system, the compiled software is Jupyter Lab, and the algorithm programming language is python 3.7.

4.2 Integration of Time-Aware Algorithms

In order to show the effects of different time decay functions, we added them to the neighbor-based collaborative filtering algorithm respectively. The dataset we used is dataset ml–100K. The results were evaluated using precision and recall, which were shown in Table 2.

Table 2. The impact of different decay functions.

Decay function	$f_1'(t) = e^{\frac{t}{\lambda}} + b$	$f_2(t) = \frac{2}{1+t^k}$	$f_3(t) = \begin{cases} 1, & t < k \\ \left(\frac{t}{k}\right)^{-a}, & t < k \end{cases}$	$f_4(t) = \frac{1}{1+e^{\frac{t}{k}-b}}$
Precision	0.221	0.220	0.213	0.207
Recall	0.168	0.167	0.162	0.158

In Latent factor model (LFM), the ratio of negative samples to positive samples has a great influence on the performance of LFM. As can be seen from Table 2, $f_1'(t)$ proposed by us has the highest accuracy. Compared with other functions, this function is more similar to the memory forgetting curve. The recommendation effect is a better than the other functions as well. Therefore, in the following experiments, $f_1'(t)$ is selected as the time-aware function to be added to the algorithms. UBCF and IBCF represent user-based collaborative filtering algorithm and item-based collaborative filtering algorithm.

We used dataset ml–100K, set the number of hidden features, learning rate and regularization parameters, and alter the ratio of negative samples and positive.

Table 3. The impact of increasing the proportion of negative samples.

Negative samples/positive samples	1	2	5	10	20	50
Precision		0.129	0.175	0.210	0.227	0.244	0.236
Recall		0.096	0.130	0.156	0.169	0.181	0.176

It can be seen from Table 3 that when the ratio of negative samples to the positive samples is 20, the precision and recall values are the highest. The data sparsity of dataset ml–100K is 0.063, and the number of users who did not give a rating is far greater than that of users who give a rating. Therefore, an appropriate increase in the proportion of negative samples is helpful to improve the accuracy of prediction. In the latter experiments, we used the ratio 20 as the standard for algorithm input.

The third experiment was designed to compare precision of different algorithms. The time-aware user-based, item-based collaborative filtering algorithms Latent factor model are represented as T-UBCF, T-IBCF and T-LFM, respectively. We validate our algorithm using two different data sets ml–100K and Netflix. The weights used in the final fusion algorithm are given (Table 4).

As can be seen in the left part of Fig. 1, after adding the time-aware function, user-based collaborative filtering algorithm is improved by 9.4%, item-based collaborative filtering algorithm is increased by 11.1%, latent factor model algorithm is improved by 5.3%, and the integrated algorithm improved by 9.2%. It can be concluded that the addition of the time factor has a significant improvement on the recommendation effect of collaborative filtering.

Table 4. Weights of integration of time-aware algorithms.

Weight	θ_0	θ_1	θ_2	θ_3
Ml–100K	0.11	0.31	0.34	0.38
Netflix	0.19	0.39	0.46	0.06

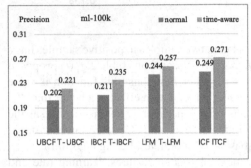
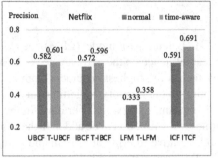

Fig. 1. Comparison of results produced by different algorithms in datasets ml–100K and Netflix

As can be seen in the right part of Fig. 1, after adding the time-aware function, user-based collaborative filtering algorithm, item-based collaborative filtering algorithm, latent factor model algorithm, and integrated algorithm is improved by 3.2%, 2.9%, 10.8%, and 4.9%, respectively. Since the sparseness of dataset Netflix is more serious than dataset ml-100K, the performance of latent factor model is not as good as the neighbor-based collaborative filtering.

5 Conclusion

In this paper, we studied how to add time factors in collaborative filtering algorithms to improve the recommendation effect, and proposed two time-aware algorithms for user&item-based collaborative filtering and latent factor model. These two algorithms reflect the time dynamics from different points. In order to take advantage of the characteristics of both algorithms, an integrated time-aware collaborative filtering algorithm ITCF is proposed. In this algorithm, the weight of the two types of methods can be flexibly adjusted. The experiment proved the effectiveness of the integrated algorithm.

References

1. Sarwar, B.M., Karypis, G., Konstan, J.A., Riedl, J.: Item-based collaborative filtering recommendation algorithms. Www **1**, 285–295 (2001)
2. Linden, G., Smith, B., York, J.: Amazon. com recommendations: Item-to-item collaborative filtering. IEEE Internet Comput. **1**, 76–80 (2003)
3. Zhang, Y., Liu, Y.: A collaborative filtering algorithm based on time period partition. In 2010 Third International Symposium on Intelligent Information Technology and Security Informatics, pp. 777–780. IEEE (2010)

4. Ren, Y., Zhu, T., Li, G., Zhou, W.: Top-N recommendations by learning user preference dynamics. In: Pacific-Asia Conference on Knowledge Discovery and Data Mining, pp. 390–401. Springer, Heidelberg (2013)
5. Xiong, L., Chen, X., Huang, T.K., Schneider, J., Carbonell, J.G.: Temporal collaborative filtering with bayesian probabilistic tensor factorization. In: Proceedings of the 2010 SIAM International Conference on Data Mining, pp. 211–222. Society for Industrial and Applied Mathematics (2010)
6. Liu, Q., Chen, E., Xiong, H., Ding, C.H., Chen, J.: Enhancing collaborative filtering by user interest expansion via personalized ranking. IEEE Trans. Syst. Man Cybern. Part B (Cybernetics) 42(1), 218–233 (2011)
7. Adomavicius, G., Tuzhilin, A.: Toward the next generation of recommender systems: a survey of the state-of-the-art and possible extensions. IEEE Trans. Knowl. Data Eng. 6, 734–749 (2005)
8. Xu, H.L., Wu, X., Li, X.D., Yan, B.P.: Comparison study of internet recommendation system. J. Softw. 20(2), 350–362 (2009)
9. Ungar, L.H., Foster, D.P.: Clustering methods for collaborative filtering. In: AAAI workshop on recommendation systems, vol. 1, pp. 114–129 (1998)
10. Getoor, L., Sahami, M.: Using probabilistic relational models for collaborative filtering. In: Workshop on Web Usage Analysis and User Profiling (WEBKDD'99), pp. 1–6 (1999)
11. Hofmann, T.: Collaborative filtering via gaussian probabilistic latent semantic analysis. In: Proceedings of the 26th Annual International ACM SIGIR Conference on Research and Development in Informaion Retrieval, pp. 259–266. ACM (2003)
12. Chien, Y.H., George, E.I.: A bayesian model for collaborative filtering. In: AISTATS (1999)
13. Mnih, A., Salakhutdinov, R.R.: Probabilistic matrix factorization. In: Advances in Neural Information Processing Systems, pp. 1257–1264 (2008)
14. Adomavicius, G., Tuzhilin, A.: Context-aware recommender systems. In: Recommender systems handbook, pp. 217–253. Springer, Boston, MA (2011)
15. Karahodza, B., Donko, D.: Feature enhanced time-aware recommender system. In: 2015 XXV International Conference on Information, Communication and Automation Technologies (ICAT), pp. 1–6. IEEE (2015)
16. Xia, C., Jiang, X., Liu, S., Luo, Z., Yu, Z.: Dynamic item-based recommendation algorithm with time decay. In: 2010 Sixth International Conference on Natural Computation, vol. 1, pp. 242–247 IEEE (2010)
17. Karahodza, B., Supic, H., Donko, D.: An Approach to design of time-aware recommender system based on changes in group user's preferences. In: 2014 X International Symposium on Telecommunications (BIHTEL), pp. 1–4. IEEE (2014)
18. Koren, Y.: Collaborative filtering with temporal dynamics. In: Proceedings of the 15th ACM SIGKDD International Conference on Knowledge Discovery and Data Mining, pp. 447–456. ACM (2009)
19. Khoshneshin, M., Street, W.N.: Incremental collaborative filtering via evolutionary co-clustering. In: Proceedings of the fourth ACM Conference on Recommender Systems, pp. 325–328. ACM (2010)
20. Zhao, H.Y., Wang, Y., Chen, Q.K.: Timeliness sensitive collective matrix factorization personalized recommendation. J. Chinese Comput. Syst. 38(9), 2022–2027 (2017)
21. Sun, B., Dong, L.: Dynamic model adaptive to user interest drift based on cluster and nearest neighbors. IEEE Access 5, 1682–1691 (2017)

A Contextual Multi-armed Bandit Approach Based on Implicit Feedback for Online Recommendation

Yongquan Wan[1], Junli Xian[2], and Cairong Yan[2(✉)]

[1] Department of Computer Science and Technology, Shanghai Jian Qiao University, Shanghai, China
[2] School of Computer Science and Technology, Donghua University, Shanghai, China
cryan@dhu.edu.cn

Abstract. Contextual multi-armed bandit (CMAB) problems have gained increasing attention and popularity recently due to their capability of using context information to deliver recommendation services. In this paper, we formalize e-commerce recommendations as CMAB problems and propose a novel CMAB approach based on implicit feedback data such as click and purchase records. We use product categories as arms to reduce arm size and leverage user behavior contexts to update the estimation of expected reward for each arm, and no negative samples are needed here to train model. As a core part of the approach, we design a contextual bandit recommendation algorithm based on Thompson sampling, named IF-TS, which can provide real-time response by learning user preferences online and alleviate the cold start problem by adding non-personalized actions. The experiments on three real-world datasets show that our approach can dynamically update user preferences using implicit context information and achieves a good recommendation effect. The experimental results also demonstrate that the proposed algorithm is robust in cold start environments.

Keywords: Contextual multi-armed bandit · Implicit feedback · Thompson sampling · Recommender systems

1 Introduction

There are two classic problems in recommender systems, namely exploration/exploitation trade-off (EE) problem and cold start problem. Multi-armed bandit (MAB) problem, which is a special case of reinforcement learning with only a single state, is used to study EE problem. Contextual multi-armed bandit (CMAB) problem introduces state based on MAB problem. It models a situation where, in a series of trails, an online algorithm selects an action from a set of actions based on a given context (side information) to maximize the rewards of the selected action [1]. CMAB-based algorithms are usually used in recommender systems to solve EE dilemma and cold start problem using context information [2].

© Springer Nature Switzerland AG 2021
L. Uden et al. (Eds.): KMO 2021, CCIS 1438, pp. 380–392, 2021.
https://doi.org/10.1007/978-3-030-81635-3_31

Different contextual bandit algorithms have been proposed, including LinUCB [6], LogUCB [7], Contextual Thompson sampling [8], Con-CNAME [9], etc. They have been applied to the recommendations of news [10], music [11], movies [2], e-commerce [12], etc. In the field of e-commerce, Hsieh et al. [13] modelled the query recommendation as a MAB problem and proposed an M-Independent arm Thompson sampling algorithm, in which the queries are modeled as arms, and query-suggestion pairs are used as contexts to construct recommendation candidate sets. Brodén et al. [12] proposed a bandit ensemble algorithm based on Thompson sampling (BEER [TS]), which is used to orchestrate basic contextual recommendation algorithms for e-commerce, in which a simple basic recommendation algorithm is modeled as an arm. Recently, Brodén et al. [14] added a personalized recommendation component k–Nearest Neighbors (kNN) on the basis of BEER [TS] to further improve the recommendation accuracy. There is a large amount of implicit user feedback data on e-commerce platforms, such as user interaction behavior records (click, purchase, favorite, add-to-cart). Compared with explicit user feedback, the collection cost of implicit user feedback is low and does not affect user experience [15], but the lack of negative samples in implicit user feedback makes traditional recommendation model training difficult [16, 17]. We find that the contextual bandit recommendation algorithm can directly use the interaction behaviors of implicit feedback to update user preferences without negative samples, and avoid the noise caused by artificially introducing negative samples. Therefore, it is feasible to apply CMAB to implicit feedback recommendation, but the following challenges still exist:

1) Modeling of arms. Previous works usually model products as arms [11, 13], but the number of products on e-commerce platforms is huge, thus such method will lead to excessive arms. Using a product set as an arm can alleviate this problem to some extent, but it also brings up the problem of how to classify the products. 2) Setting of rewards. Most existing works give Bernoulli reward (1 or 0) based on whether recommended product is clicked or purchased, which is unreasonable for user behavior records, because Bernoulli reward not only ignores different behaviors of users that can reflect different preferences, but also ignores the association between adjacent behaviors. 3) Use of contexts. Existing works only use simplified context information to construct recommendation candidate set, without considering its impact on the estimation of expected reward and the selection of actions.

Based on the above background, this paper studies how to apply the contextual bandit approach to implicit feedback in e-commerce. This work is dedicated to making full use of the limited context information of implicit feedback to provide users with personalized online recommendations. The main contributions include:

- Based on implicit feedback, a CMAB approach for online recommendation is proposed, which models context-based product categories as actions, updates the estimation of expected reward for each action based on behavior contexts, and then choose the action with largest expected reward to provide users with online recommendations.
- An algorithm for defining actions based on contexts and an online recommendation algorithm based on Thompson sampling are proposed to generate top-N recommendations for each time step of user interactions.
- Three experiments were performed on three public datasets. The effectiveness of the proposed approach for recommendation based on implicit feedback is verified. And

the effects of the number of contexts and actions on improving the recommendation performance and the effect of solving cold start problem are also discussed.

The rest of this paper is organized as follows. In Sect. 2, the problem formulation and the framework of CMAB approach based on implicit feedback for online recommendation are introduced. A TS-based top-N online recommendation algorithm is designed in Sect. 3. Extensive empirical evaluation results are reported in Sect. 4. Finally, Sect. 5 concludes the paper.

2   Problem Formulation and Methodology

We formalize the problem of online recommendation based on implicit feedback in e-commerce as a CMAB problem. The specific description is as follows.

E-commerce **environment** includes product catalog $I = \{i_1, i_2, \ldots, i_{|I|}\}$ and user set $U = \{u_1, u_2, \ldots, u_{|U|}\}$, where each u represents a user's behavior records within a certain time, represented as $u_j = (b_1, b_2, b_3, \ldots, b_n)$, where b_i is a behavior record at time t_i of user u_j, including user ID, item ID, timestamp and contexts. The **contexts** at time t are expressed as x_t, including user contexts x_{user} (age, gender, etc.), item contexts x_{item} (category, brand, seller, price, number of sales, etc.) and interaction behavior contexts $x_{behavior}$ (click, favorite, add-to-cart, purchase, etc.). The **action** (a.k.a. arm) is defined as a subset of I divided according to contexts, and represented as $A = \{a_1, a_2, \ldots, a_{|A|}\}$, where each $a_k \in A$ represents an action. Its role is to produce a recommended item. The **rewards** correspond to user's feedback, such as a click or purchase on a recommended item. See Sect. 3.2 for specific definitions. The reward feedback is used to update the expected reward estimation function $f(x_t, a, r_a)$ of the selected action. The recommendation **agent** is a contextual bandit recommendation algorithm with A. It selects the best action a^* based on the estimation of expected reward and generates a recommended item i, and then receives the user's feedback on i as rewards r_{a^*} to update the estimation of expected reward of a^*, and then makes the next round of best action selection. The goal of the recommendation agent is to maximize the cumulative reward $r_T = \sum_{t \leq T} r_t$, where r_t is the total rewards obtained at time t.

The proposed CMAB approach simulates the real-time interaction between user and recommendation agent in offline mode by processing the user records of implicit feedback at each time step. The difference between offline training and online training is that offline training is performed on data blocks, so it cannot use the recent user feedback information timely, and it is also one of the root causes of cold start problem [17]. However, online training is gradually trained after each observed user-item interaction. Implicit feedback data enter the system continually in the form of data streams. For each user feedback, agent can receive and update user preferences online in time to provide real-time recommendation service. This approach avoids retraining, thus it significantly improves training efficiency and achieves a fast-response online recommendation. The framework of CMAB approach based on implicit feedback for online recommendation is shown in Fig. 1. It focuses on showing the first recommended item generation process at timen t_1.

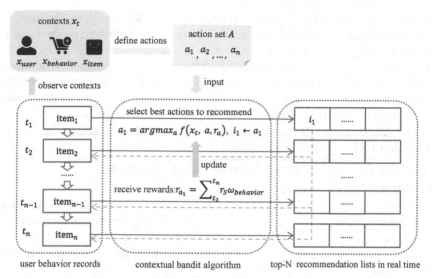

Fig. 1. Framework of CMAB approach based on implicit feedback for online recommendation. The action set based on contexts x_{t_1} is input into contextual bandit algorithm, and the algorithm selects the best action a_1 with the highest expected reward to generate a recommendation item i_1, and then observes the user's feedback on i_1 from t_2 to t_n. The obtained reward r_{a_1} is fed back to $f(x_t, a, r_a)$ of a_1 for updating. Repeat this step until the top-N list is filled.

3 Online Recommendation Algorithm

Action set and contextual bandit algorithm are the two core parts of the proposed approach. In this section, we describe the implementation details of algorithms.

3.1 Action Initialization

In contextual bandit recommendation algorithms, the action reflects user's preferences and greatly affects recommendation effect. In order to prevent large-scale problems caused by modeling products as actions, this paper proposes an algorithm that defines actions based on contexts (Algorithm 1). The details are as follows.

Single-attribute Actions. If there is lite context information in implicit feedback data, single-attribute is used to classify products. For example, assuming that the contexts only have click and purchase interaction behaviors and product category attribute, we can define the purchase set of other users who have purchased current product as an action, or all products that belong to the same category as current product as an action.

Interactive-attribute Actions. If the implicit feedback data has a lot of context information, such as rich user behavior information, user personal information, and rich product attributes, we use a combination of attributes to divide the products, which increases the similarity of the products within the product set and makes the action more refined. Choosing two attributes to interact can prevent too many attributes interaction from generating excessive empty sets or product sets with few products. The method of attribute interaction is to find the intersection of two single-attribute product sets and define the intersection as an action.

An action is a recommendation candidate set that randomly generates a recommended item each time. Context-based actions change dynamically with user interaction behaviors, which not only captures user preferences timely to make recommendations accurate and diverse, but also ensures the interpretability of recommendations.

Algorithm 1. Get context-based actions

Input: $U = \{u_1, u_2, ..., u_{|U|}\}$, u_j: behavior records of each user
Output: $A = \{a_1, a_2, ..., a_{|A|}\}$
1: $A \leftarrow \emptyset$ // initialize actions set
2: **if** $|v| < 3$ **then**   // v is all attributes in implicit feedback
3:      **for** all v **do**
4:          $a_i = divide(v)$ // divide product sets based on single attribute
5:          $A \leftarrow A \cup a_i$
6: **else**
7:      **for** all $(v_a, v_b) \in C(|v|,2)$ **do**   // combine two attributes together
8:          $a_i = divide(v_a, v_b)$ // divide product sets based on two attributes
9:          $A \leftarrow A \cup a_i$
10: **return** A

Assuming that the number of contexts in implicit feedback is n, the time complexity of Algorithm 1 is $O(C(n, 2)) = O(n!/2(n - 2)!) = O(n^2)$. Since the number of contexts in implicit feedback is generally small, the time complexity of the algorithm is relatively low.

3.2 Reward Feedback and Expected Reward Estimation

Thompson sampling (TS) is one of oldest heuristics for solving MAB problem. The basic idea is to choose an arm to play according to its probability of being the best arm. Whether it is the stochastic MAB problem [3], CMAB problem [11], Bernoulli TS [4] or TS with complex action rewards [5] it has been proven to have low regret. That is why we chose TS as the basic algorithm.

In standard Bernoulli TS, each action represents the selection of an arm. The probability that action a produces an average reward θ is unknown, but it is fixed over time. The prior distribution of expected rewards for each action is usually modeled as a Beta distribution $P(\theta) \sim Beta(\alpha_0, \beta_0)$, where $\alpha_0 = \beta_0 = 1$. In each round, TS samples θ_a from the posterior distribution $Beta(\alpha_0 + S, \beta_0 + F)$ of expected reward for each action, where S is the number of successes and F is the number of failures. Then the best action a^* with the largest θ_{a^*} can be selected to recommend item. Finally, S_{a^*} and F_{a^*} can be observed for updating the posterior distribution. Under Bernoulli reward settings, if $r_{a^*} = 1$, then $S_{a^*} = 1$, and if $r_{a^*} = 0$, then $F_{a^*} = 1$.

In this paper, we change the Bernoulli rewards to the sum of rewards for whether users interact with the recommended item. Specifically, different weights $\omega_{behavior}$ are set according to the behavior contexts of the user to recommended item. User behavior contexts $x_{behavior}$ in implicit feedback from large e-commerce platforms (such as Taobao and Tmall) usually include: click, favorite, add-to-cart, and purchase. We set the weights respectively:$\omega_{click} = 1$, $\omega_{fav} = 2$, $\omega_{cart} = 3$, $\omega_{buy} = 4$, $\omega_{no\_behavior} = 2$. Assuming that the recommended item generated by action a at time t_i interacts with user, then $S_a = \sum_{t_{i+1}}^{t_n} r_S \omega_{no\_behavior}$, where $r_S = 1$ means successful reward, $\omega_{behavior}$ is the weight corresponding to the interaction behavior contexts. If the user does not interact with the recommended item,$F_a = r_F \omega_{no\_behavior}$, where $r_F = 1$ means failure reward. After selecting an action for recommendation each time, the S_a or F_a obtained by a is observed and fed back to the estimated reward distribution $Beta\left(\alpha_0^{(a)} + S_a, \beta_0^{(a)} + F_a\right)$ to update the posterior distribution.

Our method considers not only the impact of different types of user interactions on rewards, but also the correlation between user behaviors. In addition, the behavior contexts in implicit feedback are used to directly update the expected reward distributions of the actions, avoiding the use of negative samples. According to the characteristics of $Beta(\alpha, \beta)$ distribution, if $\beta \geq 1$ is a constant (that is, $\omega_{no\_behavior}$ can be set to any positive constant), the average value $\alpha/(\alpha + \beta)$ increases with α, and the distribution becomes more concentrated and closer to the true average reward. Actions with more rewards have a higher probability of being selected, and actions with fewer rewards also have the opportunity to be selected during random sampling, thereby solving the EE problem in recommendation process.

3.3 IF-TS Algorithm

Based on the above improvements, an implicit feedback based TS online recommendation algorithm (IF-TS) is proposed. This algorithm generates a recommendation list L_t of size N for users in real time. Figure 2 shows the steps of the algorithm.

Cold Start Problem. For new users without history of shopping behaviors, only a small modification to our algorithm can solve cold start problem. Specifically, adding non-personalized actions (such as best-selling list) makes the first recommendation for new users. In particular, for a new user with personal information, the user's personal information can be added to the non-personalized actions during the first recommendation to make recommendation more accurate. With the increase of user behavior records, the proposed algorithm can make online recommendations based on user's current records. In order to further improve the recommendation effect, follow-up recommendations are made to the user by training the historical records of other users to obtain a set of well-performing actions, where the action rewards are set according to whether the new user currently interacts with the recommended item.

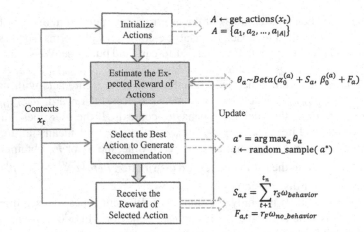

Fig. 2. Flowchart of IF-TS algorithm. The algorithm takes context information into the entire process to better extract user preferences and provide accurate recommendation services. The estimation of the expected reward of actions is the core step of the algorithm.

Algorithm 2 gives the TS-based online recommendation algorithm IF-TS.

Algorithm 2. IF-TS

Input: α_0, β_0: prior parameters, N: size of recommendations, $b_u = (u, i, t, x_t)$: a behavior record of user u for item i at time t // default: $\alpha_0 = \beta_0 = 1$

Output: top-N recommendations L_t

1: $A \leftarrow get\_actions(U)$ // use Algorithm 1 to define actions
2: **for** $j = 1, ... N$ **do**
3:     **for all** $a \in A$ **do**
4:         **if** $|a| = 0$ **then**
5:             continue   // skip unresponsive actions
6:         **else**
7:             $\theta_a \sim Beta(\alpha_0^{(a)} + S_a, \beta_0^{(a)} + F_a)$ // sample θ_a
8:         $a^* \leftarrow arg\,max_a\,\theta_a$
9:         $L_t[j] \leftarrow random\_sample(a^*)$
10:         **for** $k = t + 1, ..., t_n$ **do**
11:             **if** $L_t[j] = i_k$ **then**   // observe reward feedback
12:                 $r_S^{(a^*)} = r_S^{(a^*)} + r_S\omega_{behavior}$
13:             **else**
14:                 $r_F^{(a^*)} = r_F^{(a^*)} + r_F\omega_{no\_behavior}$
15:         $S_{a^*} \leftarrow S_{a^*} + r_S^{(a^*)}$ // update parameters
16:         $F_{a^*} \leftarrow F_{a^*} + r_F^{(a^*)}$
17: **return** L_t // output recommendations at time t

Let the length of the recommendation list at time t be n, the numbers of actions be m, and the total record length of user u be l. Since $l > m > n$ and n is a small constant, the time complexity of IF-TS is $O(l)$.

4 Experimental Settings and Results

4.1 Dataset and Evaluation Metrics

In order to verify the effectiveness of the proposed approach and the performance of the algorithms, we selected three public datasets from different e-commerce platform, namely Yoochoose[1], UserBehavior[2], and IJCAI-15[3]. These three datasets have different context information, which can be used to verify the impact of contexts on the performance of the algorithms. The data size of the e-commerce dataset is huge. For example, UserBehavior dataset contains hundreds of millions of user records. Due to limited operating hardware conditions, in this paper we resample the datasets by removing invalid users, invalid products, and non-representative data. A detailed description of each dataset after processing is shown in Table 1.

Table 1. Dataset summary

Dataset	User context	Behavior context	Item context	Experimental data size
1. Yoochoose	None	click, buy	category, price, brand	Sessions:1,000 Interactions: 8,556
2. UserBehavior	None	click, add-to-cart, favourite, buy	category	Users:1,000 Interactions: 14,000
3. IJCAI-15	age, gender	click, add-to-cart, favourite, buy	category, saler, brand,	Users:1,000 Interactions: 10,887

In all our experiments, the top-N recommendation list is set to $N = 5$ and the results are the average of 5 runs. In order to ensure that there is sufficient feedback information for each recommendation, the length of the recommendation time for each user is set to the first half of the length of the user behavior records. The evaluation metrics of the experimental results include cumulative rewards $r_{T,U}$, *precision* and *recall*, which respectively measure the quality of the algorithm, the accuracy and diversity of recommendations. The definition is as follows:

$$r_{T,U} = \sum_{u=1}^{U} \sum_{t=1}^{T} r_{u,t} \qquad (1)$$

---

[1] http://2015.recsyschallenge.com/challenge.html.
[2] https://tianchi.aliyun.com/dataset/dataDetail?dataId=649.
[3] https://tianchi.aliyun.com/dataset/dataDetail?dataId=47.

where U represents all experimental users, T is the entire recommendation time length of user u, and $r_{u,t}$ is the sum of rewards obtained by user u at time t.

$$precision = \frac{\sum_u q_u}{\sum_u n_u} \quad (2)$$

where q_u represents the number of interactions between user u and the recommended item, and n_u is the number of recommendations to user u.

$$recall = \frac{\sum_u p_u}{\sum_u m_u} \quad (3)$$

where p_u represents the number of distinct recommended items that interact with user u, and m_u represents the number of all items that interact with user u.

4.2 Experimental Results

Experiment 1: IF-TS vs. BEER [TS]. The bandit ensemble algorithm based on TS (BEER [TS]) proposed by Brodén et al. is the closest to the idea in this paper. It models simple recommendation algorithms such as best sellers and those-who-bought-also-bought as actions [12]. To verify the advantages of the proposed algorithm, we select 1,000 sessions on the same dataset, Yoochoose, to compare the three evaluation metrics of IF-TS and BEER [TS]. The results are shown in Fig. 3(a) and (b).

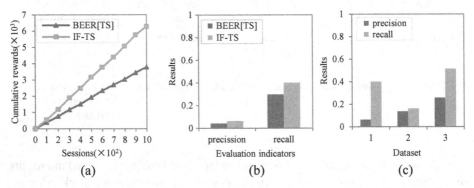

Fig. 3. (a) Comparison of cumulative rewards results of the two algorithms; (b) Comparison of precision and recall results of the two algorithms; (c) Analysis of the effect of contexts.

Figure 3(a) and (b) show that our IF-TS algorithm is significantly higher than BEER [TS] in terms of cumulative rewards, precision, and recall. The results show that the proposed IF-TS algorithm can make full use of the context information of implicit feedback to update user preferences in real time and provide users with accurate and diverse personalized recommendations.

In addition, we compare the performance of the IF-TS algorithm on three datasets with different context information. We select 1,000 users or sessions on three datasets, and define 6, 6, and 15 actions based on contexts. It can be seen from Fig. 3(c) that the richer the contexts of the dataset, the higher the precision of the recommendation, and the richer the item contexts of the dataset, the higher the recall. The results are reasonable and prove the generalization of our algorithm.

During the experiment, it takes about 1.2s to make a recommendation. According to the webpage response time test standard, when the operation gets a response within 2s, the user will feel that the system responds quickly. Therefore, the proposed online recommendation algorithm also has the advantage of fast response.

Experiment 2: Further Improve Recommendation Performance. The   algorithm may choose a poorly performing action multiple times during the exploration phase, resulting in low recommendation accuracy. This experiment verifies whether the recommendation effect can be improved by reducing invalid exploration. first, we define a *hit* rate to evaluate the quality of actions. A hit indicates that the recommended item interacts with user.

$$hit = \frac{\sum_u h_{a,\,u}}{\sum_u n_{a,u}} \tag{4}$$

where $h_{a,u}$ represents the number of times that action a hits user u, and $n_{a,u}$ represents the number of times that action a is selected as the best action.

In this experiment, the action with the lowest hit rate is sequentially removed from the three datasets, and the changes of the three evaluation metrics are observed. The results are shown in the following figures.

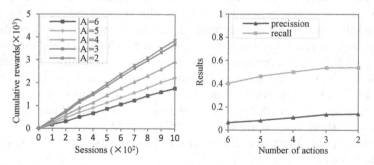

Fig. 4. Results after removing poorly performing actions in Yoochoose dataset

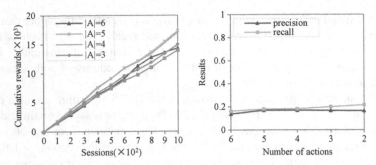

Fig. 5. Results after removing poorly performing actions in UserBehavior dataset

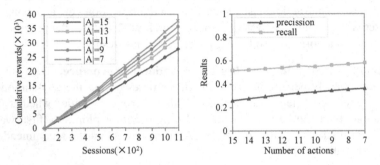

Fig. 6. Results after removing poorly performing actions in IJCAI-15 dataset

It can be seen from the figures that by removing actions with a low hit rate, the recommendation can be effectively improved, but when the actions are reduced to a certain amount, the recommendation performance will deteriorate or change slightly. Thus, the number of actions is also a factor affecting the recommendation effect.

Experiment 3: Cold Start Problem. For new users in Yoochoose and UserBehavior datasets, we use best-selling list for the first recommendation, and for new users in IJCAI-15 dataset, we use personal information plus the best-selling list for the first recommendation. According to Experiment 2, we can use user history records to pre-train to get the best action set that is most suitable for each dataset, and use this action set to provide follow-up recommendations for new users to improve the accuracy of recommendations. We select another 1,000 users or sessions from each dataset as new users for cold start testing, and compare the results of cold start with or without pre-training. In this experiment, real interactive behavior is used as user feedback.

The results show that the algorithm is robust in cold start environment. In addition, using the pre-training best action set has significantly improved the cold start recommendation effect.

Table 2. Cold-start with pre-training and without pre-training

Dataset	Implement	Number of actions	Precision	Recall	Cumulative rewards
Yoochoose	with pre-training	3	**0.1415**	**0.5089**	**3,611**
	without pre-training	6	0.0641	0.4019	1,759
UserBehavior	with pre-training	4	**0.1634**	**0.1826**	**14,366**
	without pre-training	6	0.1375	0.1631	14,352
IJCAI-15	with pre-training	7	**0.3596**	0.4693	**33,903**
	without pre-training	15	0.2589	**0.5163**	27,737

5 Conclusion

In this paper, we introduce a CMAB approach based on implicit feedback for online recommendation, which uses the contexts and real-time interaction behaviors of users to dynamically extract user preferences, and solves the challenge of implicit feedback lacking of negative signals and inability to express users' explicit preferences. In this framework, a context-based action definition algorithm and TS-based online recommendation algorithm IF-TS are proposed. Modeling the product set as an arm greatly reduces the size of the arms. IF-TS algorithm can learn user preferences online, provide accurate, diverse and highly responsive real-time recommendations, and alleviate the cold start problem. Experiments on three public datasets show that the proposed approach can well solve the implicit feedback recommendation problem, and the proposed algorithms are generalized and interpretable. Further optimization of actions and processing of large-scale data is the direction we will study in the future.

References

1. Bouneffouf, D., Rish, I.: A survey on practical applications of multi-armed and contextual bandits, arXiv: 1904.10040 (2019)
2. Wang, L., Wang, C., Wang, K., et al.: Biucb: a contextual bandit algorithm for cold-start and diversified recommendation. In: International Conference on Big Knowledge (ICBK), pp. 248–253. IEEE, Piscataway, NJ (2017)
3. Agrawal, S., Goyal, N.: Analysis of Thompson sampling for the multi-armed bandit problem. In: Conference on Learning Theory (COLT), pp. 39.1–39.26. Springer, London, England (2012)
4. Kaufmann, E., Korda, N.: Thompson sampling: an asymptotically optimal finite time analysis. In: Algorithmic Learning Theory, pp. 199–213. Springer, Berlin (2012)

5. Gopalan, A., Mannor, S., Mansour, Y.: Thompson sampling for complex online problems. In: International Conference on Machine Learning, pp.100–108. ACM, New York (2014)
6. Li, L., Chu, W., Langford, J., et al.: A contextual bandit approach to personalized news article recommendation. In: 19th International Conference on World Wide Web, pp. 661–670. ACM, New York (2010)
7. Mahajan, D., Rastogi, R., Tiwari, C., et al.: LogUCB: an explore-exploit algorithm for comments recommendation. In: ACM International Conference Proceeding Series, pp. 6–15. ACM, New York (2012)
8. Agrawal, S., Goyal, N.: Thompson sampling for contextual bandits with linear payoffs. In: 30th International Conference on Machine Learning, pp. 127–135. ACM, New York, NY, USA (2013)
9. Zhang, X., Zhou, Q. He, T., et al.: Con-CNAME: a contextual multi-armed bandit algorithm for personalized recommendations. In: International Conference on Artificial Neural Networks, pp. 326–336. Springer, Cham (2018)
10. Zeng, C., Wang, Q., Mokhtari, S., et al.: Online context-aware recommendation with time varying multi-armed bandit. In: International Conference on Knowledge Discovery and Data Mining (KDD'16), pp. 2025–2034. ACM, New York (2016)
11. Hariri, N., Mobasher, B., Burke, R.: Adapting to user preference changes in interactive recommendation. In: International Conference on Artificial Intelligence (IJCAI'15), pp. 4268–4274. AAAI Press, Menlo Park (2015)
12. Brodén, B., Hammar, M., Nilsson, B.J., et al.: Ensemble recommendations via Thompson sampling: an experimental study within e-commerce. In: 23rd International Conference on Intelligent User Interfaces, pp. 19–29. ACM, New York (2018)
13. Hsieh, C.C., Neufeld, J., King, T., et al.: Efficient approximate Thompson sampling for search query recommendation. In: 30th Annual ACM Symposium on Applied Computing (SAC'15), pp. 740–746. ACM, New York (2015)
14. Brodén, B., Hammar, M., et al.: A bandit-based ensemble framework for exploration/exploitation of diverse recommendation components: an experimental study within e-commerce. ACM Trans. Interactive Intell. Syst. 9(4), 1–39 (2019)
15. Jannach, D., Lerche, L., Zanker, M.: Recommending based on implicit feedback. In: Brusilovsky, P., He, D. (eds.) Social Information Access. LNCS, vol. 10100, pp. 510–569. Springer, Cham (2018). https://doi.org/10.1007/978-3-319-90092-6_14
16. Yin, J., Wang, Z., Li, Q., et al.: Personalized recommendation based on large-scale implicit feedback. J. Softw. (in Chinese) 25(9), 1953–1966 (2014)
17. Wang, Z., Li, Q., Wang, J., et al.: Real-time personalized recommendation based on implicit user feedback data stream. Chinese J. Comput. 39(1), 52–64 (2016)

A Sentiment Classification Model Based on Deep Learning

Zijia Liu[1], Ran Tao[1(✉)], Youqun Shi[1], and Qinglan Luo[2]

[1] School of Computer Science and Technology, Donghua University, Shanghai, China
{taoran,yqshi}@dhu.edu.cn
[2] Shanghai Moule Network Technology Co., Ltd. University, Shanghai, China
steve@bugbank.cn

Abstract. Sentiment classification is an interesting and crucial research topic of opinion mining and sentiment analysis, which is used to obtain sentiment types from the text documents of numerous sources. Sentiment classification has the problems of insufficient semantic feature extraction and ignoring context information. This paper proposes a MSCNN-BiGRU model for text sentiment classification by utilizing multi-scale convolution kernels to extract rich semantic features and BiGRU to extract features containing text context information. The experimental results on the Chinese Weibo text dataset and the English e-commerce reviews dataset show that the classification accuracy of this model is 3.41% better than CNN and 3.59% better than RNN. The model proposed in this paper is not only suitable for text sentiment classification, but also helpful for expression classification research with time series information.

Keywords: Deep learning · Natural language processing · Sentiment classification · Convolutional Neural Network · Recurrent Neural Network

1 Introduction

With the rapid development of the Internet, the number of Internet users is growing rapidly. According to statistics, as of March 2020, the number of Internet users in China is 904 million, and the Internet penetration rate is 64.5% [1]. Social networking and e-commerce networks play an important role in Internet life, and huge amounts of text data are generated in these platforms every day. Effective sentiment analysis or opinion mining of network public opinion data can help decision-makers quickly respond to various events and make adjustments to adapt to the rapid changes of social environment [2]. Therefore, sentiment classification as the basic task of sentiment analysis has important practical value.

Through the ages, the methods of sentiment classification have undergone many changes, from the initial sentiment dictionary-based methods to machine learning methods, such as Support Vector Machine (SVM), Naive Bayes (NB),logistic regression, random forest, etc. [3, 4].Using these machine learning methods requires complex preprocessing and feature engineering [5], such as emotional word features, part-of-speech

© Springer Nature Switzerland AG 2021
L. Uden et al. (Eds.): KMO 2021, CCIS 1438, pp. 393–403, 2021.
https://doi.org/10.1007/978-3-030-81635-3_32

features, N-gram and location features [6]. Moreover, it is difficult to achieve acceptable classification results [7, 8]. Deep learning method does not rely on feature construction, and is widely applied to sentiment classification tasks [9]–[11]. The practical effect is usually better than the other two methods.

The features extracted by Convolutional Neural Network (CNN) have the defect of missing contextual information, and cannot well summarize the overall features of the text. At the same time, the traditional Recurrent Neural Network (RNN) also has the problem of gradient disappearance. As variants of traditional RNN, long short term memory (LSTM) and gated recurrent unit (GRU) can solve the problem of long-term dependence, but they can only get one-way information in the text.

In response to the above problems, this paper proposes a Multi-Scale Convolutional Neural Network -Bidirectional Gated Recurrent Unit model (MSCNN-BiGRU) for sentiment classification. The main contribution of this paper as follows:

1) In order to solve the limitation of single CNN in text feature extraction and enrich the semantic information of output features, multi-scale convolution kernels are used to extract word vector features of different granularities. The optimal convolution scale is determined through experiments.
2) Aiming at the context dependence of natural language structure, BiGRU network is used to extract contextual information from the output features of multi-scale convolutional neural network, so as to obtain the overall semantic features of sentences. The effectiveness of the method is verified on Chinese and English data sets.

The rest of the paper is organized as follows. Section 2 provides a brief literature review of sentiment classification. Section 3 proposes the MSCNN-BiGRU model for sentiment classification. Section 4 deals with experimental implementation and examines the results, Sect. 5 elaborates the conclusion and future work.

2 Related Literature Review

Sentiment analysis is an important subject in the field of natural language processing. It is widely used on public platforms such as social media, e-commerce reviews, hotel reviews, etc. to help government officials, companies or businesses tap users' emotional tendencies and make correct decisions. Sentiment classification is a basic task in sentiment analysis, which mainly includes sentiment dictionary-based methods, machine learning methods and deep learning methods.

The method based on the sentiment dictionary mainly relies on the construction of a dictionary with artificially labeled emotional words and phrases, such as the English dictionary WordNet [12] Chinese dictionary HowNet [13]. The sentiment tendency of the text is obtained by counting sentiment words through the dictionary. However, the dictionary needs to be constantly improved, and the emotion of a word is completely fixed. Machine learning methods need to manually extract features as the input of the machine learning model. Suchita et al. [14] used the text features constructed by the bag-of-words model to experimented on Naive Bayes and SVM for movie reviews with achieved good results.

As deep learning has achieved remarkable results in the fields of computer vision and speech recognition [15, 16], researchers have begun to apply it to natural language processing. Kim [17] applied CNN to sentence classification, using pre-trained word vectors as the input of the network, and verified the effectiveness of CNN on various classical English datasets. Jelodar [18] conducted sentiment analysis on social media related discussions during the period of COVID-19, using a two-layer LSTM network for sentiment classification, and the accuracy is better than machine learning methods.

Recently, researchers prefer to combine CNN and RNN for sentiment classification tasks. Zhou et al. [19] combined the strengths of CNN and RNN, proposed C-LSTM model, which achieved excellent performance in sentiment classification and question classification tasks. Jin et al. [20] proposed a multi-task learning model based on multi-scale convolutional neural network (MSCNN) and LSTM for multi-task sentiment classification, and verified its effectiveness on several datasets. Li Yang [21] proposed a sentiment classification model based on CNN and BiLSTM, which combined the local features extracted by CNN and the time series information obtained by BiLSTM, and the experimental results show that the classification effect of bidirectional RNN is better than unidirectional RNN. Zhao Yaou et al. [22] proposed a sentiment analysis method based on ELMo(Embedding from Language Model) and MSCNN, in which MSCNN is used to extract sentence features of different scales and find the optimal scale in the experiment. Cheng Yan et al. [23] combined the advantages of CNN and BiGRU to extract the semantic information of long text context, and improved the feature extraction ability of the model.

From the perspective of the shortcomings of a single convolutional neural network and the structural dependency of natural language, this paper proposes the MSCNN-BiGRU model, which makes the extracted text features not only have semantic features of different granular words but also have contextual meanings. It helps increase the generalization of the model and achieve higher classification accuracy.

3   The Proposed MSCNN-BiGRU Model

In order to learn the word feature information of different granularities in the text, and to make full use of the context information of the entire text, we designed a MSCNN-BIGRU model. The model structure is shown in Fig. 1.

This model is mainly composed of word embedding layer, multi-scale convolutional layer, pooling layer, concatenate layer, bidirectional GRU layer and full connect layer. Preprocessed text data as input layer, and converted into word vectors through the word embedding layer, the feature representation of the text is obtained through the joint network, and then sentiment tendency judgment is performed by the softmax function.

3.1   Word Embedding

In order to convert text into word vectors, the embedded layer of deep learning framework Keras is used to transform each word into vector with a fixed size ($w = [w_1, w_2, \ldots w_n]$, n is the dimension of the word vector), the dimension of word vector is 128. Finally, we got a word vector matrix $R^{v \times n}$ (v is the size of the vocabulary).

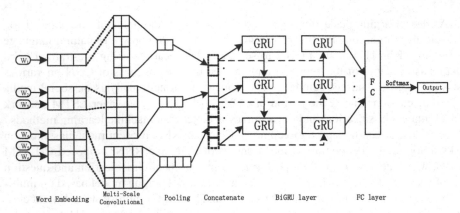

Fig. 1. The sentiment classification model based on MSCNN-BiGRU

3.2 Multi-scale Convolutional Neural Network

Sentences are composed of words, and convolution operations of different scales of convolution kernels can be used to obtain semantic vectors of different scales [22].These vectors can be more generalized to the semantic representation of the whole sentence.

CNN captures features of sentences by scanning parts of the text through a convolution kernel. However, different from the traditional convolution operation, we used multiple convolution kernels with different scales to extract features [24]. Considering the phrases, transitions, and our experimental results and other factors int the sentence, we chose 1, 2, and 3 sizes of convolution kernels to extract the features of the sentence on different scales. The calculation is shown in Eq. 1:

$$c_i = f(K \cdot w_{i:i+d-1}) + b \tag{1}$$

Where K is the size of the convolution kernel, $K \in R^{n \times d}$, d is the width of the convolution kernel; $w_{i:i+d-1}$ is composed of words from i to $i + d - 1$ vector; b is the bias term; the feature matrix $c = [c_1, c_2, \ldots, c_{m-d+1}]$ is obtained through the convolution layer.

The multi-scale CNN of our model is a stack of convolution pooling layers [25], and finally the semantic features obtained by different scale convolution kernels are concatenated. In the experiment, we determined the appropriate convolution scale, and because the features observed by max-pooling help to distinguish the categories, the pool layer uses max-pooling to take the maximum value of the entire region as the feature.

3.3 Bidirectional Gated Recurrent Unit

In view of the structural dependence of natural language, this model uses bidirectional gated recurrent unit (BiGRU) to extract contextual information. GRU can solve the problems of long-term dependence and gradient disappearance of traditional RNN [26].

As a variant of LSTM, GRU combines the forget gate and the input gate into a single update gate, mixing the cell state and the hidden state. Compared with LSTM, GRU has a simpler structure, fewer parameters and a better convergence model [27]. GRU structure is shown in Fig. 2. The calculation formulas of each gate and memory cell are shown in Eqs. 2–5.

$$r_t = \sigma\left(W_r \cdot [h_{t-1}, x_t]\right) \tag{2}$$

$$z_t = \sigma\left(W_z \cdot [h_{t-1}, x_t]\right) \tag{3}$$

$$\tilde{h}_t = tanh\left(W_{\tilde{h}} \cdot [r_t * h_{t-1}, x_t]\right) \tag{4}$$

$$h_t = (1 - z_t) * h_{t-1} + z_t * \tilde{h}_t \tag{5}$$

Where r_t represents the reset gate; z_t represents the update gate; W_r, W_z, $W_{\tilde{h}}$ represent the weight matrix of the reset gate, the weight matrix of the update gate, and the weight matrix of the candidate state respectively; $\tilde{h}_t$ represents the candidate state; h_t represents the current Hidden layer state; x_t is the input of GRU at time t; σ is the sigmoid activation function.

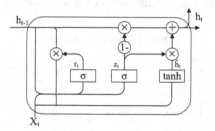

Fig. 2. GRU model structure

BiGRU is composed of a forward GRU and a backward GRU, and the sequential information of text can be obtained from two perspectives. At each time, the input provides two GRUs in opposite directions, and the output is determined by two unidirectional GRUs.

Suppose $\vec{h}_t$ is the output hidden state of the forward GRU at time t, and $\overleftarrow{h}_t$ is the output hidden state of the reverse GRU. Then the output hidden state h_t of BiGRU is calculated as shown in Eqs. 6–8.

$$\vec{h}_t = \overrightarrow{GRU}\left(\vec{h}_{t-1}, x_t\right) \tag{6}$$

$$\overleftarrow{h}_t = \overleftarrow{GRU}\left(\overleftarrow{h}_{t-1}, x_t\right) \tag{7}$$

$$h_t = \left[\vec{h}_t, \overleftarrow{h}_t\right] \tag{8}$$

3.4 Model Training and Output

In this model, the final text features extracted by the above neural network are used as input, and the emotional polarity classification results of the text are obtained through the softmax function. When the model is trained, the loss function used is the cross-entropy function. Assuming that the number of text categories is k, the probability of dividing S_i into category j in softmax is calculated as shown in Eq. 9.

$$P(y_i = j \mid x_i; \theta) = \frac{\exp\left(\theta_j^T S_i\right)}{\sum_{t=1}^{k} \exp(\theta_t^T S_i)} \qquad (9)$$

4 Experimental Implementation and Evaluation

4.1 Experimental Dataset

The Chinese data in the experiment comes from the Weibo text data on the emotion recognition of netizens during the epidemic in the 2020 Beijing Open Data Application Competition. There are a total of 100,000 artificially labeled texts. The English data comes from the dataset on e-commerce reviews on the Kaggle website. There are a total of 23,000 annotated texts. Part of the data is selected in the experiment of this article by random sampling method. The specific dataset statistics used is shown in Table 1.

Table 1. Dataset statistics

Dataset	Language	Positive	Negative	Neutral	Total
WeiBo Text	Chinese	5127	3295	11366	19788
E-Commerce Reviews	English	8984	2016	-	11000

4.2 Data Preprocessing

Preprocess the dataset with jieba word segmentation tool and remove stop words, and eliminate invalid data. The results of pretreatment of experimental data are shown in Table 2.

4.3 Experimental Parameter Setting

When using multi-scale convolution neural network for feature extraction, in order to find the most suitable convolution scale, the accuracy index is tested on Chinese and English dataset for many times. The calculation formula of accuracy is shown in Eq. 12. The experimental results are shown in Fig. 3.

It can be seen from Fig. 4 that as the convolution scale increases, the accuracy of the model is also improving. At the same time, the combination with a convolution scale of 1–3 has the highest accuracy. When the convolution scale exceeds 3, the effect is not as good as 1–3. It may be because in natural language, the semantic connection between more than 3 words is not very strong. Therefore, a convolution kernel with a convolution scale of 1–3 is used in the experiment. Other parameter settings are shown in Table 3.

Table 2. The Sample sentences after preprocessing.

Language	Original	After preprocessing
Chinese	希望2020保佑所有战斗在一线的医护人员和其他同胞们平平安安的	希望 保佑 所有 战斗 一线 医护人员 同胞们 平平安安
English	I am tall (5′11 and 3/4) and mostly leg with a shorter torso so i am always looking for longer shirts to balance my leg to torso ratio	tall mostly leg shorter torso always looking longer shirts balance leg torso ratio

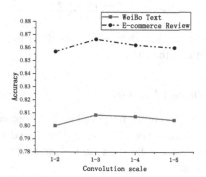

Fig. 3. The classification results of different convolution scales

Table 3. Parameter setting

Parameter	Value	Parameter	Value
Number of hidden layers	128	Learning rate	0.001
Number of convolution kernels	64,128,128	Batch_size	64
Activation function	Relu	Epoch	20

4.4 Evaluating Indicator

The evaluation indicators used in this experiment are Accuracy, Presicion, Recall, and F1 value. The calculation method is shown in formula 10–13. TP (True Positive) means true cases, FP (False Positive) means false positive cases, FN (False Negative) means false negative cases, and TN (True Negative) means true negative cases.

$$Accuracy = \frac{TP+FP}{TP+FP+TN+FN} \tag{10}$$

$$Precision = \frac{TP}{TP+FP} \tag{11}$$

$$Recall = \frac{TP}{TP+FN} \tag{12}$$

$$F1 = \frac{2 * Presion * Recall}{Precision + Recall} \quad (13)$$

In order to more effectively illustrate the effect of internal classification, this paper also uses the weighted average F1 value to evaluate the classification results. The related calculation method is shown in formula 14–16.

$$Macro_P = \sum_{i=1}^{k} \frac{n_i}{n_1 + n_2 + ... + n_k} \times P_i \quad (14)$$

$$Macro_R = \sum_{i=1}^{k} \frac{n_i}{n_1 + n_2 + ... + n_k} \times R_i \quad (15)$$

$$Macro_F = \frac{2 * Macro_P * Macro_R}{Macro_P + Macro_R} \quad (16)$$

n_i represents the quantity of the i-th type of data, P_i is the accuracy rate of the i-th type, and R_i is the recall rate of the i-th type.

4.5 Experimental Results and Analysis

In order to verify the effectiveness of the proposed model, comparative experiments with the following models are carried out on Chinese and English datasets. The experimental results on the Weibo text dataset are shown in Table 4, and the results on the e-commerce reviews are shown in Table 5.

Table 4. Test results on Weibo text dataset

Model	Accuracy	Presicion	Recall	F1
SVM [14]	0.5600	0.4626	0.5600	0.4567
CNN [17]	0.7808	0.6627	0.6705	0.6466
LSTM [28]	0.7759	0.6546	0.6605	0.6521
GRU [27]	0.7845	0.6671	0.6765	0.6559
BiGRU [26]	0.7852	0.6666	0.6765	0.6635
CNN-BiLSTM [21]	0.7866	0.6771	0.6805	0.6774
Single CNN-BiGRU	0.8015	0.7036	0.702	0.6793
MSCNN-BiGRU	**0.8118**	**0.7174**	**0.7170**	**0.7085**

Combining the comparison results of each model in Table 4 and Table 5, it can be seen that this model is better than other comparison models on data sets with different languages. The effect of the machine learning method SVM is significantly lower than that of the model using the deep learning method, and the accuracy rate differs by up to 25%, the fusion models are better than the single model.

The proposed model is superior to the single-scale CNN combined with the BiGRU model in various evaluation indicators, which proves the important role of the multi-granularity word information extracted by the multi-scale convolution kernel. At the

Table 5. Test results on e-commerce Reviews dataset

Model	Accuracy	Presicion	Recall	F1
SVM [14]	0.7860	0.7365	0.7860	0.7527
CNN [17]	0.8424	0.8342	0.8425	0.8375
LSTM [28]	0.8439	0.8344	0.8440	0.8379
GRU [27]	0.8435	0.8263	0.8435	0.8287
BiGRU [26]	0.8510	0.8356	0.8510	0.8362
CNN-BiLSTM [21]	0.8600	0.8537	0.8600	0.8562
Single CNN-BiGRU	0.8655	0.8545	0.8655	0.8500
MSCNN-BiGRU	**0.8765**	**0.8682**	**0.8765**	**0.8639**

same time, it is 2% higher than the average accuracy of the CNN-BiLSTM model. It illustrates the effectiveness of BiGRU in overall semantic representation.

In order to understand the overall effect of model classification, this paper uses the weighted average F1 value to compare models, and the results are shown in Fig. 4.

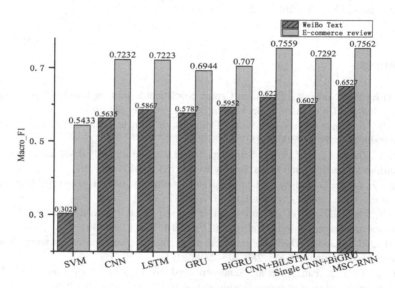

Fig. 4. Macro_ F1 value comparison results

The Macro_F1 value not only pays attention to the overall classification result, but also pays attention to the classification effect of each category in the data set, so we can see that the value in Fig. 4 is significantly lower than the normal F1 value. Compared with the SVM model, the Macro_F1 value of the proposed model on the two types of data sets is increased by 34.98% and 21.29%, respectively. It is also better than the results of other models, which reflects that the model in this paper can not only improve the overall classification effect, but also has different data sets. The classification accuracy of the categories can also achieve satisfactory results.

5 Conclusion

In this paper, we propose a deep learning model for sentiment classification of different types of online text. We use the improved optimal scale CNN to extract a sequence of different granularity phrase representations, and fed into BiGRU to obtain the sentence representation. MSCNN-BiGRU is able to capture both local features of phrases as well as global and temporal sentence semantics. Through experiments on two datasets, it is found that the model proposed in this paper outperforms the traditional CNN, LSTM, GRU and other single neural network models and CNN-RNN series hybrid neural network model.

As one of the future works, the pre-trained language model [29] will be used to further improve the sentiment classification results. Moreover, deeper convolutional neural network will help to improve the stability and accuracy of the model.

Acknowledgments. This research was supported in part by the National Key R&D Program of China under Grant No. 2020YFB1707700, and the Fundamental Research Funds for the Central Universities under Grant No. 20D111201.

References

1. China Internet Network Information Center. Statistical Report on Internet Development in China. Beijing: China Internet Network Information Center (2020)
2. Liu, B.: Sentiment Analysis: Mining Opinions, Sentiments, and Emotions. Cambridge University Press, New York (2015)
3. Yan, K., Zhong, C., Ji, Z., et al.: Semi-supervised learning for early detection and diagnosis of various air handling unit faults. Energy Build. 181 (2018)
4. Singh, J., Singh, G., Singh, R.: Optimization of sentiment analysis using machine learning classifiers. Hum.-centric Comput. Inf. Sci. 7(1), 32 (2017)
5. Yan, K., Ma, L., Dai, Y., et al.: Cost-sensitive and sequential feature selection for chiller fault detection and diagnosis. Int. J. Refrig. (2017). S0140700717304449
6. Chenlo, J.M., Losada, D.E.: An empirical study of sentence features for subjectivity and polarity classification. Inf. Sci. **280**, 275–288 (2014)
7. Xia, H., Yang, Y., Pan, X., et al.: Sentiment analysis for online reviews using conditional random fields and support vector machines. Electr. Commer. Res. 20 (2020)
8. Qu, L., Ifrim, G., Weikum, G.: The bag-of-opinions method for review rating prediction from sparse text patterns. In: Coling 2010, 23rd International Conference on Computational Linguistics, Proceedings of the Conference, 23–27 August 2010, Beijing, China. DBLP (2010)
9. Yan, X., Cui, B., Xu, Y., et al.: A method of information protection for collaborative deep learning under GAN model attack. IEEE/ACM Trans. Computat. Biol. Bioinf. (99), 1–1 (2019)
10. Deng, J., Cheng, L., Wang, Z.: Attention-based BiLSTM fused CNN with gating mechanism model for Chinese long text classification. Comput. Speech Lang. 68(6), 101182 (2021)

11. Tan, Y., Zhang, J., Xia, L.: A survey of sentiment analysis research in social media context. Data Anal. Knowl. Discov. 4(1) (2020)
12. Fellbaum, C.: WordNet. The Encyclopedia of Applied Linguistics. Blackwell Publishing Ltd, 231–243 (2012)
13. China Knowledge Network. A collection of words for sentiment analysis [EB/OL] (2007). http://www.keenage.com/html/c_bulletin_.html
14. Wawre, S.V., Deshmukh, S.N.: Sentiment classification using machine learning techniques. Int. J. Sci. Res. (IJSR) 5(4), 819–821 (2016)
15. Krizhevsky, A., Sutskever, I., Hinton, G.: ImageNet classification with deep convolutional neural networks. Adv. Neural Inf. Process. Syst. 25(2) (2012)
16. Graves, A., Mohamed, A.R., Hinton, G.: Speech recognition with deep recurrent neural networks. In: 2013 IEEE International Conference on Acoustics, Speech and Signal Processing. IEEE (2013)
17. Kim, Y.: Convolutional Neural Networks for Sentence Classification. Eprint Arxiv (2014)
18. Jelodar, H., Wang, Y., Orji, R., et al.: Deep Sentiment Classification and Topic Discovery on Novel Coronavirus or COVID-19 Online Discussions: NLP Using LSTM Recurrent Neural Network Approach. arXiv (2020)
19. Zhou, C., Sun, C., Liu, Z., et al.: A C-LSTM Neural Network for Text Classification. Comput. Sci. 1(4), 39–44 (2015)
20. Jin, N., Wu, J., Ma, X., et al.: Multi-task learning model based on Multi-scale CNN and LSTM for sentiment classification. IEEE Access, (99), 1–1 (2020)
21. Yang, L., Hongbin, D.: Text sentiment analysis based on CNN and BiLSTM network feature fusion. J. Comput. Appl. 38(11), 29–34 (2018)
22. Yaou, Z., Jiazhong, Z., Yibin, L., et al.: Sentiment analysis combining word embedding based on language model and multi-scale convolutional neural network. J. Comput. Appl. 40(3), 651–657 (2020)
23. Yan, C., et al.: Text sentiment orientation analysis of multi-channels CNN and BiGRU based on attention mechanism. Comput. Res. Dev. 57(12), 107–119 (2020)
24. Jiang, M., Huang, W., Huang, Z., et al.: Integration of global and local metrics for domain adaptation learning via dimensionality reduction. IEEE Trans. Cybern. 1–14 (2015)
25. Zhang, Y., Wallace, B.: A sensitivity analysis of (and practitioners' guide to) convolutional neural networks for sentence classification. Comput. Sci. (2015)
26. Schuster, M., Paliwal, K.K.: Bidirectional recurrent neural networks[J]. IEEE Trans. Signal Process. 45(11), 2673–2681 (1997)
27. Cho, K., Merrienboer, B.V., Gulcehre, C., et al.: Learning phrase representations using RNN encoder-decoder for statistical machine translation. Comput. Sci. (2014)
28. Hochreiter, S., Schmidhuber, J.: Long Short-Term Memory. Neural Comput. 9(8), 1735–1780 (1997)
29. Zhang, L., Wang, S., Liu, B.: Deep learning for sentiment analysis : a survey. Wiley Interdisc. Rev. Data Min. Knowl. Disc. e1253 (2018)

Etiquette Action Similarity Evaluation Based on Posture Recognition

Rui Yang[✉], Ran Tao, Zhaoyang Wang, and Xiangyang Feng

School of Computer Science and Technology, Donghua University, Shanghai 201620, China
{taoran,fengxy}@dhu.edu.cn

Abstract. At present, more and more vocational colleges set up the etiquette course. In traditional etiquette education, due to the shortage of teachers, it is not practicable to effectively manage students. In order to address this problem, this paper proposes a method based on posture recognition technology and using fuzzy comprehensive evaluation method to evaluate the similarity of etiquette action. This method can be used in action video teaching, used for individual teaching. The student can carry out real-time learning or evaluation of the etiquette action, and be given guidance, thus his resources can be accumulated in the process, so that the teacher can scientifically manage students' knowledge. The research found that the proposed method can automatically match standard and test keyframe, and can calculate similarity for skeletons of different body sizes. By comparing the similarity of different postures, the consequence shows that the method is more feasible than the European distance. This method can be used not only for etiquette action teaching, but also for the other field of action teaching.

Keywords: Etiquette · Posture recognition · Fuzzy comprehensive evaluation · Similarity · Evaluation

1 Introduction

Since ancient times, China has enjoyed the reputation of "an ancient civilization and a country of etiquette", and etiquette is the core of Chinese excellent traditional culture [1]. Vocational college, as an important training base for cultivating special talents for the country, etiquette education cannot be ignored here, and it occupy an important position and significance in a complete teaching system [2]. For the student in higher vocational college, the method of this paper can help him to carry out one-on-one learning and evaluation. So that the teacher can complete more efficient management, thereby improving the efficiency of etiquette teaching. The student can master the basic knowledge of etiquette, and cultivate etiquette behavior norms, so as to better serve the work of social production.

Human action behavior recognition is a research hotspot in the field of computer vision in recent years, and it is widely used in fields such as human-machine intelligent interaction, virtual reality, and video surveillance [3]. Posture recognition is a branch of human action recognition. With the emergence of camera monitoring equipment

© Springer Nature Switzerland AG 2021
L. Uden et al. (Eds.): KMO 2021, CCIS 1438, pp. 404–415, 2021.
https://doi.org/10.1007/978-3-030-81635-3_33

and motion capture equipment, the progress of computer technology and the rise of artificial intelligence technology, posture recognition has become a hot topic. In recent years, posture recognition has been widely used in the field of education. In reference [4], posture recognition is applied to the dance analysis and teaching, and a three-dimensional data database is established. Based on the feature plane matching the human body posture, obtained the human characteristics Google model. Apply the above data to posture teaching and analysis in the process of dance teaching. In reference [5], posture recognition is applied to Taijiquan teaching. The spatial coordinate data of the action skeleton joint points obtained by Kinect sensor are processed to construct the action test sequence and compare with the standard sequence. According to the preset scoring rules, the function of evaluating and scoring the students' actions is realized. In reference [6], posture recognition is applied to yoga training. The developed interactive system uses Kinect V2 to recognize six kinds of yoga postures with command sound to visualize the instructions and pictures about the postures to be performed. Finally, the system is used to assist the training of yoga activities to improve the performance of users. However, there is no literature on the application of posture recognition technology in etiquette teaching.

With the advancement of computer vision, automated evaluation of the similarity of students' actions has become feasible. This paper applies posture recognition technology and fuzzy comprehensive evaluation method to etiquette teaching, and proposes an action similarity evaluation method for etiquette, which achieves the effective evaluation of students' etiquette actions. Firstly, the teacher specifies standard video keyframes. Secondly, the student uploads video and extracts test keyframe sequence according to the time axis information of standard video keyframe and threshold. Furthermore, Use OpenPose to extract information about keypoints. According to 12 vector angles and foot Euclidean distance, compare standard video keyframes and test video frame sequences. The similarity is calculated by fuzzy comprehensive evaluation, and the high similarity is selected as the corresponding test keyframes of the standard keyframes. Finally, the students' etiquette postures are scored, and their actions are ultimately evaluated. It is an advanced way of assisted learning or scoring.

2 Action Similarity Evaluation

Human action similarity research is one of the important research branches of human behavior recognition [7]. The research content is to automatically analyze and recognize behavior from some unknown information.

In reference [8], Euclidean distance is used as the similarity evaluation method, but the method requires two videos to correspond to the action height at the same point in time, and when the participants are not equal in height and weight, the results of the calculation will be offset by coordinate displacement. In reference [9], Dynamic Time Warping (DTW) was used to calculate the similarity between time series, which can effectively evaluate the similarity between time series, but the height and weight of the human body still affects the similarity results. In reference [10], according to the different proportions of the human body, before the motion similarity calculation, the skeleton length information to be detected is mapped to the template skeleton length, then coordinate translation is performed, and finally the similarity is calculated. But the point recognition is continuous, that is, according to the direction of the path, if a point in the path is not identified, then all points after the point can not be identified, which has a significant hidden danger.

This paper records the time sequence of standard video keyframes to find the corresponding posture, and obtains the angle difference and the distance difference by comparing the vector angle and the foot distance. Because the etiquette action similarity is fuzzy, and there are 12 vector angles and foot distance multiple influencing factors, the fuzzy comprehensive evaluation method is used to calculate the similarity. According to the threshold, find the corresponding posture with the highest similarity, realize the registration of the standard keyframe and the test keyframe, and return the corresponding score according to the score calculation method. This method can realize the correspondence between standard video keyframes and test video keyframes, and the motion similarity calculation method is not affected by the human skeleton, which is feasible.

In order to achieve automated evaluation, this article establishes the following model. Students can choose to upload test videos or record test videos in real time. The model is divided into two parts. The first part is the similarity calculation, which calculates the similarity between the test video sequence and the standard video keyframe. The second part is the score calculation. First match the test video keyframe corresponding to the

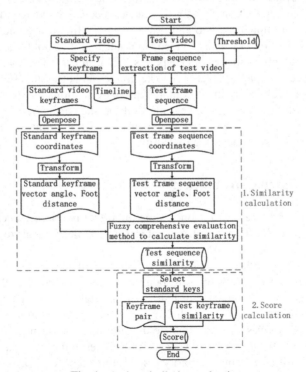

Fig. 1. Action similarity evaluation

standard video keyframe, then calculate the corresponding posture score, and finally output the action score. The flowchart is shown in Fig. 1.

The specific steps are as follows:

1) The teacher specifies standard video keyframes and records the time axis information of keyframes.
2) According to the input time axis information of the keyframe and threshold, the test video frame sequence is extracted.
3) The standard keyframe keypoints and test frame sequence keypoints are obtained by OpenPose.
4) Keypoints transformed into 12 vector angles and the foot distance.
5) The difference between the vector angle of standard keyframe and the vector angle of test frame sequence, and the difference between the foot distance of standard keyframe and the foot distance of test frame sequence is compared. The similarity of test sequence is calculated by fuzzy comprehensive evaluation method.
6) Select the test sequence with the highest similarity corresponding to the standard keyframe as the test video keyframe, and return its similarity.
7) Convert similarity to score.

3   Etiquette Feature Extraction

3.1   Extracting Vector Angle

In this paper, the body_25 model of OpenPose is used to extract the coordinates of keypoints of the human body. keypoints are shown in Fig. 2, and labels and their names of keypoints are shown in Table 1.

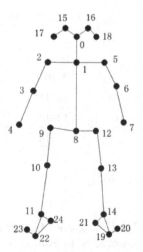

Fig. 2. The body_25 model of OpenPose

Table 1. Keypoints and names

Keypoint	Name	Keypoint	Name
0	Nose	13	LKnee
1	Neck	14	LAnkle
2	RShoulder	15	REye
3	RElbow	16	LEye
4	RWrist	17	REar
5	LShoulder	18	LEar
6	LElbow	19	LBigToe
7	LWrist	20	LSmallToe
8	MidHip	21	LHeel
9	RHip	22	RBigToe
10	RKnee	23	RSmallToe
11	RAnkle	24	RHeel
12	LHip		

Table 2. 12 key vectors.

Symbol	Vector
A_1	0–1
A_2	1–8
A_3	2–3
A_4	3–4
A_5	5–6
A_6	6–7
A_7	9–10
A_8	10–11
A_9	12–13
A_{10}	13–14
A_{11}	24–22
A_{12}	21–19

Because keypoints 15, 16, 17 and 18 have no effect on human actions, 12 key vectors composed of other keypoints are extracted to evaluate etiquette actions. The extracted 12 key vectors are shown in Table 2.

Calculate the vector angle:

$$P_i = a \tan(A_i) * \frac{180}{\pi} \quad (i = 1, 2, ..., 12)$$

Among them, A_i is the extracted key vectors, and the return value of $a \tan(A_i)$ is a radian. Multiply it by $\frac{180}{\pi}$ to get the vector angles corresponding to the key vectors.

3.2 Extracting of Foot Distance

Fig. 3. Foot comparison picture

In Fig. 3, the 12 vector angles of the human body are almost identical, but the foot posture is different, that is, the distance between the left and right heels is different. The heels of the standard posture are close together in etiquette action, but there is a distance between the left and right heels of the right test posture in the figure, so the foot distance is considered in the similarity calculation.

Calculate the Euclidean distance between the left and right heels (keypoint 21 and keypoint 24), i.e.

$$D = \sqrt{(x_{21} - x_{24})^2 + (y_{21} - y_{24})^2}$$

4 Similarity Calculation

Fuzzy comprehensive evaluation uses some concepts of fuzzy mathematics to provide some evaluation methods for actual comprehensive evaluation problems. Specifically, fuzzy comprehensive evaluation is a comprehensive evaluation method based on fuzzy mathematics, applying the principle of fuzzy relation synthesis, quantifying some factors with unclear boundary and difficult to quantify, and evaluating the subordinate level of the evaluated things from multiple factors [11]. The similarity is fuzzy, and there are many factors such as vector angles and distance, so the fuzzy comprehensive evaluation method is used to calculate the similarity.

The fuzzy comprehensive evaluation model is as follows:

(1) Establish evaluation factor set

$$SU = \{su_1, su_2, ..., su_{13}\}$$

That is, the evaluation index reflecting the factors in the similarity of the evaluated object, $su_1 \sim su_{12}$ represents the value of the 12 angle vector differences converted by the ridge membership function, su_{13} represents the value of difference of foot distance converted by trapezoidal membership function.

(2) Establish evaluation set

$$SV = \{sv_1, sv_2, ..., sv_5\}$$

Each grade can correspond to a fuzzy subset. $sv_1, sv_2, sv_3, sv_4, sv_5$ represent very similar, similar, less similar, dissimilar and very dissimilar respectively. The similarity classification and membership degrees are shown in Table 3.

Table 3. Similarity classification and membership

Classification	sv_1	sv_2	sv_3	sv_4	sv_5
Meaning	Very similar	Similar	Less similar	Dissimilar	Very dissimilar
Membership degree	1	0.8	0.55	0.25	0

(3) Establish weight set

$$SW = \{sw_1, sw_2, ..., sw_{13}\}$$

The weight vector should be determined before synthesis. In this paper, the weight is set by the teacher.

(4) Fuzzy comprehensive evaluation.

The weighted average operator is selected to combine the weight vector SW with the SR of the evaluated object to obtain the fuzzy comprehensive evaluation result vector SZ of the evaluated object.

$$
\begin{aligned}
\mathbf{SZ} &= (SZ_1, SZ_2, ..., SZ_5) \\
&= SW \circ \mathbf{SR} \\
&= (sw_1, sw_2, ..., sw_{13}) \circ
\begin{bmatrix}
sr_{11} & sr_{12} & \cdots & sr_{15} \\
sr_{21} & sr_{22} & \cdots & sr_{25} \\
\vdots & \vdots & \ddots & \vdots \\
sr_{13\times1} & sr_{13\times2} & \cdots & sr_{13\times5}
\end{bmatrix}
\end{aligned}
$$

$$SY = (1, 0.8, 0.55.0.25, 0) \times (SZ_1, SZ_2, SZ_3, SZ_4, SZ_5)^T$$

5 Score Calculation

5.1 Corresponding Frame Sequence

According to the input n standard video keyframes and threshold T, extract $2 \times T + 1$ frames corresponding to the test video $[K - T, K + T]$ for each standard video keyframe according to the frame number K, and calculate the similarity with the current frame respectively. Take the frame with the highest similarity as the final corresponding frame corresponding to the keyframe, so as to obtain the corresponding frames of the n keyframes and their corresponding similarities. The process is shown in Fig. 4:

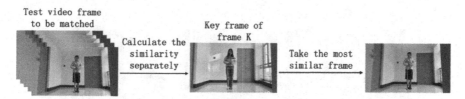

Fig. 4. Extract the test frame.

5.2 Score Calculation

According to the n pairs of keyframes and the similarity obtained by the similarity calculation, the similarity and the weight of n keyframes are entered into the score calculation module. According to the following rules, calculate the posture score, then calculate the action score, and finally output the score.

(1) Calculate posture score

$$S_i^0 = SY_i \times 100 \quad (i = 1, 2, ..., n)$$

Among them, SY_i is the pose similarity of the i-th keyframe, and its interval is $[0,1]$, so it is converted into the initial posture score of the interval $[0,100]$.

(2) Calculate action score

$$S = \sum_{i=1}^{n} We_i S_i$$

Among them, n is the number of keyframes, We_i is the weight of the i-th keyframe, and S_i is the score of the posture of the i-th keyframe.

6 Experimental Results and Analysis

The experimental platform is a PC with core i5-5200 2.2 GHz CPU and 4 [3]GB memory. Python and VS are used as the development environment. The data is collected from two volunteers in the laboratory. Take the actions of one trained person as the standard action, and the other person as the tester to score. The average execution time of each posture algorithm is about 0.86 s.

Firstly, the standard video keyframes are specified. Nine keyframes are shown in Fig. 5, which are standing posture, bow ceremony, introduction ceremony, step attention, direction guidance, product guidance, hand up ceremony, report ceremony and squatting ceremony.

Fig. 5. 9 standard etiquette keyframes

By comparing the following postures in Table 4, the comparison scores of each two postures are calculated respectively. Comparison with the Euclidean distance, scores are more reasonable. Euclidean distance score is not in line with the reality, because Euclidean distance is affected by the position of the human body and the size of the skeleton.

In Table 4, the 1/4 different contrast postures are compared with different skeletons. It can be found that the Euclidean distance is affected by the skeleton, and the score obtained is 2.39, which is very unreasonable. The method in this article has a score of 50.34, which is reasonable.

Keyframe pair scores calculated using the action similarity method in this paper are shown in Table 5. The first column is the standard keyframe. The second column is the corresponding test keyframe. The third column is the score obtained by the similarity evaluation method in this article, i.e. the score for each test keyframe. The Table 5 gives test posture scores for keyframes of 9 actions.

Table 4. Comparative posture scores

Name	Standard posture	Test posture	posture similarity evaluation score	Euclidean distance score
Same stance			100	100
Turn around			82.59	93.66
Feet			88.95	95.04
1/4 different			50.34	2.39
1/2 different			36.70	91.57
Upright and squat			35.35	89.55
Bow and squat			25.07	95.60

As shown in Table 5, in the stance posture, the A_5 vector angle of the standard frame and the test frame differs by 7 degrees, the vector angle of A_{12} differs by 6 degrees, and the remaining vector angles are basically within 5 degrees, and the foot distance difference is also less than 3. Therefore, its score is high at 99.31. In the squatting posture, the vector angle of A_4 differs by 27 degrees, the vector angle of A_6 differs by 30 degrees, the vector angle of A_8 differs by 65 degrees, the vector angle of A_9 differs by 31 degrees, and the foot distance difference is greater than 20. Therefore, its score is low at 52.67.

The tester's action score is calculated by using the action similarity evaluation method. The keyframe weight is $We = (\frac{1}{9}, \frac{1}{9}, \frac{1}{9}, \frac{1}{9}, \frac{1}{9}, \frac{1}{9}, \frac{1}{9}, \frac{1}{9}, \frac{1}{9})$, and it set by the teacher. The final action score is 80.42 points.

Table 5. Keyframe pair score.

Standard posture	Test posture	Posture similarity evaluation score	Standard posture	Test posture	Posture similarity evaluation score
		99.31			85.23
		85.58			70.88
		78.69			87.53
		80.78			52.67
		83.14			

7 Conclusions

This paper proposes an action similarity evaluation method based on posture recognition. This method can be used to assess the similarity of automated actions of human bodies with different bones. Using this method to realize the analysis of etiquette posture, apply it to etiquette teaching, realize action video teaching. The teaching system can effectively store and manage students' test data, give feedback to students in time, which realizes computer-assist management teaching, and improves teaching quality. The experimental data verifies that the method has good accuracy for the evaluation of the similarity of etiquette actions. This method can not only evaluate the similarity of etiquette actions, but also can be used in other scenarios. However, this method relies on the accuracy of OpenPose recognition, as long as there is a mask, some points can not be recognized, which also affects the accuracy of the result, and the human body's distance from the lens will also affect the result. These issues require further study.

Acknowledgments. This research was supported in part by the National Key R&D Program of China under Grant No. 2020YFB1707700, and the Fundamental Research Funds for the Central Universities under Grant No. 20D111201.

References

1. Nan, Z.: Research on university etiquette education in the internet + background. Rural Econ. Technol. **30**(08), 293–294 (2019)
2. Wanshu, W.: Research on the direction and content of etiquette education in higher vocational colleges. Contemp. Educ. Pract. Teach. Res. **01**, 84–85 (2019)
3. Ruifeng, L., Liangliang, W., Ke, W.: A review of human action behavior recognition research. Pattern Recogn. Artif. Intell. **27**(01), 35–48 (2014)

4. Weijiang, C.: Practical research on motion capture technology in dance posture analysis and teaching. Microcomput. Appl. **36**(03), 102–105 (2020)
5. Zhihong, X., Liying, Z., Zhenhua, C., Haozhi, Z., Chunhui, Y.: In-situ Taijiquan auxiliary training system based on Kinect. J. Hebei Univ. Sci. Technol. **38**(02), 183–189 (2017)
6. Trejo, E.W., Yuan, P.: Recognition of yoga poses through an interactive system with kinect device. In: 2018 2nd International Conference on Robotics and Automation Sciences (ICRAS), Wuhan, pp. 1–5 (2018). https://doi.org/10.1109/ICRAS.2018.8443267
7. Sahoo, S.P., Ari, S.: On an algorithm for human action recognition. Expert Syst. Appl. **115**, 524–534 (2019)
8. Jiang, Y.: Research on Sports Aided Training Based on Kinect. Autom. Technol. Appl. **38**(09), 151-153+157 (2019)
9. Songtao, Y., Xueqin, W.: Tai Chi video registration method based on joint angle and DTW [J]. Comput. Technol. Autom. **39**(01), 117–122 (2020)
10. Li, S., Ma, Y., Huang, H., Li, S.: A skeleton adaptive human motion similarity calculation method [A]. Institute of Management Science and Industrial Engineering. In: Proceedings of 2019 9th International Conference on Education and Social Science (ICESS 2019)[C]. Institute of Management Science and Industrial Engineering:Computer Science and Electronic Technology International Society, 7 (2019)
11. Zailuo, S., Wei, Z.: The application of fuzzy comprehensive evaluation method in teaching quality evaluation of university teachers. Technol. Innovation Manage. **35**(01), 58–61 (2014)

AI&New Trends in KM

The Impact of Artificial Intelligence on Work and Human Value: Views from Social Researchers

Chu-Chen Rosa Yeh, Wei-Wen Chang$^{(\boxtimes)}$, and Cze Chiun Wong

Graduate Institute of International Human Resource Development, National Taiwan Normal University, 162, Section 1, Heping E. Rd., Taipei, Taiwan, ROC
changw@ntnu.edu.tw

Abstract. The rise of artificial intelligence (AI) and related new technologies have been widely discussed in recent years, especially on its benefits and threats to society. This study aims to explore the impact of AI on work and human value at different levels of AI capability. Adopting a qualitative approach, we conducted a focus group discussion with six scholars who have AI research experience in different social disciplines and in various global regions. Four main topics were discussed in the focus group, which are: (1) attitude toward AI, (2) types of businesses, industries, or workers that benefit or are threatened the most by AI, (3) willingness to work with a robot with different levels of intelligence, and (4) how to find human's value and get prepared for future workplace. The discussion was recorded under the consent of participants and transcribed verbatim. ATLAS.ti version 8 software was used for the textual data analysis. The findings reveal that scholars: (1) are optimistic toward AI in general, (2) believe that most industries will benefit from AI, (3) are divided in attitude toward robots with empathetic intelligence, (4) argue that humans need to get prepared for the future workplace. Implications and future research suggestions are provided.

Keywords: Artificial intelligence · Qualitative study · Social impact · Workforce · Human value

1 Introduction

Artificial Intelligence (AI) is the hottest topic in the world nowadays. Its reputation was built by the victory of Deep Blue and AlphaGo over the human player in 1997 and 2016. In 1956, McCarthy and his colleagues [1] announced their idea about AI and suggested that it is a science of making machines and programs intelligent. Lee and Wang [2] defined AI as a program which imitates human's behavior and is capable of self-learning and reacting to the environment.

The outstanding development of AI today is facilitated by the advancement of big data, machine learning, and deep learning [3, 4], after several evolutions in the past, from logical computation, complex problem-solving [5] to expert system [3]. The support

© Springer Nature Switzerland AG 2021
L. Uden et al. (Eds.): KMO 2021, CCIS 1438, pp. 419–428, 2021.
https://doi.org/10.1007/978-3-030-81635-3_34

from the government, especially the financial investment and the relevant national policy development are also the factors contributing to the development of AI.

Nowadays, AI is represented in a virtual or physical form. The chat-bot is a human daily dialogue simulation, which works through audio or text. It is one of the virtual AI examples and has been widely implemented in services, especially the customer service [6]. The examples of physical forms of AI usually found in the smart medical care industry are care-giving or companion robots and surgical assistants [7]. The discussion of AI can also be found in other industries, for instance counseling psychology [8], manufacturing [9], and services [10]. Therefore, the utilization of AI is believed to be an influencer on the current labor market and has profound impact on the human workforce.

Although various points of views were asserted by scholars in the literature, most work on the social impact of AI remain conceptual. Few empirical research can be found in this specific issue. Hence, the present study aims to collect the views from social scholars who are experienced in AI research, in order to pave the way for more empirical studies on the impact of AI on human workforce in the future.

2 Literature Review

The rapid development and utilization of new technologies have changed the original organizational structure and raise new issues on human resources deployment, specifically the substitution, assistance, and improvement of human workers' work process and efficiency [11]. In the literature, scholars have expressed three general views toward AI, which are positive, negative, and neutral [12].

Scholars who hold a positive attitude toward AI believed that it would bring benefits rather than negative impact to the society or labor market. New jobs or expanded job opportunities will arise in this wave of AI [13]. According to Linkedin [14], several AI or new technology relevant new jobs are created, for example, artificial intelligence specialists, site reliability engineers, and cybersecurity specialists, just to name a few. Additionally, the demand for non-technical jobs also increased due to accelerated AI adoption in the business, for example, behavioral health technician, customer success specialist, and sales development representative.

Another school of scholars advocated that AI technologies will take over the low-skilled workers' jobs and cause massive job loss, while lower the salary standard and destruct the employment structure. As Graetz & Michaels predicted in 2018, jobs requiring skills at a low level will be substituted by technologies [15], particularly those who are middle-level white-collar and blue-collar employees [16]. The other societal issues will also occur as well, such as a polarization of employment structure [17, 18] and salary reduction [19, 20].

In the neutralist's view, the time has not arrived yet to conclude the impact of AI on the society and the labor market [21]. Although the development and implementation of this new technology seem to be flourishing in many fields, AI is still in its infancy. Many uncertainties and problems still exist which require AI developers to constantly deal with and resolve [22, 23].

3 Methodology

For the purpose of examining what were the societal impact caused by new technology implementation, an international focus group interview was conducted to collect data. The focus group took place in Taipei, Taiwan.

3.1 Participants

A total of six international scholars, including four professors and two lecturers, participated in this study. They came from the field of hospitality business management, human resource development, digital and cultural policy, and journalism. Four of the participants were male and two were female. Three of them worked in a western country and the other three in Asian countries. The participants were invited to speak at an AI International Forum because of their rich experiences in the research of AI technology and its applications in various industries.

3.2 Focus Group Interview Implementation Process

The international focus group interview was moderated by a researcher with rich qualitative research experience. An interview outline was developed in advance by the research team and presented to the participants ahead of time. The moderator guided the discussion and asked additional questions to probe for more insights. The main discussion topics in the focus group were as follows: (1) attitude toward AI, (2) the types of businesses, industries, or workers who benefit or are threatened the most from the implementation of AI or similar technology in the future, (3) working with a robot designed with empathetic intelligence, and (4) how to find human's value and get prepared to avoid being replaced by robots. For data analysis, the interview was recorded and videotaped under the consent of all interviewees.

3.3 Data Analysis

Verbatim transcription and analysis were conducted in the process of data analysis. In the first phase, a team of master students was in charge of transcribing the verbal audio into transcripts. Then, cross-checks were conducted for ensuring the accuracy of each transcript in presenting interviewees' points of view. The analysis phase was conducted by an analysis team, which consisted of two master level graduate students and two researchers. The analysis team used ATLAS.ti version 8 software and followed Corbin and Strauss's [24] open coding and axial coding methods to code the verbatim transcripts. The analysis team read through the full transcription and highlighted important sentences as units of meaning repeatedly and carefully until no new code was found. Afterwards, the analysis team explored, linked, and summarized the codes generated in the previous step to form themes. Table 1 showed the example of the coding process.

Table 1. Demonstration of data analysis in the present study

Semantic unit	Coding label	Theme
A5: AI takes over the human job slowly and increase the technological unemployment	Take over job; Unemployment	Impact of AI
A2: So, basically, would those robots eventually substitute human in the workplace? To this case, we think it's a NO. But the challenges are real because AI will change the structure, modify the process, adjust the operation with good number of things in the workplace which we had already mentioned before	Won't entirely replace human's job; Change of workflow; Change of working mode	

4   Findings

4.1   Positive Versus Negative Attitude Toward AI

In discussing the societal impact of AI, optimists and pessimists are always found in the literature [12]. The optimists think that the rise of AI and other technology improves the quality of our life and work. On the other hand, pessimists think that AI takes over jobs and increases unemployment.

Participants in the present study in general represented the school of optimists and believed that AI in turn will provide humans a better quality of life and enhance work performance. Participant A4 had taken the aging society as the example and claimed that AI is important for providing services for the elders, he said:

> *Someone will have to look after the old folks. AI is crucial and an important role; it is maintaining and providing the services to all the population.*

Another participant (A2) from the journalism field indicated that using AI and new technology will gain a better performance on the job, he said:

> *AI can check customers by chat-bot, analyze client data, especially journalizing a media where we are highly involved. AI can compose different news, like weather forecasts or sport events and many breaking news, and sharing, holding and classifying information for target audience. In addition, AI can be made to mediate platforms, such as network analyze on what news which certainly pick reader's current interests. As a result, top of news office can increase the news output with the demanded volume for the least cost. It saves time for the reporter and the news partition at the top to do the different news writing, content creating, so they can focus on more complex issues.*

Against the optimistic perspective, one of the participants (A5) indicated himself as a pessimist toward AI. He said:

I might be the pessimist. AI takes over the human job slowly and increase the technological unemployment. Many Koreans have some panic about the job needs in future, however...including my position,...

Participants A5 further explained that the labor market in the future might become very tricky since the intelligent machine will gradually take over the job and humans are getting panic about losing their job as a consequence. Other issues of concern toward the use of AI are ethics, trust in AI devices, and inequality in using AI.

4.2 Most Industries Will Benefit from AI

Participants agreed that most industries will benefit by AI, especially the industries which are currently facing labor shortage or high labor cost issue, for instances services, senior healthcare, and journalism. Participant A3 indicated that AI does bring benefits to senior healthcare industry in taking care of the elders. She said:

I think healthcare is another industry which would be hugely impacted by AI. I'm thinking of, in the US, they have shortage of nurses and a shortage of the people who want to work with the seniors. We actually in our school have a senior living concentration, but they have been trying to build it for many years, still cannot get many young students. So generation X and Y are really not interested in working with senior living. So AI can really help in that sense.

Another benefit of the implementation of AI discussed by participant A2 and A4 is that AI will affect and change the workflow, operation, and job structure. Specifically, the repetitive tasks or tasks that don't require high skill and human interaction can be taken over by AI, so that labor is released. Participant A2 illustrated:

For example, we have the Washington Post, we have the Mount Board, we have the capability to work, as many as fourteen news editors at one time just to check the comments of an article. So basically AI is quite beneficial for the repetitive tasks. Which tasks of the business or the industry or workers are threatened by AI or similar technology? I think also of those that are beneficial but due to the employment, AI can replace the human resources in those tasks, so the workers who are responsible for this aspects is the most vulnerable to this.

4.3 Willingness to Work with Empathetic Intelligence Robots

According to Huang & Rust's (2018) view of AI development, machines or robots equipped with the ability to carry out consistent and rule-based tasks, or to perform contextual interactive tasks have already existed. The next will be machines or robots with emotional reading and reacting ability. However, a debate was found in this hypothesized proposal.

Participant A3 doubted that someday technology would be advanced enough to detect emotions. She felt distressed if a human lost their connection or interaction with society and can only share the emotion with a robot, she said:

I actually wonder if the technology can one day be that advanced, you can detect the difference of all different emotions that human can experience. And also, it's really sad, when you like say you have to go to the, u know, a robot, to share with the robot...your emotions.

Opposite to A3, participant A1 believed that it is possible to get an emotion-readable and reactive robot. Participant A5 agreed with participant A1's opinions and suggested that AI is useful when taking it as a companion for the elders who are lonely and living independently, he said *"they have sometimes talked to the AI to be free from loneliness by using, by communicating with AI"*. However, participant A1 also highlighted the right of a human to choose the way to receive empathy and that different types of relationships will express such. He took the communication between him and his father as an example, and said:

I promised my dad that I will send him a postcard by the end of the week. I also speak to him on skype once a week and I email. But, what is it about this form of communication that has more meaning to him than my email and my skype-call? I think it has something to do with empathetic intelligence, and I think whatever our version of a postcard to our father, we will choose this for certain types of communication over communicating with a robot, regardless of its level of hypothetical empathetic intelligence.

4.4 Human's Value in the Future Workplace

There is a difference between humans and robots, which was emphasized during the discussion. The development of AI is growing rapidly, nonetheless it is programmed by codes as humans want it to be and can be terminated by humans anytime. Therefore, participant A4 considered humans as a final decision maker since humans are able to judge and choose the right thing, he said *"You can always put stops. They are computer programs. I think one thing we forget about AI is that they are computer programs"*. Participant A1 sided with A4, he believed that humans do have the choice of selecting how robots should behave in our life.

As participant A4 denoted, since *"We will be dealing with them, living with them"*, coexisting with AI is an undeniable trend in the future. Therefore, preparation for getting along with AI is necessary, no matter in skills or abilities. Participant A2 suggested that *"human should prepare themselves with interdisciplinary knowledge; computational skills and algorithmization are the most vital, others like the human understanding and study the mechanical too"*.

5   Conclusions and Discussion

This study aims to explore the impact of AI on the workforce at different levels of AI capability. Adopting a qualitative approach, a focus group discussion was conducted with six scholars who have AI research experience in different social disciplines and in various global regions. The findings reveal that scholars: (1) are optimistic toward AI in general, (2) believe that most industries will benefit from AI, (3) are divided in attitude toward robots with empathetic intelligence, (4) argue that humans need to get prepared for the future workplace.

Most participants in the present study held a generally optimistic attitude toward AI and a high willingness in working with AI, especially in the belief that AI can further enhance the quality of life and work efficiency. Although the scholars in the focus group came from different fields, such as tourism, media, and organization management, most of them agreed that AI has two effects, first to release humans from repetitive tasks and second to fill a labor shortage in service fields or to substitute for low-skilled tasks in these fields. However, they also raised the issues related to human-machine substitution, ethics, trust in AI devices, and inequality in using AI. The trust in AI and the ethics in using AI were the most prominent issues when facing the hypothetical scenario of working with empathetic intelligence robots someday. Inequality on using AI was also mentioned in the aspect of a re-distribution of power, since it is expected that those who own more AI capability (individuals, corporations, countries, etc.) will gain more access to power.

The findings in the present study reveal two different attitudes toward empathetic AI, the optimists and the pessimists. An interesting regional divide was observed between the two views, in that the optimists in the focus group discussion came mostly from the western background, while the pessimists from East Asian. Hofstede's [25] cultural dimensions may help explain this difference in the participants, specifically long-term versus short-term orientation. According to Hofstede, short-term orientation is focused on the present time, personal steadiness and stability, and providing services to others. On the other hand, the characteristic of long-term orientation concentrates on the future, changeable environment, and individual's adaption. The typical representatives of the long-term and the short-term orientations are respectively the East Asian countries and the western countries such as the U.S. In the present study, the scholars who stood on the optimistic side of working with an empathetic robot were from a western background, who might have higher level of trust in new and advanced technologies because they provided instant return in the short run by delivering a better service or improving human quality of life. On the opposite side, the scholars from East Asian countries appeared to be more skeptical and more reserved on the benefit of working with an empathetic intelligent robot. They would prefer to wait and see how things evolve before taking a stand.

6 Implications and Future Research Suggestions

The present study revealed that not everyone satisfies with the current technological advancement and its outcomes. AI development and applications are still in their infancy, and as such some uncertainty and anxiety were expressed in the focus group discussion. These concerns when left unchecked may impede the development of AI and tarnish its potential to benefit the society. To alleviate these uncertainty and anxiety, the government and educational institutes must work together to create an environment where AI can fulfill its promise to improve the quality of life of human beings while minimizing the potential harm to the society.

To successfully promote and incorporate AI in the society to minimize potential negative impacts, the government is an important catalyst. The government needs to take a leading role in the development of AI as a national plan, provide guidelines in its development, and facilitate multilateral cooperation, such as those between the government and the industries or between education institutes and the industries. Providing financial support and taking stocks of the country's resources are methods for building an innovative and open environment for the AI developers, managers, and users.

As reported by Smith in 2019 [26], and echoed by scholars in our study, the demand will increase dramatically in the next ten years for a workforce that is technology-savvy and can work comfortably alongside AI. The government, business organizations, and education institutes should start making and implementing talent training plans to produce more AI talents.

At the same time, the academic community can exert research effort on investigating the influence of present technological advancement on humans in order to provide empirical evidence for the public policy makers for better decision making in regulating AI development. Furthermore, the government, business organizations, and education institutes can also adjust the talent training plans in accordance with the research results.

More research is needed for the purpose of fully understanding the impact of AI on human workforce. One important research agenda is the future talent demand. An exploration on the changes of a job and its workflow is important for knowing what the must-get new competencies are in the AI era. Moreover, job analysis research on a regional basis will help track new occupational titles being created due to technological application and adoption rate in the region. Lastly, empirical evidence that leads to better explanation of regional or cultural difference in AI adoption attitude and behavior will help contribute a more holistic view in the line of technology acceptance research.

7 Limitations

The present study aims to explore the current opinion of social scholars on the new technologies, from their experience in doing AI research. Though the focus group discussion generated substantial in-depth understanding of various issues through dialogue and debates, these views are mostly personal experiences of a small group of scholars and by no means can be generalized to all social research community. Another limitation of the study is the fact that our participants are all social scholars who do not have a technical background and therefore may not have a full understanding of the current capability of AI.

Acknowledgement. This research was supported by the Ministry of Science and Technology of Taiwan, ROC (MOST 109-2634-F-003-008 -).

References

1. McCarthy, J.: What is artificial intelligence? http://jmc.stanford.edu/artificial-intelligence/what-is-ai/index.html. Accessed 26 Dec 2019
2. Lee, K.F., Wang, Y.G.: The Advent of Artificial Intelligence. Commonwealth Publishing Co., Ltd, Taiwan (2017). [Text in Chinese]

3. Haenlein, M., Kaplan, A.: A brief history of artificial intelligence: on the past, present, and future of artificial intelligence. Calif. Manage. Rev. **61**(4), 5–14 (2019). https://doi.org/10.1177/0008125619864925

4. Huang, M.-H., Rust, R.T., Maksimovic, V.: The feeling economy: managing in the next generation of artificial intelligence (AI). Calif. Manage. Rev. **61**(4), 43–65 (2019). https://doi.org/10.1177/0008125619863436

5. Council of Europe [COE]: History of Artificial Intelligence. https://www.coe.int/en/web/artificial-intelligence/history-of-ai. Accessed 25 Dec 2019

6. Luo, X., Tong, S., Fang, Z., Qu, Z.: Frontiers: machines vs. humans: the impact of artificial intelligence chatbot disclosure on customer purchases. Mark. Sci. **38**(6), 937–947 (2019). https://doi.org/10.1287/mksc.2019.1192

7. Hamet, P., Tremblay, J.: Artificial intelligence in medicine. Metabolism **69**, S36–S40 (2017). https://doi.org/10.1016/j.metabol.2017.01.011

8. Fulmer, R.: Artificial intelligence and counseling: four levels of implementation. Theory Psychol. **29**(6), 807–819 (2019). https://doi.org/10.1177/0959354319853045

9. Veila, J.W., Kiel, D., Müller, J.M., Voigt, K.: Lessons learned from industry 4.0 implementation in the German manufacturing industry. J. Manuf. Technol. Manage. (2019). https://doi.org/10.1108/jmtm-08-2018-0270

10. Huang, M.-H., Rust, R.T.: Artificial intelligence in service. J. Serv. Res. **21**(2), 155–172 (2018). https://doi.org/10.1177/1094670517752459

11. Makridakis, S.: The forthcoming artificial intelligence (AI) revolution: its impact on society and firms. Futures **90**, 46–60 (2017). https://doi.org/10.1016/j.futures.2017.03.006

12. Yeh, C.-C., Wong, C.C., Chang, W.-W., Lai, C.-C.: Labor displacement in artificial intelligence era: a systematic literature review. Taiwan J. East Asian Stud. **17**(2), 25–75 (2020). https://doi.org/10.6163/tjeas.202012_17(2).0002

13. Borland, J., Coelli, M.: Are Robots Taking Our Jobs? Aust. Econ. Rev. **50**(4), 377–397 (2017). https://doi.org/10.1111/1467-8462.12245

14. Linkedin: Emerging Jobs Report. https://business.linkedin.com/content/dam/me/business/en-us/talent-solutions/emerging-jobs-report/Emerging_Jobs_Report_U.S._FINAL.pdf. Accessed 10 Sept 2020

15. Graetz, G., Michaels, G.: Robots at work. Rev. Econ. Stat. **100**(5), 753–768 (2018). https://doi.org/10.1162/rest_a_00754

16. Gallie, D.: The quality of work in a changing labour market. Soc. Policy Adm. **51**(2), 226–243 (2017). https://doi.org/10.1111/spol.12285

17. Levy, F.: Computers and populism: artificial intelligence, jobs, and politics in the near term. Oxf. Rev. Econ. Policy **34**(3), 393–417 (2018). https://doi.org/10.1093/oxrep/gry004

18. Wolnicki, M., Piasecki, R.: The new luddite scare: the impact of artificial intelligence on labor, capital and business competition between U.S. and China. J. Int. Manage. **11**(2), 5–20 (2019). https://doi.org/10.2478/joim-2019-0007

19. DeCanio, S.J.: Robots and humans-complements or subsititutes? J. Macroecon. **49**, 280–291 (2016). https://doi.org/10.1016/j.jmacro.2016.08.003

20. Korinek, A.: Labor in the age of automation and artificial intelligence. Econ. Inclusive Prosperity Res. Brief 1–9 (2019)

21. Acemoglu, D., Restrepo, P.: Automation and new tasks: how technology displaces and reinstates labor. J. Econ. Perspect. **33**(2), 3–30 (2019). https://doi.org/10.1257/jep.33.2.3

22. Frank, M.R., Autor, D., Bessen, J.E., Brynjolfsson, E., et al.: Toward understanding the impact of artificial intelligence on labor. Proc. Natl. Acad. Sci. USA **116**(14), 6531–6539 (2019). https://doi.org/10.1073/pnas.1900949116

23. Grace, K., Salvatier, J., Dafoe, A., Zhang, B., Evans, O.: Viewpoint: when will ai exceed human performance? Evidence from AI experts. J. Artif. Intell. Res. **62**, 729–754 (2018). https://doi.org/10.1613/jair.1.11222

24. Corbin, J., Strauss, A.: Basics of Qualitative Research: Techniques and Procedures for Developing Grounded Theory. Sage Publications, New York (2014)
25. Hofstede, G.: Dimensionalizing cultures: the hofstede model in context. Online Read. Psychol. Cult. **2**(1), 2307-0919 (2011)
26. Smith, E.: The growing demand for digital skills in global development, Devex. https://www.devex.com/news/the-growing-demand-for-digital-skills-in-global-development-94971. Accessed 7 Sept 2020

Data Quality Categories with a First Exploration Towards Agility

Christian Ploder(✉), Reinhard Bernsteiner, Stephan Schlögl,
Rebecca Weichelt, and Sofia Herfert

Management, Communication and IT, MCI Entrepreneurial School,
Universitätsstrasse 15, 6020 Innsbruck, Austria
christian.ploder@mci.edu

Abstract. Currently, data quality is in the spotlight of research and organizations. It derives from new technological developments, such as the Internet of Things (IoT), which provides unprecedented amounts of data and enables new ways of creating knowledge. The interim value is hidden in the flood of data and has already received many industries such as construction, manufacturing, and healthcare. These organizations adopt data applications to extract critical information to understand its purpose better, leading to a competitive advantage. In parallel to gain these positive effects based on struggling around with the data, the quality of data and the decisions are neglected very often. Decisions must be made quickly in response to changing requirements. Thereby, agile methods and approaches can be successfully and profitably applied. The decisive factor for success is the holistic view of architecture, organization, technology, and adapted process models. Due to the given ideas, research on data quality combined with agile companies is still in its infancy. This paper presents categories for data quality in combination agility based on literature and expert interviews to close this gap and establish a foundation for future research.

Keywords: Data quality · Agile methods · Data quality audit

1 Introduction

The main challenges companies face today are the pressures of globalized and digitized markets, in combination with the need to adapt continuously [30]. Since the beginning of the 21st century, the world has experienced several significant changes in information technology, such as the Internet of Things, cloud computing, or social networks [22]. While rapidly increasing processing power, communication speed, and ubiquitous device connections, these technological innovations are new vital factors for competitive advantage [21]. As such, they all produce and process enormous amounts of data. This phenomenon is called "Datafication" and describes the ability to transform aspects of daily life into

© Springer Nature Switzerland AG 2021
L. Uden et al. (Eds.): KMO 2021, CCIS 1438, pp. 429–443, 2021.
https://doi.org/10.1007/978-3-030-81635-3_35

data to maximize utilization [10]. Data quality challenges include diverse data sources producing heterogeneous data types, a massive volume of data leading to difficulties in assessing data quality in a reasonable time, very short timeliness of data, and a lack of standards for data quality [22]. Data quality is not just a one-dimensional concept. It instead can be described as the superset of all data quality dimensions [7,99,103]. Data quality consists of (i) inherent quality attributes that relate directly to the data (accuracy, timeliness, consistency or completeness), and (ii) surrounding quality attributes for the design that are intended to meet the user needs (e.g., accessibility) [85]. Thus, a holistic framework is required, comprising data and corresponding technological innovations, focusing on data storage, provision, formats, processing, and analytics [21]. As data becomes less structured, data quality techniques are becoming increasingly complex [15] and new data storage solutions have to be developed. As such, the data warehouse provides a complex structure, for which data must be cleaned before storage [18,41]. However, the advantage is that the IT department has full control over all data, and only qualified data is in the repository. A data lake offers more flexibility and no restrictions on data storage [67,71].[1] Since the data is not prepared until it is read out, it is available more quickly [49]. However, one difficulty is to keep track of the analyses and ensure that users handle the data with care. In practice, therefore, a combination of both approaches is being applied more often. These three architecture parts are critical components for the data infrastructure and main challenges combined with long-term data quality. In addition to the ideal technology setup, companies need agile structures that adapt to change, innovations, and customer requirements and that effectively acquire and implement knowledge [80]. The concept of agile incorporates recurring cycles, allowing for iterative development [29]. Further, cross organizational teams organize themselves while including frequent customer feedback [102]. Agile methods are characterized by flexibility [64], speed [101], competence [64,82], leanness [60,73,75], resuability [63,66], scalability [83] and responsiveness [20]. The necessity to introduce agile concepts in companies can also be justified by the VUCA model [65]. VUCA stands for central aspects of the changes, such as volatility, uncertainty, complexity, and ambiguity. In any case, recent exogenous developments seem to provide sufficient reason to take a more systematic reactive or proactive approach to change. The circular construction of agile processes thereby might allow to inspect data quality regularly. Building on previous research findings on data quality and agility, the main objective is to investigate the relationship between the two topics of interest. Therefore, the research question is formulated as *Which influencing categories enable a combination of long-term data quality and agility?* After describing the methodological approach in Sect. 2 the results are presented and discussed (Sect. 3). Lastly, the research question will be answered within a summary given in Sect. 4. In Sect. 5 the limitations of this work are given.

---

[1] Brunet, P. (2018). Data Lakes: Just a swamp without data governance and catalog. Retrieved 08 January 2021 from: https://www.infoworld.com/article/3290433/data-lakes-just-a-swamp-without-data-governance-and-catalog.html.

2   Methodology

This chapter presents the methodological approach used to conduct this research study. First, the literature analysis is shown, followed by the detailed guidelines of the interviews.

2.1   Literature Review

The search strategy for collecting relevant studies includes using standard electronic databases, which were suggested for conducting a systematic literature review [53]. The data used in this work was collected from different electronic databases, being Web of Science, IEEE Xplore Digital Library, ACM Digital Library, Science Direct, and Google Scholar. The search strings are visible in Table 1. The applied search strategy included capturing keywords by reading the papers found in an initial search and by using the PICOC (Population-Intervention Comparison-Outcome) criteria [53]. Second, the notion of backward and forward search from Webster and Watson (2002) [100] was applied. The criteria to include papers to the review are defined as follows: Academic papers and business articles focusing on the research question and topic (Standards on Data Quality and Agility), written in English and published after 2014. The instructions of Guyatt, Rennie, Meade, and Cook (2002) [46] were followed to evaluate the quality of the selected primary studies. Carefully applying the screening and excluding unrelated research from full-text reading, a total number of 85 sources were taken into consideration.

Table 1. Population and Intervention for search string

Population	Intervention
"Data quality" AND	("data quality requirements" OR "data quality attributes" OR "data quality challenges" OR "data quality assurance" OR "data quality dimensions" OR "good data quality")
"Data quality" AND	("data management" OR "agility management" OR "agile management" OR "metadata management")
"Data quality" AND	("long-term" OR "short-term" OR "maintenance" OR "lasting" OR "lifelong" OR "continuing" OR "extended")
"Data quality" AND	("agility" OR "agile" OR "agile analytics")
"Data quality" AND	("dynamic" OR "flexible")
"Data quality" AND	("data-driven" OR "decision making") AND ("agile" OR "agility")

2.2   Interviews

As an expansion of the literature review, additional interviews were conducted to gain more insights into long-term data quality and agility. The guideline for the semi-structured interviews were divided into four sections: (i) purpose of the interviews, (ii) providing an understanding of high quality and agile business processes, (iii) implementation of the questionnaire, and (iv) discussion of the drivers that describe the different terms. All expert interviews were recorded, manually transcribed, and encoded, following Mayrings (2004) approach [68]. The three experts were selected from different companies to represent a broader group of experts. The specialists are top players either in the field of data quality or agility, since we could not find experts in both fields. Nonetheless, the participants were carefully selected while ensuring their expertise in one of the research fields of interest. The average age of the participants is 38 years. The selection of the different professional roles provides a solid basis for expert interviews: one start-up CEO, one team leader, and one agility specialist. The two latter experts work in a medium-sized construction or industrial company. The start-up company is from Finland, and the other companies are located in Germany. The participants were either suggested by companies or contacted via LinkedIn. Participation in the interview was voluntary and lasted 30 min. Two interviews could be conducted in the office, one via Microsoft teams. The interviews took place from May to June 2020.

3   Results

In this section, first the results of the literature review are presented. This is followed by the findings of the interviews. In particular, the main topics of data quality and agility are addressed, and their particular quality characteristics are successively explained.

3.1   Literature Findings

The literature was classified according to components or services that are relevant to data quality. Therefrom the categories of Management (26 papers), Data Source (11 papers), Data Fitness (30 papers), Tools and Technologies (13 papers), Organizational Agility (2 papers), Organizational Environment (3 papers), Organizational Analytics (14 papers) and People Aspect (7 papers) could be identified. Some of the papers even belong into multiple categories as visible in Table 2.

Management. The categories of data quality management, data governance, and metadata can all be grouped under the primary term of Management. Under this term, the focus is on data life cycle management, analysis procedures, integration of information in panels, data transformation into knowledge, the definition of guidelines, and organizational management structures. These

Table 2. Reviewed literature

Data quality components	Papers
Data quality management	$[1,2,26,45,61,69,88]^a$
Data governance	$[3–5,14,52,61,72,76,79]^b$
Metadata	$[10,32,48,55,58,78,86,98]$
Data source	$[1,10,16,22,24,25,35,36,43,86,106]$
Data profiling	$[13,24,28,74,88]$
Data pre-processing	$[36,42,50,86,87,90,91,96]$
Data assessment	$[10,22,27,33,44,48,55,70,77,81,86,88,91,92]$
Data assurance	$[11,34,38,105]$
Tools and technology	$[19,29,38,47,54,56,59,62,67,74,94,95,105]$
Organizational agility	$[47,97]$
Organizational environment	$[8,12,93]$
Organizational analytics	$[6,8,17,23,31,37,39,40,42,54,57,59,81,93]$
People aspect	$[9,23,31,51,84,89]^c$

[a] Lebied, M. (2018). Ultimate Guide to Modern Data Quality Management (DQM) For An Effective Data Quality Control Driven by The Right Metrics. Retrieved 08 January 2021, from Datapine website: https://www.datapine.com/blog/data-quality-management-and-metrics/

[b] Brunet, P. (2018). Data Lakes: Just a swa mp without data governance and catalog. Retrieved 08 January 2021 from: https://www.infoworld.com/article/3290433/data-lakes-just-a-swamp-without-data-governance-and-catalog.html

[c] Valentine, C., & Merchan, W. (2016). DataOps: An Agile Methodology for Data-Driven Organizations Data Science and Machine Learning in the Enterprise. Retrieved 08. January 2021 from Oracle, Datasience.com website: https://www.oracle.com/cn/a/ocom/docs/oracleds-data-ops-map-r.pdf

challenges relate to the need to define an enterprise data strategy and configure the ideal model for the administration and management of enterprise data to facilitate the value-added processes [69]. Data quality is not solely related to data but also to how information is used, influenced, and supported by data management. Thereto, different frameworks exist [45,88]. In this context, Cichy, and Rass (2019) [26] provide decision support among different methods to identify the most appropriate framework for the company. Lillie and Eybers (2019) [61] review in their paper the importance of data management in the context of agility. They found that incremental development requires the initiation of measures at an early stage to steer projects in the desired direction. Besides, data governance and agility can be described as symbiotic twins. Skill relies on proactively maintaining its operational integrity to redirect resources into proactive decision-making rather than responding to external and internal threats. That's why governance enables agility - especially when it comes to data. Finding the right balance between agility and governance can be difficult, but maintaining that balance equals increased revenue from your data insights. Further, the supply of metadata provides additional information about data and thus supports the understandability of data structure, quality, and origin [10, 78, 98]. Metadata management should be present in every project, so increase the understandability and interoperability of data to lead to declining costs and time [48, 55, 58]. Besides, the concept must be worked out early in the project to be carried out promptly during the activities. After all, outdated metadata harbors the great danger of drawing the wrong conclusions.

Data Source. The challenges posed by the diversity of data are mainly storage problems, leading to outgrown standards [24, 43, 86, 106]. In the current discussion about building efficient architectures that can cope with the heterogeneity of structures, data, agility requirements, and cost reduction for development are increasingly relevant. The needs of the entire company must already be taken into consideration when collecting and originating data to ensure data quality and to be able to define appropriate measures from a holistic perspective.

Data Fitness. The categories of data profiling, data pre-processing, data assessment, and data assurance can be grouped under data fitness.

Data profiling includes the processes, tools, and skilled resources required to identify characteristics and understand the meaning and structure of critical data, conduct root-causes, and impact analyses [28]. This leads to the benefits of understanding whether the data is fit for purpose, reduced cycle times for critical projects, and the possibility to compare the data with user expectations [28]. Certain data pre-processing and improvement techniques are required to avoid costly consequences from low data quality. Frequent pre-processing activities according to Taleb, Dssouli, and Serhani (2015) [90] are: Data integration, outlier detection, interpolation, data enhancements or enrichment, data transformation, data reduction, data discretization, data de-duplication, and data cleaning. The pre-processing of data is crucial for data quality. It can be seen as the activity of making data "fit for purpose". Additionally data assessment is a set of methods, analyses, and data quality rules applied to measure the quality of critical data. In the context of agility, this means ensuring scalable data storage and processing performance, e.g., for real-time data quality assessment, and the ability to store heterogeneous data structures. Data quality assurance ensures the quality of the data in the context of quality characteristics [38]. Artač et al. (2016) [11] combine model-based quality assurance and agility by introducing DICER, a model-driven framework for continuous deployment based on Model-Driven Engineering (MDE) and DevOps. Model-driven approaches can lead to ultimate flexibility, system quality, and maintainability in the long run by making changes to software components (i.e., extensions) more accessible and less expensive. Furthermore, some authors, such as Yu and Zhang (2017) [104] already define model-driven approaches as crucial prerequisites for quality assurance of data applications.

Tools and Technologies. Scalability can be described as a critical requirement [54,59,74]. Scalability should ensure a flexible expansion or deduction of data storage and processing performance, e.g., for real-time data quality assessment and the ability to store heterogeneous data structures [62,67]. Model-driven approaches and cloud solutions are the technologies of choice based on their flexibility and cost-efficiency [38,105].

Organizational Agility. Agility, sometimes flexibility, refers to rapid adaptation to change, which seems crucial in the fast-paced environment of companies and requirements [47,97]. Organizations need to identify and react to transactions in real-time. They must also reflect deeply on what is being monitored to identify critical weak signals and nascent patterns (agility implies the ability to deliver efficient decisions; this efficiency arises from profound reflection supported and influenced by the analysis of massive amounts of data). As this feedback loop becomes closer, it drastically improves detection (agility necessitates a quick reaction, relying on analytical insight and a lean operational structure).

Organizational Environment. The commitment to agility extends far beyond merely recommending new guidelines and processes; it demands that management reconsiders organizational structures, functionalities, and time-intensive management practices, including planning, budgeting, reward and measurement systems with a deep focus on the status quo [8]. By looking at agility in the context of dynamic capabilities, one can conclude that agility should only be pursued following the requirements of the business environment and corporate strategy. The type of agility that (entrepreneurial) managers choose should depend on their strategy and market positioning and their desire to prepare for both negative and positive developments [93]. Three leading practices, including the analysis of past data, monitoring current activity, and predicting the future, should be given high priority [12].

Organizational Analytics. Comprehensive data analysis based business process management systems can promote ambidextrous organizations' agility by enabling the monitoring of consumer behavior patterns and internal processes while providing evidence of the flow of information to the actors involved in process management. Therefore, they could increase the speed of the decision-making process, which is consistent with the quest for ambidextrous organizations [8]. Agile skills, combined with leadership capabilities, provide improved control and management of the impact of environmental and moderation facilities [61].

People Aspect. Agility is a cultural characteristic of employees throughout the organization. An agile culture improves employees' abilities and skills to manage decision-making resting on technology and analysis. According to

ISO/IEC 27002:2017, roles must be defined and documented to protect information resources from unauthorized access, modification, or destruction [89]. Both roles and responsibilities should be considered in the application design to define the proper access controls and audits. Further, the cooperation between teams, team members, and customers are decisive for a successful performance. Also, the collaboration with the client is another factor to be considered. Using agile methods, the employees have regular touchpoints with the customer through the scheduled reviews.

3.2   Results of the Interviews

In this section, the results are presented in chronological congruence to the theoretical background.

Business Value. Agility's value contribution is seen in the generation and maintenance of competitive advantages: to react to changes faster than the competition and generate new changes from within the company. Thus, agility becomes very important. Further, it is mentioned that data quality is an essential driver for correct decision-making, reinforced by agility. A change towards agility usually involves both hard and soft factors and often requires extensive cultural adjustments. It, therefore, represents a demanding, comprehensive, and long-term project for the company. Therefore, utilizing successfully integrated agility, change processes can be continuously initiated and integrated into everyday life.

Business Needs. The respondents noted that many companies have difficulties in collecting decision-specific data and data collection. Organizations need to establish data courier processes related to the active management of data throughout its life cycle to ensure that it meets data quality requirements for practical use. This step is often neglected because users of data applications, e.g., executives, misinterpret them as static. The user carries out the evaluation of the data and information regarding their individual quality at the moment of use and the moment to understand the problem to be solved, which allows deciding which data will be used to tackle the problem. Thus, the origin and use of the data plays a decisive role for him. However, all experts agreed that several factors play together to increase quality and agility.

Process and Technology. The interviewees freely named a wide variety of actions, with which the goal of increasing data quality and agility in their company is being addressed. Exemplary actions are: "Elimination of parallelism, redundancy, harmonization, and centralization", "flat hierarchies", "lean and lean management", "standardization, and "silos". In contrast to what many expect, standardization is a crucial criterion and a critical prerequisite and component for accelerating agility and data quality. Standardization enables fast and structured actions that are also flexibly scalable at any time. Simultaneously, the interviews also show that agility in companies cannot be controlled to a sufficient degree. When asked about the extent to which agility is already being measured in companies, almost all participants stated that they do not use any metrics to measure agility.

People. Accountability is required for data that is accessible and used by many people, which requires roles and responsibilities that should be embedded in the application. Data Accountability is essential to define access control and authorization of data or to perform granular checks. "Data quality is not a one-man show - data quality concerns the whole organization" as stated by an expert. An expert has a dedicated team that regularly incorporates data quality change measures. Currently, the technology used is only as efficient as the people. Therefore, there are multiple data quality management roles that need to be staffed. Data quality is not just about tools and technology; it has an enormous need for people, knowledge workers who understand their business, data, and aligning data with the company. Furthermore, everyone agrees that flat hierarchies and diversity increase agility.

4   Summary

Concerning the research question, the authors could identify that many factors influence the application of agility while maintaining long-term data quality. The decisive factor for success is the holistic view of architecture, organization, technology, and adapted process models. These results indicate that long-term data quality from the point of view of agility holds an enormous value potential for managers of industrial companies and provides opportunities for better and faster responses to change and decisions.

5   Limitations and Potential Future Work

The most significant limitation of this work is the evaluation part. The required information is compiled from various web articles and papers. However, we could not find any publications in the literature within the domain of agility and data quality in combination. Unfortunately, the various methods presented cannot be further validated in the context of this paper and should be tested based on a use case or a study. Also, the extent to which organizations need to adopt agile methods cannot be addressed in this framework. Besides, other researchers' further classifications could lead to a better understanding of the completeness and value of this paper. An increase in the reviewed literature, including other standards, using different search methods to identify studies, or a greater focus on real-world applications in defining such a classification might provide future directions for new research.

References

1. Abbasi, A., Sarker, S., Chiang, R.H.: Big data research in information systems: toward an inclusive research agenda. J. Assoc. Inf. Syst. **17**(2), 3 (2016)
2. Abdallah, M.: Big data quality challenges. In: 2019 International Conference on Big Data and Computational Intelligence (ICBDCI), pp. 1–3. IEEE (2019)
3. Abraham, R., Schneider, J., vom Brocke, J.: Data governance: a conceptual framework, structured review, and research agenda. J. Assoc. Inf. Syst. **49**, 424–438 (2019)
4. Al-Badi, A., Tarhini, A., Khan, A.I.: Exploring big data governance frameworks. Procedia Comput. Sci. **141**, 271–277 (2018)
5. Aljumaili, M., Karim, R., Tretten, P.: Data quality assessment using multi-attribute maintenance perspective. Int. J. Inf. Dec. Sci. **10**(2), 147–161 (2018)
6. Ambler, S.W., Lines, M.: The disciplined agile process decision framework. In: Winkler, D., Biffl, S., Bergsmann, J. (eds.) SWQD 2016. LNBIP, vol. 238, pp. 3–14. Springer, Cham (2016). https://doi.org/10.1007/978-3-319-27033-3_1
7. Apel, D., Behme, W., Eberlein, R., Merighi, C.: Successfully control data quality: Practice solutions for business intelligence projects. Heidelberg: dpunkt. verlag (2015)
8. Appelbaum, S.H., Calla, R., Desautels, D., Hasan, L.: The challenges of organizational agility (part 1). Industrial and Commercial Training (2017)
9. Appelbaum, S.H., Calla, R., Desautels, D., Hasan, L.N.: The challenges of organizational agility: part 2. Industrial and Commercial Training (2017)
10. Ardagna, D., Cappiello, C., Samá, W., Vitali, M.: Context-aware data quality assessment for big data. Futur. Gener. Comput. Syst. **89**, 548–562 (2018)
11. Artač, M., Borovšak, T., Di Nitto, E., Guerriero, M., Tamburri, D.A.: Model-driven continuous deployment for quality DevOps. In: Proceedings of the 2nd International Workshop on Quality-Aware DevOps, pp. 40–41 (2016)
12. Ashrafi, A., Ravasan, A.Z., Trkman, P., Afshari, S.: The role of business analytics capabilities in bolstering firms' agility and performance. Int. J. Inf. Manage. **47**, 1–15 (2019)
13. Azeroual, O., Saake, G., Schallehn, E.: Analyzing data quality issues in research information systems via data profiling. Int. J. Inf. Manage. **41**, 50–56 (2018)
14. Barker, J.M.: Data Governance: the missing approach to improving data quality. University of Phoenix (2016)
15. Batini, C., Cappiello, C., Francalanci, C., Maurino, A.: Methodologies for data quality assessment and improvement. ACM Comput. Surveys (CSUR) **41**(3), 1–52 (2009)
16. Batini, C., Rula, A., Scannapieco, M., Viscusi, G.: From data quality to big data quality. In: Big Data: Concepts, Methodologies, Tools, and Applications, pp. 1934–1956. IGI Global (2016)
17. Batra, D.: Adapting agile practices for data warehousing, business intelligence, and analytics. J. Database Manage. (JDM) **28**(4), 1–23 (2017)
18. Bauer, A., Günzel, H.: Data-Warehouse-Systeme: Architektur. Anwendung. dpunkt. verlag, Entwicklung (2013)
19. Benkhaled, H.N., Berrabah, D.: Data quality management for data warehouse systems: state of the art. In: JERI (2019)
20. Bernardes, E.S., Hanna, M.D.: A theoretical review of flexibility, agility and responsiveness in the operations management literature: toward a conceptual definition of customer responsiveness. Int. J. Oper. Prod. Manage. **29**(1), 30–53 (2009)

21. Caballero, I., Serrano, M., Piattini, M.: A data quality in use model for big data. In: Indulska, M., Purao, S. (eds.) ER 2014. LNCS, vol. 8823, pp. 65–74. Springer, Cham (2014). https://doi.org/10.1007/978-3-319-12256-4_7

22. Cai, L., Zhu, Y.: The challenges of data quality and data quality assessment in the big data era. Data Sci. J. **14**, 1–10 (2015). https://doi.org/10.5334/dsj-2015-002

23. Chen, H.M., Kazman, R., Haziyev, S.: Agile big data analytics development: An architecture-centric approach. In: 2016 49th Hawaii International Conference on System Sciences (HICSS), pp. 5378–5387. IEEE (2016)

24. Chen, M., Mao, S., Liu, Y.: Big data: a survey. Mob. Netw. Appl. **19**(2), 171–209 (2014)

25. Cheng, G., Li, Y., Gao, Z., Liu, X.: Cloud data governance maturity model. In: 2017 8th IEEE International Conference on Software Engineering and Service Science (ICSESS), pp. 517–520. IEEE (2017)

26. Cichy, C., Rass, S.: An overview of data quality frameworks. IEEE Access **7**, 24634–24648 (2019)

27. Côrte-Real, N., Ruivo, P., Oliveira, T.: Leveraging internet of things and big data analytics initiatives in european and american firms: Is data quality a way to extract business value? Information & Management **57**(1), 103141 (2020)

28. Dai, W., Wardlaw, I., Cui, Yu., Mehdi, K., Li, Y., Long, J.: Data profiling technology of data governance regarding big data: review and rethinking. Information Technology: New Generations. AISC, vol. 448, pp. 439–450. Springer, Cham (2016). https://doi.org/10.1007/978-3-319-32467-8_39

29. De Donato, R., Ferretti, G., Marciano, A., Palmieri, G., Pirozzi, D., Scarano, V., Vicidomini, L.: Agile production of high quality open data. In: Proceedings of the 19th Annual International Conference on Digital Government Research: Governance in the Data Age, pp. 1–10 (2018)

30. Dewi, M.U., Mekaniwati, A., Nurendah, Y., Cakranegara, P., Arief, A.S.: Globalization challenges of micro small and medium enterprises. Eur. J. Mol. Clin. Med. **7**(11), 1909–1915 (2020)

31. Dharmapal, S.R., Sikamani, K.T.: Big data analytics using agile model. In: 2016 International Conference on Electrical, Electronics, and Optimization Techniques (ICEEOT), pp. 1088–1091. IEEE (2016)

32. Dinter, B., Gluchowski, P., Schieder, C.: A stakeholder lens on metadata management in business intelligence and big data-results of an empirical investigation (2015)

33. El Alaoui, I., Gahi, Y., Messoussi, R.: Big data quality metrics for sentiment analysis approaches. In: Proceedings of the 2019 International Conference on Big Data Engineering, pp. 36–43 (2019)

34. El Bekri, N., Peinsipp-Byma, E.: Assuring data quality by placing the user in the loop. In: 2016 International Conference on Computational Science and Computational Intelligence (CSCI), pp. 468–471. IEEE (2016)

35. Fang, W., Wen, X.Z., Zheng, Y., Zhou, M.: A survey of big data security and privacy preserving. IETE Tech. Rev. **34**(5), 544–560 (2017)

36. Framework, D.N.B.D.I.: Draft nist big data interoperability framework: Volume 6, reference architecture. NIST Special Publication 1500, 6 (2015)

37. Franková, P., Drahošová, M., Balco, P.: Agile project management approach and its use in big data management. In: ANT/SEIT, pp. 576–583 (2016)

38. Gao, J., Xie, C., Tao, C.: Big data validation and quality assurance-issues, challenges, and needs. In: 2016 IEEE Symposium on Service-Oriented System Engineering (SOSE), pp. 433–441. IEEE (2016)

39. Ghasemaghaei, M., Hassanein, K., Turel, O.: Increasing firm agility through the use of data analytics: the role of fit. Decis. Support Syst. **101**, 95–105 (2017)
40. Gill, A.Q., Henderson-Sellers, B., Niazi, M.: Scaling for agility: a reference model for hybrid traditional-agile software development methodologies. Inf. Syst. Front. **20**(2), 315–341 (2018)
41. Gluchowski, P., Gabriel, R., Dittmar, C.: Management support systeme und business intelligence: Computergestützte Informationssysteme für Fach-und Führungskräfte. Springer-Verlag (2007)
42. Grady, N.W., Payne, J.A., Parker, H.: Agile big data analytics: analyticsops for data science. In: 2017 IEEE International Conference on Big Data (Big Data), pp. 2331–2339. IEEE (2017)
43. Gudivada, V.N., Rao, D., Grosky, W.I.: Data quality centric application framework for big data. ALLDATA **2016**, 33 (2016)
44. Günther, L.C., Colangelo, E., Wiendahl, H.H., Bauer, C.: Data quality assessment for improved decision-making: a methodology for small and medium-sized enterprises. Procedia Manuf. **29**, 583–591 (2019)
45. Gupta, S., Modgil, S., Gunasekaran, A.: Big data in lean six sigma: a review and further research directions. Int. J. Prod. Res. **58**(3), 947–969 (2020)
46. Guyatt, G., Rennie, D., Meade, M., Cook, D., et al.: Users' guides to the medical literature: a manual for evidence-based clinical practice, vol. 706. AMA press Chicago (2002)
47. Hashem, I.A.T., Yaqoob, I., Anuar, N.B., Mokhtar, S., Gani, A., Khan, S.U.: The rise of "big data" on cloud computing: review and open research issues. Inf. Syst. **47**, 98–115 (2015)
48. Immonen, A., Pääkkönen, P., Ovaska, E.: Evaluating the quality of social media data in big data architecture. IEEE Access **3**, 2028–2043 (2015)
49. John, T., Misra, P.: Data Lake for Enterprises. Packt Publishing Ltd, Birmingham (2017)
50. Karkouch, A., Mousannif, H., Al Moatassime, H., Noel, T.: Data quality in internet of things: a state-of-the-art survey. J. Netw. Comput. Appl. **73**, 57–81 (2016)
51. Karvonen, T., Sharp, H., Barroca, L.: Enterprise agility: why is transformation so hard? In: Garbajosa, J., Wang, X., Aguiar, A. (eds.) XP 2018. LNBIP, vol. 314, pp. 131–145. Springer, Cham (2018). https://doi.org/10.1007/978-3-319-91602-6_9
52. Kim, H.Y., Cho, J.S.: Data governance framework for big data implementation with NPS case analysis in Korea. J. Bus. Retail Manage. Res. **12**(3), 36–46 (2018)
53. Kitchenham, B., Charters, S.: Guidelines for performing systematic literature reviews in software engineering (2007)
54. Kitchens, B., Dobolyi, D., Li, J., Abbasi, A.: Advanced customer analytics: strategic value through integration of relationship-oriented big data. J. Manag. Inf. Syst. **35**(2), 540–574 (2018)
55. Kläs, M., Putz, W., Lutz, T.: Quality evaluation for big data: a scalable assessment approach and first evaluation results. In: 2016 Joint Conference of the International Workshop on Software Measurement and the International Conference on Software Process and Product Measurement (IWSM-MENSURA), pp. 115–124. IEEE (2016)
56. Kousalya, D.R., Sindhupriya, T.: Review on big data analytics and Hadoop framework. Int. J. Innov. Sci. Eng. Res. (IJISER), ISSN: 2347–9728 (print) **4**(3MAR), 101 (2017)

57. Krawatzeck, R., Dinter, B., Thi, D.A.P.: How to make business intelligence agile: the agile bi actions catalog. In: 2015 48th Hawaii International Conference on System Sciences, pp. 4762–4771. IEEE (2015)
58. Kulkarni, A.: A study on metadata management and quality evaluation in big data management. Int. J. Res. Appl. Sci. Eng. Technol. (IJRASET) 4(VII) (2016)
59. Larson, D., Chang, V.: A review and future direction of agile, business intelligence, analytics and data science. Int. J. Inf. Manage. 36(5), 700–710 (2016)
60. Li, S., Rao, S.S., Ragu-Nathan, T., Ragu-Nathan, B.: Development and validation of a measurement instrument for studying supply chain management practices. J. Oper. Manage. 23(6), 618–641 (2005)
61. Lillie, T., Eybers, S.: Identifying the constructs and agile capabilities of data governance and data management: a review of the literature. In: Krauss, K., Turpin, M., Naude, F. (eds.) IDIA 2018. CCIS, vol. 933, pp. 313–326. Springer, Cham (2019). https://doi.org/10.1007/978-3-030-11235-6_20
62. Llave, M.R.: Data lakes in business intelligence: reporting from the trenches. Procedia computer science 138, 516–524 (2018)
63. Luna, A.J.D.O., Kruchten, P., de Moura, H.P.: Agile governance theory: conceptual development. arXiv preprint arXiv:1505.06701 (2015)
64. Luna, A.J.D.O., Kruchten, P., Pedrosa, M.L.D.E., Neto, H.R., de Moura, H.P.: State of the art of agile governance: a systematic review. arXiv preprint arXiv:1411.1922 (2014)
65. Mack, O., Khare, A., Krämer, A., Burgartz, T.: Managing in a VUCA World. Springer, Heidelberg (2015). https://doi.org/10.1007/978-3-319-16889-0
66. Martini, A., Pareto, L., Bosch, J.: Enablers and inhibitors for speed with reuse. In: Proceedings of the 16th International Software Product Line Conference, vol. 1, pp. 116–125 (2012)
67. Mathis, C.: Data lakes. Datenbank-Spektrum 17(3), 289–293 (2017)
68. Mayring, P.: Qualitative content analysis. A Companion Qual. Res. 1(2004), 159–176 (2004)
69. de Medeiros, M.M., Hoppen, N., Maçada, A.C.G.: Data science for business: benefits, challenges and opportunities. The Bottom Line (2020)
70. Merino, J., Caballero, I., Rivas, B., Serrano, M., Piattini, M.: A data quality in use model for big data. Futur. Gener. Comput. Syst. 63, 123–130 (2016)
71. Miloslavskaya, N., Tolstoy, A.: Big data, fast data and data lake concepts. Procedia Comput. Sci. 88(300–305), 63 (2016)
72. Morabito, V.: Big data and analytics. Strategic and organisational impacts (2015)
73. Motwani, J.: A business process change framework for examining lean manufacturing: a case study. Ind. Manage. Data Syst. 94, 17–21 (2003)
74. Münzberg, A., Sauer, J., Hein, A., Rösch, N.: The use of ETL and data profiling to integrate data and improve quality in food databases. In: 2018 14th International Conference on Wireless and Mobile Computing, Networking and Communications (WiMob), pp. 231–238. IEEE (2018)
75. Nafei, W.A.: Organizational agility: the key to organizational success. Int. J. Bus. Manage. 11(5), 296–309 (2016)
76. Otto, B.: Quality and value of the data resource in large enterprises. Inf. Syst. Manag. 32(3), 234–251 (2015)
77. Otto, B., Österle, H.: Corporate Data Quality: Prerequisite for Successful Business Models. epubli (2015)
78. Pawar, S.H., Thakore, D.: An assessment model to evaluate quality attributes in big data quality. Int. J. Comput. Sci. Trends Technol. 5(2), 373–376 (2017)

79. Rau, K.G.: Effective governance of it: design objectives, roles, and relationships. Inf. Syst. Manag. **21**(4), 35–42 (2004)
80. Ravichandran, T.: Exploring the relationships between it competence, innovation capacity and organizational agility. J. Strateg. Inf. Syst. **27**(1), 22–42 (2018)
81. Ji-fan Ren, S., Fosso Wamba, S., Akter, S., Dubey, R., Childe, S.J.: Modelling quality dynamics, business value and firm performance in a big data analytics environment. Int. J. Prod. Res. **55**(17), 5011–5026 (2017)
82. Rick, U., Vossen, R., Richert, A., Henning, K.: Designing agile processes in information management. In: 2010 2nd IEEE International Conference on Information Management and Engineering, pp. 156–160. IEEE (2010)
83. Rys, M.: Scalable SQL. Commun. ACM **54**(6), 48–53 (2011)
84. Sanaa, H., Afifi, W.A., Darwish, N.R.: The goal questions metrics for agile business intelligence. Egyptian Comput. Sci. J. **40**(2), 24–42 (2016)
85. Scannapieco, M., Catarci, T.: Data quality under a computer science perspective. Archivi Comput. **2**, 1–15 (2002)
86. Serhani, M.A., El Kassabi, H.T., Taleb, I., Nujum, A.: An hybrid approach to quality evaluation across big data value chain. In: 2016 IEEE International Congress on Big Data (BigData Congress), pp. 418–425. IEEE (2016)
87. Shankaranarayanan, G., Blake, R.: From content to context: the evolution and growth of data quality research. J. Data Inf. Qual. (JDIQ) **8**(2), 1–28 (2017)
88. for Standardization, I.O.: ISO 8000–61: Data quality management: Process reference model. ISO (2016)
89. For Standardization, I.O., Commission, I.E.: Information Technology-Security Techniques-Code of Practice for Information Security Management: ISO/IEC 27002. ISO/IEC (2005)
90. Taleb, I., Dssouli, R., Serhani, M.A.: Big data pre-processing: a quality framework. In: 2015 IEEE International Congress on Big Data, pp. 191–198. IEEE (2015)
91. Taleb, I., Serhani, M.A.: Big data pre-processing: Closing the data quality enforcement loop. In: 2017 IEEE International Congress on Big Data (BigData Congress), pp. 498–501. IEEE (2017)
92. Tantsyura, V., et al.: Impact on data management of the new definitions of data quality (DQ), risk-based approaches to quality and esource methodologies (2016)
93. Teece, D., Peteraf, M., Leih, S.: Dynamic capabilities and organizational agility: risk, uncertainty, and strategy in the innovation economy. Calif. Manage. Rev. **58**(4), 13–35 (2016)
94. Terrizzano, I.G., Schwarz, P.M., Roth, M., Colino, J.E.: Data wrangling: The challenging yourney from the wild to the lake. In: CIDR (2015)
95. Theodorou, V., Abelló, A., Lehner, W., Thiele, M.: Quality measures for ETL processes: from goals to implementation. Concurrency Comput. Pract. Experience **28**(15), 3969–3993 (2016)
96. Uçaktürk, A., Uçaktürk, T., Yavuz, H.: Possibilities of usage of strategic business intelligence systems based on databases in agile manufacturing. Procedia Soc. Behav. Sci. **207**, 234–241 (2015)
97. Unhelkar, B.: Big Data Strategies for Agile Business. CRC Press, Boca Raton (2017)
98. Wahyudi, A., Kuk, G., Janssen, M.: A process pattern model for tackling and improving big data quality. Inf. Syst. Front. **20**(3), 457–469 (2018)
99. Wang, R.Y., Strong, D.M.: Beyond accuracy: what data quality means to data consumers. J. Manag. Inf. Syst. **12**(4), 5–33 (1996)
100. Webster, J., Watson, R.T.: Analyzing the past to prepare for the future: writing a literature review. MIS Q. **26**(2), xiii–xxiii (2002)

101. Wixom, B.H., Yen, B., Relich, M.: Maximizing value from business analytics. MIS Q. Executive **12**(2), 111–123 (2013)
102. Wolf, H., Bleek, W.G.: Agile softwareentwicklung: Werte, konzepte und methoden. dpunkt. verlag (2011)
103. Würthele, V.: Data Quality Metric for Information Processes. ETH Zurich, Zurich (2003)
104. Yu, H., Zhang, M.: Data pricing strategy based on data quality. Comput. Ind. Eng. **112**, 1–10 (2017)
105. Zhang, P., Zhou, X., Li, W., Gao, J.: A survey on quality assurance techniques for big data applications. In: 2017 IEEE Third International Conference on Big Data Computing Service and Applications (BigDataService), pp. 313–319. IEEE (2017)
106. Zhang, Q., et al.: Understanding the effect of data center resource disaggregation on production DBMSs. Proc. VLDB Endowment **13**(9), 1568–1581 (2020)

Will Robots Take My Job? Exploring the Effect of Artificial Intelligence in Taiwan's Labor Market

Chu-Chen Rosa Yeh, Cze Chiun Wong, Chia-Chun Amanda Liang, and Wei-Wen Chang[✉]

Graduate Institute of International Human Resource Development, National Taiwan Normal University, 162, Section 1, Heping E. Rd., Taipei, Taiwan, ROC
changw@ntnu.edu.tw

Abstract. The rise of artificial intelligence (AI) and related new technologies have received a lot of attention from the public. In Taiwan, the government and enterprises are also making efforts to develop these technologies. Against this backdrop, and with the massive unemployment that resulted from automation in the third industrial revolution, human workers are anxious about their jobs being replaced by smart robots. On the contrary, many scholars hold a positive view and suggest that technologies augment and enhance human capabilities. Therefore, in order to better understand the present situation in Taiwan, this research was designed to explore the relationship of AI and jobs by adopting a qualitative approach for data collection. Two sessions of focus group discussion were conducted with eight practitioners from different industries, in addition to three in-depth interviews with executive-level managers. All participants have rich knowledge and experience in AI development or implementation. The discussions mainly focused on: (1) examples of the impact of AI and related new technologies on the labor market, (2) the competency of future talents, and (3) suggestions for policymakers. The discussions were recorded with the consent of the participants and transcribed into textual data for further analysis. The research adopted ATLAS.ti version 8 for data analysis. The findings revealed: (1) most practitioners consider AI as a tool; (2) task replacement does happen but workers gain more benefits; (3) new jobs are created as technologies are being developed and utilized. Most participants hold an affirmative attitude toward AI and new technologies. Suggestions for the government and organizations have also been discussed.

Keywords: Artificial intelligence · Labor market · Qualitative study

1 Introduction

The term artificial intelligence (AI) was coined by John McCarthy in 1956 and defined as the technology that realizes human intelligence in an artificial way [1]. The goal is to make computers capable of reasoning, learning, perceiving, and manipulating objects with human-like abilities to learn and solve complex problems, process extreme amounts of data, and more.

© Springer Nature Switzerland AG 2021
L. Uden et al. (Eds.): KMO 2021, CCIS 1438, pp. 444–456, 2021.
https://doi.org/10.1007/978-3-030-81635-3_36

With the progress of technology, the application and effects of AI and automation are becoming more and more widespread, which will have a great impact on the whole society and economy, enterprises, and even individuals. In the face of this unstoppable trend, many workers feel anxious, especially under the rendering of various workforce reports and news, worrying that their jobs will be replaced by AI one day. This issue has also triggered extensive international discussions and initiated a wave of research on related issues. Among the many risks and social impacts that AI will cause, one issue that has received a great deal of attention is the impact of AI on the job market. That is, whether the large-scale adoption of AI technology in each industry will lead to the replacement of human labor by machines causing unemployment, thus radically changing the structure of the future labor market.

The paper reports the results of a study which was conducted with two purposes. First, it attempted to explore the current threats and opportunities of AI in the labor market in Taiwan from practitioners' perspective. The exploration meant to uncover important trends to increase governments and corporates' understanding and awareness of AI development in order to facilitate better strategic planning and policy making. Second, it aimed at uncovering the competencies required for future AI talents. Since it is difficult to avoid technology advancement in the future of work, humans need to observe and adapt to the changes in the workplace generated by AI. Therefore, it is important to know the competencies required to respond to those changes.

2 Literature Review

2.1 The Development of AI in Taiwan

To respond to the advent of the era of intelligence, countries worldwide have been investing in AI research. In 2017, the Taiwan government announced the DIGI + Plan for promoting the development of AI on the ground [2]. According to Executive Yuan of Taiwan, this plan is focused on talent incubation, cooperation between government and industry, connection with the international-bound companies, regulations making, and intelligence digitalization for facilitating the development of AI on the ground [3]. They expected to invest 16 billion dollars in semiconductor, information and communications technology, internet of things (IoT) systems and security, and unmanned equipment in the next five years [4]. On the other hand, since only a few AI talents are available in the Taiwan market, the most urgent need for Taiwan to keep up with the AI trend is to establish a good environment for cultivating talents and integrate related resource platforms. Hence, Taiwan AI Academy has been established and aims to quickly train a large number of talents who can help Taiwan's industries solve the various problems they face in the process of going smart [5]. It gathers professionals who are already specialized in a certain field, and through short-term training, they learn to use AI to solve problems in their own field in order to speedily solve the AI talent shortage in Taiwan's industry as well as bring new momentum to the industry upgrade.

Flow, an AI data service company in Taiwan, has observed that the demand for AI data processing is still dominated by smart traffic and security surveillance, especially self-driving car and vehicle identification and pedestrian flow monitoring [6]. For example, in 2019, the number of customers with cross-border tracking data processing needs has increased, they were required not only to identify the target object but also to be able to deduce the movement path of the target object. Moreover, ITRI in 2020 predicted that the main growth of global AI applications in 2020 would come from four major areas, including manufacturing, medical, financial, and retails industry and it proposed that manufacturing and medical industries will be important areas for Taiwan to develop AI applications because Taiwan has the greatest amount of data in manufacturing and medical care industries [7]. In the case of equipment maintenance in the manufacturing industry, generally, the manufacturing industry uses regular maintenance, while the "machine failure prediagnosis" developed by ITRI uses AI technology to analyze past machine failure records and predict when equipment needs to be repaired early, thereby reducing the risk and cost of sudden machine failure.

2.2 Research on AI and Labor

The discussion on AI and the labor market has been widely explored in the literature [8–11]. The works of Hislop et. al [10] and Yeh et. al [11] reviewed articles about the influence of new technology and AI on society and labor. By reviewing 184 studies, Hislop and his colleagues argued that AI and new technologies will influence knowledge, service, and also professional labor; however, it will take the role of assisting and complementing rather than replacing labor. They also mentioned that the skills gap will be a pressing issue in this emerging era, as the demand for a technically skilled workforce will increase dramatically, but lack of talents to fulfill the shortage. Therefore, it is necessary for both governmental institutions and educational institutions to be prepared for the early development of policies or related talent training strategies.

Yeh et. al examined 39 articles between 2016 and 2019 and found three schools of scholars' perspectives toward the impact of AI on the labor force, which were optimistic, pessimistic, and neutral. Scholars on the optimistic side welcome the development and implementation of AI techniques, and they believe that AI will create new jobs and augment labor. On the opposite, the pessimists claimed that AI would lead to unemployment and control over human users. However, neutral scholars believed that AI technology is still evolving and it is too early to draw conclusions. These two papers summarized how AI and new technologies are going to affect the workforce with the existing literary evidence from around the world.

2.3 Taiwan's Labor Market

Taiwan, as a semiconductor foundry and a major producer of information and communication products, has been containing and breeding a pool of technology talents. In a 2018 speech by Joe Chen, a Deputy General Manager in Taiwan's largest job bank, he indicated that Taiwan's industries were transforming from information technology to data technology [12]. He further suggested that jobs related to the digital economy would grow by 120% in the next five years. The Yes 123 report in 2018 also revealed that 31.3% of companies had plans for robotic automation or AI systems for their future operations [13]. Besides, the survey also asked respondents about the perspective of AI replacing jobs and got as many as 81.4% of workers worried that their jobs would be replaced by robots or AI. Among them, the top five that were thought to be most likely replaced jobs were ticket salespersons, production line operators, mass merchandisers or supermarket staff, customer service workers, and restaurant servers. Recently, the 104 Career Whitepaper reported that the number of full-time jobs in Taiwan's labor market grew steadily from 395,636 to 517,764 from 2015 to 2020, and showed that talent in technology-related fields has become more popular [14]. According to the investigation, six AI-related occupations were on the list of the top 10 hottest jobs. At the same time, the report also noted that as technology creates new jobs, it will weaken the demand for certain jobs and affect white-collar workers in addition to traditional blue-collar jobs. Similarly, Microsoft reported that AI could take over at least 80 journalists in June of 2020 [15–17].

From the above evidence, it is apparent that the new technology not only has an affirmative status in the labor market but also a couple of concerns. In this regard, this study aims to understand the impact of AI on the labor market in Taiwan, through conversations with practitioners to empirically explore the current state of AI development and its influence on Taiwan's labor market.

3 Methodology

In the purpose of understanding AI's impact on the labor market in Taiwan, the present research took a qualitative research approach for data collection, using the methods of focus group interview and semi-structured in-depth interview.

3.1 Participants

This research sought data from experienced participants in various positions and industries. A total of 11 interviewees participated in the present research. Two sessions of focus groups were conducted with 8 interviewees, including 5 industrial practitioners in AI application and 3 scholars in the fields of Computer Science, Information Management, and Social Science. Additionally, three in-depth interviews were also held with 3 executive-level practitioners, who are respectively from the human resource department in a Taiwan job bank, a robot team in a renowned computer brand, and an AI academy.

3.2 Data Collection Process

Two focus groups and three in-depth interviews were conducted, each lasted 120 min. These interviews were moderated by researchers with rich qualitative research experience. A discussion outline was developed by the research team and provided to participants before the interviews. During the interviews, the participants were asked to (1) introduce their experience of AI or technology-relevant projects, (2) share the example of changes in the labor market due to AI or new technology application, (3) define the competency of future talents, and (4) provide suggestions to policy makers. To facilitate data analysis, the interviews were audio-recorded and videotaped with participants' consent. The research team ended data collection after data had begun to converge and no new perspective could be found.

3.3 Data Analysis

Two phases of data analysis were executed, which were verbatim transcription and analysis. Two graduate students were assigned to transcribe the audio into verbatim, then cross-checked the accuracy to confirm that every sentence presented the interviewees' exact opinion. In the second phase, the analysis team, formed by two researchers and two graduate students, was in charge of the coding and further analysis. By following Corbin and Strauss' open coding and axial coding methods, the analysis team read through the verbatim transcript carefully and picked out those important sentences as semantic units [18]. This step was done repeatedly until no new semantic units were created. Then, the analysis team developed several main themes of the present research by exploring, linking, and gathering up the semantic units. The coding process was performed by two graduate students separately. Afterwards, the results were compared and differences in coding were resolved though discussions among the members of the analysis team.

4   Findings

4.1   Views on AI and the Workforce

This present research aimed at exploring the impact of AI on the workforce at the current stage of development. Most of the interviewees had a positive attitude toward AI, as they believed that AI is a tool to extend human capability and a solution for solving the current labor shortage issue.

AI as a Tool to Aid Human Workers.   During the discussion, most of the interviewees stood on the side of the users and advocated AI as merely a tool when asked to identify the linkage of AI and jobs (Interviewees P3, P5, and A3). Specifically, interviewee P3 said:

> *In my opinion, AI is a tool. What it creates is that you could have more opportunities or concrete information to know your customers.*

Interviewee P3 and P4 believed that new technologies are decreasing cost and maximizing production. P4 and A9 agreed to this view. A9 reported the case of an aerospace company which is currently using AI for controlling the time in producing aerospace components with hot-pressing furnaces. In this case, AI is used to alert the operator when there is any abnormity, hence it not only helps control the production time and cost but also avoid the risk of production failures.

AI as a Solution to Labor Shortage.   Labor shortage has been a main issue in Taiwan's highly competitive manufacturing business since the production lines used to require a large quantity of manual workers to maintain capacity. Therefore, robotic arms have long been introduced to the industry to partially solve this issue. Interviewee P4 claimed that robotic arms are actually doing the jobs that manual workers are dissatisfied with. Furthermore, these machines do not have the physical limitation and are able to work 24 h a day without the need to take a break. Interviewee P2 take chat-bot as an example, she said:

Its learning ability is better than a service center staff, and then its response quality... It's never wrong; it can operate 24 hours a day, doesn't need a break, and won't ask for a raise, doesn't have emotions...

AI Helps Humans Achieve the Impossible. The difference between previous technology advancement and AI is that the former mainly improves the speed or efficiency of what humans do, while the latter helps humans achieve what used to be impossible. Smart algorithms such as Google which is available at everyone's fingertip can now guide the way, provide answers to most questions, and suggest goods to buy or articles to read, all customized to the user. Facial recognition techniques together with surveillance cameras help police officers track criminals and solve cases that used to be unsolvable. Interviewee A7 further explained that this technique is widely implemented in the custom for recognizing traveler's information and also able to distinguish twins clearly. He said:

The system that we use to recognize the face at the airport has become very popular nowadays, but face recognition is actually an impossible task for human since we can't really confirm the accuracy of a person and his information by just comparing passport and his face. But if we are using a machine, we will get better accuracy. We find some twins for testing the machine and found that the machines can apparently distinguish the twins, which means that it again did what we can't see with the naked eye.

4.2   The Changes in Current Labor Market Caused by AI

This present research empirically examined the reality of AI in practice and its impact on current labor market by asking our study participants to share their experience of AI and related new technologies implemented in the Taiwanese industries. Examples of AI shared include high-resolution smart cameras which are frequently used for quality assurance particularly on checking precision instruments (interviewees P4, A9, and A10), diabetes test (interviewee A9), fast trade in the stock market (interviewee P4), autonomous driving (interviewees P3 and P5), and chat-bot in the call center (interviewee P2).

From the above examples, it can be seen that AI technology has already been adopted in many industries and certainly has caused some degree of changes in the labor market. Yeh and others identified three different schools of viewpoints in the literature, namely optimistic, pessimistic and neutral, in regards to the impact of these new technologies [11]. The following paragraphs reveal opinions of our interviewees and cases in practice.

Replacement Mostly Happened in Certain Tasks Rather than an Entire Job. According to Yeh et al., the pessimists worry about massive unemployment caused by machine or technological substitution [11]. However, interviewees P4 and A9 in the present research argued that generally speaking, AI at its current capability is not able to take over all human jobs. The AI we have today is "weak AI" which works only as programmed by humans. Therefore, as long as a job cannot be fully "programmed", AI will not be able to replace the human incumbent. Interviewee A9 said:

To me, the issue is that the popularity of AI will definitely mean the replacement of some human workers, but there is no way for it to fully replace people.

Other interviewees P6, P7, A9, and A10 also believed that only certain "pro-grammable" tasks, such as daily routine and repeated job tasks were at higher risk of being replaced by AI or automation technologies, like the assembly line operators in the third industrial revolution (Interviewees P1, P5, and P6). Additionally, interviewee P7 added that jobs involving a high safety-concern working environment would also be substituted and that this replacement is meant to avoid employees being in danger. She said:

> *I would say that it's labor-intensive and high-risk jobs that are likely to be replaced, like if you're afraid of getting blown up and robots can do...... Right! So I would argue that high labor-intensive and high risk are likely to be replaced by robots.*

Labor will Benefit from AI Techniques. Although it is an undeniable fact that a portion of jobs are taken over by AI, the workforce also benefits from AI. Interviewees suggested that we should consider the positive side of AI since it will enhance efficiency and productivity of our work allowing humans to do what humans do best (Interviewees P2, P3, P4, P5, P6, A7, and A9).

One of the interviewees took the tasks of a human resource specialist as an example, he said:

> *If you're an HR, for example, it can help the company get the right people, because if you have to rely on a recruiter to look for every candidate's LinkedIn and FB, and so on, it's too troublesome. If you use AI technology to do... Then it can help you with the initial screening, and ensure the quality of the candidates. I think it's the tasks that can be done to enhance the value of work.*

Chat-bots are also a commonly implemented technology nowadays, especially in telemarketing in the financial industry. It is able to make around a thousand calls a day, which can mean that chat-bots can be ten times more productive than human telemar-keters. However, chat-bots do not completely take over the job of telemarketers, because they still need to stand by for promoting a product once the chat-bots reach customers with high willingness to purchase, as described by interviewee P2.

> *Telemarketing is a very important part of the work in many, such as financial and insurance industries. At this time, if I ask human workers to call, they feel tired and frustrated after they get hung up 10 times. Well, the robot doesn't feel that way,... And it's very efficient.... A real person who makes one hundred calls a day may call it great, but a robot can call a thousand times. If there is one percent in the thousand calls, that is, 10 customers are interested, its performance today is definitely higher than the people. So the chat-bot becomes the first host and then [the customer is relayed to] the real people to do the second contact, which will improve employees' sense of achievement.*

New Jobs are Created Because of AI. New jobs, tasks, and service demands are being created at the moment. Examples of newly created jobs described in the discussion include technical project managers, AI project managers, AI implementation consultants, AI trainers, AI lecturers, etc. The head of the robotics team in a renowned computer brand

(Interviewee P7) noted that their company is currently in high demand for AI engineers, in particular those with expertise in developing algorithms. The increasing AI application in the high-tech manufacturing sector in Taiwan also calls for more AI related talents. This causes a pressing need to increase the supply of AI workforce. Interviewee A10 said:

Some of the jobs may work through the cooperation of humans and machines. For example, if there are ten processes in a production line, three of the processes may be replaced by machines to increase its productivity. At the same time, the three production lines will need to have an AI engineer on duty to take care of the production. This job is newly created because it had not existed before.

Expectation on AI Technology Development and Utilization. The practitioners generally stayed positive and welcomed AI. They expected that AI and new technologies are able to lend a hand to human labor in the future, such as taking care of disadvantaged groups, avoiding the occupational fatigue of social workers and assembly line operators, and creating new and innovative medical and healthcare services. Interviewee P4 further showed his confidence on AI by saying:

In my opinion, artificial intelligence and human beings should complement each other and become a better application for the benefit of mankind.

4.3 Soft and Hard Skills of Future Talents

Our participants expressed strongly the idea of human-machine collaboration or human-machine symbiosis being the trend of the future. To survive as the fittest, people are advised to put their efforts into both soft skills and hard skills from now on. Soft skills are related to interpersonal relationships, which is difficult to measure compared with hard skills. Communication, adaptability, problem-solving, and collaborations with humans or machines are considered as critical soft skills for the future (Interviewees P2, P3, A7, A9, P5, and P6).

Hard skills, on the other hand, are skills that are measurable and able to be learned from the education systems or training. The key hard skills mentioned in the discussion are domain knowledge of a professional field and programming languages. Interviewee P6, the deputy general manager of a job bank, observed that talents with interdisciplinary skills are likely to be in great demand very soon. Interviewees P5 and A9 agreed and explained that these talents have their own domain expertise and are familiar with the "language" of their colleagues in different disciplines, allowing them to work more effectively with others. As executives, interviewees P3 and A10 indicated that programming languages such as python, will be key languages in the future, and can be learned through the internet platform. *"Take a look on Git-hub every day, it is beneficial"*, said P3. He further explained that this platform includes numerous models that are well-trained by engineers all over the world and welcomes those who are interested in accessing and sharing their knowledge.

4.4   Suggestions from Practitioners to Policymakers

The Taiwan government has recently been promoting and supporting the development of AI and talent incubation. In addition to financial support, country-level related AI development strategies have also been established and announced. However, the practitioners found that some efforts are still lacking, and advocated that the government or policymakers need to pay attention to them during this period in order to effectively facilitate the strategies.

One of the interviewees who have rich experiences on labor research, interviewee A8, noticed that the existing standard occupational classification in Taiwan is too rough if compared with the U.S version. For this reason, she made further suggestions that more nuanced job and task analysis is needed, in the purpose of accurately identifying talent demands for further developing a new or adjusting the current education strategy. Interviewee P2 pointed out that the job contents of an engineer have changed in the AI era, so he or she is no longer performing the same job tasks as in the past and a new job competency may be required at this time. She said:

> There are many tools of business intelligence today. Therefore, the processing of numbers, as well as images, and the recognition of videos, images, and sounds. These are all AI-related technologies...... Therefore, in this process, we need AI engineers, but we already don't have enough traditional engineers. As a result, what are the competencies of an AI engineer? They need to be familiar with the new algorithms and new programming languages.

Data is believed as an important input for AI development, especially for training AI models. In Taiwan, where data is greatly protected, interviewees thus stated that the government as well as organizations need to see data as a vital asset for the public since it is a valuable resource today. Interviewee P4 said, *"Let's consider removing the label of data and get agreement from everyone, so that we can do data integration."* A data sharing and integration strategy could also be regarded in the future so that government and enterprises are able to enlighten each other. Table 1 summarizes the perspectives from the focus group discussions and in-depth interviews.

Table 1. Interview summary

Topic	Themes	Supporting quotes
AI and workforce	AI as a tool	- AI creates more opportunities or concrete information to know your customers (P3)
	AI as a solution to labor shortage	-Chatbot's learning ability is better than a service center staff. It's never wrong; it can operate 24 h a day and it doesn't have emotions. (P2)

(continued)

Table 1. (*continued*)

Topic	Themes	Supporting quotes
	AI can achieve the impossible	-Face recognition is actually an impossible task for humans since we can't really confirm the accuracy of a person and his information. However, the machine can get better accuracy. (A7)
Changes in current labor market	Replace certain tasks, not an entire job	-AI popularity means it will replace some human workers, but there is no way to fully replace people. (A9) -Labor-intensive and high-risk jobs are likely to be replaced. (P7)
	Labor will benefit from AI techniques	-For HR, AI can help with the initial screening, and ensure the quality of the candidates. (P4) -For telemarketing, the chatbot becomes the first host, and then the real people to do the second contact, which will improve employees' sense of achievement. (P2)
	Create new jobs	-If three processes on a production line are replaced by machines, a new position called AI engineer may be created to take care of the production. (A10)
	Expectation on AI development and utilization	-AI and human beings should complement each other and become a better application for the benefit of mankind. (P4)
The competency of future talents	Soft and hard skills of future talents	-Talents with interdisciplinary skills are likely to be in great demand very soon. (P6) -Python will be key languages in the future. (P3 & A10) -It is beneficial to take a look on Git-hub. (P3)
Suggestions to policymakers	Suggestions to policymakers	-Existing standard occupational classification is too rough, and the more nuanced job and task analysis is needed, in the purpose of accurately identifying talent demands for further developing a new or adjusting the current education strategy. (A8) -Since there are many tools of business intelligence today, we need AI engineers, and need them to be familiar with the new algorithms and new programming languages. (P2) -Consider removing the label of data and get agreement from everyone, so that we can do data integration. (P4)

5   Conclusions and Discussion

The current research indicated that most practitioners interviewed in Taiwan have an affirmative attitude toward AI and new technologies implementation and consider AI as a tool. They believe that while AI certainly has the ability to replace some human labor, they also gain benefits from the application of the technology, such as a more developed economy due to increased efficiency and productivity. As new technological advances such as AI are inevitable, future talents are encouraged to cultivate soft and hard skills, including communication, adaptability, problem-solving, programming language, and more. Besides, while strategies like financial support or more opened policy are implemented by the government at the present, practitioners raised the issues on job analysis and data management in order to expedite the development of AI and its application in Taiwan.

The current AI's capability is to learn how to deal with affairs from existing experience but is not good at work that requires creativity and feeling emotions. For this reason, human beings are still better at solving major problems by their own observation, judgment, and making the final decision. Furthermore, AI can be used to handle tasks that humans cannot perform and to help solve professional tasks that a human is not currently doing well enough, because AI can achieve constant quality, without the need for rest, and is non-sensory. Executive Vice President Yu in ITRI Taiwan also pointed out that AI can do the job that people do not want to do or to help share the workload [19]. For example, AI can be used in the night shift, so that human labor can properly rest, and the output can be increased without the necessity to reduce human labor.

Technology sometimes works in mysterious ways in influencing human behavior and economic activities, and therefore its impact on the labor market is also hard to predict. Looking at one example of technology development in the past, when Uber was invented, people thought that taxi drivers were going to lose their jobs, but instead, the profession of Uber driver emerged. It appears the same for the development of AI, which may create more new types of jobs. It can be noticed that the technology may replace some jobs, but it can also create new jobs and enhance the existing ones. Likewise, the labor market has changed over the past decade, but some aspects have remained the same. Technology and innovation are increasing the demand for new skills, knowledge and work experience, so it is essential that skills are constantly being updated to keep up with the changing workforce needs and work patterns of the world of tomorrow.

6   Limitations

The purpose of this paper is to explore the current status of the labor market in Taiwan under the influence of AI and new technologies, from the practitioners' perspective. Limitations were identified in the present study. One of the limitations is that the findings are synthesized from the personal experiences of a small group of practitioners and may not generalize to all industries or the entire country. Moreover, although the majority of the interviewees had practical experiences in applying or developing AI, the majority held a managerial level of focus in this study. Therefore, their views may not represent those of the general workforce. Finally, as this study was conducted in Taiwan with a purpose to reveal its current labor conditions under the influence of AI, the findings may not apply to other regions which are at a different stage of AI development.

Acknowledgement. This research was supported by the Ministry of Science and Technology of Taiwan, ROC. (MOST 109–2634-F-003–008 -).

References

1. McCarthy, J.: What is Artificial Intelligence? http://jmc.stanford.edu/artificial-intelligence/what-is-ai/index.html. Accessed 26 Dec 2019
2. Executive Yuan, DIGI+: Digital Nation and Innovative Economic Development Program. https://english.ey.gov.tw/News3/9E5540D592A5FECD/659df63b-dad4-47e3-80ab-c62cb4 0a62cd. Accessed 9 Sep 2019
3. Executive Yuan, AI Taiwan Action Plan. https://english.ey.gov.tw/News3/9E5540D592A5 FECD/1dec0902-e02a-49c6-870d-e77208481667. Accessed 7 Aug 2019
4. Executive Yuan, AI innovation: Grand strategy for a small country. https://www.ey.gov.tw/ Page/5A8A0CB5B41DA11E/50a08776-e33a-4be2-a07c-a6e523f5031b. Accessed 16 Oct 2018
5. Taiwan AI Academy, Vision and Mission of Taiwan AI Academy. https://aiacademy.tw/vis ion/. Accessed 29 Dec 2020
6. Flow, See the trend of Taiwan's AI industry from data processing. The Guide Book of AI. https://ai-blog.flow.tw/ai-strategy-10. Accessed 20 Jan 2021
7. ITRI, 2020 AI Trend Analysis! Taiwan's AI development first in the manufacturing and medical industries. https://www.itri.org.tw/ListStyle.aspx?DisplayStyle=01_content&SiteID=1& MmmID=1036276263153520257. Accessed 29 Jan 2020
8. Arntz, M., Gregory, T., Zierahn, U.: Revisiting the risk of automation. Econ. Lett. **159**, 157–160 (2017)
9. Frey, C.B., Osborne, M.A.: The future of employment: How susceptible are jobs to computerisation? Technol. Forecast. Soc. Chang. **114**, 254–280 (2017)
10. Hislop, D., Coombs, C., Taneva, S., Barnard, S.: Impact of Artificial Intelligence, Robotics and Automation Technologies on Work (London: Chartered Institute of Personnel and Development, 2017), 1–30 (2017). https://www.voced.edu.au/content/ngv%3A80279
11. Yeh, C.-C., Wong, C.C., Chang, W.-W., Lai, C.-C.: Labor displacement in artificial intelligence Era: A systematic literature review. Taiwan J. East Asian Stud. **17**(2), 25–75 (2020). https:// doi.org/10.6163/tjeas.202012_17(2).0002
12. Chen, J., The Future Trends of the industry and Key Competency. http://assistance.sa.ntnu. edu.tw/ezfiles/1/1001/img/61/400290657.pdf. Accessed 7 Mar 2018
13. Yes 123, Slashies vs. Expert workplace survey with AI. Whitepaper. https://www.yes123. com.tw/admin/white_paper/article.asp?id=20180523182446. Accessed 23 May 2018
14. Job Bank, 104 Career Whitepaper, March 2020. https://www.104.com.tw/jobs/career_whitep aper/. Accessed 31 Mar 2020
15. Business Insider, Microsoft News just cut dozens of editorial workers as it moves towards a robot-driven system of selecting stories. https://www.businessinsider.com/microsoft-news-cuts-dozens-of-staffers-in-shift-to-ai-2020-5?utm_source=feedly&utm_medium=web feeds&r=US&IR=T. Accessed 1 June 2020
16. Business next, MSN news editor lost his job! Microsoft to replace at least 80 employees with AI, all to AI to deal with no problem? https://www.bnext.com.tw/article/57923/microsoft-msn-ai-news. Accessed 2 Jan 2020

17. Guardian, Microsoft sacks journalists to replace them with robots. https://www.theguardian.com/technology/2020/may/30/microsoft-sacks-journalists-to-replace-them-with-robots. Accessed 30 May 2020
18. Corbin, J., Strauss, A.: Basics of Qualitative Research: Techniques and Procedures for Developing Grounded Theory. Sage Publications, New York (2014)
19. China Times, Shiaw-Shian Yu, Never be tired of playing AI. https://turnnewsapp.com/tw/wangwang/135427.html. Accessed 6 Dec 2016

An Analysis of an Augmented Reality Application to Support Service Staff in Industrial Maintenance

Reinhard Bernsteiner[✉], Christian Ploder, Thomas Dilger, Johannes Nigg, Teresa Spieß, and Rebecca Weichelt

Department Management, Communication and IT, Management Center Innsbruck, Innsbruck, Austria
reinhard.bernsteiner@mci.edu

Abstract. Augmented Reality is an emerging technology and gains in importance. With AR, the physical world can be extended with virtual content. Especially AR-applications for industrial maintenance are experiencing an upswing. AR-technologies for maintenance aim to improve human performance by providing relevant information for a specific task. This information can be provided by sensor data from machines, software systems, or human experts. Currently, there are not many industry-ready AR-applications on the market. This lack raises the question if AR-applications can effectively support service staff in the field.

An experimental investigation was carried out to explore this field. Two industrial maintenance cases with different levels of difficulty were simulated, whereby service staff had to solve these real-life problems. Support from an expert was provided via an AR-application. In addition, the Affinity for Technology Interaction score was assessed in order to identify the target group for AR-applications.

The results clearly show that AR-applications can effectively support service staff in the field. The research also reveals that a high Affinity for Technology Interaction score of the service technician leads to a higher acceptance of the AR-application. The application offers many potentials, but there are still some limitations concerning the user interface and technological aspects.

Keywords: Augmented Reality · Expert support · Affinity for Technology Interaction · Industrial maintenance support · Experiment · Empirical study

1 Introduction

To keep up in the highly competitive market, companies have to improve their product quality and reduce their maintenance time. Technological developments are continually providing companies with new and innovative solutions to meet these challenges in a better way. Especially in the service sector, particularly in industrial maintenance, Augmented Reality (AR) technologies offer numerous application areas [1].

Maintenance tasks in the industrial environment are becoming increasingly complex and require more and more know-how, which service specialists have to acquire an expensive and time-consuming training [2, 3].

© Springer Nature Switzerland AG 2021
L. Uden et al. (Eds.): KMO 2021, CCIS 1438, pp. 457–467, 2021.
https://doi.org/10.1007/978-3-030-81635-3_37

This causes enormous costs for companies. Training is therefore often provided only to selected service specialists. In the case of maintenance tasks, it is more common for the service technicians on-site to get stuck on a problem. They have to contact a more experienced and better-trained expert.

Communication usually takes place via a telephone call. In the industrial environment, complex issues are difficult to present and explain via purely verbal communication, which often leads to misunderstandings and ambiguities. As a result, in practice, the experienced expert is usually called in to solve the problem on-site. Especially in rural areas, the expert's trip causes a high expenditure of time and money for the company and, in turn, for the customers [4].

AR represents a way to provide expert support to service workers in the field. However, this technology may not be suitable for the entire service staff universally [5]. Therefore, the research question arises if an already existing metric as the Affinity for Technology Interaction (ATI) scale can be used to identify the target group of AR in an industrial setting quickly and accurately. To explore the eligibility of the ATI-scale as a predictor, an experimental setting was designed, including a questionnaire to collect data ATI scale data.

The next section provides a literature review followed by a description of the methodology. Section 4 presents the results of the empirical survey. The last section provides a summary, limitations, and ideas for further research.

2   Literature Review

In this section, the central terms and concepts relevant to the empirical study are presented. First, AR and its application in the industrial service sector are described, followed by Affinity for Technology Interaction. This chapter ends with the aim and the hypothesis for this contribution.

2.1   Augmented Reality

Augmented Reality (AR) is a technology that adds virtual content to the real world. AR creates an additional layer of information through computer-aided graphics, which is intended to simplify the user interaction in and with the physical world [6].

For this paper, AR is defined as "a set of human-computer interaction techniques that enriches user's real-world experience by embedding contextualized information into user's space in coexistence with real-world objects" [7].

Most AR-applications are available on mobile devices, like smartphones or tablet computers. In recent years, hands-free wearable devices, like smart glasses and displays that can be worn on the head, gained importance [8].

As depicted in Fig. 1, the Reality-Virtuality (RV) continuum can be used to integrate AR in a broader context [9].

The Reality-Virtuality continuum can be used to explain the difference between AR and Virtual Reality (VR). On the left side of the continuum is the real world, which consists exclusively of real objects. On the other side is the virtual environment, which consists solely of virtual and simulated objects. Between these two extremes, Mixed

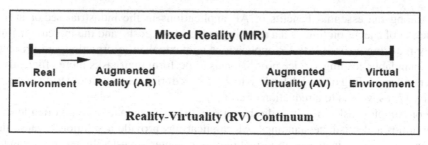

Fig. 1. Reality-virtuality continuum [8]

Reality (MR) is located. AR is a part of MR and is placed more on the left edge of the continuum. The basis of AR is the real environment with overlays of virtual objects or data.

VR, on the other hand, is entirely in the virtual environment. VR is computer-generated, three-dimensional, and interactive reality. In VR, the user is put into an immersive, virtual world and is cut off from the real world. When virtual reality is combined with parts of the real world, it is referred to as Augmented Virtuality (AV). An example would be a VR environment in which users can see their own hands [9].

AR is a very versatile technology that can be used in a wide variety of domains, e.g. in education [10–12], tourism [13–16], or marketing [17–19]. Visualizing information, receiving and following instructions, and interacting with products are the three central functions of AR-applications [8].

Currently, one of the most common uses of AR-systems are applications for instructing and training people. The potential use cases of AR-applications in this area are wide and varied. For example, there are promising experiments that deal with tennis training through real-time instructions via AR [20]. Another example is to use AR-applications to find the way out of buildings in an evacuation event [21].

AR has versatile use cases in the industrial sector. In the aviation industry, many activities are already supported by AR-systems. This includes the training of skilled workers or the support of staff in assembly and maintenance activities [22–24].

2.2 AR Support for Industrial Services

Research on AR-technologies for the industrial service sector focuses mainly on four categories: assembly and disassembly, repair, inspection or diagnosis, and training. The first category uses AR-applications virtual content to guide the service professional through the assembly or disassembly process. For repairs, AR is used to assist in the reconstruction or replacement of components. When inspecting and diagnosing equipment, AR-systems can assess the current condition of a product and analyze the causality of the defect. AR-applications for the training of service professionals provide a better understanding of maintenance activities [25].

In their research, Mourtzis et al. describe an AR-system that efficiently combines and integrates real-time data from various sensors implemented in machines to get an overview of the current condition of this machine. These results are displayed in an AR-application used by the machine operator [26].

Among the essential benefits of AR-applications in the industrial sector are the reduction of execution time and a resulting reduction in costs, and the increase in quality by reducing errors [27]. AR-applications contextualize information and present it understandably, leading service professionals to perform their tasks more efficiently. A better understanding of the job leads to fewer errors during execution and to an increased quality [7] as well as to a reduction of cost [28].

For complex tasks, purely audio-based support (e.g. via phone calls) often leads to ambiguities and misunderstandings. AR-applications provide a solution because they can extend communication with virtual real-time content that facilitates understanding and dissolves communication barriers [29].

2.3 Affinity for Technology Interaction

Increasing digitization means that interaction with new and sometimes complex technologies must be made low-threshold and straightforward. System developers try to solve this problem by developing systems that are user-friendly and intuitive. To that extend, user acceptance models can be applied. At the beginning of the 21st century, the Unified Theory of Acceptance and Use of Technology (UTAUT) was developed out of previous user acceptance models [30]. The fast changing world however demands for new models that allow facing current challenges.

The recent Affinity for Technology Interaction (ATI) describes the individually varying tendency of people's interaction with technical systems [31]. ATI is defined as "the tendency to actively engage in intensive technology interaction, as a key personal resource for coping with technology" [5]. The ATI scale was developed to measure this concept. The scale consists of nine items and uses a six-point Likert scale. The reliability and construct validity of the ATI scale as a measurement instrument has already been verified [5].

Further, Lezhnina and Kismihók conducted a multi-method psychometric evaluation of the ATI scale and described it as a valid, reliable, and recommendable instrument for human-technology interaction research [32].

We assume that the ATI-scale is a suitable predictor and helps to identify the right workforce, which should be provided with the AR tools in the first phase of the deployment. Thus, the central aim of this work is to explore if the ATI-scale is a suitable predictor to identify the right workforce for the first phase of AR deployment.

This leads to the hypothesis: The higher the ATI-score the better an AR-tool supports to solve problems in the field.

3 Methodology

An experimental setting was designed to collect data for the empirical study. The following section describes the design and execution of the experiment.

3.1 Design of the Experiment

The following situation was simulated as a scenario for the experiment: a service employee is on-site to maintain or repair a machine in a construction area. The service employee has to perform work for which the employee is not qualified. Consequently, the service employee has to contact a more experienced and better-trained specialist in the company. An AR-application is used for communication purposes. Within the distinct case of this experiment, PTC Chalk was applied.[1] The software allows experts to remotely assist technicians based on VR (see Fig. 2).

Specialist   Service technician

Fig. 2. AR-application functionality[2]

[2] Image retrieved from: https://www.ptc.com/en/products/vuforia/vuforia-chalk [last checked on 12th of April 2021].

To simulate the maintenance case as good as possible, the experiment was conducted in two separate rooms. The experienced expert was located in one room, while the service employee with the machine that has to be repaired was in the other room. The expert had a tablet, and the service employee used a regular smartphone, both with the AR-application installed.

In all runs of the experiment, the expert stayed, whereas the service staff changed. The expert's instructions for solving the problem were always the same. This ensured that the experiment was always carried out under consistent conditions.

One experiment consisted of two runs with different service cases. Each participant was given two maintenance cases (one easier and one more difficult) that had to be solved with the support of an expert and the AR-application.

To be transparent and provide similar initial situations for all participants, they were informed about the study and the experiment's design. Furthermore, they received a short introduction to the AR-tool.

The experimental study was conducted at two different companies. The test subjects came from the service sector. Thus, the experiment must be classified as a quasi-experiment, since the assignment of participants was not randomized. Based on the objective of the research project, the participants were deliberately chosen from the service sector, as this allocation gives the results more relevance.

[1] https://www.ptc.com/en/products/vuforia/vuforia-chalk [last checked on 12th of April 2021].

3.2 Used AR-Application

A commercial and professional tool was used in the experiment. This tool is an app, which runs on regular smartphones. A camera and an internet connection are required. The application has to be installed on the smartphone of the worker in the field and on the experts tablet.

This tool combines AR-technologies with real-time video communication function-alities. In a first step, the tool scans the environment (e.g. a machine) for which support is required. On the screen of the smartphone, marks (text, symbols, drawings, etc.) can be associated with objects of the environment (e.g. one specific component of a machine). These marks are stuck to these components. With that mechanism, the worker can move around in the environment, and marks are only displayed when the associated component is visible on the screen. Both the worker and the expert can draw marks. The session can be recorded (video and voice), or screenshots can be made. This helps to document all activities.

3.3 Data Collection

After the two runs of the experiment, each participant had to fill out a questionnaire printed on paper. The questions of the first section are related to personal data, like gender, age, highest educational attainment, current position in the company. In section two, the ATI-scale had to be filled out by the participants to measure the Affinity for Technology Interaction. The section asks if the AR-application supported the service employee without unnecessary burdens. They had to indicate if they would use the AR-tool again regarding the two different difficulty levels.

At the end of the questionnaire, an open-ended question was available. The partic-ipants were asked to provide further feedback and make personal remarks about the AR-application.

4 Results

Due to the Covid-19 pandemic, it was not possible to recruit more than 25 participants from two different companies for the experiment. From company one, seven and from company two 18 staff members participated.

The evaluation was not company-specific. The age of the subjects ranges from 16 to 47 years. The average age of the sample is 32.88 years, with a standard deviation of 8.67. The gender distribution is very unbalanced. There is only one female participant. The uneven gender distribution can be explained by the industry in which the experimental study was conducted. The proportion of men and women in technically focused industries is still very unevenly distributed. For mechatronics, energy, and electrical occupations, 89% of employees in Germany are male [33].

This uneven distribution is represented in the sample. The companies and participants have their focus in technical fields. Technicians, mechatronics engineers, and machine operators are significantly frequently represented in the sample. The vast majority of participants had an apprenticeship diploma or a master craftsman's diploma.

4.1 Affinity for Technology Interaction

Comparing the results of the two service cases showed that the AR-application provided better support in solving the more difficult problem. The support for the more manageable problem was rated less high.

As the following Table 1 shows, for service case two, the more complicated use case, 20 participants indicated that the application facilitated problem-solving. For service case one, only 17 held this opinion.

Table 1. Support for both use cases

The AR-application supports solving the service case	Frequency use case one	Frequency use case two
Do not agree at all	1	0
Strongly disagree	0	0
Neutral	7	5
Strongly agree	8	10
Fully agree	9	10
Total	**25**	**25**

4.2 Evaluation of the Hypothesis

The following hypothesis was formulated: The higher the ATI-score the better an AR-tool supports solving problems in the field.

This hypothesis tests whether there is a correlation between the measured ATI-score and the degree of support provided by the AR-application in solving the problem. Spearman's bivariate correlation with a two-sided test for significance is used for evaluation. The results differ among the use cases. As shown in the following Table 2, there is no significant correlation ($r = -.139$; $p > .05$) for the first use case.

Thus, there is no significant correlation between interaction-related technology affinity and the degree of support.

Table 2. Evaluation of hypothesis

	Correlation
The AR-application supports solving service case one	$-.139$
The AR-application supports solving service case two	409*
$n = 25$; *$p <,05$; **$p <,01$	

The evaluation shows that there is a significant correlation ($r = .409$; $p < .05$) with a medium effect for the second, more difficult use case. Consequently, there is a significant positive correlation between the user's ATI-score and the degree of support that the AR-application offered.

It can be concluded that the more tech-savvy the service employee is, the more likely the AR-application is to provide support to solve challenging tasks. Conversely, however, we might deduce that users with a lower affinity for technology tend to perceive the application as less helpful in solving serious problems.

4.3 Analysis of the Open-Ended Questions

The results of the open-ended question are associated with four categories: user-interface design, additional functions, technical limitations, and other. The category other includes all other suggestions that could not be assigned to any of the other categories.

Most of the suggestions for improvement are related to technical limitations of the application. These include the reduction in image quality when the bandwidth of the Internet connection is low or the limited availability of the application on different end devices. The used AR-application is only available on smartphones or tablets, but not on laptops or personal computers. In the meantime, a newer version of the AR-application is already available, and it can be used on laptops or personal computers as well.

Most of the comments in the category technical limitations refer to the calibration of the AR-application. Before the application can be used, the environment must be scanned using the camera of the mobile device. This just takes some seconds. The smartphone or tablet has to be moved around slowly until all required objects for the service task are covered. Only when the scanning process is successful, symbols and graphical content (e.g. marks or symbols) can be drawn in.

If the environment changes significantly during the session or the user changes location, the AR-application no longer finds its way around, and the environment has to be rescanned. This recalibration bothered many participants.

The second most named suggestions can be associated with category user-interface design. Again, most of the recommendations relate to calibration. However, this is more about the wish for a dedicated button for manual recalibration than about the calibration function's general technical problem. The AR-application currently does not offer a way to restart the calibration manually. Only when the environment is no longer recognized, the AR-application prompts the user to rescan the environment.

One respondent describes that a remote zoom function would be a nice feature for the AR-application. Another suggestion refers to integrating a chat function, which can be used if it was too loud for voice communication. These suggestions are summarized in the category additional functions. Under the category other, there are further suggestions, like the wish for voice output in several languages.

5 Summary, Limitations and Further Research

84% of the participants agreed that the AR-application supported them to solve relatively simple service cases. In the case of the more complex services tasks, 88% of the service employees were of this opinion. 76% of the participants stated that they would use the application in their daily work. This can clearly be evaluated as a positive aspect of the AR-application, as employee acceptance is a critical success factor in implementing AR-technologies [34]. It can be concluded that the used AR-application support service staff in the field when further assistance by experts is required.

The future for AR-systems in the service sector is promising, and new technologies in particular, such as the 5G networks, offer new opportunities for future developments. However, system usability evaluations of new systems should take the user's interaction-related affinity for technology into account. This score has a significant influence on user support when solving especially more complex problems.

In turn, this results in the problem that users with a lower ATI-score tend to perceive the AR-application as less helpful in solving difficult problems. Consequently, when implementing AR-applications, it is essential to evaluate the technical affinity first. Staff with a lower ATI-value should receive intensive training.

The application offers many potentials but still has some limitations in terms of technology and user interface.

5.1 Limitations and Generalization

The sample size of 25 participants is very small and cannot be representative of the population. Further, only one female service employee participated, and only two cases were considered. Besides, the experiment was not conducted in a real world setting, but in an experimental one. Therefore, a generalization is rather difficult. Furthermore, the age distribution of the sample is uneven and is rather in the lower range with an average age of 32.88 years. Also, the average ATI-score of the participants is above average and is 4.82. However, the uneven distribution of the subjects' occupational orientation was deliberately chosen because the AR-application in this study is primarily relevant to individuals in technical occupations in the industrial sector.

Lastly, the biggest challenge in the experimental study was the international Covid-19 pandemic. This significantly delayed and complicated parts of the experimental study.

5.2 Further Research

One of the first activities would be to repeat this experiment with more participants from more companies. The gender distribution should be more balanced.

Since the technical development of AR-tools is growing rapidly, a newer version of the used AR-tool or AR-tools from different manufacturers could be used. In this study, a regular tablet and smartphone were used. From a technical perspective, it would be interesting to use a combination of AR-glasses and smartphones. Another approach could be to compare two settings, one group supported with an AR-application and a second group supported with regular voice support from experts.

References

1. de Pace, F., Manuri, F., Sanna, A., Zappia, D.: A comparison between two different approaches for a collaborative mixed-virtual environment in industrial maintenance. Front. Robot. AI (2019). https://doi.org/10.3389/frobt.2019.00018

2. Martinetti, A., Rajabalinejad, M., van Dongen, L.: Shaping the future maintenance operations: reflections on the adoptions of augmented reality through problems and opportunities. Procedia CIRP (2017). https://doi.org/10.1016/j.procir.2016.10.130
3. Palmarini, R., Erkoyuncu, J.A., Roy, R.: An innovative process to select Augmented Reality (AR) technology for maintenance. Procedia CIRP (2017). https://doi.org/10.1016/j.procir.2016.10.001
4. Masoni, R., et al.: Supporting remote maintenance in industry 4.0 through augmented reality. Procedia Manuf. (2017). https://doi.org/10.1016/j.promfg.2017.07.257
5. Franke, T., Attig, C., Wessel, D.: A Personal resource for technology interaction: development and validation of the Affinity for Technology Interaction (ATI) scale. Int. J. Hum.-Comput. Interact. (2018). https://doi.org/10.1080/10447318.2018.1456150
6. Amin, D., Govilkar, S.: Comparative study of augmented reality Sdk's. IJCSA (2015). https://doi.org/10.5121/ijcsa.2015.5102
7. del Amo, I.F, Erkoyuncu, J.A., Roy, R., Palmarini, R., Onoufriou, D.: A systematic review of augmented reality content-related techniques for knowledge transfer in maintenance applications. Comput. Ind. (2018). https://doi.org/10.1016/j.compind.2018.08.007
8. Porter, M.E., Heppelmann, J.E.: Why every organization needs an augmented reality strategy. Harv. Bus. Rev. **95**, 46–57 (2017)
9. Milgram, P., Takemura, H., Utsumi, A., Kishino, F.: Augmented reality: a class of displays on the reality-virtuality continuum. Proc. SPIE – Int. Soc. Opt. Eng. (1994). https://doi.org/10.1117/12.197321
10. Ferrer-Torregrosa, J., Jiménez-Rodríguez, M.Á., Torralba-Estelles, J., Garzón-Farinós, F., Pérez-Bermejo, M., Fernández-Ehrling, N.: Distance learning ects and flipped classroom in the anatomy learning: comparative study of the use of augmented reality, video and notes. BMC Med. Educ. (2016).https://doi.org/10.1186/s12909-016-0757-3
11. Garzón, J., Kinshuk, S.B., Gutiérrez, J., Pavón, J.: How do pedagogical approaches affect the impact of augmented reality on education? A meta-analysis and research synthesis. Educ. Res. Rev. **31**, 100334 (2020). https://doi.org/10.1016/j.edurev.2020.100334
12. Sahin, D., Yilmaz, R.M.: The effect of augmented reality technology on middle school students' achievements and attitudes towards science education. Comput. Educ. (2020). https://doi.org/10.1016/j.compedu.2019.103710
13. Mesároš, P., et al.: Use of augmented reality and gamification techniques in tourism. E-Rev. Tour. **13**, 366–381 (2016)
14. Cranmer, E.E., tom Dieck, M.C., Fountoulaki, P.: Exploring the value of augmented reality for tourism. Tour. Manage. Perspect. (2020). https://doi.org/10.1016/j.tmp.2020.100672
15. Jingen, L.L., Elliot, S.: A systematic review of augmented reality tourism research: what is now and what is next? Tour. Hospitality Res. (2021). https://doi.org/10.1177/1467358420941913
16. Tsai, S.-P.: Augmented reality enhancing place satisfaction for heritage tourism marketing. Curr. Issues Tour. **23**(9), 1078–1083 (2020). https://doi.org/10.1080/13683500.2019.1598950
17. Ozdemir, M.A.: Virtual Reality (VR) and Augmented Reality (AR) technologies for accessibility and marketing in the tourism industry. In: Korstanje, M., Eusébio, C., Teixeira, L., Carneiro, M.J. (eds.) ICT Tools and Applications for Accessible Tourism. Advances in Hospitality, Tourism, and the Services Industry, pp. 277–301. IGI Global (2021)
18. Huh, J.-H., Seo, Y.-S.: A location-based solution for social network service and android marketing using augmented reality. In: Park, J.J., Fong, S.J., Pan, Yi., Sung, Y. (eds.) Advances in Computer Science and Ubiquitous Computing. LNEE, vol. 715, pp. 569–573. Springer, Singapore (2021). https://doi.org/10.1007/978-981-15-9343-7_80
19. Chylinski, M., Heller, J., Hilken, T., Keeling, D.I., Mahr, D., de Ruyter, K.: Augmented reality marketing: a technology-enabled approach to situated customer experience. Australas. Mark. J. (2020). https://doi.org/10.1016/j.ausmj.2020.04.004

20. Kim, Y., Hong, S., Kim, G.J.: Augmented reality-based remote coaching for fast-paced physical task. Virtual Reality **22**(1), 25–36 (2017). https://doi.org/10.1007/s10055-017-0315-2
21. Lovreglio, R., Kinateder, M.: Augmented reality for pedestrian evacuation research: promises and limitations. Saf. Sci. (2020). https://doi.org/10.1016/j.ssci.2020.104750
22. Ceruti, A., Marzocca, P., Liverani, A., Bil, C.: Maintenance in aeronautics in an Industry 4.0 context: The role of Augmented Reality and Additive Manufacturing. Journal of Computational Design and Engineering **6**(4), 516–526 (2019). https://doi.org/10.1016/j.jcde.2019.02.001
23. Safi, M., Chung, J., Pradhan, P.: Review of augmented reality in aerospace industry. AEAT (2019). https://doi.org/10.1108/AEAT-09-2018-0241
24. Eschen, H., Kötter, T., Rodeck, R., Harnisch, M., Schüppstuhl, T.: Augmented and virtual reality for inspection and maintenance processes in the aviation industry. Procedia Manuf. (2018). https://doi.org/10.1016/j.promfg.2018.01.022
25. Palmarini, R., Erkoyuncu, J.A., Roy, R., Torabmostaedi, H.: A systematic review of augmented reality applications in maintenance. Robot. Comput.-Integr. Manuf. (2018). https://doi.org/10.1016/j.rcim.2017.06.002
26. Mourtzis, D., Vlachou, E., Zogopoulos, V., Fotini, X.: Integrated production and maintenance scheduling through machine monitoring and augmented reality: an industry 4.0 approach. In: Lödding, H., Riedel, R., Thoben, K.-D., Cieminski, G. von Kiritsis, D. (eds.) Advances in Production Management Systems. The Path to Intelligent, Collaborative and Sustainable Manufacturing, vol. 513. IFIP Advances in Information and Communication Technology, vol. 513, pp. 354–362. Springer International Publishing, Cham (2017).https://doi.org/10.1007/978-3-319-66923-6_42
27. Cardoso, L.F.S., de, Mariano, F.C.M.Q., Zorzal, E.R.: A survey of industrial augmented reality. Comput. Ind. Eng. (2020). https://doi.org/10.1016/j.cie.2019.106159
28. Mourtzis, D., Siatras, V., Angelopoulos, J.: Real-time remote maintenance support based on Augmented Reality (AR). Appl. Sci. (2020). https://doi.org/10.3390/app10051855
29. Fang, D., Xu, H., Yang, X., Bian, M.: An augmented reality-based method for remote collaborative real-time assistance: from a system perspective. Mobile Networks Appl. **25**(2), 412–425 (2019). https://doi.org/10.1007/s11036-019-01244-4
30. Venkatesh, M.D.: User acceptance of information technology: toward a unified view. MIS Q. (2003). https://doi.org/10.2307/30036540
31. Wessel, D., Heine, M., Attig, C., Franke, T.: Affinity for technology interaction and fields of study. In: Preim, B., Nürnberger, A., Hansen, C. (eds.) Proceedings of the Conference on Mensch und Computer. MuC'20: Mensch und Computer 2020, Magdeburg Germany, 06 09 2020 09 09 2020, pp. 383–386. ACM, New York, NY, USA (09062020). https://doi.org/10.1145/3404983.3410020
32. Lezhnina, O., Kismihók, G.: A multi-method psychometric assessment of the affinity for technology interaction (ATI) scale. Comput. Hum. Behav. Rep. (2020). https://doi.org/10.1016/j.chbr.2020.100004
33. Bundesagentur für Arbeit: Anteil von Frauen und Männern in verschiedenen Berufsgruppen in Deutschland am 30. Juni 2019 (sozialversicherungspflichtig und geringfügig Beschäftigte) (2020). https://de.statista.com/statistik/daten/studie/167555/umfrage/frauenanteil-in-verschiedenen-berufsgruppen-in-deutschland/. Accessed 30 Dec 2020
34. Sorko, S.R., Trattner, C., Komar, J.: Implementing AR/MR – learning factories as protected learning space to rise the acceptance for mixed and augmented reality devices in production. Procedia Manuf. (2020). https://doi.org/10.1016/j.promfg.2020.04.037

Author Index

Printed in the United States
by Baker & Taylor Publisher Services